World Trade and Biological Exchange Before 1492

Revised and Expanded Edition

By

Professor Emeritus John L. Sorenson, Anthropologist

Professor Emeritus Carl L. Johannessen, Biogeographer

Edited by
Jerrid M. Wolflick
Kethleen Wheeler

World Trade and Biological Exchanges Before 1492, Revised and Expanded Edition

Copyright © 2013 Dr. John Sorenson and Dr. Carl Johannessen.

All rights reserved. No part of this book may be used or reproduced by any means, graphic, electronic, or mechanical, including photocopying, recording, taping, or by any information retrieval system without the written permission of the publisher except in the case of brief quotations embodied in critical articles or reviews.

This book may be ordered from www.amazon.com (both print and Kindle editions) or by contacting the authorized author:

Carl L. Johannessen
1284 East 21st Avenue
Eugene, Oregon 97403

Due to the dynamic nature of the Internet, any Web addresses or links contained in this book may have changed since publication and may no longer be valid. The views in this work are solely those of the author and do not necessarily reflect the views of the publisher, and the publisher hereby disclaims any responsibility for them.

ISBN-10: 148208760X (pbk.)
ISBN-13: 978 1482087604 (pbk)

DEDICATION

This book is dedicated to all the tireless researchers in the world looking fearlessly for truth; for all those flying in the face of convention and received wisdom.

TABLE OF CONTENTS

Acknowledgements	i
Preface	1
Introduction	3
Method	7
Sailing Evidence	8
Plant Evidence	10
Some Salient Cases	11
Other Species Of Flora From Table 1	25
Microfauna	52
Other Fauna	65
Turning Parsimony Around	72
Cultural Freight	74
Summary Points	78
Appendix 1	80 - 308
Flora	81
Microfauna	260
Other Fauna	294
Appendix 2	309 - 317
Appendix 3	318 - 334
Illustrations	335
Bibliography	351
Index	416
Biographical Information	440

John L. Sorenosn and Carl L. Johannessen

List Of Tables

Table 1 – Flora, Decisive Evidence .... 21 - 24
Table 2 – Flora, Significant But Not Decisive Evidence 50
Table 3 – Flora Needing Further Research 50-51
Table 4 – Microfauna, Decisive Evidence 63-64
Table 5 – Microfauna, Significant But Not Decisive Evidence 64
Table 6 – Other Fauna, Decisive Evidence 71
Table 7 – Other Fauna Needing Further Research 71

List Of Illustrations

Illustration 1 – Wall Sculpture, Maize (India) 335
Illustration 2 – Wall Sculpture, Maize "J" Curl (India) 336
Illustration 3 – Wall Sculpture, Maize (India) 337
Illustration 4 – Wall Sculpture, Maize (India) 338
Illustration 5 – Pottery Effigy, Maize Cob (China) 339
Illustration 6 – Maize Plants Bas-Relief (Java) 340
Illustration 7 – Balustrade, Cashew Nuts (India) 341
Illustration 8 – Pineapple Sculpture (India) 342
Illustration 9 – Balustrade, Annona (India) 343
Illustration 10 – Wall Sculpture, Annona (India) 344
Illustration 11 – Bas-Relief, Chili Pepper Plants (Java) 345
Illustration 12 – Teapot, Moschata Squash (China) 346
Illustration 13 – Nandi Sculpture, Sunflower (India) 347
Illustration 14 – Sculpture, Parrot On Sunflower Head (India) 348
Illustration 15 – Wall Sculpture, Monstera Deliciosa (India) 349
Illustration 16 – Pottery Effigy, Chicken (Lima, Peru) 350

ACKNOWLEDGMENTS

We appreciate the insight provided by Victor H. Mair that resulted in the initiation of the preparation and presentation of this book. We express our gratitude for assistance in its preparation to the Center for Ancient Studies, University of Pennsylvania, and the Institute for the Study and Preservation of Ancient Religious Texts and Foundation for Ancient Research and Mormon Studies at Brigham Young University. The Foundation of the University of Oregon assisted in this research early on and continue to provide working space and technical assistance.

We thank Victor H. Mair for assistance in modernizing the reading of certain Chinese names.

We appreciate the assistance with photographs from the American Institute of Indian Studies, the Archaeological Survey of India and Shakti M Gupta. for photos from her book, Plants in Indian Temple Art. Eve McConnaughey provided the Indonesian photos.

The following organizations assisted financially in Johannessen's early field research in India and China: National Science Foundation (Grant #2187), Foundation for Ancient Research and Mormon Studies, University of Oregon Research Services and the University of Oregon Foundation, Caterpillar Tractor Co., Brookhurst Mill, Alpine Map Co., Jerry's Home Improvement Center, Furrow Building Materials, Northrup Seed Co., Charles A. Lily Co., Imus Cartographics Co., and others.

The people who have helped Johannessen with finances for field study are: John Sorenson, George Carter, Robert and Sharon Wilson, Gordon Swoffer, Rob Lewis, and Casey Dale and the kind people who have assisted in the reading and editing the manuscript: Jeneen Beckett, Steve Jett, Hugh Iltis, Greg Howard, Ronald Wixman, Aimee Yogi and many more contributed their time and efforts.

Johanessen thanks the people who have been with him in the field: Doris Johannessen, Anne Z. Parker, Barbara Northrup, Grace Schneiders, Linda McElroy, Jane Pyle, S. G. Samak, Wang Siming and Bruce and Laura Johannessen. I am especially grateful for the assistance in the research in India and China: Zhang Kai, Sun Bisin, Hu Zhihao, K. S. Saraswat, Mahadev Katti, C. Margabandhu, J. C. Joshi, K. V. Ramesh, K. P. Poonacha, Shitala P. Tewari, T. Dayananda Patel, P. D. Mahadev, Joginder Singh, K. Venkatesh. Thank you all.

Lastly, we would like to thank Jerrid M. Wolflick for his tireless work doing the final edit, creating the Table of Contents and Indices, and insuring that the formatting was correct for the iUniverse publication, the Create Space publication, and The Kindle epublication.

PREFACE

Professors John L. Sorenson and Carl L. Johannessen have been working and researching in the field of early diffusion models for over forty years. Both professors have published numerous articles on discoveries relating to various specific species that were transported across the early oceans; *Zea mays*, or corn, being especially important to Dr. Johannessen. These articles were regularly published in peer-review journals.

The original book was an expanded version of a presentation given at the conference, "Contact and Exchange in the Ancient World," held at the University of Pennsylvania, Philadelphia, May 5, 2001. The conference was organized by Victor H. Mair of the Department of Asian and Middle Eastern Studies at the University of Pennsylvania. He is also editor of the volume of papers from that conference published by the University of Hawaii Press in 2006.

Since the time we submitted our paper for inclusion in that volume, we have made further discoveries. Some additions were included in an electronic version entitled "Scientific Evidence for Pre-Columbian Transoceanic Voyages to and from the Americas" (Sino-Platonic Papers, No. 133, CD-ROM edition, April 2004), published by the Department of Asian and Middle Eastern Studies, University of Pennsylvania, Philadelphia. The present book incorporates further material. Because much of the literature in this book is interpreted in ways other than biologists conventionally have, for readers' convenience we give in Appendix 1 a précis of our reference materials on each species discussed. Appendix 2 is a list of the species categorized by their common uses. Appendix 3 summarizes the most salient types of evidence we have used in relation to India. Selected illustrations and a bibliography for both the text proper and the appendices follow.

The current edition of the book reflects continued research and discoveries in the field of early transoceanic diffusion. The bibliography has been expanded to include articles and books published in the last 10 years. The tables have been reformatted for easier use. Information not available at the time of the original publication has been added to the relevant species.

Support for this work has been provided by the Institute for the Study and Preservation of Ancient Religious Texts at Brigham Young University and The Center for Ancient Studies of the University of Pennsylvania. We express gratitude to those organizations, but, of course, we alone are responsible for the views expressed and for any errors. We are also grateful to Victor H. Mair for his constant encouragement. Our appreciation also goes to Linda S. Mcelroy for her helpful preparation of the manuscript and Jerrid M. Wolflick for his extensive editorial services and preparation of the electronic kindle edition and Create Space manuscript edition.

INTRODUCTION

After examining the published literature, both peer-reviewed and popular, of the last 150 years we have discovered conclusive evidence that nearly 100 species of plants, a majority of them cultivars (plants intentionally cultivated for use by a group of people), were present in both the Eastern and Western Hemispheres prior to Columbus' first voyage to the Americas. The evidence comes from archaeological, historical and linguistic sources; ancient art materials; and conventional natural science studies. Additionally, 19 species of micro-predators and seven other species of fauna were shared by the Old and New Worlds. The evidence further suggests that an additional 75 organisms be given further study as probably or possibly bi-hemispheric in pre-Columbian times. This distribution could not have been due to natural transfer mechanisms such as bird flight or seed floatation. Nor can it be explained by early human migrations to the New World via the Bering Strait route, since there are no remains or evidence for many of the presented species in the Northern Hemisphere of the Americas. Over half the plant transfers consisted of flora of American origin that spread to Eurasia or Oceania, some at surprisingly early dates.

The only plausible explanation for these findings is that a considerable number of transoceanic voyages across both major oceans in both directions were completed between the sixth millennium B.C.E. and the European Age of Discovery. Scientists' growing knowledge of early maritime technology and its accomplishments increasingly give us confidence that both the vessels and the nautical skills capable of the long-distance travels were developed by the dates indicated in the manuscript. These voyages put a new light on the extensive Old World/New World cultural parallels that have long been considered controversial and explained through the idea of parallel evolution.

Scholars concerned with the ancient cultural history of the Americas generally believe that there were no culturally or biologically significant connections between the Old and New Worlds as a result of transoceanic voyaging before 1492. This book presents, explains, and documents the evidence for our position. We believe researchers of the past are now obliged to adopt a new paradigm for the role of long-distance sea communication in world history and culture.

In the past, arguments for transoceanic contacts have relied mainly on evidence from cultural parallels (Sorenson and Raish 1996). Some of those are indeed striking, but scholars generally have rejected their value as evidence that significant pre-Columbian human contacts took place across the oceans (see, e.g., Kroeber 1948, 538–71; Rands and Riley 1958; Willey 1985).

Over a century ago, Tylor (1896) compared details of the Aztec board game, patolli (e.g., the board's layout, the sequence of moves, and cosmic associations of the pieces and moves), with the game called pachisi in India. Even Robert Lowie, an influential anthropologist who was usually critical of voyage-dependent diffusionist explanations for such similarities, accepted that in this case "the concatenation of details puts the parallels far outside any probability [of having been invented independently]" (1951, 13). However, tentative acceptance by some influential observers, like Lowie, of the possible historical significance of some cultural parallels has always ended up being negated in academic circles by a demand from critics for 'hard,' or 'scientific' evidence for voyaging. The sort of evidence often demanded was demonstration that a substantial number of domesticated plants were known and used on both sides of the oceans before Columbus' day (e.g., Kidder et al. 1946, 2).

Data, primarily from the life sciences, now provide that evidence, not only for the researched flora, but for fauna and micro-organisms as well. The majority of our data is on plants (Tables 1, 2, and 3, below). We also look at shared human disease-associated organisms (germs, viruses and parasites) as evidence for voyaging (Tables 4 and 5). Lastly, we point out some larger animals that were also likely transported across the tropical oceans before Columbus (Tables 6 and 7).

An example from the history of health-damaging organisms demonstrates our approach while illustrating the power this kind of evidence provides in the study of human history and prehistory. The hookworm *Ancylostoma duodenale* causes one of the most widespread human ailments. The long-term prevalence of the hookworm in East and Southeast Asia makes that area the obvious source from which the organism reached the Americas.

A. duodenale was at first assumed to have been introduced to the New World by slaves brought from Africa. Early in the 20th century, Fonseca (not fully published until 1970) discovered the parasite in an isolated Amerindian population in the Amazon basin. Shortly afterward, microbiologist Samuel Darling (1920) pointed out that the hookworm apparently had infested South American tropical forest peoples long before Columbus arrived. If a date for the parasite in the Americas before European discovery could be proven, he observed, then the only explanation for the parasite in the New World would be that it had arrived anciently via infected humans who had crossed the ocean - "storm-tossed fishermen," he ventured.

His reasoning sprang from facts about the life cycle of this worm. In one stage it must inhabit warm, moist soil (in a climate no colder than that of North Carolina today). At a later stage, larvae from the soil penetrate a human host's body and settle in the digestive tract. Immigrants who came to the New World in slow stages via Beringia would have arrived hookworm-free because the cold ambient conditions would have killed the parasite in the soil (Soper 1927; Ferreira et al. 1988).

The hookworm's pre-Columbian presence in the Americas was established authoritatively by Allison et al. (1973), who found traces of the pest in a Peruvian mummy dated about 900 C.E. Evidence from other mummies and human coprolites has since repeatedly confirmed the initial find (Araújo 1988; Reinhard 1992). In 1988, Brazilian scientists identified this parasite from remains excavated in eastern Brazil (Ferreira et al. 1980; 1988). A series of radiocarbon dates fixed the age at about 7,200 years ago. Given the inland remoteness of the site, the organism's arrival on the coast of the continent must have occurred centuries earlier.

Can these findings be said to establish conclusively that early human voyagers crossed the ocean to the Americas? Is there some explanation for the presence of the worm in the New World due to natural forces, independent of human beings? Absolutely not. There is no alternative explanation. Modern microbiologists continue to assure us that Darling's assessment was correct. Ferreira et al. (1982, 39) say, "Transpacific migrants from Asia by sea must be one component of the ancient American population." Fonseca (1970, 306) asserts, "shared species of parasite ... make it inescapable that voyagers reached South America directly from Oceania or Southeast Asia." Ferreira et al. (1988, 39) agree: "We must suppose that [the human hosts for the parasite] arrived by sea." Araújo (1988, 149) confirms, "The evidence points only to maritime contacts" (emphases added).

This kind of fact, or secure inference, is vital in our present study. First, since *A. duodenale* could have arrived in the Americas only in the bodies of (presumably) Asians who came by sea, we can be certain that elements of some particular culture, as well as a set of Asian genes, arrived with them. Second, we know that vessels capable of crossing or skirting the Pacific were already in use by the sixth millennium B.C.E., and at least one of those craft actually reached South America, where its occupants passed the hookworm on to subsequent inhabitants.

A second species, *Necator americanus*, also called 'hookworm,' has been found in Brazil in human remains of the same age (Ferreira et al. 1980, 65–7). Its reproductive cycle is similar to that of *A. duodenale*. The presence of this second organism confirms what the facts about *A. duodenale* told us. It is important to note that *N. americanus* is not named after its origin point. It is named the New World hookworm or 'American Killer' because it has a far more damaging effect on the Caucasian population in America than it did on the African slaves.

Subsequently, archaeologists and microbiologists have found decisive evidence in the Americas for the presence of 17 other infectious organisms from the Old World (see Table 4). Most of them could not have come with early Bering Strait migrants, and the others in fact did not. They include additional micro-predators—parasites, bacteria, viruses, and fungi. Beyond the primary 19, there is enough evidence of transfer across the ocean of another 18 disease-causing organisms to call for further research on their possible pre-Columbian bi-hemispheric distribution. The zoological literature also identifies six animal forms (see Table 6) documented as present in both hemispheres, and possibly at least nine others (see Table 7).

Since the amount of available evidence about plants greatly exceeds the evidence about fauna, we will first present salient data on transported fauna. Prior to presenting the bulk of our evidence we will explain our methodology.

* * *

Organisms, whether plant or animal, have special significance for the history and study of long-distance human movements. Biologists believe that any given species arises only once in the course of evolution because any new species develops within a unique set of environmental parameters that is found in only a single geographical location (see Zohary 1996, 156; for changes in thought on this topic, see Blumler 1992; 1996). Plant geographer N. Polunin (1960, 6) stated the governing principle very clearly: "The chances that two isolated populations will evolve in exactly the same way are incalculably low," since, as Wulff (1943, 56) put it, "no two localities on earth are exactly alike in all … physico-geographical conditions" governing the evolutionary process. Stephen Gould (1994, 3) echoed the thought: "I regard each species as a contingent item of history …. [A] species will arise in a single place [and time] …."

When we find evidence that the same species lived before Columbus in the New World as well as an ocean apart in Oceania, Asia, Europe, or Africa, the paradox demands rational explanation. One might hurriedly conclude that certain seeds moved inter-continentally by the actions of winds or waves; however, few seeds are equipped to survive long while floating or moving great distances via wind, and no disease organism spreads that way. The odds for successful natural transport of plants are so slim (Guppy 1906, following De Candolle; Fosberg 1951) that anyone who claims a passive, natural mode of transport is obliged to demonstrate the possibility in the immediate case rather than merely assuming or asserting it.

METHOD

Our search for evidence of the mechanical or intentional transport of plants, microorganisms, and animals involved an exhaustive search of the literature already assembled in the Sorenson and Raish (1996) annotated bibliography, the largest annotated list of articles and books on the subject of transoceanic voyaging. Further study revealed additional, updated sources. We searched primarily for dated archaeological evidence, historical literature, lexicons, first records of the discovery of sites by Europeans, local art work, and biochemical data.

We know that we must have missed some evidence in the vast array of published works in most languages of the world. Recognizing this, we provide our findings even when the results do not totally meet our criteria for conclusive evidence. These inconclusive references are assembled as tables in the text and as write-ups in Appendix 1 to assist others, who may wish to expand this knowledge. We provide a record of our inconclusive findings on literature that can be utilized as a basis for continuing the search. We also include the written opinions of past writers on the subject of diffusion, even when they disagree with us so that the reader can see some of the causes for concern by many traditional scientists on our mutual subject.

Researchers published from Asian sources and in languages other than English have proved a particularly valuable. Indian and Chinese publications have significantly increased the number of species that we now record as having definite evidence of diffusion through early intentional transoceanic methods. Since they are specialists in the languages and cultures of many of the prominent areas where diffusion took place, they made interpretation of ancient text and artwork more reasonable and realistic. We hope that in the near future an exhaustive search of the Asian and Indian publications can be completed by scholars who fluently speak the languages, since we do not. We can be certain that there is much more evidence in these works than we were able to uncover.

SAILING EDIVENCE

From the point of view of nautical history we must, think of watercraft as capable of trans- or peri-oceanic voyaging as early as the 5th millennium B.C.E. In recent years, serious proposals about early sailing capability have been made by archaeologists and others involved in research on the question of the early settlement of the Americas. Some see early voyages around the North Pacific to be thoroughly plausible (Dixon 1993; Erickson et al. 2005, 18319; Erlandson et al. 2007, 161). Data on navigation in Near Oceania and Australasia have shown that there was a spectacularly early capability to cross stretches of open ocean. Australia was reached from Papua New Guinea or Timor more than 50,000 years ago. The Solomon Islands were inhabited nearly 27,000 B.C.E. after an open-sea crossing of over 100 miles (Gamble 1993, 214–30). Bednarik (1997, 360) has argued convincingly that Homo erectus living on island Southeast Asia had "almost habitual use of navigation" of some sort by 840,000 years ago! He and his associates constructed a craft on the island of Timor using only 'Lower Pleistocene' stone-tool technology. They used the craft to cross to Australia (2001). For more recent times, researchers have established that trading voyages of thousands of miles were carried out in the Pacific millennia ago (Science News 1996; Service 1996; Jett 1998; Dickinson et al. 1999).

Nautical history and modern experimental voyages have demonstrated that oceanic voyaging in early times was not as daunting as many modern researchers have supposed; at least it did not intimidate certain types of people (Jett 1971, 16–19; Helms 1988). In modern days, oceans have been crossed hundreds of times in unlikely craft ranging from midget and small boats, rafts, rowboats, and canoes to even less conventional vessels (see, for example, Anthony 1930; Barton 1962; Borden 1967). The ocean is not nearly as severe and fearsome a barrier to technologically limited voyagers as landlubbers have been wont to suppose. One experienced sailor of small craft in the tropics went so far as to assert, "It takes a damn fool to sink a [small] boat on the high seas" (Lindemann 1957, 21). Despite well-documented evidence of ancient capability for oceanic travel, a negative attitude has persisted among scholars that has been labeled "American thalassophobia" (illogical aversion to considering the sea as a possible route) (Elkin and MacIntosh 1974, 181) and "intellectual mal de mer" (Easton 1992, 39). This phobia "cannot abide sea-travel as a mode of communication" (Meggers 1976, 638); and has kept virtually all New World archaeologists from even inquiring whether shipping could have spread ancient cultures and people over long distances (Chard 1958).

Recently, however, up-to-date scholars have begun to realize that voyagers using simple technology could have reached the New World millennia ago. Over 40 years ago, archaeologist G. Bushnell (1961) granted that there was nothing physically impossible about vessels coasting around the North Pacific at any time after 8000 B.C.E. Since then, Fladmark has argued repeatedly for a similar thesis (1979; 1983; 1986). James Dixon considered it "not unreasonable" (1993, 119) to assume that watercraft were capable of moving along the coast from Asia by 11,000 B.C.E. Six years later (1999, 31), he had changed that estimate to 14,000 B.C.E. Nowadays, the coastal voyaging position is supported with increasing frequency (Engelbrecht and Seyfert 1994; Gamble 1993; Borg 1997; Dillehay 2000; Erlandson et al. 2007, 161). A respected archaeologist, Dennis Stanford of the Smithsonian, has even proposed that Late Paleolithic (Solutrean) hunting people from Western Europe made their way around the ice-bound edge of the North Atlantic to settle in Late Pleistocene North America (Holden 1999a).

A more restrained support has continued for the idea of voyages directly across the Pacific. The hypothesis, put forward 40 years ago, that voyagers bearing ceramics of the Jomon culture of Japan reached Ecuador around 3000 B.C.E. (Estrada and Meggers 1961) was accepted by a number of prominent archaeologists (e.g., Willey 1971, 16; Kidder II 1964, 474; Jennings 1968, 176, but all with some subsequent hedging). Edwards (1965; 1969) and Doran (1971; 1978) presented details about the nautical capability of Chinese sea-going rafts and made evident that the rafts of coastal Peru and Ecuador were explicitly parallel in form and capability to those of China, Indochina, and India (cf. Needham and Lu 1985, 48–9). The work of Edwards and Doran has been readily available but widely ignored. There is no question that those rafts (more accurately 'ships') were capable of direct transpacific voyages. Although the date for historical documentation on these Chinese and Southeast Asian ocean-going vessels goes back only to the first century B.C.E. (Ling Shun-shêng 1956), the craft are likely to prove much older (Edwards 1965, 98–100; Needham et al. 1971, 542–43).

In Peru, balsa rafts similar to those of bamboo in use on the coast of China reached off-shore islands by 2500 B.C.E., and ocean-going craft were developed well before the first century B.C.E. (Norton 1987). Alsar (1973; 1974) demonstrated the feasibility of crossing the Pacific, from east to west at least, by sailing a fleet of three Ecuadorean-built rafts with a crew of 12 over 9200 miles to Australia (the rafts even exchanged crew members at rendezvous points en route). Various forms of such rafts, in addition to large canoes, were used throughout much of Oceania (Clissold 1959). Our present state of knowledge about ancient nautical capabilities allows for voyages that could account for the early presence of amaranth, maize, the peanut, and other crops in both Asia and the Americas.

PLANT EVIDENCE

In this section we will focus on the evidence available for eight fauna species. Table 1 lists 99 plants for which there is definitive evidence that the organism was present in both the Eastern and Western Hemispheres before Columbus' first voyage. Table 2 gives 19 more species for which the evidence is significant, though less than decisive, and Table 3 adds 21 more that deserve further research to determine the possibility of their pre-Columbian transfer.

What do we consider decisive evidence? It can come from the archeological discovery of plant remains – macrofossils, pollen, phytoliths, and DNA – that indicates that a particular species was present before 1492 C.E. in the hemisphere where, according to plant geographers and botanists, the species did not originate. A second source of decisive or conclusive evidence comes from historical documents – references to or descriptions of plants in ancient texts, explorers' reports, or lexicons of appropriate date that show knowledge of the species in the hemisphere where it did not originate. Depictions of plants in ancient art can also be determinative. Conclusive information may also come through well-reasoned inferences by botanists, based on such data as where a plant's relatives and possible wild ancestor grew (Zohary and Hopf 1993, chap. 1). However, we have not usually considered any single datum sufficient; typically we combine at least two types of evidence to arrive at our conclusion of 'decisive' evidence.

Of course, tables provide only a spare summary of our data. Our next task is to present the chief points of our argument as to why we consider each species a transoceanic transfer backed by decisive evidence. The text sketches the major components of our argument, species by species. For the fullest presentation of each species see Appendix 1.

Some Particularly Salient Cases

We have not treated all the species at equal length. Data on species of lesser interest are postponed in the interest of clear presentation of the primary argument. Note that 'sp.' means two species of the genus and 'spp.' means more than two species in the genus.

Amaranthus spp. in general (a cereal grain)

The most important grain amaranths, *Amaranthus hypochondriacus* and *A. caudatus*, are both native to the New World (Sauer, J. 1950, 612–13; 1967; Brücher 1989, 54–6) where they constituted important cereal crops. These plants have been grown for a long time in Asia as well.

Some of the significance of this American/Asian distribution was first presented in Jonathan Sauer's monograph on grain amaranths, published in 1950 (588–614). He concluded (page 613) that "... there is a great, vaguely delimited grain amaranth region stretching all the way from Manchuria through interior China and the Himalaya to Afghanistan and Persia. *A. leucocarpus* [now known as *A. hypochondriacus*, from Mexico; see Brücher 1989, 56] and *A. caudatus* [from the Andes] are both grown throughout this [Asian] area." Culinary uses were similar in Asia and the Americas. After being parched or popped, "the seeds were sometimes made into balls, like popcorn, using a syrup or other binder, or the seeds were ground and the flour was stirred into a drink or baked in small cakes."

Sauer also observed (page 588) that, "The crop is scattered so widely through Asia and is so firmly entrenched among remote peoples that it gives a powerful impression of great antiquity in the area;" in fact, it would seem to have been present "from time immemorial." Yet, "the available Old World specimens represent nothing but a small sample of the diversity present in the American grain amaranths." Hence, "The conclusion appears inescapable that the grain amaranths are all of New World origin."

However, species of amaranths that are used as potherbs or for decoration or that are weeds are another matter; those that grow in Asia are probably Asian natives (Sauer 1967). In his later publications, Sauer showed reluctance to accept the early transoceanic contact that his first results implied, although the facts of the matter remained unchanged.

In Mesoamerica, the cultivation of a grain amaranth began as early as 4000 B.C.E. (García-Bárcena 2000, 14). Wild species provide plausible ancestors for the earliest domesticated amaranths. No comparable ancestors for the grain amaranths are known in Asia. Even though, on the basis of the evidence presented by Sauer, grain amaranths appear to be old in Asia, exactly when the transfer of the grain amaranths from their American area of origin took place went unspecified in the literature for many years.

Jonathon Sauer (1950) was impressed that Bretschneider (1896, 406) presented "what seems to be a clear reference to a grain amaranth" in a

Chinese text. The reference was to the *Kiu Huang Pen Ts'ao* (*Jiu huang bencao*) (Bretschneider 1882, 49). This volume includes descriptions and woodcut illustrations of 414 plants, based on older printed works as well as the author's own observations. The editor/author, Zhou Ding Wang died in 1425 C.E. The source of his citation for amaranth was a document written about 950 C.E. for the Prince of Shu, in modern Sichuan. It recognized six kinds of *hien* (*xian*), a generic name for a group of related plants. A "modern record of grain amaranths from the same area ... gives the same name," Sauer adds (p. 613). The pre-Columbian presence of grain amaranths in Asia that was indicated by their wide distribution is thus confirmed by this 10th Century mention.

Archaeology now has confirmed a dramatically earlier date for the grain amaranths in Asia. Seeds of *A. caudatus*, along with *A. spinosus*, a thorny weed that also grew in pre-Columbian Mesoamerica (Sauer 1967, 1007; Miranda 1952–53, I, 215), have been excavated in India. These date to the 1000–800 B.C.E. period at the site of Narhan (Gorakhpur Dist., Uttar Pradesh) (Saraswat et al. 1994, 282, 284, 331). Such a date is in general agreement with the distributional evidence in Asia as interpreted by Sauer.

The idea of an early movement of amaranths to Asia is supported by information on maize (*Zea mays*). In the 1960s a "primitive maize" was found in cultivation in the Himalayan country of Sikkim. Botanists judged that it most closely resembled the "wild maize" of "ancient Mexico, a fossil specimen of which was uncovered [in 1960] in a lower level of San Marcos Cave in [the Tehuacán Valley of] Mexico" (Marszewski 1975–1978, 132–34, cf. 162; Dhawan 1964; Gupta and Jain 1973). The date for maize of this type in Mexico is not entirely clear; it could be as early as the fifth millennium B.C.E., or it may fall in the third millennium (Johnson and MacNeish 1972, 21ff.; Long et al. 1989). (See more on maize in Asia below.)

Arachis hypogaea (the peanut)

Early specimens of *Arachis hypogaea*, the peanut, have been found by archaeologists in China. Because the plant is a South American native, when nuts were found over 40 years ago at Neolithic-age sites in China, some biologists and archaeologists claimed that the specimens were misidentified or that the dates attributed to them were in error (Harlan and de Wet 1973; Peng 1961). But the critics failed to examine the evidence carefully enough; it turned out that the specimens were unquestionably peanuts, and the archaeology was sound (Johannessen and Wang 1998, 18).

The peanut has since been discovered in archaeological excavation in caves on the island of Timor in Indonesia (Glover 1977, 43, 46). The nuts were found along with two other American plant species, the *Annona squamosa* (custard apple) and *Zea mays* (maize); these were dated loosely after the third millennium B.C.E. but earlier than 1000 C.E., the time at which the caves were no longer inhabited by humans.

Safford had observed (1917, 17) that the variety of peanut found in graves at Ancón, Peru, was the same as that cultivated in China, Formosa, and India. Anderson (1952, 167) noted that "until the Peruvian excavations, the experts were certain that it [the peanut] came from the Old World, so widely is it disseminated there, with every appearance of having been grown for a very long time in Asia and Africa." More specifically, he added that "The most primitive type of peanut, the same narrow little shoestrings which are found in the Peruvian tombs, are commonly grown today, not in Peru, but in South China." Towle (1961, 42–3) later noted that one of two kinds of peanuts from the [Peruvian] tombs found in coastal sites is "similar to one grown in the Orient today."

Any uncertainty that Sinologists might have retained about the pre-Columbian presence of peanuts in China has been put to rest by more recent digging on the mainland. Some "10 or more" additional specimens of nuts have been found in the third-century B.C.E. tomb of Western Han emperor Yang Ling in Xianyang, Saanxi (Chen Wenhua 1994, 59–60). Radiocarbon dates associated with the original two finds mentioned above put them as early as around 2800 B.C.E. uncalibrated (Chang 1973, 527). The more recent discoveries show the crop was still being grown two and one half millennia later, and use of the cultigen continues into modern times, as Anderson (1945b) observed.

Krapovickas (1969) compiled names for the peanut from Native American peoples in the Amazon Basin, the area where botanists think the plant was first domesticated. There, it bears such names as, in the Tupí language: *mandobi*, *manobi*, *mandowi*, *mundubi*, and *munui*; in the Pilagá language: *mandovi*; in the Chiriguano language: *manduvi*; and in the Guaraní language: *manubi*. Black (1988) compared these terms with names for the peanut in India (taken from Kirtikar and Basu 1935, 754–65) and found Sanskrit *andapi*; Hindi *munghali*; and Gujarati *mandavi*. These obvious lexical parallels, together with the discovery of early plant remains in Asia, mean that transoceanic voyaging was surely responsible for the plants and the names reaching Asia

Gossypium spp. in general (cotton plants)

The early history of cotton (*Gossypium* spp.) in the New World is found, on the basis of cytogenetic analysis, to be tied directly to Asian cotton. For over half a century most botanical models for the origin of the American cottons have depended heavily on the work by a group of cotton scientists led by Joseph Hutchinson with colleagues Silow and Stephens (1947). They argued that in order to rationalize the facts about the chromosome structure of later cottons, we must suppose that a diploid species, either *Gossypium arboreum* or *G. herbaceum*, had been carried from India to the Americas at an early date. There, it hybridized with a Native American diploid lintless species to yield a tetraploid cotton (one having double the number of chromosomes of the original diploid) that had longer, more useful fibers. The genetic composition of all subsequent domesticated American cottons incorporates the Old World chromosomes of *G. arboreum* (or it might have been *G. herbaceum*) (the D genome) with A genome chromosomes from a wild American ancestor. Hutchinson et al. (1947) postulated that the first American hybrid subsequently became extinct, but two of its descendant species, *G. hirsutum* and *G. barbadense*, became the bases for all subsequent domesticated cotton varieties in the New World.

So when did Asiatic cotton first reach the Americas? Archaeologists have found Mesoamerican specimens of *G. hirsutum* dating to the fourth or fifth millennium B.C.E. (MacNeish et al. 1967, 191), and *G. barbadense* was being grown in Peru by the mid-third millennium B.C.E. (Yen 1963, 112; Shady Solís 1997). So the time of arrival of their ancestral Asian diploid had to be earlier still, perhaps as early as the fifth millennium B.C.E.

Before Columbus' time, American cottons were carried across the oceans to parts of the Old World. Historical documents from the Cape Verde Islands show that *G. hirsutum*, the Mexican species, had apparently reached the Guinea Coast of Africa, by means of some unrecorded voyage, before Columbus' first voyage. We know that because Cape Verdean records report that a cotton arrived there from West Africa some 25 years prior to 1492. Apparent remnants of that cotton turn out to have the American tetraploid genetic structure (Stephens 1971, 413–14). It was suggested by Jeffreys (1976) that Arab sailors may have carried *G. barbadense* from the Americas to Africa, perhaps along with corn. This suggests that tetraploidal cotton, *G. hirsutum*, arrived in West Africa from the Americas some time before that.

Cottons that evolved from the American tetraploid species were also found by the earliest European explorers when they reached islands in eastern Polynesia (Stephens 1947; 1963; Merrill 1954; Wendel 1989; Langdon 1982). Johnson and Decker (1980) show that languages across the entire Pacific Basin have terms for cotton that also signify (fish)line.

Recent genetic research has also shown that a portion of the gene sequence of a local cotton species in southern Mexico, *G. gossypioides*, had one genetic component that comes directly from an African cotton (Wendel et al. 1995, 308–9). The genetic argument is, then, that some unknown African cotton must have been introduced in ancient times to Mesoamerica in order to account for the African genes. They would have been incorporated by introgression into an existing American species to yield *G. gossypioides*. While we do not have direct evidence for that transatlantic transfer, we can conceive of no sequence of purely natural events to otherwise explain the arrival of the African genetic signature. Stephens (1971, 406–8) explained why an accidental, passive scenario for the spread by ocean drift of any variety of domesticated cotton is highly unlikely. This, therefore, suggests that an African cotton was transported to the Americas at some early point in time, then later it was transported back to West Africa where it eventually was taken to the Cape Verde Islands, arriving there at least 25 years before the first voyage of Columbus.

Despite the notable discoveries of the past half-century about the history of cottons, the comings and goings of *Gossypium* across the oceans still pose complex questions. The only answers that make sense, we feel, involve voyagers crossing the oceans to an extent that no one anticipated 60 or so years ago.

Ipomoea batatas (the sweet potato)

The problem of the dispersion of the sweet potato has produced a huge literature over the past 75 years, but at last we have resolution of several facets of the issue.

Ipomoea batatas has been found fossilized in a Peruvian cave dated perhaps as early as 8,000 B.C.E. (Brücher 1989, 5). The domesticated sweet potato was being grown at the precocious pre-ceramic city of Caral in the Supe Valley of Peru, a few miles from the coast, between 2700 and 2100 B.C.E. (from calibrated radiocarbon dates) (Shady Solís et al. 2001, 725). A name for *I. batatas*, in the Proto-Mayan language of Guatemala before 1000 B.C.E has been reconstructed (Bronson 1966, 262 ff.). Later, common names for the plant in the Peruvian and Ecuadorian Andes, and probably on the coast as well, included variants of *cumara* or *cumal* (Patiño 1976, 62; Heyerdahl 1963, 29), or *k^{h}umara* in Quechua (Peruvian); speakers of the Chibchan family of languages in Colombia and Panama used a cognate name (Kelley 1998, 73). Very similar names (see Appendix 3) were applied later to the sweet potato in Polynesia, mostly variants on *kumara*. Although the claim was made as much as 75 years ago that the sweet potato spread into Polynesia only via Spanish exploring ships (Laufer 1929), traditions, linguistic studies among the island peoples, and explorers' historical records contradicted that position. Rather, those sources painted a picture of early islanders apparently carrying tubers with them from the mainland to the islands (Dixon 1932), or else Amerindians carried them westward. As late as the 1970s, passionate but ill-informed arguments (Brand. 1971; O'Brien 1972) were still being posed to stifle the idea that the sweet potato reached the islands in pre-Columbian times.

Yen (1974) capped a comprehensive investigation of the dispersion question by concluding that the data require that the transfer of the sweet potato from South America to Polynesia happen between 400 and 700 C.E. to be able to account for its known distribution. Since his study, archaeology has confirmed that view. For example, burnt tubers were found on Easter Island dated "early C.E." by radiocarbon, while other evidence has also come to light for a transfer to Polynesia prior to European exploration (Hather and Kirch 1991, 169; Yen 1998). Moreover, new linguistic studies have shown that American names for the tuber were brought into the eastern Pacific with the plant (Rensch 1991, 108; Kelley 1998). Rensch found on the basis of plant names that the sweet potato reached Polynesia at least twice, once via Hawaii and once through Easter Island. Barthel (1971, 1165–86) claimed to decipher an Easter Island text that refers to a directional model where the "path of the sweet potato" was from the east, while a "path of the breadfruit tree" was from the west. Both fit botanical reality.

The sweet potato also reached Asia long ago, as Baker (1971) had thought. Bretschneider (1882, 38) reported that the Chinese document _Nan Fang Ts'ao Mu Chang_ mentions the *I. batatas* plant. The author was Ki Han during the Tsin (Jin) Dynasty, between 290 and 307 C.E. We note now complementary evidence from India. Aiyer (1956, 71) cites the Sanskrit name, *valli*, and Pullaiah (2002, II, 307) gives two more names in that ancient tongue: *pindalah* and *raktaluh*. Aiyer also reports mention of *I. batatas* in the Hindu text _Silappadikaram_. Yen, in a 1996 personal communication to Johannessen, reported that the sweet potato had the same name in Sanskrit as it had in "northwestern South America," although he did not supply the terms. Kelley (1998, 72) has studied plant names for sweet potato and concludes that "An Indonesian word for 'yam,' **kumadjang*, appears to have been borrowed by Quechuan and by Chibchan languages (of northwestern South America) and reapplied to 'sweet potato.'" From Quechuan it (the name) was "transferred to southern Polynesia, and from Chibchan it seems to have gone to Hawaii." It would seem that the voyages and botanical movements involving the sweet potato were complex, and that we have detected them only in part so far.

Nicotiana tabacum (the tobacco plant)

The question of whether tobacco (*Nicotiana tabacum*), a plant native to the Americas, was found in ancient Egypt has arisen in the last quarter-century as a result of museum research. Fragments of tobacco were found about 30 years ago in the abdominal cavity of the mummy of Ramses II in a European museum (Bucaille 1990). In the intervening years, a large literature has arisen about the resulting controversy (the best survey is found in Jett 2002a). In 1992 Forensic Toxicologist Svetla Balabanova and a team of other scientists in Germany used sophisticated instrumentation to examine nine Egyptian mummies in order to learn about the ancient use of hallucinogenic or narcotic substances. Unexpectedly, they found the chemical residues for tobacco, cocaine, and hashish in the hair, soft tissues, skin, and bones of eight of the nine mummies, including metabolically processed derivatives of the drugs, signifying that the drugs were ingested while the subjects were alive. (Cocaine and hashish, but not tobacco, were found in the ninth mummy.) The historical dates of the mummies ranged from 1070 B.C.E. to 395 C.E. (Balabanova et al. 1992a), indicating that the plants yielding the drugs were apparently continuously available, at least to Egyptian royalty, for over 1400 years. Investigators have since found evidence of the drugs in many additional Egyptian mummies from museums across Europe (Nerlich et al. 1995; Parsche and Nerlich 1995; Balabanova et al. 1997). The researchers suspected error so took an additional 3000 samples from the Egyptian mummies across Europe and found similar results. Other researchers corroborated their evidence. Despite charges by critics that the analyses must have been faulty, the scientists involved vigorously defended their work, and recent independent critiques give them good marks (Wells 2000; Pollmer 2000). All attempts to explain the unexpected findings without granting that voyagers intentionally transferred the American plants to the Old World have serious flaws (see, e.g., Buckland and Panagiotakopulu 2001, the critiques in Jett 2002a and 2004, and Wells 2000).

The nub of the controversy is, of course, that according to the standard paradigm of plant history, tobacco 'should not' appear at all in Egypt or anywhere else in the Old World until after Columbus. Extravagant claims by Leo Wiener (1920–1922) about pre-Columbian tobacco in the Old World had been dismissed curtly by anthropologists and historians (e.g., Dixon 1920; 1921). But Ashraf (1985) found that textual and artistic materials in India as far back as medieval times show the presence and use of tobacco. The evidence includes a Sanskrit name, *tanbaku* (and *támrakúta* according to Nadkarni (1914, 257), along with representations or mentions of the water-cooled pipe (*huqqa*, or *hookah*) for smoking, but other scholars do not seem to have paid attention to Ashraf's evidence. Now, the facts obtained from study of the Egyptian mummies leave no plausible explanation other than that *N. tabacum* was indeed used long ago in the Old World, and that could only be so if the plant (or at least its leaves) was taken there at some early point in history by voyagers.

Erythroxylon novagranatense (the coca plant) and *Cannabis sativa* (the marijuana plant)

In western South America the leaves of the coca plant have been chewed for their chemical effect for more than 4000 years (Plowman 1984; Shady Solís 1997), although outside the Andean area where it is grown there has been little evidence for consuming it. Yet definitive evidence has come forth that the plant reached Egypt (Balabanova et al. 1992, 358). The chemistry involved is unequivocal. Coca's chemical signature appears in

Egyptian mummies along with that of tobacco and hashish.

It remains to be clarified just how coca reached Egypt. A few years ago all logical scenarios, biological and historical, to account for its presence there seemed far-fetched, including the voyaging hypothesis. But in light of the evidence for transoceanic movements demonstrated herein of so many other plants, the reality of ships conveying tobacco and coca to the central Old World and hashish to the New need no longer be doubted.

As strange as coca's presence and use in the Near East is the fact that Peruvian mummies dating to before 200 C.E. have been found to contain not only tobacco and coca, but also hashish (*Cannabis sativa*) (Parsche et al. 1993). Hashish was, of course, ancient in Eurasia. (For the fullest discussion of the evidence on tobacco, coca, and hashish; see Jett 2002a.)

Despite the discomfort of having a hoary paradigm upset, scientists must now accept that the evidence is convincing that humans were ingesting tobacco, coca, and hashish in both Egypt and Andean South America many centuries before Columbus.

Zea mays (corn or maize)

The literature on the question of whether maize (*Zea mays*) appeared in Eurasia before the time of Columbus has become large and contentious. Few botanists and even fewer archaeologists or historians have examined that literature exhaustively.

Field investigations have discovered odd sorts of maize growing in Asia (especially Sikkim Primitive in the remote Himalayas and 'waxy' varieties from Myanmar (Burma)). The waxy forms range across China to the Korean peninsula, mostly away from coastal areas where 16th-century Iberian sailors are supposed to have first introduced maize. The characteristics and distribution of these grains cannot be explained in terms of a post-Columbian introduction, because waxy varieties were not known in the Americas in recent centuries (if ever). Also the 'Primitive' variety to which that of Sikkim was likened has been extinct in Mexico for millennia (Marszewski 1975–1978, 1987; Johannessen and Wang 1998; Collins 1909; Stonor and Anderson 1949; Suto and Yoshida 1956; Dhawan 1964; Thapa 1966; Chiba 1968, 1969, 1970; Gupta and Jain 1973; The Wealth of India 1974). Yet, some unusual traits exhibited in these Asian maizes have close matches to corn known archaeologically from Peru (Towle 1961, 21–5) or that is still being grown by native groups in Peru, Colombia, Chile, Bolivia, and Argentina (Anderson 1945b; Sarkar et al. 1974).

In recent years decisive evidence for the presence of American maize in the Old World has been found in Asian art and archaeology. Johannessen and colleagues (Johannessen 1998a; Johannessen and Parker 1989a) were the first to document extensively that maize ears were represented in sculptures—hundreds of them—on original temple walls in Karnataka

State, southern India (details are given in Appendix 3). The art usually dates from the 11th to the 13th centuries C.E., but some representations are much older.

Gupta. independently identified maize, as well as a number of other plants of American origin, sculpted on Indian temples and monuments. For example, at the Lakshmi Narasimha Temple, Karnataka, "Nuggehalli, the eight-armed dancing Vishnu in his female form Mohini, is holding a corn cob [ear] in one of her left hands, and the other hands hold the usual emblems of Vishnu" (Gupta. 1996, 176). At least one maize representation dates from the Fifth Century C.E. (Cave Temple III, Badami, where, uniquely, the cob is held horizontally and the stem of the ear shows; Johannessen and Parker 1987a, 4).

In India, four Sanskrit words for maize have been recorded (Watt 1888–1893, VI, Pt. IV, 327; Balfour 1871–73, V, s.v. "Zea"), which show that the crop was present long before modern times. An early date is shown also by the mention of maize in the *Garuda Purana* (1980, 925, 947, 1128), as well as the Linga Purana (1973, 58, 85), texts of the fifth century C.E. Moreover, the commonest name for maize throughout most of India is similar to one of the names for the same plant among Arawak-language speakers of lowland South America (Johannessen 1992).

From the museum at Xinxiang near Zhenghou, Henan province, China, comes a ceramic effigy of a bird that was found in an excavation of an imperial tomb of the Han Dynasty. Impressions left on the interior of the figure show that a de-grained corncob had been used as an armature around which wet clay was modeled in avian form and then fired (See Illustration 5). The cob had, of course, burned up in the kiln. The tomb is over 2000 years old (Johannessen and Wang 1998, 28). The same authors have published a photograph of a bas-relief that patently exhibits entire maize plants. This bas relief stone sculpture comes from the Prambanan Temple complex, east of Jogjakarta, Java, dating before 1000 C.E. (See Figure 6). Glover's excavation of maize in Indonesia has already been noted; although the exact date is uncertain, the age has been interpreted as at least two millennia (Pokharia and Saraswat 1999, 101).

In the Middle East, also, maize was grown by medieval times, as Jeffreys long argued (1953a; 1953b; 1971; 1975; 1976). An Arabian juridical tradition, recorded in Yahya ben Adam's *Kitab al Karaj* (about 800 C.E.) lists maize among other grain and pulse crops (legumes used as foodstuff) on which a tax could justly be levied (Ben Shemesh. 1958, 77). Meanwhile, there is good reason to believe that maize was in Europe before Columbus' time (see, e.g., Finan 1948; C. Sauer 1962; Sauer in Newcomb 1963).

Overall, there is not the slightest question remaining that maize was carried from the Americas to Asia long ago—at least once and perhaps multiple times. The evidence for transoceanic transfer of the other plants discussed so far is also conclusive.

World Trade and Biologocal Exchanges Before 1492

Table 1
Plants with Decisive Evidence for Transoceanic Movement

Species	Common Name	Origin	Moved To	Moved by
Agave sp.	agave	Americas	Mediterranean	300 B.C.E.
Agave Americana	agave	Americas	India	1000 C.E.
Agave angustifolia	agave	Americas	India	1000 C.E.
Agave cantala	agave	Americas	India	1000 C.E.
Ageratum conyzoides	goat weed	Americas	India, Marquesas?	1500 C.E.
Alternanthera philoxeroides	Alligator weed	Americas	India	1000 C.E.
Amaranthus caudatus	love-lies-bleeding	Americas	Asia	800 B.C.E.
Amaranthus cruentus	amaranth	Americas	Asia	1000 C.E.
Amaranthus hypochondriacus	amaranth	Americas	Asia	1000 C.E.
Amaranthus spinosus	spiked amaranth	Americas	South Asia	800 B.C.E.
Anacardium occidentale	cashew	Americas	India	100 B.C.E.
Ananas comosus	pineapple	Americas	India, Polynesia	600 B.C.E.
Annona cherimolia	large annona	Americas	India	1200 C.E.
Annona reticulata	custard apple	Americas	India	100 B.C.E.
Annona squamosa	sweetsop	Americas	India, Timor	700 B.C.E.
Arachis hypogaea	peanut	Americas	China, India	2800 B.C.E.
Argemone Mexicana	Mexican poppy	Americas	China, India	1100 B.C.E.
Aristida subspicata		Americas	Polynesia	1500 C.E.
Artemisia vulgaris	mugwort	E. Hemisphere	Mexico	1500 C.E.
Asclepias curassavica	milkweed	Americas	China, India	1000 C.E.
Aster divaricates	Heart-shaped aster	Americas	Hawaii	1500 C.E.
Bixa orellana	achiote, *annatto*	Americas	Oceania, Asia	1000 C.E.
Canavalia sp.	jackbean, swordbean	Americas	Asia	1600 B.C.E.
Canna edulis	Indian shot	Americas	India, China	300 C.E.
Cannabis sativa	marijuana	E. Hemisphere	Peru	100 C.E.
Capsicum annuum	chili pepper	Americas	India,	800 C.E.

John L. Sorenosn and Carl L. Johannessen

			Polynesia	
Capsicum frutescens	chili pepper	Americas	India	800 C.E.
Carica papaya	papaya	Americas	Polynesia	1500 C.E.
Ceiba pentandra	silk cotton tree, kapok	Americas	Asia	900 C.E.
Chenopodium ambrosioides	Mexican tea, apazote	E. Hemisphere	Mesoamerica	1000 C.E.
Cocos nucifera	coconut	E. Hemisphere	Colombia to Mexico	400 C.E.
Couroupita guianensis	cannonball tree	Americas	India	1000 C.E.
Cucurbita ficifolia	chilacayote	Americas	Asia	1500 C.E.
Cucurbita maxima	Hubbard squash	Americas	India, China	900 C.E.
Cucurbita moschata	butternut squash	Americas	India, China	900 C.E.
Cucurbita pepo	pumpkin	Americas	India, China	500 C.E.
Curcuma longa	turmeric	E. Hemisphere	Andes	1500 C.E.
Cyperus esculentus	sedge	Americas	Eurasia	B.C.E.?
Cyperus vegetus	edible sedge	Americas	Easter Island, India	1000 C.E.
Datura metel	datura, jimsonweed	Americas	Eurasia	B.C.E.
Datura stramonium	datura, thorn apple	Americas	Eurasia	B.C.E.
Diospyros ebenaster	black sapote	Americas	Eurasia	1500 C.E.
Erigeron canadensis	Fleabane	Americas	India	1000 C.E.
Erythroxylon novagranatense	Coca Plant	Americas	Egypt	1200 B.C.E.
Garcinia mangostana	mangosteen	E. Hemisphere	Peru	B.C.E.?
Gossypium arboretum	a cotton	E. Hemisphere	South America	3000? B.C.E.
Gossypium barbadense	a cotton	Americas	Marquesas Islands	1500 C.E.
Gossypium gossypioides	a cotton (genes)	Africa	Mexico	1500 C.E.
Gossypium hirsutum	a cotton	Mexico	Africa, Polynesia	1475 C.E.
Gossypium tomentosum	a cotton	Americas	Hawaii	1500 C.E.
Helianthus annuus	sunflower	Americas	India	200 B.C.E.
Heliconia bihai	Balisier	Americas	Oceania, Asia	1500 C.E.
Hibiscus tiliaceus	linden hibiscus	Americas	Polynesia	1500 C.E.
Ipomoea batatas	sweet potato	Americas	Polynesia, China	300 C.E.
Lagenaria siceraria	bottle gourd	Americas	Eastern Polynesia	1500 C.E.
Luffa acutangula	ribbed gourd	Americas	India	B.C.E.?

World Trade and Biologocal Exchanges Before 1492

Luffa cylindrical	vegetable gourd, loofa	Americas?	India, China	1200 B.C.E.
Lycium carolinianum	Christmasberry	Americas	Easter Island	1500 C.E.
Manihot sp.	manioc	Americas	Easter Island	1500 C.E.
Macroptilium lathyroides	phasey bean	Americas	India	1600 B.C.E.
Manihot sp	manioc	Americas	Easter Island	1500 C.E.
Maranta arundinacea	arrowroot	Americas	Easter Island, India	1000 C.E.
Mimosa pudica	sensitive plant	Americas	India, China	B.C.E.?
Mirabilis jalapa	four-o'clock	Americas	India	B.C.E.?
Mollugo verticillata	carpetweed	E. Hemisphere	North America	B.C.E.?
Monstera deliciosa	a climbing aroid	Americas	India	1100 C.E.
Morus alba	mulberry tree	E. Hemisphere	Middle America	1500 C.E.
Mucuna pruriens	cowhage	Americas	India, Hawaii	B.C.E.?
Musa x paradisiaca	banana, plantain	E. Hemisphere	Tropical America	B.C.E.?
Myrica gale	bog myrtle	E. Hemisphere	North America	1000 C.E.
Nicotiana tabacum	tobacco	Americas	South China, Egypt	1200 B.C.E.
Ocimum basilicum	basil	Americas	India	1000 C.E.
Opuntia dillenii	prickly pear cactus	Americas	India	B.C.E.?
Osteomeles anthyllidifolia	'Ulei (Hawaiian Rose)	Americas	China, Oceania	1500 C.E.
Pachyrhizus erosus	jicama	Americas	Asia	1000 C.E.
Pachyrhizus tuberosus	jicama, yam bean	Americas	India, China, Oceania	1500 C.E.
Pharbitis hederacea	ivy-leaf morning glory	Americas	India, China	1000 C.E.
Phaseolus lunatus	lima bean	Americas	India	1600 B.C.E.
Phaseolus vulgaris	kidney bean	Americas	India	1600 B.C.E.
Physalis lanceifolia	ground cherry	Americas	China	B.C.E.?
Physalis peruviana	husk tomato	Americas	East Polynesia	1000 C.E.
Plumeria rubra	frangipani	Americas	South Asia	1000 C.E.
Polygonum acuminatum	a knotweed	Americas	Easter Island	1500 C.E.
Portulaca oleracea	purslane	Americas	Eurasia	B.C.E.
Psidium guajava	guava	Americas	China,	B.C.E.?

			Polynesia	
Saccharum officinarum	sugarcane	Oceania	South America	1500 C.E.
Sapindus saponaria	soapberry	Americas	East Polynesia, India	B.C.E.?
Schoenoplectus californicus	totora reed, bulrush	Americas	Easter Island	1300 C.E.
Sisyrhynchium angustifolium	blue-eyed 'grass'	Americas	Greenland	1500 C.E.
Smilax sp.	sarsparilla	Central America	E. Hemisphere	B.C.E.
Solanum candidum/S. lasiocarpum	naranjillo	Americas	Southeast Asia, Oceania,	1500 C.E.
Solanum nigrum	black nightshade	E. Hemisphere?	Mesoamerica	B.C.E.?
Solanum repandum/S. sessiliflorum	Pacific tomato / peach tomato	Americas	Oceania	1500 C.E.
Solanum tuberosum	potato	Americas	Easter Island	1500 C.E.
Sonchus oleraceus	sow thistle	Americas	China	1500 C.E.
Sophora toromiro	toromiro tree	Americas	Easter Island	1300 C.E.
Tagetes erecta	marigold	Americas	India, China	B.C.E.?
Tagetes patula	dwarf marigold	Americas	India, Persia	1000 C.E.
Zea mays	corn, maize	Americas	Eurasia, Africa?	B.C.E.

Where only the name of a genus plus 'sp.' is given, the meaning is that our sources do not provide sufficient information to identify which of two or more species of the genus was transferred, although one assuredly was.

Other Species of Flora from Table 1

We next present summaries of the evidence for 46 other plant species which also have sufficient documentation for decisive transfer. For discussion and documentation of the all investigate flora species, whether accepted ort not, see Appendix I.

Agave sp.

The entire genus *Agave* is of American origin, yet it was represented in Old World biotas of several regions. Already by 1809, Lord Valentia, a traveler in India, observed that agave plants were "in such profusion that it is hardly possible to suppose it could have been introduced from America [i.e., after Columbus]" (Desmond 1992, 201).

When agave plants have been observed growing in Eurasia in recent centuries, scientists have assumed that they were imports via Iberian ships after 1500 C.E. Thus, the shock was understandable when Steffy (1985) reported in the American Journal of Archaeology the discovery of 'agave' fibers mixed with pine resin that served as watertight caulking (between the hull and a sheet of lead covering) in a fourth-century B.C.E. Greek ship that had sunk at Kyrenia, Cyprus. When we asked him about the apparent geographical anomaly of agave in the Mediterranean, Steffy responded (e-mail, 2001), "You wouldn't believe how many people have protested that statement, but I was only repeating the identifications made by professionals [botanists] in respectable laboratories," starting with the Royal Botanic Gardens, Kew. (Only the genus, but no particular species, could be identified.) Furthermore, he has been told by other Mediterranean archaeologists that they too have discovered agave specimens but have not reported them in print (probably because they anticipated hostility from colleagues to the implication of transoceanic voyaging). Some feel that a plant of this genus must have been growing somewhere in the Mediterranean basin, Steffy continued, although no specific botanical evidence for that view has been put forward.

The plausibility of Steffy's find was recently supported by data from a discovery first reported over 70 years ago. At that time, a Mexican archaeologist discovered an apparent Roman figurine head while excavating a site of Aztec Age in central Mexico (García-Payón 1961). Two Mexican scholars recently tracked down that object, along with the archived excavation notes. They established beyond question that the head had indeed come from beneath sealed floors where it had been buried no later than the 1400s, at least a generation before Cortez arrived. A thermoluminescence dating test on the terracotta head put its age at many centuries before Columbus. Stylistic analysis by experts on Roman art has confirmed its manufacture around the second century C.E. (Hristov and Genovés 1999). At the least, this information shows that a (presumably)

Roman ship very probably reached Mexico; a return trip could have carried agave plants, or at least a supply of the fiber, to the Mediterranean.

Anacardium occidentale

A. occidentale is the cashew nut. This tree, native to the Americas, was taken to India in the 16th century by the Portuguese, but it is now clear that it was present long before. The distinctive fruit was clearly represented on a bas-relief at the Bharhut Stupa (second century B.C.E.). Images of the nut had been carved adjacent to renderings of annona (the custard apple), another American fruit (Gupta. 1996, 17; Watt 1888–1893, I, 259; Cunningham 1879). In addition, the cashew bore a name in Sanskrit, *bijara sala* (Balfour 1871–1873, I, 107; III, 409). Sanskritwas only a literary language by the 10th Century C.E.; crop names would not have been absorbed into the lexicon after that time. Since many of our plants had multiple Sanskrit names, this shows that they were common to India long before 1492.

Ananas comosus (syn. *sativa*)

The pineapple originated in Brazil, yet it is shown in a sculpture dated to the fifth century C.E. at a cave temple in Madhya Pradesh, India, as well as at a site in Gujarat, India (Gupta. 1996, 18). A pineapple fruit pictured in an Assyrian bas-relief of the seventh century B.C.E. was confidently identified by the Assyriologist Rawlinson ("The representation is so exact that I can scarcely doubt the pineapple being intended") and was confirmed by Layard, the excavator of the relief (Collins 1951). The fruit is also represented on artifacts from Egypt (Wilkinson 1879) and in an Ankara museum (seen by Johannessen in 1998). An Iron Age monument in the museum at Haifa also shows a pineapple. Zena Halpern of Syosset, NY, (personal communication to Sorenson 2003) has furnished a photograph of a carved stone in a museum in Haifa, Israel, that displays a pineapple on it, although a part of the fruit representation is broken off, rendering the identification less than final. The carving is probably from the Iron Age). Appearance of the fruit in Pompeiian art is firmly documented in the writings of Casella and others published in the December 2002 issue of Pre-Columbiana (322-343).

Annona spp.

At least three species of the annona have been identified in art and referenced in the mythic literature of India. Images of the fruit and leaves of *Annona squamosa* at Bharhut Stupa place the plant in India by the second century B.C.E. (Gupta. 1996, 19–20; Cunningham 1879). The fruit is also seen carved on the gateway at Sanchi, on sculptures excavated from Mathura (Pokharia and Saraswat 1998–1999), and at the Ajanta Caves (Watt

1888–1893, I, 259). Johannessen and Wang (1998, 16–17) illustrate an *A. squamosa* fruit in the hands of a goddess sculpted on the 10th-century C.E. Durga Temple at Aihole, Karnataka, India. The fruit is also depicted at other Hindu and Buddhist temples in the states of Madhya Pradesh, Karnataka, Bengal, and Andhra Pradesh. For example, Bussagli and Sivartamamurti (1978, 189, Fig. 216) picture an eighth-century sculpture of Varuna, lord of the waters, seated with his consort on a makara monster and holding in his hand an annona fruit. Archaeological discovery of annona seeds in a cave on Timor, prior to 1000 C.E., further confirms the Indian art (Glover 1977, 43, 46). Casella 2002b thoroughly documents the presence of *Annona squamosa* in art at Pompeii.

The plant is also mentioned in the traditional literature of India, where it is widely called *sitaphala*, 'the fruit of Sita,' because of a popular belief that Sita, wife of Ramachandra of the Ramayana epic, subsisted on the fruit of this tree while in exile (Gupta. 1996, 19). In Kerala, the tree is called *Ramachakkamaram*, "tree bearing the fruit of Lord Rama" (Nicolson et al. 1988, 50). In Sanskrit, a short name of the tree is *sita* (Watson 1868, 527); it also has a second Sanskrit name, *gunda-gutra*, or *gunda-gatra* (Watson 1868, 181, 527), and Nadkarni (1914, 38) lists two other Sanskrit names, *shubhâ* and *suda*.

Annona reticulata and *A. cherimolia* were also present in India. In Sanskrit, the former was also called *rama-sita* in addition to three other names (Watt 1888–1893, I, 125; Watson 1868; Torkelson 1999, 1646; Int. Lib. Assoc. 1996, 559). Bishagratna (1907, 72) reads it in a text assigned to the sixth century B.C.E. It is still widely cultivated in Kerala, where it bears the name *Ramachakkamaram* (Nicolson et al. 1988, 50). Johannessen (Johannessen and Wang 1998, 156–57, Fig. 7) reports that annona, including *A. cherimolia*, are shown in the hands of multiple sculpted figures on the walls of Indian temples, including the Hoysala temple at Somnathpur, Karnataka (1268 C.E.). Yet, as noted earlier, the annona originated in South America, where *A. cherimolia* is known archaeologically in Peru before the beginning of our era (Towle 1961, 38–9).

Argemone mexicana

The Mexican prickle poppy is another plant of American origin. Today, it is widespread in India. Saraswat et al. (1994, 262, 333, 334) report mention of this plant in the Sanskrit medical treatise *Bhava Prakasha* by Sushrutha (first and second centuries C.E.). An archaeological find of *A. mexicana* seeds at Narhan in Uttar Pradesh shows that the plant was being grown in India, possibly as a medicinal drug, as early as 1100 B.C.E. (Pokharia and Saraswat 1998–1999, 90, 100).

Artemisia vulgaris

This fragrant shrub was well known anciently in Europe and Asia. It was also present in Mexico, where it shared parallel cultural meanings (including medicinal uses) associated particularly with the goddesses Artemis (Greece) and Chalchiuhtlicue (Mexico). Both of them were especially concerned with women and childbirth, as well as being associated with water and marshes (Mackenzie 1924, 201–4; Roys 1931, 310).

Asclepias curassavica

The milkweed, *Asclepias curassavica*, originated in America. In India, it is thoroughly naturalized and occurs commonly as a weed (Chopra et al. 1956, 28). Some Indianists have considered it to be the soma plant of antiquity (Watt 1888–1893, I, 343). A Sanskrit name attests to its age (Int. Lib. Assoc. 1996, 560). In both areas it is much used medicinally.

Bixa orellana

The small tree *Bixa orellana* serves widely in the tropics as a flavorant for food and as a red colorant for food, body paint, and dye (Donkin 1974). It originated in Brazil (Newcomb 1963, 41). We know it was used very early in Peru as shown by excavations at the phenomenal pre-ceramic city of Caral on the central coast, which dates to 2700–2100 B.C.E. (Shady Solís et al. 2001). Early botanists in India assumed this was an indigenous plant because it was so completely naturalized (Donkin 1974). It is not surprising that they should think so, for its having a Sanskrit name (Balfour 1871–1873, I, 177) means that it has been present in India for at least 1000 years and probably much longer.

Capsicum spp.

Chile peppers, *Capsicum* spp., are also American plants. They are mentioned in the *Siva Purana* and *Vamana Purana*, Indian sacred texts dated to the sixth through eighth centuries C.E. (Banerji 1980, 9–10). The Sanskrit name *marichiphalam* was applied to both *C. annuum* and *C. frutescens* (Nadkarni 1914, 86). The *C. annuum* plant and its fruit are naturalistically depicted in stone carvings both at a Shiva temple at Tiruchirapalli, Tamil Nadu (Gupta. 1996, 50), and on a bas-relief dated earlier than the 10th century C.E. at the Prambanan temple complex east of Jogyakarta, Java (Johannessen and Wang, 1998, 28).

Furthermore, in Oceania chili peppers were reported growing in Tahiti in 1768 by Bougainville, who reached that island only eight months after Wallis, its European discoverer (Langdon 1988, 334).

Carica papaya

One variety of papaya was grown in the Marquesas Islands before the arrival of Europeans (Brown 1935, 190). Its name signified 'papaya of the people,' as distinct from a larger, 'Hawaiian papaya,' that Christian missionaries had brought from Hawaii. Brown was confident that the former fruit was pre-European. Because this species is of American origin (Safford 1905, 215–16; Zeven and de Wet 1982, 188), the implication is that native voyagers may have brought it to Polynesia from the east.

Several interesting lines of evidence support voyaging as the mechanism for the plant's arrival. The ethnographer Handy (1930, 131) reported a Marquesan legend to the effect that a double canoe of great size left the islands anciently in search of lands to the east. They were said to have reached a large land called 'Jefiti,' where they left some of their crew before returning to the islands. Sinoto's (1983) excavations in the Marquesas revealed that "great vessels" were being built there in the ninth century C.E. Gifford (1924) considered that the use in the Marquesas of knotted cords as mnemonic devices is "strongly reminiscent of the Peruvian *kipu*," an idea previously put forward by Von den Steinen (1903). Pérez de Barradas (1954) also saw parallels in sculptural styles and in an unusual type of stone bead shared between San Agustín, Colombia, and the Marquesas. Heyerdahl (1996, 149–57) came across a stone statue in the Marquesas (Hivaoa) of a non-Polynesian style (stone sculpture in Polynesia is otherwise virtually unknown except for Easter Island) that Von den Steinen had earlier discovered. It showed long-tailed quadrupeds—felines—(Polynesia had no cats) whose nearest analogues, according to Heyerdahl, were on the monuments of San Agustín, Colombia. A radiocarbon date on charcoal from beneath the Marquesan statue was dated ca. 1300 C.E. The papaya very likely was carried across the 4400-mile ocean gap from the American mainland in the voyage(s) around 1300 C.E. that brought to this eastern Polynesian outpost the mainland notion of a large cat as well as the papaya.

Ceiba pentandra (syn. *Bombax malabaricum*)

Commonly known as the kapok or silk-cotton tree, this plant is of American origin. Brücher (1989, 146–47) considers the center of radiation for the species to be Central America, where it played a significant role in the cosmological myths of the Maya people. A name for the tree has been reconstructed in the proto-Mayan language of the second millennium B.C.E. (Bronson 1966, 262 ff.). It also grew in Peru (Yacovleff and Herrera 1934–1935, 283).

In 1935, De Prez published a representation of the ceiba carved on a monument from Djalatounda, near Sourabaya, Java. This led him to characterize the species as "Indo-American." That Javanese monument is considered to date to 977 C.E. Moreover, Chinese records report the tree growing during the Tang Dynasty (618–907 C.E.) on Hainan Island, where its fibers were being woven into fabric by the Li people (Schafer 1970, 64). At least five Sanskrit names for this species have been reported in India (e.g., Nadkarni 1914, 59; Pullaiah 2002, I, 147) including *sveta salmali* and *kutashalmali*.

Chenopodium ambrosioides

Commonly known as 'Mexican tea,' *C. ambrosioides* has a clear record of ancient cultivation in Asia. When Fa Hien returned to his Chinese homeland in 414 C.E. from a long journey to Buddhist countries, his spotting of this species under cultivation was one of the assurances by which he knew he was actually in China again (Bretschneider 1892, 261–62). But the plant was also ancient in India, for it has three Sanskrit names (Chopra et al. 1956, 61; Torkelson 1999, 1684; Int. Lib. Assoc. 1996, 562), including *sugandhavastuk*. Furthermore, the plant was known in Mesopotamia under the Arabic name *natna* (Thompson 1949, I, 416–36). Yet the species was widespread in Mesoamerica. It has been found archaeologically in southern Mexico as early as the beginning of our era (Martínez 1978, 123), and it bore a pre-Columbian name in Yucatec Mayan (Roys 1931, 262).

Cocos nucifera

The place of origin of the coconut, *Cocos nucifera*, has long been controversial. Early on, Cook (1901, 261–87) argued that the species was native to the Americas, and some other botanists agreed (Guppy 1906, 67; Bailey 1935). Counter arguments, however, later persuaded most plant historians that Asia or the western Pacific was its home (Hill 1929; MacNeish 1992, 259).

Those favoring an Asian homeland extended their argument to claim that the tree was wholly absent from the Western Hemisphere until the Spaniards introduced it. However, Heyerdahl (1965, 461) presented evidence that the tree was being planted for economic purposes on Cocos Island, near the west coast of Panama, before the first Europeans arrived there. Furthermore, traces of coconut fiber had been found in tombs at Ancón, Peru (Harms 1922), and representations of the coconut palm are seen in Peruvian art (Heyerdahl (1965, 461).

Patiño (1976, 54) documented at least five locations on the Pacific coast of the Americas where the coconut was reported by Spanish chroniclers to have been growing shortly after the Conquest and, presumably, before also. Hernández, the 16th-century Spanish naturalist, casually reported the coconut in Peru and Mexico as being the same as in the Old World (1942–1946 [before 1580], II, 507–10). Balboa found coconuts on the Pacific Ocean side of Panama in 1513 (Mendez P. 1944). Even anti-diffusionist Merrill (1954, 267) judged the presence of the nut in pre-Columbian America to be "most certain," agreeing with cultural historian Julian Steward (1949), who accepted the ancient American occurrence of the coconut to have been "established beyond reasonable doubt." Most recently, and most definitively, Robinson et al. (2000) excavated coconut remains in southern Guatemala dated around 700 C.E., confirming a previous archaeological find at Copán, Honduras, that dated it three centuries earlier. These data leave no question that the coconut was grown in the Americas before Columbus' time.

But might the tree have reached the Americas from across the Pacific by drift nuts that washed ashore and sprouted? Despite off-the-cuff claims that coconuts can drift long distances and remain viable when cast ashore, experimental research has shown that there is a limit of viability of about 3000 miles (Dennis and Gunn 1971). (Coconuts were carried both atop the raft, Kon-Tiki, and attached to the vessel, floating in the water, but only those that were on top germinated after the voyage (Heyerdahl 1950, 104, 204). Pacific islands with coconuts are all more distant from the Americas than that. Ward and Brookfield (1992) did the definitive review of the literature, but they remained inconclusive on this particular question. They also did an extensive computer simulation of patterns of coconut drift that shows that it is highly unlikely that drift nuts would have reached the Americas from the nearest Pacific Island loci. (The coconut was absent from the Atlantic Ocean/Caribbean region until introduced there by the Portuguese.) Whether drift nuts could successfully sprout and mature into trees on the strand has also been disputed contentiously. Accordingly, no cases are known of coconuts having grown on Australian shores (Ward and Brookfield 1992). Carriage of the nuts by Pacific voyagers and intentional planting at an American destination is the explanation now preferred by the best-informed scientists (Harries 1978, 271; Dennis and Gunn 1971), and we consider it the only convincing scenario.

Couroupita guianensis

The 'cannon-ball tree,' *Couroupita guianensis*, is native to South America or the West Indies. It now grows in South India where it is called *naga lingam* and has a unique meaning in Hindu symbolism. The tree bears flowers that grow directly out of the trunk and main limbs. Stamens and pistil of the blossom fuse in a manner that gives the appearance of a miniature lingam (stylized penis, symbol of cosmic generative power) facing the hovering hood of a naga (cobra). *Naga lingam* flowers in India today are left as offerings before sacred stone lingams in temples to honor Shiva (Johannessen, personal observation, 1996). The only reason one can imagine for transporting this New World tree to India would be that a worshipper of Shiva visited the Americas, where he saw the unique flower (no doubt with astonishment) and felt that it ought to grow in India, the homeland of Shiva. No non-Shivaite would have paid particular attention to the blossom, and indeed the plant plays no role in Mesoamerican iconography as far as we know.

Gupta. (1996, 58) names four temples in Tamil Nadu state where the *naga lingam* flower is carved in stone. On the basis of this art, she considers that the plant reached India in "very early times."

Cucurbita spp.

Four species of American cucurbits were present in Asia before Columbus' day: *Cucurbita ficifolia*, the chilacayote; *C. moschata*, the crookneck squash; *C. pepo*, the pumpkin; and *C. maxima*, the winter, or Hubbard squash.

That the moschata was an inter-hemispheric transfer has unusually clear evidence. The species' American origin is unquestioned. Archaeological remains in Peru go back to the fifth millennium before the present (Yarnell 1970, 225; Towle 1961, 69), and the plant may go back even further in Mexico (Brücher 1989, 260–61).

C. moschata (Chinese, *nangua*) is mentioned in medieval Chinese medical recipes, for example, as recorded by Jia Ming (1966) in a text dated to 1473 C.E. (Johannessen and Wang 1998, 25). Furthermore, the moschata squash shows up in Chinese paintings by Shen Zhou, who died in 1509 (before Magellan's arrival in Asia). Effigy pots modeled in the characteristic shape of moschata squash date to the Song (960–1279 C.E.) and Tang (618–905 C.E.) Dynasties (Johannessen and Wang 1998, 25, Fig. 10).

Vernacular names in use in India in the 19th century for this economically important plant included *kumhra* and *kumra* (Watt 1888–1892, II, 640), while from Yucatan we find the Mayan botanical term "*Kum*, or *Kuum, Cucurbita moschata*, Duch." (Roys 1931, 258). Roys quotes an early Spanish record that, "There are [in Yucatan] the calabazas [bottle gourds] of Spain, and there is also another sort of native ones [sic], which the Indians call kum," that is, the cucurbits (Roys 1931, 258). The similarities of names for the same species in Mexico and India strongly suggest, although of course they do not prove, that direct contact tied the areas together linguistically as well as botanically.

For another American cucurbit, *C. pepo*, the pumpkin, there is also good evidence that it grew in both hemispheres. Levey (1966, 315) discovered in a ninth-century medical text from India mention of the pumpkin as an ingredient (at least the term that was used for the ingredient was the one later applied to the pumpkin). Furthermore, the plant had three Sanskrit names (Watson 1868, 319, 327). Common names for the pumpkin in India also echo the *kum* root in Mayan: *cumbuly, kumbala, kumhra, kúmara* (Watt 1888–1893, II, 641; Watson 1868, 92, 119, 310, 311). And texts by the 16th-century Chinese botanist Li Shizhen, which were based on classic Chinese botanical and medical texts (Bretschneider 1882, 59), also mention the pumpkin. The writing of Jia Sixie in the sixth century also mentions the pumpkin. (Bretschneider 1882, 77–79).

Cucurbita ficifolia was once thought to be of Afro-Asiatic origin, but Bronson (1966, 262 ff.) reported that a name for the species has been reconstructed for the proto-Mayan language dating to the second millennium B.C.E. Excavated specimens were found dated to the third or fourth millennium B.C.E. at Huaca Prieta, Peru (Yarnell 1970, 225; Towle 1961, 90).

C. O. Sauer discussed *C. ficifolia* presence as a crop (often grown for yak feed) in India, Tibet, and western China (Newcomb 1963, 29). In Asia, it is grown over an extraordinary range of environmental conditions, and accordingly its forms vary greatly, suggesting a long period of adaptation. The New World cucurbit does not vary so much. The Old and New World plants are morphologically indistinguishable and are fertile when crossbred. How and when did this cucurbit reach Asia, and how long did it take to adapt to such a wide range of environments there? Quite surely, that process required more than the four or five centuries since it might have been introduced to Asia by 16th-century European ships (Newcomb 1963, 29). The most believable explanation for the transfer involves a transpacific voyage to India that carried *C. ficifolia* along incidentally with more valuable cucurbits.

Cucurbita maxima is another plant that originated in the Americas but was grown in Asia. Its remains have been found by archaeologists in Peru dating before the beginning of our era (Towle 1961, 90), and Brücher (1989, 262–64) speaks of "irrefutable proofs" of its South American origin.

Nadkarni (1914, 129) gives Sanskrit, *punyalatha* and *dadhiphala*, for *C. maxima*, and its widespread cultivation and adaptation in Asia confirm its considerable antiquity. Levey (1966, 315) confirms *C. maxima*'s pre-Columbian presence by finding the species mentioned in a ninth-century medical text in India.

Mellén Blanco (1986, 211) interprets the wording of the account of the 18th-century González expedition to Easter Island as showing that *C. maxima* was growing there at the time of European discovery. That seems assured by the fact that altogether some 13 other species of American plants were present on Easter Island.

Curcuma longa

Curcuma longa, the turmeric plant, is of Southeast Asian origin (Newcomb 1963, 61; Brown 1931, 162–63). In Asia, it carried Sanskrit names (including *haridra*, *nisha*, and *rajani*), as well as names in Hebrew, Arabic, and Chinese (Watson 1868, 189, 205–6, 248; Watt 1888–1892, II, 659; 1892, 1–3, 231, 417, 432; U. Melbourne). Nevertheless, the plant was grown by people in the remote eastern Andes in South America, where it was used in the same ways as in Asia (Sopher 1950).

Datura spp.

One or more American species of Datura were used in Eurasia from ancient times as a medicinal, aphrodisiac, and hallucinogenic drug. The taxonomy of this genus has been confused, as historical sources have referred to its several species variously and imprecisely. But at least *Datura metel* (*meteloides, innoxia, fastuosa, alba*) and *D. stramonium* (*tatula, patula*) were definitely present (Watt 1888, III, 40–1; Burkill 1966, I, 778–79). At least five Sanskrit names are known for one form or another of datura (Nadkarni 1914, 140–45; Chopra et al. 1956, 91; Chopra et al. 1958, 134; Torkelson 1999, 1711–12; Int. Lib. Assoc. 1996, 564; Watson 1868, 257) including *dhattura, dusthara, unmatta, durdhura*. A fragment of a datura plant was excavated from the site of Sanghol in the Punjab that dates between the first and third centuries C.E. (Pokharia and Saraswat 1998–1999, 90). The Greeks are thought by some (despite the argument to the contrary by Symon and Haegi 1991) to have used a datura at Delphi to induce oracular visions, and the Romans are also believed to have used *D. metel* (Burkill 1966, I, 778–79).

Datura use was commonplace in western North America and Mesoamerica (Hernandez 1942–43 [before 1580], II, 442; Ramírez 2003) and one or more species are recognized as having originated in the latter area (Luna Cavazos et al. 2000; Nicolson et al. 1988, 247). Reko (1919, 115) saw significance in the similarity between the Náhuatl (Aztec) name, *toloache*, and Chinese *tolo-wan* for *Datura* spp., while Kroeber considered that a coastal California cult that involved the practice of ingesting datura might have arrived from "islands of the Pacific" (Kroeber 1928, 395; DuBois 1908, 72).

Helianthus annuus

This is the sunflower, an American native. Its time depth is suggested by the occurrence of a name for sunflower in the Proto-Mayan language perhaps of the third millennium B.C.E. (England 1992, 161). Archaeological finds of plant remains in southern Mexico (of the third millennium B.C.E.; see Lentz et al. 2001) fix the domestication of *H. annuus* in Mesoamerica. Previously it had been supposed first domesticated in eastern North America at a somewhat later date.

Images of sunflower blossoms have been discovered by Johannnessen and Wang in the sacred sculptural art of India (Johannessen 1998b). In both the art and references in texts—some going back as much as two millennia—there is a strong association of this plant and its flower with the sun.

When sculpted in Hindu art, the flower played a role in the cultural context of solar observations, where it marked iconographically pivotal moments in the annual cycle of the sun. Shivaite Hindu temples, especially those of the 11th to 13th centuries C.E., were sometimes oriented to sunrise or sunset points on the horizon on key calendar dates. Given this ritual setting for the sunflower, it is no surprise that a Sanskrit name for the plant, *suria-mukhi*, was known (Watt 1888–1893, IV, 209; Torkelson 1999, 1749; Chopra et al. 1956, 131); also *adityabhakta, adityabhakta, divaakaraha, suuryakamalaha, suuryakaanti*, and *arkakantha* (U. of Melbourne). The flowers were also engraved on temple doorways and on images of Nandi, the bull that served as Shiva's steed, and by association symbolized Shiva himself (Johannessen 1998b). (The fact that Heyerdahl (1986, 2, 176) found carved sunflower designs on stones in the Maldives, located precisely at the equator, also could be part of this South Asian complex of ideas.)

Live sunflowers were known to Indian artists, which is particularly confirmed by a carving on a temple pillar at Pattadakal, Karnataka State (Johannessen and Wang 1998, 15–6). A long-tailed Indian parrot is shown sitting atop a large seed head from the edge of which the bird has plucked a few seeds. No other seed-head looks like this nor has a stem capable of supporting a parrot. Gupta. (1996) also discusses and illustrates these flowers decorating 11th–13th century Indian temples.

Johannessen has observed that maize images occur in temple statuary along with sunflowers, tying two American species together in a single ritual context. In Karnataka, sculptured female figures on temples are depicted holding ears of maize (see the discussion above), and they also have sunflower blooms below the bottoms of their skirts. (Different figures show whole, half, or quarter images of the flowers; Johannessen suggests that these images communicated information about the ritual calendar – see Johannessen and Wang 1998.) Moreover, a sunflower carved beneath the tail of a sculpted, recumbent Nandi in the doorway of Halebid Temple in Karnataka is fully illuminated at each solstice sunrise (from alternate sides, winter and summer). The same Nandi is placed so as to allow dawn light to pass over the sunflower between the bull's left horn and above the ear so as to penetrate deep into the temple at equinox and shine on the Shiva lingam in the inner sanctum. Also, the carved blooms on the support for the tail of Nandi are completely shaded on the equinox (Johannessen 1998b, 354–60). At other Shiva temples, the solar azimuths differ, but the sculpted art typically involves the sunflower at sunrise or sunset as a calendrical indicator.

Lagenaria siceraria

The bottle gourd, *Lagenaria siceraria*, was discovered by Bird (1948) in pre-ceramic levels dating to the Third Millennium B.C.E. on the coast of Peru. Its discovery was hailed by diffusionists as proof that ancient voyagers had crossed the Pacific (Carter 1950). Botanists previously had assumed that the species had not reached the Americas until imported by the Spaniards. Whitaker was the botanist who first identified *L. siceraria* at the archaeological site of Huaca Prieta, Peru (Whitaker and Bird 1949). He considered that, since bottle gourd plants from both hemispheres are closely comparable and occurred early in Peru, the burden of proof lay on those who, until then, had claimed that it had been colonial-era Europeans who introduced it from the Old World. It is also reported that the bottle gourd appeared in Mexico as early as perhaps 9000 B.C.E. and in Peru at about the same time, according to other researchers (Brücher 1989, 265; Heiser 1989, 475).

However, the species was found in Fifth-Dynasty Egyptian tombs (Whitaker and Carter 1954, 697–700), and in India it bears Sanskrit names (Nadkarni 1914, 213; Pullaiah 2002, II, 323), *tiktalabu*. Lathrap (1977) and Schwerin (1970) proposed that fishing boats bearing gourds drifted westward from Africa to South America at a very early date (14,000 B.C.E. according to Lathrop and 5700 B.C.E. according Schwerin). But there is no evidence for domesticated plants in West Africa at times even close to those dates. Patiño (1976, 244) and also Mangelsdorf, MacNeish, and Willey (1964, 441) doubted an Atlantic natural drift hypothesis because the bottle gourd was unknown in the Antilles or eastern South America. Brücher (1989, 265–66) wondered rhetorically "why it did not arrive before the Pleistocene, if the natural dispersal of floating fruits was so easy." Furthermore, "if *Lagenaria* had in one or another way come from Africa, the puzzling question remains how it crossed the whole American continent and appeared so early [in pre-2500 B.C.E. Peru] on the Pacific side?" Clearly, there is no good answer to Brücher's questions, so the plant's arrival via Pacific voyaging remains the superior explanation.

Considerable experimentation has gone into the question of whether the bottle gourd could have floated across the ocean, arrived in viable condition, and become self-established on shore (Towle 1952; Carter 1953; Whitaker and Carter 1954). Results of experiments on how long floating gourds remain viable have been inconclusive, perhaps because some experiments were carried out in tanks, where a gourd would not have been subjected to the boring organisms that are encountered in the open sea. The results are summarized by Camp (1954) to the effect that, while a gourd might have crossed from Africa and might have sprouted on shore in the Americas, there would still be no satisfactory explanation of how the offspring became established in the plant's normal habitat, which is inland.

Whistler (1990, 120; 1991) concluded that, contrary to the old picture of a slow spread from island group to island group eastward across the Pacific, which resulted from early misidentifications of the bottle gourd in western Polynesia, *L. siceraria* never grew there, while it was common in eastern Polynesia. "The most likely hypothesis," Whistler concluded, "is that it was introduced [by voyagers] to eastern Polynesia from South America." The coconut "may have moved eastward on the same roundtrip Polynesian voyage as the bottle gourd."

Most recently, Erickson et al. (2005) have established on the basis of new genetic studies that African bottle gourds could not be ancestral to the American plants. They propose that the Asiatic ancestor, rather, was brought to the Americas via Beringia on the order of 10,000 years ago, either by land migrants or coastal voyagers. (Given conditions and times needed for travel in that area the former suggestion is incredible.) But coastal voyaging is plausible and in agreement with the proposals of Fladmark, Dixon, and others (see above). If such travel proves to be the means by which this gourd came from Asia to the Americas, the idea of a mid-latitude crossing is unnecessary to account for the two-continent distribution. But this still leaves the western Polynesian gap pointed out by Whistler unexplained. If drift had been the primary mechanism in the gourd's spread, that gap would not have occurred. The only acceptable explanation seems to be that a voyage was made from the Americas to eastern Polynesia bearing the gourd, along with up to a dozen other plants discussed in this document. It is this implied transfer that leads us to list *Lagenaria siceraria* in Table 1.

Luffa cylindrica (syn. aegyptiaca)

Luffa cylindrica is an Old World plant known as the 'vegetable sponge.' It was grown in South and Southeast Asia (Brücher 1989, 267) where it played a significant role in medicine (Nayar and Singh 1998, 14–15). It has also been cultivated for a long time in the Americas, according to Heiser (1989; 1985); he allows that it might have traveled by ship across the Pacific. Kosakowsky et al. (2000, 199) excavated pottery on the Pacific coast of Guatemala dating around 1200 B.C.E. that had been decorated by daubing the pot's surface with paint using as a tool the unique cut stem end of *L. cylindrica*.

Macroptilum lathyroides

The minor pulse *Macroptilum lathyroides* has the English vernacular name of 'phasey bean.' It has been considered part of a distinct group within the genus *Phaseolus* but has recently been made a separate genus. Like several species of *Phaseolus*, which we will discuss below, the phasey bean is of American origin (Smartt 1969, 452). Along with two other American beans, *M. lathyroides* has been excavated by Pokharia and Saraswat (1998–1999, 99) at several Neolithic and Chalcolithic sites in India of the second millennium B.C.E. Phasey bean specimens have also been recorded by Vishnu-Mittre, Sharma, and Chanchala (1986) from deposits of the Malwa and Jorwe cultures (1600–1000 B.C.E.) at Diamabad in Ahmednagar Dist.,

Maharashtra State, India.

Manihot sp.

Pullaiah (2002, II, 346–47) points out two Sanskrit names, *darukandah* and *kalpakandah*, for *Manihot esculenta*, i.e., manioc, or cassava. This is surprising since there is no other sort of evidence yet for its pre-Columbian transfer to India. A third Sanskrit name for *M. esculenta* is *karrapendalamu* according to the Multilingual Multiscript Plant Name Database at http://www.plantnames.unimelb.edu.au/Sorting/Manihot.html maintained by the University of Melbourne.

The first European botanists to discover it growing on Easter Island found that it was called by the same name, *yuca*, by which it was known widely in the Americas (Langdon 1988, 326–28; Mellén Blanco 1986, 13). We suppose that a voyage carried the plant there from the continent (Heyerdahl 1964, 126). It may also have been known in the Marquesas, for in 1939, young Heyerdahl and his bride, living on rustic Hivaoa, were taught by relatively unacculturated natives how to grow bitter manioc and process its starch (Heyerdahl 1996).

Maranta arundinacea

The tuberous shrub *Maranta arundinacea*, or arrowroot, was grown in Central America up to 6000 years ago (Piperno 1999, 126). It is a vegetatively reproduced plant, so it could not have crossed the Pacific by floating. Yet in India, Aiyer (1956, 44) has recorded the Sanskrit term, *kuvai*, for the species, and Pullaiah (2002, 348) gives *tavakshiri* and *tugaksiri*. Furthermore, it is mentioned in South India in the Tamil-language texts, *Malaipadukadam* and *Mathuraikanji*, that were written long preceding the arrival of Portuguese ships in India.

Mimosa pudica

Mimosa pudica, the 'sensitive plant,' was probably native to Brazil. It is called 'sensitive' because its leaves abruptly fold up when they are touched. It was known to the pre-Spanish Maya (Roys 1931, 267). But there were seven Sanskrit names for it (Watson 1868, 347; Nadkarni 1914, 233; MMPND) *lajjalu, samipatra, samanga, jalakarika, rakthapadi, namaskari*, and *khadiraka*. That means that it was known in India centuries before European voyagers could have brought it from the Americas. The same plant was present in the Marquesas, though perhaps nowhere else in the eastern Pacific. It very likely reached those islands by a separate voyage from the Americas.

Mirabilis jalapa

The widely appreciated flower, *Mirabilis jalapa*, is called the 'four o'clock' from its habit of opening its blossoms only in the late afternoon. Zeven and de Wet (1982, 177) report that South America is the center of this genus' diversity and its apparent place of origin. Roys (1931, 291) documented a pre-Columbian Mayan-language name for it, and Hernandez (1942 [before 1580], I, 194–95) identified two varieties that were growing on the Mexican Mesa Central in the 16th century.

Once again, we find a plant of American origin in ancient India. Five or six Sanskrit names were in use for the four o'clock. Torkelson (1999, 1786) provides *krishnakeli*; Balfour (1871–1873, III, 282) and Watson (1868) give *bahu-bumi* and *sundia-ragum*; and Pullaiah (2002, 361) reports *sandhya-rāga, trisandh*, and *krsnakeli* (sic). To explain such a proliferation of names, we must suppose that the four o'clock was present in India from an early time. It is not credible to suppose that its presence in India was due to fortuitous oceanic drift from half way around the world. Ayurvedic medical practioners also report *sandhyakuli*.

Mollugo verticillata

The carpetweed, *Mollugo verticillata*, was shown by Chapman et al. (1974, 411–12) to have been found in archaeological digs at early sites in both the Americas (it was distributed in North, Middle, and South America) and Europe, yet the plant's origin is said to be China (MOBOT 2003). It is one of those weeds whose favorite habitat is the disturbed ground that results from husbandry.

Monstera deliciosa

The large climbing aroid, *Monstera deliciosa*, is native to Central America. It is represented on sculptures of medieval age in India. Gupta. (1996, 108–9) describes and pictures temple scenes where not only do the distinctive leaves of this giant philodendron provide background for scenes of sacred art, but the distinctive fruit is also visible. In one such scene, the fruit is shown on a plate held by an aide alongside Vishnu. The fruit tastes like a mixture of pineapple and banana and was much esteemed in both hemispheres (Lundell 1937, 35; Burkill 1966, II, 151).

Morus alba

The white mulberry, *Morus alba*, has long been one of the plants essential to Chinese civilization. Its leaves have been used to feed silkworms for at least 3000 years, and mulberry bark was used to manufacture paper (Bretschneider 1892, 128; Watt 1888–1893, V, 280). The genus originated in the Old World.

Soon after the Spaniards subdued the native people of the Antilles, they launched a plan to raise silkworms there in order to take advantage of the strong European market for silk. In central Mexico, too, the conquistadors launched a silk industry, utilizing worms and trees imported from the Mediterranean area (Borah 1943, 5–14). Nevertheless, Las Casas, who died in 1522, said, concerning the Antilles, where he was a planter before his ordination as a priest, that there were "as many mulberries as weeds" already growing in those islands before the intentional importation of the European trees (1875–1876, IV, 379–80). Presumably, they grew on the mainland also. So at least one species of *Morus* was in Middle America before the Spaniards arrived, although its modern botanical identification is uncertain. Nevertheless, Von Hagen (1944, 67) considered that all three of the *Morus* species most often recognized, *M. alba*, *M. nigra*, and *M. rubra*, "may ... have been present in Mexico and used for their bark." Tozzer (1941, 195) translated Bishop Landa's account (ca. 1566) of life in Yucatan as reporting the presence of "two kinds of mulberry plant, very fresh and fine." The two kinds he referred to may have been *M. alba* (the most common species) and either *M. nigra* or *M. rubra*.

Making paper from bark had a long history in Mesoamerica. Von Hagen noted that trees whose bark was made into paper (in colonial days) by the Otomí Indians, a relatively unacculturated native people of central Mexico, included one "which has been identified [in the taxonomy of over 60 years ago] as *Morus celtifolia*, a paper mulberry similar to the plant used by many Asiatic papermakers" (1944, 50, 51, 58–59, 67).

Making bark cloth and paper of mulberry bark is of particular significance because of a pair of exemplary studies by Paul Tolstoy (1963, 1966). He demonstrated that the bark cloth/paper complex of Mesoamerica was parallel in great detail to bark-processing methods in island Southeast Asia. Meanwhile, MacNeish et al. (1967, 85) excavated a stone bark beater in the Tehuacán Valley of Mexico that they considered so similar to beaters of Java and the Celebes that they found it "extremely difficult" to account for the degree of similarity by "independent invention" (the only alternative explanation for the similarity being transmission of the artifact form and function across the Pacific). Mulberry tree starts probably accompanied the bark-beater when Asian voyagers carried knowledge of the complex process across the Pacific in "the early part of the first millennium B.C.E." (Tolstoy 1963). (When ancestors of the Maori left central Polynesia to settle New Zealand, they considered bark cloth so essential, they carried mulberry starts with them; see Von Hagen 1944, 23.) While the *Morus* species involved in the Mesoamerican industry still need to be identified definitively, it is evident that at least one species reached the Americas with Asian or Oceanian voyagers who not only brought the plant but also carried the complex technology of turning bark into cloth and paper. We are supposing here that the most likely species was the Chinese mainstay, *M. alba*.

Meanwhile, if, as Brücher (1989, 132) suggests, *Morus rubra* had an

American origin, then the question arises, how did it reach Asia, where it was not uncommon?

Mucuna pruriens

M. pruriens (syn. prurita) is commonly called 'cowhage,' or 'cow-itch' in English (Oxford English Dictionary, 2nd ed., 1082). The pods are covered with barbed hairs that cause severe itching. The hairy part was sometimes ingested as a vermifuge, while the plant's roots served to make a tonic. The seeds have been considered aphrodisiac in India since Sanskritic times (Watt 1888–1893, V, 286; Watson 1868, 263). Balfour (1871–1873, III, 394–95) listed the Sanskrit name *atmagupta* (the secret self) for cowhage; Watson (1868, 11) added *alkushee*, and Nadkarni (1914, 242–43) gave *kapikachchu*. Banerji (1980, 26, v, vii) also has *adhyanda*. Such a varied lexicon indicates that the plant was long familiar in India. That is further confirmed by Banerji's note of its mention in the <u>Satapatha Brahmana</u>, a text dated in its earliest form before the rise of Buddhism.

However, the plant is of tropical American origin. For Mayan, Roys (1931, 235) gives the name, *chiican*, for it and says, "This is the English cow-itch."

Musa spp.

The terms 'banana' and 'plantain' have been a source of confusion in botanical discussions because the two supposed 'species,' *Musa sapientum* and *Musa paradisiaca*, were never established as bona fide species. Cytogenetic analysis demonstrated in the 1950s that most of the bananas or plantains commonly grown contain varying proportions of genomic contributions by hybridization from two base species, *M. balbisiana* (B-genome) and *M. acuminata* (A-genome) (Simmonds 1966; Nicolson et al. 1988, 297). In this publication, we speak of a single species, *Musa balbisiana* x *acuminata*, covering what the earlier literature termed both 'bananas' and 'plantains.' (Some other 'bananas,' however, did not originate from those two genomes.)

A notion commonly held by scientists and historians is that there were no bananas or plantains in the Americas before the Spaniards introduced them. However, when Sapper (1934) studied Native American names for *Musa*, he concluded that bananas/plantains had to have been present in South America no later than the first millennium C.E. to account for the diversity and distribution of names. Smole (1980) reached about the same conclusion from ethnographic and ecological study of plantains among peoples of Brazil and Venezuela. Moreover, a word has been reconstructed in the proto-Mayan language dating to the second millennium B.C.E. that is glossed by Kaufman and Norman (1984; followed by England 1992, 25) as *plátano*, banana. Ethnohistorical documents also attest to pre-Columbian cultivation of "bananas" in Mexico and Guatemala (McBryde 1945, 36; Spores 1965, 971–72; Roys 1931, 218). Archaeological finds of probable banana leaves from Peruvian tombs (Harms 1922, 166) seem to confirm these data.

The invalidity of the claimed isolation of the New World in relation to the banana/plantain was clear enough to persuade the anti-diffusionist critic E. D. Merrill (1954; see also Heyerdahl 1964, 123) to grant that "We may reasonably admit that one, or a few, of the numerous Polynesian plantain varieties may have ... " reached the Amazon Basin before Columbus. Considering its source, this statement constitutes an admission of the strength of the evidence for the pre-Columbian presence of the genus *Musa* in the New World.

Myrica gale

Bog myrtle, *Myrica gale*, is found on both sides of the North Atlantic, although it is now absent from Iceland and Greenland. Its pollen is found in Iceland in excavated strata from Norse saga times, and possibly also in Greenland (Thorarinsson 1942, 46). It is often supposed by biogeographers that various plants growing on both sides of the North Atlantic, including this species, date back to Cretaceous times, before continental drift widened the North Atlantic Ocean gap. Nevertheless, Thorarinsson supposes that the Norse brought this particular plant to North America because they sometimes used it instead of hops to brew their beer. Since no other scenario for the plant's North American distribution made sense to him, he suggested medieval voyaging as the means. We find his argument convincing.

Pachyrhizus spp.

Data are unavailable to allow us to distinguish consistently and certainly in the literature between *Pachyrhizus erosus* (called 'yam,' but of the family Fabaceae, not Dioscoreaceae) and *P. tuberosus* 'yam bean'), both of which are called *jícama* in Hispanic America. Today's favored view is that *P. tuberosus* was native to the headwaters of the Amazon in northwestern South America (Brücher 1989, 44). It was commonly cultivated in ancient Peru, fossil remains having come from tombs at Paracas (before our era). The plant is also shown in Nazca-period art (Yacovleff and Herrera 1934–1935, 281–82). Several biotypes of *P. erosus* grow wild in Mesoamerica (Brücher 1989, 84–85). The Mayan name is *chicam* (from which the word *jícama* was derived). From the earliest accounts Patiño (1976, 33) mapped the distribution of both species in South America at the time of the Spaniard's arrival.

One or the other species is cultivated in the Philippines and China to such an extent that it has been claimed to be of East Asiatic origin

(MacNeish 1992, 260). Watt (1888–1893, VI, Pt. 1, 3) said the same thing for *P. angulatus* (syn. *erosus*), based in part on the fact that the plant bore a Sanskrit name, *sankhálu*. Both data suggest that transfer from the Americas took place anciently.

P. tuberosus is called *doushu*, or *tugua*, in modern China (Johannessen and Wang 1998, 26–27). A text dated 1736 C.E. describes this plant as having a "root ... quite big, greenish-white in color" which "tastes sweet and fragile or soft-crunchy to eat." The name of the plant was already in use in the Song Dynasty (before 1182 C.E.) to denote a plant whose description was so similar that it cannot be anything but this currently recognized species. Archaeologist K. C. Chang (1970, 177) and other Chinese scholars accept that *P. tuberosus* was present in China in pre-Columbian times.

Phaseolus spp.

The common, or kidney, bean, *Phaseolus vulgaris*, and the lima bean, *P. lunatus*, also had an American origin. Specimens of *P. vulgaris* are known at ca. 4000 B.C.E. in Mexico (Pickersgill and Heiser 1977, 810–11) and before 2000 B.C.E. in Peru (Yen 1963, 112). The orthodox view is that they reached the Old World only when Portuguese traders brought them to Asia around 1500 C.E.

All botanists have not agreed, however, that these beans were absent from the Eastern Hemisphere. In connection with their landmark research on cotton, Hutchinson, Silow, and Stephens (1947, 138) accepted a bi-hemispheric distribution of *Phaseolus* and considered the widespread use of beans in Asia to constitute satisfactory evidence for pre-Columbian contact. Hutchinson was reported in 1961 to be still "working on the genetics of American beans" (Bushnell 1961), but his research was never published.

However, now the problem is resolved definitively. *Phaseolus vulgaris*, *P. lunatus*, and the phasey bean, *Phaseolus lathyroides* (reclassified as *Macroptilium lathyroides*, per Walker 1976, 598), have all been discovered in multiple archaeological sites in India of the second millennium B.C.E. Pokharia and Saraswat (1998–1999, 99) report that *Phaseolus* "... beans of American origin have been encountered from proto-historic sites in peninsular India." *P. vulgaris* was recorded from the pre-Prabhas and Prabhas cultures at Prabhas Patan, Junagadh Dist., Gujarat, dated from 1800 B.C.E. to 600 C.E. They also came from Chalcolithic Inamgaon (about 1600 B.C.E.), Pune Dist., Maharashtra, and from Neolithic Tekkalkota, Bellary Dist., Karnataka, with a radiocarbon date of 1620 B.C.E. *P. vulgaris*, *P. lunatus*, and the phasey bean have also been recorded by Vishnu-Mittre, Sharma, and Chanchala (1986) in deposits of the Malwa and Jorwe cultures (1600–1000 B.C.E.) at Diamabad in Ahmednagar Dist., Maharashtra. The phasey bean was also found at the Sanghol site (Pokharia and Saraswat 1998–1999, 99), dated in early C.E. times. Plant names provide supportive data. Levey

(1973, 55; 1966, 16) found that "The medieval Arabic term for kidney bean [i.e., *P. vulgaris*] is *lubiya*. It is *lubbu* in Akkadian and *lu.úb* in Sumerian .... In Sanskrit and Hindustani, however, it is *simbi* and *sim* respectively ...."

It may be of interest at this point to mention that we have noted direct evidence for the presence in Asia long before Columbus of the four classic foods in the Mesoamerican diet: maize, cucurbits, chiles, and beans.

Physalis spp. in general

The ground cherry, or winter cherry (or husk tomato), seems to refer, at least in the older literature, to more than one species of *Physalis*. The sources are not consistent in their terminology (see the sources cited under *Physalis lanceifolia* in the Appendix). *P. lanceifolia*, *P. philadelphica* (Hernández 1942–1946 [before 1580], I, 283; Brücher 1989, 276), *P. pubescens*, *P. lanceolata* (Index Kewensis), *P. indica* (Nadkarni 1914, 298), *P. alkekengi* (Bretschneider 1882, 32), *P. angula* (MOBOT 2003; Roys 1931), and perhaps *P. minima* (Gunther 1934, 468–71) sometimes may be conspecific. Although the origin of the genus was unquestionably in the Americas as a protected weed, these fruits were also known in India (Bretschneider 1882, 32; 1892, 43; the plant had a Sanskrit name, *rajaputrika*, *mrdukunjika*, *upakunjika*, and *cheerapotha* according to Chopra et al. 1956, 191; Torkelson 1999, 1808; and Ayurvedic Medicinal Plants, 2012), in China (Bretschneider 1882, 1892), and in Greece (Gunther 1934, 468–71). At least some of these cultivars are descriptively equivalent and leave questions of how the taxonomy and distribution of the 'ground cherry' are to be explained. The cultivated species and presumably the genus originated in the Americas (see Brown 1935, 257-5; Brücher 1989, 275–77, and Zeven and de Wet 1982, 181). To us, the field identifications fall into two species that had Old and New World distributions.

Physalis lanceifolia and *Physalis peruviana*

The former (ground cherry, winter cherry) is synonymized by Index Kewensis with *P. lanceolata* and by MOBOT with *P. angulata*.

Chopra et al. (1956, 191–92) provide a pair of Sanskrit names: *rajaputrika* (also Torkelson 1999, 1808), and *lakshmipriya*, the latter said specifically to be from "tropical America." We take the Sanskrit name to mean that *P. lanceifolia* was known in India while the language was colloquially active.

P. peruviana, the winter cherry, also called the 'Cape gooseberry,' or 'Brazil cherry,' seems to have reached both Asia and Polynesia before European influence could have carried it there. Balfour (1871–1873, IV, 562) cites *P. peruviana* as growing in India, while noting its American origin. Furthermore, this particular species had a Sanskrit name of its own, different from that for *P. lanceifolia* (Chopra et al. 1956, 192).

Occurrence of *P. peruviana* in the Marquesas, Easter Island (Heyerdahl 1996; 1964, 126), and Hawaii (Hillebrand 1888, 310) was most plausibly due to voyages from the Americas to the islands (Brown 1935, 257–58).

Plumeria rubra
This plant grew and had a native name of great linguistic and mythological depth on Rotuma in the Fijian archipelago. "The Plumeria ... is a New World plant; its presence in Rotuma is certainly due to introduction [from abroad] at some [ancient] period ...." (Kelley 1957, 236).

Bakhuizen van den Brink identified a 12th-century bas-relief representation of a plant from Borobudur, Java, as *Plumeria acuminata*, which occurred widely in temple contexts in India, amidst several other flowers of Mesoamerican origin. This suggests the need for further investigation of the history and distribution of that species along with *P. rubra*. But at least the linguistic link is certain for an Oceanic transfer from the Americas.

P. rubra and *P. acuminate* both appear in India prior to the 15th Century C.E. (Parotta, 2001; Pullaiah 2002; Lancaster,1965). There are seven Sanskrit names for this plant, *ksirachampaka, devaganagalu, kshira*, and four others (Parotta, 2001; Pullaiah 2002).

Polygonum acuminatum
P. acuminatum is an aquatic species native to the Americas but found on Easter Island, where it floats on the surface of the lakes inside two volcanic craters (Heyerdahl 1961, 26) and nowhere else in Polynesia. It is used for medicinal purposes on the island, as it is in the Titicaca Basin, Bolivia.

Of the island flora, Skottsberg (1920, I, 412) said, "The presence of a neo-tropical (i.e., American) element (on Juan Fernández and Easter Island) is surprising." The "mode of occurrence and ecology oblige us to regard" *P. acuminatum* as "truly indigenous," or else "intentionally introduced in prehistoric time during one of the mythical [sic] cruises which, according to Heyerdahl, put Easter Island in contact with Peru. A direct transport of seeds across the ocean without man's assistance is difficult to imagine ...." Skottsberg adds (page 425) that, contrarily, for the Marquesas "there is no neo-tropical element in spite of the prevailing direction of winds and currents." Dumont et al. (1998) update the matter by reporting analysis of a core taken from Rano Raraku crater lake on Easter Island. Five (stratigraphic) zones are identified. The last three of these are separated by waves of human immigration. The researchers argue that a first, or South American wave, dated to the second half of the 14th century by Carbon-14 dating, may represent a visit by South American Indians. They found the top 85 cm. of sediment to include *Polygonum acuminatum*. Because of the synchronous appearance of multiple floral taxa from the Americas, Dumont rules out passive introduction. "The island is so remote, and such a small target, that mechanisms of passive dispersal were ineffective for populating it" (with flora). Besides, there are no freshwater birds on the island whose migration might have brought the seeds. "We therefore propose that humans introduced these neo-tropical biota, in one single event."

Portulaca oleracea

Purslane, *Portulaca oleracea*, was common in Roman gardens in Pliny's day (Leach 1982, 2). It grew throughout the warmer parts of the Old World and was also mentioned in Egyptian texts. Nevertheless, Gray and Trumbell (1883, 253; cf. Danin et al. 1978, 201, 209) demonstrated over a century ago that the species is actually of American origin. In North America, it was growing as early as 2500–3000 years ago (Chapman et al. 1974, 412). It thrives best in the disturbed soils of gardens, which indicates that the plant may well have accompanied a transoceanic movement by horticulturists.

A number of Sanskrit names for purslane are known: *lonika*, or *loonia* (Balfour 1871–1873, IV, 660); *ghotika* (Pullaiah 2002, II, 426); and *mansala* (Chopra et al. 1958, 521–23). Furthermore, Bretschneider (1882, 49–53, 57–61) notes the mention of the plant in a Chinese treatise by Zhou Ding wang, an imperial prince who died in 1425 C.E.; he had seen the plant growing in Henan province (Bretschneider 1892, 428). Another work, Zhu Xi yulei, by the famous Song-period neo-Confucian scholar, Zhu Xi (1130–1200 C.E.), mentions purslane as *machixian*, a term that is still used for it in China today (personal communication from V. Mair, 2002).

Psidium guajava

More than 100 species of the genus *Psidium*, which includes the guava, are native to Tropical America (Brown 1935, 200). Bailey (1935, III, 284) concurred that the genus originated wholly in the Americas. Towle (1961, 73) documented a fruit of *P. guajava* having been found in a burial at Ancón, Peru (dated B.C.E.), and fruits have also been found in remains from the Gallinazo phase (early centuries C.E.) and the following Mochica phase. Johannessen has seen *Psidium* woven as a design in Mochica cloth; this observation places the plant in the Americas back several hundred years before Columbus.

Historically documented names provide evidence for the pre-Columbian presence of the guava in India. In Sanskrit, it was known as *amruta-phalam* (cf. Arabic and Persian: both *amrúd*) (Watt 1888–1893, VI, Pt. 1, 351–53). Pullaiah (2002, 433) has Sanskrit *péràlà* as well as *mansala* for this species. Sharma and Dash (1983, 518) identify the guava as the 'Paravata fruit' mentioned in the <u>Caraka Samhita</u> text (between 900 B.C.E. and the fourth century C.E.) (Aiyer 1956, 36; Pullaiah 2002, 2). Of linguistic interest is the fact that the name of the guava in the Mysore area of India involves the root *bidji* (Watson 1868, 134), while in Yucatec Mayan, the same fruit is called by the near equivalent *pichi* (Roys, 1931, 231, 276).

Sapindus saponaria

The soapberry tree, *Sapindus saponaria*, is another Native American species (Zeven and de Wet 1982, 178; Knoche 1925, 102–23) that has spread throughout the tropics. Its antiquity in the Americas is certain (Tozzer 1941, 197; Hernández 1943 [by 1580], II, 529–30). In the Casma Valley of northern Peru it has been found in middens, radiocarbon-dated to ca. 1785 B.C.E. (Ugent et al. 1986).

An equivalent tree was common in India under the scientific name *S. mukorossi* in northern India and *S. trifoliatus* in the south. They are now equated with *S. saponaria* by Index Kewensis. Three Sanskrit names are known: *phenila* and *arushta* for *S. trifoliatus* (Nadkarni 1914, 350; Int. Lib. Assoc. 1996, 572), and *urista* for *S. mukorossi* (Int. Lib. Assoc. 1996, 572). The soapberry trees of India are also distributed in China (Watt 1889, VI, Part II, 468).

The same American tree was in use on Easter Island at discovery, and it was widespread in some other Polynesian islands as well (Heyerdahl 1963, 31; Langdon and Tryon 1983, 43; Brown 1935, 160–61).

Schoenoplectus californicus

A bulrush, or sedge, *Schoenoplectus californicus*, grows on Easter Island in close association with *Polygonum acuminatum* (see above) on the surface of the island's crater lakes. It too is of American origin and is found up and down the Pacific Coast of both American continents. The same species grows in Hawaii with a name nearly parallel phonetically to that on Easter Island (Rapanui, *nga?atu*; Hawaiian, *nanaku*) (Langdon 1988, 330, 334; Langdon and Tryon 1983, 43). The uses to which it was put were very nearly the same as in South America and Easter Island (Heyerdahl 1961, 23–5; Towle 1961, 26–7). As with *P. acuminatum*, Dumont et al. (1998, 410, 418) conclude that the evidence is strong that this plant was brought from the mainland in the 14th century by voyagers, while no other explanation stands up.

Sisyrhynchium angustifolium

A small lily (commonly called a 'grass'), *Sisyrhynchium angustifolium*, is fundamentally North American in distribution, although it has also been found at the site of the ruins of Norse settlements in Greenland (Faeggri 1964, 344–51; Polunin 1960, 181; Thorarinsson 1942, 45–6). Here is botanical evidence in support of the historical and archaeological facts on the Norse migration to and from the American Vinland.

Solanum spp.

Solanum candidum is one of a set of fruit-bearing trees that inhabit Middle and South America, Oceania, and Asia and that overlap taxonomically in an intriguing way. American *S. candidum* is so close to *S. lasiocarpum* of Western Oceania that they may be the same species, and the two areas share certain uses of the fruit. On the American side, *S. candidum* is virtually conspecific with *S. quitoense*. *S. candidum* has so nearly the same characteristics as the Asian *S. lasiocarpum* that their relationship demands an historical explanation. No plausible one has been offered from the perspective of the botany alone.

Solanum repandum, which is spread from Fiji to the Marquesas, is so similar to South American *S. sessiliflorum* that Whalen et al. (1981; cf. 1991, 41–66) suspect the two may be conspecific. The uses to which each is put are essentially the same. (See details in the Appendix.). Moreover, the name of *S. repandum* in the Marquesas, *kokoua* or *koko'u*, is enough like a South American name for the species, *cocona*, that on the basis of the name alone one may be justified in seeing a direct transfer before Europeans came on the scene. We agree with Whalen and Whistler that voyages between the Americas and the islands make more sense than any other possible explanation for these relationships. The similarities are such that two transoceanic transfers must have been accomplished, *S. candidum* and *S. lasiocarpum* requiring one voyage to account for similarities between them and *S. repandum* and *S. sessiliflorum* being linked by another. (See Whalen et al. 1981; Heiser 1985).

Solanum nigrum, known as 'black nightshade,' today is widely distributed throughout temperate and tropical regions of the world. In the Americas, the Maya knew *S. nigrum* as *ich-can*, or *pahal-can* (Roys 1931, 248, 272). It was also used medicinally in Peru (Yacovleff and Herrera 1934–1935, 281). After mentioning medicinal uses of the nightshade in ancient Assyria, India, and China, Thompson (1949, 143) observed, "it is obvious that the *S. nigrum* is a very popular drug in the East." Watt (1888–1893, VI, Pt. III, 263–64) reported *S. nigrum* growing throughout India and Ceylon. Pokharia and Saraswat (1998–1999, 90) found nightshade seeds in material excavated from the Sanghol site in India (first to third centuries C.E.). Its berries are described in Sanskrit works of medicine where the plant's name is *kákamáchai* (Nadkarni 1914, 373), or a variant thereof. Dioscorides' first century C.E. Greek herbal catalog identified the plant there (Gunther 1934, 467). Maimonides (1974; Meyerhof and Sobhy 1932) described it in 12th-century Egypt. We can imagine no way to account for such a distribution and the inter-hemispheric transfer that it indicates except that voyagers carried the plant across an ocean over two millennia ago.

Solanum tuberosum, the potato, was found on Easter Island by early

European visitors, as Mellén Blanco (1986, 133) demonstrate using explorers' accounts. Of course, the potato is very old on the mainland, but it is absent elsewhere in Polynesia and points west.

Sonchus oleraceus

Sonchus oleraceus in some sources is called 'chicory' although true chicory is *Cichorium intybus*. *S. oleracues* plant was a potherb and source of medicine among the Maya (Tozzer 1941, 146) and in Peru (Yacovleff and Herrera 1933–1934, 299). Chroniclers' accounts place it so early in the Americas that there is no question of the Spaniards having brought it. Actually, it was an Old World native that was extensively cultivated in Europe and Asia (Balfour 1871–1873, V, 482–83; Bretschneider 1892, 179; Watson 1868, 259; Watt 1888–1893, II, 285). Those facts can only be explained by supposing that it was carried from Eurasia to the Americas long before Columbus.

Sophora toromiro

S. toromiro was the only wild tree in the flora of Easter Island. Its wood served the islanders for constructing canoes and to make other carved items. Knoche (1919) considered it to have been introduced from the outside and to be a 'cultivated' plant (syn. *S. tetraptera*). A native tradition told to the early Christian missionaries (Mellén Blanco 1986, 135; cf. Heyerdahl 1963a, 26–7) said that this toromiro tree was among the plants brought by ancestral settler/voyager Hotu Matu'a. It is now extinct. According to Skottsberg (1920, 421) it, or a close relative, has been recorded by botanists only from Chile, Juan Fernandez Island, Easter Island, and New Zealand. He also thought its natural transport to Easter Island was not a satisfactory explanation for its presence there.

Tagetes spp.

Tagetes erecta is the common marigold and *T. patula* the dwarf marigold. They both originated in Mexico (MacNeish 1992). Hernández (1943 [before 1580], II, 644-52) illustrated ten varieties of *Tagetes* in 16th-century Mexico, including one that Linnaeus later would dub *T. erecta*. The botanists who prepared the 1943 edition of Hernández suggested two of the other nine varieties that could represent *T. patula*. Roys (1931, 279) added that the dwarf species grew abundantly in the Maya area as a weed.

Levey and Al-Khaledy (1967, 192) identify one or more of the marigolds in texts from Persia and India dated to the 13th century C.E. The blossom is known as the 'flower of the dead' in both Mexico and India today. Neher (1968) has published an eyewitness account by Harlan of a harvest festival in an Indian village whose ritual and symbolism revolve around the marigold and directly recall Mexican customs. It is hard to believe that the transfer of European influence on India in the past 500 years could explain those conditions, let alone account for two Sanskrit names for the marigold, *zanduga* (Chopra et al. 1956, 239) and *sthulapushpa* (Int. Lib. Assoc. 1996, 574) and *sandu* (Kew Garden Plant Culture site, 2012). Rather, it is evident that the genus has been on the subcontinent for many centuries. Since both *Tagetes* species are widespread and naturalized in India today and had Sanskrit names (Pandey 2000), they probably both arrived together anciently and are thoroughly integrated in Indian culture(s).

Table 2
Flora for which Evidence is Significant but not Decisive

Species	Common Name	Old World	New World
Adenostemma viscosum	Boton, Tia juana	India	Origin
Amanita muscaria	fly agaric	Origin	Middle America
Chenopodium quinoa	Quinoa	Easter Island	Origin
Erigeron albidus	Horseweed	Hawaii	Origin
Gnaphalium purpureum	Purple Cudweed	Hawaii	Origin
Gossypium religiosum	a cotton	Hawaii	Mesoamerica
Indigofera tinctoria	Indigo	Polynesia, Asia?	Mexico, Peru
Ipomoea acetosaefolia		Hawaii	Origin
Lycopersicon esculentum	Tomato	India, Hawaii	Mexico, Middle America
Magnolia grandiflor	magnolia	India	Origin
Mangifera indica	Mango	Origin	Middle America
Musa coccinea	Chinese banana	China	South America
Polianthes tuberose	tuberose	Origin	South America
Salvia coccinea	scarlet salvia	India	Origin
Salvia occidentalis	a salvia	Marquesas	Origin
Smilax sp.	sarsaparilla	Eurasia	Middle America
Tamarindus indicus	tamarind tree	South Asia	Tropical America
Triumfetta semitriloba	Sacremento burbark	Easter Island	South America
Verbesina encelioides	Golden crown-beard	Hawaii	Origin
Vitis vinifera	Grape	Eurasia	Mexico

For species in Table 2 we have discovered one strong source of evidence that there is a strong likelihood of trnasoceeanic transfer.

Table 3
Flora for which Evidence Justifies Further Study

Species	Common Name	Species	Common Name
Acorus calamus	sweet flag	*Indigofera suffruticosa*	indigo
Ageratum houstonianum	floss flower	*Lonchocarpus sericeus*	a fish poison
Alternanthera	khakiweed	*Lupinus cruickshanksii*	field lupine

pungens			
Alternanthera sessilis	Sessile joyweed	*Momordica balsamin*	Balsam apple
Alternanthera tonella		*Morus rubra*	Mulberry
Annona glabra	pond apple	*Nelumbo* sp.	Lotus
Cajanus cajan	pigeon pea	*Nicotiana rustica*	wild tobacco
Cassia fistula	purging cassia	*Nymphaea* sp.	Lotus
Cinchona officinialis	quinine (bark)	*Ocimum americanum*	hoary basil
Colocasia esculenta	dry-land taro	*Paullinia* sp.	a fish poison
Cucumis sp.		*Phaseolus adenanthus*	a bean
Cyclanthera pedata	pepino hueco	*Sagittaria sagittifolia*	Wapatoo
Datura sanguinea	datura, Jimson weed	*Sesamum orientale*	sesame
Derris sp.	a fish poison	*Sisyrhynchium acre*	a grass
Dioscorea alata	yam	*Spondias lutyea*	Hog plum
Dioscorea cayenensis	guinea yam	*Spondias purpurea*	Hog plum
Dolichos lablab	a bean	*Synedrella nodiflora*	pantropic weed
Elaeis guineensis	guinea oil palm	*Tephrosia* spp.	a fish poison
Gossypium brasiliense	a cotton	*Trapa natans*	water chestnut
Gossypium drynarioides	a cotton	*Vigna sinensis*	Cow peas
Hibiscus youngianus	hibiscus		

For species in Table 3 we have found some anomalous information that leads us to believe that there may have been transoceanic transfer, but the information does not qualify as strong or definitive. These plants need to be researched further to either find more evidence of transfer or to determine that they were not transferred.

Species of flora listed in Tables 1, 2, and 3 that have not been discussed to this point are treated in Appendix 1.

MICROFAUNA EVIDENCE

In the Introduction to this book we established that two species of hookworm, *Ancylostoma duodenale* and *Necator americanus*, were brought to South America by voyagers in the sixth millennium B.C.E. or before. Those, along with 17 other species of infectious organisms that appear to have crossed with voyagers are listed in Table 4. The occurrence of the consequent disease demonstrates that actual human beings, as hosts of the disease agents, landed in the Americas and passed on the imported organisms to their descendants (in addition to making contributions to the New World gene pool). We next discuss those organisms in Table 4. In addition, 20 more of those species of microfauna that possibly were transported by ship are included in Table 5, but they are discussed only in Appendix I. Using the exacting science of paleopathology, these diseases have been discovered in ancient populations across the oceans from where the disease originated.

Ascaris lumbricoides
 A. lumbricoides is the large roundworm known to have infested Egyptian mummies, such as Pum II, dating to ca. 170 B.C.E. The roundworm has also been found in other Old World locations in antiquity (Cockburn et al. 1998, 79–80). Pictorial evidence exists for ascariasis in ancient Mesopotamia, and prescriptions in ancient Egypt have *A. lumbricoides* as a target of treatment (Kuhnke 1993, 457). Moreover, this nematode was known to ancient pre-Columbian writers in China, India, and Europe. It was also present in pre-Columbian America (Patterson 1993, 603). Although it was once thought to be a post-Columbian arrival, it has been shown recently to have plagued pre-Columbian South American populations (Verano 1998, 221).

Bordetella pertussis
 This is the bacterium that causes whooping cough. It originated in the Old World, as did all the other species discussed in this section. However, a century ago antibodies for pertussis bacilli were found in the blood of isolated, unacculturated Brazilian Indians. Furthermore, it "may have been present in the Southwest [of the United States] before arrival of the Spaniards" (Stodder and Martin 1991, 62). Van Blerkom (1985, 46–47) concludes, "If not pertussis, then some close relative of it probably occurred in the New World as well as the Old .... Perhaps different strains existed in the two hemispheres." But what "close relative" would that be unless one that also arrived from the Eastern Hemisphere where alone it would have evolved? To Hare (1967, 119, 122), "It is highly improbable

that any of these organisms would have become established in a scattered community with a Palaeolithic culture" and thus that they could have crossed to the Americas with early hunters via Beringia. The transfer of *B. pertussis* would of necessity have waited until an infected person, from a more densely populated Old World society voyaged across the ocean.

Borrelia recurrentis

Relapsing fever is caused by the spirochete *Borrelia recurrentis*. It is vector-borne, not transmitted from person to person. The infection is usually acquired by crushing an infected louse, *Pediculus humanus corporis*, so that its body fluids contaminate a bite wound or a skin abrasion (Chin 2000, 421–22).

Since *B. recurrentis* occurred initially in the Old World, our primary question becomes, how did the vector organism reach the New World? Van Blerkom (1985, 62–5) concluded that louse-borne relapsing fever dated only to the rise of urban centers in the Old World (ca. 3000 B.C.E.?). Hare (1967, 118) says that cases closely resembling relapsing fever were described by Hippocrates, ca. 400 B.C.E. The arrival of the disease by early Beringian migrants is apparently ruled out because louse infestation of such a population would not be maintained under the existing social and demographic conditions. Yet Alchon (1991, 22, 25) found that relapsing fever, both the endemic type (transmitted by ticks) and the epidemic type (carried by lice), was present in pre-Hispanic coastal Ecuador. The only plausible scenario for this occurrence is the arrival in the Americas of lice (and ticks?) with human transoceanic voyagers. We will see below that such immigration is directly confirmed.

Entamoeba hystolytica

Amoebic dysentery is caused by *Entamoeba hystolytica*. Transmission is mainly by ingestion of fecally-contaminated food or water (Chin 2000, 11–13). Van Blerkom (1985, 19) maps the historical incidence of amoebic dysentery, which reached Persia from India by 480 B.C.E. then spreading to Africa. Again, the key issue is how this particular amoeba reached pre-Columbian America. Stodder and Martin (1992, 62) believe that amoebic dysentery was probably present before European contact. Saunders et al. (1992, 118) approvingly cite Newman (1976) who considered that pre-European-contact diseases included both bacillary and amoebic dysentery.

Alchon's (1991, 20) detailed study using ethnohistoric sources that report diseases in Ecuador at or near the Conquest concluded that amebiasis was present before the Spaniards arrived. An unidentified (as to species) Entamoeba cyst was found in a Peruvian mummy dating to about 1500 C.E. (Pike 1967, 185). Van Blerkom considered that this date leaves the case in the range of possible Spanish contamination. Most Andeanists, however, suppose that Spanish influence was unlikely to have had any effect in the case of this desiccated body (Pike 1967). Moreover, Van Blerkom observed (1985, 19), it is now known that the amoeba alone is incapable of inducing the disease state, which requires the concomitant presence of a certain bacterium (citing Schwabe 1964). She thinks it is likely that the amoeba, but not the bacterium, was present in the New World. From our non-epidemiological point of view, the only question is, did an organism reach the New World from the Old, not whether the disease was manifest? The sources convince us that the amoeba arrived in the Americas. Again, we cannot imagine any means for that transfer except by an infected voyager.

Herpes zoster, varicella-zoster virus VZV

Human (alpha) herpes virus 3 is the cause of chicken pox, shingles, etc. Chicken pox (*varicella*) is an acute, generalized viral disease. *Herpes zoster*, or shingles, is a local manifestation of latent varicella infection. The infectious agent for both chicken pox and shingles is human (alpha) herpes virus 3 (Chin 2000, 91–93). Transmission from person to person is by direct contact or airborne (droplet) spread of fluids from an infected person.

Human (gamma) herpes virus 4

This is the Epstein-Barr virus, which is involved in infectious mononucleosis and other disease manifestations such as simplex (cold sores) and cytomegalovirus, a mononucleosis-like infection. Type 4 is closely related to other herpes viruses, that is, it is similar morphologically but distinct serologically (Chin 2000, 350–51). The agents for both type 3 and 4 can remain latent within the human body for years after the initial attack (Alchon 1991, 23).

To Hare (1967, 121), "It is highly improbable that any of this class of organisms would have become established in a scattered community with a Palaeolithic culture." (In his day herpes viruses had not yet been identified in the Americas.) Actually, while little is known about the early history of chickenpox, there is no doubt about its comparative antiquity in the Old World. It was reported by the first century C.E. (Hare 1967, 120). Still, these viruses were endemic in the pre-Spanish population that occupied the area of modern Ecuador according to Alchon (1991). They leave no evidence on skeletons, thus their existence cannot be checked archaeologically. But they have been found in isolated populations of Amazonian natives, implying pre-Columbian incidence. Stodder and Martin (1992) also believe that herpes was present in the Southwest of the United States before the Spaniards arrived.

Van Blerkom (1985, 27–9) thought that since varicella is endemic in Brazilian tribes and is also known in wild primates, that *Herpes zoster* in humans in the Americas must have been derived from the ancient primate virus. But because the wild primate population in the Americas had limited interaction with humans, one would hope for real evidence that native populations did receive the infection from those primates. It is far more persuasive to us that one of the voyages from the Old World to the New, such as those that brought hookworms, probably tuberculosis, and also Old World plants to South America, was the medium by which these organisms from the Eastern Hemisphere reached the Americas.

Microsporum spp.
Several fungi cause ringworm on the human body. The causal species differ depending on the area of the human body infested (head, beard, groin, body, foot, or nails) (Chin 2000, 147–53). For the most common forms of the disease, *tinea corporis* (ringworm of the body) and *tinea cruris* (ringworm of the groin and perianal region), the reservoir for the agents is humans. Most species of *Microsporum* and *Trichophyton* (as well as *Epidermophyton floccosum*, *Scytalidium dimidiatum*, and *S. hyalinum*) cause 'dry type' *tinea corporis* in tropical areas of the Americas as well as in the Old World; thus they are potential additional species that could demonstrate transfer by voyagers.

Fonseca (1970, 40–5, 147 ff.), the discoverer of the disease in South American indigenes, called it *tinha* (or *tinea*) *imbricada* as well as, in the older literature, *toquelau*, or *tokelau* (a name used for the disease in Oceania) and *chimbêrê* (in Brazil). European explorers in Brazil reported its presence from the beginning. The disease is also known in central Mexico, Guatemala, and El Salvador, but it is totally absent among native peoples of North America, Alaska, and Canada. The area of incidence in the Old World is most of Polynesia, Micronesia, Melanesia, and Malaysia, as well as the indigenous population of Formosa and Indochina, and, with less frequency, south China, Sri Lanka, and the south of India but not to Africa.

Fonseca (1970, 44–5, 195–96, 216–17) presented a ten-point argument supporting the proposition that this parasite was introduced to South America by ancient immigrants. The Brazilian tribes who were first discovered (by Fonseca, in 1924) bearing the disease were virtually isolated and untouched by European influence.

Mycobacterium tuberculosis
Tuberculosis is caused by *M. tuberculosis*. It is one of a complex of organisms that includes *M. africanum*, found primarily in humans, and *M. bovis*, mainly in cattle (Chin 2000, 523–24). Transmission is by exposure to tubercle bacilli in airborne droplet nuclei produced by people with pulmonary or laryngeal tuberculosis when coughing or sneezing.

The origin and history of tuberculosis in the Old World is but dimly understood. Hare (1967, 117) points out that *M. tuberculosis* has never been isolated from wild animals, nor has it ever become established as a human parasite. It has infected (Old World) dairy herds since before the Christian era. Because Paleolithic societies did not have domesticated cattle, it is impossible that this organism caused infection in humans at the time when migrants to the Americas presumably entered via Beringia. But the disease could have existed in Neolithic and more recent societies when domesticated cattle were kept. The earliest sure evidence for pulmonary tuberculosis in the Old World is late in the second millennium B.C.E.—in India, China, and Egypt. Bones with lesions suggestive of tuberculosis may go back as early as 3700 B.C.E., although that date may somehow be deceptive. "It was never found in the thousands of mummies from Egypt and Nubia examined by Dawson, Smith et al. (Hare 1967, 125–26)." Klepinger (1987, 52–3) says that "Current paleopathological evidence would suggest that the mycobacteria responsible for the New World disease were not carried over by the Beringian trans-migrants but more likely arose *de novo* in the Western Hemisphere." However, to accept a '*de novo*' origin of a particular species separately in each hemisphere requires more faith in parallel evolutionary processes than we can muster.

Allison et al. (1973) first established the presence of *M. tuberculosis* in a Peruvian mummy. Since then, additional cases in the Americas have been documented beyond any question (Allison et al. 1981; Karasch 1993, 537; Salo et al. 1994; Verano 1998, 217–19). In fact, Alchon (1991, 23–4) maintains that archaeological evidence indicates that acute respiratory infections (no doubt including tuberculosis) were the most frequent cause of death among pre-Columbian Andean residents, the same as today.

So how are we to explain the existence of *M. tuberculosis* in the Americas? Buikstra (1981, 13) says, "In the absence of appropriately-timed migrations from the Old World, we must develop and defend a reasonable model for the origin of this disease in the absence of [New World reservoirs of] domestic herd animals such as cattle." No such model has been offered that does not contradict vital facts. So Lovell's (1987, 53) interrogative stands: "But where did that organism come from?" We are confident that the answer involves voyagers from the Old World who intruded into pre-Columbian America carrying *M. tuberculosis* bacilli in their lungs.

Pediculus humanus spp.

Two species of lice, *P. humanus capitis* and *P. humanus corporis*, were shared by Native American peoples and those in Oceania. The only sensible explanation for these insects to arrive in the Americas is by sea voyaging. Lice are host specific; those of lower animals do not infest humans. Transmission is by direct contact with infested persons or objects used by them. Lice can survive for only a week without a food source (Chin 2000,

372–73).

Fonseca (1970), particularly, has discussed the distribution of *"Pediculus pseudohumanus,"* as *P. humanus* was once known. It is "a form of louse found solely in indigenes of the Americas and of Oceania and in American macaques." Fonseca quotes Ferris (1935), who described its distribution as "extremely peculiar" (see also Ferris 1951, 275) —specimens from the Marquesas and Tahiti in Polynesia were identical down to the morphological details to lice from Guatemalan and Panamanian villagers and from mummified heads found in Ecuador and Yucatan. More modern writers assure us of similarities on an even wider scale. Sandison (1967, 178–83) says lice of the same species are known from pre-Columbian Mexico and Peru and are the same as those distributed from the Mediterranean through China. Karasch (1993, 538) notes that lice have been identified on mummies from Chile and Peru. According to chroniclers, the poor in the Inca Empire (as a control measure) had to "pay tribute in the form of small containers of lice." "Not surprisingly," Karasch continues, typhus was "a very common disease in ancient Peru." Alchon (1991, 22) believes "One can build a strong case for the existence of both endemic (flea-borne) and epidemic (louse-borne) typhus in the New World, based on lice on Peruvian and Chilean mummies." (Compare Zinsser (1960, 254–61), who also believed that historical evidence involving lice found on mummies, indicates that typhus was present in South America.) Meanwhile, Van Blerkom (1985, 4) summarizes: "The lice found on pre-Columbian American mummies are of the same species (with only slight differences, on the order of a subspecies) as those on Old World humans (El-Najjar and Mulinski 1980, 111)."

Linguistic evidence anchors the case for the transfer of lice by direct maritime contact from Oceania or beyond. Roys (1931, 341) cites the authoritative 16th Century Mayan Motul dictionary for the term "*Uk*. The louse found on man and quadrupeds." Meanwhile, Schumacher et al. (1992, 18) report from Oceania that the ethnically-Papuan, Austronesian-speaking Buma tribe, on Vanikoro, eastern Solomon Islands, have *uka* for the louse, while in the western Solomons, the Austronesian Ontong Java people call the louse *uku*. In Hawaii the name of the musical instrument ukulele comes from Hawaiian *uku*, flea, and *lele*, jumping (Merriam Webster's Collegiate Dictionary, 10th edition). (Recall that a Hawaiian term for sweet potato was effectively identical to a South American word [see above]).

Piedreaia hortai

This fungus causes piedra (negra), a disease of the hair. "Piedra is characterized by black, hard 'gritty' nodules on hair shafts" (Chin 2000, 147–48). According to Fonseca (1970, 262), the disease is especially characteristic of South American natives in the interior of the continent. It is found very rarely in North America. On page 264, Fonseca observed that this disease is also found in Southeast Asia – Thailand, Vietnam, Burma, Malaya, and Indonesia. In those regions it presents with exactly the same clinical, epidemiological, and parasitological characteristics as it appears on the South American continent. Based on a variety of evidence, Fonseca concluded that this disease was introduced to the Americas by pre-Columbian migrations from Oceania. It is missing in northern Asia and North America, so any migration across the Bering Strait would not have brought it. Nor does the disease exist in Europe or Africa. Because it was widely distributed in South America, among many language groups, it must have arrived long ago as Fonseca wrote.

Rickettsia prowazekii

The body louse can be infected with *R. prowazekii* by feeding on the blood of a host with acute typhus fever. People in turn are infected by rubbing louse feces or crushed lice into a bite or superficial abrasion. The body louse is involved not only in outbreaks of epidemic typhus but also epidemic relapsing fever caused by *Borrelia recurrentis* (Chin 2000, 372, 541–42).

As noted above, Alchon (1991, 22) argued that both endemic (flea-borne) and epidemic (louse-borne) typhus probably were present in the New World, based on the fact that Peruvian mummies were infested with lice. Head and body lice were common on mummified remains. Most native households (at least in the Andes) included several guinea pigs in the family's living quarters; these animals can be reservoirs for the *typhus rickettsiae*. Infected fleas can easily jump from rodent to human, thereby transmitting the endemic form of the disease. There are pre-Conquest traditions of epidemics occurring during periods of social turmoil – wars, famines, and natural disasters – supporting the assertion that typhus existed in the Americas before the 16th century. For example, Peruvian chronicler, Guaman Poma, described two epidemics that took place long before the Spanish Conquest. Cabieses (1979) believes that typhus was common in pre-Columbian Peru. Guerra (1966, 330–32) maintained that the two most important aboriginal Aztec disease entities were *matlazahuatl* and *cocolitztli*. They caused major epidemics. Translation of the terms remains unclear, but Guerra's analysis of the symptoms indicated that the former was exanthematic typhus. Ackerknecht (1965, 53) interpreted the reported (by tradition) epidemic of 1454 on the plateau of Mexico as in all probability typhus. Goldstein (1969) agreed with Ackerknecht, Bruce-Chwatt (1965), Sandison (1967), and Villacorta C. (1976) who said that typhus definitely occurred in the Americas before Columbus.

Where did the infectious organism come from? It may have been earlier in the Old World than in the New, but even that is uncertain. Hare (1967,

118) believed the first outbreaks known in European medical history occurred in Italy only in 1505. Epidemic typhus is therefore a comparatively modern disease and, on chronological grounds alone, is very unlikely to have come across Bering Strait. However, typhus was much older in Asia and Oceania than in Europe, judging from the wide distribution. Nicolle (1932) drew attention to the Asian/Oceanic distribution of typhus and considered that that fact supported the idea that pre-Columbian migrations reached the Americas from Oceania, bringing typhus (along with fleas and lice). Fonseca cited a large literature (Mooser, Gay, Miranda, Gaitán, Nicolle) representing what he (1970) referred to as "most authors" who have written on this point, to conclude that exanthematic typhus indeed existed in pre-Columbian America.

In the nature of the evidence of ancient epidemiology, we cannot be absolutely certain of the presence of many diseases, including typhus, because they leave no physical indication visible on skeletal remains to prove that the corpse had been infected. Nevertheless, we agree with Alchon that the evidence is strong for the presence of this rickettsial organism in the ancient Americas. No explanation for the presence of *R. prowazekii* other than human voyaging, is apparent. From the plant evidence already cited, it is clear that numerous transoceanic voyages to the Americas took place from the Asian home where so many diseases were endemic.

Rickettsia rickettsii

Rickettsia rickettsii is the infectious agent that causes spotted fever. According to Chin (2000, 372), the disease is one of a group of clinically similar diseases caused by closely related *rickettsiae* that probably originated in Asia. They are transmitted by ixodid (hard) ticks, the tick species differing by geographic area.

Newman (1976, 669) considered that pre-European-contact diseases in the Americas included rickettsial fevers. Saunders et al. (1992, 118) agree. Ackerknecht (1965) considered that petechial typhus (spotted fever) was at least as old as 1083 C.E. in Mexico, according to his reading of the Aztec traditions.

Rickettsia typhi (ex. *Rickettsia mooseri*)

This organism produces typhus murine, i.e., endemic typhus. Murine typhus is similar to louse-borne typhus but milder. It is found where humans and rats live together. Rats, mice, and other small mammals form the reservoir. (See below on the presence of *Rattus* sp. in Mesoamerica.) Infective rat fleas (usually *Xenopsylla cheopis*) defecate rickettsiae while sucking blood, which contaminates the bite site and other skin wounds. Once infected, fleas remain so for up to their one year of life (Chin 2000, 544–45).

Fonseca (1970, 333–36) said that murine typhus was at first assigned primarily to two geographic areas: (1) certain regions of North America (Mexico, Guatemala, and the southern United States), and (2) the Far East and Pacific—India, Malaysia, China, Manchuria, Formosa, Australia, New Guinea, New Zealand, and Hawaii. Nicolle (1932) recognized the presence of murine typhus in Mexico and Guatemala that was the same as in Southeast Asia. He considered the possibility that typhus murine might have come via the Vikings, yet thought it far more logical that it reached the Americas via rats on Polynesian vessels. Alchon (1991, 22) also accepted the pre-Columbian presence of the disease in Ecuador, again based on ethnohistoric records.

Among diseases Newman (1976, 669) thought were "part of man's primate ancestry" and that either crossed the Bering Strait cold-screen or "were acquired" in the Americas were "various rickettsial fevers," including typhus. He thought so because the Aztecs had a name, *matlazahuatl*, for the disease, and depicted it in conventionalized pictures of suffering Indians. But we cannot see how the typhus vector could have passed the Arctic cold-screen, and neither is it apparent from where the supposed settlers of the Americas via Alaska could have "acquired" the disease. Transmission by transoceanic voyagers is once more the only plausible source. (But see now Stutz 2006 for a report of Acuña-Soto's thesis that this disease was not typhus.)

T cell lymphotropic (retro) virus (HTLV-I)
Only a small number of peoples in Tropical America show infection with this virus. The group studied in the greatest detail is the Noanama Amerindians in the high mountains of southwestern Colombia. Their geographical and social isolation reduces the chance of any contact with the slaves of African origin brought to Colombia by the Spaniards (León et al. 1996). The study by León's group combined sero-epidemiologic, genetic, virologic, molecular, anthropological, archaeological, and oceanographic data that led the authors to conclude that this virus could have arrived from Kyushu Island in Japan more than 5000 years ago through direct voyaging. No other explanation stands up to criticism.

An earlier study of 13 genetic markers around the world revealed that the Noanama had very close relations with Samoans on the one hand, and Japanese – especially Ainu – on the other. Furthermore, recent genetic studies on native South Americans showed that their ancestors possessed genetic markers related to the histo-compatible leucocyte antigen (HLA), as do the Japanese of Kyushu. A direct voyage from Japan to Colombia would explain this relationship, because populations of North and Central America are totally without the HLA markers. At a mitochondrial DNA level, study of the deletion 9 bp in the human genome has shown it to be

Asiatic in origin; however, it is being found in North American Amerindians and Polynesians (citing Torroni). Yet it is not present in the (Jomon-derived) Ainu people, and the 9 bp deletion is also absent among the Noanama (as well as on the coasts of Chile and Peru a thousand years earlier according to studies of mummies). All this suggests an intrusion of people from Japan. León et al. (1995) cite the proposal of Meggers et al. (1965) concerning the intrusive Valdivia culture of Ecuador as confirming their position about the disease.

Finally, León et al (1995) point out that Japanese investigators have voyaged across the Pacific to Colombia by the North Pacific route, which the authors suppose was used anciently; the Japanese researchers used vessels similar to those of prehistoric times. This nautical experiment demonstrates that it was possible to make such a voyage, which is seen as bearing this disease (Errazurriz and Alvarado 1993).

Trichophyton spp.

In the genus *Trichophyton*, there are eleven species of fungi that are cosmopolitan, seven of which are anthropophilic (Ajello 1960, 30). The *Trichophyton concentricum* fungus is a cause of a ringworm of the body. *T. concentricum* (the cause of *tinea imbricata* as Fonseca called the disease) is endemic in Southeast Asia and also widespread among the inhabitants of Polynesia and countries bordering the western shores of the Pacific. However, it only occurs sporadically among Indians living in the tropical forests of Brazil, Guatemala, and Mexico. The disparity in prevalence between the Asian endemic areas and those of Latin America has led to the interpretation that the fungus was introduced from Asia into the New World (Ajello 1960, 30). Since the fungus can only have been transferred on a human body, no other explanation than the arrival of voyagers can be accepted for its American incidence. The Bering Strait migrations could not have spread this disease as it does not appear in North American tribal groups.

Trichosporon ovoides

T. ovoides is present in Brazil and Asia. It is a fungus that causes a disease (known in Brazil as piedra branca) consisting of white or clear nodules that develop on individual hairs of the beard or scalp. Fonseca (1970) described it, gave its distribution, and argued that it could only have arrived by seaborne travelers from across the Pacific.

Trichuris trichiura

The whipworm, *Trichuris trichiura*, like the hookworm, requires warm, moist climatic conditions for the completion of its life cycle and reproduction. It is particularly incident in Asia and Oceania. Finding the human-specific parasites in the Americas is circumstantial evidence for transpacific contact (Reinhard 1992, 231–45), because the cold of the Bering Strait route would kill the organism in the stage when it is excreted from the human host. Coprolites from coastal Peru show the whipworm present by 2700 B.C.E. (Verano 1991, 15–24). According to Ferreira et al. (1988, 65–7), the whipworm has been identified along with the two hookworm species (see above) in human coprolites from Boqueirão do Sitio da Pedra Furada, Brazil, in the same stratum as the hookworms, around 7320±80 BP.

Yersinia pestis

Some epidemiologists might assert that *Yersinia pestis*, the plague bacillus, is simply zoonotic in origin and as such has no relevance to the history of humans in the Americas. But that dodges the question of how the infectious bacillus came to be in the Americas at all. Either an infected animal or an infected human must have come carrying it from its original home in the Old World. Chin (2000, 381–83) says it is endemic in East and South Asia and sub-Saharan Africa. The reservoir is wild rodents, especially ground squirrels, rats, and also rabbits and hares. Transmission occurs as a result of human intrusion into the zoonotic (sylvan or rural) cycle, or by the entry of sylvatic rodents or their infected fleas into human habitats. Domestic pets may carry plague-infected wild rodent fleas into homes. The most frequent source of exposure that results in human disease has been the bite of infected fleas (especially *Xenopsylla cheopis*, the oriental rat-flea). Although human plague is commonly zoonotic in origin, it can be transmitted from man to man, with or without the agency of vector fleas, and humans can also act as a reservoir of the disease (Van Blerkom 1985, 48, 50–9). Person to person transmission by *Pulex irritans*, the flea that infests humans, is presumed important in the Andes area (Chin 2000, 381–82).

Many (Schwabe (1969, 282) calls it a consensus) believe that sylvatic plague is indigenous in the Americas. Van Blerkom considers the most compelling evidence in favor of pre-Columbian plague to be the existence of several sylvatic foci in both North and South America, with the largest being in western North America in rodents. Also, it is focused in eastern Siberia and western Canada. This distribution suggests that plague is an ancient and widely distributed disease of rodents diffused across the Bering Strait. But Van Blerkom disagrees. Besides, Hare (1967) reports that there is no evidence that the disease occurred in the Eastern Hemisphere at any time during the pre-Christian era. Therefore, it could not have reached the Western Hemisphere via early Holocene settlers traversing the Bering Strait.

How it was transmitted to the Americas is clarified by Van Blerkom's (1985, 58) observation about the distribution of this organism. There are three subspecies: *Y. p. orientalis*, endemic in India, Burma, and South China; *Y. p. antiqua*, carried by rodents in Central Asia and Africa; and *Y. p. mediaevalis*, or the Black Death in Europe, which is today found only in West Africa. If New World sylvatic plague was an indigenous disease of the rodents of this hemisphere, one would expect it to be the same strain found on the other side of the Bering Strait, *Y. p. antiqua*, the parent of the other strains. However, American plague is derived from the urban strain found in Southeast Asian seaports, *Y. p. orientalis* (Alland 1970, 101–2; Hull 1963, 534). This suggests that plague was carried by ship to the Americas from Southeast Asia. In fact, any other explanation seems impossible.

Van Blerkom (1985, 58) believes that transmission to the Americas occurred only during the last pandemic. That was in China in 1855. She supposes that only later was plague found in wild American rodents, and it seems to have spread rapidly into wild reservoirs from the original murine foci in seaports (Hull 1963, 547–54). But her scenario presumes an unbelievable rate of spread since 1855 to a wide variety of rodents (up to 200 species in the New World; so, Van Blerkom 1985, 56) over a wide geographical range. That seems impossible. But the extensive presence of *Y. p. orientalis* in the Americas can be explained economically by supposing its arrival via a pre-Columbian voyage from some seaport in Southeast Asia. That would allow sufficient time to spread to the many New World rodents. This seems to be the only scenario that takes account of all the parameters of the case.

Table 4
Microfauna for Which There is Decisive Evidence

Species	Common Name or Caused Disease
Ancylostoma duodenale	a hookworm
Ascaris lumbricoides	Roundworm
Bordetella pertussis	whooping cough bacterium
Borrelia recurrentis	relapsing fever spirochete
Entamoeba hystolytica	amoeba that causes dysentery
Enterobius vermicularis	pinworms
Human (alpha) herpes virus 3	cause of shingles, chicken pox, etc.
Human (gamma) herpes virus 4	cause of mononucleosis, etc.
Microsporum spp.	cause of ringworm of the body
Mycobacterium tuberculosis	bacterium causing tuberculosis
Necator americanus	a hookworm
Pediculus humanus capitis	the scalp louse
Pediculus humanus corporis	the body louse
Piedreaia hortai	a fungus that infests the hair
Rickettsia prowazekii	bacterium that causes typhus
Rickettsia rickettsii	bacterium that causes spotted fever
Rickettsia typhi	bacterium causing typhus murine
T cell lymphotropic (retro) virus	lymphotropic virus

(HTLV-I)	
Treponema pallidum	Cause of syphilis, yaws, and pinta
Trichosporon ovoides	a fungus infesting hair of scalp or beard
Trichuris trichiura	whipworm
Yersinia pestis	the plague bacillus

The evidence for all the microfaunal species in Table 4 is definitive using the same scale of measure used for the plant species in Table 1.

Table 5
Microfauna for Which Evidence Is less than Decisive

Species	Common Name or Caused Disease
Diplococcus pneumoniae	bacterium that causes pneumonia in humans and mice
Flavivirus spp.	organism causing yellow fever
Giardia lamblia	protozoan causing giardiasis
Influenza viruses	sources of influenza
Leishmania sp.	protozoan causing Leishmaniasis
Mycobacterium leprae	bacterium causing leprosy
Onchocerca volvulus	nematode causing onchocerciasis
Plasmodium falciparum	sporozoan causing malaria
Salmonella enterica serovar Typhi	typhoid bacillus
Schistosoma sp.	liver fluke
Shigella dysenteriae	cause of bacillary dysentery
Staphylococcus x aureus	bacillus causing impetigo, carbuncles
Streptococcus pneumoniae	a bacterial cause of pneumonia
Streptococcus pyogenes	cause of scarlet and rheumatic fever, etc.
Strongyloides sp.	threadworm nematode
Trichophyton concentricum	a fungus causing ringworm of the body
Trychostrongylus sp.	a helminthic parasite
Tunga penetrans	chigoe, chigger
Wuchereria bancrofti	a nematode causing filiariasis

For the microfaunal species in Table 5 we have discovered one strong source of evidence that there is a strong likelihood of trnasoceeanic transfer.

OTHER FAUNA

In addition to the flora and the microfauna already discussed, evidence of communication across the oceans also comes from the distribution of various faunal species that are not agents of disease. As a simple term of reference for this miscellany we use "Other Fauna." The six species with the necessary evidence to constitute a definitive transfer are listed in Table 6. Nine further possibilities to be investigated are in Table 7.

Alphitobius diaperinus
This pest native to the Old World has been discovered in a similar mortuary context in the New World as well. It is called, in the vernacular, the 'lesser meal worm.' Panagiotakopulu (2001, 16) reports it in the British Isles in a second-century C.E. burial and in Egypt with a mummy at 1350 B.C.E. In Peru, the same worm has been found in a 1240 C.E. mummy bundle (Riddle and Vreeland 1982).

This association of pests with burial practices in both hemispheres appears less startling when we recall the mortuary context of the discovery of tobacco and coca plants in Egyptian mummies dating from the second millennium B.C.E. to the fifth century C.E. (see above). Also, residues of *Cannabis sativa*, an Old World plant, have been found in Peruvian corpses. It is not so surprising then, that a beetle and a worm from Eurasia should show up in graves in Peru. Humans traveling on boats provide the only plausible means by which the two areas, halfway around the world from each other, could have been so linked both biologically and, apparently, culturally.

Canis familiaris
The dog is commonly assumed to have been brought to the New World by early hunter-gatherers via Beringia, but there is very slim evidence for this. Mair's (1998) round-up of data from Asia suggest that dog-in-the-company-of-humans in the Old World is not particularly ancient. The earliest record of morphologically small dogs for which we have archaeological evidence occurred in the Near East during the Natufian era only around 12,000 years ago. Current research has found evidence of the dog with humans in Belgian caves 31,000 years ago (Parker, 2010). Dogs in the European Mesolithic period date on the order of 7,000–5,000 B.C.E. The earliest dog remains in China are around 4,000 B.C.E. Moreover, the common hypothetical root words for dog in ancestral language groupings like Nostratic and Afro-Asiatic appear to date "closer to 6000 B.C.E. than to 10,000 B.C.E." (Mair 1998, 22–3). Turner (2002, 144) says a dog skull dated to 12,000 B.C.E. was found in a cave in the Altai Mountains, but it

was not associated with evidence for human presence in the area. These data mean that it is a stretch to imagine domesticated dogs being available in northeastern Asia to accompany the presumed early migrants to the New World via Bering Strait. So where did the American dogs come from? (Of course, they might have been independently domesticated in the Americas from wild canids, although evidence – even hints – of that are all but absent, cf. Turner 2002 144–45).

As many as three varieties, or breeds, of canines might have reached the New World from the Old as a result of ocean travel.

1. **The voiceless, hairless dog**. Covarrubias (1957, 93) reported that early in the first millennium B.C.E., or before, an edible dog was known in both China and at Tlatilco, Mexico, of identical appearance. Coe (1968, 59) found physical evidence for consumption of small dogs at the site of San Lorenzo in southern Mexico around 1000 B.C.E. Fiennes and Fiennes (1968, 26, 53–55, 103–110) told of a special breed of hairless, or 'toy,' dog that was kept and bred in China and also in west Mexico and Peru as temple and sacrificial animals, as well as for food. Campbell (1989, 360–367, 385) noted the presence of dogs for eating in the Chorrera phase in coastal Ecuador about 1500–500 B.C.E.; they appeared alongside such Asiatic cultural traits as house effigies, roller and flat stamps, and ceramic pillows. Tolstoy (1974) considered the hairless dog of Mexico to have been derived by direct contact from Asia (along with chickens and several plants).

2. **A Viking dog?** Friant and Reichlen (1950,1–18) concluded that "the Inca dog was not domesticated from a South American wild form but was brought from elsewhere already domesticated." Subsequently Friant (1964–1965, 130–35) examined mummified dog remains, including skulls in Inca burials, and found that they compared closely with dog remains in Denmark from the late Neolithic. They postulated that the similarity must be due to the hybridization of Viking dogs with those of the 'Indians' (Incidentally, Adelsteinen and Blumenberg (1983) suggest on genetic grounds the possibility that certain cat populations of the northeastern United States originated from a Viking/Norse introduction. Further research may or may not confirm their speculation.)

3. **Dogs kept for wool**. Lord (1866, II, 215–17) discovered on the American Northwest Coast a few tribes that kept peculiar dogs "differing in every specific detail from all the other breeds of dogs belonging to either coast or inland Indians." They were kept on secluded islands where they could not interbreed with regular canines. These special dogs had long white hair that was shorn

annually. The hair was then woven into rugs, sometimes mixed with wool of a mountain goat, or duck feathers, or finely carded wild hemp. The practice dated from before European contact. Lord was sure these dogs were not indigenous but had been brought from elsewhere. He thought they were likely from Japan, where a small, long-haired dog had been reported. It is not clear to us how more evidence might be obtained to adjudicate this notion, but DNA sequencing probably could solve the problem soon.

The most logical explanation for the 'toy' edible dog of the Americas is, again, transfer by voyage from Asia. It is highly unlikely that such a breed would have been developed separately in two areas and used for the same purpose. A mechanism for how transfer could have taken place is suggested by Xu's (2002) report of a Chinese inscription in Shang Dynasty characters on an artifact from La Venta (the Olmec site in southern Veracruz). This inscription was first noted by other Chinese scholars while inspecting artifacts in a museum in southern Mexico. Xu had previously discovered Chinese characters, also specifically like those of the Shang era in China, on other ceremonial objects from La Venta (Xu 1996; 2002). Chinese experts on Shang-period writing have confirmed some of Xu's readings (personal communication to Sorenson from Xu 2002).

Gallus gallus

Conventional wisdom among zoologists holds that chickens were absent in the New World until introduced by the Spaniards. If that had been the case, the chickens in the hands of Amerindians after the Conquest ought to have been strictly of the Mediterranean type, as Carter (1971; 1998) pointed out, but they were not. Many of them looked like Chinese or Malay chickens, very different in appearance, color of eggs, and behavior from the Mediterranean variety of chicken. Evidence from physical characteristics of fowls, documentary history and ethnography, the uses to which the fowls were put, and the distribution of vernacular names combine to establish that the reputed introduction of the chicken by the Spaniards is contrary to the facts. Instead, multiple introductions of fowls across the oceans, in addition to the Spanish importation, are indicated.

Latcham (1922, 175) observed that in Chile, Bolivia, and Peru, at least three indigenous domesticated varieties or species of chickens were known. The Spanish terms for 'cock,' or 'chicken,' had not been adopted for those birds by the Amerindians "because they have their own names." Their three kinds were definitely present before the Spanish Conquest and are still represented among the fowls kept by the Araucanian Indians of Chile. Some lay blue and olive-green eggs, some are tailless, and have tufts of feathers in the form of a ball at the sides of their heads, as do fowls in China that also lay blue eggs. Johannessen also examined chickens in Chile and found fowl similar to those just described. Finsterbusch (1931) agreed that these were pre-Columbian chickens. Castello (1924) went so far as to identify four types of Chilean chickens which differed from the common European fowl but showed Asiatic features. Blue-egg layers are distributed from Chile to Ecuador and Mexico, he reported. Hartman (1973) surveyed the literature, paying particular attention to cultural meanings of fowl and their uses in Asia and throughout the Americas. She also concluded that Asiatic voyagers probably introduced black-boned, black-meated (BB/BM) chickens to the New World before Columbus.

C. O. Sauer (1952) summarized some of the evidence for the aboriginal presence in South America of a BB/BM chicken. Its breast meat is dark, a melanotic sheath surrounds the bones, and it bears tufts on the side of its head. It also has raised hackles, a black tongue and legs, and characteristic coloring of the feathers that mark it as distinctively Southeast Asian.

Johannessen's fieldwork found that the BB/BM type was still being kept in several locations (Johannessen 1981; Johannessen and Fogg 1982; Johannessen, Fogg, and Fogg 1984). The recent distribution of the melanotic fowl, he reported, is from Mexico southward to Brazil, Peru, and Chile. This is a non-flocking chicken, displaying the social psychology characteristic of the chickens of Southeast Asia that leads them to stay apart from others when feeding.

At least among the groups that speak Mayan languages, the BB/BM chicken is not normally eaten but is used ritualistically in divination or medicinal treatments in essentially the same manner as the Chinese recorded in 1530 C.E. in their Chinese encyclopedia of medicine. These treatments are esoteric. For instance, in highland Guatemala the chicken is cut sagitally, bound against the soles of the feet of an ill person, and left there for two or more hours during which time it is said to absorb the pulmonary problems resulting from an asthma attack. It is also used to cure 'women's problems.' The curer intones specific incantations that are in a non-Mayan jargon recited while candles and copal incense are burned and rum is blown onto the patient's bare skin. Other rituals involving the BB/BM chicken take the fowl's blood and life in order to protect a house, family members, tools, and even ships against hexes. These beliefs and practices also correspond to Chinese ways with BB/BM fowls in Asia.

It seems likely that successful transfer of these cultural patterns must have involved explicit teaching over a considerable period by Asian carriers of the original bird stock. Such rites and beliefs could hardly have been imported via ephemeral contact, say with people off the 17th-century Manila galleons. And it is only speakers of Mayan who received, or at least have carried on, the practices involving the BB/BM chickens. No Chinese (or any other non-Catholics) were legally allowed to settle in early colonial Mexico or Central America, so these esoteric practices appear to have originated earlier.

A very ancient presence of chickens in the Americas has recently been pointed out by a historical linguistic study (Wichmann 1995, 76). Wichmann reconstructed the proto-Mixe-Zoquean language of southern Mexico, which is widely considered to date to the second millennium B.C.E. in the area occupied at that time by the Olmec civilization, and which contained the term *ce:we(kv?)(n) 'chicken, hen.' The same term continued in the succeeding proto-Zoquean language in the following millennium, when it was glossed as 'hen.' The linguist also reconstructed the expression *ná'w-ce:wy for 'cock.' (The word for 'turkey' is completely different from either of the above.) Guillemaud's (Sancho Castro 1947, 112) list of Mixe terms is generally confirmatory, giving *tseuk* for Spanish *gallina*, 'hen.' Furthermore, Kaufman's (1972, 110) reconstructed Proto-Tzeltal-Tzotzil (Mayan) language (ca. 1400 BP) shows *me?-mut [orthography incomplete] for *gallina*, 'chicken.'

Archaeological specimens of purported chicken bones in the Americas have been reported. However, until recently, none of the few tested had been positively dated to before the time of Columbus. There is one Mayan site, Caracol, Belize, where the archaeologists attribute *Gallus gallus* to the Classic era. (Teeter 2004.) At the Cozumel, Mexico dig, archeologists found 4 chicken bones (Hamblin 1985). Storey et al. (2007) found 50 chicken bones, that represent at least five different chickens, at the archeological site El Arenal-1 on the Arauco Penniula in Chile. From one bone they were able to successfully extract a DNA sample that indicates this chicken DNA is similar to Polynesian chicken DNA. The archeological site dates from 700 C.E. to 1390 C.E. This date is arrived at through thermoluminescent analysis of the ceramic object. The chicken bones themselves were Carbon-14 dated and were found to be from 622±35 C.E. (uncalibrated) which results in a calibrated date of 500 C.E. The mDNA was tested agains both DNA obtained from chicken bones dug in ancient Polynesian sites and modern Araucanian chickens.

Littorina littorea

The mollusk *Littorina littorea* is native to Northern European waters. Spjeldnaes and Henningsmoen (1938) suggest that it was introduced to North America by Norse settlers about 1000 C.E. There is no other way to account for its presence on both sides of the Atlantic. They noted that it is a hardy species that could survive for a long time in water in the bottom of an open boat.

Meleagris gallopavo

It is now clear that that quintessentially American fowl, the turkey, was being kept in Europe in the late Medieval Period. In 1940, an observer claimed that an American turkey could be seen in a painted frieze at Schleswig Cathedral, which had been built about 1280 C.E. (Hennig 1940). That claim was rebutted by Stresemann (1940; Rieth 1967) who showed that the mural had been restored in the 1800s and 1900s; hence the rendering of the turkey as it existed in 1940 could have depended on knowledge acquired after Columbus (Bökönyi and Jánossy 1959; Varshavsky 1961). Nevertheless, findings since that time have restored the possibility of a pre-Columbian origin for the Schleswig representation. Hungarian archaeologists found bones of a turkey in the 14th-century royal castle at Buda. Turkey bones have also been excavated from a carefully dated 14th-century-site in Switzerland (Bökönyi and Jánossy 1959). Other Hungarian sites of the 10th to 13th centuries have yielded signet rings engraved with images of this fowl that show the fleshy pendant growth on the turkey's neck. Furthermore, a letter written in 1490 by Hungarian King Matthias, who died later that year, requested through an envoy that the Duke of Milan send him turkeys (*"galine de Indie"*). The king wanted to acclimatize the bird in Hungary. He also asked that a man who knew how to care for turkeys be sent with the birds (Bökönyi and Jánossy 1959). Obviously, the fowl was in Europe before Columbus' first voyage.

Confirmation of the late medieval European distribution of the turkey appears in a comment in a Relación (report of inspection) from Mérida, Yucatan, from about 1579. "There are many turkeys in the mountains which differ little from those in Spain, very good to eat, very timid birds" (Tozzer 1941, viii, 186; emphasis added). The conventional view is that the turkey was brought from the Americas to Spain by the returning conquistadors probably no earlier than 1523. It seems doubtful that their progeny in Iberia would have multiplied in 50 years to such an extent as to be spoken of in the off-handed manner of this Spaniard.

Mya arenaria

The case of *Mya arenaria*, the soft-shelled clam, is probably tied to the Norse voyages in the North Atlantic. Previously thought only to occur in American waters, this species was recently found offshore of Denmark (Peterson et al. 1992). A radiocarbon date on the shells falls in the 13th century, leaving only a slight possibility that the clam could have reached European waters after Columbus. Of course, the transfer to European waters had to have been by ship (perhaps in bilge). Not surprisingly, the investigating scientists decided that the mollusk "could have been transferred from North America to Europe by the Vikings." In the absence of credible alternative scenarios, we think the case should be put more firmly than that.

Stegobium paniceum

The beetle species, *Stegobium paniceum*, a pest usually found in dried, stored vegetable matter, is documented in both Egyptian and Peruvian burials. Greater incidence and earlier recognition of the species in the Old World favors that hemisphere as the place of origin. In Peru, *S. paniceum* was found with mummies dated at least to the 13th century C.E. (Riddle and Vreeland 1982). Burials in Egypt as early as 3400 B.C.E. have revealed this same 'drugstore,' or 'biscuit,' beetle (Buckland and Panagiotakopulu 2001, 6), and it was present also in both Roman (Hall and Kenward 1990) and Bronze Age England (Panagiotakopulu 2000, 16).

Additional evidence for other possible bi-hemispheric species of fauna can be found in Appendix 1.

Table 6
Other Fauna for Which There is Decisive Evidence

Species	Common Name
Alphitobius diaperinus	lesser mealworm
Canis familiaris	edible dog
Gallus gallus	chicken
Littorina littorea	a mollusk
Meleagris gallopavo	turkey
Mya arenaria	American soft-shell clam
Stegobium paniceum	drugstore beetle

The evidence for all the larger faunal species in Table 6 is definitive using the same scale of measure used for the plant species in Table 1.

Table 7
Other Fauna Needing Additional Study

Species	Common Name
Cairina moschata	Muscovy duck
Crax globicera	curassow
Cicada sp.	cicada
Dendrocygna bicolor	fulvous tree duck
Felis catus	cat
Lasioderma serricorne	tobacco or cigarette beetle
Mus musculus	mouse
Rattus rattus	rat
Oryctolagus cuniculus	a rabbit
Rhyzopertha dominica	lesser grain borer

For larger faunal species in Table 7 we have found some anomalous information that leads us to believe that there may have been transoceanic transfer, but the information does not qualify as strong or definitive. These plants need to be researched further to either find more evidence of transfer or to determine that they were not transferred.

TURNING PARSIMONY AROUND

As we view all the evidence, it becomes quite apparent that a large number of plant and animal species were transported across the ocean to or from the Americas before 1492. Furthermore, it is plausible that additional plants will be shown to have crossed as well. There is no reason to think that our present list is exhaustive. Tables 2 and 3 list additional candidates from the flora that ought to be further researched. Of the microfauna, 19 species show decisive evidence of prehistoric transoceanic movement, and another 20 deserve more study (shown in Table 5). Of other species of fauna, we count six as conclusively demonstrated to have been distributed in both hemispheres, and nine others are possible (shown in Table 7).

This evidence puts a new complexion on long-standing questions about transoceanic movements of humans and associated flora and fauna. The outdated stance was illustrated by Spinden's statement (1933, 219) that, "the fact that no food plant is common to the two hemispheres is enough to offset any number of petty puzzles in arts and myths" [such as the patolli/pachisi game]. Thirty-eight years later the same argument was still being invoked: "There is no hard and fast evidence for any pre-Columbian human introduction of any single plant or animal across the ocean from the Old World to the New World, or vice-versa" (Riley et al. 1971, 452–53). The logic of those days held that since "the bulk of the evidence" from biology was generally construed as being against any direct interhemispheric contact, every item of evidence in apparent contradiction to the orthodox view ought to be ignored or held in prejudiced abeyance.

As late as 1985 (p. 361), Willey tried to tighten screws on the evidence even further by insisting that, "No Old World manufactured object has yet been found in an indisputable, undisturbed New World context. If nothing concrete can be shown in the next 50 years, proponents should stop talking about it." Of course by the usual criteria any purported imported object is automatically considered "disputable" or from a "disturbed" context. But no arbitrary stricture like this can be imposed on the question. The evidence speaks for itself, whether it consists of a shared "manufactured object" or a natural feature, and intelligent students of the topic will make up their own minds.

In the light of our findings, parsimony should now be interpreted quite differently from what it formerly was. Given that so many organisms were demonstrably shared between the hemispheres before Columbus, "the bulk of the evidence" today actually supports a voyaging explanation. Not only can we expect additional confirmation to come from study of the flora and fauna (including DNA studies, archaeology, and more careful study of ancient art), but we may also find that many of the "petty puzzles" in culture formerly rejected as proof of contact will now turn out to be in agreement with "the bulk of the [newer] evidence." The facts demand careful consideration instead of perfunctory dismissal.

CULTURAL FREIGHT

It is obvious that cultural, as well as human genetic, features had to have been transported with the flora and fauna on transoceanic voyages. A full discussion of the significance of the biological facts will have to take account of concomitant cultural sharing.

Domesticated plants and animals are almost never successfully transplanted by human agency to a strange area without appropriate care being given to the specimens being moved. Cultural norms for the preservation and exploitation of new organisms must be transmitted along with domesticated plants and animals if they are to survive and flourish in their new setting. That essential knowledge comprises botanical data, agricultural practices, culinary technology, and other measures needed to ensure that the transported organisms are correctly cultivated and usefully employed on the new scene.

Moreover, the skills essential for making ocean voyages generally involve navigational, astronomical, and calendrical lore – concepts that could well survive at the destination. We can be confident also that a substantial body of myth, beliefs, and ritual practices would have accompanied the voyagers. A new linguistic and artistic repertoire would also have been introduced by the newcomers.

Fortunately for solid science, we do have a few archaeologists such as Torber Rick and Jon Erlandson (2008) who have started their science on a path of examining the actual history of the movement of modern humans by ocean voyages into the Americas. They look for early remains along the coasts that indicate the very likely entrance of humans who were following the abundant fishery resource around the shores of the North Pacific Ocean. Erlandson (2002 68) records that the earliest voyaging on the sea was likely by Homo erectus traveling over ocean expanses to Flores, Indonesia, 700,000 to 800,000 years ago. The next oldest voyages recorded are up to 60,000 years BP between New Guinea and Australia. The Channel Islands off Southern California were reached by boat or raft 11,000 to 10,000 years ago for certain. How much earlier people came down the coast by floating craft from the Arctic is probably much in excess of this travel off the coast 10 km. to the islands, visible from the mainland shore. As pointed out earlier, an increasing number of archaeologists see early coastal voyages as probable in the settling of humans in the Americas.

Speculation that people arriving from abroad would automatically be killed or their cultural baggage rejected is not supported by historical cases. The notion that such would have been the fate of voyagers probably owes more to Victorian stereotypes about 'cannibals' eating missionaries than to ethnographic reality. Curiosity is the response, at least as often as hostility, to new arrivals in a land.

Thus, not only does our documentation of the transport of flora and fauna across the oceans open the door for further studies in biological science -- for example, we have noted few of the possibly large number of weeds inadvertently transported by voyagers -- it also demands reconsideration of cultural parallels that have heretofore been categorically thrown out of court by almost all scholars when treating the issue of Old World/New World contacts.

Let us examine a single geographically focused setting for inter-hemispheric contact in order to appreciate how biological facts might connect to cultural data. The data in this book show that as many as 55 species of plants definitely, or very likely, were transferred between the American tropics and India, or vice versa, before Columbus' day. The time of introduction to India was as early as the third millennium B.C.E. While we cannot tell how many voyages this long process involved, there must have been several score – or maybe several hundred – stretched over a period of millennia. Given the apparent scale of biological contact, one would a priori expect substantial cultural interchange as well. For decades researchers have been spelling out data that they consider show a connection between ancient civilizations in India and Mesoamerica and the Andean region, although the nature, timing, and significance of the influences at play have remained vague. We recognize that a certain amount of the cultural evidence that has been offered has been of poor quality and deserves to be ignored unless carefully reconsidered.

As mentioned earlier, in the case of India and the New World, Tylor's 19th-century (1896) identification of striking parallels between the South Asian pachisi and the Mexican patolli board games has never had a satisfactory explanation in terms of parallel, independent invention. In the 1920s, G. Elliot Smith added more cultural parallels between the two areas (see especially his 1924 book that treated elephant symbolism; the Mexican and Buddhist 'purgatory' ordeal; the makara, or 'dragon;' and miniature ritual vehicles bearing sacred figures drawn by animals). A series of articles by Milewski (1959, 1960, 1961, 1966) pointed to many conceptual parallels between deity names in Sanskrit on the one hand, and Aztec (Nahuatl) and Zapotec names on the other. Giesing went on (1984) to compile 50 pages of names and epithets for the Hindu god Siva/Shiva with which names and titles for the Aztec god Tezcatlipoca prove to be congruent. The fire-god complexes of India (Agni) and of central Mexico (Xiuhtecuhtli) were meticulously compared by Cronk (1973), who found extensive and startlingly detailed parallels.

Kelley (1960; Moran and Kelley 1969) argued that much that was basic in Mesoamerican calendrics, cosmology, and mythology is traceable to India of the last centuries B.C.E. and to nowhere else as clearly. Durbin (1971) was sufficiently impressed with Kelley's proposals that he suggested a set of lexical links between Prakrit, Sanskrit-derived languages of India, and proto-Mayan in Central America. Mukerji (1936) claimed to demonstrate specific astronomical correlations between the Mayan and Hindu calendars. Kirchhoff (1964a, 1964b) laid out large blocks of material on conceptual and structural features of the calendar and mythology of Eastern and Southern Asia, also apparently in Mesoamerica. Barthel (1975a, 1975b, 1981, 1982, 1984) did a series of intricate studies of Mesoamerican codices and calendars which he believed confirm that a Hindu 'missionary' effort reached Mexico, only to be obscured by a later 're-barbarization' of the transplanted concepts. The sacred figures who hold ears of corn on temple sculptures in India do so with hands in symbolic positions, or mudra gestures, while Mesoamericanists have noted a repertoire of mudras shared by Indian and Mesoamerican art (Martí 1971; Medvedov 1982). And Compton (1997) has pointed out elaborate parallels between Aztec and Buddhist etiological myths involving the rabbit and the moon.

These studies, plus many more that could be cited, have typically been presented by diffusionists at a high level of abstraction, as though disembodied elements of 'Indian culture' or 'Mesoamerican civilization' were somehow wafted across the ocean where they lodged in the minds of the locals. Protagonists of diffusion have rarely proposed, let alone documented, plausible historical scenarios that would account for the parallels they cite. That is, they have not hypothesized actual voyages in which culturally knowledgeable persons with believable motives are supposed to have boarded specific kinds of vessels to travel along nautically feasible routes and then arrive at particular locations in the opposite hemisphere, where they significantly affected existing cultures. But the time is at hand when such plausible scenarios can be proposed.

Concrete data on biology has the potential to help relate cultural features to dates and locations. The degree of concreteness this would furnish to investigations of cultural parallels may allow researchers to formulate focused and convincing hypotheses about when, where, and how sharing took place. For example, the fact that important American crops were represented in Indian art, mentioned in texts, and found in excavations, might provide concrete chronological and material settings to relate to, say, Kelley's, Cronk's, and Barthel's hypotheses about Indian intellectual and religious influence on Mesoamerica in the late B.C.E. centuries. Yet India is only one area of influence to which the evidence points.

We emphasize that by momentarily focusing on the India/America interchange, we do not consider other origin/destination pairs non-credible. The evidence is particularly strong for South America/Polynesia, Mesoamerica/Hawaii, several American scenes connected to Southeast (especially Indonesia) and East Asia, and Mediterranean/Mesoamerican links. But those are matters yet to be explored and delineated.

We are also convinced that our study by no means resolves all questions about the evidence from the life sciences in regard to voyaging. More needs to be known about all possible species that might have been transported in both directions. But of even greater importance will be the discovery of facts about the processes of diffusion. Who was willing to risk his vessel, his reputation and his life on sailing off into the little-known? How was lore about past seafaring, both successes and failures, passed on through time? What ancient nautical technology and culture have we failed to discover? Were natural resources accumulated for a voyage from a wide or narrow area? (Our list of transported plants, for example, show that they were drawn from a variety of ecological situations – moist lowlands, cool highlands, hot and arid zones, etc.) Did voyagers have to reach a destination with an ecology similar to that of the departure point in order to successfully transfer plants or animals taken along? What economic and ecological consequences did the introduction of novel resources produce in receiving areas? And what were the demographic results of introduced disease agents? Were any voyages planned as outright colonizations? How many different voyages would have had to be carried out to complete the demonstrated plant transfers?

Rather than having discovered a new set of answers to old questions, we prefer to consider this paper a potential source of provocative new questions.

SUMMARY POINTS

Aside from questions for the future, the following points summarize what we have learned from the data in this paper. Each bypasses old conceptions and opens up new avenues of inquiry.

1. A wide variety of mostly tropical floral and faunal materials was carried across the oceans by voyages carried out over a long period of time. The movements must have had significant ecological and economic impacts on the receiving areas.
2. A considerable number of voyages were required to accomplish these transfers. Our views of nautical history quite surely must expand.
3. Travel crossed the oceans in both directions. At least a large number of American plants reached Asia. That fact challenges not just previous interpretations of the American past but also ideas about the history of various Old World areas.
4. The evidence for transoceanic interchange of fauna and flora imply also human gene exchanges and generally a more complex biological history of humankind than has been considered until now. The history of disease is a connected subject that calls for new lines of investigation in the light of our findings about the unexpected ancient distribution of microfauna.
5. It has frequently been postulated – and more frequently assumed – that parallel cultural or social evolutionary processes moved societies independently in Eastern and Western Hemispheres toward the same basic form of 'civilization.' But since developments in both hemispheres must now be seen to have been significantly interconnected, theoreticians would be on weak ground to continue supposing that what transpired in the New World can serve as a separate control by which it is possible to identify general principles or 'laws' of sociocultural evolutionary process. There have been many cultures and civilizations, but it is now apparent that there was to a considerable degree a single ecumene (Sorenson 1971) spread over not just Eurasia but much of the world in pre-Columbian times. Consequently, after five centuries of use, the expressions 'Old World' and 'New World' may have outlived whatever usefulness they initially possessed or at least their accuracy in cultural/historical discourse. We need to move on to clearer geographical, as well as cultural/historical, specification.
6. The time-depth of many cultural developments is probably greater than has been thought. For example, the evidence presented above – of major plant and, by inference, cultural transfers between the

Americas and Asia by the third, or even the fourth, millennium B.C.E. – renders highly unlikely the prevailing view that the impetus toward civilization in Mesoamerica and the Andean zone began only in the late second millennium B.C.E. The challenge to archaeology is obvious.
7. If there is to be further progress toward a truthful history of humankind, greater curiosity needs to be manifested by investigators. Most of the evidence we have utilized here has been around in the literature for years (illustrating A. N. Whitehead's dictum, "Everything of importance has been said before by somebody who did not discover it.") Why the importance of these data has not been grasped previously can be attributed largely to the constriction imposed on scientific and scholarly thought by dogmatic acceptance of a single, unchallenged paradigm for the history of human development. Scholars have accepted sociocultural evolution as representing historical 'truth' instead of as a heuristic device.
8. At the level of public awareness and education, the fact that we have established that ocean-spanning voyages were many and took place both early and late, as well as from multiple origin points to numerous destinations, casts a new light on the inherent capabilities of the world's varied peoples. The transoceanic movements that we have identified do not show 'superior' folks diffusing 'civilization' to benighted 'primitives.' Rather, the facts reveal a poly-cultural tapestry, although still but dimly perceived. It was woven by people of courage and wit of many origins and skin shades. The tapestry's integration came from the fact that from time to time voyagers undertook history-changing communication with lands distant from their own.

We do not intend that our findings spawn new dogmas of any kind. Rather, we hope that intellectual curiosity and openness, disciplined by sound research and logic, will prevail among the next generation of investigators so that they may go beyond, not only where the old paradigm of culture-history allowed, but also beyond the perspective we offer.

APPENDIX 1

In Appendix I the first portion lists the plant species in alphabetical order. Following that, the species of microfauna are presented in alphabetical order, and finally other fauna are listed, again in alphabetical order.

Detailed Documentation

We give references and abstracts or paraphrases of relevant contents in sources used in constructing the argument in the preceding text.

It is obvious that the main text already presented required weighing the value of the data on the various species as evidence for transoceanic voyaging. In that evaluation we tried to utilize a semi-objective framework by reverting to a procedure familiar to us as professors who have had to grade student papers. That is, we laid out a scheme of factors we thought significant in arriving at the worth of information on each species. We then agreed on a score reflecting how convincing each element of information is to us personally. Naturally, the two of us disagreed in places but proceeded to negotiate until we agreed.

Definitive archaeological work demonstrating the appearance of the species in the hemisphere where it did not originate was of course assigned a high score. Other ratings were positive:

1. If a pre-Columbian historical document mentioned the (imported) species.
2. If a lexical source assured us that the species name was known anciently.
3. If pre-Columbian art clearly represented the species in the hemisphere where it did not originate, etc.

We then added those factorial scores together to yield an overall grade. Those species which we graded with an A, A-, B+, or B we considered to have been supported by 'decisive' evidence; we have listed them in Table 1. Tables 2 and 3 list species deemed to rate less than 'decisively evidenced.' A similar procedure was followed to grade the fauna.

The same species could have traveled to more than one destination from more than one origin point. Where that possibility is likely, in our judgment, we have spoken of more than one 'case.' Each case involves different judgments about the applicable evidence; hence, different grades are given for the evidence on a case by case basis.

For each species, we also give a short summary of the logic followed in the grading process. For the convenience of those wishing to evaluate the evidence for themselves, we have included abstracts of the relevant data in each source. The order in which the source abstracts are presented has no particular logic to it.

Since we are not expert in either floral or faunal systematics, our judgment on some points is, of course, subject to correction. We are prepared to be shown how we may be in error of fact or judgment. However, we have no reason to believe that our overall conclusions would need revision as a result of any such corrections.

FLORA

Acorus calamus
Origin: South Asia (?)
Summary: This plant had a long history of cultivation and use in Asia. C. Sauer (1969, 56) reported the tuber to have been used among (North) American Indians at the time of European discovery, and Pullaiah (2002) says, for whatever it means, that the plant is a native of both Asia and Western North America. However, information on its American occurrence that we have encountered is too limited to arrive at any secure conclusion about its significance.
Transfer: Asia to the Americas
Time of transfer: pre-Columbian
Grade: incomplete
Sources: *Acorus calamus* – sweet flag
    Pullaiah 2002, I, 27. "Native of South Asia, and cent. and west North America"
    C. Sauer 1969, 56. One of several plants associated with man in the Americas, which also grew in Asia.

Adenostemma viscosum
Origin: the Americas
Summary: The plant was found in Hawaii by Hillebrand (1888), who considered it to have grown there before Europeans arrived, because it was growing throughout the low-elevation woods on all the islands of the archipelago within 75 years after Capt. Cook's arrival. A legitimate native name and established native medicinal usage confirm its pre-Cookian age. Furthermore, Chopra et al. (1956) describe its distribution as "throughout India" with no hint that it could have been a modern introduction and still be able to account for that distribution.
    Case 1: Transfer: the Americas to Hawaii
    Time of transfer: pre-European discovery
    Grade: Incomplete
    Case 2: Transfer: the Americas to India
    Time of transfer: pre-European, sufficient centuries ago to explain distribution "throughout India."
    Grade: C
Sources: *Adenostemma viscosum*
    Hillebrand 1888, 192. A. viscosum, Forst. "A genus of few American species, of which the following is spread over many warm countries." Under the species entry he also notes: "Common in the lower woods of all [Hawaiian] islands. Nat. name: Kamanamana. An infusion of the leaves is

used as a remedy in fevers by the natives. The species is widely spread over the Americas, Polynesia, N. Australia, Asia, and Africa." Not marked to indicate a post-Capt. Cook import.

Chopra et al. 1956, 6–7. Adena lavenia (syn. A. viscosum). "Throughout India."

Agave spp.
Origin: the Americas
Summary: Since the plant is usually vegetatively reproduced, transoceanic movement must have been human-aided. Finding Agave (species not identified) fiber in the ancient wreck of a Greek ship is conclusive evidence for America-to-Mediterranean transport of the genus. But we do not know which species this is, and it could have been any of seven or eight. This entry covers the indeterminate case meant to show that a minimum of one species was transferred. The widespread distribution of agave plants in India by 1800 is additional evidence for a pre-Columbian transfer. To simplify matters, we assume for the moment that the agave used in the Greek ship was probably one also growing in India, but we still do not know what species that was. (If the agave fibers from the Kyrenia ship can be located for further examination by botanists, we might be able to learn the exact species it represents.)

Transfer: from the Americas to the eastern Mediterranean
Time of transfer: before 300 B.C.E.
Grade: A
Sources: *Agave* spp.

Desmond 1992, 201. Re. Agave, Lord Valentia in 1809 observed that "it is in such profusion [in India] that it is hardly possible to suppose it could have been introduced from America" [by Europeans in recent centuries].

Steffy (1985) reported in a premier archaeological journal the discovery of agave fibers mixed with pine resin serving as watertight caulking on the fourth-century B.C.E. Greek ship that had sunk at Kyrenia, Cyprus. The hull was covered on the outside with large sheets of lead that were held in place by a compound of pine resin and agave fibers.

Steffy (2001) E-mail message. Date: Wed., 18 April 2001, 16:40:06–0500. From: "J. R. Steffy" rsteffy@pop.tamu.edu. Subject: Agave. To: John Sorenson john_sorenson@byu.edu. "You wouldn't believe how many people have protested that statement, but I was only repeating the identifications made by professionals in respectable laboratories. I am long retired and have given most of my records from the 1970s [when the Kyrenia ship was excavated] to the university [Texas A&M]. I will have to contact Michael Katzev to find out the names of the biologists who identified the agave, but I remember the first samples were identified by Kew Gardens in England. A second set was done later in the U. S. with the same results, but I can't remember which lab did it. At a conference a couple of years ago, I heard there were similar ancient analyses, but they couldn't tell me where they were published. I have also heard that one form of agave was native to the eastern Mediterranean. I am a ship construction specialist, not a biologist, so I can only repeat the information given to me in such cases. All I can confirm is that this stringy substance, when mixed with pine resin, makes a marvelous watertight underlayment; that was the only point I was trying to make."

J. Sauer 1993, 177. Two kinds of agave, henequen and sisal, have become important commercial fiber crops. They have been named as species, A. fourcroydes and A. sisalana, respectively, although they are really clones. Both were developed as cultivars in prehistoric Yucatan.

Carter 2002, 254. "…agave leaves were used anciently in a matrix of pitch to form a protective coat against shipworms," citing Steffy (1994, 56). "The huge leaves [used in the Kyrenia ship] must have been flattened and then woven into mats. There had to be a large quantity readily at hand to supply enough matting to cover a ship's bottom up to its waterline. The excavator, the late Michael Katzev, told me (personal communications) that there are piles more of the material still available for inspection" [at Texas A & M University, where both Katzev and Carter were professors]. The sophisticated development of this technique indicates that many ships would have been treated in this manner earlier, not just the one Kyrenia vessel.]

Beyond the evidence for simply some species having been transferred, the sources tell us about particular species. We list these separately.

Agave americana - (Maybe in addition to or the same as the "unidentified" species above.)
Origin: the Americas
Transfer: the Americas to India
Time of transfer: while Sanskrit was still lexically active (before 1000 C.E.)
Grade: A-
Sources: *Agave americana*

Balfour 1871–1873, I, 51–2. Common all over India, useful as a hedge plant and for fiber. 52. Sanskrit: *kala kantala*. I, 84. Two species of agave, the *A. americana* and *A. vivipera*, have become so naturalized in many countries and in India as to seem indigenous.

Reference to the Flora of China: this species is listed as "native" to China (presumably because of distribution}.

MOBOT 2003. Distribution of *A. americana*, N., M., S. America and Carib. according to the MOBOT and traditions indicating a long history in country.

Torkelson 1999, 1634. *A. americana*, Sanskrit: *kantala*

Watson 1868, 250. *A. americana*, Sanskrit: *kantala*

Nadkarni 1914, 23. *A. americana*, Sanskrit: *kantala*; Eng.: "American aloe" (the vernacular English term used in India for *A. americana*, although in strict taxonomic terms, it is not an aloe.) Naturalized in many parts of India.

Pullaiah 2002, I, 34–5. *A. americanum*, Sanskrit: *kalakantala*. Century plant, aloe plant. It is propagated by suckers [which rules out any transfer across the ocean by natural means].

Agave angustifolia - (This species may be in addition to or the same as the "unidentified" *Agave* sp. above.)
Origin: the Americas
Transfer: the Americas to India
Time of transfer: while Sanskrit was lexically active (before 1000 C.E.)
Grade: A-
Sources: *Agave angustifolia* (syn. vivipera)
> Chopra et al. 1956, 9. *A. vivipera*. Naturalized in the sub-Himalayan tract, the outer Himalayas, and many other parts of India. Sanskrit: *kantala*.
> Balfour 1871–1873, I, 51–2. Common all over India, useful as a hedge-plant and for fiber. 52. Sanskrit: *kala kantala*. I, 84. *A. vivipera* has become so naturalized in many countries and in India as to seem indigenous.
> MOBOT 2003. Distribution of *A. vivipera*, Middle and South America.

Agave cantala - (May be in addition to or the same as the *Agave* sp. discussed initially above.)
Origin: the Americas
Transfer: the Americas to India
Time of transfer: while Sanskrit was lexically active (before 1000 C.E.)
Grade: A-
Sources: *Agave cantala*
> Chopra et al. 1969, 3. Sanskrit: *kantala*. Naturalized on the east and west coast, upper Gangetic plain, and parts of Punjab.
> Chopra et al. 1956, 9. Sanskrit: *kantala*. "A native of America."
> Zeven and de Wet 1982, 185. They treat as distinct species: *A. americana, A. atrovirons*, A. *cantala*, A. fourcroydes, A. sisalana, and others. The origin of the scientific species term *'cantala,'* which is obviously parallel to Sanskrit *'kantala,'* remains to be investigated. We guess that the addition to Linnaean nomenclature came from an Indian botanist.
> Balfour 1871–1873, I, 51–2. Common all over India, useful as a hedge-plant and for fiber. Sanskrit: *kala kantala*.

Ageratum conyzoides
Origin: the Americas
Summary: This weed would probably have been introduced by sailors inadvertently. According to both Brown and Hillebrand, it was in Hawaii (and had a native name) before European explorers arrived there. In India, it was so widely grown that Balfour considered it indigenous, and Pandey says it is "naturalized throughout India."
> Case 1: Transfer: the Americas to Hawaii
> Time of transfer: pre-European contact with Hawaii
> Grade: B
> Case 2: Transfer: the Americas to India
> Time of transfer: pre-European contact
> Grade: B

Sources: *Ageratum conyzoides*—goatweed

Brown 1935, 336. The (Hawaiian) native name is *meie parari*, or *mei rore*; used for leis, scent, and medicine. "Pantropic; of American origin, probably unintentionally introduced by early man in southeastern Polynesia."

Safford 1905, 176. *Ageratum conyzoides* ('goatweed'). "It is of American origin, but is now widely spread throughout the Pacific and has found its way to many tropical countries."

Balfour 1871–73, I, 52. Mentions *Ageratum coerulium* and *A. Mexicanum*, exotic flowering plants. "*A. conyzoides* is a native of India." [To be so considered would require naturalization over more centuries than since the Portuguese.]

Pandey 2000, 271. *Ageratum conyzoides*, from South America, is one species "naturalized throughout India."

Pullaiah 2002 I, 35. Sanskrit: *visamustih*. Used in the system of Ayurvedic medicine.

Chopra et al. 1956, 9. Throughout India up to 5,000 ft.

Hillebrand 1888, XCIII. The editor, W. F. Hillebrand (son of the author), noted that in the course of completing the book, his father changed his mind about some plants which he had assumed to have been introduced into Hawaii since Cook. Although he changed his mind – ending up of the opinion that they "may in reality have been of earlier [pre-Cookian] introduction" – he failed to go back and change the symbols [in the manuscript] indicating that fact. Here, young Hillebrand says, "Of 9 non-endemic species which existed before the discovery, 6, [including] one *Ageratum* (now diffused over most tropical countries) [plus five other species] are American ...."

Ageratum houstonianum
Origin: the Americas
Summary: This plant was naturalized in parts of India and China. Assuming that *A. conyzoides* is an imported weed, the accidental transport of this second *Ageratum* at the same time would be plausible, although we cannot be sure at this time.
Grade: incomplete
Sources: *Ageratum houstonianum* – floss flower

Pandey 2000, 272. A. houstonianum, from Mexico, is another species "naturalized in some parts of India." 284. Called the floss-flower.

MOBOT 2003. A. houstonianum is naturalized in China.

Alternanthera philoxeroides
Origin: Brazil
Summary: Four species of this genus, which is from South America, are naturalized in India and Southeast Asia generally. One of those is *A. philoxeroides*, which has two Sanskrit names. While botanists have assumed a recent introduction of the genus, there is no specific information to support that speculation. Rather, the mention by Rheede of the genus being in Malabar in the 17th century, along with the existence of the Sanskrit names, points to a much longer history of the genus in South Asia.
Transfer: South America to South Asia

Time of transfer: apparently while Sanskrit was still active, that is, before 1000 C.E.
Grade: B
Sources: *Alternanthera philoxeroides* – alligator weed
   Sivarajan and Mathew 1984, 49, 51. They deal with the species of
      Alternanthera Forsk. Five species of the genus have been reported.
      Another tropical American species, A. tenella, is reported here for the first
      time from India. These may be reduced to four good species because of
      duplication. Several explanations for the distribution are offered: (1) *A.
      sessilis* is commonly distributed in the tropics and subtropics of both the
      New and Old World and is common throughout India and thrives in a
      variety of habitats. [This is not an explanation.] (2) The Brazilian species,
      A. philoxeroides, commonly called 'alligator weed,' is of recent introduction
      to India, being first noted in 1964. (3) *A. sessilis* was suggested by Govindu
      as "brought to India by horses imported from the Middle East during the
      First World War. Since then, this [species] has spread to various other
      parts and is now fairly common throughout India." [Yet, these authors
      note, disjunctively, that A sessilis "has been illustrated by Rheede in his
      Hortus Malabaricus as early as in 1692."] (4) *A. pungens*, "a tropical
      American weed now widely distributed in the tropics and subtropics of
      the world. In India it is naturalized." (5) *A. philoxeroides* is "an American
      weed introduced into the Old World Tropics long ago and reported from
      Malesia [sic], Indonesia, Burma, and India."
   Pullaiah 2002, I, 47. *A. philoxeroides*. Sanskrit: *matsyahi, lonika*.

Alternanthera pungens
Origin: tropical America
Summary: A tropical American weed now naturalized in India. One or more of the species in this genus appear to have been ancient in India, therefore this plant too should be investigated further to see whether it was introduced early.
Grade: incomplete
Source: See source and information under *A. philoxeroides*

Alternanthera sessilis
Origin: tropical America
Summary: A tropical American weed now naturalized in India. One or more of the species in this genus appear to have been ancient in India, therefore this plant too should be investigated further to see whether it was introduced early.
Grade: incomplete
Source: *A. sessilis* was "illustrated by Rheede in his 'Hortus Malabaricus' as early as 1692." See source and information under *A. philoxeroides*.

Alternanthera tonella
Origin: tropical America
Summary: A tropical American weed now naturalized in India. One or more of the species in this genus appear to have been ancient in India, therefore this plant too should be investigated further to see whether it was introduced early.
Grade: incomplete

Source: See information under *A. philoxeroides*

Amanita muscaria
Origin: unclear
Summary: Whether the *Amanita muscaria* forest mushroom was transported by humans or discovered in place, uses and connotations for it are so much alike in Mexico and Asia, (as well as in North America) that it is plausible that at least the cultural complexes involving it are connected historically. Unless further study comes up with an alternative plausible scenario, we consider it probable that only a physical transfer of this fungus by a human group can explain how transfer between the hemispheres took place anciently. That may have occurred by spores borne on the wind were the plant present in boreal regions, but the distances involved make a tropical passage by wind even less likely. However, human voyagers, whose existence we have established, could have moved the mushroom to Mexico along with accompanying beliefs and rites.
Transfer: Asia to Mesoamerica
Time of transfer: since the time when a detailed cultural complex involving mushroom ingestion developed in the Old World (no earlier than 500 B.C.E.?)
Grade: C
Sources: *Amanita muscaria* – fly agaric, fly amanita (a fungus)
- Aguilar 2003, 80. The pharmacopeia of Maya shamans included the *Amanita muscaria* and various members of the *Psilocybe* genus. In India, the 'Soma' (the *Amanita muscaria* mushroom) was considered a sacred plant in the Rig Veda. Medieval Europeans were familiar with *Amanita muscaria* and considered it demoniac.
- Wasson 1980. In his 1968 book on Soma (page 163) he noted the general similarity of northern Eurasian and Middle American mushroom usages and beliefs but could not bring himself to imagine any historical connection between the two. Now, in 1980, guided by Levi-Strauss, who supposed that a connection was likely, he considers the evidence to show the circumpolar extent (including Siberia and the Algonkian Indians) of at least fly agaric usage.
- (Wasson 1980 cont'd.) The Quiché of Guatemala equate *Amanita muscaria* with the thunderbolt ('mushroom of the lightning-bolt'), although they do not eat it, preferring the *Psilocybe* species. The same belief in the connection of lightning to the Amanita was present in Eurasia (and among the Algonkian-speaking Ojibway). 185. *A. muscaria* was in use among Basques, in France, and among the Chinese. 189. The association of toad, mushroom, and female genitalia must be very ancient and probably crossed Bering Strait with early immigrants to the Americas. [That is, of course, purely speculative, in light of the restricted distribution of the plant and the cultural complex in the Americas.]
- 43. Parallels are cited between Santal (a language of India), which preserves a derivative of the Sanskrit, *putika*, the first surrogate for the sacred Soma of Vedic hymns, and Náhuatl (Mexico) as follows: (1) divinity glows in a mushroom giving it a soul; (2) the mushroom speaks; it is "the Word." *Amanita muscaria* was the Soma plant of the Vedas. 57. Parallels between

Mesoamerican and Siberian/Eurasian mushroom lore: (1) the mushroom evokes an imaginary world of Little People which are the spirits of the mushrooms; (2) it speaks through a shaman's voice; (3) it is connected to lightning bolts. 228–99. *Amanita muscaria* is all around in the Chiapas highlands and highland Guatemala, but avoided by today's dwellers. In Quiché, its name is kakuljá, "lightning bolt." 185. "In Mesoamerica, *A. muscaria* must have been replaced by the superior *Psilocybe* series" of mushrooms.

Wasson and Wasson 1957, 317. Ancestors of the Zapotecs, Greeks, Semites, Polynesians, and Chinese all had the notion of a connection of lightning to mushrooms. 318. There are "startling parallels" between the use of fly amanita in Siberia and the divine mushrooms of Middle America: for example, the substance is said to "speak" to the eater.

González Calderón 1991, 44–5. (This source has text in English that sometimes is difficult to understand, and the author rarely cites references; we suppose, however, that a competent Sinicist could provide primary documentation, if it exists, for the following assertions.) "When we checked the old Chinese texts, we found that the first historical narrations on the first sea travels of Chinese ships occurred during" the Han period. In the book Shih-Chi we can read that "there were miraculous drugs in the Peng-Lai Islands." Speaking now of Quin-Shi-Wang-Di, the first unifier of China, after the Chow [Chou] Dynasty: He unified China into a single big nation. He heard of some remote, mysterious islands located in the East Sea, where there used to exist some wonderful herbs, which were able to produce the effect of eternal youth and immortality. The gods who watched over those islands, he was told, demanded a tribute of children. Constructing a fleet of ships, he placed aboard 3000 girls and boys from good families, plus gifts, like seeds of the five types of grains. The fleet was under the leadership of Hsi-Fu. They set sail in the year 219 B.C.E., according to the Shih-Chi book. The expedition failed. Hsi-Fu arrived in Ping-Yuang and Kuangtsu and stayed there, making himself king of the region, but never returned to China. In the year 104 B.C.E., another trip into the ocean was begun, to search for the Islands of Fortune and the Sacred Mountains. The emperor was Wu, and the commander of the expedition was the magician Li-Sho-Shun. There is also another narration during the Han period that could involve a return trip. "The kings of the Barbarians from the East crossed the great ocean to offer tribute from their country to the emperor."

See also Barthel 1985 for a possible transfer mechanism.

Amaranthus spp.
Sources: *Amaranthus* spp. information in general (Index Kewensis has the following synonymies: *A. caudatus*, syn. *paniculatus*, syn. *frumentaceus*(?). Also, *A. hypochondriacus*, syn. *leucocarpus*.)

According to K. T. Harper (emeritus professor of botany, BYU), personal communication, 2004, amaranths and chenopods provide a "complete" diet of amino acids for humans without the addition of animal protein.

People with a practical, traditional knowledge of the dietary value of amaranths might have considered those grains especially appealing to parties of migrants sailing to new and largely unknown environments.

Roys 1931, 232. Mayan *chac-tez* is *Amaranthus* sp. "See *x-tez*." 242. Mayan *e-c* [pronounced etzen]. Quotes Motul, the oldest Mayan dictionary of Yucatan: "A species of *Amaranthus* of this land, resembling the Mercurialis of Spain." [That statement deserves investigation in re. origin and affiliation of mercuriali of Spain.] 285. *Amaranthus* sp., *bledo* (Motul dictionary). *Xx-tez*. *Tez* is a generic name for the species.

A published source in some ways superior to Roys 1931 is Bradburn 1998, which came to our attention too late to incorporate here in detail. It lists 50 species of flora from among those treated herein, with over 75 Mayan terms for them as used in one Yucatan village.

Bretschneider 1892, 411. Lists five species of *Amaranthus* having Chinese characters used in Japan (from Matsumura; the Chinese-character names may or may not be pre-European in usage): *A. caudatus* (an American grain), *A. mangostanus* [Asian native], *A. melancholicus* (var. tricolor) [Asian native], *A. spinosus* [see below], and *A. viridis* [Asian native].

Index Kewensis has the following synonymies: *A. caudatus*, syn. *paniculatus*, syn. *frumentaceus*(?). Also, *A. hypochondriacus*, syn. *leucocarpus*.

Balfour 1871–1873, I, 92–3. *A. caudatus*, English: 'Love Lies Bleeding.' Commonly cultivated for ornament. *A. cruentus*, in Persian *batu zard*, a common food, used for bread, cakes, among peasants of the Himalayas. *A. frumentaceus* Buch. (syn. *A. caudatus* [American origin]). Panjab [sic]: *bathú*, which is ground into flour and is a principal article of diet for hill people. *A. spinosus*, Linn. Roxb., "thorny amaranth." A very troublesome weed all over southern India and Burma.

Brücher 1989, 54–5. Taxonomically, the genus is difficult. Aellen (1967) and J. Sauer (1967) tried to order its systematics. They recommended two sections: *Blitopsis* and *Amaranthotypus*. The former has "mainly" n=17 chromosomes, the latter n=16. Most are wild-growing cosmopolites. These potherbs originated in Asia and Africa. Citing Pal et al. (1974), the species *A. caudatus*, *A. cruentus*, and *A. hypochondriacus* are closer related among themselves than to any putative weedy progenitor (Kulakov et al. 1985). 56. *A. hypochondriacus*, syn. *leucocarpus*, hispanic names, *bledo*, *huautli*. *A. cruentus*, purple amaranth, of Central American origin (so also *leucocarpus*). [In America] *A. cruentus* is known earliest, 4000 BP (citing MacNeish 1992, 57). *A. caudatus* is in northern Argentina, Bolivia, Peru. The early European herbals also depict this plant. In Argentina, it comes from 4–5000-year-old sites.

J. Sauer 1950, 612. "The grain amaranths belong to several distinct but closely-related species, cultivated by a curiously diverse and scattered group of peoples since immemorially ancient times." 613. Four regions each have their own species cultivated: *A. leucocarpus* [syn. *hypochondriacus*] in Mexico, *A. cruentus* in Guatemala, *A. caudatus* in the Andes. On the whole, the ranges of the species in the New World are distinct [which means that when different species show up in Asia, quite certainly they came from different locations in the Americas]. "In Asia, there is a great, vaguely delimited grain amaranth region stretching all the way from Manchuria through interior China and the Himalaya to Afghanistan and Persia. *A. leucocarpus* and *A. caudatus* are both grown throughout this area. The poorly known grain crop of Africa is probably also *A. caudatus*." "In mode of cultivation and use, the Old and New World crops are strikingly similar. In both areas, the crop shows a special affinity for the highlands, so far as I know, its concentration at high elevations is not explainable by any natural barriers." "In both the Old and New World, the plants are usually grown on a small scale, mixed in the plantings of maize and other crops. The grain is ordinarily consumed by the growers and is prepared in similar ways almost everywhere. The seeds are first parched or popped; then they are either made into balls like popcorn, with a syrup binder, or they are ground to meal, which is stirred into a drink or baked into little cakes."

(J. Sauer contd.) Taxonomically, all of the grain amaranths cultivated in the Old World are indistinguishable from certain of those cultivated in the New World. Not only in terms of species, but also in terms of sub-specific entities, the available Old World specimens represent nothing but a small sample of the diversity present in the American grain amaranths. There are amaranths grown in Asia for potherbs or ornamentals, but never for seeds, which [the former] are obviously natives of Asia. This entire Asiatic potherb group is easily distinguishable from the grain group by important technical characters. The non-cultivated amaranths closely related to the grain species also show a striking concentration in the New World. No evidence was found of any non-cultivated entity closely related to the grain amaranths which are peculiar to the Old World. 614. "The conclusion appears inescapable that the grain amaranths are all of New World origin." "A well-developed grain amaranth produces such an enormous quantity of seed, though the seeds are individually minute, that the yield of the crop per unit area often exceeds that of maize." "Development of these stable entities so distinct from their wild relatives would be expected to require long selection. The antiquity of the crop is also indicated by other evidence." "The grain amaranths were one of the great food staples of Mexico at the time of the Conquest, regarded by the people as among their most ancient crops, and fantastically important in legend and ritual."

(J. Sauer cont'd.) "The question as to whether the crop reached Asia before the European expansion cannot be answered with certainty. There is the 10th-century Chinese document [see below] that seems to refer to grain amaranths, but this is hardly absolute proof. If the crop was introduced into Asia after Columbus, it must be credited with a remarkable achievement in making itself very much at home among strangers within a few generations." "Strangely enough, plants resembling *A. leucocarpus* do not appear in the European herbals until about 1700, more than a century after *A. caudatus* had been brought to Europe as an ornamental."

(J. Sauer cont'd.) 588. "The crop is scattered so widely through Asia and is so firmly entrenched among remote peoples that it gives a powerful impression of great antiquity in the area. Many investigators, from De Candolle ... to Merrill (1950, 16–17), have concluded that the crop has certainly been cultivated in southern Asia from time immemorial and probably originated there." "The best hope of finding early records would seem to be in India." 589. "It is startling to find that Bretschneider (1896, 405) presents what seems to be a clear reference to a grain amaranth in an ancient Chinese Materia Medica. This work, written about 950 C.E. for the Prince of Shu, modern Szechwan, lists six kinds of *hien*, a generic name for a group of related plants, mostly indigenous amaranths cultivated as potherbs. Among these were two whose seeds were used in medicine, one was called *jen* (meaning, man) *hien*, possibly because it grew tall and erect." "... A modern record of grain amaranths from the same area ... gives the same name." A. was collected in the early nineteenth century in hills [in] south India where it was cultivated for seed which was ground for flour. 590. There are non-specific reports of cultivation of amaranths in Ceylon. Also, it was grown widely in northern India. They have been recorded repeatedly along the whole length of the Himalaya from Kashmir to Bhutan. 593. Also in Afghanistan and Persia, as well as in mountainous western China and Manchuria.

Anderson 1960, 70–1. Praises J. Sauer's thesis. He has "demonstrated beyond all reasonable doubt" that Asiatic and American amaranths "are identical." Even E.D. Merrill went out of his way to give it a clean bill of health.

Roys 1931, 285. Mayan "X-tez. *Amaranthus* sp. *bledo*. (Motul dictionary.)"

Bretschneider 1882, 32. Shen Nung, an emperor [purportedly, not actually] of the eighth century B.C.E., authored a famous classic of materia medica. He mentions this plant in the document attributed to him. 49–53. From a treatise, Kiu Huang Pen Ts'ao, by Chou Ting Wang, an imperial prince under the first Ming Emperor (the prince died in 1425). He had seen this plant in Honan province.

Pal and Khoshoo 1974, 130. Description of uses in places where the seed is in the staple diet of the people. The most common use is in the form of sweetmeats. The popped grains are mixed with brown cane sugar and converted into balls or cakes. 132. Theories of origin: Citing Purseglove 1968 as authority, they assert there is no valid evidence of the movement of crops by man between the Old and the New World in pre-Columbian times. Most of the grain amaranths reached Asia in the eighth century and early in the ninth century. The grain amaranths, although an accepted food of the Hindus and Buddhists on religious days, they say, do not have a Sanskrit name [this is contradicted now by Chopra, see above, and implicitly by archaeological sources, such as Saraswat et al.], but such names exist for vegetable amaranths indigenous to Southeast Asia and India. They set out to test the cross compatibility of species experimentally. Evidently the differentiation between the three groups of species is very great [contradict J. Sauer on this point]. Contrary to general belief, a variety of isolating mechanisms prevents hybridization. All these facts indicate that the theories of introgression in the history of the grain amaranths put forward by J. Sauer are not substantiated. Three groups are differentiated by chromosome numbers (one type covers *A. caudatus* and *A. edulis* with weedy *A. quitensis*. Central and North American species divide on chromosome number with one type consisting of *A. hypochondriacus* and the wild *A. hybridus*, while cultivated *A. cruentus* and wild *A. powellii* form the third type.)

Amaranthus caudatus
Origin: Andean region
Summary: The Asian forms of the plant are clearly within the norms for *A. caudatus* in the Americas. The grain has been recovered at an archaeological site in India dated to before 800 B.C.E. Moreover, it bore a Sanskrit name. The food uses to which the grain is put are the same in the Himalayan area as in Middle America.
Transfer: South America to India
Time of transfer: by 800 B.C.E.
Grade: A
Sources: *Amaranthus caudatus* – amaranth, *bledo*, love-lies-bleeding
  Chopra et al. 1956, 17. Sanskrit: *rajagiri*. Cultivated throughout India, chiefly in mountainous tracts, up to 9000 ft. in the Himalayas.
  Torkelson 1999, 1641. Sanskrit: *rajagiri*
  Int. Lib. Assoc. 1996, 559. Sanskrit: *rajagiri*
  Saraswat, Sharma, and Saini 1994, 282, 284, 331. *A. caudatus* excavated in India at the Narhan site (1000–800 B.C.E.).
  Towle 1961, 37. Cook says that the seeds will pop like kernels of maize and taste is similar. No archaeological specimens have been recovered, but it is thought this plant was economically significant.
  Bretschneider 1892, 411. Lists five species of *Amaranthus* labeled with Chinese characters in Japan (after Matsumura, not necessarily classic Chinese): *A. caudatus, A. mangostanus, A. melancholicus* (var. tricolor), *A. spinosus,* and *A. viridis*.
  J. Sauer 1967, 127. It probably originated by domestication of *A. quitensis* as an ancient Andean grain crop. In South America, it is superficially similar to *Chenopodium lupinus*.
See also the material under *Amaranthus* spp. in general.

Amaranthus cruentus
Origin: Guatemala or thereabouts
Summary: It is so widespread throughout Asia that it must have been introduced there at a fairly remote historical period. The plant fits readily into the range of the American species. Uses are the same in both hemispheres.
Time of transfer: 1000 C.E.
Re. plausibility of alternative explanations for its distribution: J. Sauer said, "If the crop was introduced into Asia after Columbus, it must be credited with a remarkable achievement in making itself very much at home among strangers within a few generations."
Grade: A
Sources: *Amaranthus cruentus* (syn. *paniculatus*) – amaranth, *huauhtli*, alegría

Pickersgill and Heiser 1978, 808. *A. cruentus* dates to 5500–4300 BP in
Tehuacán Valley. [Compare divergent date by Sauer, below.]

Johannessen and Wang 1998, 29. In 1986, he and Anne Parker observed
Buddhist priests in eastern Bhutan perform an annual eucharist-like
service involving popped amaranth seed mixed with honey, an offering
that the local population insisted had to be continued to ensure their well-
being. The Aztecs had a similar rite.

J. Sauer 1967, 123. Evidently originated as a domesticated grain crop in
southern Mexico or Guatemala. Progenitor is *A. hybridus*. 125. In the Old
World tropics, the chronology and geography of the species' immigration
are quite mysterious. Attributed to China and India in eighth-century
literature. By 1850, it was common in south India. 126. Asiatic cultivation
of *A. cruentus* is mostly outside the grain amaranth regions and extends
through the tropical and warm temperate parts of India, Indo-China,
China, Japan, Philippines, Indonesia, New Guinea, and Fiji. "In African
botanical literature, *A. cruentus* usually masquerades as *A. caudatus*."

See also materials on *Amaranthus* spp. in general.

Amaranthus hypochondriacus
Origin: highland Mexico
Summary: This third grain amaranth shares with *A. caudatus* and *A. cruentus* an
extended distribution in Asia. Again, food uses are similar. Sauer: "All specimens
examined from Nepal appear to be identical to common Latin American forms."
Time of transfer: by 1000 C.E.
Grade: A
Sources: *Amaranthus hypochondriacus* (now the preferred taxon; syn. *leucocarpus*) –
amaranth, *huauhtli*

J. Sauer 1950, 561–632. There were four species in the Americas cultivated for
grain. *A. leucocarpus* in Mexico and the U.S. Southwest, *A. cruentus* in
Guatemala, *A. caudatus* in the Andean region, and *A. edulis* in Argentina.
The first and third are widely cultivated in Asia over a large area extending
from Manchuria through interior China and the Himalayas to India,
Afghanistan, and Iran. Carter cites him as showing that the Chinese
character that today represents the word for grain amaranth was known as
early as the 10th century in China. The Asian plants are not only nearly
identical but also part of a complex of traits involving methods of
cultivation, preparation, and use. (The most common method of
utilization was popping the seeds and adding syrup as a binder to form
cakes in China, Mexico, Nepal, and Argentina.)

J. Sauer 1969, 80–1. Grown in the Tehuacán Valley, Mexico, Upper Palo
Blanco phase, 200 B.C.E.—700 C.E. Also in Arizona in the fourth
century.

J. Sauer 1967, 127–8. "Post-Columbian introduction [to Eurasia] is hard to
imagine." "*A. caudatus* was taken to Europe in the sixteenth century and
historically dispersed, yet "other races from the Andean complex are also
in the Old World and are harder to explain; one was first found by

European botanists in Kashmir and Ethiopia, where it is planted for grain."

Sasuke and Sauer, J. 1956, 141. There are two closely related species in Asia: *Amaranthus caudatus*, a native of the Andes, and *A. leucocarpus*, a native of the Mexican highlands. No information available indicates that these two species are distinguished by Nepalese, although they are planted separately. "All specimens examined from Nepal appear to be identical to common Latin American forms." Local names reported are: marcha in northwest Nepal, nana in central Nepal in general, pilim among Sherpa of central Nepal, latav in Katmandu. No name is recorded among Tibetans in Nepal. Sometimes inter-planted with maize, maturing after harvest of the corn ears. Occasionally, some of the young plant leaves are boiled as potherbs, a common practice with various amaranth species in the plains of India and many other parts of the world. Amaranth grain is used exclusively for human food, not fed to livestock. In western and central Nepal the grain is ground into flour, then boiled into gruel. At Katmandu and Madwanpur on the pilgrim way to Katmandu, amaranth grain is popped and made into little cakes or balls held together with sugar syrup. These cakes are associated with a special winter festival during which they are offered to a particular god and eaten by the people.

(Sasuke and Sauer cont'd.) "In many respects – the species involved, the methods of planting, preparing for food, and ceremonial use – the grain amaranth pattern of Nepal is similar to that found over a tremendous area of the highlands of Asia and Latin America. The reason for the parallels between America and Asia is not understood, nor is it known how or when amaranths were introduced to Asia. The first botanists who recorded the crop in Asia believed it was an ancient native domesticate and this belief has persisted until quite recently. Since it has become clear that the wild relatives of the grain amaranth species are strictly American and that the crop is certainly ancient in America, the antiquity of the crop in Asia has naturally been called into question. It has been suggested recently that the plants were introduced from Brazil to India by early Portuguese traders (Merrill 1954, 301). This explanation is not completely satisfying because there is no evidence that amaranths were ever cultivated for grain in Brazil or any other Portuguese areas of the New World, nor is their distribution in Asia correlated with areas of Portuguese activity ... ; grain amaranths are not the sort of crop that the early European voyagers would be expected to promote. The Spanish invaders of the grain amaranth regions of the New World generally regarded the crop with contempt or hostility because of its intimate association with what they regarded as the devilish ceremonials of the Indians. No European colonists are known to have adopted the crop. Could Europeans have introduced these as ornamentals? "[Reasons are given why this is unlikely.] ... The possibility remains that at least one species, *A. leucocarpus*, was introduced to Asia as a crop in pre-Columbian times."

J. Sauer 1967, 110–3. There are three domesticated species: *A. hypochondriacus* L.; evidently from *A. powellii* by selection as a grain crop in North

America; syn. *A. frumentaceus*, syn. *A. hybridus*, syn. *A. leucocarpus*. Its "distribution as a grain crop in Asia, although perhaps old, is clearly secondary and its wide dispersal as an ornamental is recent." 113. In Mexico, at the Conquest, *A. hypochondriacus* was probably the main if not the only species cultivated for grain. 115. For at least a hundred years, the species has been a far more widespread and important crop in Asia than in its homeland. Early botanists generally took it for an indigenous domesticate because it was so well established in subsistence agriculture, more often than not in remote regions. (Other American Indian crops followed the same pattern: *A. caudatus*, and perhaps *Chenopodium quinoa* Willd., a tall chenopod of uncertain identity which strongly resembles the latter, has long been grown as a grain crop in the hills of northwest India, where it shares the name bathú with grain amaranths (citing Thompson 1852 and Singh 1961)). 120, 122. Some seen in Manchuria in 1945–1946.
See also the materials on *Amaranthus* spp. in general.

Amaranthus spinosus
Origin: tropical New World
Summary: A troublesome weed that grew also in pre-Columbian India. Multiple Sanskrit names attest its presence in India at least one and, more probably, two or more millennia ago; that agrees with its wide distribution "throughout southern India" and beyond. Since it is elsewhere apparent that the grain amaranths were transported by humans from the Americas to Asia, it is reasonable to suppose that *A. spinosus* seeds accidentally accompanied them.
Transfer: Americas to Asia (or the reverse if origin proves Asiatic)
Time of transfer: probably at least two millennia ago
Grade: A
Sources: *Amaranthus spinosus* – spiked amaranth (a weed)
    J. Sauer 1967, 107. One of the commonest weedy amaranths of the New World tropical lowlands, where it presumably originated. By 1700 C.E., *A. spinosus* was spreading rapidly through the warmer parts of the world, both as a weed and as a sporadically planted potherb.
    Miranda 1952–1953, I, 215. Grows in Chiapas.
    Torkelson 1999, 1641. Sanskrit: *tanduliya*
    Chopra et al. 1956, 15. Sanskrit: *tanduliya*, "a field weed"
    Int. Lib. Assoc. 1996, 559. Sanskrit: *alpamarisha, tandula*
    Pullaiah 2002, I, 48. Sanskrit: *tandaluya, kataib, chaulai*. Medicinal uses in India. "Prickly amaranth"
    Bretschneider 1892, 411. Lists five species of *Amaranthus* labeled by Chinese characters used in Japan (from Matsumura; the Chinese-character names may or may not be pre-European in usage): Three Asian species plus *A. caudatus* (American) and *A. spinosus* (both hemispheres).
    Balfour 1871–1873, I, 92–3. *A. spinosus* Linn. Roxb., "thorny amaranth." A very troublesome weed all over southern India and Burma.
See also material under *Amaranthus* spp. in general.

Anacardium occidentale

Origin: Brazil or Venezuela
Summary: A representation of the cashew fruit and nut were carved at Bharhut Stupa, India, adjacent to images of the annona, also an American fruit. The structure, and thus the plant, is dated to the second century B.C.E. At least two Sanskrit names for the cashew confirm that date.
Time of transfer: before the second century B.C.E.
Grade: A
Sources: *Anacardium occidentale* – cashew
- Nadkarni 1914, 32. *A. occidentale*. Sanskrit: *shoephahara*. Eng.: cachew nut (sic). Established in the coast forests of India and all over South India.
- Watson 1868, 251. *A. occidentale*. In the Hortus Malabaricus as *kapa-mava*, all vowels long.
- Balfour 1871–1873, III, 409. Cashew-nut tree, called "Cashoo Apple" in English. Sanskrit: *beejara sula*. I, 107. Sanskrit: *bijara sala*.
- Pullaiah 2002, I, 52. Sanskrit: *kajutaka*
- Kirtikar and Basu, 1987, I:658-59. Chinese, three names. Sanskrit: eleven names.
- Bretschneider 1882, 94. Condemns Balfour for accepting botanical names of plants in the ancient Sanskrit vocabulary; Amara Cosha [ca. 600 C.E.], and other writings in the classical language of the Hindus, which was a dead language, not spoken even at the time of Buddha. "The author [Balfour] does not hesitate to admit the existence of Sanskrit names for such plants as ... *Anacardium occidentale* ... which, as is well known, have been introduced into Asia from the Americas, since the discovery of the New World."
- Brücher 1989, 215–6. Portuguese navigators in the sixth century took seeds to India and Mozambique. The cashew is native to the semi-arid coasts of Venezuela and Brazil, where one still finds many biotypes wild.
- Pandey 2000, 272. *A. occidentale*, a native of Brazil, is one species "naturalized in some parts of India."
- Dressler 1953, 122. Appears that it may be native from Brazil to the Antilles, especially as a strand plant. Also occurs naturally in southern Yucatan and may possibly have been cultivated there.
- Gupta. 1996, 17. A native of Brazil, it was introduced into India in the sixteenth century C.E. by the Portuguese. The only depiction of the plant complete with flowers and fruits is at the Jambukeshvara temple, Tiruchirapalli in Tamil Nadu (see plate). The depiction of the fruit, the cashew nut, is slightly stylized. Whereas the sanctum sanctorum and the inner portions of the temple, according to tradition, legend, and the temple priests, was built 2500 years ago, the outer pillared hall is much more recent. And the Archaeological Survey of India dates it to the seventh century C.E., by which time the cashew nut plant had been introduced to India and was already a hundred years old. But the earliest sculpture of the cashew nut is from the Bharhut Stupa balustrade relief, dated ca. the second century B.C.E. The relief is a broken fragment depicting two fruits of the custard apple on the left and two cashew nuts on the right side of the panel. Yet, "... it is not offered in worship at

temples. Since the plant has no religious associations, the pillar decoration showing the cashew nut plant motif is purely decorative."

Newcomb 1963, 41. The cashew is a New World species but today is most abundant in the Old World. Its major production is concentrated in South India.

Watt 1871–1873, I, 232. Originally introduced from South America. Indigenous to the West Indies. Now one of six species of the genus is naturalized in coastal forests in India. It bore a name in Sanskrit, *bijara sala* (Balfour 1871–1873, I, 107; III, 409).

J. Sauer 1993, 15. A native of Brazil, apparently. Natives made use of both nuts and wine made from the cashew apple. "The Portuguese introduced it to India in the 1560s, perhaps more as a source of wine and brandy than for the nuts."

Ananas comosus
Origin: Brazil, although long cultivated in Middle America
Summary: Found on Easter Island, the Marquesas, Tahiti, and Hawaii, providing good evidence for its pre-European presence. Gupta. reports images sculpted on Indian temples, one dating to the fifth century C.E. Pineapples are also shown in the art of Assyria, Egypt, Anatolia, and perhaps Israel, at Haifa.
Time of transfer: by the eighth century B.C.E. (Assyria) and by the fifth century C.E. (India, presumed to have been by way of the Middle East)
Grade: A
Sources: *A. comosus* (syn. *sativus*) – pineapple

England 1992, 160. A word for this plant existed in proto-Mayan, pre-1000 B.C.E.

Langdon 1988, 329. Found by W. Knoche, one of first Chilean scientists to visit Easter Island in 1911. "Small, semi-wild," and "scrubby." Found by first missionary in the Marquesas (ca. 1800) with the same name as in Tahiti. Hawaiians claimed pineapple was present there since pre-European times (citing Handy and Handy 1972).

Heyerdahl 1996, 149–57. In the Marquesas (Hivaoa), Von den Steinen, Linton, and Heyerdahl discovered and then rediscovered large, non-Polynesian stone carvings showing long-tailed quadrupeds that could represent only felids and whose nearest analogs were on the monuments of San Agustín, Colombia. He connects these (radiocarbon-dated by charcoal beneath the statues at ca. 1300 C.E.) with several plant species of American origin that have been identified in remote locations in the Marquesas. They can only be accounted for by the arrival of voyagers. 218. The faa-hoka pineapple of the Marquesas was a South American plant. It could not have spread across an ocean without human aid. Brown (1935) reported that in addition to the large pineapple brought by missionaries from Hawaii in the 1800s, there were six local varieties that grew semi-wild, which Brown considered pre-European introductions from South America.

McBryde 1945, 141. Probably a native of Brazil but long cultivated in Mesoamerica. Aztec word is matzalli. He considers a possible Central American or Mexican origin for those in Mesoamerica.

Simmonds 1976, 16. Pineapple is old in the New World on distributional grounds but the only archaeological record for it consists of seeds and bracts found in coprolites from caves in Tehuacán Valley of Mexico dated to the period from about 100 B.C.E. to 700 C.E.

Heyerdahl 1964, 126. A semi-wild pineapple was found in deserted areas of Easter Island when the flora was first recorded by Europeans. Bertoni in 1919 suggested that the American pineapple seems to have spread into the Pacific in pre-Columbian times (Bertoni 1919). Macmillan Brown argued a very strong case for pre-European growth of Ananas in the Marquesas (Brown, 1931, 137). Degener stated that the Hawaiians had grown a poor variety of the plant in a semi-wild state long before the first recorded introduction by Europeans (Degener 1930, 88).

Collins, 1948, 376-7. He is puzzled over the following three references [note that this information is omitted in the largely identical article that he published in the Southwestern Journal of Anthropology in 1951]. Layard (1849) and Rawlinson both describe stone carvings at Nineveh that show food served at a banquet, one of which both writers list as representing a pineapple. Rawlinson stated: "The representation is so exact that I can scarcely doubt the pineapple being intended." Layard also had doubts that the Assyrians knew the fruit, but "the leaves sprouting from the top proved that it was not the cone of a pine tree or fir." A third reference is Wilkinson (1879, II, 213): "Among the numerous productions of India met with in Egypt which tend to prove an intercourse with that country may be mentioned the pineapple, models of which are found in the tombs, of glazed pottery. One was in the possession of Sir Richard Westmacott."

Krauss n.d. 188. "Extraordinarily, fossils of pineapple have been found in Switzerland, it has been reported."

Johannessen reports his personal experience seeing a representation of pineapple on a piece of jewelry in the museum at Ankara, and K. Harper (a professor of botany) has seen another pineapple on an object in the museum in Cairo.

Pickersgill 1976. Cites Merrill against Heyerdahl's claim for pineapple in the Marquesas. She resists claims of Assyrian, Egyptian, and Pompeiian representations of the pineapple, asserting magisterially that "the reproductions that have been published are not convincing." [Contrast Rawlinson above in Collins.]

Brown 1931, 137. *Ananas sativus* Schultes. Pineapple. Marquesan names are compounded from ha'a hoka or fa'a hoka. The fruit is small but extremely fragrant and superior in flavor. Six named and cultivated varieties are listed "all of which were an integral part of the ancient material culture, [and] were evidently originated by the Marquesans from the single Brazilian species. This fact seems fairly positive evidence that the early Polynesians, through contact with the Americas, obtained their original stock long before the discovery of the Marquesas by Europeans." 138. Anciently, the fruits were used more extensively for leis and for scenting coconut oil than for food. Planted usually in dry areas, in all inhabited valleys, where nothing else useful grew; plants flourished without human care.

Gupta. 1996, 18. Clearly depicted on the vanamala of Vishnu in his Varaha avatara in the Udayagiri cave temples, Madhya Pradesh, dated ca. fifth century C.E. (plate 10). This depiction shows that the plant must have been growing in India at that early date. For "there is no evidence of artisans having come from Brazil at any point in Indian history and the local artisans could not have sculpted it without being familiar with it." The only other temple where there is a depiction of the pineapple fruit is at Moti-Shah-Ka-Tuk, Shatrunjaya hill complex, Palitana, Gujarat. The small shrine where it is sculpted is white washed and difficult to date. The Shatrunjaya hill Jain temple complex consists of nearly 863 Jain temples and is believed to be more than 1000 years old.

Pullaiah 2002, I, 53. Sanskrit: *anamnasam, bahunetraphalam*. Medicinal uses in India.

Bertoni 1919, 280ff. He believed Polynesians carried pineapples from the Americas.

Watt 1888–1893, I, 236. The genus has five or six species, inhabitants of tropical America. "From the vernacular names one would suppose it came to India via Persia." It was not found in Europe, Asia, or Africa before Columbus (sic). Its introduction is "expressly mentioned by Indian authors." "The rapidity with which it spread through Europe, Asia, and Africa is unparalleled in the history of any other fruit." [Unless, of course, it had already spread in pre-Columbian times, as is now certain.]

Zena Halpern of Syosset, NY, (personal communication 2003) has furnished us with a photograph of a carved stone in a museum in Haifa, Israel, that displays a pineapple on the stone, although a part of the fruit representation is broken off, rendering the identification less than final. The carving is probably from the Iron Age.

Addenda: Too late to enter in detail: Casella 2002a; Casella 2002b; Casella 2002c; Ciferri 2002; Jett 2002c; Merrill 2002. All these, published together by Jett in the Dec. 2002 issue of Pre-Columbiana, combine to demonstrate unequivocally that the pineapple was indeed represented in Pompeiian art.

Annona spp. in general
Sources: *Annona* spp. in general

Roys, 1931, 271. Mayan language: "Op. *Annona reticulata*, L. Custard-apple, Anona colorada."

Schoenhals 1988. *A. cherimola*, custard apple, cherimola. *A. glabra*, pond apple, alligator apple. *A. muricata*, guanábana, soursop. *A. purpurea*, custard apple. *A. reticulata*, custard apple.

Steentoft 1988, 72. *Annonaceae*—soursop family. "A pantropical but especially Old World family of woody plants." 74. [Yet] Annona (West Indian name) is largely an American genus, with only three species in West Africa (i.e., *A. senegalensis, A. glabra*, and *A. glauca*, which replaces *A. glabra* in Ghana).

Balfour 1871–1873, I, 125. *Annonaceae*. A tropical order of plants, chiefly
inhabiting the Americas and the East Indies. The order includes about 15
genera and 250 species, more than half of which occur in India.

Brücher 1989, 218. In the Americas more than 70 *Annona* species exist, of
which at least a dozen have been domesticated for their aromatic fruits.

Addenda: Too late to enter in detail: Casella 2002a; Casella 2002b; Ciferri 2002; Casella 2002c; Jett 2002c; Marcus 1982 Several of these, published together by Jett in the Dec. 2002 issue of Pre-Columbiana, combine to demonstrate unequivocally that the annona was represented in Pompeiian art.

Annona cherimolia
Origin: the Americas
Summary: This Annona is especially characteristic of the highlands of Colombia, Ecuador [and] Peru, [but also occurs in] Mesoamerica.
The fruit of *A. cherimolia* is shown held by a sculpted goddess figure on a wall of a Hoysala Dynasty temple, Karnataka State, India, dated to the 13th century.
Transfer: the Americas to India
Time of transfer: by the 13th century C.E.
Grade: B
Sources: *Annona cherimolia* – large annona, custard apple

Shady Solís 1997, 18. *A. cherimolia* remains have been found at the Los
Gavilanes site in the Huarmey valley, Peru, dating to the Late Archaic
(3000–1500 B.C.E.).

Towle 1961, 38–9. A small tree bearing edible, heart-shaped fruits. Remains
have also come from graves at Ancón (dated in B.C.E. times). Also one
prehistoric funeral vase depicts a fruit.

Johannessen and Wang 1998, 16–7. Held in the hands of sculpted figures on
temples in India, as in the hand of a goddess statue on an 1268 C.E.
Hoysala Dynasty temple at Somnathpur, Karnataka State (illustrated).
Johannessen comments: the image of the fruit shown at Somnathpur is a
general, but not a perfect, match with *A. cherimolia*.

Roys 1931, 279. Mayan. "Pox. *Annona cherimola*, Mill. Cherimoya." Often called
the custard apple in English.

Balfour 1871–1873, I, 125. *A. cherimolia*. A tree of Peru, introduced into India
in 1820.

Bailey 1935, I, 294. From the Andes of Peru and adjacent regions but
naturalized at a very early date in Mexico and Central America.

Dressler 1953, 123. Wild cherimoyas grow in Ecuador. There is archaeological
evidence for the early occurrence of *A. cherimolia* in Peru, yet Cobo wrote
of introducing it from Guatemala about 1630 and implies that it was
previously unknown [another 'historical' fable].

Brücher 1989, 219. He considers *A. cherimolia* "the most attractive fruit of
America." Characteristic of the tropical mountains (800–2000 m.) of
Colombia, Ecuador, and Peru.

Annona glabra
Origin: West Indies, South America

Summary: Reports differ as to the value of this *Annona* as an edible fruit, yet it was used in some areas and apparently occasionally cultivated. It grew wild on shorelands of the West Indies and South America. It had a name in the Yucatec Mayan language. Also found in West Africa and in Kerala, the southwest coast of India, and (recently) islands in the Indian Ocean.

Since other species of *Annona* reached South and Southeast Asia as early as the third millennium B.C.E., it is not unreasonable to suppose that *A. glabra* shared in the same transfer process as those earlier manifested, even if it was an inferior fruit. Oceanic drift over such a vast distance (and from the Atlantic side of the Americas at that) to South Asia is out of the question (the tree is also entirely missing in the Pacific Ocean area).

Transfer: the Americas to South Asia.
Time of transfer: pre-Columbian (?)
Grade: incomplete
Sources: *Annona glabra* – pond apple

> Bailey 1935, I, 293. Pond-Apple, Alligator-Apple, Monkey-Apple, Mangrove-annona, Mamin, etc. Fruit considered not edible except by animals. Found in Florida and also along tropical shores of the Americas, West Indies, the west coast of Africa, and the Galapagos Islands.
>
> Dressler 1953, 123. Reports as to quality and cultivation of this species do not agree. Appears to have a very wide natural distribution as a strand plant.
>
> Roys 1931, 263. Mayan. "*H-maak. Annona glabra*, L."
>
> Brücher 1989, 218. *A. glabra* L. grows wild (he has seen it in Panama) but fruit is often collected. It cannot be excluded that this is an ancestral form of some of the domesticates.
>
> Sreekumar et al. 1996. *A. glabra*, previously known in India only from the west coast of Kerala, is recorded (wild) for the first time from the Andaman and Nicobar Islands. It has potential value as an edible fruit.

Annona reticulata
Origin: tropical America
Summary: It was known by at least four Sanskrit names, besides being shown on sculpture at the Bharhut Stupa of the second century B.C.E. Its name on the Malabar Coast incorporates Rama's name and thus seems to have a connection to the ancient legends. Moreover, common names of the fruit can be construed as related between Mexico and Asia.
Transfer: the Americas to India
Time of transfer: by the sixth century B.C.E.
Grade: A
Sources: *Annona reticulata* – custard apple

> Roys, 1931. 271. Mayan. "Op. *Annona reticulata* L. Custard-apple, Anona colorada."
>
> Balfour 1871–1873, I, 125. English name: Bullock Heart. Sanskrit: *Rama sita*.
>
> Pullaiah 2002, I, 60. Sanskrit: *ramphal*. Medicinal uses in India.
>
> Watson (1868) reports an additional Sanskrit name, *luvunee*, (citing Roxburgh 1814 and other early botanical researchers in India).
>
> Torkelson 1999, 1646. Sanskrit: *ramphala*.

Chopra et al. 1956, 19–20. Sanskrit: *ramphala*. Cultivated in India, naturalized in Bengal and South India.

Int. Lib. Assoc. 1996, 559. Sanskrit: *krishnabeejam, ramphal*.

Watt 1888–1893, I, 256. Naturalized in India, supposed imported from the Americas. But considered by some authors a native of Asia.

Bishagratna 1907, 72. Reads *A. reticulata* in a text assigned to the sixth century B.C.E.

Bailey 1935, I, 294. Common Custard Apple, Bullock's-Heart. At home in tropical America, now widely spread throughout the tropics of both hemispheres. A robust tree which has spread spontaneously in the forests of the Philippines, the island of Guam, and the East Indies, while its congeners, *A. muricata* and *A. squamosa*, occur usually only where planted. It is essentially tropical while the *cherimoya*, with the smooth-fruited forms with which it has often been confused, is subtropical. Fruit of *reticulata* is inferior in flavor to both *cherimoya* and *squamosa*. 295. Produces fruit only once per year while *squamosa* has multiple fruitings

Nicolson et al. 1988, 50. In Hortus Malabaricus (1682) this appears as *anona-maram*. "Today the tree is called Ramachakkamaram (tree, maram, with the fruit, chakka, of Lord Rama)." It bears the same name as *A. squamosa*. Cultivated throughout Kerala.

Pokharia and Saraswat 1999, 97. "The fruit is called *ata* in Malabar, *ahata* or *ate* in Mexico, and *ate* or *atte* in the Philippines. But *Annona reticulata* (bullock's heart) was called *parangi* ('foreigner') or Portuguese Jack fruit. These facts seem to suggest that the name *ata* came to India from Hispaniola via the Cape" [sic – of Good Hope?] (end-note 129). They take these data to indicate a Portuguese (re-?) introduction. Yet Sitholey's drawings of sculpted plants at Bhárhut show that the "dazzling presence of custard-apple has been confirmed, as claimed by Cunningham in 1879." (Custard-apple argument is continued on p. 99.)

Panagiotakopulu 2000, 35. Different substances used as insecticides in storerooms against insects and other pests (in Eurasia). Include *Annona reticulata*.

Annona squamosa
Origin: tropical America
Summary: At least four Sanskrit names were used for the tree, and its fruit is associated with the sacred figure, the wife of Lord Rama, in the Ramayana record. It is mentioned in another literary source dated near the beginning of our era. The fruit is sculpted at Bhárhut Stupa, second century B.C.E., and at Ajanta Cave, and in other sacred art since then. Seeds have been excavated from a cave site in the island of Timor dated (perhaps) to the middle of the third millennium B.C.E. (together with two other plants of American origin) and excavated also in India from 700 B.C.E.
Transfer: the Americas to South Asia
Time of the transfer: by 700 B.C.E.
Grade: A
Sources: *Annona squamosa* – sweetsop, sugar-apple, annona

Parotta 2001, 70. Referred to or depicted in ancient literature, painting, and sculpture. 84–88ff. Sanskrit: *gandhgataram, gandagatra, krishnabija.*
Nadkarni 1914, 38. *Annona squamosa.* Sanskrit: *shubhâ, suda.* Eng.: custard apple. Hindi: *sharifah.* Bengali, Gujerati, others: *sitâphal.* Cultivated in gardens all over India for its fruit.
Torkelson 1999, 1646–7. Sanskrit: *sitaphalam.*
Chopra et al. 1956, 19–20. Sanskrit: *gandagatra, sitaphala.*
Pullaiah 2002, I, 60. Sanskrit: *sitaphalam, gandhagathra, shubha.*
Bretschneider 1892, 412. Japanese source gives (Chinese) characters for the name of *Annona squamosa* (may not be from classic Chinese sources, however).
Brücher 1989, 220. A native of Central America and the Antilles. The species is now dispersed in all tropical countries, especially in India, which is erroneously considered as its homeland.
Nicolson et al. 1988, 50. "In the market, the fruit is called *seethachakka*, the fruit of Seetha (wife of Lord Rama)." Cultivated mostly in drier areas.
Pandey 2000, 271. *A. squamosa*, from tropical America and West Indies, is a species "naturalized in some parts of India".
Johannessen and Wang 1998, 16–17. Fruit is held in the hands of sculpted figures on temples in India, as in the hand of a goddess statue in the 10th-century Durga temple at Aihole, Karnataka State (illustrated).
Gupta. 1996, 19. Thrives in Karnataka and Maharashtra. Grows in the wild in Madhya Pradesh. The tree is called Sitaphala because of a popular belief that Sita, wife of Ramachandra of the epic Ramayana, when in exile with her husband, used to eat fruits of this tree. Yet there is no religious significance attached to the plant. But it could symbolize fertility, as from one composite fruit a large number of seeds are produced, at least in some fruits.
(Gupta cont'd.) Sculpted on both Hindu and Buddhist temples in Madhya Pradesh, Karnataka, Bengal, and Andhra Pradesh. Held in the hands of Vishnu in Bengal (plate 11); Murugan (plate 12); Kubera from Karnataka Hoysaleshvara temple, 12th century C.E. He sits on a pedestal under a canopy from which bunches of mangoes are hanging, and is holding a custard apple in his left hand and an akshamala in his right hand. As well as in the lower left hand of Shiva on a lintel sculpture showing the Trinity, Kakatiya, 12th century C.E., Warangal, Andhra Pradesh, and in the hands of various other deities. The best depiction of the Sitaphala is from Bhárhut in Madhya Pradesh (plate 13), on the Kalpalata, the wish-fulfilling creeper, where not only the fruit, but also the leaves are sculpted. According to Randhawa, the custard apple was introduced into India by the Portuguese in the 16th century. But the tree must have been growing in India from very early times considering that it is mentioned in the Ramayana, ca. 2000–1000 B.C.E. up to 200 C.E. [misprinted in Gupta. as 2000 C.E.], and sculpted at Bhárhut, ca. the second century B.C.E.
Bussagli and Sivartamamurti 1978, 189, Fig. 216. Varuna, lord of the waters, with his consort, mounted on a makara monster, is shown holding an annona in his hand. From Gurjara Pratihara, eighth century C.E.

Towle 1961, 39. In Peruvian archaeological materials, the fruit is said to be modeled in pottery jars.

Roys 1931, 271. Mayan. 312. *"Zuli-pox. Annona reticulata,* L. Anona colorada." 313. "Calmuy (C = plosive tz). *Annona squamosa,* L. Saramuyo."

Watt 1888–1893, I, 259–60. Custard apple of Europeans in India; sweet-sop or sugar apple of the West Indies and the Americas. Gives vernacular names. Common in areas of India indicated here and in Burma. Custard apples have been identified among the sculptures of the Ajanta caves as well as of the Bhárhut Stupa. This opposes theory of late introduction. General Cunningham remarks: "My identification of this fruit amongst the Máthura sculptures has been contested on the ground that the tree was introduced into India by the Portuguese. I do not dispute the fact that the Portuguese brought the custard apple into India, as I am aware that the East India Company imported hundreds of grindstones into the fort of Chunár, as if to illustrate the proverb about carrying coals to Newcastle. I have now travelled over a great part of India, and I have found such extensive and such widely distant tracts covered with the wild custard apple, that I can not help suspecting the tree to be indigenous. I can now appeal to one of the Bhárhut sculptures for a very exact representation of the fruit and leaves of the custard apple." Further, he said, "The names of the two varieties of custard apple, Rámphal and Sítaphal, are in themselves almost enough to show that from very early times the trees have been grown and honoured by the Hindus." Watt notes: "... Although there seems hardly any doubt as to *Annona squamosa* being an introduced plant, the date of its introduction is, however, very obscure."

Glover 1977, 43. Annona remains were excavated from a cave on the island of Timor that might have dated soon after 3000 B.C.E.

Watson 1868, 181, 527. It also has a second Sanskrit name, *gunda-gutra* or *gunda-gatra.* Meanwhile, in the Malayalam language, the annona fruit is called *Seethachakka,* the fruit of Seetha (Nicolson et al. 1988, 50). Its mention in the Ramayana epic could mean that the species was present in B.C.E. times, simultaneously with or earlier than the artwork at Bhárhut Stupa.

Nadkarni (1914, 38) notes two other Sanskrit names: *shubhâ* and *suda.*

Bretschneider 1892, 413, deserves further study, since the antiquity of Chinese knowledge of the fruit is hinted at by the early presence of the annona representations in India. The species was recognized early in Bhárhut and Sanchi sculptures in Madhya Pradesh and carvings dug up at Mathura (second–first century B.C.E.) by Gen. Cunningham (1879).

Pokharia and Saraswat 1999, 101. A series of caves in Timor, Indonesia, have yielded a continuous sequence of occupation from 12,000 B.C.E. to the time of Christ [sic; the cited source, Glover 1977, says, rather, that the terminal date is no later than the middle of the third millennium.] Interestingly, in the top layers several introduced New World crops occur, such as peanuts (*Arachis*), custard-apple/sweetsop (*Annona*), and maize (*Zea mays*) together with Southeast Asian or generally Asian natives, including coconut, mangosteen, and almond (endnote 176). Seeds of *Annona* have also been found in a stratigraphic sequence of an iron-using culture at Raja Nal-Ka-Tila, Sonbhadra Dist., U.P., India, radiocarbon-dated to about 700 B.C.E.

Arachis hypogaea
Origin: South America
Summary: Archaeological finds place it in use in Peru by earlier than 700 B.C.E. Archaeology shows the peanut by 2800 B.C.E. (uncalibrated radiocarbon date [calibrated date: 3588 B.C.E.]) in China and by the 10th Century C.E. on the island of Timor. There is strong evidence for a link between names of the nut in lowland South America and India. There are also several names in Sanskrit (probably dated in B.C.E. times). In morphology, there are very detailed similarities, if not identities, between Asian and South American peanuts.
Transfer: the Americas to Southeast Asia
Time of transfer: fourth millennium B.C.E.?
Grade: A
Sources: *Arachis hypogaea* – peanut, ground nut
- Shady Solís 1997, 18. Peanuts have been found in three sites of the Late Archaic (3000–1500 B.C.E.) on the coast of Peru.
- J. Sauer 1993, 800–83. Was being grown in Peru before 2000 B.C.E. 881. The name *mandubi* (see Krapovickas, et al. below) was reported from the coast of Brazil about 1550. 882. The 'Peruvian' variety of peanut (Arachis asiatica) was taken to the Philippines by Spanish galleons and from there to southeastern China before 1600.
- Nadkarni 1914, 39. *Arachis hypogaea*. Sanskrit: *buchanaka*.
- Torkelson 1999, 1646. Sanskrit: *buchanaka*.
- Chopra et al. 1956, 22. Sanskrit: *buchanaka*.
- Pullaiah 2002, I, 65. Sanskrit: *bhueanakah, mandapi*. Medicinal uses.
- Kirtikar and Basu, 2nd ed., 1999, 754. "Brazil: *Jarere, Mandobi, Mandubi, Mandupiliu, Manobi*." 755. "Sanskrit: *Bhuchanaka, Bhumija, Bhushimbika, Bhustha, Mandap, Raktabija, Snehabijaka, Tribija*."
- Pokharia and Saraswat 1999, 101. Caves in Timor, Indonesia, show a continuous sequence of occupation from 12,000 B.C.E. to the time of Christ [sic., see, rather, Glover 1977, whom they cite; the latter seems to say the occupation referred to by Pokharia and Saraswat belongs to the third millennium B.C.E.] (endnote 175). In the top layers, a culture introduced from the northwest (Indonesia) is manifested which includes introduced New World crops, the peanut (*Arachis*), custard-apple/soursop (*Annona*) and maize (*Zea mays*), together with Southeast Asian or generally Asian natives, including coconut, mangosteen, and almond (endnote 176). Glover says before 1000 C.E.
- Zeven and de Wet 1982, 172–3. *Arachis hypogaea*. Primary gene center is in Argentina and Bolivia. (Subspecies *hypogaea* var. hirsute Kohler is synonymous with *A. asiatica* Lour., reportedly introduced by the Spaniards to the Philippines.)
- Watson 1969, 400. "At the site of Chien Shan Yang in Chekiang, in addition to rice, the following [was] identified:" *Arachis hypogaea*. (Also *Trapa natans*).

(Citing, in endnote 17, Chekiang Province Cultural Properties Control 1960.)

Pickersgill and Heiser 1978. 813. In Tehuacán, Mexico, from Palo Blanco phase (2200–1250 BP) and later. It is much older in Peru.

Carter 1974, 213–4. Cites a report of archaeological specimens, Chang 1963. At a named site in Chekiang excavated in 1956 and 1958, two carbonized peanuts were found in a Lungshanoid association (i.e., from ca. 2000 B.C.E. to perhaps 1500 B.C.E.). They were identified by the Laboratory of Plant Seeds of the College of Agriculture of Chekiang as *Arachis hypogaea*. The second site was near the village of Shan-pei, northwest Kiangsi, and the archaeological association was again Lungshanoid. Chinese documentary sources attribute the origin of the peanut to the south, from overseas. Chekiang is said to have obtained peanuts from Fukhien, its southern neighbor, toward the end of the sixth century. (This is only the date for local borrowing, not necessarily for the arrival in China initially.) Bretschneider (in Burkhill 1935) quoted a Chinese source that attributed the introduction of the peanut to the Sung (960–1280) or Yuan (1260–1368) Dynasty. Bretschneider rejected the date, probably because he did not believe any American plant could be in China then.

Chang Kwang-Chih 1970, 179. The groundnut (peanut), generally thought to be native to South America, came from a Lungshanoid site in North China.

Chang Kwang-Chih 1968, 491, 421. The peanut quite surely was known in Lungshanoid pottery times [i.e., pre-Shang], regardless of claims of critics that the stratigraphy of the specimens had been confused. For the criticisms, see Harlan and de Wet (1973, 51–62) and Bayard, (1975, 167–70).

Jeffreys 1976, 9–28. Among crops he believed to be present in Africa before the Portuguese could have brought them, he included the groundnut.

Laufer 1907. He claimed the peanut reached China from the Malay Archipelago or Philippines via Chinese sailors or the traders of Fukien. The earliest date is 1573 C.E. he concluded.

Patiño 1976, II. Shows on map on p. 163 distribution of plantings of this at the time of the Conquest. Oviedo stigmatized the plant: "The Indians in this island of Hispaniola, have a fruit that they call mani [and] that they sow and reap, and it is a very ordinary plant .... Christians [Europeans] use it very little and then only some low fellows and children and slaves .... It is of mediocre aroma and little substance, but a very common vegetable to the Indians ...." (Oviedo 1851, I, 274; II, 165). Patiño observed, "We don't know if the majority of Spaniards had the same taste as Oviedo and disdained the peanut in early times. Food habits are difficult to change." [Sounds like the kind of plant no Spaniard would have bothered to carry to Goa or the Philippines.]

Towle 1961, 42–3. Remains of the pod are among the most commonly encountered plant remains in Peru, and in addition, we find pottery vessels decorated with representations of the pods, and there are textile designs depicting parts of the peanut plant. A larger variety of nut in coastal sites is similar to one grown in the Orient today (Ames 1939, 46–8). A smaller variety is also found, as from a site at Supe, belonging to the Early Ancón Period (ca. 700 B.C.E.). Also from the Cupisnique levels at Huaca Priéta. Well-preserved peanuts were found in a mummy bundle from Paracas Necropolis. Plant and pods were depicted on Early Nazca textiles.

Steward 1949, 742–3. Considers that the quality of evidence for diffusion is maximal in "actual American domesticated plants, whose identity and genetic connection with Old World species can be established beyond reasonable doubt." These include "perhaps peanuts."

Pickersgill and Heiser 1978, 813. In Tehuacán, Mexico, from Palo Blanco phase (2200–1250 BP) and later. It is much older in Peru.

Anderson 1952, 167. Primitive forms of the peanut have come from ancient Peruvian tombs. "Yet up until the Peruvian excavations the experts were certain that it came from the Old World, so widely is it disseminated there, with every appearance of having been grown for a very long time in Asia and Africa. In fact, the old argument used to be whether it came from Africa or from Asia." "The most primitive type of peanut, the same narrow little shoestrings which are found in the Peruvian tombs, are commonly grown today, not in Peru, but in South China. How did they get there?"

Skvortzov 1920, 142–5. Considered the peanut present in Asia before European influence.

Krapovickas 1969, 527. Despite diffusionists' claims for the peanut in China before European discovery, Merrill's anti-diffusionist interpretation has been generally accepted. Krapovickas compiled names for the nut from Native American groups in the Amazon Basin, the area where botanists think the plant was first domesticated. There it bears such names as: *tupí*, *mandobi*, *manobi*, *mandowi*, *mundubi*, and *munui*; Pilagá, *mandovi*; Chiriguano, *manduvi*; and Guaraní, *manubi*. Black (1988) compared these with names for the peanut in India (from Kirtikar et al. 1953, 754–65), Sanskrit, *andapi*; Hindi, *munghali*; and Gujarati, *mandavi*.

Ping-ti Ho 1955, 191–201. No earlier (pre-European) diffusion of such crops, including the peanut, is justified by the evidence from China.

Johannessen and Wang 1998, 18. Some government archaeologists in Beijing accept a date for peanuts of ca. 300 C.E. as well as two finds of Neolithic age peanuts. 22–4. Johannessen has examined the two excavated specimens of early peanuts and describes them. One was from Jiangxi province, found in a Neolithic house site between two pots (Chinese source citations) and dated ca. 4400 BP, presumably uncalibrated. It is virtually impossible that these specimens were modern and 'accidentally' came to rest in this position by falling down a rodent hole or that they were introduced by plowing of the surface, as suggested by at least one botanist. A second peanut is also Neolithic in age, from Zhejiang province. Although K. C. Chang several times referred to these two Neolithic specimens, he also, paradoxically, asserted at one point a "post-European" date for them. A written record of the peanut is found in a

300-C.E. volume on the flora of South China and North Vietnam, although there are some problems with the description. Also, some Chinese scientists acknowledge (personal communications) that the peanut is old, but insist it was domesticated in China (all wild relatives of the peanut are from South America). 25. Safford (1917) found peanuts of the same type as those from Ancón, Peru, to be present in modern China. Johannessen found that the same Ancón varieties still are found in farmers' markets in China.

Chen Wenhua 1994, 59. Reports not only basic facts regarding the two Neolithic discoveries from the 1960s, but also that subsequently 10 or more peanuts came from the tomb of a Western Han emperor (before 200 C.E.).

Safford 1917, 17. The species of peanut found in graves at Ancón, Peru, resembles specimens collected in southern Mexico by Collins. The same form is cultivated in China, Formosa, and India, "where it was probably introduced at a very early date."

Bretschneider 1882, 64. In the midst of a discussion of how Chinese characters expressing a plant name often relate to the appearance of the plant, etc., he cites "*Arachis hypogaea*, the ground-nut, is called [3 Chinese characters] lo hua sheng ('the flowers fall down and grow'), the same concept as its Greek name also denotes; the fruit growing (seemingly) in the ground."

Bretschneider (1892, 167) gives a Chinese name for *A. hypogaea* from a Japanese source (Matsumura) which may or may not reflect usage in classical Chinese sources.

Balfour 1871–1873, I, 153–4. *Arachis hypogaea*, Linn. syn. A. Africana Loureir and *A. asiatica* Loureir. English: American earth-nut, groundnut, earthnut, manilla-nut, pea-nut. Sanskrit: *buchanaka*. Indigenous to South America; extensively cultivated in India for oil.

Argemone mexicana
Origin: Mexico
Summary: At least six Sanskrit names for the plant are known, and Chinese names may also have been identified. The plant is mentioned in an Indian medical treatise dated to the first or second century C.E. Seeds have been recovered by archaeologists in sites in India dated 1100 B.C.E., before 800 B.C.E., and 100 – 300 C.E. Overlapping medical uses are documented for Mexico and India.
Transfer: Asia from Mexico
Time of transfer: before 1100 B.C.E.
Grade: A
Sources: *Argemone Mexicana* – Mexican poppy, prickle poppy

Nadkarni 1914, 41. *Argemone mexicana*. Sanskrit: *brahmadandi*. Eng.: yellow thistle; prickly or Mexican poppy. Common everywhere in India on roadsides and waste places. Much medical use is discussed.

Watt 1888–1893, I, 305–6. Reports Sanskrit names (*srigála kantá* and *brahmadandi*). The second is confirmed by Nadkarni (1914, 910), and cf. *bramadundie* and *bramhadundie* in Watson 1868, 78, as well as *bramhie* or *bramh* in Balfour 1871–1873, I, 177.

Chopra et al. 1956, 23. Sanskrit: *srigala-kantaka*. Naturalized throughout India up to 5000 ft.

Torkelson 1999, 1646. Sanskrit: *satyanasi, srigala-kantaka*.

Kirtikar and Basu 1999, I:131. Sanskrit: *brahmadandi* and nineteen other names.

Int. Lib. Assoc. 1996, 559. Sanskrit: *bhramhadandi, swarnaksiri*.

Pullaiah 2002, I, 66. Sanskrit: *swarnakshiri, bhramadendi*. Medicinal uses.

Saraswat, Sharma, and Saini (1994, 262, 333, 334) report mention of this plant in the medical treatise Bhava Prakasha in the Sushruta Samhita (first/second century C.E.) where two Sanskrit names of the plant are given as *swarnakshiri* and *kauparni*.

Saraswat et al. (1994) also report archaeological finds of *A. mexicana* seeds at the Narhan site in Uttar Pradesh belonging to the Black-and-Red-Ware phase (ca. 1300–800 B.C.E.) and also the Black-Slipped-Ware phase (ca. 800–600 B.C.E.). Moreover, Saraswat et al. (1981, 284) found charred seeds of the plant at a site in the Punjab that yielded radiocarbon dates of 1100 B.C.E. and 1060 B.C.E. (Pokharia and Saraswat 1998–1999, 90, 100).

Pandey 2000, 271. "The Mexican prickle poppy, is naturalized throughout India."

Balfour explained its presence as due to introduction from Mexico in modern ship ballast (1871–1873, I, 177). However, Watt (1888–1893, I, 305–6) was puzzled by the supposition that it was only recently acquired, noting, "But for its known history [sic], no one could hesitate in pronouncing it wild and indigenous .... It has even received by adaptation vernacular names known to oriental literature before the introduction of the plant," that is, before the era of European discovery.

Aristida subspicata
Origin: South America
Summary: *Aristida subspicata* was found dominant in areas near Nukuhiva, the Marquesas Islands, where it was credited by Brown with having been inadvertently imported by pre-European Polynesians. Embeddedness of the plant in local custom confirms his judgment.
Transfer: the Americas to the Marquesas Islands
Time of transfer: before European discovery in the eight century
Grade: B
Source: *Aristida subspicata*

Brown 1931, 79. "The presence of this American grass [*Aristida subspicata*] as a dominant element in the prairie of Nukuhiva [the Marquesas] is of interest. It is not unlikely that it was unintentionally brought in by the early inhabitants, possibly at the same time that the wild pineapple was introduced" (i.e., before European discovery).

Artemisia vulgaris
Origin: temperate Eurasia
Summary: This plant was widely distributed in Eurasia as well as in Mesoamerica and Peru. It was closely associated with the Greek goddess Artemis, with detailed

similarities in customs involving the medical treatment of women and children and the process of childbirth. Also, the plant served as magical protection of travelers on the water.
Transfer: to nuclear America
Time of transfer: pre-Columbian
Grade: B+
Sources: *Artemisia vulgaris* (syn. mexicana) – mugwort, wormwood
- Roys 1931, 310. Mayan: "*zizim*. *Artemisia mexicana*, Willd. Agenjo del país. *A. vulgaris*, L." [Apparently considered equivalent.] The Motul dictionary says: "There are wormwood plants much fresher and more fragrant than these here (in Spain). Their little leaves are longer and more slender. The Indians grow them for their fragrance and to please" (from Landa, Tozzer 1941, 194, which depends on Lundell's botanical judgment: "This is probably *Artemisia vulgaris* L. zizim").
- Hernandez 1942 [before 1580], I, 291. In his *Anonima mechoacanense*, his modern botanical editors identify "*Artemisia mexicana*?," "Iztauhyatl."
- Zeven and de Wet 1982, 150. Center of maximum diversity, "temperate N. Hemisphere."
- Pullaiah 2002, I, 73. (syn. *nilagirica*). Sanskrit: *barha grnthika* (sic), *vishirnakhya*. Medicinal uses.
- Bretschneider 1892, 247. A name that occurs in the Shi king (document) has been correctly identified by Legge with the mugwort, *Artemisia vulgaris*, L. It is one of the plants that the Chinese employ for their moxa.
- Mackenzie 1924, 201–4. The plant representing, and even being, the goddess Artemis among the Greeks was mugwort or wormwood. Her Mexican equivalent was Chalchiuhtlicue. Her mountain near Mexico City was called Yauhqueme, which signifies "covered with mugwort." She dwelt on that mountain. In like manner Artemis dwelt on Mount Taygetus and her herb Artemisia grew there. One of the Greek names for the plant is *taygetes*. (Citing Rendel Harris, The Ascent of Olympus, 75.) She was a furnisher of medicinal herbs, she assisted at childbirth, and the herb was a child's medicine as well as a woman's medicine. The herb was also supposed to protect, especially mariners, against tempests. Chalchiuhtlicue did the same and had the same water/marsh associations, herbal connections, and childbirth links. Artemisia was also in use in China as a medicinal herb "from time immemorial." The mugwort cure and associated goddess also reached Kamchatka. The lotus in Asia and the white waterlily in the Americas were cult symbols associated with (Aztec) Chalchiuhtlicue.
- Yacovleff and Herrera 1934–1935, 280. Artemisia (*Franseria artemisioides* Willd.) A four-foot-high bush in Peru. The whole plant exhales a soft perfume. Mixed with alcohol, the leaves are used as an anti-rheumatic, or in hot baths for the feet. Also used anciently in preparation of textile dye.
- According to K. T. Harper (personal communication 2004), Chinese scientists have recently extracted a useful anti-malarial chemical from a green, herbaceous mugwort very similar to *vulgaris*.

Panagiotakopulu 2000, 35. Substances used as insecticides in storerooms against insects and other pests (in Eurasia) include *Artemisia* spp.

Asclepias curassavica
Origin: the Americas
Summary: A Sanskrit name in India, where the plant is now naturalized, puts it there one or two millennia ago. It was also considered to be pre-European in Hawaii and the Marquesas, which would probably mean transfer from the Americas (although one desires further confirmatory evidence to increase confidence).
>Case 1: Transfer: to India
>Time of transfer: before 1000 C.E.
>Grade: C
>Case 2: Transfer: to eastern Polynesia
>Time of transfer: pre-European discovery
>Grade: B+

Sources: *Asclepias curassavica* – milkweed, blood flower
>Langdon 1982. Marquesans on Fatuhiva used the word for cotton (*vevai*) to refer also to this shrub, which is of American origin and "probably of aboriginal introduction in the Marquesas" (citing Brown 1935). On the nearby island of Hivaoa another term for cotton, *uruuru*, was involved in the native name there for this same shrub.
>Safford, 1905, 191. Of American origin but has found its way to almost all tropical countries. Its root possesses emetic properties and leaf juice is a remedy for intestinal worms.
>Roys 1931, 215, 318. "Mayan: *Anal, Anal-kak, Anal-xiu. Asclepias curassavica*, L. Span. Cancerillo. Milkweed. Prescribed for an abscess of the breast." 223. May also be named *x-canzel-ak*. 228. *Chac-anal-kak* is the same. 229. "*Chac-hulubte-kak. Asclepias curassavica*, a synonym for *Anal*." 257. "*Kokob-xiu. Asclepias curassavica*, L. (?)" 277. "*Pol-kuch*, or *X-pol-cuchil. Asclepias curassavica*, L."
>Brown 1935, 237. Part of a large genus centering in the Americas. *A. curassavica* is a pantropic weed of American origin; probably of aboriginal introduction in the Marquesas. The native name is *vevai*, or *pua kirata*, or *uruuru vai kirata*.
>Hillebrand 1888, 300. Called wild ipecac. A native of Mexico and the West Indies. A native Hawaiian name may indicate pre-European presence.
>Watt 1888–1893, I, 343. According to some authors, the soma plant of Sanskrit authors is *A. curassavica*—indigenous in the West Indies, but quite naturalized in India. Found as a weed in various parts of India.
>Int. Lib. Assoc. 1996, 560. Sanskrit: *kakatundi*.
>Pullaiah 2002, I, 75–6. Sanskrit: *kakatundi*. Vernacular: blood flower, false ipecac.
>Chopra et al. 1956, 28. Naturalized in many parts of India.

Aster divaricates
Origin: the Americas

Summary: This is one of the species that Hillebrand identified that was imported to Hawaii in pre-European (aboriginal) days.
Transfer: to Hawaii
Time of transfer: before European discovery of Hawaii
Grade: B
Source: *Aster divaricates* – heart-shaped aster
> Hillebrand 1888, XCIII. The editor, W. F. Hillebrand, notes that his father changed his mind about some plants that he had assumed to be introduced after Cook but finally concluded they "may in reality have been of earlier introduction." But he failed to go back and change the symbols in the manuscript indicating the fact. Here young Hillebrand says "Of nine non-endemic species which existed before the discovery ... one" was Aster divaricatus [sic]. "Not common; collected first by Chamisso. The species to which Gray (cit.) refers our plant is found in many of the warmer portions of the American Continent, both east and west."

Bixa orellana
Origin: Brazil
Summary: This plant was distributed in Peruvian archaeological sites before our era and in Mesoamerica at the Conquest. It is also found on Pacific islands and in Southeast Asia, India, and Africa. At first it was assumed by Indian botanists to be native to India because it was so thoroughly naturalized. It was used as a colorant and as medicine. It has nine Sanskrit names, implying a considerable age in India.
Transfer: assumed to have reached the Pacific islands, Southeast Asia, and then India as a progressive series of movements, and then on to East Africa from India.
Time of transfer: reaching India in time to enter the Sanskrit lexicon, no later than 1000 C.E.
Grade: A-
Sources: *Bixa orellana* – achiote, *arnatto*, *annatto*
> McBryde 1945, 148. Widely used in Guatemala for food coloring.
> Towle 1961, 67. Found in Peru in a burial at Ancón and elsewhere. Not native to Peru.
> Donkin 1974, 33–56. He assumes post-Columbian distribution to Africa, India, Southeast Asia, and the Pacific islands. In 1832, Roxburgh thought the plant indigenous to India.
> Newcomb 1963, 41. A monotypic genus of Brazil, used as a coloring agent and flavorer. Occurs in the Pacific Islands and Southeast Asia also.
> Roys 1931. Mayan: *kuxub*. Achiote, *arnatto*.
> Balfour 1871–1873, I, 177. Sanskrit: *brahmi*. Grows luxuriantly in many parts of India, wild. Seeds and milk-like sap are used in native medicine. "The plant was introduced from Mexico in (ships') ballast." [Johannessen notes: This plant is commonly reproduced by inserting a branch in soil where it grows without further care.]
> Pullaiah 2002, I, 97. Sanskrit: *sinduri*. Medicinal uses. Vernacular name: *annatto*.
> Kirtikar and Basu, 1999, I:217-18. *Sinduri* and eight other names.

Shady Solís and Levya 2003. Achiote was among the species of domesticated plants excavated at the ancient site of Caral in coastal Peru, which is radiocarbon-dated between ca. 2700 and 2000 B.C.E.

Cajanus cajan
Origin: India
Summary: Despite its Old World origin, the plant is widely distributed in native agriculture in the tropical New World, and C. Sauer suspected its pre-Columbian presence. Further information is required.
Transfer: the Americas from Old World
Time of transfer: uncertain
Grade: incomplete
Sources: *Cajanus cajan* (syn. *C. indicus*; syn. *Cytisus cajan*) – pigeon pea
    Newcomb 1963, 40. Originally of the Old World, yet in the New World tropics it is a widely spread shrub. Grows in native gardens in the West Indies, the Amazon, and tropical South America in general. Maybe it was introduced (to the Americas) by Europeans, but, if that explanation is adopted, the plant's present wide dissemination in the hemisphere is strange.
    Watt 1888–1893, VI, Part I, 364. *Cajanus indicus.* Pigeon-pea. Apparently a native of equatorial Africa. Cultivated in most areas of India.
    Zeven and de Wet 1982, 76. Center of maximum gene diversity: India.
    Pullaiah 2002, I, 108. Sanskrit: *adhaki, tuvari.*

Canavalia sp.
Origin: New World or Old World
Summary: There are two species, *C. ensiformis* and *C. obtusifolia*, that are domesticated, but since reports sometimes are by non-biologists, they do not give us much confidence in the accuracy of their distinction, so we refer only to *Canavalia* sp. The two species are said to be from the Old World according to some and the New World according to others, with the American evidence somewhat stronger. Vavilov assigned it to his Mexican/Central American center of origin, and there are twice as many American species of *Canavalia* as in the Old World. On the other hand, there is a Sanskrit name for *Canavalia ensiformis* in India, and the genus is found by botanists distributed throughout the eastern part of India from the Himalaya to Ceylon and Siam.

    At pre-ceramic Huaca Priéta, Peru (2500 B.C.E.), there may have been two species of *Canavalia* found, together with *Phaseolus lunatus.* Abundant seeds assigned to *Canavalia* sp. were also recovered from the cemetery at Paracas, Peru (late B.C.E. times). However, one botanist in the late 19th century dismissed the possibility of these being jackbeans because of color differences in the seeds. In absence of comparative plant material from Peru (in that day), he noted a similarity in color between his specimens and the seeds of *C. obtusifolia*, a species he considered "native to Asia." [Note that the actual radiocarbon date at Huaca Priéta for the plant layer is 2578 to 2470 B.C.E., according to Yen (1963), which calibrates to 3200–3070 B.C.E.]

It has been claimed that a wild strand species, *C. maritima*, is spread easily by sea and thus could have reached the opposite hemisphere by natural means. The supposition is that *C. maritima* was ancestral to domesticated *Canavalia*. But even if dispersion of *C. maritima* by sea were a fact, accounting for the same domesticated species in both Old and New Worlds would require two separate domestication events in which the strand plant was carried by sea to shore, then picked up by humans and taken to the inland habitat preferred by the domesticates, where evolutionary processes (including selection by cultivators) continued in exact parallel to produce identical outcomes. Those seem highly unlikely assumptions. On the other hand, we already know (see below) that *Phaseolus lunatus*, which was associated with *Canavalia* spp. in early Peru, was also present with Canavalia seeds in an archaeological site in India dated to 1600 B.C.E. (which accounts for a Sanskrit name). It is a far more economical explanation to suppose that the voyagers who carried the lima bean from Peru to India, also carried *Canavalia ensiformis* (or *C. obtusifolia*).

Transfer: the Americas to South Asia (or possibly vice versa)
Time of transfer: before 1600 B.C.E.
Grade: A-
Sources: *Canavalia* spp. – swordbean, jackbean

- Bretschneider 1892, 164. Among pulses illustrated, especially in a Japanese compilation (that may be following classic Chinese precedent) was *C. ensiformis*.
- Dressler 1953, 126. Piper considers it "practically certain that the plant is native to the Americas." Its nearest relatives appear to be Mexican, Central American, and West Indian in distribution. Vavilov assigns it to the Mexican/Central American center of origin (on the basis of diversity) with a query.
- McBryde 1945, 147–8. Its origin has been subject to much disagreement. Some say Old World. McBryde has seen archaeological evidence in Peru that seems to indicate that this was the commonest bean of that region in pre-Columbian times, dating from pre-ceramic cultures and probably antedating the lima bean. According to Bukasov (1930) 24 of the species of Canavalia are American and only 13 from the Old World.
- Martínez M. 1978, 110–11. Miranda (1976, II, 19) reports only one wild species of Canavalia from Chiapas in his collections, *C. villosa*, a wild species. Yet *C. ensiformis* is one of the most abundant plants found in Martínez' archaeological remains. It was usually mixed with the regular bean, *Phaseolus vulgaris*, which it resembles.
- C. Sauer 1952, VI, 499. The problem (of pre-Columbian distribution in Asia) is raised by the jackbean, or swordbean, widely cultivated throughout the Pacific and "always considered to be of Old World origin." It "is now known from prehistoric sites along the coasts of both South America and Mexico." He now considers the jackbean a New World domesticate.
- Schwerin 1970. Proposes that African farmer/fishermen blown across the Atlantic introduced cotton, bottle gourds, and jackbeans between 8000–5700 B.C.E.

Shady Solís 1997, 18. The jackbean (*Canavalia* sp.) has been excavated at nine different Late Archaic (3000–1500 B.C.E.) sites in Peru.

Towle 1961, 45. L. Kaplan reported that *Canavalia* sp. was present with *Phaseolus lunatus* from the early pre-ceramic levels through those of the ceramic-bearing Cupisnique Period at Huaca Priéta. Three species [sic] of Canavalia were found at Huaca Priéta, Peru. Seeds of this [sic] species were also recovered from Paracas and another site; however, Harms (1922) dismissed the possibility of some of these being jackbean because of color differences. "In lieu of comparative plant material from Peru, he [Kaplan] notes a similarity in color between his specimens and the seeds of *Canavalia obtusifolia*, a species native to Asia."

Newcomb 1963, 35. J. Sauer worked on this genus, which produces a large pod in the wild plant (*C. maritima*?). Sauer believes this to be pan-tropic, and it is a strand plant. There is evidence for separate domestications in New and Old Worlds. Lends itself to natural dispersal by reason of its growth habitat. 61–62. J. Sauer has studied this genus. Both New and Old World cultivated types derive from a strand plant, *C. maritima*, which has large edible beans. In both hemispheres "somebody got interested in this plant" and carried it inland from its native habitat. But strand plants are different because they are pan-tropic. Other plants with similar species or the same species occurring in both Old and New Worlds are more difficult to explain. Genera that occur in both hemispheres are much easier to account for than species. [Note that the actual radiocarabon date at Huaca Priéta for the plant layer 2578–2470 B.C.E., according to Yen (1963), calibrates to 3201–3068 B.C.E.]

Watt 1888–1893, II, 197. Swordbean. Sanskrit: *shimbí*. Found in the eastern part of India from the Himalayas to Ceylon and Siam, wild or cultivated. Both green pods and beans are eaten.

Kirtikar and Basu 1999, I, 791. Give eight Sanskrit names.

Canna edulis
Origin: South America
Summary: This species is cultivated for its edible starchy rootstock. The stock is pictured in ceramic effigies and also drawn on pots in coastal Peru. Macrofossil remains have been excavated from as early as 4300 BP. *C. edulis* has a pre-Columbian name in Mayan and grows wild in Yucatan, where it may have been cultivated. It may also have grown on Easter Island before discovery.

It was reported in China in 300 C.E., and in India early enough to bear Sanskrit names. In India and Bhutan the tuber is eaten, and it also has medicinal uses. It grew in Polynesia and as far west as Fiji. In Burma, its hard seeds were used as sacred beads; in Mexico in colonial times as rosary beads. In Mexico, Hernandez (pre-1580) pictured a plant with a Náhuatl (Mexican) name that appears to be the same as *C. indica*.

Case 1: Transfer: to Eastern and Central Pacific islands
Time of transfer: pre-Columbian
Grade: B
Case 2: Transfer: the Americas to East and South Asia

Time of transfer: before 300 C.E.
Grade: A-

Sources: *Canna edulis* (syn. *indica*, syn. *patens*, syn. *orientalis*) – *achira, platonillo*, Indian shot

- Towle 1961, 132. Used in the Nazca era (ca. first–ninth century C.E.). 33. Both this *C. edulis* and *C. indica* go under the name *achira*. (Today both are considered synonymous.) Cultivated for edible tubers. Vases of unspecified date representing the rootstocks have been found in archaeological sites on the coast.
- Shady Solís 1997, 18. Excavated at seven different sites of the Late Archaic (3000–1500 B.C.E.) in Peru. [Note that the actual radiocarbon date at Huaca Priéta for the plant layer is 2578–2470 B.C.E., according to Yen (1963), which calibrates to 3200–3070 B.C.E.]
- Bronson 1966, 256. *Canna edulis* grows wild in the Mexican Peten, and he thinks it possible that the root was cultivated or utilized by early Maya.
- Roys 1931, 233. "*Chankalá. Canna edulis*, Ker-Gawl. *Lengua de dragón.*"
- Brücher 1989, 40–1. There are no Mesoamerican archaeological finds, but remains have been found in Peru (citing Ugent and Pozorski) at 4300 BP.
- Zeven and de Wet 1982, 168. Center of diversity was probably northwestern South America.
- Nadkarni 1914, 77. *Canna indica*. Sanskrit: *sarvajaya*. Eng.: Indian shot. Common all over India in gardens.
- Pullaiah 2002, I, 116. *Canna indica*. Sanskrit: *devakuli*.
- Balfour 1871–1873, I, 43. Sanskrit: *silarumba*. Much cultivated by the Burmese for the seeds, which they use for sacred beads.
- Yacovleff and Herrera, 311–12. *Achira, Canna indica*. Shown in Nazca and Chimú art.
- Brown 1931, 169–170. Throughout Polynesia to Fiji. "Native of tropical America; pantropic; of rather late introduction in the Marquesas, where it occurs both naturalized and cultivated in nearly every inhabited valley." [Unclear what he intends by "rather late."]
- Watt 1888–1893, II, 102. Sanskrit: *Sarvajayá, silarumba*. Related to chiefly Hindi names. Several varieties are common all over India and Ceylon, mainly in gardens. Medicinal uses. Rootstock is edible in almost all the species. "From the root of one kind, *C. edulis*, a nutritious aliment is prepared," according to Drury.
- Bretschneider (1882, 38) lists plants in the document Nan fang Ts'ao Mu Chang. The author was Ki Han, a Minister of State in the Tsin (Jin) Dynasty, 290–307 C.E., who had previously been Governor of Canton. The 80-species list includes: banana, *Canna indica*, and "sweet-potato (batatas)."
- Hernandez 1942–1946, III, 735–7. His *tozcuitlapilxochitl*, which others call *cocoyotzin*, is an herb that was taken some time ago to Spain. It is called there *litospermo arundináceo* because it has leaves and fruit that are white at first and then (turn) black. The *lithospermum arundinaceum* of the sixth century is *Coix lacryma-jobi* L., it seems, from the East Indies, and notable for its hard, spherical fruits. (*Coix lacryma-jobi* is a medicinal plant

cultivated in South Asia under the Sanskrit name *jargadi*—see Int. Lib. Assoc. 1996, 563). "It is extraordinary, if the plant was introduced by the Spaniards, that already by the time of Hernandez' [16th-century] visit to Mexico it had common Mexican (Náhuatl) names." Actually, of the two figures shown by Hernandez under this name, one is, it appears [according to the modern botanists who edited this edition of Hernandez], a species of *Canna* ("*C. indica* L?"). Both genera, *Coix* and *Canna*, were anciently cultivated in Spain. [Johannessen observes: *Coix* is a broad leaved grass and, in the hand, would not have had its leaves confused with *Canna*.]

Mellén B. 1986, 133. "*Achira*" was found by Spanish visitors from South America as being present on Easter Island.

Cannabis sativa
Origin: Central Asia
Summary: Long used as a psychoactive drug in Asia, a signature chemical from the metabolic breakdown of this plant in the human body has been identified in Peruvian mummies dated from 100 to 1500 C.E.
Transfer: either India (via the Pacific?) or the Middle East (via the Atlantic?) to the Americas
Time of transfer: no later than 100 C.E.
Grade: A
Sources: *Cannabis sativa* – hashish, marijuana, Indian hemp

Int. Lib. Assoc. 1996, 561. Sanskrit: *bhanga, vijaya*

Chopra et al. 1956, 48. Sanskrit: *ganjika, bhanga*

Nadkarni 1914, 77. *Cannabis sativa*. Sanskrit: *vijayâ, siddhapatri*. Hindi: *ganja*. Arabic: *kinnab*. Native of western and central Asia. Now cultivated all over India and wild in the western Himalayas and Kashmir. The plant is sacred to the Hindus.

Zeven and de Wet 1982, 71. Center of maximum diversity in Central Asia. 149. There is a wild form in Central Asia.

Jett (2004) reprises the literature on evidence for the mortuary use of hashish in the New World: "Hashish or Indian hemp (*Cannabis sativa*), a native of western Asia, carried the alkaloid delta-9-tetrahydrocannibinol (THC). The plant (commonly called 'marijuana'), which has long been popular in the Middle East for its psychoactive effects, is generally assumed to have been a post-Columbian introduction to the warmer parts of the New World. However, Parsche, Balabanova, and Pirsig (1992b) found THC (along with cocaine and nicotine) in the tissues, teeth, and hair of ancient naturally mummified bodies from both the North Coast and the South Coast of Peru—in 39 of the 60 cadavers tested and in a corporal distribution indicating ante-mortem use. These mummies ranged in date from about 115 to 1500 C.E."

Balabanova, Parsche, and Pirsig 1992b. Residues from hashish and cannabis were identified chemically in cranial hair of pre-Columbian Peruvian mummies.

Parsche, Balabanova, and Pirsig 1993, 503. They analyzed hair, skin, muscle, brain, teeth, and bones from 72 Peruvian (as well as 11 Egyptian) mummies and found chemical residues of cocaine, nicotine, and hashish and their metabolites in both sets of mummies (16 of the Peruvian corpses revealed cocaine; 26 had tobacco traces; and 20 showed hashish).

Díaz 2003, 80. Marijuana (cannabis) may have been introduced to Mexico during the colonial period as a source of fiber. Shortly afterward, the plant was used for ritual purposes by indigenous groups. Famous Mexican scientist Alzate described its ritual use with a beautiful Náhuatl name, *pipiltzintzintli* [which actually implies a pre-Columbian use, although it does not guarantee it].

Capsicum spp. in general
Sources: *Capsicum* spp. in general

Nicolson et al. 1988, 246. They believe that "the taxonomy of *Capsicum* is still far from resolution." The <u>Hortus Malabaricus</u> name for *C. annuum*, *capomolago*, occurs in Kerala today as *kappamulaku* (*kappa* meaning 'ship,' i.e., introduced by Europeans, and *mulaku*, a general term for 'hot chilies.'

Brücher 1989, 166. A *capsicum*, flowers and fruits, appears on a stela from Chavin, Peru, first millennium B.C.E. 168. The genus *Capsicum* includes 30 wild-growing species, five of which were domesticated by distinct Indian tribes. Soviets claim a Central American gene center for *Capsicum*. Others suppose concentration in the low mountain region of South Brazil, where a dozen species grow, 8 more from Bolivia/NW Argentina, 7 from Peru/Ecuador, 4 more from Mexico. Phylogeny is complicated.

Bailey 1935, I, s. v. *Capsicum* (page not noted). Originally from tropical America, but escaped from cultivation in the Old World tropics where it was once supposed to be indigenous [a sign that it was thoroughly naturalized and thus old].

Yarnell 1970, 225. Earliest archaeological remains: Peru, 4000 BP; Southern Mexico, 8000; Northern Mexico, 9000.

Shady Solís 1997, 18. *Capsicum* sp. has been excavated at nine different sites of the Late Archaic (3000–1500 B.C.E.) in Peru.

Bronson, 1966, 262. McQuown and Kaufmann have reconstructed ten plant names in proto-Mayan, perhaps at about 2600 B.C.E. [more likely somewhat later]. Among them is 'chili'.

Langdon 1988, 334. *Capsicum* was reported in Tahiti as far back as 1768 by Bougainville, who reached that island only eight months after its European discoverer, Wallis.

Heyerdahl 1963b, 31. The chili plant was listed by Knoche (1919, 169) as one of the aboriginal cultigens on Easter Island, known as *poro-poro*.

Newcomb 1963, 41. In the Solomon Islands, chilies are used, and there is grown a curious form of a very primitive botanical kind. 'Turkish' area usage is also very strong. This includes paprika, which does not have a known equivalent in the New World. Names are very confused. Spaniards did not consume much chili and the Portuguese even less. So how did the chili get into S.E. Europe and the adjacent Near East, India, and southwestern China? Note the difficult question of some of the peppers of the Guinea Coast, e.g. *malagueta* or 'grains of paradise.' The term *pimienta* is used in South America for black pepper. This probably has Brazilian ties. Note the wide usage of *Capsicum* in Korea; also old in parts of East Asia such as West China, which is remote and inaccessible. Yet, chilies are not used in coastal China, which was more accessible to the New World. This is a curious pattern if one assumes Iberian introduction to the Far East.

Johannessen and Wang 1998, 27. A Chinese written character of pre-European occurrence designates 'chili pepper.' The plant is feral. One form in south Yunnan develops into a moderate-sized tree (citing personal communication from a biologist at Yunnan University, 1996). [Cf. the sculpture shown by S. Gupta. of a tree-sized *capsicum* plant in India.] Furthermore, the chili pepper plant is shown in Java on ancient panels on a temple wall constructed before the 10th century C.E. at the Prambanan Temple complex, east of Yogyakarta (see Johannessen and Wang, Fig. 11). Besides, a considerable age for this plant in Asia is implied to account for its use in the daily cuisine of almost the entire Chinese population, especially in the south. The use of the same condiment in the diet of South India implies similar antiquity there.

For additional references to *Capsicum* species in the medieval literature of India and Egypt, see Johannessen and Parker 1989b, 16.

Capsicum annuum
Origin: the Americas
Summary: Three Sanskrit names were used for one or another *Capsicum*. It is mentioned in the Siva and Vamana Puranas, dated ca. the sixth–eighth century C.E. The plant and fruit are shown in sculpted art of Java and India in medieval times. The species was also found growing in Tahiti and Easter Island at a time indicating aboriginal cultivation of the crop. Both *C. annuum* and *C. frutescens* are cultivated very widely and play key roles in the cuisines of East, South, and Southeast Asia.

    Case 1: Transfer: to South and Southeast Asia
    Time of transfer: no later than the eighth century
    Grade: A
    Case 2: Transfer: to eastern Polynesia
    Time of transfer: pre-Columbian
    Grade: B+

Sources: *Capsicum annuum* – chili pepper

García-Bárcena 2000, 14. *C. annuum* was found domesticated in the Tehuacán Valley of Mexico from 4100 B.C.E., although it was being collected in the wild long before that.

Gupta., 1996. 49–50. Quotes Heiser, re. arrival of *Capsicum* in tropical Asia from the Americas after Columbus. Regarding the 16th century C.E. introduction of chilies by the Portuguese, "this obviously is not true. Chilies have been grown and used in India much earlier, as chilies are mentioned in Siva and Vamana Puranas, which are dated ca. Sixth–Eighth century C.E." Mention is made in <u>Siva Purana</u> that chilies (*Capsicum*) are an ingredient in a remedy for consumption. In spite of the importance of this plant in the diet, the author has seen them depicted only at Jambukeshvara Shiva temple at Tiruchirapalli, Karnataka. In all panels showing *Capsicum*, the flowers and leaves are true to nature (plates 55, 56) and not only show fully developed fruits but also the different stages in their development. In plate 55, the only discrepancy is regarding the large size of the plant motif showing a *rishi* [figure] sitting under it. The *Capsicum* plant is usually not more than 70–80 cms. in height." [Note above, Johannessen's mention of a Yunnan *Capsicum* growing as large as a "moderate-sized tree."]

Towle 1961, 132. Used in Nazca era (first–ninth centuries C.E.).

Roys 1931, 229. Chac-ic in Mayan. 247. "Ic. *Capsicum annuum*, L. Chile."

Watt 1888–1893, II, 134–9. "The greatest confusion exists in Indian literature as to the cultivated species of *Capsicum*." "Much remains still to be done in order to clear up the ambiguities which exist in the literature of the Indian Capsicums." Sanskrit: *marich-phalam*. Arabic and Persian terms are related: *filfile* and *filfile-surkh, pilpile-surkh*. This annual is cultivated throughout India. Supposed to have been recently, comparatively speaking, introduced from South America. According to the best authorities, this and the other species of *Capsicum*, now cultivated in India, have no Sanskrit names (sic). "Although not natives of India, the cultivated forms, at the present date, are everywhere met with and constitute an indispensable ingredient in native curry."

Nadkarni 1914, 86. *Capsicum annuum* and *C. frutescens*. Sanskrit: *marichiphalam*. Eng.: Spanish pepper, red pepper, cayenne pepper. Very largely cultivated throughout the plains of India and in the hills in some districts.

Torkelson 1999, 1675. Sanskrit: *katuvira, marichi-phalam*

Pullaiah 2002, I, 121. Sanskrit: *katuvirah, rakta maricha*. Used medicinally.

For references to *Capsicum* in additional historical sources from India and Egypt, see Johannessen and Parker 1989b, 16.

See also material under *Capsicum* ssp. in general.

Capsicum frutescens
Origin: Mesoamerica
Summary: Art in India display and ethnographic reports in China document Capsicums so tall they can only be perennials, and *C. frutescens* is perennial. A Sanskrit name is recorded. The plant is widely cultivated in Asia today.
Transfer: Asia from the Americas
Time of transfer: by medieval times
Grade: A
Sources: *Capsicum frutescens* (syn. *C. minimum*) – chili pepper

Pickersgill and Heiser 1977, 823. Unequivocally a domesticated plant in the Tehuacán Valley, Mexico, from the Santa Maria period, 2900–2200 BP.

Martínez M. 1978, 122. Miranda's survey of flora of Chiapas found this species. *Capsicum* spp. was found lightly in Martinez' archaeological remains of first century date.

Roys 1931, 264. Mayan. "*Max, Max-ic,* or *Putun-ic. Capsicum frutescens,* L. *Chile del monte.*"

Brücher 1989, 46. *C. frutescens* is widespread, from the southeasterm U.S. to Argentina. It has a wide distribution as a wild or semi-domesticated plant in lowland tropical America and, secondarily, in southeastern Asia. It is also grown in India and throughout the islands of Polynesia. 170. Probably domesticated in Costa Rica and Nicaragua.

Nicolson et al. 1988, 246. The Kerala name for this particular species is *valiyakappamulaku,* or more commonly, *valiyamulaku.* (*Kappa* in the former means 'ship,' i.e., 'foreign.')

Pullaiah 2002, I, 122–3. Sanskrit: *katuvirah.* (One source makes this name *katuirah,* one consonant different from the name for *Capsicum annuum*).

In general, it may be noted that when sources refer to large or tree-sized Capsicums, as they occasionally do in Asia, they probably are speaking of *C. frutescens,* because only a perennial would reach such a size, and the perennial species is frutescens.

See also material under *C. annuum.*

Carica papaya
Origin: Central America
Summary: Found in the Marquesas Islands, and evidence indicates its cultivation/use was aboriginal. Presence of (multiple) Sanskrit, Hindi, Arabic, and Persian names for the papaya, plus the plant's widespread naturalization in South Asia, strongly indicates that it had also spread to Asia long before 16th century European commerce commenced.

    Case 1: Transfer: the Americas to Polynesia
    Time of transfer: pre-Columbian
    Grade: B+
    Case 2: Transfer: to South Asia, uncertain
    Time of transfer: uncertain
    Grade: B

Sources: *Carica papaya* – papaya, pawpaw

Zeven and de Wet 1982, 188. Lowlands of Central America somewhere between southern Mexico and Nicaragua. Not known wild. [However, Johannessen notes that wild—feral?—papaya does occur and is used commercially as a meat tenderizer in Central America.]

Nadkarni 1914, 87. *Carica papaya.* Eng.: papaw tree. Hindi: *popaiyah.* Pers. and Arab: *amba-hindi.*

Pullaiah 2002, I, 125–6. Sanskrit: *Brahmairandah, eranda, karkati.* Medicinal uses.

Heyerdahl 1964, 127. A native of the New World. A large form grew from Mexico to Peru. A smaller, poorly known lot of indigenous South American species were cultivated through the Andean area to northern Chile.

Brown 1935, 190. *Carica papaya.* At least two varieties are present in the Marquesas. *Vi inana* (or *inata,* 'papaya of the people') is recognized by Marquesans as an ancient food plant, doubtless of aboriginal introduction. Its fruit is smaller and less palatable than the *vi oahu* which is claimed by the natives to have been introduced from Hawaii by early missionaries. Sap of the papaya is used as a poultice. "A native of tropical America; of aboriginal introduction in Polynesia."

Tozzer 1941, 199. The papaya tree and fruit are described as in common use among the Maya, and Footnote 1085 identifies it as *C. papaya* L.

Lundell 1938, 43. "It must have been known to the ancient Maya."

Safford 1905, 215–6. A native of tropical America, but it has become established throughout the entire tropical world.

Roys 1931, 236. *Chich-put* (the h's in chich indicate 'ch explosive'). *C. papaya*. This is the wild form. Fruit said to be inedible. 280. "Put. *Carica papaya*, L. Papayo."

Pandey 2000, 280. *C. papaya*, from Central America, is one species "naturalized throughout India."

Bretschneider 1892, 300. Legge takes the *mu kua* to be the papaya, but he is mistaken. The *mu kua* of the (Chinese) classics is undoubtedly the quince.

Heyerdahl 1996, 149–57. In the Marquesas (Hivaoa), Von den Steinen discovered and then Linton and Heyerdahl both re-discovered, large, non-Polynesian stone carvings (radiocarbon-dated by charcoal beneath the statues at ca. 1300 C.E.) showing long-tailed quadrupeds that could represent only felids and whose nearest analogs were on the monuments of San Agustín, Colombia. He connects these with several plant species of American origin that have been identified in remote locations in the Marquesas. They can only be accounted for by the arrival of voyagers. 219. Among these plants was the papaya (cf. Brown (1935) above).

Parotta 2001, 202. Sanskrit: *eranda, karkati*.

Cassia fistula
Origin: Old World
Summary: This well-known medicinal plant (laxative) was used throughout Eurasia. Yet it also grew in North, South, and Middle America, as well as in Africa. Details of chronology and distribution in the Americas deserve further investigation.
Grade: incomplete
Sources: *Cassia fistula* – purging cassia

MOBOT 2003. Distribution: North, South, and Middle America, and Africa.

Gupta. 1996, 51. Represented in art as early as the Bhárhut Stupa, second century B.C.E.

Pullaiah 2002, I, 133. Sanskrit: *aragvadha, suvarnaka*. Medicinal uses.

Ceiba pentandra
Origin: the Americas
Summary: It grew and was utilized in Java and South China by the 10th century. Its growth was also intentional and its utilization was widespread in Malabar, India, where two names in Sanskrit were used for the tree. Apparently, it was also grown in the Marquesas Islands before Europeans arrived there.

    Case 1: Transfer: the Americas to Southeast Asia
    Time of transfer: by the fourth century
    Grade: A

Case 2: Transfer: the Americas to the Marquesas
Time of transfer: pre-Columbian
Grade: C

Sources: *Ceiba pentandra*, (syn. *Eriodendron anfructuosum*, *Bombax malabaricum*, *B. ceiba*)—kapok, silk cotton tree, white silk cotton tree

Miranda 1952–1953, I, 268. The kapok of Java is *Ceiba pentandra*.

Aiyer 1956, 31. Listed as *Bombax malabaricum*. Mentioned in the *Charaka Samhita* as the silk cotton tree, no later than the fourth century C.E. (and possibly as early as 900 B.C.E.).

Zeven and de Wet 1982, 187. Toxopeus (1948) believed that this tree originated in an area later divided by the Atlantic, so it is native both to the Americas and Africa. However, Bakhuizen van den Brink (1933) and Chevalier (1949) thought that seeds may have come from the Americas in prehistoric times. Its chromosome number (2n=72) suggest a polyploid origin, and, if this is correct, the kapok tree can only have arisen in the area where its parents occur. As all other *Ceiba* species are restricted to the Americas, this would indicate an American origin.

Nicolson et al. 1988, 74. *Bombax ceiba* is called *mulelavu* still today. *Mul* means 'spines' or 'thorns,' and *elavu* means 'silk cotton tree,' i.e., spiny elavu. Known wild in Kerala. *C. pentandra* is discussed also, with equivalents *B. pentandrum* and *Eriodendron anfratuosum* (*anfructuosum*?). *Panjimaram* is still used as a name. *Panji* (the nj is pronounced as nasalized 'y') refers to cotton, and *maram* means 'tree.' Tree is only known in cultivation in Kerala.

Carter 1974, 212. This tree is portrayed in a Javanese sculpture at about 977 C.E.

Schafer 1970, 64. In the Tang era (600–900 C.E.), the people of Hainan Island spun and wove kapok. It was called 'tree floss,' or 'silk cotton,' and was frequently mentioned in the historical sources as woven into blue and red fabrics by women of the Li people. It seems to have been 'simal' rather than a perennial cotton, "and indeed, this fiber, so difficult to weave and usually considered suitable only for stuffing quilts and pillows, is still spun and woven by the Li tribeswomen."

Towle 1961, 65–6. "Much confusion has arisen as to the identity of the several genera involved." Both Saffray (1876) and Rochebrune (1879, 345, 355) identify the fibers used for stuffing dolls and for wrapping small objects as the floss of *Bombax ceiba*. This species was earlier attributed to the tropical regions of Asia, but recently has been described as native to the Americas. However, the plant is not reported from Peru [?]. Harms (1922, 181), considering *Bombax ceiba* as a native of Asia, suggested that the fibers examined by Saffray and Rochebrune were those of *Ceiba pentandra*, a species of a related genus [now synonymous] and the source of the kapok of commerce. Again, this species, although a native of the Americas, like *B. ceiba*, is not found in Peru. However, two other bombacaceous species, *B. ruizii* and *Chorisia insignis*, are found in northern Peru and the valleys of the central Andes. Both of these produce floss, that of the latter closely resembling the fibers of *Ceiba pentandra*. It is quite probable [sic; this suggestion is not defended by Towle] that the fibers examined by Saffray and Rochebrune were from one of the other of these two plants.

De Prez 1935, 60. Kapok trees are represented on four Javanese monuments dating to different periods of time. Particularly, two reliefs from the pool of Djalatounda, situated at the residence of Sourabaya, are dated to about 977 C.E. (see one illustrated as his Fig. 19). Those trees bear undeniable resemblance to the Javanese kapok tree, *Ceiba pentandra* (L) Gaertn. var. indica. Also known under the name *Eriodendron anfractuosum*, D.D. The resemblance is very striking as seen also in the sketch of that tree according to the <u>Historia plantarum</u> of Bontius (1658) (reproduced as De Prez' Figure 23). These bas-reliefs from Djalatounda offer very probably the most ancient representation of the ('Indo-American') kapok tree known in Java and perhaps in Asia. 61. This representation confirms the opinion of Bakhuizen van den Brink in his study on the flora of the Indies and on the elements of American origin where he mentions among others the intrusion of the *Ceiba pentandra*. This shows that the kapok tree was present in Asia and in the Malay Archipelago before the discovery of the New World.

Bronson 1966, 262ff. McQuown and Kaufmann have reconstructed ten plant names apparently present in proto-Mayan, perhaps at about 2600 B.C.E. [More likely somewhat later]. Among them is ceiba.

Yacovleff and Herrera 1934–1935, 283. Common in Peru. (Species not mentioned, but their description of the tree-cotton fits.)

Safford 1905, 221. There is some difference between trees growing in the East Indies and in the West Indies, and some botanists have regarded them as distinct species. "No difference, however, can be discovered in herbarium specimens great enough to warrant their being separated."

Newcomb 1963, 41. Herbert Baker has been collecting them and is doing genetic work on them. This genus was not disseminated by ocean currents. *C. pentandra* is from the Guinea Coast (of Africa) (sic). The ceiba of Sinaloa is a 'shadow stealer' in local lore of the New World, but it occupies a similar spot in African lore. *Ceiba* sp. in Nigeria is a holy tree cared for by man. The Southeast Asian kapok is not a simple *C. pentandra*, but is a subspecies of the African temple Ceiba. Baker sees a dispersal route of tropical America to Guinea Coast to Southeast Asia. What is the story in tropical East Africa, C. O. Sauer asks?

Miranda 1952–1953, 268. Nearly all commercial kapok today comes from the East Indies, especially Java. "There are several trees of the Bombacaceae that produce it; the so-called kapok of Java derives from the same *Ceiba pentrandra*."

Brown 1935, 179. The native names are *uru uru* and *urupuato* in the Marquesas. Of "recent introduction" in the Marquesas [but his usage of that expression means pre-European contact?].

Watt (1888–1893, III, 258–60) lists *Eriodendron anfractuosum* as The White Cotton Tree; Kapok floss. Synonym *Bombax pentandrum*, Linn.; and *Ceiba pentandra*, Gaertn.. Various vernacular names are given, none Sanskrit. Acording to the <u>Flora of British India</u> it occurs "in the forests throughout the hotter parts of India and Ceylon; distributed to South America, the West Indies, and Tropical Africa." Not common in India. "In southern Malabar there is little trade in the silk cotton, such trade as there is being more often in the cotton of the *Bombax malabaricum*."

Gupta. 1996, 38–40. The *Bombax ceiba* is the salmali tree in India. It is sacred. In Nadia, Sirohi Dist., Rajasthan, a seventh-century temple shows deities with flowers of this tree in the background.

Brücher 1989, 146–7. Radiation center of the genus is probably Central America.

Roys 1931, 298. Mayan Yax-che. Silk-cotton tree. (Important in Maya mythology.)

Nadkarni 1914, 59. *Bombax malabaricum*. Sanskrit: *shalmali, mocha*. Eng.: silk cotton tree.

Pullaiah 2002, I, 147. Sanskrit: *swetha salmali*. He distinguishes *Ceiba pentandra*, the white silk cotton tree (syn. *Eriodendron anfructuosum*), from *Bombax ceiba*, the red silk cotton tree (pp. 98–99), which has distinct Sanskrit names, *nirgandha pushpi* and *panchaparni*.

Kirtikar and Basu 1999, I: 358-60. List eight Sanskrit names.

Tagare 1982, 408; 1983, 179. There are references to the silk cotton tree in the <u>Kurma Purana</u> of the fifth century C.E. and the <u>Brahmanda Purana</u> of the 10th century.

Chenopodium ambrosioides
Origin: Old World?
Summary: Distributed in China, Mesopotamia (there is an Arabic name), and India. It was grown in Mexico at the beginning of our era and at the time of the Conquest among the Maya.
Transfer: Old World to Mexico, or vice versa
Time of transfer: pre-Columbian
Grade: A
Sources: *Chenopodium ambrosioides* – apazote, Mexican tea, goosefoot

Bretschneider 1892, 261–2. Fa Hien, when he returned in 414 C.E. by sea from his long journey to the Buddhist countries, landed in the province of Shantung. Upon seeing the *li ho* vegetable (*Chenopodium album*) he was confident that this was indeed the land of Han (i.e., China). Also mentions *C. ambrosioides*.

Thompson 1949, I, 416–36. *Chenopodium ambrosioides* L. In Mesopotamia, the Arabic equivalent is *natna*.

Safford 1905, 224. Called Mexican tea. In Mexico, a medicinal tea is made of it.

Martínez M. 1978, 123. Miranda speaks of only this one species in Chiapas. It is sometimes cultivated. 106. Leaves are cooked as a condiment. 107. Also the cooked fruit is useful for medicinal purposes. Archaeological remains have a proto-Classic date (ca. 1st century B.C.E. or C.E.). One variety (species not told) is used for anti-intestinal parasite therapy.

Roys 1931, 262. Mayan. "Lucum-xiu. *Chenopodium ambrosioides*, L. Apasote." A vermifuge.

Watt (1888–1893, II, 267) says, "An Old World, widely-spread species, now [?] introduced into the Americas, common in many parts of India;" also, "This plant affords the Mexican tea." He says (265, under the genus heading), "There are about 50 species of the genus met with in the world. These are distributed in all climates. India possesses seven species, with perhaps numerous varieties and cultivated forms of most of these."

Bretschneider 1892, 406. One of the names unchanged from classic times to today is *li*. Chenopodium. 261–2. Chenopodium has several Chinese names: *C. ambrosioides* is mentioned in Matsumura citing Japanese sources.

Note that Chopra et al. (1956, 61) and Torkelson (1999, 1684) both give Sanskrit *vastuk* for *C. ambrosioides*, while Torkelson has Sanskrit *sugandhavastuk* for *C. ambrosioides*, and Int. Lib. Assoc. (1996, 562) has *kshetravastuk* for it. Sanskrit nomenclature evidently recognized the relationship (in effect, recognizing the genus), although *album* is now credited with an Old World origin and *ambrosioides* with an American origin.

Chenopodium quinoa
Origin: South America
Summary: Langdon makes a fairly strong argument that this chenopod grew on Easter Island before European presence there, although facts are scarce.
Transfer: South America to Easter Island
Time of transfer: pre-Columbian
Grade: C
Sources: *Chenopodium quinoa* – quinoa

Langdon 1988, 327–9. Was present on Easter Island under cultivation by 1776 as documented in visitors' accounts. (Roggeveen had discovered the island in 1722. Nobody had visited from then until the Gonzalez expedition out of Peru in 1771. There is some possibility of confusion in naming with taro, but Langdon explains why he thinks this is not likely.)

J. Sauer 1993, 33–6. Earliest archaeological occurrence of quinoa is from before 1500 B.C.E. in the northern Chilean desert, but it is basically a high Andean crop.

Towle 1961, 36. Seeds of this plant are a staple food in Peru, replacing maize in higher altitudes. Found in numerous archaeological contexts including mummy bundles at Ancón.

Shady Solís 1997, 18. Excavated at three sites of the Late Archaic (3000–1500 B.C.E.) in Peru.

J. Sauer 1967, 115. A tall chenopod of uncertain identity (perhaps *Chenopodium quinoa* Willd.), which strongly resembles quinoa, has long been grown as a grain crop in the hills of northwest India, where it shares the name *bathú* with grain amaranths (citing Thompson 1852 and Singh 1961). (Needs more research.)

Cichorium intybus
See *Sonchus oleraceus*; the two species are confused by some of our sources.

Cinchona officianalis
Origin: South America
Summary: This American species appears in India with Sanskrit names, one of which may be of Spanish origin. How that could be needs further investigation.
Grade: incomplete
Sources: *Cinchona officianalis* – quinine bark, Peruvian bark
   Pullaiah 2002, 158. Pullaiah lists both *C. officianalis* and *C. cinchona calisaya*, which is called 'Peruvian bark' in India, but the latter has no Sanskrit name. *C. officianalis* is given as Sanskrit *sinkona* and *kunayanah*. The term *cinchona* is said in Peru to come from the name of the wife of a 17th-century (Spanish) Peruvian governor (Markham 1874)); thus, *sinkona* is suspicious appearing in Sanskrit. Nevertheless, the fact that there is an additional Sanskrit name, *kunayanah*, suggests a pre-C.E. 1000 date for the presence of the plant, whatever is to be made of *sinkona*.
   Brücher 1989, 172–3. The generic name is related to the family name of the Viceroy of Peru (1629), Conde de Chinchon, whose wife fell ill with malaria and was saved from the disease by Indian '*curanderos*,' who knew about the anti-fever qualities of cinchona bark. The successful treatment of the illness of Chinchon's wife with a native Indian remedy caused much publicity at the time, and Linné used the name of Cinchon (sic) for the botanical classification of the marvelous 'fever tree.' It is true that the bark of several cinchona trees contains a potent drug against feverish diseases, among them malaria. Modern pharmaceutical analysis has determined 30 different alkaloids in Cinchona species. The most important is quinine. It acts as a protoplasm poison in the cells of *Plasmodium*, the cause of malaria. The genus is represented by many species and natural hybrids in the rain forest of the Andes and Central American mountains. Brücher mentions five species that have been exploited for their quinine content. The nomenclature is, however, still confused and complicated by the existence of natural crosses.
   Bruce-Chwatt 1965, 379. Therapeutic virtues of cinchona bark are believed to have been known to the native Indians of Peru, who confided their knowledge to Jesuit missionaries after the Conquest. However, there is no native written reference (including in Mesoamerica) to such a medicinal plant (called quina-quina indigenously in Peru).

Cocos nucifera
Origin: Asia (?)
Summary: Ethnohistoric and archaeological data ensure the presence of the nut in Mesoamerica at least by 400 C.E. and perhaps earlier in Peruvian graves. The odds are strongly against a drift origin from across the Pacific to the coast of the Americas. The ocean-spanning voyages that moved other plants between the hemispheres (as demonstrated in this paper) provide a plausible medium for transmission of this plant.
Transfer: Pacific islands to the Americas
Time of transfer: no later than 400 C.E.
Grade: A

Sources: *Cocos nucifera* – coconut

> Robinson et al. 2000, 43. From an archaeological site in the Antigua Valley of Guatemala, remains of flora demonstrate the use of the coyol palm and the coconut ('*la carne de coco*') in subsistence in the Late Classic [i.e., ca. 600–850 C.E.] (the coconut was also found at Copán, Honduras, dated 400 C.E.).
>
> Bailey 1935, III, 2437. Palms probably do not greatly exceed 1200 species. Most of the genera are small, and many of them are monotypic. *Calamus* genus has about 200 species, all Old World, mostly Asian. *Geonoma*, about 100 species, of which all are American, and *Chamaedorea*, about 60. *Cocos*, 30 species, all confined to the Americas except the coconut, which is now cosmopolitan. Many of the species, particularly in the small genera, are restricted to a very small geographical region, often to one island or to a group of islands (which suggests that they do not spread far nor readily by natural means).
>
> Heyerdahl 1964, 121–2. The numerous species of the sub-family (*Cocoinae*) to which the coconut belongs are characteristic of tropical America; none occurs in Asia, and only the cultivated and highly useful species, *Cocos nucifera*, is found from Mesoamerica in aboriginal settlements all the way across the Pacific to Indonesia and coastal Asia. It was long supposed that the coconut came from Asia. Experiments had been conducted with coconuts in Hawaii by 1941. The results disproved the old belief that a nut could float across almost any ocean gap and germinate when washed ashore at the other end. Rather, the eyes will be attacked by fouling organisms and lose viability. Further research has also shown documented evidence that the coconut grew in Mesoamerica at the arrival of Columbus and the early Spaniards. The nut is also reproduced in Peruvian effigy jars. Merrill (1954, 267) granted that the coconut was "thoroughly established along the wet Pacific coast of Panama and adjacent Colombia before the arrival of the Spaniards." 131. The coconut was present in Indonesia at the beginning of the Christian era.
>
> Heyerdahl 1950, 460–1. Coconuts kept in the ocean water between the logs of the Kon-Tiki raft were covered with microorganisms and many clusters of pelagic crabs and [the coconuts] deteriorated seriously. Other nuts were kept in baskets on the deck; they remained edible to the end of the voyage and many sprouted early in the voyage. Heyerdahl planted the remaining nuts at the end of the voyage, and only those that had been on the deck germinated and grew as trees.
>
> Cook 1901, 261–87. Presents *in extenso* the case for the coconut being widespread in tropical America before the Spaniards arrived, particularly citing chroniclers.
>
> Bruman 1944, 220–43. After a review of the historical data, he concluded that the coconut did occur in Colima and probably elsewhere on the west coast of Mexico when the first Europeans arrived [he supposed that coconuts reached the coast due to drift from Pacific islands on the Equatorial Counter Current, although the reality of that current has been called into question].

Spriggs 1984, 71–6. Radiocarbon dates on coconut remains excavated on Aneityum Island, Vanuatu, reach the fourth millennium B.C.E., (presumed to be) prior to human settlement. Other possible early coconut remains are discussed. The dates indicate that coconuts were distributed by natural means [at least in the western Pacific]. They also suggest an Indo-Pacific source for this plant rather than a Central American one with human carriage of the seed to the islands as claimed by Heyerdahl.

Dennis and Gunn 1971, 407–13. Evidence from the distribution of the coconut in the Indian Ocean shows that 3000 miles is the effective limit for sea dispersion. It survives on the strand of coral islands much better than on a continent. Cook's and Heyerdahl's notion of an American origin for the coconut has long been discredited. It is a western-Pacific plant rather. But how it reached the islands off Panama is puzzling since no island with the tree was within the required distance. "The mystery of how the coconut reached western America, if it was brought by man, remains unresolved. But it seems far more reasonable to believe that primitive man, and not ocean currents, was involved."

Harries 1978, 271. Bruman (1944) considered that specimens could have reached Central America by drift from Palmyra atoll, the easternmost location in the Pacific islands where coconuts grow, but re-evaluation of the data on survivability now raises questions about that view. Apparently the coast of the Americas was just at or beyond the limit for viability of the nuts after sea drift. Furthermore, there is a question about whether nuts will sprout and become established naturally where they land or whether humans must assist them; the latter view is the general consensus today.

Heyerdahl 1965, 461–7. Heyerdahl's brief visit to the (Cocos) island (off Panama) provided evidence which he reviews here. He shows it to be consistent with the view that prehistoric people (presumably from the mainland) cleared areas and planted coconut groves on them, and thus that the coconut palm was present and economically significant off the Panama coast before European discovery.

Heyerdahl 1965, 461. Specific references in an early document establishes the presence of the coconut on Cocos Island, west of Panama. Also cites Edmondson 1941 re. controlled tests on Oahu by floating coconuts in sea-water. Short-term sea-exposed nuts sprouted successfully only if planted in soil, not sand. 458. "If Sellergren's analysis (1898, 27) of certain vegetable fibers found in prehistoric graves at Ancón, north of Callao, is correct, then these included material plaited from pre-Columbian coconut husk. Wienter (1880, 601) too, supported by the botanist André and later quoted by Harms (1922, 165), lists the coconut among plants reproduced in ancient Peruvian effigy jars.

Mahan 1983, 106. The Yuchi Indians of the southeastern U.S. had a tradition that their ancestors used rattles made of coconut shells.

Merrill 1954, 267. It is "most certain" that Polynesians introduced the coconut to the west coast of the Americas not long before the Spaniards arrived.

De Prez 1935, 58, Fig. 4. Coconut trees are shown at Borobudur (India) in bas-relief ca. 700–900 C.E.

Newcomb 1963, 57. If it is true that the coconut in West Africa was late in comparison to introduction of the coconut into East Africa, no one is going to suggest that the coconut moved overland between the two shores of the continent. Could Austronesians have rounded Cape of Good Hope?

Mangelsdorf, MacNeish, and Willey 1964, 434. Accept the coconut as one of "the cultivated plants of Middle America."

Robinson et al. 2000, 843. At the site of Urías in the Valley of Antigua, Guatemala, they have archaeological remains of a coconut in the Late Classic, ca. 700; the same plant was found at Copán, Honduras, around 400 C.E.

Lunde 1992, 50–5. A plant definitely shared between the two hemispheres was the coconut.

Patiño 1976, 54. Statements of the chroniclers about palms are relatively few. The coconut, although it was found by the Spaniards on their arrival in the Americas, cannot be considered rigorously as an American plant. Other than the oil palm (*Elaeis guinensis* Jacq.) and two others, originally from Africa, the rest of the *Cocoinae* are American. Patiño goes on to cite literature pro and con in relation to Cook's claim of American presence of the coconut when Europeans arrived. He also gives much historical information on additional species of palms cultivated in South America [some of these might prove to be distributed in both Old and New Worlds, but we have not investigated any besides the coconut]. 58–90. Extensive treatment of the historical sources in re. the nomenclature and early occurrences of the coconut, show its slow dispersion, even in colonial times. Map on p. 61 shows five localities in Colombia and isthmian Panama (including Cocos Island) where the coconut was present upon European discovery. Documents at least five locations on the Pacific coast of the Americas where the coconut was reported by Spanish chroniclers to have been in cultivation.

Guppy 1906, 62–69. Discusses the question of what plants and conditions lead to sea-borne transmission of seeds. 63. "It must be admitted that the effectual operations of the currents as plant-dispersers are limited to the shore-plants with buoyant seeds or fruits." The total of these worldwide would not reach 200 species. 64. For example, the number of littoral plants introduced into Hawaii only comes to about 16. And some of them include trees that are useful to the natives and that were probably introduced by them. This number declines from the western Pacific (e.g. Fiji, about 65) as one moves eastward. Easter Island has few [any?] Indo-Malayan beach trees, and, on Juan Fernandez and the Galapagos, no Indo-Malayan strand-plants are represented at all. 67. "The Coco-nut palm has been carried around the world through the agencies of man and the currents, whilst the home of the genus is in America" based on the principle that where the species are most numerous there is the home of the genus.

Parkes 1991. Archaeological evidence for coconuts has been found on Atiu Island (the Cooks) by 7820±70 BP.
Lepofsky et al 1992. Anaerobically-preserved domesticated coconuts have been found in the Society Islands, dated 600 C.E.
Bailey 1935, I, s.v. "Coconut" (9-15). The coconut is the most important of cultivated palms. "Its nearest relatives, whether or not regarded as in the same genus, are natives of tropical America. For this and for other reasons which have been presented by Cook, it must be believed that the coconut is a native of America, and that it was carried westward across the Pacific in prehistoric times. While the nut will float and retain its power of germination for a considerable time, its propagation from island to island in known cases has practically always been the deliberate work of men, and it is probable that men were ..." the normal agents of dispersion.
MacNeish 1992, 259. Lists *Cocos nucifera* as one of the "native cultivated and/or domesticated plants of Southeastern Asia."
J. Sauer 1993, 186. The coconut evidently evolved in the Indo-Pacific Ocean region where Tertiary and Quarternary fossils have been found. This remains the region of greatest genetic diversity and of its parasites, including many totally dependent insect species. Coconuts are known to be capable of remaining viable while floating in the sea for over 6 months, no maximum limit being established." [sic] [To the contrary, see Harries and Dennis and Gunn above]. 187. "During Holocene time, the range of sea-dispersed wild coconut palms probably spanned the tropical Indian and Pacific Oceans from East Africa to the Pacific coast of Panama and Costa Rica. 188. "*C. nucifera* was absent from the Atlantic-Caribbean region until introduced by the Portuguese."
Bretschneider (1882, 38) lists plants in the <u>Nan fang Ts'ao Mu Chang</u>. The author was Ki Han, a Minister of State in the Tsin [Jin] dynasty, 290–307 C.E., who had previously been Governor of Canton. The 80-species list includes the coconut.
Hernandez 1942–1943 [before 1580], II, 507–10. In a long piece on the coconut: "This, which the hindues vulgarly call *maron*, and Strabo (as some say) called *palma*, and which gives a fruit that the Mexicans call *coyolli*, by the Portuguese *coco*, because of certain eyes that seem like those of a monkey, and by the Persians and Arabs *narel*, is a tall tree ...." Pictured.
Heyerdahl 1965, 461. He presents persuasive evidence that the tree was being planted for economic purposes on Cocos Island, near the west coast of Panama, before the first Europeans visited there. He also noted that traces of coconut fiber had been found in ancient tombs at Ancón, Peru, while representations of the coconut palm could be seen in Peruvian art.
Heyerdahl 1996, 220. The early voyager Captain Porter was told by Marquesans that the coconut came to them by voyagers from the east on rafts.
Ward and Brookfield (1992) provide the definitive review of the literature on the drift of coconuts. They also report on an extensive computer simulation of coconut drift from which they conclude that it is highly unlikely that drift nuts would have reached the Americas from the nearest

Pacific Island loci. The question of whether drift nuts would successfully sprout and mature to trees on the strand has also been contentious. (For example, no coconuts that have drifted to Australian shores are known to have survived.) Some biologists suppose that humans would have had to be involved to protect and plant or transplant germinating nuts to soil mixed with sand rather than sand alone, and especially to keep them safe from land crabs (Harries 1978, 271). Nevertheless, Spriggs (1984) reported coconuts from Vanuatu that dated to the fourth millennium BP, probably before any humans inhabited those islands.

    Méndez P. 1944, 14–5, 50. Balboa encountered natives growing and using the nuts in 1513 when he arrived with the first Spaniards on the Pacific coast of Panama.

Colocasia esculenta
Origin: Americas?
Summary: "Dry-land taro," found on Easter Island, is described by Heyerdahl as an American species. More detailed information is required to assess the botanical reliability of this statement.
Grade: incomplete
Sources: *Colocasia esculenta* – dry-land taro

    Heyerdahl 1963b, 31. Polynesian wet-land taro, *Colocasia antiquorum*, is grown in wet land in central and western Polynesia, whereas the rare Easter Island taro is grown between closely packed stones in entirely arid, eroded, lava-flows, and may perhaps be a dry-land taro such as is reported common to both east Polynesia and the Americas.

    Kirch 2000, 79. *C. esculenta* "was once thought to be a Southeast Asian domesticate, but recent cytological research suggests multiple origins, one in the New Guinea region."

Couroupita guianensis
Origin: tropical America
Summary: The unique flower of this tree is interpreted in Indian iconography, as shown in temple sculptures, as denoting the god Shiva. The tree originated in Middle America and grows only there and in India.
Transfer: the Americas to India
Time of transfer: Medieval?
Grade: A
Sources: *Couroupita guianensis* – cannonball tree, *naga lingam*

    Gupta. 1996, 58. *Naga lingam* is a large tree, native of South America and the West Indies, but planted in South India "from very early times." The tree bears curious flowers that grow directly out of the trunk and main limbs. Stamens and pistil fuse in such a manner that the flower gives the appearance of a miniature lingam (symbol of the male generative organ) facing the hovering hood of a naga (cobra). For this reason, the tree is cultivated in Shiva temples, and its flowers are offered in worship before the sacred stone lingam in temples devoted to Shiva. Gupta. names four temples in Tamil Nadu and one in Karnataka where the plant and flowers are shown in sculpture. *Naga lingam* flowers are left as offerings before stone lingams in Shivaite temples. [The only scenario one can imagine for anybody's transporting this New World tree to India would be that a worshipper of Shiva visited Mesoamerica, where he saw the tree's unique flower (no doubt with great astonishment) and felt that it ought to grow in India, the homeland of Shiva. No non-Shivaite would have paid particular attention to the blossom, and indeed the plant plays no role in Mesoamerican iconography.]

> Pullaiah 2002, I, 186. Telugu name is *nagalingam*, but no name in Sanskrit is reported. It has medicinal uses.
>
> Lancaster 1965, 4. Called in South India *sivalingam* or *nagalingam* and is especially sacred to the god Shiva. "The tree, however, was introduced to India not more than 100 years ago and its habitat is Guiana and South America" [sic].

Cucumis sp.

Origin: Old World
Summary: A poorly preserved *cucurbitaceous* seed was found in a nineteenth-century excavation in Peru and initially was considered to represent a possible *Cucumis* species, but the identification was later given up. Further examination would be desirable.
Grade: incomplete
Source: *Cucumis* sp.

> Towle 1961, 96. Poorly-preserved *cucurbitaceous* seeds are mentioned by Constantin and Bois as possibly those of a species of the genus *Cucumis*. This is an Old World genus not otherwise represented in pre-Columbian Peruvian sites; these seeds were excluded from discussion in Towle's monograph.

Cucurbita ficifolia

Origin: Central America
Summary: Archaeologically, it was at Huaca Priéta in Peru before 2500 B.C.E. [Note that the actual radiocarbon date at Huaca Priéta for the plant layer is 2578–2470 B.C.E., according to Yen (1963), which calibrates to 3200–3070 B.C.E.] Also widespread through much of western India and up into the Himalayas and Tibet as far as western China. The differentiation of the species evident in Asia would have required a much longer period of time than the few centuries since the Portuguese advent.
Transfer: the Americas to Asia
Time of transfer: several millennia ago
Grade: A
Sources: *Cucurbita ficifolia* – chilacayote, Malabar gourd

> Brücher 1989, 258–60. One seed was found ca. 700 C.E. in the Valley of Oaxaca. The only other American find is from Huaca Priéta, Peru, set at 3000 B.C.E. [See note in brackets above]. He gives names as *C. ficifolia* Bouché, Malabar gourd, chilacayote, or chayote. It was considered of Afro-Asiatic origin ('Malabar') until Whitaker established its home

definitively in Central America. There, it is closely related to the wild species *C. lundelliana* Bailey.

McBryde 1945, 137. Says Standley and Calderón (1925) suppose an Asiatic origin for this, but it is probably of Mexican origin, based on the existence of Aztec names.

Towle 1961, 90. The only archaeological find was at Huaca Priéta in the pre-ceramic levels (with other plants of Asian origin) and in the following Cupisnique period.

Whitaker and Bird 1949. *C. ficifolia* was present in Peru from the pre-ceramic period (ca. "2500 B.C.E."). It had never previously been reported from a South American archaeological collection. [See note above.]

Newcomb 1963, 29. C. Sauer says this is a perennial of Southern Mexico, Bolivia, Malabar, and Tibet, "the fig-leaf cucurbit." 31. The Malabar gourd is widely cultivated in Malabar, India, and on into the agricultural valleys of Tibet, and again east of there into the high country of Western China, where it is used as yak feed. This plant ranges over an extraordinary area of varying environmental conditions and its forms vary greatly, whereas the New World cucurbits do not vary too much from the common watermelon in shape, color, or markings. Surprisingly, the Malabar gourd is an American plant, identical with *C. ficifolia*. *C. ficifolia* originated in the Yucatan/Guatemala borderlands, says Sauer. It was introduced early into the Peruvian coastal area, based on archaeological evidence, and possibly into the Andes. But how did it reach India and thence the Himalayas and China? This plant was of no interest to Spaniards or Portuguese, so they provide no explanation. We are certain of the species' identity from Old to New World on morphological grounds. Malabar gourds are fertile when bred with New World stocks of *C. ficifolia*. Moreover, there are no wild cucurbits in the Old World. Nor, was it carried around by ocean currents. Perhaps it was taken along on voyages. Insufficient time has elapsed since the Columbian era for the plant to have been disseminated so extensively in Asia and differentiated so much. 35. This is the only perennial species of the cucurbits. There is archaeological evidence of its growth at sea level in coastal Peru, but today it is [also] found in upland sites. Also ranging from the Malabar coast of India, which is humid, to the Tibetan/Chinese borderlands, in the uplands. It is an odd and minimally useful vegetable with a strange distribution.

Cucurbita maxima
Origin: the Americas
Summary: In India, there were at least three Sanskrit names for this. Vernacular names in India are patently related to Mayan names. In China, there is great varietal differentiation, indicating long presence and cultivation. In India, a medical text of the eighth century mentions this species as an ingredient. Some scholars consider the texts of reports by European explorers of Easter Island also to refer to this cucurbit.

    Case 1: Transfer: to Asia
    Time of transfer: probably two millennia or more ago

Grade: A
Case 2: Transfer: to Easter Island
Time of transfer: pre-Columbian
Grade: C

Sources: *Cucurbita maxima* – squash, winter squash, Hubbard squash, giant squash

Nadkarni 1914,129. *Cucurbita maxima*. Sanskrit: *punyalatha, dadhiphala*. Eng.: squash, gourd.

Pullaiah 2002, I, 194. Sanskrit: *pitakusmandah*. Medicinal uses.

Johannessen and Wang 1998, 26. Easter Island had acquired red-fleshed squashes (probably *Cucurbita maxima* and *moschata*—see Mellén B. 1986, 211).

Yarnell 1970, 225. Earliest remains in Peru, 2000 BP.

Towle 1961, 90. Represented in Mochica and Chimu pottery, one an exact reproduction of a warty Hubbard squash. Seeds were found in remains at Ancón (before our era).

Bronson 1966, 262ff. McQuown and Kaufmann have reconstructed plant names for proto-Mayan. Among them is a term for yellow squash. Maybe as early as 2600 B.C.E. [but more likely somewhat later.]

Watt 1888, II, 638–41. Under discussion of the genus: "The very greatest confusion exists in the Indian publications that deal with Gourds, Pumpkins, and Vegetable Marrows ...." "All the forms met with exist in a state of cultivation only." De Candolle seems to incline to the opinion that *Cucurbita maxima* may be a truly Asiatic species and the origin of "the pumpkins cultivated by the Romans, and in the Middle Ages" in Europe generally; but that *Cucurbita pepo* is most probably a native of America ...." He has not ventured to assign a habitat for *C. moschata*, although he states that all writers on Asiatic and African botany describe it as cultivated, and that "Its cultivation is recent in China, and American floras rarely mention the species." *C. maxima* he calls "Squash Gourd." "Atkinson, Dutt, and others confuse the pumpkin (*C. pepo*) with the White Gourd (*Benincasa cerifera*). Roxburgh (1814) described only *C. pepo* and *C. moschata* in India, and Voigt, who wrote after Roxburgh, described only *C. maxima*. Stewart gives an account of all three. Seeds were used medicinally (cf. Levey). *C. maxima* produces the largest known *cucurbitaceous* fruit, in some cases weighing as much as 240 lb. and measuring nearly 8 feet in circumference [in India]. The fruit is wholesome" [but watery].

Bretschneider 1892, 196–8. Nowadays, the Chinese cultivate throughout the empire the *Cucurbita maxima*, or Melon Pumpkin ... the *C. Pepo*, or Pumpkin gourd, and *C. moschata*. Of the *C. maxima* they have many varieties, varying considerably in size and shape of the fruit and in the color of the skin. 197. All the *cucurbitaceous* plants now cultivated for food in China "are probably indigenous to the country" [this presumption is based on the wide cultivation and degree of adaptation of the species] with the exception of the cucumber and watermelon. He lists Chinese characters for *C. moschata* and *Luffa cylindrica*, among others.

Brücher 1989, 262–4. *C. maxima* Duch., winter squash. He wants to call it *zapallo* to eliminate the imprecision of 'squash.' There are irrefutable

proofs of South American origin and early domestication (Chimu and
Mochica ceramic effigies). It is incompatible genetically with all other
cucurbits. Descended from *C. andreana* (wild).

Levey 1966, 315. Lists *C. maxima* as referred to (along with *C. pepo*) in a
medieval medical text from India (Al-Kindi, ninth century C.E.). Levey
assumes both plants were cultivated in India at that time.

Nadkarni 1914, 129. Gives Sanskrit: *punyalatha* and *dadhiphala* for *C. maxima*,
and widespread cultivation and adaptation of this squash confirms
substantial antiquity for its presence there.

Mellén Blanco 1986, 211. Interprets the accounts of the González expedition
(1776) to Easter Island as showing that *C. maxima* was growing there at
the time of European discovery.

In India the plant had at least three Sanskrit names (Watson 1868, 319, 327).

Common names for the pumpkin current in India, as well as ones for *C.
moschata*, echo the *kum* root in Mayan: *cumbuly, kumbala, koomra, kumhra,
kúmara* (Watt 1888–1893, II, 641; Watson 1868, 92, 119, 310, 311).

Cucurbita moschata
Origin: the Americas
Summary: Painted or modeled in Chinese art as early as the seventh–tenth centuries
and later. Vernacular names in use in India are markedly similar to those in Mayan.
Reports by European explorers of Easter Island may refer to this cucurbit in
cultivation.
    Case 1: Transfer: to Asia
    Time of transfer: over one millennium ago
    Grade: A
    Case 2: Transfer: the Americas to Easter Island
    Time of transfer: pre-Columbian
    Grade: incomplete
Sources: *Cucurbita moschata* – winter squash, banana squash, butternut squash
    Schoenhals 1988, 141. Eng.: butternut squash.
    Johannessen and Wang 1998, 26. Easter Island had acquired red-fleshed
squashes (probably *Cucurbita maxima* and *moschata*, citing Mellen B. 1986,
211.) 25. Known in China as nangua. Recorded by Jia Ming (1966) in a
medicinal recipe published in 1473 C.E. A specimen is pictured in a
Chinese painting by Shen Chou, an artist whose life spanned 1427–1509
C.E. A ceramic teapot in the definitive shape of a moschata squash and
belonging to the Ming Dynasty (1368–1644 C.E.) has been published, but
the exact date is not established. Similar pots are to be found in the
Zhejiang Provincial Museum at Hangzhou dated to the Song Dynasty
(960–1279 C.E.; see Johannessen and Wang's Fig. 10). A similar porcelain
teapot of Tang Dynasty age (618–905 C.E.) has also been published.

    Bailey 1935, I, 910. *C. moschata*, Duch. Cushaw, crookneck squash. Winter
crookneck squash. Nativity undetermined. He notes the variety sylvestris,
Naudin. A form found wild in the Himalayan region [? but Watt 1888, II,
638–41, says all cucurbits are cultivated, none wild, in India] with fruit as
large as a man's head.

Yarnell 1970, 225. Earliest remains: Peru: 4000 BP; Southern Mexico: 5000 BP; Northern Mexico: 3000 BP; S.W. U.S.: 1000 BP.

Towle 1961, 91. Found in pre-ceramic levels at Huaca Priéta, ca. 2500 B.C.E. (although it is apparently of Mexican or Central American origin) and shells and seeds appear with Cupisnique pottery and maize (first millennium B.C.E.). [Note that the actual radiocarbon date at Huaca Priéta for the plant layer is 2578–2470 B.C.E., according to Yen (1963), which calibrates to 3200–3070 B.C.E.]

Shady Solís 1997, 18. *Cucurbita* sp. only identified. Excavated at several sites dating to the Late Archaic (3000–1500 B.C.E.) in Peru. (Based on the find at Huaca Priéta, below; Shady Solís probably refers to *C. moschata*.)

Whitaker and Bird 1949. *C. moschata* was present from the pre-ceramic period (2500 B.C.E.) at Huaca Priéta. (See Towle 1961, 91 above.)

Roys 1931, 258. "*Kum*, or *Kuum*. *Cucurbita moschata*, Duch." Vernacular names in use in India in the nineteenth century for this economically important genus included *kumhra* and *kumra* (Watt 1888–92, II, 640), while from Yucatan we find a homonymic Mayan term, *kum*, or *kuum*. Roys' colonial-era source continues, "there are [in Yucatan] the calabazas [bottle gourds] of Spain, and there is also another sort of native ones [sic], which the Indians call *kum*. The close similarities of names for the same species in Mexico and India suggests, although, of course, it does not prove, that an historical event tied the areas together, linguistically as well as botanically.

Brücher 1989, 260–1. *C. moschata* Duch. ex Poir. pumpkin, crookneck. Remains from Ocampo caves in Mexico date to 2900–1500 B.C.E. (although his table on p. 258 gives the date for this as 4900–3500 B.C.E.—probably intending BP rather than B.C.E. – "earliest known"). Because it crosses with so many species, it is considered a basic species in the phylogeny of the American cucurbits.

Nicolson et al. 1988, 95–6. The element shown in <u>Hortus Malabaricus</u> is surely *C. moschata*, not *C. melopepo* or *C. maxima*. In Kerala today, this plant is called *mathan*.

Lancaster 1965, 25. *C. maxima* provides flowers and fruit for worship in India [implying a long time for the plant in India].

Cucurbita pepo
Origin: the Americas
Summary: The pumpkin has two Sanskrit names and is mentioned in several Hindu texts as early as the fourth century C.E. It is also listed as an ingredient in medicine in an Indian text of the ninth century and is an ingredient in Ayurvedic medicine (today). It was also mentioned in a Chinese document as early as the fifth century C.E.
Transfer: the Americas to India
Time of transfer: no later than the fourth century
Grade: A
Sources: *Cucurbita pepo* – pumpkin
Aiyer 1956, 57. Pumpkin is mentioned in the <u>Atharvaveda</u>, dating before 800 B.C.E. Also mentioned in the Buddhistic Jatakas.

Watson 1868, 310. Bengali and Hindustani have *Koomra* for *Cucurbita pepo*. The same word is also Bengali for *Benincasa cerifera*.

Pickersgill and Heiser 1977 814. From Guila Naquitz cave, Oaxaca, from 10,750–9,840 BP.

Bretschneider 1882, 77–9. From a work on Chinese agriculture, <u>Ts'i Min Yao Shu</u>, by Kia Sz' Niu (Jia Sixie) authored in the fifth century C.E., a list is published containing *C. pepo* that is framed by the heading, "Various Pumpkins and Gourds still Cultivated in China."

Newcomb 1963, 33. C. Sauer says: Linnaeus assigned this species a home in Turkestan and Western Asia. Fuchs called it the "Turkish cucurbit" and established it in southeastern Europe by the early fifth century. *C. pepo* in Asia has shapes and occurrences not known in New World forms. The ornamental gourds, the star-shaped ones, are not known in the New World. *C. pepo* does not occur in the West Indies nor South America (but it does in Mesoamerica). In the Old World, *C. pepo* inhabits the same area of North Africa, the Mediterranean, and Asia as does maize. Needs further work for clarification. 33. "*Cucurbita ficifolia* and *C. pepo* are the overseas strangers." 36. In addition to the Americas, this is distributed in Turkey and from the Balkans to Turkestan. How did it get there?

Nayar and Singh 1998, 12. *C. pepo*, L. The fruit is considered in Ayurvedic medicine to be very cooling, astringent, a cure for thirst and fatigue, and a blood purifier.

Levey 1966, 315. Lists *C. maxima* as referred to (along with *C. pepo*) in a medical text from India (Al-Kindi, ninth century C.E.). Levey assumes both plants were cultivated in India at that time.

Torkelson 1999, 1704. Sanskrit: *kurkaru, kushmanda*.

Chopra et al. 1956, 83. Sanskrit: *kurkaru*.

Watt 1888–1893, II, 641. Vernacular name in Bengali is *kumra, kúmara*, among others. Sanskrit: *kurkareú*. Cultivated over most of India, in gardens and near houses. Seeds are supposed to possess anti-helminthic properties.

Bretschneider 1882, 57–61. Author of the famous Chinese volume of materia medica. <u>Pen Ts'ao Kang Mu</u> (*Ben cao gang mu*) was Li Shizhen, born in first quarter of sixth century, begun in 1552, first published 1590. This material is mainly about medicines and includes a compilation of older materials. The list mentions several American plants including this cucurbit.

Brücher 1989, 261–2. *C. pepo* L., summer pumpkin, summer squash, marrow. Oldest find is dated at 14,000 years BP [sic], from Tamaulipas. From the Ozarks at 5000 BP. Its wild ancestor is *C. texana*.

For a score of other references to *C. pepo* in historical Greece, India, Arabia, China, Egypt, Iraq, and Persia, see Johannessen and Parker 1989b, 16–17.

Curcuma longa
Origin: Asia
Summary: It is grown among isolated tribes in Peru under conditions and with uses that can be explained only by pre-Columbian importation. It was widely planted in Polynesia.
Transfer: Asia to South America (possibly via Polynesians?)

Time of transfer: pre-Columbian
Grade: B+
Sources: *Curcuma longa* – turmeric
- Newcomb 1963, 61. Of Southeast Asian origin, it is vegetatively reproduced, hence quite certainly human-transported across the ocean. Occurs in the eastern Andes where it is used for scent and food color.
- Brown 1931, 162–3. *Curcuma longa* L. Mainly used for its yellow color. A native of India and the islands of the Indian Ocean. Of aboriginal introduction in the Marquesas. Turmeric. Marquesan *eka*, or *ena*.
- Watt 1888–1893, II, 659. Turmeric. Sanskrit and other names given. Names in Heb./Arabic: *kurkum*, and Chinese terms are also given.
- Bretschneider 1892, 231. Yü kin. The description given of this plant by several ancient authors agrees with *Curcuma longa*. Yellow root.
- Sopher 1950, 88, Map F – general summary information. 140. Linguistic and historical evidence shows the cultivation of this plant to be of great antiquity. It was probably a common cultural possession of [all] the Indonesian peoples. Botanical evidence indicates that the plant's original home was India. "Early dispersal" manifested by distribution argues for spread by man east to Polynesia and "possibly beyond." And "perhaps, also, westward to Madagascar." 84. Probably in the islands of Polynesia was where *C. domestica* had its greatest importance outside India as a dye and pigment. 86–87. Distribution throughout most Polynesian islands is discussed and documented. "It is therefore very significant that Curcuma has been reported among forest peoples on the eastern slopes of the Peruvian Andes." Tessman (1920, 161, 324; 1928) reported that a species of Curcuma, grown by the Amahuaca to the east of the Upper Ucayali R. in Peru, was a dye-plant, the color being used, together with *bixa* and *genipa*, for painting the body. He also says it is used by the Chama, while the Uitoto, nearby, use the yellow from *Curcuma* as face paint in their ceremonial dances. Sopher continues (page 88): "If these plants are indeed *Curcuma domestica*, and they can hardly be anything else because the genus *Curcuma* does not [otherwise] occur in the New World, then the evidence for a pre-European, transpacific introduction of the plant by man seems to be very strong indeed." Polynesian occurrence is important because "the plant materials taken by them in their slow progress eastward belong to an early phase of South Asiatic culture."
- Yacovleff and Herrera (1934–1935) have found turmeric being cultivated in a valley in the Urubamba region below Cuzco, and identify it tentatively with the plant referred to by Cobo in 1653 as "*azafrán de los Andes*."

Cyclanthera pedata
Origin: the Americas
Summary: The fruit is cultivated in Mexico, the Andes, Nepal, and Taiwan.
Transfer: the Americas to Asia
Time of transfer: pre-Columbian. (Needs better documentation in re. Asia.)
Grade: incomplete
Sources: *Cyclanthera pedata* – *pepino hueca*

Zeven and de Wet 1982, 189. "Cultivated in Mexico for its young fruits and shoots."

Nayar and Singh 1998, 13. *C. pedata* (L.) Schrad. grows in the Andes and, according to Herklots (1972) also in Nepal and south Taiwan. The flesh is eaten raw or cooked.

Bailey 1935, I, 935. All 30 species of this genus are tropical American. *C. pedata*: Mexico south.

Brücher 1989, 265. *Cucurbitaceae*: *Cyclanthera pedata* (L.) Schrad., *pepino hueco*. Used throughout the Andes.

Cyperus esculentus
Origin: New World ?
Summary: The modern botanical distribution is American, which presumes an American origin. Indians in the Eastern United States also used it. Yet, it had Sanskrit names and was present in the ancient Near East as well as in pre-Columbian Spain.
Grade: B+
Sources: *Cyperus esculentus* (Kew. syn. Longus; syn. rotundus (N., Middle, and S. America))—edible bulbous sedge, chufa, yellow nutsedge

Thompson 1949, 11. Mention of (ancient) Babylonian presence of *Cyperus esculentus* (Arabic: *hab el-azîz*).

Newcomb 1963, 59. Used in Spain, where it is boiled down to make a confection, or a milky, soft drink. It is a bulbous sedge, or cypress, relating to boiled chestnuts. *C. esculentus* is also reported in the Eastern U.S. among Indians "from the earliest days." This transfer is difficult to account for.

Pullaiah 2002, I, 203. Sanskrit: *bhadrmusta, nagaramustakah*. Medicinal uses.

Cyperus vegetus
Origin: New World?
Summary: Edible roots of this plant were used for food in times of extremity, as well as having other uses, in Peru and on Easter Island. A Sanskrit name in India indicates a transfer there anciently.

Case 1: Transfer: South America to Easter Island
Time of transfer: pre-Columbian
Grade: B
Case 2: Transfer: the Americas to India
Time of transfer: while Sanskrit was still an active language
Grade: B

Sources: *Cyperus vegetus* (syn. eragrostics) – edible sedge

Schoenhals 1988, 142. *Cyperus* spp., Span.: tule.

C. Sauer 1969, 56. One of a group of plants found in both the Americas and Asia.

Heyerdahl 1963, 28. Useful in the Easter Island economy, with a native name. It also grows in Peru. Edible roots were used when other food was scarce. Grows in moist places next to the *totora* and *Polygonum* (q.v.).

Towle 1961, 25-6. Under "*Cyperus* sp." Bird found small tubers of a species of *Cyperus* in pre-ceramic levels at Huaca Priéta. Rhizomes used for food in

Peru. 16. Leaves of a certain species of *Cyperus* are also used on the coast in the manufacture of matting, basketry, cordage, 'reed' rafts and small boats, along with Scirpus and Typha (q.v.)

Skottsberg 1934. Three American, non-endemic species, *Cyperus eragrostics*, *Scirpus riparius*, and *Polygonum acuminatum*, remain to have their origin on Easter Island accounted for.

Chopra et al. 1956, 88. Sanskrit: *kaseruka*

Torkelson 1999, 1709. Sanskrit: *kaseruka*

Datura spp. in general

Origin: Although opinions have varied greatly, the home of the entire genus is likely Mexico or Central America.

Summary: The synonymies of species have been quite unsettled until Hadkins et al. (1997), but the fact of the genus' presence in Asia for a long time is well established by its being so abundant that early botanists (including De Candolle) considered some species native to the Old World. At least eight Sanskrit names for Datura are known, and sacred Hindu texts mention medicinal uses. Furthermore, Pokharia and Saraswat (1999, 90) recently excavated specimens of *Datura* (exact species not determinable) dating to the first–third centuries C.E. A species (*D. ferox*, syn. *D. stramonium*) was grown in China, and Greek and Roman physicians are thought to have had the same or another species available (it has been proposed that oracles at the temple of Delphi were spoken under this drug's influence).

Sources: *Datura* spp. in general. (Kew. syn. *stramonium*, syn. *fastuosa*, syn. *trapezia*, syn. *metel*, syn. *meteloides*, syn. *ferox*) – thorn apple, datura, Jimson weed

Lancaster 1965, 45. Lists it as one of the species whose flowers are sacred in India. [The logical implication is that the "sacred plants of the Hindus" discussed by Lancaster must have been present in India for a substantial period of time to have achieved such a degree of sacredness. It is difficult to believe that this could have happened in the few centuries since the Portuguese began visiting.]

Symons and Haegi 1991. They explain references by Dioscorides and all other Old World pre-Columbian attributions as instances of misclassification or in some other way unreliable. In several places the reason given is that this and several other Native American plants are said to occur in India or some other Old World location, but, they insist, this cannot be, so the attributions are discredited. The daturas, and specifically *D. metel* and *D. stramonium*, are shown to be American species. "The sudden appearance of recognizable illustrations and accounts of Datura in the literature [i.e., of Europe] soon after the discovery of the New World ... provides strong circumstantial evidence of the Americas as a source of introduction." They note that they have not consulted Hindu or Sanskrit literature in connection with their study.

Schoenhals, 1988, 142. *Datura* spp. Span.: *toloache*.

Nadkarni 1914, 140–5. *Datura alba* and *D. fastuosa*. Sanskrit: *dhustoora, unmatta*. Eng.: thorn apple, datura. Pers.: *kouzmasab*. Found growing in waste places throughout India. The different species of this plant possess the same medicinal properties. Stupefies, has narcotic, anodyne, and anti-spasmodic properties. It has properties analogous to those of belladonna. Seeds have a strong aphrodisiac effect.

Chopra et al. 1956, 91. *D. metel.* Sanskrit: *dhustura. D. stramonium.* Sanskrit: *dhattura.* A native of Mexico introduced into India. In appearance, D. innoxia resembles it closely. 123. Sanskrit: *dhattura, dhustura.* Cultivated on the west coast.

Torkelson 1999, 1711–12. *D. metel.* Sanskrit: *dhattura, dhustura.* 1740. *D. fastuosa.* Sanskrit: *dhattura, dhustura.*

Int. Lib. Assoc. 1996, 564. *D. metel.* Sanskrit: *dhustur.*

Watson 1868, 257. Sanskrit: *khrishna-dhattura, D. fastuosa.* 280. *Khunubhon-mutta-shiva, D. metel.*

Pullaiah 2002, I, 207. *Datura innoxia* (syn. metel); Sanskrit: *dhatturah. Datura metel* (syn. fastuosa); Sanskrit: *dhatura. Datura stramonium;* Sanskrit: *dhattura, madakara.*

Pokharia and Saraswat 1999, 90. At ancient Sanghol, Punjab (Ludhiana Dist.), first–third centuries C.E., they excavated remains of *Datura* (Dhatura); species could not be determined. The genus is represented today in their area of the Punjab only by *D. innoxia,* but five species are grown in adjoining regions of Pakistan. (See endnotes 59 and 60.)

Pandey 2000, 271. *D. innoxia* Mill., from Mexico, and *D. metel,* from tropical America, are species "naturalized throughout India."

Nicolson et al. 1988, 247. Under this plant, they make clear there are "three confused species of Datura known to occur in South India:" *D. innoxia* Mill. (New World), *D. metel,* and *D. stramonium.* 248. Although *D. stramonium* is supposed to be a neo-tropical [i.e., an American] species, Safford (1931) noted that it was "introduced at a very early date into the warmer regions of Europe, Asia, and Africa." They identify here for the first time one of the plates in Hortus Malabaricus as *D. stramonium.*

Hernandez 1942–1943 [before 1580], II, 442. Hernandez' *tecomaxóchitl* is identified by Mociño y Sess as *Datura maxima* Moc. y Sessé. They also call it *D. patula* Don., which the Kew Index has corresponding to *D. stramonium.* Standley says it is commonly cultivated in *tierras calientes* of Mexico.

Hillebrand 1888, 311. "A small genus, common to both worlds." *D. stramonium* is a "troublesome weed" and spread over many of the islands, i.e., Hawaii. "... As the plant rarely produces seed, its presence ... is probably due to the agency of man."

DuBois 1908, 72. Introduction by A. L. Kroeber. Characteristics of a Datura cult in southern California. "The succession of births or existences [believed in by this religion], some of them psychic, evidences an unusual point of view for an American people, and is reminiscent of Oceanic and Asiatic ways of thought." 76. "The religion of Chungichnish was a genuine missionary movement in a primitive Indian religion." It involved ingestion of *Datura meteloides* (Jimson weed, *toloache,* Luiseño: *naktamush*), obedience, fasting, self-sacrifice, tattooing, treading on fire, and sand painting. The Milky Way was considered a symbol of where spirits go when humans die, and the raven was a sacred bird. 99. She considers this complex of ideas and practices to have come from "one of the islands of the sea."

Watt (1888–1893, III, 40–1) calls it Thorn Apple. Grows in the temperate Himalayas from Baluchistan and Kashmir to Sikkim. In some areas, it is hard to know whether *D. fastuosa* or *D. stramonium* is present. The Flora of British India regards it as indigenous to India, but De Candolle considered *D. stramonium*, L. only to be indigenous to the Old World, probably the borders of the Caspian Sea or nearby, but not native to India. It is very doubtful that it was in Europe in Roman times but spread to there before 1500 C.E. De Candolle held that *D. tatula*, "a form most writers express the strongest hesitation in accepting as specifically distinct from *D. stramonium*," is a native of Central America. Much used medicinally in India. Leaves are "smoked with tobacco for asthma." Also, "its value as a curative in asthma is known both to Europeans and Natives, who smoke the seed in their hukas when so afflicted." (Quote from Baden Powell). 42. *D. metel* grows wild in every part of the country and seeds are used extensively. 43. Var. *tatula* (of *D. stramonium*). Young fruits imported into India from Persia. Common everywhere around villages in Afghanistan. The name *Tatula* is the Turkish corruption of *dhatura*, through the Persian, the Sanskrit being *dhattura*, or *dhustura*; it would be equally applicable to any form of datura. He quotes O'Shaughnessy (Beng. Disp.): "It [i.e., *D. metel*] is a native of North America, very nearly the same as *D. stramonium* ...." "But in this opinion [Watt says], he was most probably in error, the plant he regarded as *D. tatula* being more likely a cultivated state of *D. metel*. De Candolle appears, however, to consider *D. tatula* to be of Central American origin, and if that be so its Turkish name would be a most misleading accident ...."

Burkill 1966, I, 778–9. A rather small genus of herbs, shrubs, and little trees of the family *Solanaceae*, found throughout the tropics, but chiefly in Central America. Safford (1921, 173) maintained that *D. stramonium*, Linn., now common in Europe, was introduced from the Americas at an early date after Columbus. If that is so, the Greek and Roman physicians, who had one datura or other, cannot have employed it (i.e., *stramonium*). The similar *D. ferox*, Linn., he admits as native of the Old World, but as it is Chinese, it is scarcely likely to have reached the Levant during the Roman Empire. *D. metel*, Linn., for which *D. fastuosa* and *D. alba* are but other names, he admits as occurring naturally in Asia and Africa. This species the Greeks and Romans had. It is supposed that as a drug it was used in the temple of Delphi. Apart from these species, the rest of the genus is American. If Safford's view is accepted, interest in the genus in the East is concentrated upon *D. metel*, which is in Malaya. But of *D. stramonium*, which does not occur in Malaya, a few words must be said. *D. stramonium* may be found in parts of Asia very remote from ports, and for that reason it is possible to argue in favor of its occurrence in the Old World before the discovery of the New World.

Chopra et al. 1958, 134. (1) *D. innoxia* is a native of Mexico now found growing in the western parts of the Deccan Peninsula and a few other places in India. Used in India for the same purposes as *D. stramonium*. 134–5. (2) *D. metel* (syn. *D. fastuosa* Linn.; syn. *D. alba* Nees.) occurs throughout India. (3) *D. stramonium* (syn. *D. tatula* Linn.) Vernacular names: Jimson weed, stink weed, mad apple, thorn apple, stramonium. Sanskrit: *dhattura, unmatta, kanaka, Shivapriya*. Known to ancient Hindu physicians; smoking seeds was a treatment for asthma and was known during the Vedic period. The drug is frequently mentioned in the literature in its use for suicidal and homicidal purposes. "*D. stramonium* is indigenous to India and grows abundantly throughout the temperate Himalayas from Kashmir to Sikkim."

Reko 1919, 115. In Mexico, "The name *toloache*, which coincides with the Chinese name *tolo-wan*, for the same plant (*Datura stramonium*), could indicate transpacific communications."

Lozoya 2003, 89. Psychotropic plants are those that guide the soul (from the Greek roots). The origin in our territory (Mexico) of these plants goes back, probably, to very ancient times. For example, among the ancient writers of the world (and, among those, the Chinese were truly the most ancient), a Chinese geographer of the sixth century B.C.E., Guo Pu, stated in his work called *Shan jing* (Book of the Mountains and the Seas) that the sea on their east, the Pacific Ocean, was crossed by Chinese navigators as they headed towards the origin of the sun, America. He adds that the emperors of the Zhou era sent great ships bearing their *fangshi*, or alchemists, astrologers, and founders of Taoism, to this eastern region, called the White Coast, in search of *busicao*, or 'plants of undying.' It was believed that ingesting these plants would cleanse the senses, clarify the perception of the world, and provide immortality. All of these properties were acquired by consuming *busicao*. The two intangible forces in the substance circulate through the channels of the human body, performing a revitalizing function that prolongs human life and permits plenitude. These ancient Asian travelers may have sought *busicao* in the Americas; prevailing currents would surely have brought them to the coasts of northern America. If this was not the case, how can we explain the fact that plants (some of them also present in Asia) now classified as psychotropic, are in the Americas? Plants like *Amanita muscaria, Datura* spp., *Brugmansia* spp., *Lophophora* spp., and *Ipomoea* spp., among others, gradually became part of the rituals, later termed as ecstatic, that were performed by American peoples many centuries later.

Ancient Mesoamericans believed that the human body consisted of flesh and bone as well as two intangible, luminous entities known as *tonalli* and *yályotl*. They had received this knowledge from enigmatic Toltec sages, a people who also came from over the sea. These substances were administered in sacred contexts. Among them, *Nicotiana rustica*, tobacco chewed or smoked to induce a trance, and the *tolohuaxíhuitl*, or *toloaches*, 'the revered lord' (i.e., *Datura stramonium, D. inoxia, D. metel*) that allowed them to "see clearly." Also used were *péyotl*, or *peyote*, (*Lophophora williamsii*) and *teonanácatl*, 'flesh of god' (*Psilocybe mexicana, P. semperviva, P. yungensis, P. caerulescens*).

In the captions accompanying this article's illustrations the following hallucinogens are discussed: *Trichocereum* sp., a cactus, endemic in South America and rich in mescaline; *Turbina corymbosa, ololiuhqui; Ipomoea violacea, tlitliltzin* (one of the principal hallucinogens in Oaxaca); and *Pasiflora incarnata*, passion flower. One might check all these plants for Asian equivalents.

Ramírez 2003, 88. Indigenous peoples in northern Mexico and Southwestern United States used datura medicinally for diagnostic purposes, to have visions, as an amulet to win bets, as an aid in hunting (success), and in initiation rites.

Díaz 2003, 80. The Náhuatl name of *Datura stramonium* is *tlápatl*, or *toloache*. It is classed as a deliriogen. Those plants cloud and reduce consciousness and can be described as true narcotics. In high doses, they produce delirium similar to that caused by fever. "These are plants of a dark and secret tradition, used in rites of witchcraft, occasionally to harm enemies, or to confuse an unfaithful spouse."

At least two species of Datura are identified specifically in both Asian and American sources:
Datura metel (syn. *meteloides*, syn. *innoxia*, syn. *fastuosa*, syn. *alba*)
Origin: the Americas
Transfer: to Asia
Time of transfer: B.C.E.
Grade: A
Sources: *Datura metel*

Luna Cavazos, Jiao, and Bye 2000 find that *Datura metel*, the domesticated species of the Datura group, had its source in Yucatan and the Isthmus of Tehuantepec where it depended on the hawk moth for pollination. The source of the domesticated species is *D. lamosa* whose proposed location is coastal Sonora and Sinaloa (Luna Cavazos, Jiao, and Bye 2000; Jiao, Luna-Cavazos, and Bye 2002, 157).

Parotta 2001, 670. Sanskrit: *senmatla*

Lancaster 1965, 37. The flowers of *Datura metel* are especially enjoined for worshipping the Lord Shiva.

Datura sanguinea
Origin: South America.
Summary: Needs further research, but this additional narcotic species that is used to induce prophetic states in Peru may have been a pre-Columbian transfer to Asia along with the other daturas.
Grade: incomplete
Sources: *Datura sanguinea*

Bailey, 1935, I, 970. The seeds of this plant are said to have been used by Peruvian priests that were believed to have prophetic power. Plant is native to Peru.

Pandey 2000, 283. *D. sanguinea*, an import from South America to India, is one species "naturalized throughout India." [But when?]

See also the material under Datura spp. in general.

Datura stramonium (syn. *tatula*, syn. *patula*)
Origin: the Americas
Summary: Since these two cannot be untangled historically on recent data, we suppose that their transfer from the Americas to Asia (pre-eminently India) took place either via a single transoceanic boat passage that brought both the species at once, or by separate voyages perhaps to separate destinations. Inasmuch as the transport across the ocean between Eurasia and the Americas of at least four other drugs (*Argemone mexicana, Cannabis sativa, Erythroxylon novagranatense,* and *Nicotiana tabacum*) has been established (see above and below), it would not be surprising for the Daturas to have been part of the movement (one name in India for *A. mexicana* means 'foreign datura').
Time of transfer: of the Daturas would probably be on the order of two or three millennia ago in order to account for their Sanskrit names, references to the plants in ancient Hindu texts, and the archaeological find.
Grade: A

Derris sp.
Origin: tropical Old World (?)
Summary: On the basis of the extensive questions raised by Quigley about the piscicidal plants shared between Africa and South America, it seems advisable to look further into the question of whether there may have been a transatlantic link. More research is obviously required.
Grade: incomplete
Sources: *Derris* sp.
- Burkill 1966, I, 798. The root is used to make a piscicide. Its use extends throughout Indo-China and Malaysia to Australia and Fiji, and throughout tropical South America. "It is obvious when the distribution of the species of *Derris* is studied that sometimes one species is used and sometimes another; but the choice is limited to a few species."
- Quigley 1957. Raises general questions about the use of this genus for fish poisoning in both Africa and South America. The taxonomy is so confused that one cannot tell from the ethnographic accounts whether the parallels and the substances are specific or not. [Johannessen observes: Since these plants are reproduced by placing pieces of the stem in the ground, any mutagens that are reproduced may give only the appearance of different species.]

Dioscorea alata
Origin: Southeast Asia
Summary: The sources have a number of references to the presumed presence of this species at and immediately after the Conquest. Modern botanists, however, generally accept that only certain native American species of Dioscorea were present in the Western Hemisphere. Further research is needed to reconcile the disparate views.
Grade: incomplete

Sources: *Dioscorea alata* – yam

Heyerdahl 1964, 128. The yam had acquired a truly transpacific distribution in pre-Columbian times, with edible forms cultivated from the Americas to Indonesia. A spread from Melanesia to Polynesia has been generally assumed, but if the use of the yam bean in conjunction with cultivation of yams is assumed (sic) then a spread from the Americas may also be postulated. The New World tropics hold a number of wild species of *Dioscorea*, some with edible tubers, but it is not known whether the domesticated American forms have been developed out of wild American parents.

Alexander 1970. The genus is found wild in Africa, Asia, and the Americas in 600 species. It is agreed by botanists that cultigens have been developed from local wild forms on the three continents. Southeast Asia: *D. alata* and *D. esculenta* are held to be of Asian origin, and a third, *D. bulbifera*, originated either there or in the islands. On literary evidence, yams were known and presumably domesticated in South China by the third century C.E. and India by the sixth century (but in India not much earlier). Direct archaeological evidence does not exist. In the Pacific islands, yams are a major and perhaps a staple crop. Botanically, the island species are those of the Asiatic mainland. In the farther islands, where wild yams are not found, arrival of domestic species are recorded in oral tradition and dated to the first and second millennia C.E. Groups with equipment similar to that possessed by farmers on the mainland have been found and dated, as on the mainland, to the second and first millennia B.C.E. In Madagascar and the East African Coastal Plain, Southeast Asian species are grown. On linguistic and physical anthropological grounds, settlement of Madagascar is considered to be of Southeast Asian origin, and movement of peoples and plants across and around the Indian Ocean in the first millennium C.E. is generally accepted. In Africa, a comparable body of evidence has been accumulated. Two important cultigens and several minor forms have developed from indigenous species. Several yam pests exist in Africa in four species, which may be significant in relation to age of the crop. In South America, wild yams are found in Brazil and Venezuela and at least one cultigen, *D. trifida*, is accepted by botanists as derived from local wild forms. Equipment like that used by later cultivators is present in the area in the second, or possibly even the third, millennium B.C.E. These facts do not square with the general theories so far advanced by Burkill and Sauer.

Piperno 1999, 126–7. Phytolith spectra from pre-maize (pre-7000 BP) archaeological evidence is reprised supporting the hypothesis that arrowroot and other native plants such as *Dioscorea* spp. were cultivated in Panama before the introduction of maize.

Tozzer 1941, 196. Discussing the four root crops mentioned by Landa, Stewart (in W. Gates 1937) suggests that one of them was the yam, *Dioscorea alata*; in Náhuatl: mexcal, macal. It is "not native to America."

Hernandez 1942–1946 [before 1580], II, 487–8. For this plant, *Tepactli*, or *Tepatli*, found in Panuco province, the editors suggest "*Dioscorea alata*?" M.

Martínez in *Plantas Medicinales de Mexico*, 546, thinks that this plant is *maaxcal*, which is sometimes glossed as *D. alata*.

Hatt 1951, 853–914. Myths and rituals in Asia associated with the cultivation of cereals, including maize, and of the origin of the yam (*Dioscorea*), agree with origin myths in the Americas.

Canals Frau 1956–1957, 28–42. Multiple species of Dioscoreas have a long history of use in South and Southeast Asia, from which they extended into Oceania. The ancient word for the plant and its valuable edible root, *ubi*, ended up as uhi in Eastern Polynesia. *D. trifida*, a different species, was domesticated in the Antilles and lowland South America in pre-Columbian times, and in Colombia, its name is also *uhi* (and obvious variants, cited, including those among the Huitoto, Sumu, and Miskito Indians). Furthermore, a myth on the origin of the plant's name is the same in Southeast Asia and the Americas. E. D. Merrill has finally given up his absolute opposition to [transoceanic] transfer of this plant and considers *Dioscorea* a possibility.

Mellén B. 1986, 129. Hervé's early diary in re. Easter Island mentions *uhi*, or *D. alata*. Martínez (1913) identified names of 41 varieties. Spaniards called all these *ñame*.

Johannessen observes (source cannot be recalled) that Stanton Cook's research concluded that *D. alata* had been growing on Trinidad at the time of Spanish contact.

Newcomb 1963, 55-7. Canals Frau suggested that the *D. trifida* of the Caribbean may have derived from *D. alata*, due to the plant dropping out of cultivation with disruptions resulting from the Conquest. *D. bulbifera* is grown for bulbs that form on axials between stems. It is supposed to be of Chinese origin, but shows up in coastal Mexico and South America; not at all in Africa.

Roys 1931, 262. "Macal. *Dioscorea alata*, L. Ñame. This, of course, is an Old World importation, but the name macal, designated a native plant originally." In a 16th-century account we read of "a root which they call macal and which directly resembles the root of a lily. These are eaten boiled." "This description suggests one of the Araceae, possibly Xanthosoma violaceum, Schott., a well known food plant of Central America which apparently appears in Yucatan." (Citing a letter from Standley.)

Patiño 1976, 26–9. Re. the name ñame: This name was diffused from the west coast of Africa by Hispano/Portuguese navigators. It is known that the principal ñames cultivated nowadays in the circum-Caribbean area, *D. alata* L. and *D. cayenensis* Lam., are species of African origin, or at least were introduced to the Americas from Africa. But it seems that the name ñame was applied not only to *Dioscorea* but to tuberous plants of other families. There exist in the Americas several native species of *Dioscorea*, of which some can be and were domesticated or utilized by the aborigines. In recent years, since the discovery of the existence in these plants of the hormone cortisone, search for them has intensified. He goes on to discuss native names of *Dioscorea* plants in various localities.

Dioscorea bulbifera
Origin: Asian tropics
Summary: Upon C. Sauer's observation, this species needs further research on its place of origin and possible transfer. It may have been a transoceanic immigrant.
Transfer: to tropical America
Time of transfer: by 1500 C.E.
Grade: C
Sources: *Dioscorea bulbifera*
> Newcomb 1963, 57. C. Sauer observed *D. bulbifera* is grown for bulbs which form on axials between stems. It is supposed to be of Chinese origin but shows up in coastal Mexico and South America; not at all in Africa.
> Parotta 2001, 266. A native of the Old World tropics. Two Sanskrit names: *varahi, varahikanda*.

Dioscorea cayenensis
Origin: Africa
Summary: The ambiguous historical position of *D. cayenensis* in Africa, South America, and the Marquesas leaves questions that cannot yet be answered. More study needs to be given to the distribution of this species in order to determine whether there was a possible transfer (either Polynesia/Americas or Africa/South America).
> Case 1: Transfer: Africa to South America
> Grade: incomplete
> Case 2: Transfer: the Americas to Polynesia
> Grade: incomplete
Sources: *Dioscorea cayenensis* – guinea yam
> Newcomb 1963, 56. Murdock reported D. rotundata and *D. cayenensis* in West Africa. Burkill calls these 'guinea yams,' of white and yellow type. Yams were undoubtedly taken out of the wild and cultivated in the West African tropics. They occur in the New World too. *D. cayenensis* was described by Linnaeus from Guiana and given the name 'cayenne,' the same as the West African yam. Why then is the (South American) Guiana yam said to be morphologically distinguishable from the *D. cayenensis* of Africa? [Work needs to be done to resolve this question.]
> Baker 1970, 155–6. There are approximately 450 species [sic; varieties?] of *Dioscorea* widely distributed in the tropics; two or three species are widely distributed in Polynesia and are probably of aboriginal introduction. 157–8. His fourth species of *Dioscorea* he gives as simply D. sp., from a single specimen found on Fatuhiva, the Marquesas. "The material is not sufficient for accurate determination, but it appears to be near to, if not identical with, *D. cayenensis* Lamarck, a native of Africa, widely cultivated at an early date in tropical America. ... Doubtless of early aboriginal introduction in the Marquesas, and, if *D. cayenensis*, which it closely resembles, it would further indicate contact with America."

Diospyros ebenaster
Origin: the Americas (?)
Summary: Despite some confusion in the taxonomy, there is little question that *D. ebenaster* was present both in Tropical America and in India and China.
Transfer: to Asia from the Americas (?)
Time of transfer: pre-Columbian
Grade: B
Sources: *Diospyros ebenaster* – black sapote (Kew. syn. *ebenum*)

    Schoenhals 1988, 142. *Diospyros digyna*, black sapote (synonymy?; see Watt below), Indian ebony persimmon.

    Zeven and de Wet 1982, 189. Probably Mexico is the center of gene diversity.

    Dressler 1953, 132. A popular fruit in parts of Mexico. Related to the better-known persimmon and produces fruit of good size. Some have thought it a native of the East Indies, but the evidence seems to indicate a Mexican origin (citing Merrill 1918).

    Roys 1931, 284. "*Tauch*, or *Tauch-ya*. *Diospyros ebenaster*, Retz." Sapote negro. 297. Achras Zapota. Chicozapote, Zapote. Bears the sapodilla fruit. Its gum, tzicte, is the chicle of commerce; Mayan: ya."

    Newcomb 1963, 61. C. Sauer said: "A common garden tree in Mexico and Central America, it was called *tlilzapote* in Nahuan." Also cultivated in the Philippines and in Southeast Asia. However, there is no suggestion of its having been introduced from one area into the other. "A mysterious question of its nativity remains. Some botanists suggest that it is New World, but others say Old World. It is a little more likely to be Old World in origin, because there are so many persimmons in East Asia. In Mexico and Guatemala, it is always associated with human habitations. There is a native cast to it. .... It is deeply embedded in native use."

    Chopra et al. 1958, 505. Grown throughout practically all India.

    Watt 1888–1893, III, 138–40. *D. ebenaster* is taken as synonymous with *D. ebenum*, ebony. Found in South India, Ceylon, Malaya. "The utmost confusion exists in the writings of popular authors regarding this tree ...." Apparently, the term 'ebony' is used for woods of several trees.

    Bretschneider 1892, 407. Name unchanged from [Chinese] Classic times to today, *she, Diospyros*.

    Brücher 1989, 227–8. *Diospyros* spp. This is a rare botanical family with few (5–6) genera distributed in all tropical hemispheres [sic]. The best known is the Asiatic *D. kaki* L., now widely cultivated as a prolific fruit tree. In the Americas, four species are native: *D. virginiana* L., *D. digyna* Jacq., *D. ebenaster* Retz., and *D. inconstans* Jacq. Origin in Central America (Guat. and Mexico) and grows also in the Antilles. In the south of the U.S., the fruits are more appreciated than the local *D. virginiana*, both called 'persimmon,' or black sapote.

    Balfour 1871–1873, I, 23. *Achra Sapota*, Eilld., syn. Diospyros sapota. Eng. terms: 'bulli,' or 'buily tree,' common sapota, sapodilla plum. "A native of China, cultivated in the West Indies and South America." In India, it is grown only as a fruit tree. Balfour, II, D–105. Achra sapota, syn. *D. ebenaster*, Retz., English ebony.

Dolichos lablab
Origin: Old World
Summary: A possibility seems to exist that the Peruvian specimen originally assigned to this species might prove, on further study, indeed to be this bean. The Peruvian coast in the third (or fourth) millennium B.C.E. seems to have been a zone of interchange of Old and New World flora, making it conceivable that this bean was present.
Grade: incomplete
Source: *Dolichos lablab*
> Kelly 1951, 208–9. This Old World bean was originally reported from Huaca Priéta, Peru, as an early cultivar, but the identification was subsequently changed. 29. One of the Old World pulses with others listed, including *Dolichos lablab* and *Lupinus albus*. 39. An African plant. It is a possible Negro African introduction before Columbus, although missing from Arab Africa. It was supposed to have had a New World origin until De Candolle studied it.

Elaeis guineensis
Origin: Africa
Summary: Since two species of the same genus face each other across the narrow part of the South Atlantic ocean, it may be desirable to know more about how the anomalous South American species reached its position. While that distribution is thought by some to result from continental drift, that is not, of course, known for a fact. DNA examination might reveal how long since the African and South American taxa have been apart. We know that Africa split from South America 50,000,000 years ago.
Grade: incomplete
Sources: *Elaeis guineensis* – Guinea oil palm
> Newcomb 1963. 60–1. The guinea oil palm and a black-seeded species in Brazil are of note. L. H. Bailey claimed that the Guinea oil palm (see more by him under *Cocos nucifera*) had been carried into West Africa from the New World.
> Steentoft 1988, 223. *Palmae* (*Arecaceae*)—palm family. There are 12 genera of indigenous plants in West Africa. Of these, only *Elaeis* and *Raphia* also have New World species.
> Patiño 1963, 54. Statements of the chroniclers about palms are relatively few. The oil palm (*Elaeis guineensis* Jacq.) and two others were originally from Africa.
> Bailey 1935, III, 2438. "As a rule, the members of any single genus of palms are found in one hemisphere, either the Eastern or Western as the case may be, probably the greater number of species being of Asiatic and American origin, rather than African."
> J. Sauer 1993, 189–92. *Elaeis* includes two wild species, *E. oleifera* of Central and South America, and *E. guineensis* of West Africa. 190. *Elaeis* is monoecious, so dispersal of a single seed is enough to start a new colony.

Aboriginal use of *E. oleifera* in the American tropics was very minor, and the species has never become a plantation crop.

Erigeron albidus
Origin: the Americas
Summary: The fact of the plant's native name plus its ubiquitous distribution in Hawaii suggests that it had reached there before Europeans. (Even in early historical times as a weed this is an unlikely transfer.)
Transfer: the Americas to Hawaii
Time of transfer: pre-Columbian
Grade: B
Source: *Erigeron albidus* – (Kew, syn. *bonariensis*)
> Hillebrand 1888, 196. Interspersed with *E. canadensis*, gregarious in parts of Molokai and Maui. A native of Tropical America, but now a common weed in many countries of the warmer zones. The editor, W. F. Hillebrand (son), explains on page XCIII that his father at first considered this species introduced after Capt. Cook but changed his mind and ended up concluding that it had arrived before that event.

Erigeron canadensis
Origin: the Americas
Summary: The presence of *E. canadensis* in India must be old to have naturalized quite completely, as it has, in addition to bearing two Sanskrit names.
> Case 1: Transfer: the Americas to India
> Time of transfer: more than one millennium ago and probably two
> Grade: B+
> Case 2: Transfer: the Americas to Hawaii
> Time of transfer: pre-Columbian
> Grade: C

Sources: *Erigeron canadensis* – (syn. and preferred modern taxon is *Conyza canadensis* (L.) Cronq.) - fleabane
> Hillebrand 1888, 196. A common weed on all Hawaiian islands. Native name: *iliohe*. "Of American origin, but now naturalized in most parts of the globe, particularly in the temperate latitudes" The editor, W. F. Hillebrand (son), explains on page XCIII that his father at first considered this species introduced post-Capt. Cook but changed his mind and concluded that it was pre-European.
> Pandey 2000, 272. *E. canadensis*, from North America, is a species "naturalized throughout India."
> Torkelson 1999, 1726. Sanskrit: *jarayupriya, makshikavisha*
> Chopra et al. 1958, 556. An annual herb found in the western Himalayas, and Punjab to an altitude of 4000 ft. Plentiful in Kashmir. Also in Shillong (Assam), the Western Ghats, and the Nilgiris up to 6000 ft. Leaves produce irritation of parts of the body they touch.
> K. T. Harper (personal communication 2004). This species is a follower and close associate of man, highly unlikely to have dispersed by natural means across an ocean. It is everywhere a common garden weed, so its seeds

could be expected to be found in any soil used to sustain crop rootstocks that early humans might have carried on colonizing voyages.

Erythroxylon novagranatense
Origin: South America
Summary: The evidence for early Egyptian use makes inescapable acceptance of the fact that coca plants were being grown in Eurasia; their use for many centuries precludes the possibility that a continuing supply of leaves was imported from the Americas.
Transfer: South America to at least Egypt
Time of transfer: as early as the second millennium B.C.E.
Grade: A
Sources: *Erythroxylon* sp. – coca
> Balabanova et al. 1992, 358. Nine Egyptian mummies, dated from approximately 1070 B.C.E.–395 C.E., were examined by radioimunoassay and gas chromatography/mass spectrometry. Cocaine and hashish were found in all nine mummies, and nicotine in the hair, soft tissue, and bones of eight. That 1992 article educed letters critical of the authors and their findings; see <u>Naturwissenschaften</u> 80 (1993), 243ff. Parsche responded that, "our analysis provides clear evidence for the presence of [the reported] alkaloids" and is not due to post-discovery contamination.
> Plowman 1984, 135–6. The archaeological record of the use of *Huánuco coca*. Earlier investigators did not distinguish among different species and varieties of cultivated coca. Re-examination of extant archaeological coca leaves from coastal Peru revealed that they all represent *Trujillo coca*, *E. novogranatense* var. truxillense. Gold and ceramic artifacts depicting coca chewers have been discovered at Tiwanaku. They suggest that coca was in use there perhaps as early as the fourth century C.E. (that is a quote from Carter et al. 1980). 138. *Erythroxlum novogranatense* has two well-defined varieties, var. *truxillense*, *Trujillo coca*, and var. *novogranatense*, Colombian coca. They are chemically different from *E. coca* var. *coca*. 140. The archaeological record of Trujillo coca starts by suggesting that coca-chewing on the Peruvian coast began in Late pre-Ceramic Period 6 (2500–1800 B.C.E., species undetermined) from a site dated around 2000 B.C.E.; also at ca. 1800 B.C.E., 1750–1900 B.C.E., and 1800–1400 B.C.E. Archaeological coca leaves from much later sites on the Peruvian coast have been available for study; all belong to *E. novogranatense* var. truxillense. From 600–1000 C.E., etc. 144. "There is sufficient evidence now to postulate that Trujillo coca was cultivated and chewed on the Peruvian coast at least by 2000 B.C.E. and possibly earlier." 146. Perhaps the earliest known record for coca chewing comes from the Valdivia culture in southwestern coastal Ecuador. Lime containers (lime is typically chewed along with coca leaves) have been found there that date to Valdivia Phase 4, about 2100 B.C.E. (uncalibrated radiocarbon dating). In Machalilla and Chorrera periods (1000–300 B.C.E.). "Based on the archaeological evidence [but not on actual plant remains], it appears that

coca cultivation and the habit of coca-chewing were fully established in the Valdivia area by 3000 B.C.E."

Towle 1961, 58–60. Widely recovered from archaeological sites; both Nazca and Mochica jars picture men with distended cheeks or dipping lime. Also, there are many finds of bags of leaves and lime pellets, as at Ancón, Paracas Cavernas, and Paracas Necropolis.

Shady Solís et al. 2001. At Caral (ca. 2600–2000 Cal B.C.E.) near the Peruvian coast, excavations revealed actual coca seeds as well as lime containers like those later used by consumers of coca.

Cartmell et al. 1991. Coca was in use in northern Chile (implying trade of the substance) determined from analysis of human hair.

Jett 2004 reprises the growing literature on chemical identification of cocaine as evidenced in mummies in Egypt, Nubia, etc.

Addenda, too late to enter: Jett. 2002a; Guthrie 2002.

Garcinia mangostana
Origin: Southeast Asia
Summary: The evidence for transfer to the Americas consists of remains of the fruit that have been recovered from tombs in Peru.
Transfer: Asia to Peru
Time of transfer: The tombs where the fruits were found are probably those at Ancón or Paracas, which means the late B.C.E. centuries.
Grade: B
Sources: *Garcinia mangostana* – mangosteen

Nadkarni 1914, 166. *Garcinia mangostana*. Eng.: mangosteen. Hind. and Ben.: *mangustin*. A native of the Straits Settlement and Singapore.

Pullaiah 2002, I, 264. Surprisingly, no Sanskrit name is given.

Chopra et al. 1956, 123. Cultivated on the West Coast of India.

Towle 1961, 97. Rochebrune (1879, 346, 351) reported that fruits of this plant, usually cut in half, had been found in string bags recovered from graves in Peru. His identification, however, was questioned by Wittmack (1888, 341) (only?), since mangosteen is considered a native of Asia and was brought to the New World as a horticultural importation well after the period of discovery.

De Prez 1935, 61. He pictures a sculpture at Borobudur (ca. 700–900 C.E.) that shows mangosteen fruit (simultaneously with the mango, *Mangifera indica*).

Watt (1888–1893, III, 470–1) calls this a native of Malaya ("the Strait"), cultivated in Burma for its fruit. Its distribution was very localized; it does not grow successfully if transplanted to most of India. [Hence, it could easily fail to stay on in Peru even if transferred to there across the Pacific.] "A congenial amount of heat and moisture throughout the year seems to be necessary for its successful cultivation." Used as a remedy for diarrhea and dysentery.

Bailey 1967, II, 1312–3. Genus has upward of 150 species in the tropics of Asia, Africa, and Polynesia. The name mangostana is credited to the Malay region.

Gnaphalium purpureum
Origin: the Americas
Summary: In Hillebrand's expert opinion this species reached Hawaii in pre-European times, but he does not provide confirmatory data on distribution in the islands, native uses, etc. In light of its widespread distribution in India, one wishes to know more about when the species was introduced there.
>Case 1: Transfer: to Hawaii
>Time of transfer: before European discovery
>Grade: C
>Case 2: Transfer: to India
>Time of transfer: unknown
>Grade: incomplete

Source: *Gnaphalium purpureum* – (syn. *americana*, syn. *spicata*) - purple cudweed
>Hillebrand 1888, page XCIII. The editor, W. F. Hillebrand, notes that in his father's tabulation of plant species from Hawaii that were introduced after Capt. Cook's arrival, his father changed his mind about some plants which he had assumed were introduced after Cook's visit but which "may in reality have been of earlier introduction" (in the elder Hillebrand's judgment). "Of 9 non-endemic species which existed before the discovery … one, *Gnaphalium*, [among others is] American …." 201. "A native of the American Continent, on which it extends under a variety of names from the United States East and West to the southern extremity. Has migrated also to Hongkong [sic] and a few other places of the Old World."

>Pandey 2000, 271. *G. purpureum*, a native of Tropical America, is one species "naturalized throughout India".

Gossypium spp. in general
Sources: *Gossypium* spp. in general
>Brücher 1989, 149. Old World cottons, going back to Mohenjo-Daro and Egypt, were only diploid species. "The situation in the New World in ancient times was quite different. Many thousands of years ago a unique phylogenetic event occurred there: a combination, followed by polyploidy of the Old World A-genome with a New World D-genome. Until now, nobody has been able to explain how and where it happened; but that this genome fusion took place on American soil is without doubt."

>Wendel 1995, 362. The earliest cotton cloth documented by archaeology in Asia is 4300 years old, from sites in India and Pakistan [specimens from the Americas, given on p. 362 as 5500 years in Peru, for *barbadense*; the earliest *hirsutum* finds are between 4000 and 5000 BP in the Tehuacán valley of Mexico]. Which species is represented in these earliest remains is not clear. *G. arboreum* is known only as a cultivated plant with a center of diversity in India and a range from China and Korea westward into northern Africa. Wild ancestral forms have not been verified.

Yarnell 1970, 225. Earliest remains, Peru: 4000 BP; Southern Mexico: 8000 BP; Northern Mexico: 9000 BP. [The latter two are probably excessively early, given the re-dating of MacNeish's maize specimens reported in Long, et al. 1989, 1035–40].

Yen 1963, 112. At Huaca Priéta, Peru, Bird (1948) found seeds of *Gossypium*, dated ca. 2578–2470 B.C.E. (Calibrated to 3200–3070 B.C.E.)

Johnson 1975, 340, 348. Opponents of the concept of an agricultural origin of the tetraploids point to the difficulty of explaining how Old World cotton could have been transported to the New World in prehistoric times, and to the illogic of assuming that man would have brought cotton, but not his basic food plants (Purseglove 1968). [That argument is passé in the light of the present data.] At least "With respect to the latter one, however, there is little reason to believe that biologically and culturally unadapted food plants from the Old World would survive long in Mesoamerica, an area already rich in improved food-producing species. On the other hand, the known absence in that area of a comparable fiber plant would make cotton a prized addition to the culture." Note also that "An A-genome cotton indigenous to the Americas has never been found, either living or in archaeological contexts, yet such a cotton clearly was involved in the origin of the tetraploids [on genetic grounds]. This inconsistency is explainable assuming that the A donor was an unadapted type capable of existing only under agricultural conditions (Stephens 1947) as long as the needs of man placed a premium upon its survival, and that it became extinct, or nearly so, when supplanted by better-adapted tetraploids of competing quality. Furthermore, "The idea that the tetraploids could have survived geological epochs [i.e., since the Cretaceous] as adapted species only to vanish as such since the rise of agriculture, and yet that they could have produced successful escapes from cultivation, seems highly improbable."

Wendel 1989, 4132–4136. A major conclusion of this paper is that the chloroplast genome of New World tetraploid *Gossypium* is derived from an Old World diploid cotton. Concludes that the initial hybridization and polyploidization events that led to the evolution of tetraploid cotton were "relatively recent." 4136. The low level of sequence divergence argues against a Cretaceous age for the origin of the tetraploids, but suggests occurrence "relatively recently," perhaps within "the last 1–2 million years."

Townsend 1925, 3. The major insect enemies of the plant point to the Americas as this plant's native home. The Mexican boll weevil and the Peruvian square weevil, which attack no other plant in nature, have evidently been adapted to cotton and close American allies for "tens of thousands of years." They are not carried in the seed and hence were not transported to the Eastern Hemisphere when the seed was taken there from America [sic]." Had cotton seed been brought by the ancients from India to the Americas, it is certain that the pink bollworm would have been introduced here at that time. [This author is not very reliable, generally.]

Merrill 1954, 165–385. Gives reasons for thinking that more than one form of *Gossypium* was present in the Society Islands soon after European contact and refers to "numerous hybrids between New World and Old World cotton species" which might well have reached Tahiti through the agency of man "before the long voyages of the Polynesians had ceased."

Hutchinson 1962, 5–15. Updates the research on cottons that he had carried on with Silow and Stephens from 1934 to 1947 and reaffirms their conclusion that the two key American cottons are from a hybrid involving Old World cotton, which arrived in the New World long before Columbus. The Bering Strait could not have been the route.

Silow 1949, 112–8. A major synthesis of the geography and cytogenetics of New World cottons. Diploid *Gossypium arboreum* came from South Asia, most likely from India, to the Americas, where it hybridized with a native diploid cotton, from which the two tetraploid domesticated species (*G. hirsutum* and *G. barbadense*) in the Americas sprang. Furthermore, it is significant that the domesticated American cottons occurred exclusively along with the same type of spindle "used by the fine spinners of Dacca muslin in India, and the looms also are identical with those used in the Old World." Those looms "involv[ed] at least eleven independent technical inventions." To him, then, "It seems most unlikely that such an assemblage of developments ... should have appeared in the New World by independent invention." He gives decisive arguments why chance transfer by seed floating from Asia to the Americas is not an acceptable explanation. Only one American species (of eight wild species), *G. raimondi*, has characteristics of the subsequent hybrid-domesticated, tetraploid cottons. And *raimondi* is limited to northwestern South America, which must then be the home of the earliest tetraploid hybrid. The most plausible explanation is the transference of the Asiatic diploid (linted) parent by humans across the Pacific Ocean.

Stephens 1971, 401–15. Wild cottons existed on all continents with suitable climates. If seeds could thus be naturally carried [sic], then presumably natural means could also have carried cultivated species [not so, Stephens, 1947, himself argued]. Moreover, the Spaniards and other discoverers in the Pacific islands quickly spread cottons, further complicating a reading of history from distribution. Difficulties in reliable identification of cotton varieties from archaeological materials are also discussed. In two situations, the Cape Verdes and the Marquesas, the presence of wild cottons of American origin suggests human transmission in pre-Columbian times, although the evidence is not conclusive.

Stephens 1963, 1–22. Wild *G. hirsutum*, scattered in southern Polynesia, was much more recent. It is difficult to account for its disjunct distribution (Caribbean, Central America, and South Pacific) by ocean drift alone. Possibly it was brought by Spanish expeditions some of which actually planted cotton. [But what could be the source in the Americas from which they picked up *tomentosum*? There is no trace of it as such anywhere on the mainland. Since genetically it has characteristics like *hirsutum* and *barbadense*, it appears to have descended from the ancestral tetraploid in parallel with the latter two. See Wendel, Schnabel, and Seelanan 1995.]

Stephens 1947, 431–2. It is believed that South America was where chromosomes doubled to produce the American forms. *G. tomentosum* in Hawaii is the only remaining proposed endemic cotton in Polynesia after eliminating those of the Marquesas, Fiji, and Galapagos. (Those three are actually descended from American cottons, he had noted.) A chance crossing by air or ocean currents is possible but seems unlikely over such immense distances as would be required. Cotton seed loses viability quickly in moist air. And *Gossypium* does not survive in the wild [taken to mean that domesticated species do not, as far as he knows, survive as the same species in the wild]. The facts all suggest that American cottons may have been used by man at their outset and not independently developed from wild ancestral species.

Johnson 1975, 340. The data indicate that *G. barbadense* (AADbetaDbeta) originated in northern South America from *G. herbaceum* x. *G. raimondii* and that the cultivated races of *G. hirsutum* represent various degrees of introgression involving *G. barbadense* and the Mexican *hirsutum* complex.

Schwerin 1970. A possibility is that Africans were blown to the New World between 8000 and 5700 B.C.E. and brought cotton. [Such a date is highly doubtful for cotton in West Africa. No agriculture is known to have existed anywhere near either date.]

Lathrap 1977, 713–51. Proposes that West African fishermen were carried to sea to Brazil by 16,000 years ago, bringing with them *Lagenaria*, fish poisons, watercraft, two-toned log signalling, and cotton. [There is no sign of *Lagenaria* or cotton use in Africa at that date.]

C. Sauer 1969, 229. It is "generally accepted" that the common polyploid species of *Gossypium hirsutum* originated in the Pleistocene by hybridization on tropical American seacoasts between native diploids and an African diploid whose seeds had dispersed by ocean currents. [Such a position is not "generally accepted;" it is actually incredible. Cf. Silow on *G. arboreum* as the Asian diploid source. There is no direct evidence that it was in existence in the Pleistocene, at least not in Africa. And if the D-genome came from Africa, how did it meet up with *G. raimondi*, which is in Northwest South America? Further, if the hybridization took place in the Pleistocene and dispersal was by oceanic drift, why did tetraploids not float to all other continents in the intervening millennia?]

MacNeish and Smith 1964, 675–6. Cotton finds are so early from the Tehuacán Valley that the idea of importation by human voyaging is unacceptable. [Reflects an outdated view of nautical capabilities; in any case, the dates there may not now be as old as originally claimed. Cf. Long et al. 1989.]

Mellén B. 1986, 134. References have been made to cotton being on the (Easter) Island. That is an error, coming from a statement in a letter that spoke of a plant fiber (*háu*, or *mahúte*) being used somewhat as if it were cotton.

Wendel 1989, 4132. Current classifications recognize approximately 42 species, comprising either 5 or 6 tetraploid taxa and about 36 diploid species divided into 7 cytogenetic groups or genomes. Asian/African diploids, *Gossypium arboreum* L. and *Gossypium herbaceum* L., differ from the New World tetraploids *G. barbadense* L. and *G. hirsutum* L. Pioneering cytogenetic investigations by Beasly and others demonstrated that the New World tetraploid cottons are allopolyploids containing one genome of the Old World diploids (the A-genome) and one genome similar to those found in New World diploids (the D-genome). This textbook example of allopolyploid speciation has been studied and corroborated from many perspectives (citations on all points). "Yet, the identity of the ancestral parental taxa remains unresolved. *G. raimondii* is considered by most authors (but not all) as the likely D-genome donor. There is also uncertainty regarding the identity of the A-genome donor. *G. herbaceum* is slightly more congenial in that role. The tetraploids are highly heterogeneous inter se, including *G. tomentosum* (Hawaii), the species from the Galapagos (*G. darwinii*), and other specimens from the Pacific islands, Central America, tropical South America, and the Caribbean. The literature contains a plethora of scenarios concerning the time and place of origin of the tetraploids (one of those cited is that of Hutchinson, Silow, and Stephens). Here, he re-examines the evolution of tetraploid cottons using new DNA data. Table 1 gives taxa and other information on multiple specimens from 17 species examined in the study. 4135. Concludes that the chloroplast genome of New World tetraploid G. is derived from an Old World diploid cotton. Time involved: views have ranged widely from Cretaceaous, arising from separation of continents, to suggestions of very recent origins in archaeological times involving transoceanic human transport (citing Hutchinson et al. and Johnson 1975). Only came up with 12 mutations out of a total of 3920 restriction sites assayed among 7 species of A-genome and tetraploid cottons. This suggests that the initial hybridization and polyploidization events that led to the evolution of tetraploid cotton were "relatively recent." 4134. The data they obtained are interpreted as evidence that the ancestral plastid donor of tetraploid cottons was a plant with a chloroplast genome that is similar to present day Old World cotton. He cannot determine whether *G. arboreum* or *G. herbaceum* was more likely. 4136. Time [based solely on the apparent mutation rate]: "Perhaps within the last 1–2 million years."

Newcomb 1963, 42–4. C. Sauer's observations here are based mainly on Hutchinson et al.'s work at the Empire Cotton Growing Corporation Cotton Research Station, Trinidad. *Gossypium* goes back into the Tertiary, with species in North and South America, Australia, and Africa. The three groups each have distinctive chromosome patterns and shapes: American, Australian, and African. All wild spp. are lintless. Linting came with domestication. How did man become interested in it? The Australian *Gossypium* is not exploited. African strains—*G. arboreum* and[/or] *G. terrestrium* are the progenitors of cultivated Old World cottons. But the Africans are not cotton growers, even in Ethiopia (until late). Species taken into Asia and India were developed into Old World diploids but with unblemished African ancestry.

(Newcomb cont'd.) The American wild cotton that qualified to hybridize to produce later cottons looks to be in the Peruvian highlands, namely the diploid *G. raimondii*. Found in lower valleys on the west coast from Trujillo northward. It is not an escaped cotton. Mexican cotton is ancestral to most of today's cottons. Polynesian cottons: the plant found in Tahiti is [closest to] *G. barbadense* (i.e., South American). Hawaiian is of Mexican, not South American, ancestry. It was formed by the introduction of a *hirsutum* strain out of Mexico. This has bothered S. G. Stephens no end, for how are we to account for this distribution: by a Spanish vessel shipwrecked in Hawaii? Hutchinson is also puzzled by it. A stray Manila galleon? But a ship returning from Manila to Mexico would be unlikely to have Mexican cotton seed aboard. Besides, Hawaii is far from the usual route. Galapagos cotton is *barbadense* type and almost lintless.

Roys 1931, 282. Mayan "Taman. *Gossypium herbaceum*, L." [sic.; probable error]

Johnson and Decker 1980, 249–307. 250. "Unless data are incomplete, Polynesian [terms for cotton,] vavae to vavai, are lacking in Melanesia and Micronesia." Stephens (1963) and Fryxell (1965) both "pointed to the presence of indisputably wild and probably indigenous species scattered across the Pacific from the Galapagos to northern Australia and Saipan." Summarize three points from Stephens from which Stephens concluded that the wild *Gossypium* species were known to and effectively used by Polynesians before the arrival of Europeans. 251–2. Austroasiatic languages farther west in mainland Southeast Asia do provide proto-forms for *vavae/vavai* that are reflected in the languages of Ceram and Polynesia. (See their Table 2). 256ff. The Relationship between Austronesian, Austroasiatic, and Indo-European Words for "Cotton": A Case for Affinity.

(Johnson and Decker, cont'd) 288. Amerindian Words for Cotton. "... the semantic set for 'cotton' in 'cloth' or 'weaving,' as of 'cotton' and 'hemp' (maguey), the forms appear to be very similar to the South Indian *bat-pat* and Austroasiatic *baç-paç* (Crau, Table 5) forms for 'cloth' that were particularly connected with 'cotton' (Table 35)." The table cites Amerindian forms for 'cotton.' From Goajiro (Arawak), Jicaques (Honduras), Arawak, Tlappanecan, Inca, Kayuvava (Bolivia), Pochutla (Oaxaca), Mexican, Timote (Paez), Maku (Brazil), and Arawak. Table 35 on p. 289 lists South American Indian Forms for 'Cloth' (but includes Mexican Otomian, and Central American Xinca and Miskito, as well as "Proto-Amerindian and Fox." Table 36 is also on p. 289: American Indian Proto-Forms Connected with the Spinning of Thread (Chipaya of Bolivia, Uru-Chipaya, Chol, Yunga, and Proto-Mayan). "Inasmuch as we have previously argued a possible connection between 'grass' (i.e., as 'cane,' 'reed,' 'bamboo') in the fiber set for 'cordage' and also in tools for weaving, we encounter a remarkable similarity between the forms for 'cotton' in connection with 'hay,' 'grass,' and 'down,' and those for 'fire' [because, as shown earlier, cotton was used for 'wick'.], "particularly found in North American Indian languages" (see Table 38 on p. 290: Dakota-Teton, Ponca, Osage, Pilox (?), Oto, Siouan, Arawakan). Also on p. 290 is Table 37: Additional American Indian Forms for Cloth and Cotton (for Tzeltal, Paez, Proto-Amerindian, Proto-Arawak, Proto Piro-Apuriná, Culina, Proto-Tacanan, and Amahuaca). On p. 291: Table 39: Forms for Cane and Loom Comb in South America (includes Proto-Aztecan, Zoque-Mixe, and languages from Honduras and Brazil-Uruguay). Table 40: American Indian Forms for Cloth, Thread, Kindle (includes Quechua, Inca, Atakapa-Chitimacha, Mexico [sic], Fox, Miskito, Coeur d'Alene, Shoshone). 293. Wild *hirsutum* varieties [rather *barbadense*, probably?] that resemble their Central American and Caribbean relatives are known from the South Pacific part of Polynesia, Melanesia, Micronesia, the Sulu Islands, south coastal New Guinea, northern Australia, and in the Indian Ocean as far west as Madagascar. The lexical evidence we have summarized suggests that knowledge of cotton predates European influence in the Pacific island cultures that did not spin or weave, and farther west, knowledge of cotton predates introduction of cotton-weaving [assumed to be] over 2000 years ago.

Gossypium arboreum or *herbaceum*
Origin: Old World
Summary: In order to account for the genetic history of American cottons, by any scenario, one or the other of these Old World diploids (there are arguments for each) must have been transported to the Americas to provide the D-genome that was in all succeeding tetraploid American species.
Transfer: Asia to Tropical America (preferentially northwest South America).
Time of transfer: Guesses range from 1–2 million years ago to agricultural times. We consider the scenarios that depend upon purely natural means of transfer (ocean drift) of domesticated cotton to include fatal flaws. We accept as most credible the original reasoning of Hutchinson et al. to the effect that human beings from South Asia must have sailed across the Pacific bringing about the first A-genome-to-D-genome transfer, ca. the fourth millennium B.C.E.
Grade: A-
Sources: *Gossypium arboreum* or herbaceum
See material in *Gossypium* spp. in general.

Gossypium barbadense
Origin: South America
Summary: 1. This species is credited as the genetic source of the cottons that were discovered on several Polynesian islands. The explanation must involve transfer of *G. barbadense* from the American mainland (it was on the coast of Peru by ca. 2500 B.C.E.) to one or more of the islands of Polynesia where it suffered mutation sufficient to set it apart (at least) subspecifically from *barbadense*. 2. Hillebrand found in Hawaii not only variant cottons (*G. tomentosum* and *G. drynarioides* and perhaps his "*G. peruvianum*") that are or could be derivative from *G. barbadense*, but *G. barbadense* itself, he says. If not post-Cookian, that find might be the result of

transfer of *barbadense*, directly from the continent. 3. Additionally, the presence in India of *G. barbadense* with a Sanskrit name (Chopra et al. 1956, 127; Torkelson 1999, 1745) indicates the actual transfer of the American tetraploid across the Pacific to South Asia while Sanskrit was in active use.

    Case 1: Transfer: the Americas to Polynesia
    Time of transfer: pre-Columbian
    Grade: A
    Case 2: Transfer: the Americas to Hawaii
    Time of transfer: pre-Columbian
    Grade: incomplete
    Case 3: Transfer: the Americas to India
    Time of transfer: before 1000 C.E.
    Grade: B

Sources: *Gossypium barbadense* – (syn. *vitifolium*)

> Langdon 1988, 329. Fuentes, a botanist, spent a year on Easter Island in 1911 and reported finding a few "isolated and semi-wild specimens" of this cotton (1913, 325, 334). The first missionary (ca. 1800) in the Marquesas found cotton (which proved to be of American tetraploid ancestry). The first visitors to Tahiti found cotton there too. (It too proved to be of American ancestry).

> J. Sauer 1993, 101. The oldest cotton textiles in South America, presumably made from *G. barbadense*, are from 3600 B.C.E. uncalibrated at Quiani in the northern Chilean desert. On the Peruvian coast, *G. barbadense* also enters the archaeological record from the pre-agricultural fishing village of Huaca Priéta, Peru. Cotton bolls from about 2500 B.C.E. in northern Peru show transitional forms between the wild [?] forms and the improved cultivar forms. [Note that the actual radiocarbon date at Huaca Priéta for the plant layer is 2578–2470 B.C.E., according to Yen (1963), which calibrates to 3200–3070 B.C.E.]

> Shady Solís 1997, 18. Great amounts of cotton (considered *G. barbadense*) were grown at the site of Caral, Peru, 2700–2000 B.C.E.

> Langdon 1982, 179. Hutchinson, Silow, and Stephens (1947) claimed that Marquesan and Society Island cotton was a variety of *G. hirsutum*. Langdon now points out that that is probably incorrect; the Pacific forms are from *G. barbadense*, whose center of distribution is Ecuador. Wild forms derived from that species are in the Galapagos Islands. [Hillebrand (1888, 51) referred to "*G. religiosum*, L., which grows on the islands of the Society group." (Kew: *religiosum*, syn. *barbadense*). Kew also calls it "*G. Tahitense*, Parlat." But that variety (?) is not found in Hawaii.] [Note Kew: *G. tatlense* (Ins. Tahiti). I consider this spelling to be a scribal error for *G. tahitense*, perhaps from the days of handwritten records at Kew.] 183–7. Langdon explains why he concludes that "a wild form of a cultivated New World cotton was present in only two Pacific groups—the Marquesas and Society Islands—when European contact began in the eighteenth century. But there is some evidence that it might have been growing on Easter Island." [This, Mellén B. denies.]

Stephens 1971, 406–8. Explains why the seeds of wild cottons could easily be dispersed by natural means, while the seeds of the cultivated forms would be far less likely to survive exposure to seawater, because the seed fibers of the latter are aggregated into "compact locks" which greatly reduce their natural portability. Stephens felt that such portability was minimized to the point that only human carriage of cultivated cottons was feasible. But would birds carry cotton seeds? 181. Sauer reported that birds of the area he studied do not eat cotton seeds [that should be simple enough to determine for anywhere else, since there are few, if any, species of birds that fly the several thousand miles from the cotton-growing portion of the mainland to a Polynesian island.] Furthermore, cotton seeds of domesticated species stay buoyant for no more than about 1000 miles.

Wendel, Schnabel, and Seelanan 1995, 298–313. *G. barbadense* (Bolivia, Peru) and *G. darwinii* (one of two species from Galapagos) are immediately related and both relate at further genetic distance to *G. hirsutum* (Mexico) and *G. tomentosum* (Hawaii).

Towle 1961, 64–5. The cotton used to make string, from pre-ceramic Huaca Priéta, is considered one of the earliest cultivated *barbadense* cottons. [Note that the actual radiocarbon date at Huaca Priéta for the plant layer is 2578–2470 B.C.E., according to Yen (1963), which calibrates to 3200–3070 B.C.E.)

Hillebrand (1888, 50–1) reports that besides *G. tomentosum* and *G. drynarioides*, "there are or have been in cultivation [in Hawaii] *G. barbadense*, L., with its smooth-seeded variety, the Sea-Island Cotton" and also *G. peruvianum*, Cav." [Since Hillebrand worked less than a century after Capt. Cook's discovery of the islands and was meticulous in attending to when plants arrived, it is questionable that he is referring unwittingly to the post-Cook-imported *G. barbadense*.]

Chopra et al. 1956, 127. Sanskrit: *maghani* (*G. barbadense*)

Kirtikar and Basu 1999, I:348. Sanskrit: *maghani* and *purvam*.

Torkelson 1999, 1745. Sanskrit: *maghani* (*G. barbadense*) [Note: The two Sanskrit names that are reported specific to *G. barbadense* indicate that the American tetraploid, *G. barbadense*, made the trip back across the Pacific to India. But this would have had to be while Sanskrit was an active language, no later than ca. 1000 C.E. and probably much earlier.]

See also material under under *Gossypium* spp. in general.

Gossypium brasiliense Macfadyen
Origin: South America
Summary: Were it not for Brown's puzzling report (just below under sources), we would ignore *G. brasiliense* as being simply a subspecies of *G. barbadense*. But if Brown intended that this odd, distant, South American cotton species was transferred to the Marquesas Islands in pre-European times, it becomes of interest and possibly of some moment. We need to know more, of course.
Grade: incomplete
Sources: *Gossypium brasiliense*

Brown 1935, 177. Re. Marquesas. [This species is] "Indigenous to Tropical America; widely cultivated in the Tropics; of late introduction in the Marquesas. The native name is *uru* in Nukuhiva." [What is intended by his expression "late introduction"? His monograph typically discusses native fauna, not obvious imports of modern times.]

Burkill 1966, I, 1124. *G. brasiliense*, Macfad., was found in Brazil, both in a wild state and in cultivation, by the early European voyagers. Watt (Wild and Cultivated Cottons of the World, 1907, 296) gives quotes on this species, beginning with Jean de Léry, who went to Brazil with a French Huguenot colony in 1557, 1126). Some botanists claim that *G. brasiliense* should be classified under *G. barbadense*. (Fryxell 1973, 91–2). Fryxell gives, authoritatively, *G. barbadense* Linnaeus var. braziliense (Rafinesque) Fryxell.

See also material under *Gossypium* spp. in general.

Gossypium drynarioides
Origin: Hawaii (?)
Summary: This species has not previously been connected with American cotton, but, given the presence in the Hawaiian Islands of *G. tomentosum*, with its tetraploid genetic structure, as well as other cottons of eastern Polynesia that are American-derived, we infer that the source for *G. drynarioides* is not likely to be anything but American, although it may refer to an episode of voyaging to Hawaii distinct from those involving other American cottons.

Obviously more information is needed, but the question of the source of *G. drynarioides* should not just be ignored.

Grade: incomplete

Source: *Gossypium drynarioides* – a cotton

Hillebrand (1888, 50–1) reports this as "truly indigenous," along with *G. tomentosum*, in Hawaii. It was imperfectly described by Seeman from a specimen in the British Museum collected by Nelson, the companion of Capt. Cook. Hillebrand's specimens of this came from R. Meyer, who discovered three trees of *G. drynarioides* (12–15 feet height) on the western end of Molokai. Native name: Kokio. Hillebrand found a variant of this species (two surviving trees only) on the eastern end of Oahu in cattle-grazing territory; fearing that they would be destroyed, he took other specimens on the big island of Hawaii.

Gossypium gossypioides
Origin: Mexico
Summary: This species, confined to a limited area in Oaxaca, Mexico, provides in its ribosomal DNA internal transcribed spacer (ITS) region "robust" evidence of phylogenetic placement of its ITS sequence as a member of the African clade of cottons. *G. gossypioides* may be implicated in the initial polyploidization of the A-genome and D-genome that was ancestral to American cultivated cottons. The notion that this presence of the African ITS sequence in Mexico was purely a result of natural means of transport of an African cotton which reached (only) remote Oaxaca we find utterly incredible. Its presence can be explained more economically by supposing that transoceanic voyagers brought the cotton that contained the D-

genome. This agrees with significant cultural data supporting the proposition that a transfer of Old World elements to southern Mexico took place at some early historical moment.
Transfer: to Old World (Asia or Africa)
Time of transfer: pre-Columbian
Grade: B
Sources: *Gossypium gossypioides* – a cotton

Wendel, Schnabel, and Seelanan 1995, 298–313. The New World allopolyploid (AD-genome) cottons originated through hybridization of ancestral diploid species that presently have allopatric ranges in Africa and Asia (the A–genome) and the American tropics and subtropics (the D-genome). Phylogenetic analysis of sequence data from the ribosomal DNA internal transcribed spacer (ITS) region ... reveals two strongly supported clades, one corresponding to African species and the other containing all American D-genome species except *Gossypium gossypioides*. *G. gossypioides* is narrowly distributed in Oaxaca. 308. "The central observation of this study is the unexpected phylogenetic placement of the *G. gossypioides* ITS sequence as a member of the African clade." [This is a "robust result".] 309. Their favorite proposal to account for the data and relationships places the introgression (via hybridization and recombination with an A-genome ITS sequence) as having taken place in the American tropics, perhaps in the vicinity of the state of Oaxaca, Mexico. 310. One might suggest that introgression took place as recently as during the last several thousand years, subsequent to the origin of domesticated *G. hirsutum* and its spread into Oaxaca, but they view this as unlikely. Alternatively, it could have happened prior to domestication. [But how then would the Africa-to-America transport – to Mexico, not, say, Brazil – be accounted for? Since the cotton that contained the original D-genome from which American tetraploids sprang probably had an African beginning, although perhaps shaped in Asia as *G. herbaceum* enroute, it might have been transported across the ocean either from Asia or Africa.]

Wendel et al. 1995, cont'd. 298, abstract. Probably the preferred explanation for their data "involves an ancient hybridization event whereby *G. gossypioides* experienced contact with an A-genome ... as a consequence of hybridization with a New World allopolyploid and repeated backcrossing of the hybrid into the *G. gossypioides* lineage." They suggest that this process may implicate *G. gossypioides* rather than *G. raimondii* as the closest living descendant of the ancestral D-genome parent of the allopolyploids. 306. Fig. 5 is a descent tree based on the three most parsimonious trees from analysis of G. ITS sequences. Among relevant data shown in this manner: *G. gossypioides* is basally related to the clade including *G. arboreum* (Asia) and *G. herbaceum* (South Africa and India), but also *G. mustelinum* (northeast Brazil) is closely related to those two. In another clade, *G. barbadense* (Bolivia, Peru) and *G. darwinii* (one of two species from Galapagos) are immediately related and both relate at further genetic distance to *G. hirsutum* (Mexico) and *G. tomentosum* (Hawaii).

Zeven and de Wet 1982, 194. It crosses poorly with most of the species of the D genome. However, it is similar to the pattern of *G. klotzschianum* (a cotton from the Galapagos).

Foster 1992b. "... The Mixe-Zoque languages of southern Mexico [which includes the area where *G. gossypioides* grows] ... are demonstrably closely related to, and probably descended from, ancient Egyptian." "An ... Egyptian influence in the New World is very probable ... perhaps introduced through successive oceanic crossings" (Foster 1992a, 1998).

Xu 2002. Gives specific inscriptional evidences that Chinese arrived by sea in the Isthmus of Tehuantepec area, near where *G. gossypioides* grows.

Gossypium hirsutum
Origin: Mexico
Summary: Stephens presents historical information demonstrating that this American tetraploid must have reached West Africa before Columbus in order to have shown up historically in the Cape Verde Islands by 1466.
Transfer: the Americas to West Africa and thence to the Cape Verde Islands
Time of transfer: no later than 1466 C.E.
Grade: B+
Sources: *Gossypium hirsutum* – a cotton

Johnson 1975, 340. Using 50 collectons of the commonly recognized tetraploid New World cotton species, *G. barbadense*, *G. hirsutum*, and *G. tomentosum*, from South and Central America, the Caribbean, and Pacific Islands, they gave identical seed protein electrophoretic patterns. Among 44 collections of the Mexican tetraploid *G. palmerii*, included in *G. hirsutum*, six gave patterns like that of the recognized species, while 38 gave a uniform but different pattern. Other indigenous Mexican cultigens suggested that *G. hirsutum* may have originated from more than one primary amphiploid including *G. palmeri*. Transitional forms between indigenous cultigens and the cultivated *G. hirsutum* are abundant in southern Mexico, and intermediate forms between *G. hirsutum* and *G. barbadense* are widespread under cultivation. The data indicate that *G. barbadense* (AADbetaDbeta) originated in northern South America from *G. herbaceum* x *G. raimondii* and that the cultivated races of *G. hirsutum* represent various degrees of introgression involving *G. barbadense* and the Mexican *hirsutum* complex. 297. "Out of the Americas several tetraploid species have dispersed from time immemorial." Noteworthy are the varieties *G. hirsutum*, which occur as far west as Madagascar. Their occurrence west of Polynesia before 1700 C.E. is suspected but not confirmed by existing evidence.

Pickersgill and Heiser 1978, 825. In the Tehuacán Valley from about 5000 BP [species assumed; it is nowhere specified in the source].

Brücher 1989, 151–2. Relative similarity of *G. vitifolium* and *G. hirsutum* Lam. leads him to treat them together. The two taxa can be distinguished by presence or absence of "fringed hairs" surrounding the floral nectary. *G. vitifolium* does not have them. 152. *G. vitifolium* is generally called *G. barbadense* by archaeologists. Var. darwinii of *G. vitifolium*, found on the

Galapagos. 153. *G. hirsutum* had its main range on the eastern coast of South America, Caribbean islands, and Central America. Pickersgill et al. (1975) found a "wild cotton in Northeast Brazil," raising again the old question whether *G. mustelinum* Miers and Watt, which had been collected in 1838 in the state of Ceara as a "wild species," and 100+ years later was described as tetraploid *G. cicoense*, may be a real ancestor in the evolutionary history of the tetraploid cottons. It has an AADD-genome. Pickersgill et al. conclude it is perhaps genetically descended from both *G. hirsutum* and *G. barbadense*.

MacNeish, Nelken-Turner, and Johnson 1967, 191. Found this plant dated to before 5000 B.C.E. in the Tehuacán Valley of Mexico. (Some of the early dates from their studies have now been called into question; Long et al. 1989.)

Stephens 1971, 413–4. The Cape Verde Islands were discovered around 1460, at which time there were no signs of former habitations. By 1466 cottons from Guinea had been introduced and had already become semiferal. During the subsequent colonial period, cotton was collected in the wild and also grown under primitive cultivation for export. Modern botanists have found it growing feral in areas of most of the islands. It is a New World cotton, *G. hirsutum*, var. *punctatum*. If these feral cottons today are descended from the cottons introduced from Guinea between 1462 and 1466, then New World cotton must have been established in Africa approximately thirty years before Columbus' first voyage. Of course we do not know where today's feral cottons came from. [But] one would not expect the original, well-established feral form to have disappeared completely.

Chopra et al. 1956, 127. "Cultivated in India" (meaning only modern?)
See also the material under *Gossypium* spp. in general

Gossypium religiosum, Roxb.
Origin: of genetic affiliation from *G. barbadense*, i.e., American ancestry
Summary: Hillebrand reported *G. religiosum* in Hawaii, while Roys gives it for the Yucatec Maya ("*Gossypium religiosum* L Algodon sagrado (Standl.; Gaumer.)"). The specificity of these designations invites, or demands, more careful study of the facts behind them.
Grade: incomplete
Sources: *Gossypium religiosum* – a cotton (Kew. syn. *G. barbadense*)

Hillebrand (1888, 51) seems to give this as (?) equivalent of *G. tomentosum*, yet notes that "*G. religiosum* L., which grows on the islands of the Society group," differs in specified ways. "This form (*G. tahitense*, Parlat.) has not, to my knowledge, been found on our group [Hawaii], although Mann (Enum. no. 43) enumerates it, besides *G. tomentosum*." Referred to "*G. religiosum*, L., which grows on the islands of the Society group." Kew also calls it "*G. tahitense*, Parlat.," [which is not found in Hawaii.]

Roys, 1931, 311. Mayan word "zooh. *Gossypium religiosum* L. Algodon sagrado. (Standl.; Gaumer.)" Reported from the suburbs of Merida. ("Millsp. I, 377.")

Langdon 1982,179. Hutchinson, Silow, and Stephens (1947) claimed that
Marquesan and Society Island cotton was a variety of *G. hirsutum*.
Langdon now points out that is probably incorrect, that the Pacific forms
are *G. barbadense*, whose center of distribution is Ecuador. Wild (meaning
feral—it is a tetraploid) forms of it are found in the Galapagos Islands.

Beaudry-Corbett and McCafferty 2002, 54, Table 4.1. Fibers spun in
Mesoamerica lists cotton (*Gossypium*) and then in a footnote: "Three
varieties [sic] (*G. barbadensis, G. hirsutum, G. religiosum*)."

Gossypium tomentosum
Origin: Hawaii
Summary: This species occurs only in Hawaii but is genetically grouped with American tetraploid cottons. It must be descended from *G. hirsutum* or from the original American tetraploid (now extinct), and its germ plasm must have been carried by voyagers; we consider transmission by purely natural means to such a small island target not to be direct (there is no credible evidence – only speculation – of oceanic drift of plants used by humans from the Americas to any other Pacific islands).
Transfer: the Americas to Hawaii
Time of transfer: pre-Columbian
Grade: B
Sources: *Gossypium tomentosum*

Stephens 1947, 431–2. *G. tomentosum* in Hawaii is the only remaining proposed endemic cotton in Polynesia after eliminating those of the Marquesas, Fiji, and Galapagos. (Those three are actually American cottons, he notes.) A chance crossing by air or ocean currents is possible but seems unlikely over such immense distances as would be required. Cotton seed loses viability quickly in moist air. And *Gossypium* does not survive in the wild [meaning that domesticated *hirsutum* and *barbadense* do not?] The facts all suggest that American cottons may have been used by man at their outset and not independently developed from wild ancestral species.

Johnson 1975, 340. Using 50 collections of the commonly recognized tetraploid New World cotton species, *G. barbadense, G. hirsutum*, and *G. tomentosum* from South and Central America, the Caribbean and Pacific Islands, he found that they gave identical seed protein electrophoretic patterns. Among 44 collections of the Mexican tetraploid, *G. palmeri*, included in *G. hirsutum*, six gave patterns like those of the recognized species, while 38 gave a uniform but different pattern. Other indigenous Mexican cultigens suggested that *G. hirsutum* may have originated from more than one primary amphiploid, including *G. palmeri*. Transitional forms between indigenous cultigens and the cultivated *G. hirsutum* are abundant in southern Mexico, and intermediate forms between *G. hirsutum* and *G. barbadense* are widespread under cultivation. The data indicate that *G. barbadense* (AADbetaDbeta) originated in northern South America from *G. herbaceum* x *G. raimondii* and that the cultivated races of *G. hirsutum* represent various degrees of introgression involving *G. barbadense* and the Mexican *hirsutum* complex.

Johnson cont'd. 348–49. The proposed polyphyletic origin does not minimize the difficulty of accounting for the presence of *G. tomentosum* in the Hawaiian Islands. But, in the course of a tetraploid history of more than 4000 years, it is not impossible for that species to have been transported from the Mexico/Central American area with the aid of man or ocean currents. Elsewhere, of course, he discounts the latter possibility. Opponents of the concepts of an agricultural origin of the tetraploids point to the difficulty of explaining how Old World cotton could have been transported to the New World in prehistoric times, and to the illogic of assuming that man would have brought cotton but not his basic food plants (citing Purseglove 1968). [But these arguments are moot as of the year 2000.] This study sheds no light on these questions.

Wendel 1989, 4132. The tetraploids are highly heterogeneous inter se, including *G. tomentosum* (Hawaii), the Galapagos (*G. darwinii*), other specimens from other Pacific islands, Central America, tropical South America, and the Caribbean.

Newcomb 1963, 42–4. C. Sauer says: Based mainly on Hutchinson et al. research at Empire Cotton Growing Corporation, Cotton Research Station, Trinidad. Concerning Polynesian cottons: The Tahitian plant is *G. barbadense*. The Hawaiian is of Mexican, not South American, ancestry. It was formed by introduction of a *hirsutum* strain out of Mexico. This has bothered S. G. Stephens no end, for how are we to account for this distribution, he asks, by a Spanish vessel shipwrecked in Hawaii? Hutchinson is also puzzled by it. A stray Manila galleon? But a ship returning from Asia would be unlikely to have Mexican cotton aboard. Besides, Hawaii is far from the Manila route. Galapagos cotton is *barbadense* type but almost lintless.

Fosberg (1951, 204–206), contra Silow's statement that *G. tomentosum* of Hawaii is closely related to cultivated cottons, finds little similarity.

Langdon 1982, 189. *G. tomentosum* is a problem entirely unrelated to the cotton of the Marquesas. 186. Cotton spread in colonial times from the Society Group to Rarotonga and then to Samoa, Tonga, Niue, and then Futuna and Wallis Islands.

Heyerdahl 1964, 124. The American cottons, including the Polynesian, are the only tetraploids in the entire cotton genus. On genetic grounds, therefore, Hutchinson, Silow, and Stephens (1947) were forced to suggest that the linted cotton had necessarily reached Polynesia "since the establishment of civilization in Tropical America." J. Sauer showed in 1950 that birds do not eat *Gossypium* seeds, while cotton is most unsuited to long dispersal by sea. In his last publication before his death, Merrill wrote: "That there were occasional and accidental associations between the peoples of Polynesia and America, and even occasional ones between the American Indians and the eastern Polynesian islands, actually must be accepted ... " (1954, 190). "We may admit ... that natives of South America may have reached some of the Pacific islands on balsa rafts" (Merrill 1954, 242).

Silow 1949, 112–8. This Hawaiian wild tetraploid can be explained only as derived from American cotton "which reached Hawaii only after the establishment of civilization in Tropical America" being "perhaps a degenerated escape from early attempts at cultivation [in Hawaii]."

Stephens 1963, 1–22. The earliest introduction was *G. tomentosum*, which came into the Hawaiian Islands, most likely by oceanic drift (perhaps on a 'natural island' of vegetation such as a mass of trees), where it became endemic. [Editorial observation: Such "islands" could come only from the temperate American coast (northern California or farther north), where alone there was sufficient biomass to form a jetsam "island," but no cotton grew there. The arid coast of most of western Mexico would not yield "a (floating) mass of trees" of the type hypothesized by Stephens. Pacific currents would have swept such masses westerly not northwesterly, and therefore could not have reached Hawaii.]

Hillebrand 1888, 50–1. Reports this cotton along the seacoast here and there on all the Hawaiian islands. Native names: mao and huluhulu. Occurs also in Fiji. "The species is unfit for cultivation on account of the short staple" (although it is a tetraploid).

Burkill 1976, I, 1120. In a way that is interesting phytogeographically, Pacific species are attached to the American group.

Helianthus annuus
Origin: the Americas
Summary: Art of India represents the sunflower blossom in a context that signifies the sun's cyclic, calendrical significance. This plant was mentioned in a Hindu text prior to 400 C.E. and also had a pair of Sanskrit names.
Transfer: India from the Americas; thence elsewhere in Asia
Time of transfer: by 100 B.C.E.
Grade: A
Sources: *Helianthus annuus* – sunflower

Lentz et al. 2001. Review of all known early American specimens of *H. annuus* shows that the earliest domestic sunflower was growing in Tabasco by around 2600 B.C.E.

Patiño 1976,179. This involves the difficulties of constructing a history of plants using common names. Since girasol and heliotropo were plants known to the Europeans before the discovery, it is not possible to know, for example, to what species Oviedo might have referred when he mentions in the Indies "*tornasol, girasol o helitoropia*" (citing Oviedo 1851, I, 375).

Nadkarni 1914,177–8. *Helianthus annuses* (sic) (i.e., *annuus*). Sanskrit: *suriya-mukhi*.

Pullaiah 2002, II, 282. Sanskrit: *adityabhakta, suryamukhi*. Medicinal uses.

Aiyer 1956, 67. The sunflower, *H. annuus*, is mentioned in the Hindu <u>Charaka Sahmita</u> dated no later than the fourth century C.E.

Torkelson 1999, 1749. Sanskrit: *suriya-mukhi*

Chopra et al. 1956, 131. Sanskrit: *surya-mukhi*. "A native of America."

Johannessen and Wang 1998, 14–6. Carvings of sunflowers are found on the same Indian temples where maize is shown in the sculpted decoration. The representation of sunflowers can be readily distinguished from those of the lotus flower. Sunflowers also, almost always, relate to solar directions. For example, sunflowers are carved on the heads of statues of Nandi, the bull, which is Lord Shiva's transport, or signature, at the entrance to the interior holy of holies in Shiva temples. The sunflowers are placed in a fashion such that the rising sun passes over the sunflower carving so as to illuminate the statue of Shiva beyond, within the inner sanctum, for a few minutes on solsticial, equinoctial, or half- or quarter-term dates, depending on orientation of temple. Sunflower carvings also exist at the feet of the gods and goddesses who hold maize ears. Moreover, a carving on a stone pillar of a temple shows a parrot perched on a sunflower seed head in a position as if it had just eaten the several seeds that are visibly missing from the edge of the seed head.

Addendum by Johannessen 2004: At the Gaviganga Deschvara temple in Bangalore, Karnataka State, a sunflower symbol is etched on the back wall in the garden, where it is aligned at equinox sunset with another sunflower image carved into the door sill at the holy of holies of the temple.

Gupta. 1996, 86. Sunflowers are native to Central and South [sic] America but have been cultivated in India "from very early times," which is proved by a graphic depiction of the plant in flower in the Rani Gumpha cave, Udaigiri, dated to the second century B.C.E. (see her plate 29). The panel shows a hunting scene. On the extreme right is a breadfruit tree, and a woman has climbed it out of fear. The sunflower plant with five large capitula can be seen on the right of the hunter. The variety of the sunflower floral heads depicted is the large type where the plant reaches a height of 5–6 metres and the capitula have a circumference up to 80 cms. In plate 104, the panel from Sanchi shows a bunch of sunflower capitula, or some other member of the same family, that resembles a sunflower present between two mythical animals. The capitula appear to be of *Helianthus* and the panel is purely decorative. One of the best depictions of the sunflower capitula is from Sanchi (her plate 222), showing a pastoral scene with parrots, buffalos, a mango tree, grapes, a kadamba tree, and on the extreme left are three large capitula of a sunflower.

Heyerdahl 1986, 2, 176. He found what he considers images of sunflowers and other sun symbols carved on pre-Islamic worked stones in the Maldives. They are situated precisely at the equator, which he considers significant.

Watt 1888, IV, 209. The genus has no species indigenous to India. Two, however, are much cultivated, and are very important economically. One is *H. annuus*, Linn. Names: Sanskrit: *Suria-mukhi*; Hind.: *Surajmúkhí*.

Balfour 1871–1873, II, 492. Sanskrit: *suria mukhi* is the sunflower.

Brücher 1989, 118. Soviet agrobiologists found so much variation in sunflowers in the USSR that they claimed a "secondary centre of variability" there. [Implies long presence of the plant.]

Arias and Rieseberg 1995. The variation in DNA in sunflowers in Russia and Turkey has a distribution that is different by at least a standard deviation from the wild and cultivated sunflowers from the Americas in their chart. In China, the size of the seed is significantly larger than almost all commercial sunflowers of the U.S. Both these phenomena point to substantial age for adaptation since *H. annuus* was introduced into Asia.

Tewari (1987) found the name *ashtapushpika* as Sanskrit for the sunflower; it means eight flowers, or eight-parted flower (or multiples of eight-parted flowers). Flowers so named are properly offered to the god Shiva. The lotus, whose representation might possibly be confused with the sunflower in art, is not offered to Shiva, so no confusion can be expected in Ishvara (Shiva-worshipping) temples.

Heliconia bihai
Origin: the Americas
Summary: By the Age of Discovery this species was found spread to Pacific Islands.
Transfer: Pacific islands from the Americas
Time of transfer: pre-Columbian
Grade: B
Sources: *Heliconia bihai* – platonillo, balisier

Cook 1904, 490. *H. bihai*, the leaves of which are used for plaiting, is somewhat similar to banana but without an edible fruit; it reached the islands of the Pacific in prehistoric times and is now found, though no longer cultivated, in New Caledonia. This prehistoric transfer was recognized by Schumann and Lauterbach (1901, 224).

Newcomb 1963, 41. Used for flowers and shade leaves. A relative of the banana. Origin: the Americas. Also in the Pacific islands. Was it carried thence by Spaniards, who had no interest in it, to islands which they never saw?

Heyerdahl 1964, 127. Natives of the West Indies and into South America use the starchy rootstocks of this plant for food, and the leaves served for roof- and wall-thatch, as well as for making hats, mats, and baskets. Baker showed that this plant was native to Tropical America, and that the Pacific island *Heliconia* appeared to him to be only a cultivated form closely related to the Mexican and Peruvian species. Cook (1903, 490) supported Schumann, who inferred a prehistoric introduction of this American plant to the islands: "Though no longer cultivated by the Polynesians, it has become established in the mountains of Samoa and in many of the more western archipelagoes. In New Caledonia the tough leaves are still woven into hats, but the *Pandanus*, native in the Malay region, affords a better material for general purposes and has displaced *Heliconia* in cultivation among the Polynesians."

Bailey 1935, II, 1450–1. There are perhaps 35 species in Tropical America. Many additional species are being described from Tropical Asia [as of 1935]. *H. bihai*, Linn. is called balisier, or 'wild plantain.' "It is naturalized in the Old World tropics and is the parent of many horticultural forms ...."

Hibiscus tiliaceus
Origin: China (?) or America (?)
Summary: A name in Sanskrit seems to place it in India a minimum of 1000 years ago. China is credited as its place of origin. Yet it was widespread in the Americas. It was also cultivated in pre-European Polynesia. Its uses are similar in both the Americas and Polynesia, and vernacular names are rather similar, enough so that we consider human transfer the preferred scenario.

>Case 1: Transfer: Asia to the Americas (? or possibly vice versa)
>Time of transfer: pre-Columbian
>Grade: B
>Case 2: Transfer: the Americas to Polynesia (? or possibly vice versa)
>Time of transfer: pre-Columbian
>Grade: B

Sources: *Hibiscus tiliaceus* – linden hibiscus, beach hibiscus

>Heyerdahl 1963a, 482–5. Gives a rounded summary of the evidence in the literature, pro and con, regarding *H. tiliaceus* as a transfer between the Americas and Oceania.

>Heyerdahl 1964, 129. *H. tiliaceus* has seeds adapted for natural dissemination by sea, yet it is discussed due to its deliberate cultivation in Polynesia, combined with data from linguistics. Cook and Cook (1918, 156) discussed it thus: "Though many botanists have written of the *maho* as a cosmopolitan seashore plant, its wide dissemination may be due largely to human agency, as with the coconut palm." In Middle America, it is widespread, even a dominant species in many localities, [southward] to the banks of the Guayaquil River, where it was used by natives for bark-cloth manufacture, to make water-resistant cordage and strings, and for kindling fire. Both the special uses and names of this plant were much the same among the Polynesians. In Tropical America, the tree was known as *maho*, or *mahagua*, or something close to that, while in Polynesia it was known as *mao, mau, vau, fau, hau*, or *au*. Cook and Cook (169) say: "Though considered a native of America, the *maho* appears to have been distributed over the islands and shores of the Pacific and Indian oceans before the arrival of Europeans." "The names of the *maho* afford almost as definite indications of human contacts as in the case of *kumara* [i.e. the sweet potato]." "The making of fire by friction of wood, and of cloth by beating the bark of trees with grooved mallets, are specialized arts which may have been carried with the *maho* from the Americas across the tropical regions of the Old World" [cf. Tolstoy on the bark cloth/paper complex?].

>Whistler 1991, 64–5. Because of its seawater-dispersed seeds, it is probably native over most of its range, but because of its great utility, the tree may have been introduced [by humans] to much of Polynesia (especially Hawaii).

>Carter 1950, 164–5. Recapitulates Cook's arguments for, and Merrill's arguments against, the idea that this plant was human carried. Contra Merrill, Carter concludes that "man carried the name for the plant and

quite possibly the usages across the ... seas. It even seems probable that he carried the plant also."

Cook and Cook 1918, 156. *H. tiliaceus*, while capable of natural dissemination by sea, had both particular uses and names in common between Polynesia and Middle and South America. (Merrill rejects the argument from names.)

Torkelson 1999, 1752. Sanskrit: *bala*

Chopra et al. 1956, 134. Sanskrit: *bala*.

MOBOT 2003. A native of China according to the Flora of China

Hibiscus youngianus
Origin: Hawaii
Summary: This species is confined to Hawaii but is said to be closely related to the Middle and South American species *H. bifurcatus* from which it may be derived. More information is needed to clarify a possible transfer.
Grade: incomplete
Sources: *Hibiscus youngianus* – a hibiscus (Kew. (apparently confined to) Hawaii)
Hillebrand (1888, 47, 49) says this plant occurs in marshes and abandoned taro patches here and there on all Hawaiian islands. Native name: *akiohala*. The plant "Is nearly [i.e., closely] related to the American *H. bifurcatus*, Cav." Hillebrand considered it part of the pre-European flora. *H. youngianus* was commonly found in old planted areas on all the Hawaiian islands, suggesting that it was dependent on ecological disturbance owing to horticulture.
Miranda 1952–1953, Pt. I, 184. *Hibiscus bifurcatus* Cav. Found in the high tropical forest of Chiapas, Mexico.
MOBOT 2003. *H. bifurcatus* is distributed in Middle and South America.

Indigofera suffruticosa
Origin: Asia, ultimately (depending on synonymy, which apprears confused by some sources)
Summary: This case is of interest only if *Indigofera anil* is synonymous with *I. tinctoria*, which is not certain to us but might be.
Grade: incomplete
Sources: *Indigofera suffruticosa* (=*I. anil*) (Kew =*anil*=*guatemalensi*=*tinctoria*) – Indigo
Townsend 1925. *Indigofera anil* is only a derivative from the Indian *I. tinctoria* introduced into the Americas some 2000 or 3000 years ago. The habits of the American form indicate that it is not native.
Towle 1961, 46. This plant is a source of the *añil* of commerce, obtained primarily from *I. tinctoria* of Asia and *I. suffruticosa*, a native of the American tropics. Wittmack (1888, 347) states that in pre-Columbian times, Peruvians used as a dye indigo obtained from a wild species ordinarily designated as *I. anil*.
Langdon 1988, 185. A 1767 visitor to the Marquesas reported the presence of cotton and also of the plant "indego." Marquesan cotton turns out to be of American derivation (i.e. *Gossypium barbadense*).

McBryde 1945, 143. The origin of American indigo (both *Indigofera suffruticosa* and *I. guatemalensis* are used) is probably Mexican. An Old World species was later introduced (*I. tinctoria*) and is much used today.

Roys 1931, 238. Mayan: "*Choh* (the first 'h' has a line through the upper stem meaning explosive 'ch'). *Indogofera anil.* L."

Jett 1998, 143. Indigo has been identified at Nazca, Peru, in the seventh century B.C.E. and at Paracas Necropolis, ca. 450–175 B.C.E. At least three other species are used to produce indigo dye: *Fuchsia parviflora*, *Cybistax antisyphilitica*, and *Muehlenbakia hastiuta rupestris* (*mullaka*) (citations given).

Indigofera tinctoria
Origin: Asia
Summary: Arnold presents a comprehensive case for the introduction of Indigofera on the west coast of Mexico two or three thousand years ago. However, he does not provide clear evidence on any area from which such a transfer might plausibly have come. He assumes that the introduced plant, *I. tinctoria*, gave rise to the New World *I. anil*, but the evidence for that is not strong. In the case of the Marquesas, a slim case can be made that an *Indigofera* plant may have been transferred from the Americas.

Case 1: Transfer: Oceania or Asia to Americas
Time of transfer: two millennia ago?
Grade: C
Case 2. Transfer: Americas to the Marquesas Islands
Time of transfer: pre-Columbian
Grade: incomplete

Sources: *Indigofera tinctoria* – Indigo (Kew. syn. *añil*, syn. *guatemalensis*, syn.? *tinctoria*)

Townsend 1925. (American) *Indigofera añil* is only a derivative from the Indian *I. tinctoria* introduced into the Americas some 2000 or 3000 years ago. The habits of the American form indicate that it is not native. [Caution: Townsend reveals in his article considerable botanical naivete.]

Towle 1961, 46. This plant is a source of the *añil* of commerce, obtained primarily from *I. tinctoria* of Asia and *I. suffruticosa*, a native of the American tropics. Wittmack (1888, 347) states that in pre-Columbian times, Peruvians used it as an indigo dye obtained from a wild species ordinarily designated as I. añil.

Langdon 1988, 185. A 1767 visitor to the Marquesas reported the presence of cotton and also of a plant, "indego." [Where did they come from? From the Americas is more plausible than from anywhere else, especially since Marquesan cotton proves to be genetically descended from American *G. barbadense.*]

Jett 1998, 143. Indigo has been identified at Nazca, Peru (seventh century B.C.E.), and at Paracas Necropolis (ca. 450–175 B.C.E.).

Chopra et al. 1956, 141. Sanskrit: *nilika*. Widely cultivated in India.

Torkelson 1999, 1759. Sanskrit: *nilika*

Int. Lib. Assoc. 1996, 567. Sanskrit: *nili*

Pullaiah 2002, II, 305. Sanskrit: *nilini, nilika*, comon indigo

Zeven and de Wet 1982, 174. *Indigofera añil* (syn. suffruticosa Mill.). Center of maximum gene diversity is in South America.
MOBOT 2003. *I. tinctoria* (syn. *indica*)
Arnold 1987, 53–84. Compares the morphology of the *Indigofera* plants in the Old and New World and finds great similarity between them. They have the same number of chromosomes, which suggests a common origin. The introduction of the genus *Indigofera* must have occurred in the zone where the largest number of species belonging to this genus are found.
Michoacán possesses 11 species and Guerrero 10, while Brazil and the U.S. have only four species. These data support the thesis of a marine introduction of indigo in the west of Mexico, someplace in Guerrero or Michoacán, several millennia ago. A voyage by sea between Asia and the American coasts, some 5000 or 6000 years ago, seems improbable given the developmental level of that period, but recent studies have found human inhabitation of Australia since at least 32,000 years ago, which makes the time of possible marine voyaging much earlier than had been thought.
See also the data from Heyerdahl (1996) below under *Mangifera indica*.

Ipomoea acetosaefolia
Origin: Tropical America
Summary: It was in Hawaii before European discovery of the island.
Transfer: the Americas to Hawaii
Time of transfer: pre-Columbian
Grade: B-
Source: *Ipomoea acetosaefolia* – (Kew. syn. carnosa)
 Hillebrand 1888, 314. Native of West Indies, Guiana, or Brazil. Hillebrand considers this plant of pre-Cook age in Hawaii.

Ipomoea batatas
Origin: South America
Summary: In addition to archaeological evidence recapped here that shows that the sweet potato spread from the Americas to Polynesia, apparently two separate times, a variety of other evidence – linguistic and historical – confirms that position.
Further, a document puts the plant in China in early C.E. times, and Sanskrit names are recorded confirming such a date for South Asia.
 Case 1: Transfer: the Americas to Polynesia via Hawaii
 Time of transfer: 400–700 C.E.
 Grade: A
 Case 2: Transfer: South America to Polynesia via Easter Island
 Time of transfer: early C.E. centuries
 Grade: A-
 Case 3: Transfer: the Americas to South/East Asia
 Time of transfer: early C.E. centuries
 Grade: A
Sources: *Ipomoea batatas* – sweet potato

Brücher 1989, 5. The claim for a South American center of origin is supported more by archaeological and historical evidence than by botany. Fossil *batatas* from the cave, Puna de Chilca in Peru, have been dated by Engels at 10,000 BP. There are no wild-growing plants [known] in South America that could be ancestral. "The hypothesis of a Central American origin has a weak basis." [No source or supporting evidence is cited for this statement.]

Patiño 1976, 62. Gives a lengthy list with references to native South American names of sweet potato. Gives *cumara, cjumara, cumal, comal,* names used in certain sectors of the Peruvian and Ecuadorian Andes for one variety of sweet potato.

Langdon 1988, 326, 333. Reporting the first lengthy visit to Easter Island, in 1770. A lengthy survey of chroniclers' references indicates *I. batatas*' presence.

Shady Solís 1997, 18. *I. batatas* remains have been excavated at two Late Archaic (3000–1500 B.C.E.) sites on or near the coast of Peru.

Shady Solís et al. 2001, 725. The phenomenal city of Caral in the Supe Valley of Peru, radiocarbon-dated between 2627 and 2020 B.C.E. (calibrated), yielded remains of *Ipomoea batatas* among other domesticated plants.

Bronson 1966, 262ff. McQuown and Kaufmann have reconstructed ten plant names apparently present in proto-Mayan in the second millennium B.C.E. Among them is sweet potato.

Rensch 1991, 108. Linguistic study of the names for sweet potato result in "the hypothesis that the sweet potato reached Polynesia at least twice: once via a northern route through Hawaii under the guise of **kuara/*kuala*, and once via a southern route under the guise of **kumara*, with Easter Island as its point of entry." In both places, a great number of varieties of sweet potato are attested, "pointing to the antiquity of cultivation."

Yen 1974. Tests three hypotheses for the distribution of the sweet potato in the Pacific. On the basis of his especially comprehensive investigation of sources for plant history, he concludes that the plant was probably transfered from South America to Polynesia between 400 and 700 C.E.

Brand. 1971, 343–65. An extensive review and critique of the literature. He maintains that mistaken identification of plants by early explorers in the Pacific makes unreliable the common conclusion that the sweet potato was present in Polynesia before Spanish transfer of the plant from South America. He also claims that the name *kumara* in Ecuador was known only in the highlands and that only if we had the name attested on "the coast" could he accept that name in relation to the Polynesian name [lexicons surviving for coastal tongues are almost nil; moreover the "highlands" are less than 60 miles from the coast].

Langdon and Tryon 1983, 40–1. Early explorers did not record existence of sweet potato in Western Polynesia. No evidence suggests that it had arrived in Western Polynesia in pre-European times, while certain evidence strongly suggests that it had not. For example, it has no place in traditional ceremonies in Tonga, and there are no local names for varieties of it.

Heyerdahl 1963b, 29. It was cultivated under the aboriginal name of *kumara* in the Urubamba Valley of Peru, a Cuzco variety was known as *cusi-kumara*, and in various parts of early Peru the name of this plant has been recorded as *kuymar, kumar, cumar, umar,* and *kumal*. It was grown in highland Ecuador under the name of *cumar*, and in Colombia as *umala* and *kuala*, the latter name extending as far north as the Cuna language. Cites on this Markham, Seemann, Hillebrand, Middendorf, Cook, Imbelloni, Hornell, Merrill, and Bingham. (A majority of these were not cited by Brand..) Dried tubers have been excavated from early tombs in coastal Peru, including Paracas.

Johannessen and Wang 1998, 27–8. Douglas Yen in a personal communication (1996) acknowledges that the sweet potato has the same name in Sanskrit as in northwestern South America.

Herbert Baker (1971) acknowledged the pre-Columbian presence of the sweet potato in Asia but thought it of limited consequence.

Murdock 1959, 217–18. In reconstructing the culture history of Madagascar, the author notes that the Malaysian food complex (rice, taro, bananas, yams, manioc, sugarcane, and sweet potato) is basic to agriculture in much of central Africa. Plants of American origin are also of much or considerable significance (manioc, maize, peanuts, haricot, and lima beans, pumpkins, and tobacco). 222–3. Indonesian ancestors of the later Malagasy of Madagascar immediately preceding or following the time of Christ introduced the Malaysian plants on the Azanian coast – Kenya, Zanzibar. (The plants are referred to as being there in the document, *The Periplus of the Erythraean Sea*, dated 60 C.E.). They became basic to agriculture across Central Africa ('the Yam Belt') all the way to the Guinea Coast.

Here, Murdock explodes a 'bombshell' – he asserts that the sweet potato was part of this Malaysian food complex and once introduced on the east coast quickly diffused across the continent to West Africa. Murdock knows about the American origin of the sweet potato. Furthermore, the distribution of the sweet potato in many parts of West Africa coincides in distribution with other American root crops, notably *malanga* (arrowroot) and *manioc*, so as to suggest that it arrived with those others (via the Portuguese or Spaniards). He is also aware of the controversy over the question of the spread of the sweet potato from South America into Polynesia and Melanesia "as far west as New Guinea, where it has long been established as the staple crop in the mountainous interior." But most authorities have supposed it did not reach Indonesia or the Philippines until the beginning of the colonial period. If the sweet potato actually arrived in East Africa across the Indian Ocean along with bananas, sugarcane, taro, and yams, then "its transpacific spread must have taken place very much earlier than even the most uninhibited theorists have as yet dared to assume." We are quite sure, on linguistic grounds, that the Indonesian source for the voyages to Malagasy, and the resulting terminology, was Borneo, where the sweet potato could have joined the Malaysian food complex. Murdock is reluctant to accept such an early date for the spread of sweet potato westward across the Pacific as this implies, but feels the evidence must be faced. He also notes that in societies in the area (Africa) who segregate their crops into groups with differential ritual associations, sweet potatoes receive the same ceremonial treatment as plants that were unquestionably introduced across the Indian Ocean and are differentiated in this ritual respect from other crops that were brought to Africa by Europeans. Incidentally, he further observes, among the Chaga, near Mt. Kilimanjaro, the only other American crop of consequence is maize, and this falls into the most recent grouping of crops in terms of ritual treatment.

Fage 1962, 299–309. In general, he believes that Murdock handles the sources on Africa inappropriately. He gently refers to Murdock's dogmatism and lack of experience of Africa (309). 308. In regard to the date of the Indo-Malaysian crop complex arriving in East Africa, Murdock depends upon the *Periplus of the Erythraean Sea*, but, Fage says, the Periplus is not an easy document to interpret. "It is not easy to be categorical about what crops were and were not cultivated in eastern Africa at this time."

Newcomb 1963, 42. Murdock's African hypothesis is "off base" in respect to this plant, C. Sauer feels.

Merrill 1954. The sweet potato must have been transmitted (from South America) consciously and with much care, in fact it would have been packed in soil in order to remain viable on a voyage to Polynesia from South America.

Mellén B. 1986, 131. Easter Island: *kumára*. At least 20 varieties existed according to Metraux. [This degree of differentiation either required a long period of cultivation on the island or else the importation of many varieties.]

Darlington 1973, 147. While some species of *Ipomoea* are distributed by sea, the hexaploidy of *I. batatas* in both Peru and Polynesia makes its identification more certain and demonstrates "the spread of the sweet potato from Peru to Polynesia, a spread which proves the meeting of Old and New World Peoples ...."

Roys 1931, 249. "Iz. *Ipomoea batatas*, L. [Mayan] *Camote*."

Evans 1998. In the process of sailing a replica Polynesian canoe from the Society Islands to New Zealand, the crew (following tradition) took with them several varieties of sweet potatoes which they presented ceremonially in the next group visited, and then received a new set of varieties when they set sail for the next destination.

Yen 1998, 168. In table: "Easter Island – early C.E., burnt tubers," citing Hather and Kirch 1991,169. They also present arguments for the sweet potato in the New Guinea highlands before European contacts. 170. On lexical grounds, Scaglion and Soto (1994) have questioned the acceptance of the supposed C.E. post-1500 introduction from the west into New Guinea. The presence of the word *kumara* and cognates in southeastern islands of New Guinea is treated as a separate set of terms for the plant, implying diffusion from Polynesia. 173–4. Quotes from Quiros, pilot on the 1595 Mendaña voyage from Peru to the Marquesas. He said they

(Spaniards) sowed maize, beans, onions, cotton, and "all the most profitable seeds and vegetables." [That is not how a Spaniard would have referred to the sweet potato in the sixteenth century. Besides, even if the sweet potato should have been among crops planted, would any of Mendaña's transplants have survived without knowledgeable care until the late 1700s when the Gonzalez expedition next reports their presence?]

Brown 1935, 238–9. Five varieties were once grown, "none of the varieties originating under cultivation in the Marquesas was of good quality ... and it seems clear that, although the sweet potato was one of the earliest food plants to be cultivated in the Marquesas, it was poorly adapted to the soil, climate, topography, and related conditions."

Barthel 1971, 1165–86. An Easter Island text deciphered by him refers to an ancient directional model of their world that included a "path of the sweet potato" (from the east) and a "path of the breadfruit tree" (from the west). These directions of course correspond to the directions of botanical origin of the plants.

Bretschneider (1882, 38) lists plants in the Chinese document *Nan fang Ts'ao Mu Chang*. The author was Ki Han, a Minister of State in the Tsin (Jin) Dynasty, C.E. 290–307, who had previously been a Governor of Canton. The 80-species list includes: Banana, *Canna indica*, Sweet-potato (*Batatas*), and Coconut. Bretschneider 1892, 418. Japanese source [Matsumura] gives (Chinese) characters for the name of the sweet potato [it might not be of pre-Europea date, however].

Chopra et al. 1956, 141. Sweet potato. Hin. and Pun.: *shakar kund*

Aiyer 1956, 71. Sanskrit: "*Valli* (*Ipomoea batates*?)" The sweet potato was mentioned in the Hindu record known as *Silappadikaram*.

Pullaiah 2002, II, 307. Sanskrit: *pindalah*, *raktaluh*. Medicinal uses.

J. Sauer 1993, 39–41. Purseglove (1968) suggests the introduction of *I. batatas* to Polynesia by natural dispersal: seeds are viable for more than 20 years and impervious to salt water; the seeds are not buoyant but the capsule is. "I doubt that the seedlings could survive in the drift zone on an ocean beach, but conceivably capsules could have been picked up by some Polynesian beachcomber or seeds might have germinated along the banks of a tidal estuary." [Is there any field evidence in support of this speculative notion?]

Kelley 1998, 73. A name for sweet potato among Chibchan speakers of Colombia or Panama precisely matches the Hawaiian spelling of the name.

Lagenaria siceraria
Origin: Hemisphere of origin uncertain
Summary: The bottle gourd is apparently in evidence in both hemispheres; from early in the Holocene, i.e., probably in the pre-agricultural era (13,000 BP in Peru, 9,000 or 10,000 BP in Mexico, 10,000 BP in Thailand), so perhaps the fruit drifted one way or the other across the ocean. However, it is now clear that the species did not occur in western Polynesia, although in eastern Polynesia the bottle gourd was

abundant. This distribution makes sense only if human-aided transfer took place into eastern Polynesia from the Americas.
Transfer: South America to eastern Polynesia
Time of transfer: pre-Columbian
Grade: B+
Sources: *Lagenaria siceraria* (syn. *vulgaris*) – bottle gourd
   Whistler 1990, 1991. He reinvestigated the identification of supposed bottle gourds in western Polynesia at the time of first European contact and found that the species was actually absent from those islands, although in eastern Polynesia it is common. This absence of specimens from western Polynesia of course casts doubt on a drift hypothesis (eastward from Asia via Oceania to the Americas) to account for *L. siceraria* in the New World. In his judgment, "The most likely hypothesis is that it was introduced [by voyagers] to eastern Polynesia from South America."
   Whitaker and Carter 1954, 697–700. *Lagenaria* experimentation by Whitaker demonstrated that the gourd could possibly have been distributed to the New World without the aid of man, but there is no proof that this happened. [Carter has observed: This experiment to assess the duration of viability was carried out in a tank that probably lacked the ocean boring-worms and other potential sources of damage that would be found in the open sea.]
Nadkarni 1914, 213. *Lagenaria vulgaris.* Sanskrit: *alâbu*. Eng.: bottlegourd. Found wild and cultivated nearly all over India.
Pullaiah 2002, II, 323. Sanskrit: *kutukumbi*. Medicinal uses.
Nayar and Singh 1998, 3. *Lagenaria siceraria* dates to earlier than 10,000 BP in both Peru and Thailand.
Yarnell 1970a, 225. *L. siceraria* dated to 3000 B.C.E. in Peru; 5500 in Southern Mexico; 7000 in Northern Mexico.
Camp 1954. Summarizes the results of experimental studies of the viability of drift specimens of bottle gourd. The possibility of a gourd remaining viable after extended floating at sea remains inconclusive. He believes that while there is some possibility that a gourd might have crossed from Africa and might have sprouted on shore in the Americas, there would still be no satisfactory explanation for how the offspring could become established in the plant's normal habitat inland.
J. Sauer 1993, 51–2. (syn. *leucantha, biconurta*). The species was taken eastward from India bearing a Sanskrit name into Malaya and the East Indies. It was in China by 100 C.E. "Comparative studies show that New World bottle gourd cultivars are derived from the African subspecies, not from *asiatica*. The puzzle of how *L. siceraria* arrived in the New World was solved long ago by Whitaker and Carter (1954). Suspecting that the species had been introduced by ancient seafarers, they experimented with flotation of gourds in [a tank of] seawater to see if the possibility of natural dispersal could be excluded. Unexpectedly, they found the gourds could float and retain viable seed for many months, no limits being established, time enough for westward drift from Africa to Tropical America, or eastward drift in high latitudes to the Pacific coast of South

America. [This is an inaccurate summary of their actual findings, as Carter (1953) makes clear.] ... The likeliest hypothesis [though purely speculative] is that drift gourds were found by ancient beachcombers, carried inland out of curiosity, and that volunteer seedlings came up in kitchen middens and other artificial habitats." "The species was taken eastward bearing a Sanskrit name into Malaysia and the East Indies. It was in New Guinea by 350 B.C.E. It was in China by 100 A.D. – (C.E.). Use and cultivation of *Lagenaria* spread prehistorically through the Pacific islands all the way to Hawaii." [Western Polynesia is left without specific reference.]

Carter 1953, 62–71. The bottle gourd could have floated to South America from Africa, but it would progressively have lost fertility under attack by boring worms and microorganisms, making sprouting on the strand unlikely.

Patiño 1976, 244. *Lagenaria siceraria* is one of three plants (the others are the coconut and cotton) which surely were present in the inter-tropical area of the world, on more than one continent, at the European discovery of the Americas. Some have suggested sea transport of the seeds from Africa; however, the gourd was unknown in the Antilles or in eastern South America, although it did appear on the Pacific side. [The plant's absence from the Antilles casts doubt on even the supposition of viable drift seeding from the mainland to those Middle American islands.]

García-Bárcena 2000, 14. *L. siceraria* dates in Tamaulipas and Oaxaca from 7000 B.C.E.

Langdon and Tryon 1983, 37. Almost invariably in Eastern Polynesia the name for gourd is *húe*. But in 1770, Easter Island had *geracona*, gourd. [This suggests a separate introduction to Easter Island?]

Lathrap 1977, 713–51. Proposes that West African fishermen were swept out to sea from Africa to Brazil by 16,000 years ago, bringing the gourd and other features. [There is no evidence of the cultivation of gourds, or any other plant, nor of fishing boats, anywhere near that date in West Africa.]

Towle 1952, 171–84. Her study of seeds from two sites with a review of the literature on the archaeological occurrence of the gourd in Peru leads her to conclude that it is likely the gourd crossed the ocean by drift.

Roys 1931, 245. Mayan: "*Homa*. Probably a large variety of *Lagenaria siceraria*" (Molina). "The large *homa* is used to store food, such as tortillas and atole ...." 61. "Lec. Probably *Lagenaria siceraria* (Molina)."

Mellén Blanco 1986, 133. For Easter Island. This plant, called *húe*, is, without doubt, one of the two plants reported in the manuscripts as "*calabaza blanca y colorada*." Fuentes (1913) identified one variety as *L. vulgaris* (syn. *siceraria*), which is white flowered and meated, and noted that they had other *cucurbitaceae* not yet classified with orange meat.

Brücher 1989, 265–6. "Biologists suppose that the fruits floated on the oceans and maintained the viability of their seeds for many months." Finds in Ocampo Caves, Mexico, at 9000 BP and the Tehuacán Valley 7500 BP is an "astonishingly early time for a cultivated plant in America." "Even if it is not very convincing that 'boat-people' from Africa brought the bottle gourd to the Western Hemisphere," he observes, "we must ask why it did not arrive before the Pleistocene if the natural dispersal of floating fruits was so easy? [And] if *Lagenaria* had in one or another way come from Africa, the puzzling question remains how it crossed the whole [South] American continent and appeared so early on the Pacific side?" Lathrap cited the caves of Pikimachay in the Ayacucho Basin (13,000 BP?) as the earliest find. [The date of 13,000 BP in Peru [doubtful?] and 10,000 BP in Thailand (see above) would seem to place the earliest transoceanic transfer as very early for human intervention. It seems that we must redate this plant, extend the time of sailing by people on the oceans, or grant the drift hypothesis.]

Also, Brücher notes "the peculiar ritual importance of *Lagenaria* fruits as penis sheaths, selected for this purpose independently [sic] in Africa, South America, and New Guinea" (citing Heiser 1973).

Addendum: Too late to enter in detail: Carter 2002, 261-3.

Lonchocarpus sericeus
Origin: Old World
Summary: Distribution on either side of the South Atlantic of a tree that can serve as fish poison raises a question of whether transfer across to the Americas was human-aided. Only further study may answer that question.
Grade: incomplete
Sources: *Lonchocarpus sericeus* (Poir.) H. B. K. (Kew. syn. palmeri) - fish poison
Quigley 1956. Two plants found on both shores of the South Atlantic are *Lonchocarpus sericeus* (Poir.) H. B. K. and *Serjania pinna* L. The former is listed by some authorities as an African native and by others as South American. Some writers list it as a piscicide, but how it might have been transferred across the ocean remains a puzzle. Similarly, *Paullinia pinnata*, L. requires explanation. This is used as a piscicide in South America but not in Africa, possibly because it was replaced by more toxic species. Chevalier's conclusion is that human groups use similar plants for similar purposes on both sides of the Atlantic due to "a truly marvelous genius of intuition."[sic] "But it would require much more than that to produce the same species of plant on both sides of the ocean." That must have been by floating or else by human agency. And the human agency cannot be the Portuguese or Negro slaves. (521.) (Fish poisoning had been outlawed by the Spanish king by 1453 and for the Portuguese in 1565.)

Luffa acutangula
Origin: in dispute; Old World more likely
Summary: This gourd has long been cultivated and used in both hemispheres. That there must have been a transfer is clear and that it might have been by purely natural means is unlikely to account for the places where it is and is not grown; hence, intentional human transport is the only logical remaining explanation. (Since *L. cylindrica* definitely was transported anciently between the hemispheres by human beings, it is not unreasonable that the two closely-related species traveled together.)
Grade: B

Sources: *Luffa acutangula* – ribbed gourd
>   Torkelson 1999, 1776. Sanskrit: *koshataki*
>   Chopra et al. 1956, 156. Sanskrit: *rajakoshataki*
>   Heiser et al. 1989, 14–5. There are two American species: *L. acutangula* and *L. cylindrica* (the latter syn. with *L. aegyptiaca* Mill). However, Brücher (1989, 267) calls both species Old World, but in any case both have been cultivated since ancient times in the Americas as well as in Asia.
>   MOBOT 2003. Distribution North and Middle America and also India.
>   Chopra et al. 1958, 354–5. There are ten Sanskrit names, including those given by Torkelson and Chopra et al. 1956. The gourds are cultivated in most parts of India and are found growing wild in northwest India, Sikkim, Assam, and East Bengal. Seeds have medicinal value. 677. One more Sanskrit name is given.
>   Pullaiah 2002, II, 323. Sanskrit: *kosataki, jalini*. Medicinal uses.
>   Zeven and de Wet 1982, 72. *L. cylindrica* was domesticated probably in tropical Asia, possibly in India, and it gave rise to *L. acutangula*.

See also the information under *L. cylindrica*.

Luffa cylindrica
Origin: Asia (others say the Americas)
Summary: Extensive use in East and South Asia can be compared with a 1200 B.C.E. occurrence in an archaeological site on the coast of Guatemala that suggests transfer across the Pacific from Asia (probably coincident with other plant transfers demonstrated in the present report), without excluding possible movement in the opposite direction. Sanskrit names testify to its early presence in India at least. The apparent absence of this plant at such an early date in many other parts of both Old and New World increases the likelihood of intentional human transmission from Asia to Mesoamerica.
Transfer: Asia to Mesoamerica
Time of transfer: before 1200 B.C.E.
Grade: A-
Sources: *Luffa cylindrica* (syn. aegyptiaca) – loofah, vegetable sponge, sponge gourd
>   Torkelson 1999, 1776. Sanskrit: *dhamargava, rajakoshataki*
>   Chopra et al. 1956, 157. *Luffa cylindrica*. Sanskrit: *rajakoshataki*
>   Aiyer 1956, 55. The flower (whose color was compared to that of gold) and fruit are mentioned in several Tamil sources (cited) of pre-modern age.
>   Watson 1868, 273. Sanskrit: *kereleh*. Hindi: *kerula*. Persian: *Luffa amara*.
>   Pullaiah 2002, II, 338–9. Sanskrit: *mahakosataki*, vegetable sponge. Medicinal use.
>   Heiser (1985, chap. 2) discusses species of *Luffa* from both the Old and New Worlds, leaving a possibility open for human transmission between the two areas.
>   Newcomb 1963, 50. This is pretty close to being a naturalized species in the American tropics. It is a plant of the field margin, that is, it thrives in land disturbed by cultivation. It is used in its youthful form as a green vegetable, and when mature, as a cheap substitute for the bath sponge or scouring pad. How and when was this plant introduced in the Americas?

Nayar and Singh 1998, 14–5. Long cultivated in South and Southeast Asia. In Japan and China it has several medicinal uses. In Guyana it is used as a poultice, while in India it has a number of uses in Ayurvedic medicine.

Heiser et al. 1989, 14–5. There are two American species: *L. acutangula* and *L. cylindrica* (syn. *L. aegyptiaca* Mill). (Brücher assigns the origin of both these to the Old World.) Vernacular names in English are sponge gourd, loofah, or vegetable sponge. Cultivated in the Americas since ancient times. Also long cultivated in South and Southeast Asia. In Japan, an extract of the stem is used to treat respiratory ailments. There were other medicinal uses in China.

Watt 1888–1893, V, 96. *L. aegyptiaca* is a native of India and naturalized in most hot countries of the world. 94. *Luffa* genus "comprises ten species, natives of the warmer regions of the Old World, and one indigenous in America."

Bretschneider 1892, 196–8. *T'ien kua* (sweet kua), nowadays the common name for melons, is also known as *kan kua*. Li Shizhen suggested that the *kua* mentioned in the passage from the *Li ki* [see I, 82] was a melon. He seems to be right. But as to the other quotations, we are left in doubt whether the *kua* there mentioned were melons or were what we call pumpkins, gourds, squashes, i.e., species of the genus *Cucurbita*. 197. "All the *cucurbitaceous* plants now cultivated for food in China are probably indigenous to the country [sic], with the exception of the cucumber and watermelon, which, as their Chinese names indicate, were introduced from the West." He gives Chinese characters for *C. moschata* and *Luffa cylindrica*, among others.

Kosakowsky et al. 2000, 199. In an Early Preclassic archaeological site of Pacific coastal Guatemala, pottery from the earliest levels (1200 B.C.E.) bears a secondary decoration of loofah (sponge) impressions and other impressions on the storage jars. ("Other impressions" on the pots include rocker stamping, a ceramic decoration feature shared with early East Asia.)

Brücher 1989, 267. *Luffa* spp., sponge gourd, luffa. The genus includes six to ten taxa that are mostly of Old World origin, but one species, *L. operculata*, is native to the neotropics (i.e., North America). Its main application is as sponges, etc. "Due to the habitual similarity of the different species which now have worldwide distribution, it is not easy to separate the different taxa." The Old World species are *L. acutangula* (L.) Roxb. and *L. cylindrica* (L.) Roem. The latter is often designated as *L. aegyptiaca* Mill.

Hernandez 1942–1946 [by 1580], I, 159. Náhuatl: *tzonayotli*.

Zeven and de Wet 1982, 72. Domesticated probably in tropical Asia, possibly in India. This plant gave rise to *L. acutangula*. Maximum gene diversity is probably in India.

Lupinus cruickshanksii
Origin: Peru (?)
Summary: The similarities between European lupines and this species of Peru invite closer investigation of their taxonomic relationship.
Grade: incomplete

Sources: *Lupinus cruickshanksii* – lupine, field lupine (Kew. cruckshanksii [sic] Peru, Chile) (syn. mutabilis.)
>   Johannessen and Wang 1998, 25. Safford (see next entry) claimed that cultivated *Lupinus* plants in the New and Old Worlds are so similar that they must have been derived from the same wild species.
>   Safford 1917, 16. *Lupinus cruickshanksii* found in Peru bears close resemblance to *L. albus* of southern France, and another lupine from Peru is also related. "The presence of these lupines in South America, so distinct from the endemic species of that continent and so very similar to those used for food in the Old World, is of great interest to the ethnologist."
>   Brücher 1989, 80–81. *Lupinus mutabilis* Sweet., syn. *L. cruickshanksii* Hooker, syn. *L. tauris* Hooker. Peru: *tarhui, chocho, ullu*. Leguminosae are worldwide, with a strong background in the New World, where 200 taxa have been established. From the Old World, only a dozen species are known, the most important being *L. luteus* and *L. albus*. Cytogenetic barriers exist between the Euro-Asiatic group with n=50 and 52 chromosomes and the American lupines, which in general have 2n=48 chromosomes. The latter are depicted in Peruvian ceramics.
>   Patiño 1976, 191. Cites *Lupinus* spp. and says in the Peruvian Andes a certain people are said in a Relación of 1586 to eat the leaves. 178–9. *Lupinus mutabilis* (Kew syn. *cruickshanski*) or *Lupinus* sp., called *tarwi*, or *tarui*, in Quechua and *chocho*, or *altramuz*, in Spanish, "because of its similitude with the European *Lupinus*." Various species of *Lupinus* are endemic in the Andean cordillera, from 1800–4000 meters. "Cobo considered the *altramuz*, or *tarui*, common to both continents."
>   Yacovleff and Herrera 1934–1935, 305. *Chochos* is the common name, for which Garcilaso gives *tarvi*; Cobo, *tarui*; and Holguin, *tarhui*. Yacovleff and Herrera identify it as *Lupinus tauris* Benth. Garcilaso says, "They have *chochos*, like those of Spain ...." Cobo: "There are to be found a great abundance of wild lupines in the countryside, that the Indians call *tar-ui*." In a footnote, Yacovleff and Herrera say: "The *tarwi* collected by Cook at Ollantaytambo, which is very similar to *Lupinus albus* L. in Europe, Safford mentions with the name *L. cruckshanskii* (sic)."

Lycium carolinianum
Origin: Americas
Summary: On Heyerdahl's authority, this plant's occurrence on Easter Island implies transfer from South America, along with a dozen other useful species. Given the evidence from Dumont and Skottsberg of American species having reached Easter Island, we see the presence of this species on the island as unsurprising, another transplant by voyaging.
Transfer: South America to Easter Island
Time of transfer: pre-Columbian
Grade: B-
Source: *Lycium carolinianum* - christmasberry
>   Heyerdahl 1963a, 28. It is the only wild Easter Island shrub, yet *J. carolinianum* is an American plant.

Lycopersicon esculentum
Origin: the Americas
Summary: There are indications that the tomato was in pre-Columbian Asia, although physical evidence remains questionable. Nevertheless, the fact that four Sanskrit names for the plant are reported cannot be explained were the tomato not known anciently. Further investigation, particularly in China, remains highly desirable.
Grade:B
Sources: *Lycopersicon esculentum* – tomato (Kew. syn. *cerasiforme*)
> Langdon 1988, 329. Thompson in 1886 found the tomato (tomatillo) growing wild on Easter Island. Langdon takes this as indication of pre-European cultivation. (This was probably (?) *Physalis peruvianum*, Langdon observes.)
> McBryde 1945, 140. Both potato and tomato were domesticated from poisonous nightshades. Apparently, those (at least in Guatemala) were little developed, being only half-wild, before white men came.
> Roys 1931, 217. Mayan: "*Beyan-chan. Lycopersicum esculentum*, Mill." 272. "Ppac. *Lycopersicum esculentum*, Mill. Tomate grande." 315. Culub [backwards C,=tz]-ppac. *Lycopersicum esculentum*, Mill. Small-fruited wild form. Tomate chico."
> Bretschneider 1892, 364. List of *Solanaceae* mentioned in <u>Matsumura</u> (Japanese) includes *Lycopersicum esculentum*, Mill. and gives Chinese characters for a name (but the source does not make clear whether the name is of pre-Columbian date in China or Japan).
> Johannessen, personal communication. He was told while visiting China of tomato seeds that had been found in a coffin in a Chinese tomb and later germinated when planted. But seeds from the purported specimens cannot now be recovered for proper examination. Without reliable archaeological documentation, it remains possible, though unlikely, Johannessen observes, that the seeds were an intrusion after the tomb/coffin was opened.
> Brücher 1989, 277. Despite the fact that it is highly probable that the tomato descended from a gene pool of wild species in South America, "remains of the tomato plant have never been found [in Peru] nor do any reproductions exist on ancient potteries in the Andean region …." Apparently, it was domesticated in the Mexico/Guatemala area, which is completely devoid of autochthonous wild-growing L. species. *L. cerasiforme* is the now-cosmopolitan 'weed tomato' that is a direct ancestor of our tomato by some theories, in spite of some morpho-genetic contradictions. *L. cerasiforme* has very small fruits, no bigger than a cherry; native to a narrow west coastal region of Peru. 279. There is a set of wild species from the coastal region and low Andean valleys of Ecuador, Peru, Bolivia, and N. Chile, all with green fruits when ripe. They are separated genetically from the red-fruited Eu-lycopersicon group, with which they do not cross. They are grown in the "Lomas," where vegetation is limited to misty months of August to November. Another wild tomato was discovered on the Galapagos Islands, called *L. cheesmanii*. The Eu-

lycopersicon (red) group includes *L. cerasiforme* and the cultivated *L. esculentum*.

Parotta 2001, 673. Sanskrit names: *raktamaci, radtavardhak, ramphala, shakstmeshdha*. [The fact that there are three other names for the tomato besides *raktamaci* removes most of the uncertainty about the possible reflection of English 'tomato' in the pronunciation of *raktamaci*.]

Pullaiah 2002, II, 339. Sanskrit: *raktamachi*. (Two local names are *tamatur* and *tamata*.) [It might be speculated that *raktamachi* somehow derived from either Náhuatl *tomatl* or else the modern English derivative word 'tomato' in recent centuries and then was somehow accepted by some authors as a Sanskrit term. Enough suspicions surround this term (along with the Sanskrit name for coca) that no conclusion about the significance of that name can be drawn at this time; but of course the other reported Sanskrit names, do not suffer from this uncertainty and are accepted as genuinely ancient.]

Macroptilium lathyroides
Origin: the Americas
Summary: Found as specimens in several early archaeological sites in India, these 'beans' can only be accounted for by human transport across the Pacific along with other species of *Phaseolus* (see below).
Transfer: the Americas to India
Time of transfer: before 1600 B.C.E.
Grade: A
Sources: *Macroptilium lathyroides* (syn. *Phaseolus lathyroides*) – phasey bean, phasemy bean

Smartt 1969, 452. *Macroptilium* is a distinct group within the "genus" *Phaseolus*, consisting of very small seeded American forms.

Pokharia and Saraswat 1999, 99. *Phaseolus* "... beans of American origin have been encountered from proto-historic sites in peninsular India." *P. vulgaris* is recorded from pre-Prabhas and Prabhas cultures at Prabhas Patan, Junagadh Dist., Gujarat, dated from 1800 B.C.E. to 600 C.E. (endnote 153). Also, these come from the Chalcolithic site of Inamgaon (about 1600 B.C.E.), and another site in Pune Dist., Maharashtra (endnote 54), and from Neolithic Tekkalkota (C14: 1620±108 B.C.E. uncalibrated), Bellary Dist., Karnataka (endnote 155). *P. vulgaris*, *P. lunatus*, and Phasey bean (*P. lathyroides*, syn. *M. lathyroides*) have also been recorded by Vishnu-Mittre, Sharma, and Chanchala (endnote 156) from deposits of Malwa and Jorwe cultures (1600–1000 B.C.E.) at Diamabad in Ahmednagar Dist., Maharashtra.

Zeven and de Wet 1982, 66. They give the name as 'Phasemy bean.'

Magnolia grandiflora
Origin: the Americas
Summary: The flowers are considered sacred in India, in common with many other native plants. This status can be taken as evidence that the tree was present anciently. More research is indicated.

Transfer: the Americas to India
Grade: incomplete
Source: *Magnolia grandiflora* – magnolia
>Lancaster 1965, 13–14. This tree is one of a class of at least 18 trees (including *Plumeria rubra*), shrubs, and vines that produce flowers of the champa class each of which is interchangeable with others for ritual purposes. [The logical implication is that all the "sacred plants of the Hindus" discussed by Lancaster must have been present in India for a substantial period of time to have achieved this degree of sacredness. It is difficult to believe that this could have happened in the few centuries since the Portuguese began visiting.]

Mangifera indica
Origin: Southeast Asia
Summary: This fruit was widely and early used in India and Southeast Asia. Landa apparently reports it from sixteenth century-Yucatan, judging by the description of the fruit: yellow, soft, and sweet, "which when eaten leaves the stone like a soft hedgehog …." Tozzer notes the fit, but cannot imagine that Spaniards could have imported the tree at that early date (the only possible origin he considered). Pending more information, we consider this fruit he spoke of as probably the mango but leave a measure of uncertainty.
>Case 1: Transfer: Southeast Asia to Mesoamerica
>Time of transfer: pre-Columbian
>Grade: C
>Case 2: Transfer: Mesoamerica to Polynesia
>Time of transfer: pre-Columbian
>Grade: incomplete

Sources: *Mangifera indica* – mango
>Tozzer 1941, 199. "Another tree [in Yucatan] bears another fruit also yellow and not as large as the other and soft[er] and sweeter than it, which when eaten leaves the stone like a soft hedgehog …." Note 1086 says, "PM suggests *Couopia dodecandra*, (DC.) Hemsl., in Maya *uzpib*. There is an Asiatic species, *Mangifera indica* L. It is evident that a foreign importation would not have been cited by Landa at the time he wrote" [sic]. [The description of the fruit fits *M. indica* so exactly, it is difficult to imagine the Yucatan fruit being of any other species. Had the plant resulted from Spanish importation (they do not mention any such introduction from Asia), there would not have been time for the imported tree to have grown and multiplied sufficiently to be noticeable as a fruiting tree by Landa.]
>Bailey 1935, II, 1984. The Malay Archipelago is home to nearly the entire genus. *M. indica* has been in cultivation since such a remote period that its exact origin is somewhat doubtful, but it has been considered by the best authorities to be indigenous to the Himalayan foothills of eastern India, extending possibly through Burma into the Malayan region. The genus has about 30 species, natives of tropical Asia. Allied distantly to the hog

plum, cashew, and pistachio. *M. indica*; Mango. Northern India, Burma, and possibly Malaya, as noted above.

Zeven and de Wet 1982, 71. The center of maximum diversity is said to be Assam and the Chittagong Hills of India.

Heyerdahl 1996, 149–57. In the Marquesas (Hivaoa), Von den Steinen, Linton, and Heyerdahl discovered and then rediscovered large, non-Polynesian stone carvings showing long-tailed quadrupeds that could represent only some form of felid and whose nearest analogues were on the monuments of San Agustín, Colombia. He connects these representations (radiocarbon-dated by charcoal taken from under the statues at ca. 1300 C.E.) with several plant species of American origin that have been identified in remote locations in the Marquesas. They can only be accounted for by the arrival of voyagers. 78. Among these species was the mango.

J. Sauer 1993, 17–20. Evidently domesticated in the northeastern India/Burma region. It was probably being planted in India by 2000 B.C.E. and is prominently recorded in ancient Sanskrit writings. It came to figure symbolically in Hindu and Buddhist mythology and ceremonies. Not widespread in the East Indies until after the European incursion. Earliest known introduction of *M. indica* to the New World was to Bahia in Brazil about 1700, with seed from West Africa. In 1742, it was successfully introduced to Barbados. A quite separate introduction had taken place across the Pacific from the Philippines to Mexico. Mangoes were not grown around Manila until over a century after trade with Mexico began.

Manihot sp.
Origin: South America
Summary: Manioc was observed by the earliest Europeans to examine Easter Island, and there is evidence that it may have been in use also in the Marquesas. The report of two Sanskrit names from India sheds a new and puzzling light on the plant's ancient distribution.

    Case 1: Transfer: South America to eastern Polynesia
    Time of transfer: pre-Columbian
    Grade: B
    Case 2: Transfer: Tropical America to Asia
    Time of transfer: While Sanskrit was an active language
    Grade: C (pending further confirmation of the Sanskrit names)

Sources: *Manihot* sp. – manioc, cassava

McBryde 1945, 139. Both varieties ('sweet' and 'bitter') were used in pre-Columbian Mesoamerica.

J. Sauer 1993, 57. "The crop is always propagated by cuttings of the woody stems, not by seed." 59. "The first records of establishment of manioc planting in the Old World were in West Africa in the mid-seventh century."

Langdon 1988, 326–8. Called *yuca* in various native languages of Peru and other Central and South American countries. Apparently, the name was derived from *mandioca*. Citing Purseglove, there is one center of speciation in Brazil and another in southern Mexico and Guatemala. It was seen in "beds" on "small plots of ground" on Easter Island in 1770 by Hervé.

Mellén Blanco 1986, 132. Hervé's *yuca*, or *mandioca*, is surely *Manihot utilissima*. Introduced into Tahiti only in the mid-nineteenth century.

Shady Solís 1997, 18. Remains of this plant have been excavated at the Late Archaic (3000–1500 B.C.E.) site of Los Gavilanes in the Huarmey Valley of Peru.

Ugent, Pozorski, and Pozorski 1985, 81–2. Manioc, a Brazilian word, was called *rumu* in ancient Peru, while Aztecs called it *guacamote*. Based on C14 assays, they now report specimens of the plant from the Casma Valley of Peru ranging in age from 1800 B.C.E. (uncalibrated) to 1532 C.E.

Martínez M. 1978, 111–3. Miranda (1952-1953, II, 277) reports five species for Chiapas, one being *M. esculenta*. It is eaten cooked or prepared in the form of bread. Heavy yield: 12–15 tons per hectare. He found at his site in Chiapas (first century C.E. or B.C.E.) two carbonized seeds (species not known) and lots of pollen, these being the only evidence from archaeology of the use of *mandioca* in Chiapas. Lowe supposed its use there anciently, based on finds of what he presumed to be obsidian grater chips.

Yarnell 1970, 225. Earliest archaeological remains: Peru, 2700 BP; Southern Mexico, 2100 BP.

Towle 1961, 132. Associated with Early, Middle, and Late Nazca ceramics (first to ninth century C.E.). 61. Found in remains of Cupisnique Period (B.C.E.) on the north coast, and there was a root of *yuca* in a burial at Ancón (B.C.E. date) and another in a Paracas (also B.C.E.) grave. Many representations can be seen on effigy pots and textiles.

Bronson 1966, 262ff. Named in the proto-Mayan language of the second or third millennium B.C.E. Among them is *manioc*, or *yucca*, *Manihot esculenta*, and *M. dulcis*, sweet yuca, *yuca dulce*, or *mandioca*.

Roys 1931, 225. "*Cici-cin* ['c' of second word pronounced 'tz']. *Manihot aipi*, Pohl. *Yuca dulce*." 314. "*Tzin. Yuca brava*." Motul dictionary: "The yucca [sic] from which they make cassave." Or sweet yucca [sic]."

Pullaiah 2002, II, 346–7. *M. esculenta*. Sanskrit: *darukandah*, *kalpakandah*. Medicinal uses.

Heyerdahl 1996. He and his bride, living on the island of Hivaoa in the Marquesas group in 1939 were taught by natives (only partly acculturated) to process this root to make it edible. [That it had to be processed means that it was a bitter not sweet manioc.]

Maranta arundinacea
Origin: the Americas
Summary: *M. arundinacea* is an old crop in Central and South America. It was also growing wild on Easter Island at the time of European discovery. It was present in India, where it bore a Sanskrit name and was referred to in Tamil (southern India) texts long before European commerce with India began.

    Case 1: Transfer: to Easter Island
    Time of transfer: pre-Columbian

Grade: B
Case 2: Transfer: to India
Time of transfer: while Sanskrit was still active
Grade: A

Sources: *Maranta arundinacea* – arrowroot
> Piperno 1999, 126. Phytolith spectra from pre-7000 BP archaeological strata in Panama are revealing the presence of *M. arundinacea*. 127. Evidence is reprised supporting the hypothesis that arrowroot and other native plants, such as *Dioscorea* spp., were cultivated here before the introduction of maize.
>
> Heyerdahl 1964, 126. This is one of the American plants present in deserted locations on Easter Island when the flora were first recorded by Europeans.
>
> Aiyer 1956, 44. Sanskrit: *kuvai*. *M. arundinacea*, arrowroot, is mentioned in the Tamil source *Malaipadukadam*, as well as in the *Mathuraikanji* (also Tamil), long preceding Portuguese arrival.
>
> Chopra et al. 1956, 162. There are names in Hin., Ben., Tam., etc. "Native of Tropical America."
>
> Pullaiah 2002, II, 348. Sanskrit: *tavakshiri*, *tugaksiri*. Medicinal uses.
>
> Patiño 1976, 22–23. *Sagú* is the name of *M. arundinacea* in various parts of South America. This name was originally that of a palm of the genus *Metroxylon*, native of Southeast Asia and the Polynesian archipelago. How it came to be applied to this tuberous plant of Venezuela and adjacent areas is not known.

Mimosa pudica
Origin: Tropical America
Summary: Known in India in time to receive at least three Sanskrit names, and also grown in the Marquesas Islands, apparently before those islands' discovery by Europeans.
> Case 1: Transfer: the Americas to India
> Time of transfer: probably two millennia ago
> Grade: A
> Case 2: Transfer: to Marquesas from the Americas
> Time of transfer: pre-Columbian
> Grade: B

Sources: *Mimosa pudica* – sensitive plant, humble plant
> Brown 1935. Approximately 250 species, centering in Tropical America. A native of Brazil. "Of early introduction in the Marquesas, where it has escaped from cultivation."
>
> Bailey 1935, II, 2053. Probably 300 species of *Mimosas*, chiefly of Tropical America. Cultivated as an annual (at least nowadays). Brazil is the possible origin, but it is widely naturalized in warm countries.
>
> Roys 1931. 267. [Mayan] *x-mutz*. Sensitiva.
>
> Watt (1892, V, 248) calls it the "sensitive plant." Probably introduced from Tropical America; it is naturalized over most of tropical and sub-tropical India.

Pandey 2000, 271. *M. pudica*, from Brazil, is one species "naturalized throughout India."
Torkelson 1999, 1785. Sanskrit: *anjalikarika, lajja*
Chopra et al. 1956. Sanskrit: *lajja*. Probably a native of Tropical America; naturalized more or less throughout India.
Int. Lib. Assoc. 1996, 569. Sanskrit: *lajja*
Nadkarni 1914, 233. *Mimosa pudica*. Sanskrit: *ajàlikalika, namaskâri*. Eng.: sensitive plant. A native of Brazil, has long been naturalized in India and is plentiful (as a forage crop) in the hotter regions.
Pullaiah 2002, II, 358–9. Sanskrit: *lajjalu, namaskari*. Medicinal uses.

Mirabilis jalapa
Origin: South America
Summary: At least four Sanskrit names for this flower combine with wide distribution in India to witness the fact of transfer from the Americas long ago.
Transfer: the Americas to India
Time of transfer: probably at least two thousand years ago
Grade: B+
Sources: *Mirabilis jalapa* – four o'clock (flower)
Roys 1931. 291. Maravilla, Four-o'clock. *Tzutzuy-xiu*. Its showy and fragrant flowers are closed during midday.
Hernandez 1942 [before 1580], I, 194–5. He identifies two varieties. Very common on the Mexican Mesa Central.
Zeven and de Wet 1982, 177. South America is the center of gene diversity for this species.
Nadkarni 1914, 235. *Mirabilis jalappa* [sic]. Sanskrit: *sandhya-rága*. Eng.: four-o'clock flower. Found in gardens.
Torkelson 1999, 1786. Sanskrit: *krishnakeli*
Chopra et al. 1956, 168. Sanskrit: *krishnakeli*. Cultivated in the greater part of India.
Int. Lib. Assoc. 1996, 569. Sanskrit: *krishnakeli*.
Pullaiah 2002], II. *Trisandhi, krsnakeli* [sic], *sandhya-raga*. Medicinal uses.
Balfour 1871–1873, III, 282. Cultivated as an ornament in gardens. Not directly useful. English name is 'Marvel of Peru.' For Sanskrit he gives two names: *bahu-bumi*, and *sundia-ragum*. (So also Watson 1868.)

Mollugo verticillata
Origin: uncertain
Summary: Archaeological specimens provide positive evidence for ancient presence of this weed in both hemispheres.
Transfer: from one hemisphere to the other (uncertain in which direction)
Time of transfer: before Roman times at least
Grade: A
Sources: *Mollugo verticillata* – carpetweed
MOBOT 2003. This plant is native to China according to Flora of China. Specimens in the herbarium are from North, South, and Middle America.

Chapman et al. 1974, 411–12. Archaeological evidence is adduced to show the presence of this weed in the eastern United States on the order of 3000 years BP. They also reprise some of the literature on its millennia-old presence in Europe. They suppose that its presence in the Americas must be connected with the agriculture of the American Indians, for the weed is garden-dependent.

Monstera deliciosa
Origin: Middle America
Summary: Temple sculptures of India establish this climbing vine from Mesoamerica as a significant element in medieval Indian art.
Transfer: India from Mesoamerica
Time of transfer: by the 11th century
Grade: A
Sources: *Monstera deliciosa* Liebm. (syn. *Philodendron pertusum* Kunth.) – ceriman
- Zeven and de Wet 1982,187. Mexico and Guatemala are the center of gene diversity.
- Lundell 1937, 35. *Monstera* sp. Probably the most conspicuous epiphytes of the humid shaded zone are the giant root-climbing aroids, species of *Monstera philodendron*. They completely surround tree trunks and extend from the tree bases to the crotches. Some of their leaves may reach a length of a meter or more. 54. He lists two different species found at Uaxactun, each given as only '*Monstera* sp.'
- Burkill 1966, II, 1515. *M. deliciosa*, Liebm. A native of Mexico, where it is wild on the western slopes of the mountains in the southern parts of the country, and is also cultivated for the sake of its delicious fruit. It has the flavor of a pineapple. Brought to Singapore (from the Americas) only in 1877.
- Bailey 1935, II, s.v. *Monstera*. From Tropical America. Called ceriman.
- Gupta. 1996, 108–9. This is a large evergreen climber, native of Central America, but it is cultivated throughout India for its foliage and edible fruit. The artisans had to be familiar with the plant in order to sculpt it. Sculpted on various Hindu and Jain temples in Gujarat and Rajasthan; sculpted mainly behind the heads of various deities dating from the 11th to the 13th century C.E. The Mandor statue of Vishnu near Jodhpur has not only the *Monstera* leaves but even the stalks of the leaves sculpted. One of two dwarf-like figures shown with Vishnu is holding a *Monstera* fruit on a plate in his left hand. Other temple sculptures are cited. Plates 136 and 137 show two, while on page 108 is a picture of the living plant.

Morus sp.
Origin: Old World
Summary: A highly important genus in Asian civilizations (for manufacturing paper and bark cloth), two species were known also from Middle America, where they were apparently used in a similar manner. A detailed analysis of parallels in the technological complex of bark-paper/cloth-processing has shown that quite

World Trade and Biologocal Exchanges Before 1492

certainly that complex passed from Southeast Asia to Mesoamerica, including a particular type of bark-beater found anciently in Mexico.
> Case 1: Transfer: *M. alba*: Asia to Middle America
> Time of transfer: first part of the first millennium B.C.E., following Tolstoy
> Grade: A-
> Case 2: Transfer: *M. rubra*: Middle America (according to Brücher) to Asia
> Time of transfer: possibly the third millennium B.C.E.
> Grade: incomplete (origin needs more definitive determination)

Sources: *Morus* sp. – mulberry tree, moral
- Pandey 2000, 281. *M. alba*, white mulberry, was introduced to India from China.
- Chopra et al. 1956, 170. Sanskrit: *tula*
- Pandey 2000, 288. *M. nigra*, from Asia, probably Persia, was introduced to India in 1795.
- Watt 1888–1893, V, 280. The antiquity of its culture in China and Japan and the number of varieties (there) led De Candolle to believe the original area extended eastward as far as Japan. Others believe it extended from Northwestern India into Asia Minor and Persia. Watt considers his *M. indica* equivalent to *M. alba*. 283. Bark in China was used for paper from very early times.
- Bretschneider 1892, 128. The Chinese mulberry is *Morus alba*, L. ... many varieties are cultivated. 203. The Lu shi [Sung Dynasty] relates a tradition according to which the Emperor Shen Nung ["eighth century B.C.E." but now known to be much later] first taught the people to cultivate the ... mulberry tree, for making ... silken cloth." (328–9) This tree is cultivated in all the provinces of China. Silk is raised wherever the tree grows. This pattern can be traced back to the remotest time of Chinese civilization. According to an ancient tradition related in Huai Nan Wang's treatise on the rearing of silk-worms [first century B.C.E.], it was Siling, Empress of Huang Ti [2697 B.C.E.] who first taught the people the art. She was consequently deified and worshipped. The mulberry trees cultivated in China for the breeding of silk-worms are all varieties of *Morus alba*, L., as also are the trees grown in Western Asia and Southern Europe for the same purposes. The name, *M. alba*, was given to the silk-worm mulberry by C. Bauhin on account of its white fruit. But in China (at Peking at least, Bretschneider observes), the fruit of *M. alba* is generally of a red color. "I have seldom seen white berries there." [The rearing of silk-worms in Japan, according to the Japanese annals, dates from the third and fourth century.]
- Burkill 1966, II, 1522. *M. indica* and *M. alba* are the mulberries grown for feeding the silk-worm. The Malays know it as *tut*, an Arabic name widely used in northern India. 1523. *M. alba* has many varieties and intergrades with *M. indica*, which some have reduced [taxonomically] to it. [See Bretschneider (1892) under *M. alba*.] *M. nigra* is the mulberry cultivated for its fruits in Europe and elsewhere. It is not found in Malaya, but is in the hills of Java.

Balfour 1871–1873, III, 357–9. *M. alba* is from all southern Asia. 359. *M. alba* is cultivated in Europe, and in all south and east Asia the leaves of it are fed to the silkworm. *M. indica*, found in southern India, is cultivated in Bengal to feed silkworms.

Von Hagen 1944, 37. Hernández (arrived 1570) discovered many species of wild fig in use in Mexico. 51. "Primitive paper or bark-cloth, wherever it is found, whether on the African coast, or in Java, the Fiji Islands, or the Tonga Islands, Sumatra, the Celebes, or Hawaii, is always made from the mulberry or its close relative, the Fig." 53. When Maoris migrated to New Zealand they brought their mulberry plant with them, but it did not grow well. 58–9. Kinds of plants used for paper-making by the Otomí (Central Mexico) were the mulberry (Spanish: moral) "which has been identified as *Morus celtifolia*, a paper-mulberry similar to the plant used by many Asiatic papermakers." 60. The Aztecs (a living remnant tribe) use almost the same papermaking plants as the Otomís, including the mulberry. 67. After naming nine species of Ficus used for paper, he says in a footnote: "Three well-known species of mulberry found in this area may also have been paper-trees: *Morus alba*, *M. nigra*, *M. rubra*."

Brücher 1989, 239. *Morus rubra* L. "This fruit tree deserves a short mention, because it is said to be of American origin, while other *Morus* species are Old World species. It extends from the southern States of the U,S, to Central America."

Tozzer 1941, 195. In Yucatan, "there are two kinds of mulberry plant, very fresh and fine." Note 1040. Lundell notes this was "probably a *Morus*." However, no species of the genus has been collected in this region.

Las Casas 1875–1876, IV, 379–80. Reported abundant mulberries growing in the Antilles.

Bretschneider 1892, 128. *M. nigra* is a native of Western Asia, where it was much cultivated for its excellent dark red fruit, but it is not fit for rearing silk worms.

Torkelson 1999, 1788. Sanskrit: *tula*

MacNeish et al. 1967, 85. They excavated a type of stone bark beater in the Tehuacán Valley of Mexico which they consider "remarkably similar" to some in Java and Celebes; they find it "extremely difficult" to believe in the beater's independent invention because the degree of complexity and similarity is so great.

Tolstoy 1963. A detailed and systematic analysis of parallels in the bark-cloth manufacturing industries of Southeast Asia and Mesoamerica provides evidence that he considers to be unequivocally indicative of historical relationship between the two areas. He thinks the technology was introduced to Mesoamerica in the early part of the first millennium B.C.E.

Mucuna pruriens
Origin: the Americas
Summary: Widespread distribution in Asia and unmistakable characteristics combine with multiple Sanskrit names to ensure the presence of this species (or two species, if *pruriens* is distinguished from *prurita*) in both hemispheres.

Importation to Polynesia directly from the Americas is more plausible than a tortuous route from Southeast Asia for which there is no evidence.
> Case 1: Transfer: the Americas to India
> Time of transfer: at least as early as the first centuries C.E.
> Grade: A
> Case 2: Transfer: the Americas to Hawaii
> Time of transfer: pre-Columbian.
> Grade: B

Sources: *Mucuna pruriens* (syn. *prurita*) – cowhage (Kew. syn. *urens*; Am., Austr. syn. *prurita*; syn. *imbricata*) [Synonymies inconsistent]

> Burkill (1966, 1528) says *M. urens* is not the same: "The plant [*M. pruriens*, DC, cowitch) was taken to the West Indies some centuries ago and occurs there alongside a very similar species—*M. urens*, DC." Boiled seeds of *M. pruriens* have been used in India from Sanskritic times as an aphrodisiac and its roots as a tonic.
>
> Cook (1901, 292) says this plant, of American origin, was in Polynesia and the Malay region in prehistoric times.
>
> Webster's Ninth New Collegiate Dictionary says: "cowhage, also cowage. From Hindi: *kavac*. A tropical leguminous woody vine (*Mucuna pruritum*) with crooked pods covered with barbed hairs that cause severe itching; also these hairs sometimes are used as a vermifuge." The same information and more can be found in the Oxford English Dictionary (OED).
>
> Roys 1931, 235. Mayan: "Chiican. *Mucuna pruriens* (L.)" *Picapica*. "This is the English cow-itch."
>
> Watt 1888–1893, V, 286. *Mucuna pruriens*. Cowhage. "It occurs commonly throughout the tropical regions of the Americas, Africa, and India. Seeds in India are considered a strong aphrodisiac."
>
> Chopra et al. 1958, 515. In the Punjab plains, from the base of the Himalayas to Ceylon and Burma. Many medicinal uses.
>
> Nicolson et al. 1988, 1238. Called *nai-corana* in <u>Hortus Malabaricus</u>. Still known throughout Kerala as *naikurana*.
>
> Hillebrand 1888, I, 101-2. "*M. urens*." Found on Maui, Hawaii. "A native of Tropical America from the West Indies to Brazil and Peru, well known as the Cow-itch plant." He considers it of pre-Cook age in Hawaii.
>
> Balfour 1871–1873, III, 394–5. Cowage, or cowitch, has medicinal uses. Found in East and West Indies and elsewhere in the American tropics (*M. urens* and *M. pruriens*). Sanskrit: *atmagupta* in general; *M. prurita*, Hook, W. & A.; Sanskrit: *copikachuand atmagapta* (sic). "Sir W. Hooker has distinguished the East India plant, M. prurita from *M. pruriens*, which is indigenous in the West Indies." Same, vol. I, 389. The species are found in hedges, thickets, on the banks of rivers, and about watercourses, in the East and West Indies, and in the Americas within the tropics. *Mucuna urens* and *M. pruriens* usually furnish the substance (i.e., the hair).
>
> Nadkarni 1914, 242–3. *Mucuna prurians* (sic). Sanskrit: *atmaguptä, kapikachchhu*. Eng.: cowhage. An annual climbing shrub wild in Bengal and common in

the forests throughout the plains. Cultivated in some parts for its velvety legumes, which are eaten as a vegetable.

Torkelson 1999, 1788. Sanskrit: *atmagupta, kapikachchha*

Chopra et al. 1956, 171. Sanskrit: *atmagupta*

Int. Lib. Assoc. 1996, 569. Sanskrit: *atmagupta*

Pullaiah 2002, II, 369–70. Sanskrit: *atmagupta, vanari*. Described in the texts in the tradition of Ayurvedic medicine.

Kirtikar and Basu, 2d ed., 1999, 780. Sanskrit: *atmagupta*, and 44 other names.

Musa x paradisiaca
Origin: South Asia
Summary: *Musa x paradisiaca* is descended from two genomes which now include 'banana' (most varieties) as well as the 'plantain.' Historical and linguistic evidence in abundance demonstrates that the traditional view among plant historians that the Spaniards first introduced bananas and plantains to the New World is in error. Archaeological finds from Peru seem to confirm the early occurrence. In any case, ethnohistoric accounts credit several Mesoamerican peoples with growing this cultivar before Columbus' arrival, and linguistic and historical documents confirm heavy pre-Columbian use by tropical South American peoples also.

Transfer: Widespread distribution in the American tropics seems to rule out a mere transfer to the hemisphere via Polynesia as too late to account for the Western Hemisphere spread. There must have been (also?) an earlier advent, either via the Pacific or Atlantic Oceans. We take one transfer as a minimum; two or more as possible.

Time of transfer: supposing the Peruvian tomb finds were legitimate, then perhaps as early as the first B.C.E. centuries, or at least on historical and linguistic evidence in South America, one millennium before the Spanish Conquest.

Grade: A

Sources: *Musa* sp. – banana, plantain

Nicolson et al. 1988, 297. *Musa x paradisiaca*. In Malabar, vazha is still used (cf. Rheede *bala*, which is the general term for all bananas and plaintains as plants). "Modern nomenclature for cultivated *Musa* is based on genome analysis. Moor "pointed out that *M. x paradisiaca* is correctly applied only to cultivars with parental genomes of *M. acuminata* ('A') and *M. balbisiana* ('B'). Thus, the genome of the cultivar Mysore is expressed as (AAB), showing it is a triploid with two complements of *M. acuminata* and one of *M. balbisiana*." [The plant is normally cooked to eat it.]

Berry 1925, 531–2. Illustrates and discusses seeds of "*Musa enseteformis* Berry, n. sp." These fossils were collected from coal beds by "an experienced naturalist" (Dr. M. A. Rollot, aka Bro. Aristé) of the Instituto de La Salle of Bogotá. Most modern bananas do not bear seeds, but of those which do, the closest to these are those of the African species *Musa ensete* Gmelin which have inedible fruits and very large seeds. 533–4. All *Musaceae* have been considered to be natives of the Old World except the large and exclusively American genus *Heliconia* and one species of the ditypic genus *Ravenala* found in northern South America, the other species of which is confined to Madagascar. The peculiar distribution of *Ravenala* and the disputed occurrence of *Musa* in the New World before the arrival of the Spanish explorers might well have discouraged dogmatism regarding the latter. 534–5. Cook says the banana was originally a root crop, and even at the present time the root and heart are eaten in some countries. Most authors (Cook the most vocal exception) have assumed an Indo-Malayan region origin. Humboldt questioned this view (Nouvelle Espagne, first ed., vol. 2, 360, 1911). He quotes a number of early authors who asserted that it was cultivated in the Americas before the Conquest and mentions its cultivation on the Orinoco and Beni rivers in regions far removed from foreign influence. Garcilaso de la Vega says the banana was one of the staple foods in Peru at the time of discovery and accurately describes several cultivated varieties. Montesinos said the same. Of supposed banana leaves from Peruvian graves, "of course leaves of *Musa* (the banana) are not distinguishable from those of the exclusively American genus *Heliconia*, so that no reliance can be placed on the leaves ...." 530. [DNA would allow the distinction to be made today.] Berry: "The great similarity of the fossils to the seeds of the existing *Musa ensete* of Africa caused me to have some doubt as to their authenticity. They are, however, undoubtedly fossil and not recent ...." "It would seem that the presence of characteristic remains of *Musa* in the Tertiary of northern South America effectually disposes of the Old World origin of the genus, and although it does not prove that the New World was the actual place of origin, it disposes one to a more ready acceptance of the arguments for such an origin. It seems further to visualize the independent cultivation of the banana by the natives of the Americas long before the advent of the Europeans, thus validating the opinion of Humboldt and the statements of Garcilaso and Prescott."

De Prez 1935, 59, Fig. 15. Bananas are shown at Borobudur (India) ca. 700–900 C.E.

Newcomb 1963, 50–2. "It is time to face up to the Banana." This genus has three sections which are differentiated on the basis of chromosome characteristics. (The *Musaceae* Family is divided into four genera, *Strelitzia*, *Ravenala*, *Heliconia*, and *Musa*.) Darlington in his Chromosome Atlas subdivides the *Musa* into three groups according to haploid numbers, which are 10, 11, and 12. The African *Musa* (Ethiopia) is cultivated not for fruit but for its stem which is boiled or baked for food. The Abaca species, *Musa textilis*, has fruit. It might have appeared in the New World "later," but this is not yet proved (see Miranda, on Chiapas). Also, the Pacific Island *fehi*, or *fe'i*, bananas are distinct. And finally, seed bananas in the New World: where do these fit? (At this seminar, Simmonds had never heard of them until told by C. Sauer.) At Ancón, Peru, investigators turned up some banana seeds. This collection was studied twice, by Wittmack and by a French botanist [Rochebrune?] Some bananas are grown there in that area now. Wittmack thought the seeds in the site could have been contaminants.

Newcomb, cont'd. Cheesman pretty well established that plantains are from Southeast Asia, specifically from the eastern side of the Bay of Bengal; the wild parentage is there. The Berlanga myth (that this Dominican priest brought the first banana rootstock to the West Indies from the Canaries) couldn't explain the tremendous number of New World forms developed in so short a time. Experience shows that banana rootstock is durable and could survive lengthy sea voyaging. African bananas were imported from Asia, not domesticated locally. [In any case plantains were already in the Americas.]

Latcham 1936. For Pacific coastal South America, he reports the practice of planting bananas in moist beds above the water level but below ground level.

Moseley 1969, 485–7. South American *mahames*, or sunken garden plots, were a supplement to canal irrigation along the arid coast in Peru & Chile because ground water kept the plants moist.

Skottsberg 1920, 13. Easter Island. Describes use of small, cultivated plots dug below ground level and used particularly to grow bananas below the prevailing winds.

Dagodag and Klee, 1973,10–5. A distributional study that maps the widely spread uses of this (*mahamaes*) form of cultivation, in Oceania, Peru, and Chile. [This cultural parallel supports the supposition of a transfer of the plant also from Eastern Polynesia to South America, or vice versa.]

Mellén Blanco 1986. 130–1. Easter Island. "*Plátanos guineos*" in early explorers' documents has to refer to one of the varieties of *Musa sapientum*, (reported in tradition) brought to the island by the first settlers. Called *maika*. Grown in pits (*manavái*) sometimes to protect from the wind. Hervé reported a banana plantation a fourth of a league long and almost half that wide, in addition to smaller plantings.

Heyerdahl 1964, 123. Stevenson, Wittmack, and Harms had pointed out that plantain [meaning generic *Musa*?] leaves had been frequently identified in aboriginal Peruvian graves and Rochebrune found a fruit of cultivated *Musa paradisiaca* in a prehistoric tomb at Ancón. Chroniclers Garcilaso de la Vega, Acosta, Montesinos, and Guaman Poma unanimously stated that the plantain was grown before the Conquest in Peru. Further, when Orellana descended the east side of the Andes and crossed South America (1540–41, the first European to do so), he found plantains growing all along the reaches of the upper Amazon. [This report is circulated in the literature, but his original account does not say anything of the kind.] In the light of this, Merrill finally granted that "We may reasonably admit that one, or a few of the numerous Polynesian plantain varieties may have" reached the Americas.

Towle 1961, 97. Leaves of the banana are said to have been found in Peruvian graves (Rochebrune, 1879, 348, 352; Pickering 1879, 663). Rochebrune, 352, also speaks of specimens of the seedless, berry-like fruits having been recovered. However, this Old World species was brought to the Americas only after the European discovery [sic, Towle]. Since the specimens are not available for study, it is not possible to determine their correct identifications.

Jeffreys 1963a, 196–7. The historical claim circulates (originally from Oviedo) that Fr. Thomas de Berlanga brought the *platano* (banana and plantain) from the Great Canaries in 1516. Jeffreys, formerly a banana planter in Cameroon, observes that the shoots brought by Berlanga to Santo Domingo in 1516 would not have been available for planting out until the end of 1517 or beginning of 1518; yet before 1525 Oviedo published that by then there were huge plantations in the islands and on the mainland. Only those who have had nothing to do with running banana plantations may be able to swallow Oviedo's assertion about the banana's origin via Berlanga. Among these is Professor Merrill (1954). 202. Cites De Candolle (1884, 304) to the effect that Garcilaso de la Vega "says distinctly that at the time of the Incas, maize, quinoa, the potato, and, in the warm temperate regions, bananas, formed the staple food of the natives. He describes the *Musa* of the valleys of the Andes; he even distinguishes the rare species [variety?] with a small fruit and sweet aromatic flavor, the *dominico*, from the common banana, or arton." [Johannessen observes on the basis of field experience in Central America that the dominico is now a fairly large cooking plantain. A small aromatic banana, the *mansana*, is the chief fresh banana with an apple aroma.]

Cook 1901, 258. "The evidence of the banana in prehistoric America is equal, if not superior, to that presented here for the coconut." American bananas have mistakenly been attributed to importation via the Manila galleons, but Oviedo describes them in the New World 40 years before that route was even discovered, and Philippine varieties of bananas were still not found in Mexico in 1901.

Harms 1922, 166. Literature is cited showing their presence in Peruvian graves.

McBryde 1945, 36. Bananas are mentioned in the tradition, <u>Annals of the Cakchiquels</u> (in Guatemala), and some varieties seem to have grown in the Americas prior to the Conquest.

Scholes and Warren 1965, 965. Bananas were being grown before the Spanish Conquest in southern Mexico.

Sapper 1934, 119ff. Gives names for the banana from many languages, from which he concludes that this plant had to have been present well before the Conquest and probably in the first millennium C.E.

Smole 1980, 47–50. His ecological and ethnographic studies among the Yanoama Indians in Brazil/Venezuela provide convincing basis that their current heavy dependence on plantain cultivation is an old, conservative feature. Cultivated plantains relate to a variety of wild *Musa* forms in the vicinity. He also considers Berry (1925) as presenting "credible evidence" for Tertiary-age bananas in Colombia. Upon his reexamining the Spanish chroniclers, he finds their statements support the indigenous view rather than that Spaniards exclusively introduced bananas. The evidence overall is not incontrovertible but does support the hypothesis.

Wittmack 1890, 325–49. Lengthy review of chroniclers and archaeology concludes that the banana was pre-Columbian in Peru.

Merrill 1954, 165–385. One or more plantain varieties may have been carried by the Polynesians to South America, where they reached the Amazon basin.

Roys 1931, 304. *Musa sapientum. Platano blanco.* (No indigenous Mayan name.) The Maya text prescribes a medicinal use for the leaf.

Spores 1965, 971–2. In the hot mountain valleys to the west of Tehuantepec, [pre-Columbian] inhabitants grew bananas among other crops.

Addenda: Too late to enter in detail: Smole 2002; Jett 2002c.

Musa coccinea
Origin: China
Summary: The find of this anomalous species (only?) in such a remote spot in the Amazon basin is impossible to explain as a post-Columbian import. It seems highly probable to have been aboriginal.
Transfer: Asia, apparently, to South America
Time of transfer: pre-Columbian
Grade: C+
Sources: *Musa coccinea* – Chinese banana (Kew. (China)).

MOBOT 2003. Native to China according to the Flora of China.

Newcomb 1963, 50–2. H. Bassler, a U.S. geologist working in the Amazon in the 1920s, wrote a description of seed-bearing bananas in the Upper Amazon (published in the Journal of the N.Y Botanical Garden). He compared it to the Chinese *Musa coccinea*. The fruit head in this specimen stands upright rather than bending over and hanging down. He speculated it might have been an early Chinese introduction, carried on into Amazon country. 52ff. "The Evidence Pro and Con Regarding the Pre-Columbian Occurrence of the Banana in the New World." Tessman found that the simpler native cultures had the seed bananas. Guaraní-related Indians, more advanced, lacked the seeded type. A fairly promising case exists that these seed-bearing bananas were indeed fehi bananas, for they had seeds, and the fruit-bearing stems were not pendent but upright. No one has followed this up. (H. J. Bruman, at the C. Sauer seminar that Newcomb reports, told of meeting Tessman in 1956 to examine the wild Amazon bananas grown in Paraná. Bruman confirmed the characteristics attributed by Tessman. These plants grew at a low elevation and in conjunction with domesticated bananas as associates.)

Myrica gale
Origin: probably Old World
Summary: Distribution on both sides of the Atlantic, combined with pollen on intervening Greenland and Iceland dated to the times of the Norse sagas, make likely that those voyagers were responsible for the transfer.
Transfer: Northern Europe to Iceland, Greenland, and North America
Time of transfer: 1000 C.E.
Grade: B
Sources: *Myrica gale* – bog myrtle

Thorarinsson 1942, 46. *M. gale* is spread on both sides of the North Atlantic, although it is now absent from Iceland and Greenland. Yet its pollen is found in Icelandic excavation layers from saga times, and possibly also in Greenland as well. The Norse sometimes used this plant instead of hops to brew beer. He finds it tempting to ask the question whether this plant could have been brought to North America by the Norse. His implied answer is that they could and apparently did, since no other scenario for the plant's distribution in North America recommends itself.

J. Sauer (1969) raises a question about how it appeared in both hemispheres.

Nicotiana rustica
Origin: the Americas
Summary: This 'wild' tobacco is found widely in India. It is unlikely to have been introduced after *N. tabacum* was available, for tabacum is far more desirable, but it may have been brought in at the same time (inadvertently?). More information is needed to determine its significance, if any. DNA can solve the identification problem if leaf is available.
Grade: incomplete
Sources: *Nicotiana rustica* (syn. rusticum) – Turkish tobacco, wild tobacco
  Chopra et al. 1956, 176. Hin. and Ben.: vilayeti tamaku. Cultivated in West Punjab, Baluchistan, Bengal, and other parts of India.
  Gupta and Jain, 1973, 414. "The tobacco plant of commercial importance was introduced into India as late as the fifthteenth century C.E. by the Portuguese, and that is perhaps why there are no Hindu myths connected with the plant, nor is it considered to be sacred by them. But a large number of tribal myths connected with the plant are current, though very likely they refer to the wild varieties of the plant." (Citing V. Elwin, Myths of Middle India, 324.)
  Chopra et al. 1958, 679. Cultivated in many parts of India. *N. rustica*, Turkish tobacco, is also cultivated in some parts of northern India. Does not list any Sanskrit name, but gives Arab.: *tanbak*; and Pers.: *tanbaku*.
  Watt 1888, V, 352. *N. rusticum*. "Turkish or East Indian tobacco." (Not named in Sanskrit, he says.) Widely cultivated throughout much of India. "The vernacular names given to it would indicate its introduction into Northern India from opposite directions." (354. Rusticum was never naturalized.)
See also material under *N. tabacum*

Nicotiana tabacum
Origin: the Americas
Summary: Use of the plant by Egyptians and others in the Old World has been demonstrated definitively by study of mummies and desiccated corpses dating from at least 1100 B.C.E. Use of the water-cooled hooka smoking device is shown in pre-Columbian art in India, along with medicinal references to tobacco in traditional forms of medical practice. Names point to the pre-Columbian presence of tobacco in Asia and perhaps in Tibet. Sanskrit, Arabic, and Persian names are recorded. The plant was also found wild on Easter Island, where tradition says it was introduced by the earliest settlers.

Case 1: Transfer: the Americas to Egypt, at least
Time of transfer: no later than 1100 B.C.E.
Grade: A
Case 2: Transfer: the Americas to Eurasia (Cases 1 and 2 may prove to be combined.)
Time of transfer: Sanskritic times, surely by 1000 C.E.
Grade: A-
Case 3: Transfer: the Americas to Easter Island
Time of transfer: pre-Columbian
Grade: C

Sources: *Nicotiana tabacum* – common tobacco

Zeven and de Wet 1982, 181. It has been shown that tobacco is a natural amphitetraploid of the New World. *N. sylvestri* and *N. tomentosiformis*. The occasional wild plants are escapes from cultivation.

Balfour 1871–1873, IV,104. *N. tabacum*. He gives the Sanskrit names as *sahastra-patra* and *dhumra-patra*. (But Hindi: *tamakhu* or *tambaku*.) "Mr. Royle mentions on the authority of the Persian works on *materia medica*, that it was introduced into India in 1605 C.E. ... though Royle quotes the authority of Pallas, Loureiro, and Rumphius, who think tobacco was used in China at a period anterior to the discovery of the New World."

Pullaiah 2002, II, 380. Sanskrit: *tamakhu*.

Heyerdahl 1964, 126. This (in a wild, or feral, state) was one of a number of plants found when Europeans first recorded the flora of Easter Island. Thomson before 1891 collected traditions that say that this plant was brought by the first ancestral settlers. Its name, *avaava* [cf. Rarotonga: *kavakava*, acc. to J. Sorenson, personal knowledge] indicates, he says, that it was chewed, not smoked (another word is applied to the latter, *odmoodmo*). This is another "reasonable suspect" to have been introduced in pre-European times.

Martínez M. 1978, 124–5. Miranda found only *N. tabacum* (growing wild?) in Chiapas. Its preparation requires much care (drying or curing by air or fire). Quotes Thompson (1970, 110) on uses—offering to gods, divination, worn as an amulet, and in burials. It was chewed with lime or smoked. Thompson (p. 118) says in Mesoamerica tobacco was considered almost a panacea for illnesses. They applied the juice on insect bites. 129. Some seeds found by archaeological flotation date to the Chiapas Proto-Classic [ca. the first century C.E.).

Yarnell 1970, 225. Earliest remains, Northern Mexico, 1600 BP.

Ashraf 1985, 91–101. It is universally accepted that tobacco began in the New World and was carried to India after its introduction into Europe by Europeans, especially the Portuguese. 92. Tobacco in *Tibb-e-Unani* (Greco-Arab medicine). *Hikmat*, or *Tibb-e-Unani*, along with Ayurveda, were the two dominant schools of medicine before the advent of modern medicine. It was practiced all over India. In that system, tobacco was one of the important plants used as a cure for a number of diseases. One of the earliest mentions of *tanbaku*, or tobacco, as a medicinal plant is found in a collection of prescriptions titled <u>*Majmua-e-Ziai*</u>, penned by the court-physician of Muhannad-bin-Tughlaq of the Delhi Sultanate. It is dated 737 AH (1329 C.E.). This ms. mentions use of tobacco as a component of a compound preparation, *nás*, used for a number of diseases. (93) Name: *tanbaku* falls in the category of names identical in Persian and Sanskrit. Hence, we suspect the tobacco tradition goes much further back than the fourth century. That is confirmed by another medieval source, a Persian translation of a Sanskrit classic of Ayurvedic medicine, completed 1512 C.E. "We find mention of tobacco in traditional Indian medicine of a period almost a millennium before the discovery of the New World and the introduction of tobacco into Europe." Not only Indian but European practitioners of Greco-Arab medicine who were residing in India and were familiar with Indian traditions of both medicine and culture, considered tobacco to be native to India and not an introduction. More details.

Ashraf cont'd. 95–96. The issue rests with identity of the substance labeled by the noun; he then documents continuity of the smoking tradition in India (which used the huqqa, or water pipe). It was present almost unchanged since the fourth century and mentioned in texts very possibly earlier. A temple in Himachal Pradesh dated to 1422–1424 C.E. shows archaeologically the use of the huqqa at that time. Photographic documentation of this depiction is also had for other temples through the Archaeological Survey of India. 96–97. Argues that prohibition of tobacco smoking in Sikh religion supports the argument so far, for there would have been no prohibition without the practice being common.

Chopra et al. 1956, 176. Sanskrit; *tamakhu*. Hin. and Bom.: *tambaku*. Cultivated throughout India.

Torkelson 1999, 1793. Sanskrit: *tamakkhu*. Arabic: *tanbak*. Pers.: *tanbaku*

Marszewski 1975–1978, 255. Pointed out on the basis of plant names a possibility of pre-Columbian cultivation of tobacco in India and Southeast Asia.

Bucaille 1990, 187–8. Fragments of American tobacco and a coleopterous parasite of tobacco were found in the abdominal cavity of the mummy of Ramses II. He reproves any speculation about possible ancient American contact with Egypt on the basis of this tobacco. The abdominal cavity was open for years while the mummy was in various locations over the past century. "This accounts for my surprise upon hearing the Museum of Anthropology [in Cairo] declare that the discovery of morsels of tobacco in the mummy's abdomen was proof that the ancient Egyptians were familiar with the plant."

Christian 1897, 138. He gives Samoan, *sai*, meaning a bundle of tobacco, in possible relationship to Quechuan (Peruvian) *sairi*, name for tobacco.

Dixon 1921, 19–50. Name study shows tobacco is American only; this follows upon his devastating review of Leo Wiener's book the previous year. [But in the light of additional findings in our book, some material in Wiener's book needs to be re-examined.]

Feinhandler, Fleming, and Monahon 1979, 213–26. Comprehensive on the diffusion of tobacco. The conventional view of exclusive New World origin followed by diffusion by the Spaniards is probably false and needs to be modified. Maps are given of the pre-Columbian distribution in Australia, New Guinea, Melanesia, and Polynesia. Some of what Lewis (see below) claimed appears right. Goodspeed gave the definitive taxonomy of *Nicotiana* and argued that one sub-genus had spread from South America to Australia long before any possible human residence in the Pacific [sic].

Balabanova et al. 1992a, 358. Nine Egyptian mummies, dated from approximately 1070 B.C.E. to 395 C.E. were examined by radioimmuno-assay and gas chromatography/mass spectrometry. Cocaine and hashish were found in all nine, and nicotine from tobacco in eight mummies in hair, soft tissue, and bones.

Balabanova et al. 1992b. Showed hashish along with cocaine and nicotine in Peruvian mummies. Balabanova, Boyuan Wei, and Krámer (1995, 68) say that 1992b demonstrated "the presence of cocaine, nicotine, and hashish in hair and soft tissue of pre-Columbian mummies," so this was not an inadvertent statement.

Balabavanova, Boyuan Wei, and M. Krámer 1995, 74. More than 60 kinds of wild tobacco plant forms are known (in the world). It "seems possible" that in past centuries nicotine was used in medicine. Or nicotine may have entered the picture as a secondary alkaloid in some other plants. Thus, e.g., in *Withania somnifera*, family nightshade, in the levels (sic) of *Prunus ceresus*, family Rosaceae, in the *Narcisse*, family amaryllidaceae, etc. Use of these plants [not demonstrated, of course] "may" be followed by accumulation of nicotine in the body. Also, possibly imported. E.g., *Withania somnifera* is the best-known drug in ancient India. "In conclusion, our results showed the presence of nicotine in ancient population (sic) of southern China, and consequently, the presence and use of the alkaloid, as principal or secondary alkaloid in native Chinese or imported plants."

Langdon 1988, 329. Thomson found tobacco growing wild in secluded spots on Easter Island in 1886, a century after Cook's visit. Langdon infers that this probably meant pre-European cultivation of toabcco.

Zeven and De Wet (1982, 181) say the plant does not grow "wild" but only as an escape.

Brücher 1989, 180–1. The species *N. tabacum* does not exist in free nature, nor does *N. rustica*. Both are allo-polyploids with hybrid origin. American wild (predecessor) forms are identified here. They are found on the western slopes of the Andes in Peru, Bolivia, and Argentina.

Laufer 1931, 138–40. He had written about the spread of American tobacco into Asia, Europe, and Africa after European discovery, but Melanesia and Australia are different. He supports Lewis (1931). There are native tobaccos in New Guinea, he is assured, and the method of smoking them there is unique and likely very old.

Lewis 1931, 134–8. He claims pre-European presence of tobacco in New Guinea while others suppose it only came via the Spaniards. He argues for independent domestication and use in New Guinea.

Jeffreys 1976, 9–28. Tobacco is one of the plants he finds present in Africa before the influence of Iberian impacts. Its presence there may be due to the Arabs.

Wiener 1924, 305–314. A summary of his three-volume work (1920–22), which was badly handled by critics. At this point, he claims that forms of the word *tubaq* are found in Semitic and Sanskrit, and the Náhuatl and Tarascan words for tobacco and pipe, he claims, are from Arabic. [Requires more critical examination.]

Watt (1888, V, 352ff.). 353. *N. tabacum.* "American or Virginian tobacco." Hindi: *tamáku, tumálk, támbáka, támbáku.*" Persian: *tanbaku.* Arabic: *tanbák.* Malayalam: *pokala, puka yila,* etc. Widely naturalized. An abundant weed. 361. The tobacco plant was introduced to India by the Portuguese about 1605.

Burkill 1966, II, 1577. *N. tabacum* often maintains itself in a wild state in the tropics, but not in the sub-tropics, whereas the reverse is the case with *N. rustica. N. tabacum* is the tobacco plant of chief interest in the Malay Peninsula.

Nadkarni 1914, 257. *Nicotiana tabacum.* Sanskrit: *támrakúta.* Eng.: tobacco. Hind., Pers., and Mah.: *tambáku.* Arab: *tanbak.*

Parotta 2001, 674. Sanskrit: *dhumapatra, kalanga, tamaku*

England 1992, 161. There was a word for tobacco in reconstructed Proto-Mayan, before 1000 B.C.E.

Balabanova, Wei, and Krämer 1995, 68, 70, 73–74. Significant nicotine and cotinine (a metabolized product of nicotine) residues were identified in five of eight naturally preserved cadavers from Guangxi state in Southern China, dating some 3750 B.C.E. – thus, significantly earlier than the oldest Egyptian mummies. The cotinine indicated ante-mortem use of the source of the alkaloid, not external contamination. *Nicotiana* is known to have been used medicinally in China during the last few centuries.

Balabanova 1994. She surveys comprehensively literature from biologists, historians, archaeologists, in re. pipes, etc., to demonstrate that a tobacco plant was cultivated and consumed in Europe long before Columbus. (Compare Benoit 1962, 1963.)

Addendum: too late to enter in detail: Jett 2002a.

Nymphaea sp.
Origin: Old World
Summary: Some observers say that Eurasian and Middle American water lilies ('lotuses') differ by very little; botanists may consider such differences of considerable significance. To non-specialists, those pictured in the Americas look essentially "the same" as some flowers in the Old. (Within the Old World, species, and even genera, differences exist also but are overlooked for iconographic purposes.) But the treatment of the motif in art and myth has such notable parallels, that one supposes the natural differences may have been overlooked by the ancient Americans who could have considered the lily they had (*Nymphaea* sp.) the 'lotus' in the same manner that horticulturists treat both *Nymphaea* and *Nelumbo* species as 'lotus.' It is impossible to know at this time whether there is an exact

species equivalence between the Mesoamerican lotus and that of the Old World, where the two genera were considered equivalent for some purposes. It is a subject worth further DNA study.

Transfer: Old World to Middle America
Time of transfer: pre-Columbian
Grade: incomplete
Sources: *Nymphaea* sp. – lotus, white water lily, blue water lily

> Aguilar 2003, 80. Maya shamans had within their pharmacopeia the white lotus flower (*Nymphaea ampla*, also known as the white water lily, or nenúfar). In Egypt, the mandragora, or blue lotus flower (*N. caerulea*), was employed, along with datura and henbane (as psychotropics).
>
> Lundell 1937, 191, 198. *Nymphaea ampla* Salisb. Mayan, nohoch naab, nape. A very common aquatic plant with large floating leaves and attractive white flowers.
>
> Pullaiah 2002, II, 377. *Nelumbo nucifera* (syn. *Nymphaea nelumbo*). The East Indian lotus. Four Sanskrit names.
>
> Gupta., 1996. 117–120. *Nelumbo nucifera*, lotus. Held sacred by Hindus, Jains, and Buddhists, is the most common floral depiction on temples. "Practically every god or goddess is sitting or standing on a lotus flower. This could be because lotus is a symbol of beauty, fertility, and purity." In Hindu and Buddhist cosmology, the lotus flower arises and unfolds from the formless, endless Ocean of Creation and represents the Universe. The regents of the eight directions are its eight opened petals. Lakshmi, the goddess of fertility, beauty, and prosperity (basically a goddess of fortune), is associated with the lotus plant and is known as Padma, the lotus Goddess.
>
> Naudou 1962, 340–7. The lotus panels from Chichen Itza are compared in some detail with those of India and Southeast Asia.
>
> Heine-Geldern 1966, 284. A lotus motif was important in the art of India in the period from second century B.C.E. to the second century C.E. It shows not only the flowers and leaves but the whole plant, including the rhizome. In Maya art, the lotus motif appears in Classic times, but at Chichen Itza of the later Toltec period [post C.E. 750] motifs correspond most closely to Indian designs, particularly to those of Amaravati in south India (second century C.E.). At Uxmal, a similar motif dates to about the seventh century.
>
> Heine-Geldern and Ekholm 1951, 306–8. Associations of the lotus are discussed, all of which are shared between the two areas.
>
> Rands, 1953, 75–153. He grants that there are "truly remarkable parallels" in representations of the water lily at Chichen Itza and Palenque, and at Amaravati, India. But a naturalistic convergent explanation for the parallels cannot be ruled out.
>
> , 1951, 61–2. Motifs shared by Hindu/Buddhist art of southern India (style of Amaravati) and of Southeast Asia, with Mexico and the Maya region are now an established fact. Among the motifs is the lotus.
>
> Díaz 2003, 81. The white water lily plant employed as a hallucinogenic (called *nenúfar*, or white lotus flower), became a symbol of a lineage often

depicted in the headdresses of Maya rulers. The white water lily flower was also seen as a link in the chain of fertility: the flowers fed fish, which subsequently fertilized the soil to permit the cultivation of corn. The *nenúfar* also symbolized death. In the Codex Dresden, the god Chac pulls this precious white flower from the water.

Newcomb 1963, 59–60. Carl Sauer observes: Lotuses occur in bayous of the Magdalena River in Colombia as well as in Cuba and possibly Mexico. Only one botanical distinction exists between the New World lotus and those of the Old World, which is a matter of flower coloration. [But see below.] Old World lotus has yellow blossoms, those in the Americas white or pink. Old World distribution is also disjunct, not explainable by reason of birds or transport via drainage systems. This suggests that man is responsible. There are records of lotuses being carried to Europe from the Orient. Lotus roots are starchy; the seeds are nutty like the *piñon*, and the flowers are edible. Flowers are also an important art motif. And how are lotus and water lily related? The former is genus *Nelumbo*, whose leaves stand well above the surface of the water. Equating *Nelumbo* sp. and the term 'lotus' is the usage of U.S. horticulturists. The water lily is the genus *Nymphaea*, or true water lily, whose leaves float on the surface of the water. These species represent the true African or Egyptian water lilies. However, the common nomenclature for 'lotus' and 'lily' is quite confused.

K. T. Harper, personal communication, 2004. The Old World lotus (*Nelumbo*) has white, pink, or blue flowers. The *Nelumbo* species also has a different leaf (peltate). The *Nuphars* and *Nymphaea* species have a very different leaf. The flower of *Nelumbo* is elevated three or four feet above the water; the *Nymphaea* flower opens at, or close to, the water surface.

Wilkinson, 1879, II, 407. Plants from Pliny: "*Nymphaea* Lotus. Arab.: *beshnín*. Footnote 2: This *Nymphaea* Lotus grows in ponds and small channels in the Delta during the inundation … but it is not found in the Nile itself. It is nearly the same as our white waterlily. Its Arabic name is *nufár*, or *nilófer*, or *beshnín*; the last being the ancient *pi-sshnn*, or *pi-shneen*, of the hieroglyphics. There are two varieties—the white, and that with a bluish tinge, or the *Nymphaea caerulea*. The Buddhists of Tibet and others call it *nenuphar*. Though the favourite flower of Egypt, there is no evidence of its having been sacred; but the god Nefer-Atum bore it on his head, and the name *nufar* is probably related to *nofar*, 'good,' and connected with his title."

Roys 1931, 267. White water lily, found in shallow ponds near Merida and elsewhere.

Rands 1953, 117. The water lily in both the Maya area (*Nymphaea ampla*) and the Hindu lotus (*Nelumbo* sp.) are members of a single family, the *Nymphaeceae*. The stalks of both rise prominently above the water. This being the case, a certain degree of resemblance in the depictions of the two related plants might well be expected. A number of conventionalizations strikingly similar to Maya floral forms must be admitted to exist in Southeastern Asiatic depictions of the lotus. 118.

"The Type C flower which occurs at Chichen Itza, Palenque, and Chinkultic ... is closely paralleled in certain representations of the lotus." He continues with additional, fine details relying on Coomaraswamy (1931) for the India comparisons. 119. "Maya associations of the water lily having correspondences in Indian art appear to be quite numerous." (Details given.) [We really need DNA analysis for comparison.]

Ocimum spp.
Origin: Old World?
Summary: We have data on three species of *Ocimum* but are uncertain of all synonymies. Nevertheless, it is clear that at least one species was shared between India and Mesoamerica.
More study is required on why a plant of a taxon called *americanum* would have two Sanskrit names. Distribution of *O. basilicum* throughout the Americas also needs explanation, since it has a long history in India, where it is said to be indigenous, bears two Sanskrit names, and probably is also mentioned in a Hindu text no later than 400 C.E. The genus (species not certain) was found in an archaeological site in India before 800 B.C.E. Yet at the time of the Spanish Conquest 'sweet basil' was growing in Mesoamerica.
Transfer: Old World to New?
Time of transfer: pre-Columbian.
Grade: B

Ocimum americanum
Sources: *Ocimum americanum* (syn. canum) – hoary basil
    Pullaiah 2002, II, 384. Sanskrit: *vanabarbarika, aranyathullasi*
See also above under *Ocimum* ssp. in general. See also Parotta 2001 under *O. basilicum* below.

Ocimum basilicum
Sources: *Ocimum basilicum* – French basil
    Chopra et al. 1958, 680. Sanskrit: *munjariki*. Herb common throughout India. 517. Medicinal uses. Indigenous to the lower hills of the Punjab. Cultivated throughout the greater part of India.
    MOBOT 2003. Distribution: North, Middle, and South America; Africa; China.
    Saraswat, Sharma, and Saini 1981, 316. *Ocimum* sp. A carbonized branch (species undetermined) was excavated from the Sanghol site in each of Periods I and II (1300–800 B.C.E. and 800–600 B.C.E. respectively).
    Pullaiah 2002, II, 385. *Ocimum basilicum*. Sanskrit: *barbari, munjarik*. ('Sweet,' or 'common' basil.). Medicinal uses.
    Parotta 2001, 438. He makes *O. americanum* syn. with *basilicum*. Sanskrit: *arjaka, arjakah, barbari*.
See also above, *Ocimum* ssp. in general.

Ocimum sanctum
Sources: *Ocimum sanctum* (?syn. *micranthum*; syn. *tenniflorum*, or *tenuiflorum*), sweet basil, holy basil.
> Tozzer 1941, 194. Sweet basil was very abundant in Yucatan. Note 1033.
> *Ocimum micranthum* Willd., *albahaca* in Spanish (in modern Spanish, *alebaca*).
> MOBOT 2003. *Alfavaca* is *O. sanctum*, holy basil.
> Aiyer 1956, 27. Species not given but 'basil' is mentioned in the <u>Ramayana</u> and in <u>Charaka Samhita</u> text, no later than 400 C.E.
> Pullaiah 2002, II, 385. *Ocimum tenniflorum* (syn. sanctum). Sanskrit: *surasa, vrinda* ("sacred basil"). *O. basilicum*, Sanskrit: *barbari, munjarik* (sweet or common basil). Medicinal uses.
> Parotta 2001, 441. A sacred plant, grown in and around temples. Sans.: *ajaka, ramatulasik tulasi, vriddhtulasi*.
> Lancaster 1965, 32. *Tulasi*, or *tulsi*, (*O. sanctum*) is the sacred basil, a small herbaceous plant with green to black-green foliage, which is strongly scented. It is venerated as a household deity, very largely in Bengal where a plant will be found in nearly every house or courtyard. Legend has it that Tulsi was a nymph beloved of the God Krishhna who transformed her into the tulsi bush. Tulsi leaves are added to offerings of flowers and fruit to make the offering more acceptable.
> Heywood 1993. This species was regularly grown near temples in southwestern Asia.
> Gupta. 1996, 131–2. The plant is called *bhutagni* (Sanskrit?) and is planted in the house so that no evil spirits come near it. It is symbolically and ritually associated with marriage. Its use is old, being mentioned in five different puranas.

See also above the material under *Ocimum* spp. in general.

Opuntia dillenii
Origin: the Americas
Summary: The fact that some cacti were considered indigenous to India, with the degree of naturalization that varieties seem to show, together hint that cactus plants may have been there before the Portuguese could have brought them. That notion is bolstered by the fact of several Sanskrit names for this cactus that is of New World nativity. In the Near East there are further hints that this species lived in the area much earlier than usually assumed. (Consider also the entry on *Agave* sp.)
Transfer: the Americas to India or the Near East
Time of transfer: While Sanskrit was still a living language, i. e., before 1000 C.E., at least.
Grade: B
Sources: *Opuntia dillenii* (syn. megacantha; streptacanth; amyclaea; ficus-indicus; *Cactus indicus*) – prickly pear cactus – (Kew. syn. ficus-indicus (Haw., Am. Austr.))
> Nadkarni 1914, 266. *O. dillenii* (syn. *Cactus indicus*). English: prickly-pear. Native of the Americas, now naturalized in India, in great tracts.
> Pullaiah 2002, II, 389. *Opuntia stricta* (syn. *dillenii*). Sanskrit: *vidara, visvasraka*.
> Torkelson 1999, 1798. (syn. *Cactus indicus*) Sanskrit: *vidara*
> Chopra et al. 1956, 178. Sanskrit: *vidara*. "Introduced in India."

Parotta 2001, (syn. stricta). Sanskrit names: *kanthari, vidara*

Jeffreys 1976, 9–28. Among the plants he suggests that were in Africa before the Portuguese was "the prickly pear."

Patiño 1963, 359. The name *tuna* is from the Taino language, generalized throughout South America. In Mexico, the name is applied only to the fruit, while the plant is called *nopal*.

Towle 1961, 71. Species of *Opuntia* are widely distributed in Peru. Plants of this genus are often reproduced on pottery vessels.

Roys 1931, 273. Mayan: "*Pakam*, or *Pakan*. *Opuntia dillenii* (Gawler) Haw. Tuna, nopal. *Pakam* is probably a general name for the prickly-pear." Motul dictionary gives "*Pakam. Tunas* on whose leaves the cochineal is bred."

Dressler 1953, 139. This species is the plant on which the early Mexicans cultivated the cochineal insect. The present[-day] cultivation of cochineal in Oaxaca is said to utilize varieties of *O. ficus-indica*.

Forbes 1956, 102. "We also have hints in later Jewish documents that the cactus *cochenillefera* was grown near Nablus, and the insect producing the red dye was fed on it." Abrahams and Edefirstein reported that analysis of Bar Kokhba-period textiles (ca. 135 C.E.) from Judea revealed the dye chemical characteristic of cochineal. [But see Robinson 1969, below.] The raising of cactus in the Near East remains unproved, although today at least two *Opuntia* species are naturalized in the Mediterranean Basin, according to Groves and di Castri (1991, 68).

Jett 1998, 143–4. True (Mexican) cochineal is generally considered post-Columbian in the Eastern Hemisphere, although, according to Wulff (1966, 189), true cochineal [probably not so; see Robinson 1969] was mentioned as early as the time of Sargon II of Assyria, in 714 B.C.E. as coming from Armenia and northern Persia.

Robinson (1969, 25) states that "Cochineal made from ... *Coccus cacti* ... came to Europe from the New World [after Columbus' discovery], but recent discoveries in the Ararat Valley and adjacent areas suggest it was known and used by the Assyrians before the seventh century B.C.E., being produced in the Armenian mountains." Others say that what was referred to was a native grass-parasite, an Armenian coccid, *Porphyrrophora hamel*.

Dhamija (1994, 841) reports that this Armenian red "is chemically similar to New World cochineal," that is, it contains carminic acid, the key colorant in cochineal. An early medieval textile from Gujarat, India, has been found in Egypt, that perhaps utilizes cochineal dye (Rosenberg et al. 1993, 93).

Townsend 1925. "'*Opuntia*' and all *Cactaceae* are of American origin, but various species of *Opuntia* have been known in Asia and Africa from remote times." [Caution: Townsend exhibits an unsophisticated knowledge of botany and entomology at some points.]

Watt (1892, VI, Part I, 109) lists *Opuntia dillenii*, Haw. Prickly pear. "Originally brought from America but now quite naturalized." No Sanskrit name is known. A separate entry is in Watt, 1892, V, 490–2. Roxburgh, who described this under the name *Cactus indicas*, believed it to be a native of India. However, no references are made by Greek or Roman writers. First mention is by Spanish and Portuguese sources. "Most probable that it was introduced by the Portuguese." The cochineal insect was brought to India in 1795. Then, this (plant) species was so prevalent in India that writers spoke of this cactus as indigenous. Insects thrived on it as much as on *Opuntia* species specifically brought with the insect.

> Pandey 2000, 272. *O. dillenii*, from South America, is a species "naturalized throughout India," while (273) *Opuntia vulgaris* is listed as naturalized in some parts of India.
>
> MOBOT 2003. Distribution of *O. dillenii* is given as North, Middle, and South America, the Caribbean, Europe, Asia, and Africa. "Indigenous in Mexico."
>
> Parotta 2001, (syn. stricta). Sanskrit: *kanthari, vidara*.
>
> Desmond 1992, 209–10. In the late 1700s, "as opuntias were widely distributed in India and especially in Bengal, it was assumed by Anderson and other naturalists that they were native to the country. They did not know that this invasive genus had been introduced from the New World, probably by the Portuguese, although for what purpose is a matter for speculation."

Osteomeles anthyllidifolia
Origin: the Americas
Summary: Distributed widely in Pacific islands and perhaps in the Far East, this positively suggests human transport from the Americas.
Transfer: the Americas into Pacific islands (as far as China?)
Time of transfer: pre-Columbian
Grade: B
Sources: *Osteomeles anthyllidifolia* Ldl. (Kew. (Ins. Pacif., China)) - *Utei*, Hawaiian Rose

> Safford 1905, 233. In a footnote under *Cocos nucifera*: "Another interesting example of the wide dissemination of a plant belonging to an American genus is that of *Osteomeles anthyllidifolia*, all save one of whose congeners are indigenous to the Andes, but also occurs in the Hawaiian Islands, Pitcairn, Rarotonga, the Bonin Islands, and the Liu-kiu [Ryukyu] group, near Formosa."
>
> Bailey 1935, II, 2414. There are three species of the genus in East Asia and Polynesia. The South American genus *Hesperomeles*, with about 10 species, of which none seems to be in cultivation, is sometimes united with *Osteomeles*. *O. anthyllidifolia*, Lindl. is spread from Hawaii to Pitcairn Island. In the Hawaiian Islands, it is known as *uhi-uhi*. (Two East Asian species are also mentioned, from China and Japan.) [Needs DNA analysis.]
>
> Bretschneider 1892, 429. A Japanese source (date uncertain) gives (Chinese) characters for the name of this plant or *Osteomeles subrotunda*, Koch (syn. *O. anthyllidifolia*, Ldl.)

Pachyrhizus erosus
Origin: the Americas

Summary: The species is long naturalized in India, so much so that it has been considered indigenous and bears a Sanskrit name.
Transfer: the Americas to India
Time of transfer: at least before 1000 C.E. and probably much earlier
Grade: A
Sources: *Pachyrhizus erosus* – jicama, yam bean, xicama
> Towle 1961, 51–2. Widely cultivated and naturalized in the tropical regions of both New and Old Worlds for its edible tuberous roots. It is disputed whether *P. erosus* or *P. tuberosus* was grown in Peru.
> Newcomb 1963, 61. A legume whose beans contain strychnine and therefore are poisonous. The large, white tuber of the Mexican plant tastes like a young turnip. The same plant occurs in Southeast Asia and a similar plant grows in Andean Valleys. The last is much more starchy and is commonly cooked in stews.
> Roys 1931, 235. "Chicam. *Pachyrhizus erosus* (L.)" Jicama. Maya: *chicam*; the *xicama* (equated in the Motul dictionary). 264. *Mehen-chicam, jicama dulce*.
> Watt 1892, VI, Part I, 3. Gives *Pachyrhizus angulatus*. Cultivated throughout India for its large edible root, but it does not occur in a wild state. Sanskrit: *sankhálu*.
> MOBOT 2003. (syn. *angulatus*)
> MacNeish 1992, 260. Lists this plant as a Southeast Asian domesticate [indicating a long period of naturalization in Asia, since it is actually of American origin].
> Brücher 1989, 84–5. It is cultivated in the Philippine Islands and in China to such a great extent that it was claimed to be of Asiatic origin. Real origin is undoubtedly Central America, where several biotypes still occur wild.

Pachyrhizus tuberosus
Origin: South America
Summary: Another Amazonian plant; old in Peru, and also grew in Western Polynesia as well as in China.
Transfer: China from the Americas, possibly by way of Polynesia
Time of transfer: pre-Columbian
Grade: B
Sources: *Pachyrhizus tuberosus* – yam bean, jicama, potato bean
> Zeven and de Wet 1982, 174. Maximum gene diversity center, headwaters of the Amazon.
> Shady Solís 1997, 18. Remains of *P. tuberosus* have been excavated from five sites of the Late Archaic (3000–1500 B.C.E.) in Peru.
> Yacovleff and Herrera 1934–1935, 281–2. *P. tuberosus*, jicama. Fig. 14 shows the *jiquima* in Nazca art. According to Standley and Vavilov, it grows spontaneously in southern Mexico and Yucatan, where it is also cultivated. Fossil remains have come from tombs at Paracas.
> Heyerdahl 1964, 120–33, 128. Clausen showed *P. tuberosus* is native to the headwaters of the Amazon and tributaries in Brazil, Peru, etc. It possesses insecticidal properties, which aid in cultivating the yam. This plant has almost disappeared from modern Peruvian agriculture, although it was

described by early chroniclers, and Yacovleff and Herrera (1934–1935) demonstrated its presence in the form of roots in tombs at Paracas (B.C.E. times). The plant also formed a decorative motif in Nazca art. Cook reported that the plant occurs in Tonga. While no longer cultivated for food, farmers there believe that planting it makes the soil capable of yielding larger and earlier crops of yams. In Fiji, the stem is used for fish lines. Steward (1949, 413) and J. Sauer (1950, 513) both considered this bi-hemispheric distribution as due to early trans-Pacific voyaging.

Johannessen and Wang 1998, 9–36, 26–27. *Pachyrhizus tuberosus* is called *dou shu*, or *tu gua*, in China. It is the same plant as Mexican *jicama*. Citations to several Chinese plant records are given, one dated to 1736 C.E., describing the 'earth squash,' or 'soil squash, characterized as having "its root ... quite big, greenish-white in color," and for which a particular Chinese character was used in writing. The same character today stands for the yam bean. It was in use during the Song Dynasty (i.e., by 1182 C.E.), when the plant was represented. It was said to grow in mountainous areas where barbarians dug it up for food. Also, "It tastes sweet and fragile or soft-crunchy to eat." Several Chinese crop specialists now accept it as present in pre-Columbian China.

Brücher 1989, 44–5. *Pachyrrhizus tuberosus* Lam. Spreng., potato bean, jicama. Originated in Upper Amazonas.

Chang 1970, 177. He accepts the yam bean as one of the early crops of China.

Paullinia sp.
Origin: the Americas
Summary: Distributed on either side of the South Atlantic, although propagated by cuttings, there seems a possibility that its African presence is to be accounted for as a result of voyaging. Requires more research, along with *Tephrosia*.
Grade: incomplete
Sources: *Paullinia* sp. – piscicidal tree (Kew. syn. *P. pinnata*)

Bailey, 1935, III, 2487. Tropical America, and sparingly in Africa; species number about 140. Propagated by cuttings.

Quigley 1956. "More directly of concern are plants found on opposite shores of the South Atlantic. One is *Paullinia pinnata*, L. This is used as a piscicide in South America but not in Africa, possibly because replaced by more toxic species. Chevalier's conclusion is that human groups use similar plants for similar purposes on both sides of the Atlantic due to 'a truly marvelous genius of intuition.'" "But it would require much more than that to produce the same species of plant on both sides of the ocean." Must be by floating or by human agency. And the human agency cannot be Portuguese or Negro slaves. 521. (Fish poisoning had been outlawed by the Spanish king by 1453 and for the Portuguese in 1565.)

Pennisetum americanum
Origin: the Americas
Summary: In India its antiquity is shown by the occurrence of a Sanskrit name.
Transfer: the Americas to India, at least

Time of transfer: before 1000 C.E.
Grade: B
Source: *Pennisetum americanum*
    Parotta 2001, 84-88. Sanskrit name given.

Pharbitis hederacea
Origin: the Americas
Summary: In India as a widely spread plant that yields a medicinal substance and has a Sanskrit name. It also was probably known in China.
Transfer: the Americas to Asia
Time of transfer: before 1000 C.E.
Grade: A
Sources: *Pharbitis hederacea* – Ivy-leaf, morning glory, (MOBOT and Kew. syn. *Ipomoea hederacea*)
    Safford 1905, 349. A twining plant. "The seeds are strongly purgative and in India are used as a drug under the name of *kaladana* (citing Trimen, Handbook: Flora of Ceylon, III, 212–3, 1885). The plant is probably of American origin."
    MOBOT 2003. Distribution (of herbarium specimens) (as *Ipomoea hederacea*) given as Bolivia, Brazil, Mexico, and the Bahamas.
    Chopra et al. 1956, 142. *Ipomoea hederacea*. Hin., Ben., and Bom.: *kaladana*. Sanskrit: *krishnabija*. Cultivated throughout India and also wild, up to 6000 ft.
    Bretschneider 1892, 349. Gives two Chinese characters as a name for *Pharbitis* which is referred to by Li Shizhen in the sixth century and is probably from a classic Chinese reference. The fruit includes a capsule containing seeds built like those of an elm tree, which the wind disperses (a short distance).

Phaseolus adenanthus
Origin: the Americas
Summary: Distribution in Hawaii and other Polynesian islands argues for an early voyage.
Transfer: the Americas to Hawaii and beyond
Time of transfer: centuries ago in order to explain pan-Polynesian spread
Grade: C
Source: *Phaseolus adenanthus* (syn. *truxillensis*) – a bean
    Hillebrand 1888, 104. *P. truxillensis*. A native probably of South America, but collected also in most Polynesian islands ... and in other tropical countries.

Phaseolus lunatus
Origin: the Americas
Summary: This fundamental American crop has been found in India (before 1600 B.C.E.) and also in China.
Transfer: the Americas to Asia
Time of transfer: before 1600 B.C.E.

Grade: A
Sources: *Phaseolus lunatus* – lima bean, sieva bean, butter bean
- Zeven and de Wet 1982, 174. Center of gene diversity: Central America and the Andes from Peru to Argentina. The large lima was first domesticated in the Andean highlands and then the small lima (*sieva*) may have arisen in the Pacific coastal foothills of Mexico. The small-seeded subspecies (ssp. *microsperma*, Sieva, or Small Lima) originated by natural selection and planting.
- J. Sauer 1993, 77. "The archaeological record strongly suggests independent domestication in Central America and northwestern South America."
- Pokharia and Saraswat 1999, 99. *Phaseolus*. "... beans of American origin have been encountered from proto-historic sites in peninsular India." *P. vulgaris* has been recorded from pre-Prabhas and Prabhas cultures at Prabhas Patan, Junagadh Dist., Gujarat, dated from 1800 B.C.E. to 600 C.E. (endnote 153). Also from Chalcolithic Inamgaon (about 1600 B.C.E.), and Pune Dist., Maharashtra (endnote 154), and from Neolithic Tekkalkota (C14: 1620±108 B.C.E.), Bellary Dist., Karnataka (endnote 155). *P. vulgaris, P. lunatus*, and the phasey bean have been recorded by Vishnu-Mittre, Sharma, and Chanchala (endnote 156) from deposits of Malwa and Jorwe cultures (1600–1000 B.C.E.) at Daimabad in Ahmednagar Dist., Maharashtra.
- Vishnu-Mittre, Sharma, and Chanchala 1986. *P. lunatus* found at the Diamabad site (1600–1000 B.C.E.).
- Brücher 1989, 91. *P. lunatus* L. has two agrotypes: var. *microcarpus* = sieva bean; var. *macrocarpus* is also lima bean.
- Pickersgill and Heiser 1977, 811. Includes large limas of South America and small sieva beans of Mesoamerica. Sievas found at Tamaulipas, Tehuacán Valley and Dzibilchaltun, Yucatan, between 1850–1150 BP.
- Chen Wenhua 1994, 59. He reports a find of lima beans in an archaeological site in Zhejiang, China.
- Chopra, et al. 1956, 189–90. Pun.: lobiya. Cultivated throughout India. Native of Brazil.
- Pullaiah 2002, I, 400. No Sanskrit names.
- Yarnell 1970, 225. Earliest remains, Peru: 3300 B.C.E.; Southern Mexico: 1400 BP; Northern Mexico: 1800 BP.
- Towle 1961, 52–3. She considers *P. lunatus* the same as *P. pallar* (sieva). 45. Discussing specimens found in Peru, Towle notes that Kaplan reported that *Canavalia* sp. was present with *Phaseolus lunatus* from the early pre-ceramic levels through those of the ceramic-bearing Cupisnique Period at Huaca Priéta. 54. Lima-shaped ideograms appear from Nazca, Paracas, and Tiahuanaco.
- Newcomb 1963, 38. C. Sauer's observation: *P. lunatus* raises a distribution question. Lima beans contain prussic acid. Old World types contain this acid, but few New World ones do except in the varieties found in the West Indies. Prussic acid content was evidently bred out under cultivation in the Americas. But around the Indian Ocean (Mauritius, Madagascar, Malaysia) dangerous types occur. Where did they come from and when?

Heyerdahl 1964. In 1950, J. Sauer pointed to certain very early genetic peculiarities of a race of lima beans of primitive characteristics long under cultivation in Indonesia and Indo-China. He says: "If, then, Southeastern Asia should prove to be a reservoir of the more primitive lima beans, long since extinct in Peru and Mexico, a further problem of the time and manner of trans-Pacific connection is raised." (Similar considerations relate to the peanut, of course.)
See also material under *P. vulgaris*, below

Phaseolus vulgaris
Origin: the Americas
Summary: Archaeologically attested in early Indian sites, and, on the basis of names, it was present in the Near East all the way back to Sumerian times and in India to a time when Sanskrit was active.
Transfer: the Americas to the Near East or India
Time of transfer: before 1600 B.C.E.
Grade: A
Sources: *Phaseolus vulgaris* – kidney bean
   J. Sauer 1993, 73. Vernacular names – common, kidney, navy, string, wax bean.
   Yen 1963, 112. Notes that at Huaca Priéta, Peru, Bird (1948) found seeds of *Phaseolus*, dated ca. 2578 to 2470 B.C.E. (calibrated, 3348–3057 B.C.E.).
   Roys 1931, 218. Mayan: "Buul. *Phaseolus vulgaris*, L. *Frijol amarillo*." *Buul* is a general term in Mayan for the kidney bean. (Cf. 'bean' (*Vicia faba*), Heb.: *pôl*, Arabic: *ful*.)
   Pickersgill and Heiser 1977, 810–11. Earliest *P. vulgaris* in Tamaulipas and Tehuacán, Mexico, domesticated from ca. 4000 B.C.E.
   Shady-Solis et al. 2001, 725. The phenomenal site of Caral in the Supe Valley of Peru, dated between 2627 and 2020 Cal B.C.E., yielded remains of *Phaseolus vulgaris*, among other domesticated plants.
   Martínez M. 1978, 113–5. This was possibly the most important crop at this (Chiapas) site (around the first century B.C.E.). Two (possibly three) specimens were recovered here, but both were burned sufficiently that species could not be established. Four beans are cultivated in Chiapas nowadays, plus numerous others wild. His specimen "*Phaseolus* 1" could be *P. vulgaris*, he suggests.
   Chopra et al. 1956, 190. Hin.: *bakla*; Pun.: *babr*. "Universally cultivated but not anywhere clearly known as a wild plant."
   Kramisch 1928, 50. Reads the kidney bean as present in an Indian text of the fifth century C.E.
   Thompson 1949, I, 416–436. Gives among Mesopotamian food-plants, "*F(aba) vulgaris* Mill. (Arab.: *ful*), as well as *Phaseolus vulgaris* L. (*lubiya ifranjiyah*), *fasulia*.
   Pokharia and Saraswat 1999, 99. *Phaseolus* "... beans of American origin have been encountered from proto-historic sites in peninsular India." *P. vulgaris* was recorded from pre-Prabhas and Prabhas cultures at Prabhas Patan, Junagadh Dist., Gujarat, dated from 1800 B.C.E. to 600 C.E. (see endnote 153). Also from Chalcolithic Inamgaon (about 1600 B.C.E.), and Pune

Dist., Maharashtra (see endnote 54), and from Neolithic Tekkalkota (C14 1620±108 B.C.E.), Bellary Dist., Karnataka (see endnote 155).

Vishnu-Mittre, Sharma, and Chanchala 1986, 600–3, 589. *P. vulgaris* specimens were identified from archaeological remains at the site of Diamabad, India, to phases dated 1400–1000 B.C.E.

Balfour 1871–1873, IV, 546. *P. vulgaris*, Linn., called in Eng., 'French bean,' 'kidney bean,' or 'haricot bean.' In Hindi: lobiya and *bakla*. "Native of Cabul and Kashmir, said to be a native of India."

Bretschneider 1892, 168. Gives a two-character Chinese name for *P. vulgaris* from a Japanese list (Matsumura). The name may or may not be of classic Chinese age.

Heyerdahl 1964, 130. In the last (nineteenth) century, Körnicke, in a paper on the home of the garden bean, pointed out that this crop was formerly generally accepted as having been cultivated in Europe by the ancient Greeks and Romans under the name of *Dolickos, Phaseolos*, etc. It was supposed that the New World bean owed its introduction to post-Columbian early Spaniards. So opinion remained until in 1880 the common bean was found in excavations at Ancón, Peru. ... But at that point in time pre-Columbian beans from Europe were no longer available for examination. So then it was supposed that Spaniards had taken the bean back to Europe from the Americas. More recently, Hutchison, Silow, and Stephens [1947] pointed out, with corroborative botanical evidence, that "*Phaseolus* beans indicate inter-hemispheric contact before Columbus." The same problem exists with *P. lunatus*, lima bean. They are in the earliest Chimu and Nazca graves. In 1950, J. Sauer pointed to certain very early genetic peculiarities of a race of lima beans of primitive characteristics long under cultivation in Indonesia and Indo-China and said: "If, then, Southeastern Asia should prove to be a reservoir of the more primitive lima beans, long since extinct in Peru and Mexico, a further problem of the time and manner of trans-Pacific connection is raised."

Yarnell 1970, 225. Earliest remains: Peru, 2500 BP; Southern Mexico, 1400 BP; Northern Mexico, 1800 BP.

Watt 1888–1893, VI, Part I, 194–5. Kidney bean. Botanists held for a long time that this was of Indian or Kashmir origin, but De Candolle proved this erroneous. He concluded that it had not been long cultivated in India, Southwestern Asia, or Egypt; it is not certain that it was known in Europe before the discovery of the Americas.

Levey 1973, 55 (see also Levey 1966, 16). "The medieval Arabic term for kidney bean [i.e., *P. vulgaris*,] is *lubiya*. It is *lubbu* in Akkadian and *LU.ÚB* in Sumerian. ... In Sanskrit and Hindustani, however, it is *simbi* and *sim* respectively ...."

Physalis lanceifolia
Origin: the Americas
Summary: The historical sources show this species' presence in India anciently where it received a Sanskrit name. It was also taken to the Marquesas from the Americas by voyagers before modern discovery.
>Case 1: Transfer: to Eastern Polynesia
>Time of transfer: pre-Columbian
>Grade: B-
>Case 2: Transfer: the Americas to India
>Time of transfer: one or two thousand years ago to account for multiple Sanskrit names
>Grade: B+

Sources: *Physalis lanceifolia* Nees – ground cherry, winter cherry (Kew. syn. lanceolata; MOBOT syn. angulata)
>Chopra et al. 1956, 191. Sanskrit: *rajaputrika*. Considered a native in the area of Southeast Europe to Japan (it was not an Asian native; naturalized in many parts of the world.)
>Torkelson 1999, 1808. Sanskrit: *rajaputrika*.
>Chopra et al. 1956, 192. Sanskrit: *lakshmipriya*. Grown in Indian gardens. [From] "Tropical America."
>Nadkarni 1914, 298. *Physalis indica* (no syn.). Eng.: winter cherry.
>Brown 1935, 257-8. Approximately 45 species of *Physalis* show a distribution centered in the Americas. Marquesan: *konini*. This species is a "Native of Tropical America; of early introduction in the Marquesas where the fragrant fruits are valued." ["Early introduction" sometimes means, in Brown's usage, aboriginal, although the meaning is not entirely clear here.] Used both cooked and uncooked as food.
>Bretschneider 1882, 32. Shen Nung, was traditionally an emperor of the eighth century B.C.E. who authored a famous classic of *materia medica* [although surely the author was not of that remote an age]. In the document attributed to him (31-2), as Bretschneider gives it, Shen Nung lists plants (for which European nomenclature is supplied by Chinese physicians who relate ancient plants with the names). One is *Physalis alkekengi*. From a description elsewhere in this Appendix, this is clearly the ground cherry (syn. *lanceifolia*?), commonly used for food (although *P. alkekengi* is not considered by modern botanists synonymous with *P. lanceifolia*.). 57–61. Li Shizhen authored a great sixth-century synthetic work on medicine, including much compiled older material, wherein he mentions several cultivars of American origin including *Solanum nigrum*, maize, *Portulacca (sic) oleracea*, and "Pumpkins," along with "*Physalis alkekengi*," giving ground for supposing them pre-European in China. He calls *P. alkekengi* (64) "the winter-cherry, *hung ku uiang*, 'red girl,'" on account of the red leafy bladder which encloses the ripe fruit.
>Bretschneider 1892, 45. Two names are given; one applies to a red fruit enclosed in a five-angled bladder resembling a lantern; this is the winter cherry, *P. alkekengi*, a common plant in North China, called also 'lantern plant' and 'red girl.' Another name is also given—for a common plant that

grows near dwelling places. "The fruit is a capsule (bladder) within which is a berry of a yellowish red colour."

Balfour 1871–1873, IV, 562. In India, *P. peruviana*, the winter-cherry, is commonly called Cape gooseberry or Brazil cherry [and is considered imported.]

Brücher 1989, 276. *Physalis philadelphica* Lam., husk tomato, tomatillo, miltomate. Indians of present Guatemala/Honduras used the wild-growing species *P. philadelphica* Lam., which has relatively large fruits, and have transformed it into a garden crop. Similar importance was given to *P. pubescens* L. (called 'tomatillo'), which after the Spanish invasion was spread over the whole pantropic belt. *Physalis* species spread also to Asia and Africa.

Hernandez 1942–1946 [before 1580], I, 283. His "*tomatl de cascabel*," or *ayacachtomatl*, the editors (who prepared the Hernandez 1942 edition) read as a species of *Solanum* or *Physalis*. Hernandez (III, 699–715) identifies a dozen of the plants pictured under one or another *tomatl*. They include *miltomatl, P. philadelphica, xitomame* is what is now known as *jitomates*, that is, *Lycopersicon esculentum* Mill. "With the name of tomame are known several species of *Physalis*." *P. peruviana, P. pubescens*. The commenting editors note that *P. pubescens* is found in both India and Tropical America. According to Sturtevant, *miltomatl*, the species figured by Hernandez would be *P. philadelphica*. [Because of uncertainties in taxonomy we cannot be certain from Hernandez himself which species of *Physalis* should be compared with which species found in Asia, but regardless of the obscurities of the formal taxonomy, the same fruit seems to be present in both hemispheres.]

Roys 1931, 272. *Physalis pubescens* L. (Standl.). Ground-cherry. *P. angula* L, *farolitos*. Ground-cherry. Mayan, *ppac-can*, according to the Pío Perez dictionary: "A sort of wild tomato ... its calyx almost covers the oval fruit, so that the latter rests, as it were, in a capsule."

Gunther 1934, 468–71. He reads a plant described by Dioscorides (first century C.E.) as *Physalis minima* ('husk tomato').

See also the material under *Physalis peruviana*.

[This section shows that while early references to species of *Physalis* in Asia are confused, quite surely this one – *P. lanceifolia* – or a closely-related American species, was shared by India and the Americas, and likely more than one species.]

Physalis peruviana
Origin: the Americas
Summary: This species was present at least in Hawaii, the Marquesas, and Easter Island, that is, throughout eastern Polynesia, as well as, apparently, India, and perhaps in more of Asia. The occurrence of a Sanskrit name clearly establishes the age of the 'ground cherry' on the western side of the Pacific. Furthermore, this

species typically grows only in areas disturbed by human cultivation, reassuring us that it did not spread by purely natural forces.

    Case 1: Transfer: the Americas to India
    Time of transfer: 1000 to 2000 years ago, while Sanskrit was still a living language
    Grade: B+
    Case 2: Transfer: the Americas to eastern Polynesia
    Time of transfer: pre-Columbian
    Grade: B

Sources: *Physalis peruviana* – husk tomato

    Chopra et al. 1956, 191. Sanskrit: *rajaputrika*. Said to be native to the area from Southeast Europe to Japan; naturalized in many parts of the world. [Actually, this *Physalis* was not an Old World native; see Brücher. The old notion of a Eurasian origin that Chopra et al. still reflect suggests the degree of the species' naturalization in Asia.]

    Torkelson 1999, 1808. Sanskrit: *rajaputrika*.

    Zeven and de Wet 1982, 181. Known as Cape gooseberry. The Andes is the center of genetic diversity. Often observed as a weed or semi-wild.

    Brücher 1989, 275–7. Most *Physalis* species (probably there are 90 taxa in all) are American, with a principal center in Mexico and a dozen taxa in South America. Only a few representatives are found in the Old World.

    Heyerdahl 1964, 126. When first recorded by Europeans, the plants of Easter I. included a small husk-tomato. It was formerly widespread in eastern Polynesia. On Easter I. and in the Marquesas, it is nearly extinct, although occasionally found growing wild in old abandoned habitation sites. Also in Hawaii, where Hillebrand in 1888 considered it part of "the important American element of the Andean regions which is apparent in the Hawaiian flora."

    Heyerdahl 1996. "Shiny red husk-tomatoes, the size of big berries," were identified in the Marquesas by Brown (1935) and considered to have come from the Americas in aboriginal times. Heyerdahl and his bride in 1939 discovered the same plant feral on old habitation sites on Fatu Hiva. It was found also on Easter Island and Hawaii. He found the same husk-tomatoes growing on the site of the Tucumé pyramids in Peru.

    Hillebrand 1888, 310. Considers it of pre-Cook age in Hawaii. Native of the Americas, but common in Hawaii in the mountains.

    Dressler 1953, 144. The cultivated *Physalis* of the Guatemalan highlands is usually referred to as *P. pubescens*, but may be *P. ixocarpa* (syn. *philadelphica*) or some other species.

    Bailey 1935, III, 2608. Husk tomato. Ground cherry. Genus contains probably 75 species, mostly American, only a few of which are in Europe and Asia. Species are variable and confusing to the systemist. 2609. *P. ixocarpa*. In Mexico, fruits used for chili sauce, "usually under the name of 'tomatoes.'" "The Mexican forms are [taxonomically] confused." *P. peruviana*, Linn. Cape Gooseberry.

Balfour 1871-1873, IV, 561. Calls *P. alkekengi*, winter cherry, "a native of Europe," and Japan. 562. *P. peruviana* is in India; the winter-cherry plant, commonly called Cape gooseberry or Brazil cherry.

Plumeria rubra
Origin: the Americas
Summary: The decorative flower is much used in Oceania. It is specifically noted by Kelley on Rotuma, an island in the Fiji group whose language is considered an early relative of Polynesian.
    Case 1: Transfer: the Americas to Oceania and perhaps Asia
    Time of transfer: pre-Columbian
    Grade: B
    Case 2: Transfer: the Americas to India
    Time of transfer: by 1000 C.E.
    Grade: B
Sources: *Plumeria rubra* – frangipanni
- Lundell 1938, 53. Commonly planted in dooryards and around churches in the Maya area. In religious celebrations and during other festivals, the red, white, and yellow flowers of the nicte are strung on cords as decorations.
- Kelley 1957, 197-201. The term *pua* is used on Rotuma Island in the Fiji group for *Plumeria* sp., while *puwa* occurs among the Huichol on the west coast of Mexico apparently as the name of the same plant. Kelley discusses the possibility from a linguistic perspective, reviewing what Merrill (1937) says (critically) on the topic. Bakhuizen van den Brink identified a 12th-century bas-relief representation of a blossom of this species, from Borobudur, Java, as showing *Plumeria acuminata*, a variety of *P. rubra*, although Merrill considered the representation too stylized to be meaningful as to genus and species. *P. acuminata* is widespread in India as a temple flower, but its antiquity there is in question. [But that is hardly in question any longer, in light of the Sanskrit names.]
- Pullaiah 2002, II, 419. A Sanskrit name for this plant is *ksirachampaka*.
- Parotta 2002, 95. *P. acuminata* is a variety of *P. rubra*. In India it is planted near temples. It is a native of tropical Central America. Sanskrit: *devaganagalu*, *kshira*, and four others.
- Lancaster 1965, 14. A tree whose sacred flowers are of the champa class and so can be substituted for ritual purposes with any of 17 other species. [The logical implication is that all the 'sacred plants of the Hindus' discussed by Lancaster must have been present in India for a substantial period of time to have achieved this degree of sacredness. It is difficult to believe that this could have happened in the few centuries since the Portuguese began visiting.]

Polianthes tuberosa
Origin: the Americas
Summary: Lancaster 1965 includes it with other American species of flowers as temple-associated in India.
Transfer: the Americas to India

Grade: incomplete
Sources: *Polianthes tuberosa*
    Lancaster 1965, 45. Lists it as one of the species whose flowers are sacred in India. [The logical implication is that all the 'sacred plants of the Hindus' discussed by Lancaster must have been present in India for a substantial period of time to have achieved such a degree of sacredness. It is difficult to believe that this could have happened in the few centuries since the Portuguese began visiting.]

Polygonum acuminatum
Origin: South America
Summary: The technical work by Skottsberg and later by Dumont et al. establish a firm basis for interpreting the co-occurrence on Easter Island as due to voyagers.
Transfer: to Easter Island
Time of transfer: 13th century
Grade: A
Sources: *Polygonum acuminatum* – Easter Island: *tavari*
    Heyerdahl 1961, 26. Mixed with *totora*, this aquatic plant on Easter I. forms a thick floating bog covering crater lakes Rano Kao and Rano Aroi. *P. acuminatum* is used for medical purposes here as it is in the Titicaca basin. It is an American plant. Skottsberg (1957, 3) considered that human introduction of both *totora* and *tavari* was likely. Neither species occurs elsewhere in Polynesia.
    Heyerdahl 1964, 126. Pollen from borings analyzed by Selling showed that *Polygonum* pollen "suddenly" began to be deposited in the crater lakes during the earliest human settlement period. (Cf. now Dumont et al. 1998 for later data.)
    Skottsberg 1920, I, 412. Because of distances to adjacent Polynesian groups and to South America, "The presence of a neo-tropical element (on Juan Fernandez and Easter Island) is surprising." *Scirpus riparius* and *Polygonum acuminatum* are American. Their mode of occurrence and ecology oblige us to regard them as truly indigenous, "unless they have been intentionally introduced in prehistoric time during one of the mythical cruises which, according to Heyerdahl, put Easter Island in contact with Peru. A direct transport of seeds across the ocean without man's assistance is difficult to imagine ...." 425. Contrarily, for the Marquesas "there is no neo-tropical element in spite of the prevailing direction of winds and currents," as far as he notes.
    Dumont et al. 1998. They report analysis of a core from Rano Raraku crater lake on Easter Island. Five (vertical) zones are identified. The last three of these are separated by waves of immigration. They argue that a first, or South American, wave, dated to the second half of the fourth century by radioactive dating, may represent a visit by South American Indians. 410. They found the top 85 cm. of sediment to include *Schoenoplectus californicus* and *Polygonum acuminatum*. Because of the synchronous appearance of multiple floral taxa, they rule out passive introduction. (418. "... the island is so remote, and such a small target, that mechanisms of passive dispersal

were ineffective for populating it" [botanically]). Besides, there are no freshwater birds on the island. "We therefore propose that humans introduced these neo-tropical biota, in one single event .... The most parsimonious explanation for the South American wave, which clearly predates the arrival of the Europeans, might be an introduction by seafaring people from Peru or Chile." Polynesians presumably [also] reached Easter Island during the fifteenth century C.E.

Portulaca oleracea
Origin: the Americas
Summary: Presence widely in the Old World in a naturalized condition combined with Sanskrit names and mention in Egyptian texts establishes the antiquity of the species in Asia and Europe.
Transfer: the Americas to East Asia
Time of transfer: while Sanskrit was an active language.
Grade: A
Sources: *Portulaca oleracea* – purslane (Kew. (Africa, India, southern China, West. U.S., Mexico, Guatemala, Peru, Brazil, Marquesas, Belize, Nicaragua)).
 Watt 1892, VI, Part I, 329–30. A number of Sanskrit names are given. De Candolle [mistakenly] thought it indigenous to the region from the Western Himalaya to the south of Russia and Greece.
 Chopra et al. 1956, 202. Sanskrit: *lonika*. Grows "all over India."
 Chopra et al. 1958, 521–3. Sanskrit: *mansala*. Cultivated and naturalized all over India.
 Pullaiah 2002, II, 426. Sanskrit: *ghotika, lonika*. Medicinal uses.
 Torkelson 1999, 1818. Sanskrit: *lonika*
 Parotta, 2001, 598. Sanskrit: *brhalloni, ghotika, loni, lonika, lunia*
 Hillebrand 1888, 39. Pigweed. Genus of 16 species, chiefly belonging to Tropical America.
 Burkill 1966, II, 1832–3. Purslane is found throughout warmer parts of the world; [the genus is] chiefly in the Americas. A vegetable from time immemorial. Appears mentioned in Egyptian texts of Pharaonic times.
 Bailey 1935, III, 766. Purslane, pusley. About 40 species in the genus in the tropical and temperate regions, mostly American. *P. oleracea* is probably native to the southwestern parts of the U.S. Gray and Trumbull (1883) argued for the nativity of purslane in North America.
 Bretschneider 1882, 49–53. From a treatise, <u>Kiu Huang Pen Ts'ao</u>, by Chou Ting Wang, an imperial prince under the first Ming Emperor (prince died in 1425). He had seen the following plant in Honan province: *Portulacca* (sic) *oleracea*. 57–61. The famous Chinese volume of materia medica, <u>Pen Ts'ao Kang Mu</u>, first published in 1590, mentions *Portulacca* (sic) *oleracea*, from which it can be inferred that the plant was present in pre-European times.
 Bretschneider 1892, 67. A (Chinese) source shows two figures, one representing an amaranth and the other *Portulacca* (sic) *oleracea*.
 Balfour 1871–1873, IV, 660. For this he gives English: common, or small, purslane; Sanskrit: *lonika*, or *loonia*. Common in India and eaten by the

Hindus. A common weed but cultivated by the market gardeners. Used as spinach and in curries.

Roys 1931, 220. Span.: *verdolaga*; Mayan: *cabal-chum*. The plant is usually called *xucul* in Mayan. 296. *Xucul*, or *H-xucal*, is the name for *P. oleracea*.

Psidium guajava
Origin: Tropical America
Summary: A number of Sanskrit names (as well as obviously cognate Arabic and Persian names) join with widespread naturalization of the plant and use of the fruit in South Asia to assure us that it was not a modern introduction. Presence of the tree in the Marquesas may also indicate an oceanic transfer.
    Case 1: Transfer: Asia from the Americas
    Time of transfer: at least 2000 years ago
    Grade: A
    Case 2: Transfer: Marquesas from the Americas
    Time of transfer: pre-Columbian
    Grade: C
Sources: *Psidium guajava* – guava

    Shady Solís et al. 2001, 725. The phenomenal site of Caral in the Supe Valley of Peru, dated between 2627 and 2020 B.C.E. calibrated, has yielded remains of guava (*Psidium guajava*), among other domesticated plants.

    Towle 1961, 73. An oblong, compressed fruit of *P. guajava* was recovered from Ancón cemetery (B.C.E. date). Whole, globular fruits were found in Gallinazo and Mochica cultural levels. Also depicted on Early Nazca embroidery.

    Tozzer 1941, 199. "There is a fruit which the Spaniards have brought [to Yucatan], good to eat and healthy, which they call *guayabas*." Footnote 1088: "*Psidium Guajava* L." [Despite Landa's statement, the plant is native to the Americas.]

    Roys, 1931, 231. Mayan:"*Chac-pichi*. Probably *Psidium guajava* L. Guava." 276. "*Pichi. Psidium guajava* L. *Guayabo*, Guava."

    Brown 1935, 200. More than 100 species of this genus are natives of Tropical America. Two horticultural varieties of the guava are present in the Marquesas. One is probably of aboriginal introduction. The other is of recent introduction.

    Watt (1892, VI, Part I, 351–3) gives Sanskrit, Arabic, and Persian names, all closely related (*amrud*). Native to the Americas, now naturalized and largely cultivated throughout India.

    Bailey 1935, 2847. Genus entirely native to the Americas. It has become naturalized in many parts of Asia and Africa. The genus is somewhat confused and in need of further study. A large number of species doubtless exist in South and Central America that have not as yet been described.

    Balfour 1871–1873, IV, 694–5. *P. pomiferum*, Linn. Eng.: red guava. No Sanskrit name is listed by him. "The guava tree of the W. Indies, Mexico, and America, is cultivated throughout the E. Indies." *P. pyriferum*, Linn., Roxb.

syn. *Guava pyriformis*, Gaertn. Eng.: white guava. Grows all over British India and all southern Asia. Probably came through the Portuguese.

Chopra et al. 1956, 205–6. Sanskrit: *mansala*. "Cultivated and naturalized throughout India."

Int. Lib. Assoc. 1996, 571. Sanskrit: *mansala*.

Nadkarni 1914, 320. *Psidium guayava* (sic). Sanskrit: *péràlà*. Hin.: *amrút*

Chopra et al. 1958, 683. Sanskrit: *amruta-phalam*; Hind.: *Amrut*. Arab.: *amrud*. Found throughout India for its fruit.

Pullaiah 2002, II, 433. Sanskrit: *perukah, mansala*. Medicinal uses.

Aiyer 1956, 36. Mentioned in the <u>Charaka Samhita</u>, no later than the fourth century C.E., and it probably was present considerably earlier. This despite the belief common among scientists that the plant was introduced to India by the Portuguese.

Sharma and Dash 1983, 518. The paravata fruit of the <u>Caraka Samhita</u> text is the guava, *Psidium guajava*.

Saccharum officinarum
Origin: Old World
Summary: Some sources from the period of exploration and colonization of South America identified sugarcane as present and later the cane in South America hybridized with imported sugar cane. Most botanists who deny that sugarcane was present assume that another plant, perhaps an unusual variety of maize, was what was seen. But maize was so well known to Spanish explorers that mistaking corn for cane does not seem possible.
Transfer: Old World across either ocean
Time of transfer: pre-Columbian.
Grade: B
Sources: *Saccharum officinarum* – sugarcane

Cook 1904. Sugarcane, he claims, was cultivated in the islands of the Pacific, coastal Asia, and America. No specific data.

Newcomb 1963, 62–3. Pigafetta (Magellan expedition) reported *caña dolce* at Guam, in the Philippines and in Brazil. [Having seen it and apparently identified it correctly in the Pacific islands it cannot be imagined that they were mistaken as to what they had seen and recorded in Brazil.] (This Pigafetta eye-witness evidence is explained away by disbelievers as a reference to a form of sweet maize in the Rio Loa area.) Early Portuguese accounts exist telling of sugarcane that was true cane and which they themselves had not introduced. Labat around 1700 in Martinique spoke of what was grown there as Carib cane, not brought from Europe. In the seventeenth century, the English on Barbados and St. Kitts found wild sugarcane growing. *Uba*, cane, from the Tupi-Guaraní word for the wild cane, proved resistant to a troublesome mosaic disease that attacked the *S. officinarum* that had been brought by the Europeans. The latter was hybridized with uba from Brazil and Paraguay to produce a variety that overcame the disease.

Lunde 1992, 50–55. Two plants that definitely were shared between the hemispheres were the coconut and sugarcane (found by the Portuguese on coastal Brazil).

Sagittaria sagittifolia
Origin: Asia
Summary: Carl Sauer considered this Asian plant to have been present in the Americas, as in China. Further information is needed.
Grade: incomplete
Sources: *Sagittaria sagittifolia* – wapatoo
    Sauer 1969, 56. One of a group of Asiatic plants found in the Americas associated with man. Found also in China. Its possible transmission should be examined further.
    Balfour 1871–1873, V, 46. Extensively cultivated among the Chinese, not for its beauty but for the sake of its edible rhizome, which fixes itself in the solid earth below the mud and constitutes an article of food.

Salvia coccinea
Origin: the Americas
Summary: Its ancient presence in India is shown by the presence of a Sanskrit name. Brown apparently also considered the plant in the Marquesas to be pre-Columbian; if so, it might have arrived there either from the west or directly from its native America. In either situation, a voyage or voyages were made involving the Americas.
    Case 1: Transfer: the Americas to Asia
    Time of transfer: no later than ca. 1000 C.E.
    Grade: C
    Case 2: Transfer: the Americas to Marquesas Islands
    Time of transfer: pre-Columbian
    Grade: B-
Sources: *Salvia coccinea* – scarlet salvia, cardinal sage
    Brown 1935, 252. Native of the West Indies and Tropical America; probably of early introduction in the Marquesas, where it has become thoroughly naturalized at middle and low altitudes.
    Bailey 1935, III, 3064. In the West Indies and Tropical America and occasionally escaped in India and Australia.
    Roys 1931, 232. Mayan: *chac-tzitz* = "*Salvia coccinea* Juss." "Cultivated under the names of scarlet sage and salvia." Prescribed for decayed tooth.
    Watson 1868, 489, 201. Sanskrit: *rosea*.
    Schoenhals 1988, 159. Eng.: cardinal sage.

Salvia occidentalis
Origin: the Americas
Summary: Brown's description of the extent of its naturalization and spread in the Marquesas Islands suggests its pre-Columbian presence.
Grade: C
Sources: *Salvia occidentalis* Swartz – a salvia

Brown 1935, 253. Is a native of the West Indies and Tropical America; probably of early introduction in the Marquesas, where it has become established at altitudes from 200–600 m.

Burkill 1979, II. *S. occidentalis* Swartz is another American plant that is established in Java, where it has been tried as a cover crop.

MOBOT 2003. Distribution: Middle and South America

Sapindus saponaria
Origin: the Americas
Summary: The berries serve as soap as well as a fish poison and also medicine for some ailments. Two regional variants have long been in India; they are both synonymous with *S. saponaria*. The species is present in the Marquesas and on Easter Island, and perhaps elsewhere in the Pacific. Sanskrit names for each of the differentiated varieties that characterize south and north India indicate the age of the tree on the subcontinent. (MOBOT does not make the Indian soapberry trees synonymous with *S. saponaria*, but their functions are identical; *Index Kewensis* does make them synonymous.)

    Case 1: Transfer: the Americas to Asia
    Time of transfer: over 2000 years ago
    Grade: B
    Case 2: Transfer: the Americas to Eastern Polynesia
    Time of transfer: pre-Columbian
    Grade: B+

Sources: *Sapindus saponaria* – soapberry (Kew. syn. *S. mukorossi* (Asia trop.); and *S. trifoliatus*)

Zeven and de Wet 1982, 178. Tropical America is center of maximum gene diversity.

Nadkarni 1914, 350. *Sapinda* (sic) *trifoliatus* (syn. *S. emarginatus*). Sanskrit: *phenila*. Eng.: soap-nut tree. Common in Southern India and cultivated in Bengal. *S. mukorossi* (syn. *S. detergens*) is the soap-nut tree of North India.

Pullaiah 2002, II, 456. *Sapindus emarginatus* (syn. *trifoliatus*). Sanskrit: *arishta*. 457. *Sapindus mukorossi*. Sanskrit: *urista, phenile*, the soap-nut tree of Northern India.

Watt 1889, VI, Part II, 468. He lists *Sapindus mukorossi*, Gaertn., the soap-nut tree of North India. Distributed also in China and Japan. Original home not clear. Separately, he gives *S. trifoliatus*, Linn. The soap-nut tree of South India. Cultivated in Bengal, South India, and Ceylon. Used medicinally by Hindus "from a very early period."

Int. Lib. Assoc. 1996, 572. *Sapindus trifoliatus* L. var. emarginatus (syn. *Sapindus emarginatus*), Sanskrit: *arishta*. *S. mukorosi*, Sanskrit: *urista*.

Brown 1935, 160–1. The Marquesas plant compares closely with the Society Islands version. Marquesan name: *kokuu*. Juice from leaves and fruit treats skin diseases. Endemic in the Marquesas.

Langdon and Tryon 1983, 43. Rapanui: *mari, kuru*, soapberry. Marquesas: *ko/ku?u*, soapberry. The 60 or so species of *Sapindus* are widely distributed in the tropics, but are best represented in the Americas, citing Macmillan Brown (1935). A variety of *Sapindus saponaria* occurs in Hawaii, where it is

called *a?e*. That variety is not found elsewhere in Polynesia. This
information in Langdon and Tryon is in a section entitled "Words
confined to RAP[anui] and the Marquesic languages, that is, words that
occur in extreme eastern Polynesia where the plant may have arrived from
the Americas." In the Casma Valley of northern Peru, it has been found in
middens with *Capsicum*, cotton, and the gourd, the middens dating to 1785
B.C.E. (see Ugent et al. 1986). "Well-represented in the Americas"
(Langdon 1988, 334).

Quigley 1956, 513. "The evidence seems clearly to show that the fish
poisoning trait did not come to the New World by way of Bering Strait."
520. Beyond the *Tephrosia* species pantropical plants of other genera which
are recorded as piscicides in at least part of their range [include] ...

Sapindus saponaria L.

McBryde 1945, 152. Much used in Guatemala for soap.

Tozzer 1941, 197. Landa reports a "small fruit ... and with the rind they wash
their clothes as with soap, and thus it lathers like it." Footnote 1060.
"*Sapindus saponaria* L."

Hernandez 1943 [by 1580], II, 529–30. His *charapu* is identified as *S. saponaria*,
from Veracruz, Oaxaca, Durango, and Tamaulipas, Mexico.

Roys 1931, 309. "*Zihom*, or *Zihum*. Probably *Sapindus saponaria*, L., soapberry."
A tree standing sometimes 50 feet high, bearing a berry acting like soap.

Heyerdahl 1963b, 31. Easter Island has this plant which served as a
constringent medicine and as soap. Knoche (1925, 102–23) lists it as being
at home in the American tropics.

Towle 1961, 62–3. A small tree, four to ten meters in height. Berries contain
the glucoside saponin, which yields a soapy lather in water and forms an
emulsion with fats and oils. Specimens quite widely known
archaeologically

Schoenoplectus californicus
Origin: the Americas
Summary: Totora (a sedge) has many uses that are similar on the coasts, in Andean
lakes, and at least on Easter Island and Hawaii.
Transfer: the Americas to eastern Polynesia
Time of transfer: by 1500 C.E.
Grade: A
Sources: *Schoenoplectus californicus* – bulrush, sedge, totora (Kew. *Scirpus californicus*;
syn. *riparius*; syn. *validus*; syn. *lacustris*; syn. *totora*)

Langdon 1988, 330, 334. While unknown in western Polynesia, it is found on
Easter I. and in Hawaii with a related name in the two places (suggesting a
single transfer to one or the other island group followed by diffusion to
the other).

Langdon and Tryon 1983, 43. Called in Rapanui: *nga?atu*. Found in the
Americas from California to Tierra del Fuego. Used on Easter Island
(Rapanui) to cover huts and to make sleeping mats, baskets, floats, and
boats. Cf. Hawaiian *nānaku* for the same plant.

Skottsberg 1920, 412. Because of distances to adjacent Polynesian groups and to South America, "The presence of a [i.e., this] neo-tropical element [in the flora] is surprising." *Scirpus riparius* and *Polygonum acuminatum* remain American. Their mode of occurrence and ecology oblige us to regard them as truly indigenous, "unless they have been intentionally introduced in prehistoric time during one of the mythical cruises which, according to Heyerdahl, put Easter Island in contact with Peru. A direct transport of seeds across the ocean without man's assistance is difficult to imagine ...."

Mellén B.1986, 135. *S. riparius*, the totora, was called *ngaátu*, and abounds in the craters. It is very old if not indigenous, and was widely used in building, etc.

Heyerdahl 1961, 23–5. Skottsberg studied the wild plants of Easter Island in 1917 and 1956. He said there were only 31 wild flowering plants, and some ferns and mosses, reported from Easter I. Of those, 11 were pantropical and could be seaborne by natural means from either direction. The remaining 20 species are in part dependent on human aid for their spread to this area. The presence of American plants among the 20 was surprising to him. The most unexpected were the two aquatic phanerogams growing in the fresh water of the three Easter Island crater lakes: *Scirpus riparius* and *Polygonum acuminatum*. They are at home in Andean lakes and in irrigated swamps on the desert coast of Peru and Chile. *Scirpus riparius*, the totora reed, was the most important wild plant in the economy of Easter I. culture. The 1770 Gonzalez expedition from Peru identified the totora as the same species as the reed grown in Callao, Peru, and used by native Peruvians to make mats. According to native tradition (on Rapanui), this reed was brought by early ancestors of the Easter Islanders and planted in the deep cauldron of Rano Kao [volcano]. 26. The pre-European presence of the plant is verified by a specimen found in a datable tomb in Ahu Tepeu. Initially described as a distinct variety, Skottsberg (1956, 407) eventually concluded that it does not deserve to be distinguished as a separate variety since it is identifiable with the American species.

Towle 1961, 26–27. She gives the species as *S. tatora*, not totora. The rhyzomes are used for food in Peru, in addition to use for cordage, baskets, etc. Closely related to *S. californicus* [now considered synonymous], it is widely distributed. Some botanists consider the two synonymous. The totora of Lake Titicaca is used to construct the famous reed boats, or 'balsas,' made and used by Aymara Indians on the Lake. Yacovleff and Herrera say that root-stocks of *S. riparius* are used for food, and the canes and leaves are also used in various ways. Archaeological specimens in Peru have been found as early as the Gallinazo period (early centuries C.E.) as well as at Paracas Cavernas (Formative, perhaps first half of first millennium B.C.E.).

Gorner 1980, 19–22. A lengthy quotation from Heiser claims that he has demonstrated that the totora reed has seeds and that birds carry the seed (the plant is known to grow on uninhabited Pacific islands). [According to

Dumont et al. , there are no freshwater birds on Easter Island, hence Heiser's claim is impossible to accept in regard to that island.]

Heiser (1985, Chapter 2) reports his extensive pursuit of the origin of the totora reed, proposed by Heyerdahl to have been transported from South America to Easter Island. After reporting a great deal of information from his field and lab studies of the plant, he concludes that nothing rules out Heyerdahl's proposal, although Heiser prefers a hypothesis of introduction to Easter Island by birds, without explaining his reasons.

Dumont et al. 1998. They report analysis of a core from Rano Raraku a crater lake on Easter Island. Five (vertical) zones are identified. The last three of these are separated by waves of immigration. They argue that a first, or South American, wave, dated to the second half of the fourth century by radioactive dating, may represent a visit by South American Indians. 410. They found the top 85 cm. of sediment to include *Schoenoplectus californicus* and *Polygonum acuminatum*. Because of the synchronous appearance of multiple floral taxa, they rule out passive introduction. (418 "... the island is so remote, and such a small target, that mechanisms of passive dispersal were ineffective for populating it" [botanically]). Besides, there are no freshwater birds on the island. "We therefore propose that humans introduced these neo-tropical biota, in one single event. ... The most parsimonious explanation for the South American wave, which clearly predates the arrival of the Europeans, might be an introduction by seafaring people from Peru or Chile." Polynesians [also] presumably reached Easter Island during the fifth century C.E.

Sesamum orientale
Origin: Old World
Summary: Roys' Mayan name for this Old World species implies that the species was present and cultivated at the time of the Spanish Conquest. There is a puzzle here that needs to be elucidated by more research.
Grade: incomplete
Sources: *Sesamum orientale* – sesame
  Roys 1931, 309. S. orientale; Mayan, zicil-puuz
  Miranda 1952–53, 2a parte, 183. The plant was found in Chiapas in field survey. *Sesamum orientale* L. *ajonjolí.*

Sisyrhynchium acre
Origin: the Americas
Summary: It could not have drifted by sea when it grew so far above sea level. Native use hints at a pre-Columbian age. Further study is necessary.
Transfer: Hawaii from the Americas
Time of transfer: pre-Columbian
Grade: C
Source: *Sisyrhynchium acre* Mann. – called 'a grass' in English, although it is not so botanically (Kew. *Sisyrinchium*, with an 'i' not a 'y' in third syllable; (Hawaii)).
  Hillebrand 1888, 436–7. This genus includes about 50 species, all except the present one are natives of temperate and tropical America. Found on high

mountains of Hawaii and Maui from 3500 ft. upward. Natives use the juice to give a blue stain to their tattoo-marks. [At such altitudes, ocean drift would be an impossible mechanism for transfer.]

Sisyrhynchium angustifolium
Origin: North America
Summary: This plant has been found in Greenland at former Norse sites; Iverson believes that no other explanation for its presence will do than Norse transfer.
Transfer: Newfoundland to Greenland
Time of transfer: ca. 1000 C.E.
Grade: B
Sources: *Sisyrhynchium angustifolium* – blue-eyed 'grass' (but not of the grass family)
  Faeggri 1964, 344–51. This plant was found on the site of the Old Norse settlement of Vestribygd in southwestern Greenland. Although considered by some biologists to have survived the glacial period in Greenland, it is more likely to have been transplanted from Vinland by visiting Norsemen.
  Polunin 1960, 181. In 1936 in southwestern Greenland, he noted living descendants of this plant that had evidently been introduced from North America by Norsemen. (The author apparently never published further on this topic.)
  Thorarinsson 1942, 45–6. Of the 6 plant species that can fairly surely be assumed to have been transported to Greenland by the Norse, there are 5 on North America's Atlantic coast, and the idea can't be excluded that some of these species were even brought there by the Norse. One has, as well, to reckon with the possibility that the plants were transported from North America to Greenland in the same way. In 1932, the Danish botanist J. Iversen found, in a now inaccessible place by Godthaab's fjord in West Greenland and near to the remains of an old Norse settlement, a North American plant, *S. angustifolium*, whose nearest place of discovery lies on Newfoundland's west coast and west of St. Lawrence Bay. In 1937, Iversen and Troels-Smith found this species in three new locales in the West District, all close to the remains of old Norse settlements. Iversen rejects the idea that this species could be an interglacial relic on Greenland, or that it could have been brought there by modern people. He finds no plausible explanation for this appearance other than that it was transported there from North America by Norsemen.
[Note that these sources fail to give the names of the other four species of plants Iverson refers to. Potentially, those four would further support the case for a voyaging transfer of *S. angustifolium* as part of a complex of transported plants.]

Smilax sp.
Origin: Central America
Summary: The sources show a cacophony of species, one or more of which were recognized by the early Spaniards as common to Central America and the Old World, although precise species identification in older sources poses some problem.

Transfer: Central America to Eurasia
Time of transfer: by the time of Dioscorides and the active use of Sanskrit
Grade: B
Sources: *Smilax* sp. – sarsparilla

>Torkelson 1999, 1843. Gives the Sanskrit name *chobachini* for *Smilax glabra*, although we do not know that that specific species occurred in the Americas.
>
>Hawkes 1998, 157. Sarsparilla, *Smilax ornata*. This is a medicinal plant from the lowland forests of Central America. According to Woodward (1971), it had arrived in Europe by the 1690s. By habit, it is a climber in tropical forests.
>
>Tozzer 1941, 195. "In the region of Bacalar there is sarsaparilla." Note 1042. "This is a *Smilax*, in Maya, *am-ak*." "If Landa means here that this is the Bacalar sarsaparilla, we would find the Maya equvalent, *x-co-ceh*, or *x-co-ceh-ak*. Standley identifies this as *Smilax mexicana* Geseb., probably *Smilax aristolochaefolia* Mill."
>
>Roys 1931, 215. Mayan, *amak*, is a *Smilax* sp. that resembles *S. mexicana*. Dondé, the Yucatecan botanist, has been quoted as stating that the *am-ak* is a variety of sarsparilla. 225–6. Mayan: *x-co-ceh*, or *x-co-ceh-ak*. 226.
>
>Chopra et al. 1958, 187–8. Sarsaparilla is obtained from *Smilax ornata*, a climbing plant indigenous to Costa Rica, and from other similar species found in Central America. It is commonly known as Jamaica sarsparilla because it was formerly exported from Jamaica to various countries. *S. officinalis* comes from Honduras, but *S. ornata* is considered to be the best commercially.
>
>The important varieties of sarsparilla and their sources as given in the U.S. Pharm. XIV (1950) are as follows (as reported by Chopra): Mexican source: *Smilax aristolochiaefolia*; Honduras source: *Smilax regelii*; Ecuadorian source: *Smilax febrifuga*; Central American source (the Costa Rican or Jamaican variety): from undetermined spp.
>
>Hernandez 1946, III, 758–69. A number of species, or varieties, of *Smilax*, 'sarsparilla,' are discussed based on H.'s drawings and descriptions. One is *chiquimecatl*, or *pahuatlanense*. This is a species of *Smilax* that Spaniards commonly call *zarza parrilla*. Roots are medically efficacious. Under *mecapatli o zarzaparrilla*, the commentaters (editors of the Hernandez edition) observed: "Thus, the Mexicans call that famous medicine what our compatriots call zarzaparrilla, and of which are found in New Spain quite a few varieties." Hernandez wrote, "I first want to describe that species that in Spain and principally in Andalucia is found in valleys and mountains, classified by the pharmaceuticalists and botanical specialists as the *Smilax ásper* described by Dioscorides, and (which is) found by me not far from the city of Mexico …." "That this is a species of zarzaparrilla (although the Spaniards who haven't come to these lands can hardly believe it), no one can doubt …." The editors who prepared this edition of Hernandez say on 760: "The species found by Hernandez in the pueblo of Santa Fe is probably *Smilax moranensis* Mart. et Gal., since this is precisely the species that abounds in the cold and mountainous places of

the Valley of Mexico. It is very similar to *Smilax aspera* of the Mediterranean region." *Smilax aristolochiaefolia* Mill (syn. *S. medica* Schlecht. et Cham.) is the principal source of *mecapatli*, or commercial zarzaparrilla. It is distributed in all regions on the slope down to the Gulf (of Mexico), from Tamaulipas to Honduras, and to this species Hernandez alludes at the end of the chapter. (A discussion follows under the name *quauhmecapatli*.) 761. Several species have the same qualities. 764–6. Further discussion. *Cozolmecatl* is *Smilax mexicana* Griseb., found in Guerrero, Yucatan, and Tamaulipas. The dry roots are made into a beverage to treat rheumatism and skin infirmities. 766–8. Still another species of *Smilax* (possibly), *olcacatzan*. 768. There is a species of (in) China, called *mechoacanense*. "The root is called 'root of China' or simply 'China,' a species of zarzaparrilla that is imported to Europe from the Orient, above all from China, and has been since ancient times." The Tarascan Indian name for [this] *Smilax bona-nox* (syn. *S. corifolia* H. et B.) is *pacas*, or *phacas*, or *phacao*.

Standley 1920–26, 101–4. *Smilax medica*. Veracruz and San Luis Potosi. "The species of *Smilax* which furnish the sarsaparilla of commerce are very imperfectly known, but this species is believed to be one of the chief sources of the drug. According to the U.S. Pharmacopoeia, *S. medica* is one of the official sources of sarsparilla. However, the species are poorly known. Sarsparilla was introduced into Spain about 1540 and was widely used as a remedy for venereal diseases. *Smilax bona-nox* is a second species known as zarzaparrilla. He does not include any reference to zarzaparailla in discussing *S. mexicana*.

Solanum spp. in general
Sources: *Solanum* spp. – naranjillo and others (Kew. candidum (Mexic.); syn. ferox; syn. repandum (Ins. Pac.); syn. variabile; syn. sessiliflorum (Brazil); syn. georgicum)

Hutchinson (1974, 158). "Whether or not there is a genetic basis to the taxonomist's concept of a species has been debated long and inconclusively. It must be accepted that a species can only be defined in terms of the available information, and the taxonomist's task is to devise a classification on what is available ...." 159. "Recent work has shown in many crop plants a closer relationship between cultivars and wild and weedy types. With the knowledge now available of the brief period over which man has been practicing agriculture, it is not surprising that so many crop species can now be seen to be conspecific ... with their nearest wild relatives."

Heiser (1985, 76–7) compares the *naranjillo* of northwestern South America with *S. lasiocarpum* of Southeast Asia. The two are so close that they may be the same species. The fruits are used for food in both areas. He assumes *S. candidum* is American, although no wild ancestor is known. Its wide dispersal in Asia needs explanation. Iberian voyagers in the sixteenth/seventeenth centuries may have been involved, he thinks. A second species, *S. repandum*, is found only on Polynesian islands and Fiji and again is so similar to *S. candidum* of the upper Amazon area that the question remains of how to explain the high degree of similarity. Again, early Spanish explorers are a possible explanation. So are birds, but if that should be so, it "would not explain why the fruits are used in similar ways in South America and on the Pacific islands." [DNA analysis can solve these problems.]

Whistler (1991, 41–66). This cultivated plant in Polynesia appears to be a South American introduction. *S. repandum* is distributed from the Marquesas to Fiji, but nowadays is rare or has disappeared over most of this range. The closest relative to *S. repandum* is a South American species, *S. sessiliflorum*, according to Whalen et al. (1981), and the two are so similar that these authors suggested they may be conspecific. Their section of the genus is predominantly South American, which suggests the origin of *S. repandum* there. In Polynesia, the plant is always associated with human activities, and is rarely, if ever, found in undisturbed habitats, which also suggests the plant is an introduction. Its wide distribution in Polynesia suggests a much earlier, Polynesian, introduction as against a Spanish introduction. "Its Polynesian names, such as *koko'u* in the Marquesas, may be cognates of its South American name, *cocona* (Whalen et al. 1981), who [meaning Whalen?] spelled the Marquesan name *kokoua*."

Whalen et al. (1981, 41–129). Spread from Sonora and Chihuahua widely into Guatemala and El Salvador, some in Central America, and in the Chocó area of Colombia and lowlands of Ecuador and northern Peru. 105. *S. lasiocarpum* is closely related to the neo-tropical *S. candidum*. The species are so similar that we are not completely at ease retaining them as separate. Differences are all quantitative and in every case there is some overlap. *S. lasiocarpum* must be of ultimate American origin and its present distribution presents a puzzling historical problem, as does that of *S. repandum*. The great variability of *S. lasiocarpum* and its morphological divergence from its American counterpart make recent (that is, modern) human introduction an unsatisfactory explanation. If dispersal was by birds or early man, it is surprising that the species is not found on intervening islands of Oceania. 109. Heiser (1972) pointed out the close relationship of *S. quitoense* to *S. candidum*, a wide-ranging species extending from Mexico to Peru. The morphological similarity between these taxa is great, and the differences between them are primarily in characters that would likely have been influenced by human selection during the process of domestication. 83. *Solanum repandum* is very closely related to *S. sessiliflorum* of the western Amazon Basin in South America, and only with some hesitation do we retain it as a species. The two are essentially identical in habit, stellate vestiture, floral morphology, and fruit morphology. Most of the differences are quantitative and there is some degree of overlap. *S. repandum* has not been recorded from primary plant associations in Polynesia. Like *S. sessiliflorum* in South America, it is found only in association with human disturbances and is often cultivated for its edible fruits. Even the uses of the two species are similar in both regions. The berries are cooked in soups and stews and in fish and meat dishes, as

well as being used fresh and for juice. Apparently, these are the only two species of section *Lasiocarpa* that are used extensively in cooked dishes.
Whalen et al. cont'd. The presence of *S. repandum* as an endemic cultivated plant of the South Pacific presents enigmatic problems concerning its origin and dispersal. All that seems certain is that the species was derived from *S. sessiliflorum* or an ancestor closely resembling that species. When first discovered by Europeans, the South American and Polynesian plants were already as distinct morphologically as they are today. Therefore, dispersal to the Pacific must have occurred much earlier (than European discovery). Either dispersal by human agency or by natural means might have been involved. Certain circumstantial evidence can be marshaled suggesting humans as the dispersal agent. (1) Pre-Columbian Ecuadorians are known to have had sailing vessels capable of long ocean voyages (Doran 1971), and the Spanish were known to have made voyages to the Pacific in early post-Columbian times. In 1595, the Mendaña-Quiros expedition sailing from Piata, Peru, landed in the Marquesas Islands, the station for *S. repandum* nearest South America. (2) The indigenous name, *cocona*, used for *S. sessiliflorum* in Ecuador and Peru is rather similar to the name, *kokou*, used for *S. repandum* in the Marquesas Islands. (3) As noted earlier, uses of the two species in the two regions are similar. (4) The apparent absence of *S. repandum* from undisturbed vegetation in Polynesia suggests a human role in its survival. Successful establishment perhaps would have been much more likely following human dispersal than after natural dispersal. 84. The objection might be raised that if the Spanish had introduced *Solanum sessiliflorum* there would not be enough time for speciation to occur. 85. However, if one assumes that one or a few seedlings became established on a Pacific island, conditions would be ideal for rapid evolution. As pointed out above, *S. repandum* is only doubtfully a distinct species, and the differences between it and *S. sessiliflorum* are hardly profound. It is probably not necessary to insist on a great length of time to bring about the necessary changes. (They also talk about how the fruits arrived from the Andes to the Pacific coast of South America. Natural means?) "This offers no fewer difficulties than does the former hypothesis—humans. Neither the fruits nor the seeds of *S. sessiliflorum* seem suited for transoceanic flotation. Birds? However, most birds that make long flights in the South Pacific are shore birds and would have been unlikely to have picked up seeds of a plant so far inland as the upper Amazon."

Solanum candidum / S. lasiocarpum
Origin: the Americas?
Summary: Studies have revealed a complex set of interrelationships among closely related and perhaps conspecific plants in South America and the Pacific islands. Similar uses in different cultures as well as parallels in vernacular native names suggest human carriage into or from the islands of one or the other of these species.
Transfer: South America to Pacific islands and Asia, or vice versa

Time of transfer: pre-Columbian
Grade: B+
Sources: See sources under *Solanum* spp. in general.

Solanum nigrum
Origin: Old World?
Summary: Regardless of its place of origin, this plant was clearly present in both hemispheres before the Columbian era of discovery. Because the seed's narcotic properties are so widely known, we suppose that its spread was due to cultural selection and voyaging. It has not been suggested to have spread naturally.
    Case 1: Transfer: one hemisphere to the other, probably Old World to the Americas
    Time of transfer: pre-Columbian
    Grade: A-
    Case 2: Transfer: American mainland to the Marquesas Islands
    Time of transfer: pre-Columbian
    Grade: C
Sources: *Solanum nigrum* – nightshade, black nightshade
    Thompson 1949, 142–3. *Solanum nigrum* (see Post 1932, ii, 379). Use in India, China, is mentioned. 143. " It is obvious that the *S. nigrum* is a very popular drug in the East." The Assyrians used it.
    Nadkarni 1914, 373. *Solanum nigrum*. Sanskrit: *kákamàchai*. Ben.: *kákmáchi*. Common throughout India.
    Chopra et al. 1958, 525. Sanskrit: *kakamach*. Many medicinal uses. Grown throughout India up to 9000 ft in the western Himalayas.
    Chopra et al. 1956. Sanskrit: *kakamachi*
    Torkelson 1999, 1845. Sanskrit: *kakamachi*
    Int. Lib. Assoc. 1996, 573. Sanskrit: *kakamachi*
    Pullaiah 2002, II, 473. Sanskrit: *kakamaci*
    Nicolson et al. 1988, 249–50. A sheet in <u>Hortus Malabaricus</u> they say has been identified generally as showing *S. nigrum*; however, now "modern workers are restricting *S. nigrum* to a hexaploid (2n=72) that may not be in India. Syumon (l.c.) commented that works on Indian botany persist in misusing *S. nigrum* for what is *S. americanum*, a diploid species with 2n=24. A key is given here to distinguish the two. "Pending firm evidence to the contrary, Rheede's (i.e., the H. Mal.) element is perhaps best treated as *S. americanum*. Names: *nilamchunda*, still used in Kerala; also called *manithakkali*.
    Roys 1931, 248. Mayan: Ich- ('ch' plosive) *can*. *Solanum nigrum*, L. "A synonym for *pahal-can*." 2723. *Pahal-can*. *Solanum nigrum*, L. Black nightshade. Yerba mora.
    Yacovleff and Herrera 1934-1935, 281. *S. nigrum*, L. called *hierba mora* in Peru. An herbaceous plant with light blue flowers. Has narcotic properties.
    Brown 1935, 255. Marquesas: *koporo*. Juice of the leaves is used as a toothache remedy. A widely distributed weed in tropical and temperate parts of the globe; possibly of aboriginal introduction in the Marquesas. Also from eastern Polynesia in general.

Watt 1888, VI, Part III, 263–4. Found throughout India and Ceylon. Distributed to all temperate and tropical regions of the world. Berries were described in Sanskrit works of medicine.

Bretschneider 1882, 57–61. The famous Chinese volume of materia medica, *Pen Ts'ao Kang Mu*, which was compiled in part from older materials, mentions *Solanum nigrum*.

Maimonides 1974. *Solanum nigrum* mentioned.

Meyerhof and Sobhy 1932. *S. nigrum* mentioned, from Maimonides.

Balfour 1871–1873, V, 461–2. English nightshade, or common nightshade. Sanskrit: *kaka machie*; Persian: *ruba tarbuc*; Hindi: *mako, mackoe, pilkak, kaknachi*. Although considered by Europeans to be poisonous, natives of India eat the fruit with impunity. Used medicinally.

Hernandez 1942–1946 [before 1580], III, 710. Discussing *Toonchichi*, this is a strange (foreign? extranjera) species of *Solanum*. Identified as *Solanum*? Under the name, *tonchichi*, it is known today in Oaxaca, according to M. Martínez (Catalogo, p. 475) as *Solanum nigrum*. "Nevertheless, this species of *Solanum*, so well-known in Spain with the name of *hierba mora*, did not seem 'strange' to Hernandez."

Standley 1920–1926, 1296–7. Widely distributed in tropical and temperate regions of both hemispheres. Black nightshade. A common weed in Mexico and the U.S. Berries commonly believed to be poisonous, yet some forms of the plant have been cultivated under the names 'wonderberry' and 'garden huckleberry.' A somewhat variable plant, and many of the forms, including several from Mexico, have been described as distinct species.

Solanum repandum or *S. sessiliflorum*
Origin: the Americas?
Summary: Such closely-related species distributed in linkable areas invites seeing one species derived from the other, in whichever direction. The similar uses suggest human carriage rather than natural passive transmission.
Tranfer: America to Oceania
Time of transfer: pre-Columbian
Grade: B+
Sources: See sources under *Solanum* spp. in general.

Solanum tuberosum
Origin: South America
Summary: Early visitors to Easter Island were shown/given tubers that appear to have been *S. tuberosum*.
Transfer: South America to Easter Island
Time of transfer: pre-Columbian
Grade: A-
Sources: *Solanum tuberosum* – potato

McBryde 1945, 139–40. There are thirty species in Mexico and Guatemala, double those of Peru or Chile. Small red ones were probably in Guatemala as a pre-Columbian introduction (from the south). McBryde had seen ceramic models in Peru of a large, well-developed potato similar to the 'Irish' potato.

Jeffreys 1963a, 11–23. Quotes from Roggeveen, the first European to visit Easter Island (1721), who said in the original log of the expedition that the natives presented them with "a good lot of potatoes" (193, citing the translation in Corney 1908, 135.) 19. In 1825, the ship Blossom visited the island and Peard's journal mentions receiving "small baskets of potatoes." (Jeffreys distinguishes these from *batatas*, sweet potatoes.)

Yarnell 1970, 225. Earliest remains: Peru, 2700 BP.

Mellén B. 1986, 133. A report from Olaondo, who investigated part of the interior of the island the same day as Hervé and others in the first Spanish expedition to Easter Island stopped elsewhere, noted that the natives had "some maize and potatoes." He is the only chronicler to note the potato. Mention of these two plants augments the evidence for an introduction of plants from the New World by South American navigators. The current Easter Island word for the *patata* (the term used by Olaondo) nowadays is *kumara putéte* (formed from the word for sweet potato, *kumara*, plus a second term apparently derived from the English word 'potato').

Sonchus oleraceus
Origin: Old World
Summary: In addition to a long history and wide distribution in Eurasia, the sources identify the same plant in pre-Columbian America. This species is often confused with *C. intybus*. Either is called 'chicory' in various sources.
Transfer: Old World to the tropics of the New World
Time of transfer: pre-Columbian
Grade: B+
Sources: *Sonchus oleraceus* – sow thistle

Tozzer 1941, 196. Landa in 16th-century Yucatan says: "There are very fresh chicories and they grow them in the cultivated lands, although they do not know how to eat them." [Probably meaning that they did not know how to process the roots to make the coffee flavorer, or coffee substitute, known as chicory.] Footnote 1058, p. 196: "Roys (268) and Lundell identify this as *Sonchus oleraceus*, L., a native of the Old World. Roys gives the Mayan name as *nabukak* and notes that while this name does not appear in any of the Yucatecan sources, "the plant is probably the one described here by Landa."

Watt 1988–1893, II, 285. He lists *Cichorium intybus*, Linn. The wild, or Indian, endive, chicory, or succory, is cultivated from the Atlantic to Punjab and Kashmir and Morocco to Lake Baikal, wild in many places. 287. The young plant is used as a vegetable. The roots are roasted, ground, and mixed with coffee to flavor it. Sometimes it serves as a substitute for coffee.

Bailey 1935, III, 3189. Of the genus of 40 or more species in the Old World, some of them were introduced in North America as weeds. In the Canaries it is considered a salad.

Balfour 1871–1873, V, 482–3. *Sonchus ciliatus*, Lam. syn *S. oleraceus*, Roxb.. W.: Ic. Eng.: sow thistle. A native of Europe, of the Punjab plains and up to 8500 ft., and of Peninsular India. Used in the Nilgherries as a potherb by natives. In Kashmir, people use it as a vegetable.

Watson 1868, 259. Persian: *Cichorium endivia, kasnee*. The seeds in Hindi and Tamil are called *kassini-verei*. 274. Ditto, *kesni*. *Cichorium intybus*, Linn. The wild, or Indian, endive, Chicory.

Bretschneider 1892, 179. *Sonchus oleraceus*, sow thistle. Chinese terms given.

Roys 1931, 268. Mayan: "*Nabukak. Sonchus oleraceus*, L. Achicoria, *lechuga silvestre* [wild lettuce]. What Landa called 'chicories.'"

Yacovleff and Herrera 1933–1934, 299. Peru. Discussion of "Cerraja; Chicoria. *Hypothoeris sonchoides*, Kth. Used in popular medicine as an antibilious and antifever remedy. *Hypochoeris stenocephola* var. subcaposa Hieron. is rather similar to the preceding species. Used for food and medicine. Quotes Contreras: "It is an herb used by the Indians in health and sickness; they eat it raw. Has the same properties as chicory. [Hence the ultimate need for DNA analysis.]

Sophora toromiro
Origin: South America
Summary: The many uses to which this valuable tree is put, the tradition that says it was introduced by a voyaging ancestor, and the highly restricted distribution argue for arrival of the tree by voyaging immigrants.
Transfer: South America to Easter Island
Time of transfer: pre-Columbian
Grade: A
Sources: *Sophora toromiro* – toromiro tree (Kew. syn. *tetraptera* (N.Z., Chile))
  Heyerdahl 1963b, 26–7. The only wild tree in the flora of Easter Island, now essentially extinct except for some bushes. Formerly the principal material for wood-carving, used for house frames, tiny canoes, for ceremonial and practical paddles and clubs, wooden images, etc. Traditions recorded by the first missionaries said that the toromiro tree was imported by the original immigrant ancestors.
  Knoche (1925) considered it a cultivated plant. Apart from a distant relative in New Zealand, related species are absent from Polynesia. Skottsberg found that its closest relative is *Sophora masafuerana* from Juan Fernández Island. The time and mode of introduction to the island is obscure, possibly having come from some South American area where it is now lost.
  Skottsberg 1920, 421. Forster (who was with Capt. Cook in 1774) mentioned 'Mimosa' (*Sophora toromiro*). On page 373, he says: "Sophora (called *tetraptera*) was recognized and recorded only from Chile, Juan Fernandez, Easter Island, and New Zealand."
  Mellén B. 1986, 135. Pascuan [Easter Island] traditions relate that ancestral settler Hotu Matu'a brought to the island different species of trees and plants, such as the *totomiro* (sic), (i.e.) *Sophora toromiro*. The indigenous name derives from totó-miro, literally translated as 'blood of wood.'

Guppy 1906, II, 64. At Easter Island he suspects South American immigration due to the presence of *Sophora tetraptera* (assumes it equals *S. toromiro*.)

Spondias lutyea
Origin: uncertain
Summary: Known essentially from Standley's comment.
Grade: incomplete
Sources: *Spondias lutyea* - hog plum
> Standley 1920–1926, 658. The species is widely distributed "in the tropics of both hemispheres." This species is rather rare in Mexico but sometimes is in cultivation. "It may be that it is not native there." Its fruit is similar to the *mombin* but of inferior quality. "This species has doubtless been confused in Mexico with *S. mombin*."
> Marcus 1982, 243. Listed in <u>Relaciones de Yucatán</u> as one of the "Sixteenth-Century Fruit-bearing Trees" in Yucatán.

Spondias purpurea
Origin: the Americas
Summary: The "mirabolanos" of the Mediterranean, and *S. mombin*, or *S. purpurea*, of Middle America appear to be the same (the early Spaniards considered them the same plant). If synonymy of *S. mangifera* and *S. purpurea/S. mombin* is confirmed, than Aiyer's evidence is decisive.
Transfer: Middle America to Eurasia
Grade: incomplete
Sources: *Spondias purpurea* (syn. *mombin*; syn. *pinnata*; syn. *acuminata*) – hog plum, golden mombin, ciruela
> Tozzer 1941, 198. *Spondias purpurea* L. 'plum,' Yucatan
> Aiyer 1956, 19. *Spondias mangifera* is the Indian hog-plum; Sanskrit: *amrataka*, mentioned in the <u>Birhat Samhita</u> and <u>Mahabharatha</u>, dated previous to 400 C.E.
> Patiño 1963, 254–5. Also called *hobos*, or *jobos*, *mirabolanos*, and other names listed. In the Antilles, the Spaniards believed that the *Spondias mombim*, or *hobo* (a 'plum'), was the same as the Asiatic *mirabolanos*. In the beginning in the Antilles, they fed them to hogs, hence 'hog plum.'
> Yacovleff and Herrera 1933–1934, 304. *Spondias purpurea* L. *ciruelo, jobo*. The fruit is an oval drupe, purple or yellow color, pleasant acidic taste, with a single seed. According to Vavilov, it grows spontaneously and is cultivated in southern Mexico. It was seen by Cabezas in Peru.
> Roys 1931, 235. "*Chi-abal. Spondias mombin*, L." *Ciruela morada*. 245. Syn. *Ciruela colorada*. 213: *abal-ac. S. purpurea*. Motul: "The wild ciruela and its fruit." English: 'hog plum.' Maya medicinal use. 312. Also *zuli-abal* ("probably *S. mombin*.")
> Bretschneider 1882, 38. In the document, <u>Nan fang Ts'ao Mu Chan</u> (China), the author, Ki Han, 290–307 C.E., lists 80 species including *Spondias*.
> García-Bárcena 2000, 14. *Spondias mombin, ciruela*, was grown in Mexico from 5000 B.C.E.

Brücher 1989, 217–8. Red mombin, *jocote*. Probably of Central American origin, native also in the Antilles. Distributed from Mexico to Paraguay. During fruiting thousands of yellow fruits cover the soil under the trees, avidly devoured by wild animals and hogs. Fruit similar to European plums.

Standley 1920–1926, 656–8. He equates *S. mombin* with *S. purpurea*. Called *jobo*, or *hobo*, in some areas, *ciruela*, etc. English name is 'hog plum.' Common in many parts of Mexico. The tree is treated by most of the early writers on the Americas. Oviedo names it *xocot*, *ciruelo* (sic) and *hobo*. *S. purpurea* is illustrated by Hernandez [by 1580] but without description, under the name *mazaxochotli*. It has fruit similar to mombin but of inferior quality. "This species has doubtless been confused in Mexico with *S. mombin*." [One of the reasons for the many varieties is that the tree can be easily reproduced; any time a new taste or shape of fruit is observed, it can be reproduced by simply placing a branch in the ground.]

Addendum: Too late to enter in detail: Carter 2002, 253.

Synedrella nodiflora
Origin: American tropics
Summary: Its distribution in at least India and the Americas raises a question about possible transfer by ancient voyagers. In the absence of better information we consider it a reasonable possibility that it spread to India and Polynesia by the same means by which other plants (above) traveled.
Grade: incomplete
Sources: *Synedrella nodiflora* (L.) Gaertn. (Kew: Am. Trop.) - pantropic weed

Brown 1935, 349. Two species of this genus are natives of the American Tropics. This one is now worldwide in the Tropics. "A pantropic weed of American origin; probably of aboriginal introduction in southeastern Polynesia."

Pandey 2000, 274. *S. nodiflora*, from Tropical America, "naturalized in some parts of India".

Pope 1968, 253. Listed by Hooker (Flora of British India, Vol. 3, 308, 1879) as distributed in the tropics of the Americas and Asia. It was recently reported growing on Christmas Island in the eastern Pacific; that island has had no modern settlers likely to have introduced the plant. [There are indications of some transient ancient visitors, although Pope supposes that the plant was introduced by floating on the ocean.]

Tagetes erecta
Origin: Mexico
Summary: Substantial evidence from several lines shows that the plant has long been in India and is used in essentially the same ways as in Mexico.
Transfer: Mexico to India
Time of transfer: in time to receive two Sanskrit names and to become firmly ensconced in the ceremonial calendar on a wide scale.
Grade: A
Sources: *Tagetes erecta* – large marigold

Zeven and de Wet 1982, 188. South-central Mexico is the place of maximum gene diversity. Probably a parent of *T. patula*.

Nadkarni 1914, 389. In India, *Tagetes erecta*. Eng.: French marigold

Pandey 2000, 287. India. *T. erecta* is a native of Africa or Mexico.

Chopra et al. 1956, 239. Sanskrit: *zanduga*

Torkelson 1999, 1853. Sanskrit: *zanduga*

Int. Lib. Assoc. 1996, 574. Sanskrit: *sthulapushpa*

Pullaiah 2002, II, 492. Sanskrit: *sandu, sthulapushpa, ganduga*. Medicinal uses.

Parotta 2001, 156. Sanskrit: *jhandu, zandu*

Hernandez 1942–1946, II, 644–52. Ten varieties of *Tagetes* are illustrated by Hernandez, including *T. erecta* (*cempoalxochitl*, or *'flor de muerto'*). Also, *macuilxochitl*, possibly a variety of *T. erecta*, or of *T. patula*, while *T. patula* may be his *tepecenpoalxochitl*. 'Flor del muerto' means flower of death.

Lancaster 1965, 33. In *T. erecta* are bracketed all the large flowered forms of marigold (called *gainda* in India, "a Mexican weed"). The flowers are largely used in worship but also to form garlands for religious and other ceremonies. "Garlands are used to decorate the representatives of the Gods in Temples and are also placed around the neck of a devotee by the priest after the due performance of the ceremony." [The implication is of greater antiquity for the plant than since the Portuguese arrived.]

Lancaster cont'd. In *T. patula* are located the selection of smaller marigolds. "The flowers are largely used in worship but also to form garlands for religious and other ceremonies." [The same implication of relative antiquity prevails for this species as for *T. erecta*.]

Neher 1968. Gives a long list of uses for each species of marigold, with country listed. 321. In India, it is an anti-nematode. Used as general coloring, same as *Bixa orellana*. *Tagetes patula* and *T. erecta* are revered for their beauty and are the species most commonly associated with observance of All Saints Day, Nov. 1, and All Souls Day, Nov. 2, in Latin America. Called *'flor del muerto.'* In Mexico, the most abundant flowering of the marigolds corresponds with the time of these religious ceremonies. Flowers are used to decorate household altars and are strewn on the graves of relatives and on paths to guide the souls of dead children to food and offerings placed on the altars. Marigolds are commonly found growing in profusion along pathways and cemeteries. 322. Both species are also used in Hindu religious ceremonies as altar decoration. An eyewitness account by Harlan is quoted of a village harvest festival when village gods were decorated with garlands of marigolds. Flowers were everywhere. The orange/yellow shade of the flowers is exactly the same as maize and peppers (grown in that village). Harlan says it seems evident that the marigold provided the model (color) for the other crops to mimic. The marigold is a sacred flower in the Kulu valley, Himachel Pradesh, and varieties of maize and peppers have been bred to match its color.

Johannessen, personal observation. There is heavy production of *Tagetes* plants and flowers of several sizes in Bhutan and Nepal for use in celebrations in adjacent regions of India, where each year rickshas and taxis are strung with marigold flowers in a riot of color from Oct. 30 - Nov. 3.

Newcomb 1963, 164. The marigold, genus *Tagetes*, is a ritual flower in Mexico and Central America that was carried early into Europe along with its same usage. It is used to deck out the icons, and in South Germany it is known as the flower of the dead. It is a domesticated plant in Mexico, where double marigolds were found

Tagetes patula
Origin: Mexico
Summary: The uses in India are nearly identical to those in Mexico for both this species and for *T. erecta*. Evidently they were transmitted as a pair.
Transfer: Mexico to India. There is insufficient data to determine whether the German use/transfer was post- or pre-Columbian.
Time of transfer: pre-Columbian; probably transferred with *T. erecta*
Grade: B
Sources: *Tagetes patula* – dwarf marigold, French marigold
    Roys 1931, 279. Mayan, x-puhuk, or maceual-puhuk. Very abundant in old fields near Izamal. See also Hernandez 1942–1944 (before 1580), III, 652. *T. patula*.
    Pandey 2000, 271. *T. minuta* (referring to dwarf?) is one species "naturalized in some parts of India." 287. *T. patula* a native of Mexico.
    Zeven and de Wet 1982, 188. South-central Mexico is the place of maximum gene diversity. Probably *T. patula* has *T. erecta* as an evolutionary parent.
    Pullaiah 2002, II, 493. Sanskrit: *taugla*.
See also the information under the Neher entry on *T. erecta*

Tamarindus indicus
Origin: Asia
Summary: Wide distribution and naturalization in Tropical America leads to the possibility of a pre-Columbian transfer for which there is no direct evidence except a native Mayan name.
Grade: C
Sources: *Tamarindus indicus* – tamarind tree
    McBryde 1945, 147. Says, in connection with its Mesoamerican presence, "presumably from India."
    Castelló Yturbide 1987, 61. The tamarind, an Asiatic tree, must have arrived very early on the Manila galleon, for it is found everywhere in *tierra caliente* (in Mexico).
    MacNeish 1992, Table 9.1. Native of Southeast Asia.
    Pandey 2000, 271. *T. indica*, a native of tropical Africa, was imported to India.
    Roys 1931, 273. "*Pah-chuhuc* ('ch' plosive). *Tamarindus indica*, L." "Although a native of the East Indies, it appears to be thoroughly naturalized in the Maya area."
    Johannessen, personal observation. Tamarind fruit is produced abundantly in Central America in the regions of hot climate where the pulp/juice, mixed with water, is used as a refreshing drink.

Tephrosia spp.
Origin: uncertain
Summary: Quigley raises questions about the reason for this tree's presence on both sides of the South Atlantic. Further study is needed.
Grade: incomplete
Source: *Tephrosia* spp. - fish poison
> 1956, 510. After discussing botanical nomenclature, which includes many synonyms for the species, he concludes, intermediately, that "In general, the wide distribution of a few plants used in the same way over an area which is known to have been in culture contact from a remote period of prehistory (sic) seems to strengthen the view that the whole Old World forms a single diffusion area." Furthermore (513), "The evidence seems clearly to show that the fish poisoning trait did not come to the New World by way of Bering Strait." On subsequent pages he presents a highly detailed treatment of the intergrading and overlapping of the species of fish-stupefying plants that has resulted in labeling what are effectively the same species, or at least the same genera, on different continents as multiples. For example (517), the worldwide range of some species of *Tephrosia*, their weed-like qualities (such as prevalence around old human habitats, showing travel as hitch-hikers with humans), their great variability, their occurrence as cultivated plants on very primitive levels, all serve to make *Tephrosia* an important plant in the study of early agriculture, prehistoric migrations, and cultural diffusion. There are about 150 species, of which 22 are used as fish poisons. However, the list of 22, because of taxonomic overlap, is actually fewer. 519. ... "It would seem that the widespread American fish-poison *Tephrosia toxicaria* and the widespread African fish-poison *Tephrosia vogelii* could, botanically speaking, have been derived by long cultivation from a common ancestor, and have passed across the Atlantic from Africa to jungle South America in the pre-Columbian period." "This view is supported by a great mass of evidence, no single piece of which is entirely convincing but whose cumulative effect is rather persuasive." 520. Beyond the *Tephrosia* species, pantropical plants of other genera, that are recorded as piscicides in at least part of their range, are *Cissampelos pareirs* [sp.?] L., *Sapindus saponaria* L. [q.v. in this study], and *Entada phaseoloides* L. (all the above with many references).

Trapa natans
Origin: Eurasia
Summary: Occurrence and use of this species in China as well as in North America, raises the question of how and when the transfer took place between the hemispheres. That needs further study.
Grade: incomplete
Sources: *Trapa natans* – water chestnut
> C. Sauer 1969. Raises a question about the plant's occurrence in both hemispheres.

Bretschneider 1892, 220. In his *Index Florae* Sin., on page 311, all the Chinese species of Trapa are referred to as varieties of *T. natans*, L.

Balfour 1871–73, V, T–186. The European species is said to be grown also in China. The seed is good to eat, somewhat like a chestnut. It was known to the Romans. Pliny said it was used on the Nile for food.

Watson 1969, 400. "At the site of Chiien Shan Yang in Chekiang, in addition to rice, the following were identified," *Arachis hypogaea* (obviously a very early American crop import), and *Trapa natans*. (Citing, in endnote 17, "Chekiang Province Cultural Properties Control Report (1960) on the first and second seasons of excavation at the site of Ch'ien-shan-Yang in Wu-hsing hsien, Chekiang, K'ao ku hsüeh pao, 2 pp. 84.7.")

Triumfetta semitriloba
Origin: the Americas
Summary: The use of this neo-tropical species on the island makes quite certain its transfer from the mainland, along with at least a dozen other plants (above).
Transfer: South America to Easter Island
Time of transfer: pre-Columbian?
Grade: C
Sources: *Triumfetta semitriloba* - Sacramento Burbark

Heyerdahl, 1963b. 31. The bark of this Easter Island plant provided material for rope.

Knoche (1925, 102, 123) lists the plant as being at home in the American tropics.

Roys 1931, 267. A shrub 10 feet high found in brush lands near Izamal, Yucatan. The small fruit is covered with spines and sticks to clothing

Verbesina encelioides
Origin: the Americas
Summary: Hillebrand's expert judgment should be respected unless it is impeached by pertinent facts. The significance of the fact that the plant is also naturalized in India needs further investigation.
Transfer: North or Middle America to Hawaii
Time of transfer: pre-Columbian
Grade: C

Sources: *Verbesina encelioides* (Cav.) Benth. & Hook, f. ex A. Gray #3 VEEN Golden Crownbeard (from biosis) (Kew. Am. No. and Austr.)

Hillebrand 1888, 204. A note under the genus statement says: "A large genus, diffused over the warmer parts of the [North]American Continent." The note following the species description says: "A native of Mexico, Arizona, and Texas." On page XCIII, the volume editor, W. F. Hillebrand, notes that his father, the author, changed his mind about some plants which he first assumed to be introduced since Capt. Cook's voyage of discovery; those plants "may in reality have been of earlier introduction," but he failed to go back and remove the symbols indicating the fact. He says, "Of nine non-endemic species which existed before the discovery ... one, *Verbesina* [is] American ...."

Pandey 2000, 241. *V. encelioides*, from Tropical America, is one species "naturalized in some parts of India."

Vigna sinensis
Origin: Africa
Summary: The American distribution deserves further research in light of other transfers from the Old World evidenced above.
Grade: incomplete
Sources: *Vigna sinensis* – cowpea
   Newcomb 1963, 40. This is African, although it was considered to be from the New World until De Candolle. It is a possible Negro African introduction before Columbus, although it was missing from Arab Africa.
   J. Sauer 1950, 500–3. Vigna sp. occurred in both hemispheres before Columbus

Vitis vinifera
Origin: Old World
Summary: Martinez' discovery of apparent *V. vinifera* seeds in archaeological remains from southern Mexico is basis enough for more careful scrutiny of other sources.
Transfer: Old World to Mesoamerica
Time of transfer: by the turn of our era
Grade: B-
Sources: *Vitis vinifera* – grape
   Bretschneider 1892, 316. The true vine, *Vitis vinifera*, L., now extensively cultivated in the northern part of China, was introduced into China from Western Asia, in about 125 B.C.E., and is known since that time under the name of *p'u t'ao*.
   J. Sauer 1993, 167. *Vitis* includes about 60 species native mainly to North and Central America and to East and Southeast Asia. *Vitis vinifera* is the Eurasian grape. It is considered by experts to have been derived from a single, fairly homogeneous wild progenitor, *V. sylvestris*. 169. In Asia, the earliest evidence of cultivation of *V. vinifera* and of wine making is from Iran and Baluchistan, dated before 2000 B.C.E. Cultivation spread very slowly into India and China.
   Scholes and Warren 1965, 784. A "grape" was in use in the Olmec area, Gulf Coast of Mexico, at Conquest (species not identified).
   Martínez M. 1978, 14, 21. The site of his study is a few miles upstream from Santa Rosa, near Laguna Francesa, on the south bank of the Grijalva River, southern Mexico. He worked primarily on the contents of two bottle-shaped cavities (chultuns) filled with trash. Dated to the Proto-Classic period (200 B.C.E. to 200 C.E.), i.e., the second half of Chiapas V through VII (ceramic periods). He used flotation to extract seeds from excavated material. On 105ff is Cuadro No. 13, classification of vegetal remains. "*Vitis*, wild, called *bejuco de agua* (vid)." Under "Estimulantes" he gives: "*Vitis silvestre* (wild), vino, fruto, fermentado ((assumed) fermented)." 121. Cites Miranda 1975–1976, I, 175–6, as reporting from

field survey in Chiapas three species: *V. bouraeana*, or watervine; *V. tiliifolia*, also called watervine; and *V. vinifera*, or '*vid europea.*' He also mentions *V. labrusca*, or '*vid americana*,' leaving it unclear if he considered this a fourth species of grape. A rather good quality wine can be made from the juice (no species pinpointed). *Vitis* is wild and only slightly represented in our materials. 125. As indicated previously, utilizing the juice of the grape, pressed and fermented, he says that it is possible to produce a good quality wine. 176. Furthermore, the sap from the stem of the grape plant is fermented (today) to make a drink called '*taberna.*'

Zea mays
Origin: Mesoamerica
Summary: Archaeological evidence demonstrates unquestionably that this species was known in pre-Columbian Asia. Of particular interest is the discovery in an archaeological site on the island of Timor of remains of maize dating to 1000 C.E. There probably were other separate examples of 'primitive' *Z. mays*. Strikingly similar plants have been found growing in the Himalaya and interior East Asia and a more developed variety of later date. Names, including Sanskrit names, as well as art representations, confirm that maize was growing in India before, as well as after, the turn of our era. A historical record also places the crop in the Middle East by 800 C.E. Maize may also have reached southern Europe, as well as Africa, in pre-Columbian times, although its immediate source may have been India/Middle East.

Case 1: Transfer: the Americas to Southeast Asia
Time of transfer: by the third millennium B.C.E.?
Grade: A

Case 2: Transfer: the Americas to India and perhaps then to China and the Middle East
Time of transfer: by the Fifth Century B.C.E. to India
Grade: A

Case 3: Transfer: the Americas to Eastern Europe
Time of transfer: pre-Columbian (may be due to an extension of Case 2)
Grade: C.

Sources: *Zea mays* – corn, maize

Zeven and de Wet 1982, 75. Secondary center of gene diversity (after Central America) is "S. Himalayas" where flint maize is common (citing Brandolini 1970).

Pokharia and Saraswat, 1999, 99. Maize. Also they note sculptures of maize-ears in 12th–13th centuries and earlier in Hoysala temples in Karnataka. Sureness of details means they had models of actual ears (see endnote 165). "… Some ancient maizes have likely existed in Asia for a long time." References to maize in the 13th century C.E. literature in China (endnote 170) and in fifth century C.E. literature in India (endnote 171) suggest much earlier introduction in Asia. 101.

Glover, 1977. A series of caves in Timor, Indonesia, have a continuous sequence of occupation from 12,000 B.C.E. In the top layers, dated to 10000 C.E., several introduced New World crops occur from the northwest, such as peanuts (*Arachis*), custard-apple/soursop (*Annona*) and maize (*Zea mays*) together with Southeast Asian, or generally Asian, natives. These three species arrived about 1000 C.E.

Balfour 1871–73, V. "Zea." Bengali: *mokka*; Panjab: *mak, makki, makkei*; Persian: *bajri*; Sanskrit: *yavanala*; Tamil.: *makka-cholum*; Telugu: *makka-jonna*. "Zea is entirely American."

Monier Williams' standard Sanskrit dictionary lacks a word for maize, yet Watt (1888–1893, VI, Pt IV, 327) reported that in his day a certain (unspecified) publication by Williams himself "furnishes three [Sanskrit] words as denoting 'maize': *sasyam, stamba-kari*, and *sasyavisesha*—the last meaning, appropriately, 'remarkable grain.'"

Chopra et al. 1956, 260. Sanskrit: *yavanala*

Torkelson 1999, 1874. Sanskrit: *yavanala*

Bretschneider 1892, 149–150. Another graminea identified by the Japanese (from Matsumura) is *Zea mays*, with a three-character identifier. [It is not clear whether the names recorded in Japan were or were not from the era before European influence reached the Far East.]

Johannessen and Wang 1998, 10–12. Well over 100 Hindu, Jain, and Buddhist temples bear sculpted depictions of maize being held in the hand of a voluptuous female figure. The images of the ears include over 40 anatomical features unique to maize (e.g., the shapes of ears or cobs, the representations of corn silk, arrangement of rows in relation to each other, arrangement of kernels, unpollinated small kernels, etc.) all of which indicate that actual maize ears had to have been models for the sculptures. Opponents of this view have suggested other objects being held rather than corn. Those explanations are not credible. Various investigators have also found ancient maize varieties in the hill country of Southeast Asia and the northern India subcontinent. Johannessen found in Bhutan and in Yunnan province, China, maize with tiny grains, four-row ears, and multiple ears per stalk.

Johannessen and Wang cont'd. 12–13. The sculptured ears studied are from numerous temples of the 11th to 13th centuries C.E., built during the Hoysala Dynasty located in what is now Karnataka state, India, whose rulers and buildings are well-documented historically. Artists generally signed their work and their biographies are known. Architectural study has shown that the sculpted sections are not additions of later date. In other statuary, of the sixth through 10th centuries, maize ears are held by males, such as a carving of Vishnu, who is shown holding a maize ear carved in a living sandstone wall of Cave III near Badami. And Kubera, god of wealth and abundance, shown as a corpulent figure holding an ear of maize, is depicted in a statue dated to the fifth century.

13–14. Some art historians have questioned whether these are ears of corn or of some other plant or object. Corn breeding experts of the U.S. Department of Agriculture in Ohio who have been shown full photographic documentation of these sculptures concur fully that maize is what is represented by all the specimens displayed on the Indian temple art. In fact, some observers have recognized particular New World ecological source regions for the maize ears used as models by some of the Indian artists, as Johannessen had suggested. Moreover, studies of names for maize in India and the Amazon Basin of South America show a distinct similarity. Also studies of names of maize from South China, Vietnam, and Indonesia in comparison with Columbia and Equador provide notable similarities.

18–19. Maize is recorded in a Chinese medical encyclopedia of ca. 1448 C.E., which gives detailed guidance on the curative use of corn silk and seeds. This would not have been true of a recently-acquired plant. According to Burkill (1966), the reported treatment with maize products is still used in Southeast Asia for renal problems.

Actual maize ears were reported taken from a tomb excavated in Sichuan Province, said to date to about 2000 BP (Han Dynasty). The only documentation was in a newspaper, but the find was known to a number of archaeologists. Because of the prevailing assumption by established scientists of the late date for maize, administrators did not allow the ears to be submitted for C14 dating as requested by the field archaeologists, and the specimens were discarded. No ears were saved!

Johannessen 1998a, 122. The sculpted figures holding maize ears make specific Hindu mudra signs (symbolic hand positions when holding maize ears). A set of temples earlier than those of Karnataka State is now reported from west-central India that date to the fifth to eighth centuries. They bear sculpted figures of male Hindu gods holding maize in their hands.

Johannessen and Parker 1989b, 9–10. They point out the possibility that maize was related to elements of Hindu philosophy. Yellow maize appears 'golden.' Vishnu, the major Hindu god, his consorts, and various forms of the goddess Lakshmi are associated with golden offerings. Corn would fit in nicely with this emphasis on gold. Other temples that have possible maize effigies include: Sravana Belagola, a Jain Temple complex of the eighth century C.E.; Boodgaya Temple, first century B.C.E.; and a Kubera Temple in Rajasthan of the eighth century C.E. 16. *Zea mays* also is mentioned in 13th-century literature in China (see Kia Ming, cited in Marzeweski 1966) and in fifth-century literature in India (see Tagare 1982, 448, 486–7, 498).

Johannessen (1992, 313–33) compares and relates several expressions for maize (*tar, hobba* or *hab, ang, mak, makai, makka* or *maka, jonar, kana*, and *Bhutta*) that appear and reappear variously in the Andes, Southeast Asia, Indonesia, China, India, Brazil, and Africa. 317. The Hindu goddess, Lakshmi, and god, Vishnu, needed to be worshipped with gold; and they are apparently associated with the temples in India where yellow maize is displayed in art. Other colors of maize seed—red, blue, black, white, spotted, and striped—also fit variously into the religious complex of India.

Jeffreys 1955, 427–432. He recapitulates documentary evidence for maize being in Asia and Africa before Columbus. For example, he quotes Idrisi, ca. 1150, about people from Senegal to Tchad using "large-grained millet" which, he shows, can only be maize. He also quotes Bonafous (1836) who reported that maize had been brought by Arabs into Spain in the 13th century. Also, Bertagnoli (1881) writes of a grain, "grano Turco," that some people think came from Asia and that first appeared in Italy during the Crusades. According to this "*Carta donationis verae Crucis et primii seminis meligae*," maize was introduced in 1204 by two captains on their return from the siege of Constantinople. Naysayers have considered this a forged document, yet Bertagnoli says he has "read all the medieval chronicles available on this matter and has found mention at least a hundred times" of 'grano Turco' (maize) before the New World was even dreamed of."

Towle 1961, 21–5. Two major types of corn are found in Peruvian archaeological sites, which she calls Group A and Group B. The former is a weak pod-corn, or primitive popcorn. Found in earlier levels, starting in the Cupisnique period, ca. 750 B.C.E., these cobs tend to be as wide as they are long. Group B resembles more elongated forms of corn typically grown in Peru today. The cylindrical ears are larger than those of Group A and bear larger kernels. Group B cobs are reported from Ancón (ca. the middle of first millennium B.C.E.) and at Paracas a little later in the Formative.

Marszewski 1975, 237–60, and 1978, 128–63. He gives a complete review of the literature in regard to the question of maize in Southeast Asia and China. 241. His map plots vernacular names of maize in Vietnam with apparent similarities in Colombia and Peru. 239. One set of maize forms is distinguished by (1) many small ears on a stalk; (2) small spherical kernels having sometimes waxy endosperm; (3) many prop-roots (p. 243); shortness of almost all organs, etc. Most of these range among the popcorn subvarieties (*Zea mays* L. var. everta) labelled as a 'Persian' race and considered the most 'primitive' (Anderson), or 'pure' (Suto and Yoshida), type of maize in the Old World. These varieties are cultivated mainly by the conservative hill peoples in Asia but not in coastal zones; they have been identified from the Pontian Mountains eastwards to the Himalaya and on southward through the western part of the Indochina, maybe all the way to Java. 240. The close counterparts of the Asiatic popcorns, particularly North Anatolian, Assamese, and Siamese forms of the 'Persian' race, show traits like short cobs with spherical kernels as known from prehistoric graves and trash-heaps on the shores of Peru, Chile, and even in Argentina (Towle's Race A). 242–3. Other characteristics of the Asiatic popcorns are linked to those growing in isolated places in Argentina, Chile, Bolivia, and Colombia.

Marszewski, cont'd., 243–5. Waxy maize. Collins (1909, 1920) collected this in Southeast China, upper Burma, and Mindanao, and considered it "of a respectable age." Kuleshov (1928) reported the varieties from a far wider area inside Asia and thought a relatively long time had to have elapsed for them to evolve and be distributed. Anderson (1945) even thought this maize evidence that *Zea mays* might have originated in Asia (247). He notes the overlap in part of area growing amaranth with Asiatic maize and the peanut. (On 255, he adds a discussion of possible presence of tobacco in India and Southeast Asia.) 250–1. Marszewski also gives maize names used by Tibeto/Burman peoples of the Himalaya in comparison to names

among the Chibchan language family of Panama and Colombia. "The degree of similitude between the above-mentioned Asiatic and American vernacular names of maize is so great, that, if the peoples under consideration were living on the adjacent territories, their maize appellations could be easily suspected to derive from a common root ...."
127. Marszewski hypothesizes that 'primitive' forms of maize "could have been picked up in one or another sector of the Pacific coast of the northern part of South America or southern part of Central America at an indefinite, as yet, time of the pre-Columbian era." Also, that this "could have been done by some aboriginal sailors coming from the shores of the northern part of South Vietnam and belonging perhaps to the Cham or other akin people." 132–134. Marszewski also discusses "The enigmatic maize forms (Sikkim Primitive 1 and 2) cultivated in some isolated pockets of Sikkim." (Cf. Dhawan 1964, and Gupta and Jain 1973). These have "strikingly primitive features." Results of experiments with those maizes and detailed study of their characteristics reveals that "these two Sikkimese races (especially SP 1) resemble astonishingly the progenitor of maize reconstructed by Mangelsdorf, and are much closer to it than any of the Mexican (Nal-Tel (Yucatan 7), Palomero-Toluqueño, Chapalote) or Colombian (Pollo Segregaciones) races considered previously to be the most primitive known" (see Marszewski 1978, 163).

Marszewski, cont'd., 137. "... Among the agriculturalists and botanists who have studied them in detail in respect to their morphology, genetics, physiology, and distribution, almost all are inclined to admit their pre-Columbian occurrence in some at least of the above-mentioned region" (South China, Himalaya, East and South Asia). The author then reprises this viewpoint for Collins, Kuleshov, Anderson, Suto and Yoshida, Gupta and Jain, Vishnu-Mittre, and Gupta., all of whom either favor or allow for pre-Columbian presence of maize. 139–162. Review of indications from written records about pre-Columbian maize. Considers Chiba (1969) on the pharmacopoeia document of Lan Mao (1397–1476 C.E.) to be the best evidence, while noting potential problems with identifying the name of the apparent maize plant there mentioned. Other indications of similar nature are noted, mainly from the sixth century. 149–158. A long discussion follows on some Tibetan sources. Pre-Columbian reference to a plant that might be maize cannot be ruled out.

Marszewski, cont'd., 162. "In the light of all botanical data accumulated here, but especially those concerning the 'primitive' maizes from Sikkim (SP 1 and SP 2), the pre-Columbian transfer of such and akin forms into the more or less isolated regions inside the Himalayan zone by some aboriginal peoples, is more plausible than its post-Columbian introduction there by the Europeans." Moreover, the Chinese written sources indicate that in the border land involving certain parts of North China, Southeast Tibet, Arunachal, Bhutan, and Sikkim, maize, most probably belonging to the 'Persian' type, had already been cultivated before the sixth century.

Marszewskiv, cont'd., Final Addendum, dated 1966, says on p. 30 that one of the Sikkim primitive races bears "the closest resemblance to the wild maize of which an actual specimen in fossil was uncovered (1960) in the lower levels of San Marcos Cave in Mexico." Further, "ancient Tibetan literature" may refer to maize, and he gives an example in a text which dates before Columbus.

Suto and Yoshida 1952–1953, volume 2, 375–530. They compare Asiatic maizes, including 20 races from North China, which reveal that 'Caribbean' types, which prevail on the coasts of China and presumably were introduced by Europeans in the 16th century, were crossed with 'Aegean' types, which now predominate in China, particularly far inland. This is suggestive that the inland maize was present in pre-Columbian times.

Marszewski 1963, 250. Humlum (*Zur Geographie*, 24, 29, 74) pointed to some evidences of maize's probable presence in Angola around the year 1500.

Jeffreys (1953, 965–6) pointed out the discovery by archaeologists of potsherds decorated by rolling a maize cob over wet clay, at Ife, Nigeria. Regarding the questioned date: Ife is traditionally supposed to have been founded by a wave of immigrants from the East between 600 and 1000 C.E.

Marszewski 1987, 203. From the English summary: concerns an early transfer of maize across the Pacific, from the Americas to Asia or the opposite way. Supportive information includes the facts that among Mizo tribes and in Bhutan, cultivation of maize precedes in time rice cultivation, and maize plays an important role in local religious rituals and ceremonies.

Johannessen reports (personal communication, 2003) that the Tibetan lamaist oral tradition, as told to Johannessen and Parker by high ranking priests in Darjeeling, holds that maize was the first agricultural crop given to the Tibetans by god. Although the altitude is too high for the production of maize near Lhasa, maize is involved in worship there in the largest temple. This consists of the placement, erect in a large basin of rice in front of the largest figure of Buddha, of the largest ear of maize that can be found in northern India (collected fresh each year).

The Wealth of India 1974. 26–9. Long list of names for maize—Hindi: *makai, makka, bhutta, junri, kukri, barajowar*. Bengali: *janar, bhutta, jonar*. Mar.: *maka, makai, buta*. Gujerat: *makkari, makkai*. Telegu: *modda-janna, makka jonnalu*. Tamil: *makka-cholam*. Kan.: *mekkejola, musukojola, goinjol*. Mal.: *cholam*. Oriya: *Maka buta*. Assam: *gomdhan, makoi*. Manipur: *chujak, nahom*. 27: Fig. 2 is a photo of prolific primitive type maize from Sikkim. Evidence from Mexico and a possible secondary center of origin in the Andean region is summarized. "Asiatic origin of maize, or at least its occurrence in the continent in the pre-Columbian times has also been proposed. Outstanding variability in maize cultivars is noted, particularly from Assam, Maghalaya, Manipur, and Arunachal Pradesh in the east and the Chamba valley of Himachal Pradesh in the northwest is outstanding. Five theories of the origin of maize are summarized. Re. Africa: Portuguese introduction on the west coast early in the sixteenth century is mentioned, "though there is said to be some evidence of a prior introduction." Some maize-cob decorated potsherds have been found in West Africa, which are believed to date several centuries before Columbus landed in the New World in 1492. This and certain other evidences point to the introduction of maize into Africa through Arab/African contacts with the Americas in the beginning of 900 C.E. Re. Asia: mention is made primarily of Portuguese introduction. "A specimen of it (maize) was collected along the Euphrates River in Iraq in 1574." "The precise date and route of the introduction of maize into India still remains a mystery." The idea that it was the Portuguese is mentioned. But "lack of subsequent spread of maize cultivation, until very recently, in peninsular India, and the use of Muslim terminology (Makka, 'Mecca') in its vernacular names, suggest the arrival of maize first in northern India through Arab/African sources ... long before the Portuguese came to India." "Further, ... the identification of some very peculiar types of maize, considered to be the most primitive, from the northeastern Himalayan region, would also suggest the probable existence of maize in India in the pre-Columbian period. Pre-Columbian contacts between India and New World, particularly Mexico, have also been postulated from varied evidences." (Citing Leonard and Martin; Stonor and Anderson; Thapa; Weatherwax.)

Hatt 1951, 853–914. Myths and rituals in Asia associated with the cultivation of cereals, including maize, and of the origin of the yam (*Dioscorea*), agree with similar complex myths in the Americas about maize and yam. Re. Laufer's notion of the Spanish introduction of maize, which he says reached western China by 1540, Hatt cannot believe that a spread from Spain to India and across the Himalaya could have taken place in the less than 50 years that Laufer assumes; hence, maize very probably was in Asia in pre-Columbian times.

Gupta. 1996,176. Mexican origin of maize is noted. "Asiatic origin of maize points to Assam, Meghalaya, Manipur, Arunachal Pradesh, and Chamba in Himachal Pradesh. This hypothesis is based on extensive studies done and recorded in various collections made from the northeastern and northwestern part of India. (Citation to The Wealth of India and Hutchinson.) "Different varieties of the corncob are extensively sculpted but only [or rather, chiefly] on the Hindu and Jain temples of Karnataka." Deities are shown carrying an ear of corn in their hands. The straight rows of the corn grains can be easily identified. The Chenna Kesava temple, Belur, and the Lakshmi Narasimha temple, Nuggehalli, are additional sites. At the latter the eight-armed dancing Vishnu in his female form of Mohini is holding a corn ear in one of her left hands and the other hands hold the usual emblems of Vishnu. Two male figures at the base are playing the mridanga (musical instrument). In the Trikuta basti, Muchamandapa, Sravana Belagola, Karnataka, a 12th century C.E. sculpture of Ambika Kushmandini sitting on a lotus seat under a canopy of mangoes holds in her left hand a corncob. Plate 223 depicting a Nayika holding a corncob in her left hand is from Nuggehalli, Karnataka. Temples where the sculptures of corncobs are found are dated [to the] 12th–13th centuries C.E. The common belief [apparently meaning among Indian crop scientists] is that maize originated in Mexico and came to

India by the 11th–12th century. By the time these temples were constructed, maize would have been fairly common in India.

Hutchinson 1974. " ... The characteristics and distribution of some forms [are] such as to lend support to the view that they reached India in pre-Columbian times."

Vishnu-Mittre 1974, 6. "A spikelet of rice and pollen of maize appear after 1500 C.E.," in the Kashmir Neolithic. 22. Impressions on a potsherd from Kaundinyapur, M. Pradesh, and dated archaeologically to about 1435 C.E., have created a difference of opinion among the experts. That the impression could be of a piece of ceramic pressed on basketry or, of course, textile or fabric has been disproved by experiments. This discovery tends to support a pre-Columbian introduction of maize. [However, Johannessen reports, on the basis of careful personal observation of the actual specimen, courtesy of Vishnu-Mittre, and the Museum of Kaundanyapur, that the marks were not made by maize but by a disc with protrusions on it that had been rolled on the clay, making impressions somewhat like kernels but showing drag marks, en echelon, in the curved clay between the rows of "kernels".] Jeffreys gives names as supporting evidence for Arab introduction. Apart from the problem of its introduction, the enigmatic living fossil maize in Sikkim suggests reconsideration of the occurrence of maize there. Several different varieties are grown by aborigines in Siam, Burma, Assam, Sikkim, China, Tibet, etc. It seems to have been grown there for a long time. It could hardly have been introduced by Arabs. [Johannessen has found small-seeded four-rowed ears of corn with waxy (sticky) starch growing in southern Yunnan and Laos, which are clearly unrelated to modern maizes from America.]

Mattingly 2000, 31–7. At an oasis zone 100 miles long and 2 to 3 miles wide located 700 miles south of Tripoli, Libya, the Garamantes people mentioned by Herodotus and Tacitus constituted such a threat to the Roman Empire that Rome sent an army against them. (Their heyday was the first to fourth centuries C.E.) The area flourished agriculturally by tapping an aquifer with a system of underground channels (the *foghara*, or chain-well, system, which also was used in the Americas) and traded with both the Roman sphere and sub-Saharan Africa. Tombs shaped like the Egyptian stepped mastaba structures, as well as pyramid tombs, were also built. Recent archaeological work has identified "a series of significant botanical horizons—including a late medieval 'maize horizon,' which represents the arrival of plant species from the Americas, as well as a 'sorghum horizon,' which represents the arrival of sorghum grain from sub-Saharan Africa, probably during the Garamantian period." The Garamantes also wrote in a Libyan script; a version of this script (called Tifinag writing) has persisted among the nomadic Tuareg people of the Sahara.

J. Sauer 1993, 232. "The possibility of pre-Columbian presence of maize in various regions of the Old World was actively debated during the 1960s and 1970s. Historical evidence was drawn from early reports now generally interpreted as references to grain sorghum." "New evidence has been drawn from stone carvings in 12th- and 13th-century temples in southern India that depict objects resembling maize ears. The resemblances are intriguing, but other possible models have been suggested, including Pandanus fruits. Moreover, the carvings may not be as old as the temples." [Various publications by Johannessen and his colleagues have demonstrated that these speculations of Sauer are inadequately informed. He simply did not get a chance to look at enough of the published pictures of maize sculptures.]

Hatt, 1951, 853–914. Myths and rituals in Asia associated with the cultivation of cereals, including maize, and of the origin of the yam (*Dioscorea*) agree with those in the Americas. Re. Laufer's notion of the Spanish introduction of maize, which he says reached western China by 1540.

Mellén Blanco 1986, 133. Maize was reported from the interior of the (Easter) island by Olaondo, part of the earliest Spanish party of exploration. On the island, maize is now called taráke.

Newcomb 1963,168. C. Sauer provides here a rich source of reviewed and new information in the section entitled "Maize into the Old World." Particularly valuable is the detailed treatment of information in the European herbals on maize, including names of the plant, comprehending the data of Finans, and much more, as well as that of Jeffreys. Highlights: 20. The term 'turkish corn' (*grano turko, sorgho turko*) is still used in Northern Italy today. J. Sauer questions the conventional answers to the following issues: (1) there were no New World/Old World contacts prior to Columbus; (2) maize was introduced into the Old World via Iberia; (3) maize was not known in the Old World prior to the Columbian voyages. He holds, rather (1) that the German herbalists who cataloged maize were competent men; (2) that the South German towns were intermediaries between Venice and the Rhine areas; (3) trade was most active over the pack routes leading between Central Europe and Genoa and Venice; (4) the Levantine trade channel was via Venice, especially during the fifth century, when there were the maximum developments of Venetian ties via the Adriatic to the Black Sea and Asia Minor; (5) Venice was in active commercial contact with the Ottoman Empire; (6) things Turkish were nowhere as well known as in Venice, and nowhere north of Venice was such information better known than in the towns of South Germany; (7) the name 'turkish corn' was affixed after the Turks had gained control of the Levant; (8) note the conspicuous and old usage of maize in the cuisine of the Po Valley even today, and this kitchen usage is not found elsewhere in Europe west of the Adriatic; (9) yet, maize is important as a food only east of the Adriatic in the Balkans and Hungary, both of which were under Turkish control for centuries; and (10) finally, maize cultivation and usage for food are seen clear into Turkish Asia Minor. 21. In South Austria and Vienna, maize is known as kukuruz, which is a widely used name also in Slavic areas, including Russia. W. Eberhard did not believe it a Turkish word. There is the suggestion that it is a transfer from the Po Valley, into South Germany, and thence as kukuruz into Eastern Europe.

21. Little evidence exists to support Laufer's theory of maize dispersal eastward from Spain. The same is true for the pumpkin, paprika, and tobacco. The Spanish colonists did not care much to eat maize, but were accustomed to wheat. 22. Hernandez in 1570 wrote about maize (*tlaolli* in Náhuatl), noting what a good grain it was and expressing curiosity as to why it had not been taken back to Spain for cultivation. Well, observes Sauer, maize was all right for the mixed (mestizo) and native people to eat, but wheat was the grain for white folks. Columbus indeed brought maize back, but it was adopted for cultivation sparsely in Iberia and then meant for animal feed. 22–25 give much detail about names of maize in Europe, especially in re. possible confusions of Martyr with names for maize, sorghum and pearl millet. 25–27 reprise Jeffreys on names in Africa. 27. "Conclusions on the question of maize introduction into the Old World:" (1) The documents belie the possibility of a Columbian introduction of the first maize into the Old World, and they refute Laufer's idea of a rapid spread of maize through the Mediterranean into Asia. Sauer is of the opinion that maize occurred in pre-Columbian times in Syria, North Italy, and Turkey; and, during post-Columbian times, the Portuguese introduced from West Africa the milho/zaburro crop. Jeffreys refers to a town of medieval date in West Africa that is notable for the prints of corncobs on tiles. This settlement was abandoned in the Middle Ages. He claims the existence of hundreds of tiles so marked. How firm is this evidence?, asks Sauer. [Cf. now Mattingly 2000.]

Johannessen and Parker 1989b, 15. (1) In remote valleys in the Himalaya, such as Tashigang in Bhutan and Ilam in eastern Nepal, farmers grow primitive popcorns with seven to nine ears per stalk, all concentrated in the upper 20% of the stalk. Similar 'Sikkim Primitive' popcorn was recorded in Sikkim by Thapa (1966), Sachan et al. (1982), and Sachan et al. (1986a and 1986b), the latter in both Sikkim and elsewhere in northeastern India. These stalks have distinctive arrangements of leaves and their tassels droop in a form atypical for American maize. (2) At Pemagatshel, eastern Bhutan, there is a winter flint maize with short, conical ears with a somewhat fattish, or pregnant, shape as in the temple carvings in Karnataka Pradesh. A high conical shape used to be considered a trait of ancient specialization in Central America and Mexico, and in highland Peru. (3) Waxy (sticky) starch maize is widespread in Asia, from Manchuria and Korea to Myanmar (Burma), but it is rare to non-existent in ancient America. Professor You Xiu-ling of Hangzhou (personal communication to Johannessen) has stated that waxy starched maize in China has a significantly distinctive isozyme distribution that is very different from New World maize's isozymes. How far these isozyme patterns extend has not yet been thoroughly explored, but Sachan et al. (1982, 1986a, and 1986b) have found that the multi-eared Sikkim primitive popcorn exhibits a similarly distinct constitutive heterochromatic phenomenon to that found in American maizes. So, some ancient maizes have likely existed in Asia for a long time. It is unclear how the characteristics noted relate to the complex of strange maize traits, including primitive popcorns and sticky starch maize of the Naga Hills and Assam reported by Stoner and Anderson (1949, 355–96).

Anderson and Brown 1952. These peculiar maizes stretch from the Aegean to the Asiatic Pacific, including Nepal, Sikkim, and North Assam. Nearest counterparts are in South America before the Incas. They consider it plausible that this corn was transferred across the Pacific, in whichever direction.

Stonor and Anderson 1949, 387. The Russians, under Vavilov, comprehensively surveyed Oriental (Asian) maize. See Kuleshov 1928. They demonstrated that primitive maize like that in Naga country (of India) was widespread in central Asia from Persia and Turkestan to Tibet and Siberia.

Bretschneider 1882, 57–61. Author of the famous Chinese volume of materia medica, *Pen Ts'ao Kang Mu*, was Li Shi chen (Shizhen), who first published it in 1590; but the information is mainly in re. medicines and is chiefly a compilation of traditional materials from classic Chinese texts. He mentions maize among other plants of American origin.

Sarkar et al. 1974, 121. "No clearly established reference to maize is found in the Indian scriptures and epics, nor is the plant known to be associated with any religious or domestic rituals. There is not even an authentic Sanskrit name for the plant. [Of course, these statements have proved inaccurate.] The Sanskrit name, *Yaba-nala* (Yaba = barley, nala = reed-like), sometimes attributed to maize, is also used for Sorghum (Watt 1892)." The most commonly occurring name, *makkai*, or *makka*, which could mean 'from Mecca,' (sic) suggests introduction from outside India. The other common name for maize in Indian languages is *bhutta*, or *bhuta*. [See above for information via Watt, citing Monier Williams on the use of three Sanskrit words for maize.] The origin of this word is obscure. The idea that maize might have been present in Asia in pre-Columbian times gained some credence with the discovery of 'waxy' maize in northeastern China as far as Korea and its description by Collins (1909). But no firm evidence is known of pre-Columbian occurrence. The issue of the antiquity of maize in India is reopened by the recent survey of primitive germ plasm as reported by Dhawan 1964 (and others). These characters (discussed) of the Himalayan primitives, together with the emergence of ears from upper joints of the stalks, reduced internode length, and the occurrence of male and female flowers in the same inflorescence, show that these varieties are closer to the progenitor corn plant reconstructed by Mangelsdorf than such American races as Chapalote, etc. These observations on the two Himalayan primitive varieties clearly establish them as distinct entities different from the advanced types as well as the American primitive types. They open up an entirely new angle on the origin, evolution, and distribution of maize." "It must be admitted that the presence of primitive races in Sikkim, Nepal, Bhutan, or Assam hills is extremely puzzling and cannot be explained on the assumption of introduction and spread of maize in the post-Columbian era." Further research is obviously needed on these primitive forms of maize in south-central Asia and their possible relationships.

MICROFAUNA

Ancylostoma duodenale
Origin: Asia
Summary: Distribution requires explanation of how a parasite in humans could be common to both the pre-Columbian Old World (Asia and the Pacific islands) and the New World (mainly South America). The answer is unequivocal: human carriers of the hookworm had to have carried the worm between the hemispheres by means of voyaging, and at a very early time (at least the sixth millennium B.C.E.).
Grade: A
Sources: *Ancylostoma duodenale* – hookworm
> Allison et al. 1973. A Tiahuanaco mummy dating ca. 900 C.E. has *A. duodenale* remains in the intestine.
> Cockburn 1980. Controversy over the pre-Columbian presence or absence of hookworms (*A. duodenale*) is now settled from a Tiahuanaco mummy. "The parasites were probably carried by the original migrants from Asia, who brought them over the Bering land bridge." [This statement shows unfamiliarity with South American parasitology studies.]
> Darling 1920. Surveys the distribution of the two genera of hookworms, *Ancylostoma* and *Necator*. 221. It is possible that either or both reached the Americas in pre-Columbian times from Asia, Indonesia, or Polynesia via voyagers. Cold on the Bering Strait route would have prevented the continuance of infection, so that migrants would arrive free from hookworm (unless the average temperature at the Strait during migration was equal to that of North Carolina today). 323–3. "If certain tribes in America are found to be infected with *A. duodenale* as well as *Necator* this will suggest their having come to this continent by way of the sea from those countries in Asia where *A. duodenale* and *Necator* are [both] found to be infecting the natives, i.e., Japan and China."
> Ferreira et al 1982. Hookworm eggs are found in pre-European mummified bodies and coprolites. Such eggs develop in one phase of their development in warm soil: thus, not all ancestors of American natives could have crossed by Bering Strait. Transpacific migrants from Asia by sea must be one component of the ancient American population.
> Fonseca 1970. A number of shared species of parasites, which are discussed with supporting data, makes inescapable that voyagers reached South America directly from Oceania or Southeast Asia. 305–31. Discusses the question of the distribution of *A. duodenale* and *Necator americanus* and what might be inferred from that regarding the date of arrival.
> Verano 1991. Coprolites from coastal Peru show intestinal parasites: tapeworm 2700 B.C.E., pinworm approximately 2300 B.C.E., whipworm by 2700

B.C.E., and roundworm. Also, hookworm (*Ancylostoma duodenale*) from a mummy.

Soper 1927. Distribution suggests that *A. duodenale* was introduced to South America by ancient migrations from Indonesia or Polynesia. Cold climate in the Arctic would have interrupted the life cycle of the parasitic organism and thus precludes the possibility that the introduction to the Americas came by way of Bering Strait.

Reinhard 1992. He reprises South American incidence of the human parasites, hookworm (*Ancylostomidae*) and whipworm (*Trichuris trichiura*). Since both hookworms and whipworms require warm, moist conditions for the completion of their life cycles, finding human-specific parasites in the Americas is circumstantial evidence for transpacific contact and against a Bering-Strait-only entry of humans to the hemisphere.

Laming-Emperaire 1980. Fonseca has convincingly demonstrated that *Ancylostoma duodenale* and other parasite-caused diseases were shared between Old World and pre-Columbian South American Indians.

Adauto J. G. de Araújo 1980. Coprolites from four archaeological sites in Minas Gerais were examined for parasites. *Ancylostomids* are established that date by C14 between 3490 and 430 BP. Incompatibility of this organism with cold climate supports a hypothesis of transoceanic migration.

Manter 1967. Hookworm might have been brought with Jomon (Japan)/Valdivia (Ecuador) voyagers, if the Meggers'/Evans' theory is sound.

Stodder and Martin 1992. At least eight species of helminthic parasites appear in coprolites.

Ferreira et al.1988. The same parasites found at Unai, Minas Gerais, Brazil (i.e., *Trichuris trichiura* and *Necator americanus*) have now been identified in human coprolites from Boqueirão do Sitio da Pedra Furada in a stratum dated to 7320±80 BP. These parasites could not have reached the Americas via Bering Strait because the larvae, which must enter the soil before being taken up again into a human body, could not exist in Arctic cold. So we must suppose that they arrived by sea.

Confalonieri 1983. Examines closely the entire subject of the limits of cold climate on the transmission of this parasite to the Americas, including Bering Strait, transglacial North Atlantic, and Antarctic routes. Could parasites have been preserved in migrating humans on vessels? Yes. Such voyages alone provide a reasonable means of transmission to the Americas.

Araújo 1988. The evidence points only to maritime contacts. A map displays areas of infestation in the Old World of *N. americanus* and of *A. duodenale*. Possible maritime routes across the Pacific and Atlantic oceans are marked on the map.

Crawford 1998, 58. Summarizes the findings of Ferreira and Araujo et al., who assert that South American hookworm infection can only be explained by transpacific contact. Crawford suggests an alternative explanation, that the hookworm could have been a disease of animals since before separation of the New and Old World land masses. [But hookworms parasitic on humans are specific to their hosts. They would not be the same as those in, say, pigs.]

Ascaris lumbricoides
Origin: Old World
Summary: The intestinal parasite could only have crossed the ocean inside a human body. The presence of the parasite in both hemispheres thus required human voyaging.
Grade: A
Sources: *Ascaris lumbricoides* – roundworm
> Cockburn, Barraco, et al. 1998, 79–80. Mummy PUM II, dating to about 170 B.C.E., had in its intestinal tissue an ovum agreed by specialists probably to be *Ascaris* and some stated definitely that it was *A. lumbricoides*. That species has already been reported from many Old World locations in antiquity, as, e.g., at Winchester, England.
> Kuhnke 1993, 457. Ascariasis, infection of the small intestine caused by *Ascaris lumbricoides*, the large intestinal roundworm. Pictorial evidence exists for ancient Mesopotamia and in prescriptions in ancient Egypt.
> Patterson 1993, 603. This nematode was known to ancient writers in China, India, Mesopotamia, and Europe, and was present in pre-Columbian America.
> Verano 1998, 221. One of the parasites previously thought to have been post-Columbian introductions from the Old World, *Ascaris lumbricoides*, roundworm, in fact plagued pre-Columbian New World populations.

Bordetella pertussis
Origin: As with practically all disease organisms, origin was the Old World.
Summary: The agent of infection had to reside in a human organism during transoceanic travel, and the only rational way for a human to make the crossing is a voyage.
Grade: A
Sources: *Bordetella pertussis* – bacterium that causes whooping cough
> Chin 2000, 375–6. Humans are believed to be the only host. Transmitted primarily by direct contact with discharges from an infected person probably by airborne droplets.
> Stodder and Martin 1992, 62. Pertussis may have been present in the Southwest U.S. before arrival of the Spaniards.
> Hare 1967, 119, 122. He classes whooping cough with measles, smallpox, and other "acute infections in which the organisms disappear when recovery or death occurs." 120. "It is highly improbable that any of these organisms would have become established in a scattered community with a Palaeolithic culture (and thus to have crossed to the Americas via Beringia)." [But pertussis was apparently present in the New World. Thus, if the source was not due to a parallel mutation in the New World, a logical near-impossibility, it must have involved transmission from the

Old World, and that would probably have been after urban life developed there—i.e., 2500 B.C.E.?.]

Van Blerkom 1985, 46–7. There are other *Bordetella* species that cause respiratory illness in man and other primates, and they are found everywhere in the world.

Antibodies for pertussis bacilli occur in the blood of relatively isolated, unacculturated Brazilian Indians. "If not pertussis, then some close relative of it probably occurred in the New World as well as the Old." Sahagun's Aztec informant knew it (the disease), although this does not prove it pre-Columbian [it virtually proves it]. "Perhaps different strains existed in the two hemispheres ...." B. is probably an ancient agent which can persist in small populations because of its long period of infectivity (three weeks or more) and its capacity to reinfect ....

Borrelia recurrentis
Origin: Old World
Summary: Again, the only answer to how there could be bi-hemispheric occurrence is a transmission by humans accompanied by lice. Those lice were known.
Grade: In the absence of any alternative scenario for the American incidence: A
Sources: *Borrelia recurrentis* – spirochete that causes relapsing fever

Chin 2000, 421–2. Cause of a systemic spirochetal disease. Epidemics occur, if louse-borne; endemic, if tick-borne. Vector-borne, not transmitted from person to person. Louse-borne infection is acquired by crushing an infective louse, *Pediculus humanus*, so that it contaminates the bite wound or an abrasion of the skin. In tick-borne disease, people are infected by the bite of an argasid tick, principally *Ornithodoros hermsi* and *O. turicata* in the U.S. (or by others of the same genus in Central and South America, Africa, or the Middle East). The actual infectious agent is a spirochete, *Borrelia recurrentis*. (303. The causative spirochete of North American Lyme disease is another *Borrelia*, *B. Burgdorferi*.). 372. The body louse (*Pediculosis humanus corporis*) is involved in outbreaks of epidemic typhus caused by *Rickettsia prowazeki*, and epidemic relapsing fever is caused by *Borrelia recurrentis*.

See also material under *Pediculosis humanus corporis*.

Alchon 1991, 19–55. 22, 25. Relapsing fever, both the endemic type, transmitted by ticks, and the epidemic type, carried by lice, were present in pre-Spanish coastal Ecuador.

Hare 1967, 118. This spirochete may have first become parasitic in ticks, probably in the eastern Mediterranean. Carried north into Europe, it ultimately underwent mutation into *B. recurrentis* and became parasitic in lice. We do not know when this happened, but cases closely resembling relapsing fever were described (first) by Hippocrates, ca. 400 B.C.E.

Van Blerkom 1985, 62–65. The zoonotic form has most likely plagued hunter-gatherers since the advent of man. Louse-borne relapsing fever may date to the rise of urban centers. Relapsing fever in the New World may have been present before the Conquest in its zoonotic, or tick-borne, form. [Alchon eliminates the "may have been" in favor of "definitely was"].

Unlike the direction its evolution took in the Old World, the spirochete never adapted itself to reproduction in human lice, so no specifically human form of relapsing fever evolved in the New World, probably due to relative lack of commensal rodents to carry it into urban areas.

Diplococcus pneumoniae
Origin: Old World
Summary: It is evident that there was a transfer of this organism. Transfer via Bering Strait immigrants is possible, but so is transfer by voyagers. If no evidence of infection is found in Palaeoindian skeletons, scientists would have to turn to voyaging for an explanation.
Grade: Incomplete
Sources: *Diplococcus pneumonia* - bacterium that causes pneumonia in humans and mice
> Hare 1967, 123. Regarding acute infections harbored in carrier humans . . ., *Streptococcus pyogenes* and *Diplococcus pneumoniae* are evidenced in pre-Columbian skulls (Hooton 1930) due to visible damage to the matoids which they produce.

Entamoeba hystolytica
Origin: Old World
Summary: The only credible way for the amoeba to reach a New World population in Ecuador or elsewhere, is by a human being who personally brought the organism to the Americas, although, granted, there is the marginal chance that that might have been via Bering Strait.
Grade: B
Sources: *Entamoeba hystolytica* – organism that causes amoebic dysentery
> Chin 2000, 11–13. Human reservoir. Transmission mainly by ingestion of fecally contaminated food or water.
> Stodder and Martin 1992, 62. Amoebic dysentery was probably present before European contact (citing Van Blerkom 1985).
> Saunders et al. 1992, 118. Newman (1976) suggests pre-European contact diseases including bacillary and amoebic dysentery.
> Alchon 1991, 20. Amebiasis was in coastal Ecuador before the Spaniards arrived.
> Newman 1976, 669. Among diseases that were part of man's primate ancestry and that either crossed the Bering Strait cold-screen or were acquired in the Americas: "amoebic dysentery." In re. 'cold-screen,' cf. Innes 1993, 521. Thought on the 'cold screen' is reprised. Given the general scenario of small parties crossing Beringia "the numbers would be far too small to sustain a human-to-human mode of infection. At least one scholar (Klepinger 1987) denies that there is any evidence of the disease being carried over by the Beringia transmigrants."
> Van Blerkom 1985, 17. The New World presence of this is problematical. An unidentified *Entamoeba* cyst was found in a Peruvian mummy dating to about 1500 C.E. (Pike 1967, 185). This cannot be construed as definitive evidence for the presence of amoebiasis in the New World for several

reasons. First, the date of this putative pre-Columbian mummy is uncertain, especially when so close to the date of contact. Secondly, there are many species of *Entamoeba* which are nonpathogenic, while amoebiasis is caused by the specific strain, *E. histolytica*. Additionally, it is now known that the amoeba alone is incapable of inducing the disease state, but requires the concomitant presence of a bacterium (citing Schwabe). It is likely that the amoeba but not the bacterium was present in the New World .... The absence of the additional agent can be inferred from the much greater severity of the infection in New World monkeys than in Old World monkeys (citing Bourned). 18. "... one can reasonably conclude with Ashburn that amoebic dysentery was probably introduced into the Americas from the Old World. ... and was brought over on the slave ships ...." Fig. 2, map on p. 19, shows amoebic dysentery reaching Persia from India by 480 B.C.E., thence to Africa. [But regardless of whether the instrumental bacterium was present to trigger the disease, the fact still remains that the amoeba had entered the Americas and there is no question that it was in a human body. How? Either via Bering Strait or by voyaging, and the concept of a cold-screen makes the latter very likely.]

Pike 1967, 185. The body of an eight- or nine-year-old Inca child from a tomb in the Andes yielded cysts of the protozoan *Entamoeba* in the rectum (species unidentifiable). The approximate age of the body was 450 years. [Van Blerkom in citing this find emphasized the date as probably after Spanish influence, but in the light of Alchon's identification of amebiasis in Ecuador before Spanish arrival, there is no reason not to accept the Inca child as pre-Columbian.]

Verano 1998, 221. "Probably present" in a mummy (in Peru).

Enterobius vermicularis
Origin:
Summary:
Grade:
Sources: *Enterobius vermicularis* - pinworms
Verano 1991. Coprolites from coastal Peru show intestinal parasites: tapeworm 2700 B.C.E., pinworm approximately 2300 B.C.E., whipworm by 2700 B.C.E., and roundworm. Also, hookworm (*Ancylostoma duodenale*) from a mummy.

Flavivirus spp.
Origin: Old World
Summary: The majority of experts say this was not present in the Americas, but a few competent epidemiologists insist otherwise. In deference to the latter we keep the option open that further evidence may be brought forward.
Grade: incomplete
Sources: *Flavivirus* spp. – causal organism for yellow fever
Chin 2000, 553–4. Yellow fever exists in nature in two transmission cycles: a sylvatic, or jungle, cycle that involves mosquitoes and non-human primates; and an urban cycle involving *Aedes aegypti* mosquitoes and

humans. Sylvatic transmission is restricted to tropical regions of Africa and Latin America, where a few hundred cases occur annually, most frequently among young adult males who are occupationally exposed in forested or transitional areas of Bolivia, Brazil, Colombia, Ecuador, and Peru. With the exception of a few cases in Trinidad in 1954, no outbreak of urban yellow fever had been transmitted by *Ae. aegypti* in the Americas since 1942. Reservoir: in urban areas, humans and *Ae. aegypti* mosquitoes. In forest areas, vertebrates other than humans, mainly monkeys and possibly marsupials, and forest mosquitoes. Transmission (sylvatic) in forests of South America is by the bite of several species of forest mosquitoes of the genus Haemagogus.

Kiple 1992. Arguments for the presence of yellow fever in the Americas have faltered in the face of immunological and entomological evidence. African animals and humans show immunity, but not in the New World. Entomological evidence strongly suggests that the most efficient vector, *Aedes aegypti*, was not present in the New World. Thus, the strong probability is that both virus and vector had to be imported. A warm climate and closely-packed humans are required for yellow fever to have effect. It is supposed that huge numbers of *Aedes aegypti* arrived in the West Indies in the holds of early slave ships, but not until 1647 was the critical mass of humans and mosquitoes reached whereupon Barbados saw yellow fever succeed in getting its first beachhead.

Guerra 1966, 330–2. The two most important aboriginal Aztec disease entities were *matlazahuatl* and *cocolitztli*. Caused major epidemics. Translation of the terms remains unclear. His analysis of the symptoms indicates that the former was exanthematic typhus, with a faint possibility that it was typhoid fever. *Cocolitztli* was a more generic term which some feel might have been yellow fever. Stutz 2006 reprises research by Acuña-Soto and colleagues that challenges this identification of the two Aztec diseases.

Denevan 1976, 5. Yellow fever has generally been believed introduced from the Old World after Columbus, but the reservoir of yellow fever among South and Central American monkeys and historical evidence suggest otherwise.

Villacorta Cifuentes 1976. Yellow fever quite certainly was present in the reservoir provided by monkeys, and there is evidence that periodically, under certain ecological conditions, it had severe effects on humans.

Bustamente 1958. A physician argues at length for the presence of yellow fever in pre-Columbian Mesoamerica.

Van Blerkom 1985, 103. Since the vectors of yellow fever require tropical conditions for growth, the infection could not have been carried into the New World across the Bering Strait. Several considerations strongly suggest that it was not indigenous to the monkeys of the New World either. Yellow fever never got out of West Africa into East Africa and Asia, for inobvious reasons.

Giardia lamblia
Origin: Old World
Summary: Supposing Alchon's evidence indicates not only the genus *Giardia*, but the species *lamblia*, the question should be asked, how did this organism reach the Americas? By humans traveling across the ocean is a plausible answer.
Grade: C
Sources: *Giardia lamblia* – protozoan that infects principally the upper small intestine
- Chin 2000, 220–1. Reservoir: humans and possibly certain wild and domestic animals. Associated with drinking water from unfiltered surface water sources. Person-to-person transmission occurs by hand to mouth transfer involving feces of an infected individual.
- Alchon 1991, 20. *Giardias* were a source of infection (giardiasis) in pre-Columbian times in coastal Ecuador.
- Pike 1967, 185. Two coprolites of human origin from a cave near the Dead Sea in a layer about 1800 years old contained cysts of *Giardia lamblia*. [Witenberg 1961, 86.]
- Reinhard 1988, 356. Small band populations and limited contact between bands would have lowered parasite diversity within each band. Only parasites with long periods of infectiveness can survive in small populations. [These considerations fit with the cold-screen hypothesis to make it very unlikely that helminths and protozoa too arrived via Beringia.]

Human (alpha) herpes virus 3
Origin: Old World
Summary: It could be that American natives received this organism from Brazilian monkeys, but in the absence of any evidence that was so, it is a much simpler explanation to see infected Asians coming by sea on one or more of the voyages which are demonstrated in this paper than to explain its presence in any other way.
Grade: B
Sources: Human (alpha) herpes virus 3 (*Herpes zoster*) (varicella-zoster virus VZV) the cause of chicken pox, shingles, etc.
- Chin 2000, 91–3. Chicken pox (varicella) an acute, generalized viral disease. *Herpes zoster*, or shingles, is a local manifestation of latent varicella infection. The infectious agent is human (alpha) herpes virus 3 (varicella-zoster virus VZV, a member of the herpes virus group). Reservoir: humans. Transmission: from person to person by direct contact or droplet or airborne spread of fluids from an infected person.
  350–1. Human (gamma) herpes virus 4, the Epstein-Barr virus, is closely related to other herpes viruses morphologically, but distinct serologically. Involved in infectious mononucleosis.
- Stodder and Martin, 1992. Herpes was present in the Southwest U.S. before the Spaniards arrived.
- Alchon 1991, 23. A family of herpes viruses, including herpes simplex (cold sores), varicella (chicken pox and shingles), and cytomegalovirus (a mononucleosis-like illness), can remain latent within the human body for

years after the initial attack. By remaining dormant for long periods and allowing their hosts a chance to recover, herpes viruses bypass the need for a constant supply of new victims or for intermediate reservoirs. These viruses were endemic in the pre-Spanish coastal Ecuadorean population. They leave no evidence on skeletons but have been found in isolated populations of Amazonian natives.

    Hare 1967,120. "It is highly improbable that any of this class of organisms would have become established in a scattered community with a Palaeolithic culture. And, certainly, none of them were present in the Americas [sic]." 121. Nothing whatever is known about the early history of chicken pox. [Nevertheless] there is no doubt about its [relative] antiquity [in the Old World]. It was known by the first century C.E.

    Van Blerkom 1985. 27–28. Causes varicella and shingles, Epstein-Barr virus, and cytomegalovirus. Varicella ('chicken pox') is endemic in Brazilian tribes as well (29) as in other primates. *Herpes zoster*, like the other herpes viruses, "is therefore [sic] an ancient primate virus."

Human (gamma) herpes virus 4
Origin: Old World
Summary: See the summary for the preceding entry.
Grade: B
Sources: Human (gamma) herpes virus 4 (syn., Epstein-Barr virus; syn., cytomegalovirus) source of infectious mononucleosis.

    Chin 2000, 91–3. Epstein-Barr virus, human (gamma) herpes virus 4, is closely related to other herpes viruses morphologically, but distinct serologically. Involved in infectious mononucleosis, etc.

    Alchon 1991, 19–55. 23. A family of herpes viruses, including herpes simplex (cold sores), varicella (= zoster, cause of chicken pox and shingles), and cytomegalovirus (a mononucleosis-like illness), can remain latent within the human body for years after the initial attack. By remaining dormant for long periods and allowing their hosts a chance to recover, herpes viruses bypass the need for a constant supply of new victims or for intermediate reservoirs. These were endemic in the pre-Spanish coastal-Ecuadorean population.

    Van Blerkom 1985, 29. Widely endemic, and a related virus is found in chimpanzees and Old World monkeys, so [?cf. Hare 1967, 119–20, under Influenza] the natural history of Epstein-Barr virus is similar to that of the other herpes viruses.

See also the material under Human (alpha) herpes virus 3.

Influenza viruses
Origin: Old World
Summary: Passage to the Americas by sea migrants is a plausible mechanism to explain its presence here, but with so little evidence we cannot determine that happened. More study is needed.
Grade: incomplete
Sources: Influenza viruses

Chin 2000, 270–1. Three types of influenza viruses are recognized: A, B, and C. Humans are the primary reservoir, although swine and birds are also in play. Transmission is mainly airborne, or by direct contact.

Newman 1976, 667–72. 669. Native American diseases included viral influenza and pneumonia.

Hare 1967, 119–20. This disease fits with other acute infectious diseases that were relatively late developing in history (i.e., in urban times) and which would quite surely not have been maintained in a Palaeolithic population and thus have crossed the Bering Strait.

Van Blerkom 1985, 30–31. Influenza was described in the writings of Hippocrates. The earliest record in the New World was not until 1647, so it could have been brought over after European contact. Brazilian Indians do not show antibodies to influenza type A but possibly some show antibodies for type B. She thinks it is unlikely that influenza was in the Americas before Columbus.

Leishmania sp.
Origin: Presumably Old World
Summary: The possibility of voyagers from Asia introducing this organism must be recognized. However, much more needs to be known about distribution in both hemispheres before any judgment could be made.
Grade: incomplete
Sources: *Leishmania*

Merriam-Webster's Collegiate Dictionary, Tenth Edition, s.v. *leishmania*. Any of a genus (*Leishmania*) of flagellate protozoans that is parasitic in the tissues of vertebrates.

Weiss 1984, 29. The endemicity in distant populations of specific infections which require contact persons or co-dwellers for their spread illustrate past (historical) contacts. The problem is a real puzzler since it treats of specific infectious agents transmitted, for example, by the same winged agent, although this is of short flight (capability) as in the case of Leishmaniasis, with its vector of the genus *Phlebotomus*. The *Leishmaniasis-Phlebotomus* Complex is mysteriously repeated even in some cases with the same species in Peru, on both sides of the Andean Cordillera, the Amazonian selva, in regions of Brazil, Colombia, Central America, Mexico, the other side of the European Mediterranean, and in distant places in Asia and Africa. He adds (33), "The autochthonous [i.e., ancient] character of American skin Leishmaniasis is demonstrated by ceramic human effigy figures and by carious lesions in the bones of the nose, manifest in skulls of the region of Peru where the disease is endemic."

Microsporum spp.
Origin: Asia
Summary: Fonseca demonstrated beyond question that both *Microsporum* and *Trychophyton* organisms were present in aboriginal South America. There is no explanation for the diseases they produced except that they were brought by sea-borne peoples. (*Trychophyton* organism is listed separately below. It remains possible

that the other infectious agents mentioned by Chin in this class—*Epidermophyton floccosum*, *Scytalidium dimidiatum*, and *S. hyalinum*—might also be identified by further research.)

Grade: A

Sources: *Microsporum* spp. – infectious fungi causing ringworm of the body.

Chin 2000, 147–53. Species differ depending on the area infested (head, beard, groin, body, foot (i.e., athlete's foot), or nails. Transmission is skin-to-skin or indirect contact through shared objects. Reservoir: humans for the most common forms of the disease, *tinea corporis* (ringworm of the body), or *tinea cruris* (ringworm of the groin and perianal region). A fungal disease of the skin other than of the scalp, bearded areas, and feet, that characteristically appears as flat, spreading, ring-shaped lesions. Infectious agents: most species of *Microsporum* and *Trichophyton*; also *Epidermophyton floccosum*. *Scytalidium dimidiatum* and *S. hyalinum* cause 'dry type' *tinea corporis* in tropical areas.

Fonseca 1970, 147ff. The disease that he called *tinha* (or *tinea*) *imbricada* is the same as earlier literature called *toquelau*, or *tokelau* (in Oceania), and *chimbêrê* (in Brazil). 148. The area of distribution is detailed: most of Polynesia, Micronesia, Melanesia, and Malaysia, as well as in the indigenous population of Formosa, and in Indochina, and, with less frequency, south China, Burma, Ceylon, and the south of India. Brazilian authors continue to maintain that the earliest focus of this disease was the Malay Archipelago and elsewhere in Southeast Asia. It is endemic among tribal Formosans, as the author found by field research in Formosa in 1927. It prevailed among the natives, being there before the Chinese or Japanese dominated that island or other areas of Southeast Asia. 216–7. Presents a systematic argument on ten points supporting the proposition that the introduction of this parasite was by infected immigrants from outside the area [anciently]. Investigators have also found cases of this disease in central Mexico, Guatemala, and El Salvador. 40–41. Ringworm is totally absent among indigenes of the north of America, Alaska, or Canada. Early Mexican sources (e.g., Las Casas) do not mention it. Similarly, the chroniclers on Peru fail to make any mention of it. But Brazil, yes, from earliest colonial times. 44–45. None in Africa. 195–196. Discusses the earliest discovery of *chimbêrê*, by him, in the Mato Grosso in 1924. Goes on to justify the assumption that the bearers of the disease were virtually isolated and untouched by European influence. 216. It is impossible that this disease was introduced from Europe after Columbus, because it did not occur in Europe.

Laming-Emperaire 1980. She accepts that Fonseca has convincingly demonstrated that *tinea imbricata* (ringworm), among other parasite-caused diseases, was shared between the Old World and pre-Columbian South America.

Mycobacterium leprae
Origin: Old World
Summary: The evidence adduced for American incidence is very weak. In the future further data might come to light, so we retain the possibility.
Grade: incomplete
Sources: *Mycobacterium leprae* – cause of leprosy
> Van Blerkom 1985, 32–37. An isolated report of pre-Columbian Mexican skeletal evidence exists (Goff 1967, 291), but the evidence is equivocal, for other conditions can produce similar changes.
>
> Van Blerkom cont'd. "Sahagun's Aztec informants described a condition similar to leprosy which they called 'disease of the gods,' but this could have been any disfiguring skin disease (Ashburn 1947, 233–4)." *Mycobacteria* similar to Hansen's bacillus have been found in Bolivian frogs and wild armadillos of Louisiana and Texas. 37. "One cannot dismiss the possibility that leprosy, like tuberculosis, is an ancient disease which has become localized because of the more successful spread of TB," a related infection. Since it depends on humidity, heat, and crowding, it is not a good candidate to have come across the Bering Strait, although we cannot be sure.
>
> Goff 1967, 281, 291. A skull is illustrated and discussed showing what may be leprosy, from Mexico (probably pre-Columbian).
>
> Sandison and Tapp 1998, 42. A case of leprosy in a Coptic Christian (sixth century) body discovered by Elliot Smith and Derry in 1910 in Nubia is unquestioned. This has been confirmed macroscopically (1960) and radiologically (1967). There is no direct evidence in the pharaonic period for leprosy, and evidence for it in the medical papyri is tenuous.

Mycobacterium tuberculosis
Origin: Old World
Summary: Tuberculosis has been established as present in the Americas anciently, but no credible theory for its origin within the hemisphere has been presented. Sea migrants, now known to be a population source, would provide a satisfactory explanation.
Grade: A-
Sources: *Mycobacterium tuberculosis* – the tuberculosis bacterium
> Chin 2000, 523–4. This complex includes *M. tuberculosis* and *M. africanum*, primarily from humans, and *M. bovis*, primarily from cattle. Other mycobacteria occasionally produce disease clinically indistinguishable from tuberculosis. Transmission is by exposure to tubercle bacilli in airborne droplet nuclei produced by people with pulmonary or laryngeal TB by coughing or sneezing. Extra-pulmonary TB (other than laryngeal) is generally not communicable.
>
> Alchon 1991, 19–55, 23–4. Archaeological evidence indicates that acute respiratory infections were the most frequent cause of death among pre-Columbian Andean residents, just as today. Paleo-pathologists have discovered "incontrovertible evidence" from mummies dating from the

eighth century demonstrating the presence of tuberculosis in South America, both pulmonary and blood-borne (miliary) tuberculosis.

Allison, Gerszten, et al. 1981. Reports on eleven Peruvian and Chilean mummies that evidence TB and range in radiocarbon dates from 800 B.C.E. to 1600 C.E., with five earlier than 300 C.E.

Karasch 1993, 537. In a study of 11 mummies from Chile and Peru, two dating from 290 C.E. had "cavitary pulmonary lesions from the walls of which acid-fast bacilli were recovered." According to William Sharpe, two of these mummies have "diagnoses of tuberculosis about as solidly established as paleo-pathologic techniques will permit" (Sharpe 1983).

Buikstra 1981, 13. "In the absence of appropriately-timed migrations from the Old World, we must develop and defend a reasonable model for the origin of this disease in the absence of [animal reservoirs in the form of] domestic herd animals such as cattle."

Powell, 1992. The earliest documented cases of tuberculosis are from Chile (160 B.C.E.). North American cases postdate 850 C.E. (Ontario, and Georgia through Arkansas to the Southwest).

Clark, Kelley, et al. 1987. 46. In order to explain the high susceptibility of Amerindian populations to many Eurasian diseases, Black (1960; see also Stewart 1960) postulates that the migrations over the Beringian and Panamanian land bridges were so rigorous that all individuals with latent infection developed overt disease and died. Accordingly, many endemic diseases including tuberculosis, found in extinct [see below Hare, who makes clear there is insufficient evidence to attribute TB to any people in the world as early as those usually supposed to have crossed the Bering Strait] and extant Eurasian populations were screened out and prevented from reaching the prehistoric Americas [the Bering 'cold barrier'].

Comment on Clark et al. by Linda L. Klepinger, 52–53. "Current paleo-pathological evidence would suggest that the mycobacteria responsible for the New World disease were not carried over by the Beringia transmigrants but more likely arose *de novo* in the Western Hemisphere. Evidence for the disease appears relatively later in North America compared to the Peruvian cases and is associated with the denser populations which arose with intensive maize agriculture. Also, temporal estimates for the arrival of the Asian immigrant place all three migrations earlier than the domestication of cattle in the Old World and earlier than any evidence of human-to-human-transmitted tuberculosis."

Comment on Clark et al. by Nancy C. Lovell, 53. "But where did that organism come from? They say that there are many theories for the origin of *M. tuberculosis* but give us only two—both of which are based on origination from the bovid infection. Why do they choose these theories? While the presence of an acid-fast bacillus in pre-Columbian South America has been demonstrated [citing Allison], this bacillus could not have derived from an infection of cattle. Cattle are not indigenous to that area. Prehistoric groups hunted camelids and deer, not bovids. We are left to conclude that (1) the acid-fast bacillus is not *M. tuberculosis*, (2) *M. tuberculosis* did not originate from the bovid infection, or (3) while *M.*

tuberculosis may have derived from *M. bovis* in the Old World it has some other origin in the New." [But she raises no possibility of voyaging as a means of introducing *M. tuberculosis* into the New World.]

Hare 1967, 117. *M. tuberculosis* has never been isolated from wild animals, nor has it ever become established as a human parasite. But it has infected dairy herds since before the Christian era. Because Palaeolithic societies did not domesticate cattle, it is improbable that this organism caused infection at that time, but it may well have done so in Neolithic and more recent societies. Actually, very little is known about the antiquity of this disease.

Hare, cont'd., 125–6. The earliest sure evidence for pulmonary tuberculosis in the Old World is late in the second millennium B.C.E. – India, China, and Egypt. Bones with lesions suggestive of tuberculosis may go back as early as 3700 B.C.E., but that may be deceptive. It was never found in the thousands of mummies from Egypt and Nubia examined by Dawson, Smith, et al. 127. Repeats dependence on the bovine source theory.

Verano 1998, 217–9. Since Allison's pioneering study, many additional cases of probable TB have been identified from skeletal and mummified remains from Peru and Chile. Recent developments in DNA recovery and amplification by polymerase chain reaction have resulted in a major advance. Salo et al. (1994) recently reported the successful extraction of DNA characteristic of *M. tuberculosis* from a Peruvian mummy. Other documentation is given.

Necator americanus
Origin: Old World
Summary: The only credible explanation for the presence of this hookworm in the Americas is arrival by boat of immigrants to (South) America.
Grade: A
Sources: *Necator americanus* – hookworm

Darling 1920. Surveys distribution of the two genera of hookworms, *Ancylostoma* spp. and *Necator*. 221. It is possible that either or both were in the Americas in pre-Columbian times from Asia, Indonesia, or Polynesia by voyagers. Cold on the Bering Strait route would have prevented the continuance of infection, so that migrants would arrive free from this hookworm. 223–3. "If certain tribes in America are found to be infected with *A. duodenale* as well as *Necator*, this will suggest their having come to this continent by way of the sea from those countries in Asia where *A. duodenale* and *Necator* are [both] found to be infecting the natives, i.e., Japan and China."

Ferreira, Araújo, and Confalonieri 1988, 65–7. Human coprolites found in a cave site in Minas Gerais state, Brazil, date between 3490 and 430 BP. Eggs of two types of ancylostomids were identified (one of which is *Necator*).

Reinhard 1992. Includes a topic headed "Transpacific Contact?" on page 241. He reprises South American incidence of the hookworm parasites

(*Ancylostomidae*), whipworm (*Trichuris trichiura*), and *Necator americanus* (long before 1492).

Onchocerca volvulus
Origin: Old World
Summary: Weiss (1984) states that *Onchocerca volvulus* might have been present in the Americas based on distribution study. Further work is needed.
Grade: incomplete
Sources: *Onchocerca volvulus* – a filarial worm (nematode) causing onchocerciasis
    Chin 2000, 363–4. The female worm discharges microfilariae that migrate through the skin. Pigment changes produce the condition known as 'leopard skin.' Upon reaching the eye, they may cause blindness. Found in Guatemala and southern Mexico, Venezuela, Colombia, Ecuador, and parts of Brazil, as well as in subsaharan Africa and Yemen. Transmitted only by the bite of infected female black flies of the genus *Simulium* (different species are involved in Central America, South America, and Africa; there are several species in Africa). Reservoir: humans.
    Hoeppli 1969. "Some of the infections introduced by Africans already occurred in the New World in pre-Columbian time." Onchocerciasis was one.
    Weiss 1984, 32. Some historians of medicine believe that onchocercosis was not brought by slaves from Africa, the common belief, but was autocthonous in the Americas. Its extensive diffusion in this continent supports this possibility for, besides Mexico, Guatemala, and Venezuela, it has been found in Peru, in the high forest Amazonian area (Chanchamayho).

Pediculus humanus capitis and *P. humanus corporis*
Origin: Old World
Summary: These lice were definitely present in both hemispheres. Only one explanation will serve: ocean voyaging that brought humans infested with the pests. The patent similarity in the name of the louse between Pacific Islands and Mayan languages is more than suggestive.
Grade: A
Sources: *P. humanus capitis* and *P. humanus corporis* – lice
    Chin 2000, 372–3. Lice are host specific; those of lower animals do not infest people. The body louse is the species involved in outbreaks of epidemic typhus caused by *Rickettsia prowazekii* and epidemic relapsing fever caused by *Borrelia recurrentis*. Transmission is by direct contact with infested persons or objects used by them. Lice can survive for only a week without a food source.
    Fonseca 1970. Following a long treatment of issues of taxonomy of *Pediculi* on 145–147, he discusses particularly matters pertaining to Old and New World distribution of *Pediculus pseudohumanus*. "A form of louse found solely in indigenes of America and of Oceania and in American macaques." Quotes Ferris (1951, 275) [Fonseca promises a bibliography but failed to present one, as far as we know, so Ferris (1935) may be what

he intended] thus: "Here we have a most extraordinary situation. The form which Ewing [the first to report this louse] described exists, without question, but its distribution is extremely peculiar. Ferris (1935) mentioned the presence in his material of specimens from Central American Indians and from natives in the Marquesas Islands in the South Pacific, which show a slight lateral lobing of certain of the paratergal plates. This is the form that Ewing ascribes to his *pseudohumanus*, and the illustration here given based upon a specimen from the Marquesas Islands almost duplicates that given by him. It may be noted that those from the South Pacific all have a noticeably larger number of setae on the dorsum of the abdomen than do those from the New World." The material of *Pediculus pseudohumanus* that Ferris had available and which serves this author for identification, comes from the Marquesas and from some natives of Tahiti. They [now] come from a household of Indians in Santa Emilia, Guatemala, and a mummified head from Ecuador. Examples also come from the head of a mummy of a Maya Indian of Xinchel, Yucatan, plus natives of Guayabelete, Panama. In his monumental monograph, Ferris (1951, 275) notes the puzzle this poses: "Here is a form that is supposed to occur both on New World monkeys and upon man. More than that, it occurs not only upon man in the region where these monkeys occur naturally, but what is apparently the same form occurs on man in the far distant South Sea Islands."

Sandison 1967, 178–83. Lice are known from pre-Columbian Mexico and Peru as well as the Mediterranean through China.

Karasch 1993, 538. Some parasite remains have been recovered in autopsies on mummies from Chile and Peru. An examination of the body of a young boy revealed those for head lice. According to chroniclers, the poor in the Inca Empire had to "pay tribute in the form of small containers of lice." Not surprisingly, typhus was "a very common disease in ancient Peru."

Alchon 1991, 22. One can build a strong case for the existence of both endemic (flea-borne) and epidemic (louse-borne) typhus in the New World, based on lice on Peruvian and Chilean mummies. (Cf. Roys 1931. 341. Mayan: "*Uk*. The louse found on man and quadrupeds." Motul dictionary).

Schuhmacher et al. 1992, 18. Ethnically-Papuan Austronesian Buma tribe, on Vanikoro, eastern Solomon Islands, *ukə* = louse. Austronesian Ontong Java (western Solomons), *uku* = louse. Maya (southern Mexico), *uk* = louse.

Zinsser 1960, 254–61. Was typhus in humans in the Americas before the Spaniards? Perhaps. Mooser found Tarascan and Aztec words relating to the disease. Much historical evidence involving lice found on mummies suggests typhus was present in South America.

Hoeppli 1969. "Some of the infections introduced by Africans already occurred in the New World in pre-Columbian time." "Lice" were present.

Van Blerkom 1985, 4. "The lice found on pre-Columbian American mummies are of the same species (with only slight differences, on the order of a subspecies) as those on Old World humans (El-Najjar and Mulinski 1980, 111; Zinsser 1964, 176–7)."

Piedreaia hortai
Origin: Old World
Summary: Fonseca's evidence is straightforward. This organism causes the same growth in the hair of occupants of Asia and Africa and of the Amazon Basin.
Grade: A
Sources: *Piedreaia hortai* – the fungus that causes piedra (negra), a disease of the hair
    Chin 2000, 147–8. Under the discussion of *Tinea capitis*, or ringworm of the scalp, he observes that *T. capitis* is "easily distinguished from piedra, a fungus infection of the hair occurring in South America and some countries of Southeast Asia and Africa. Piedra is characterized by black, hard 'gritty' nodules on hair shafts, caused by *Piedreaia hortai* ...."
    Fonseca 1970, 262. This fungal disease, commonly called piedra negra but which he wants to call *piedra ascospórica*, is especially characteristic of inner South America, although found very rarely in North America. He cites such limited literature as exists. 264. "Separated from South America by the two great ocean barriers," this disease is in both hemispheres; [for] it is also in Southeast Asia—Thailand, Vietnam, Burma, Malaya, Indonesia. "In all these regions of Oceania and of Southeast Asia, *piedra ascospórica* presents exactly the same clinical, epidemiological, and parasitological characteristics with which it appears on the American continent." 270–2. Gives names for the disease in Guaraní and Tupí languages (lowland South America). In previous works, he has concluded, and has justified the conclusion, that this disease was introduced to the Americas by pre-Columbian migrations by natives of Oceania. Argues anew why that must be so. It is missing in those parts of northern Asia and in North America that could have been involved in transmission by any migration across the Bering Strait that might have brought this disease. None of the disease existed in Europe or Africa. Because it was widely distributed in South America, among many language groups, it must have arrived long ago.
    Laming-Emperaire 1980. Fonseca has demonstrated that the disease *pierre noire* [what Fonseca calls piedra negra, or piedra ascospórica], as well as other parasite-caused diseases, were shared between Old World and pre-Columbian South American Indians.

Plasmodium falciparum
Origin: Old World
Summary: The evidence is in dispute whether malaria occurred in the Americas, but what is true is that a significant number of researchers who have investigated the matter think it was.
Grade: C
Sources: *Plasmodium falciparum* – the sporozoan parasite which causes malaria
    Chin 2000, 310–12. There are four human malarias which can present sufficiently similar symptoms to make species differentiation generally impossible without lab studies. The most serious malarial infection is

falciparum malaria. The others (vivax, malariae, and ovale) are generally not life-threatening. Humans are the only important reservoir of human malaria. Nonhuman primates are naturally infected by many (other) malarial species, which can infect humans experimentally, but natural transmission to humans is rare. Transmission is by the bite of an infective female *Anopheles* mosquito.

Bruce-Chwatt 1965. Argues from physical remains, epidemiology of living native groups, names of disease and use of cinchona bark, plus ethno-historical/chronicle sources that malaria was present in pre-Columbian times. A personal communication to the author from Fonseca says the latter believes that several diseases were imported to the Americas from Polynesia, Micronesia, and Melanesia, and that malaria might have been included. Bruce-Chwatt is confident that malaria was present. Today, the judgment regarding its presence in pre-Columbian America should not be "improbable though not impossible" (so Jarcho 1964) but "probable but not proved."

Cabieses 1979, 539. Malaria may have been indigenous and hence may have been the reason ancient Peruvians built their houses far from the rivers; it also might have been one of the 'fevers' that attacked the Inca armies as they invaded the Upper Amazon.

Hoeppli 1959. Emphatic that malaria was pre-Columbian in the New World.

Jaramillo-Arango 1950. Includes a "critical review of the basic facts in the history of cinchona." Malaria was known among American Indians from earliest times and cinchon was familiar to them as a remedy.

Sandison 1967, 182. "Probably malaria also occurred in pre-Columbian America."

Villacorta Cifuentes 1976. The preponderance of evidence is against malaria being present; however, the fact that the Peruvians knew of the value of quinine as an agent against it in colonial times leaves a question.

Goldstein 1969. Ackerknecht, Bruce-Chwatt, and Sandison say that malaria probably occurred in the Americas before Columbus, although malaria probably originated in the Old World. Goldstein tends to agree with them.

Alchon 1991, 63. By 1630, when malaria had become a serious problem in Quito, the Spaniards had recognized the value of cinchona bark, the remedy for malaria. [Whether that remedy had been used earlier (by natives) is somewhat uncertain.]

Van Blerkom 1985, 37–42. "Malaria has been widespread in the Old World since most ancient times." Many species of simian plasmodia exist which can be transmitted to man. Angel suggested the human infection may have been present at Çatal Huyuk in Anatolia by 6000 B.C.E. It is also manifest in the oldest Egyptian mummies. 40. However, malaria in humans was probably not in the Americas in pre-Columbian times. Furthermore, the New World simian malaria is severe, not a condition to be expected in a long-present disease. Some think it was present, including Bruce-Chwatt (1965) and T. D. Stewart (1973, 38–40).

Millet et al. 1998, 192. A 3200-year-old Egyptian mummy had had malaria at one point in his life as shown by a test for a protein antigen of *P. falciparum*.

Sandison and Tapp, 1998. Millet and his colleagues (1994) recently detected an antigen produced by *Plasmodium falciparum* in Egyptian mummies from all the periods they tested, indicating the presence of malaria.

Dunn 1993, 860. Malaria could have reached the New World before 1492 only as an infection of migrants from northeast Asia or by pre-Columbian sea-borne introductions. The possibility that humans brought malaria overland into North America from Siberia can almost certainly be discounted.... Similarly, any voyagers landing on American shores from the central or eastern Pacific could not have carried the parasites with them because islands in that region are free of anopheline vectors and thus of locally transmitted malaria. Voyagers reaching the American coasts from eastern Asia (e.g., fishermen adrift from Japan) could conceivably have introduced malaria, but this possibility too is remote. Moreover, colonial records indicate that malaria was almost certainly unknown to the indigenous peoples. Also, absence of any blood genetic polymorphisms associated with malaria elsewhere in the world is evidence consistent with American absence.

Rickettsia prowazekii
Origin: Old World
Summary: Fairly clearly, epidemic typhus, and of course with it the human body louse, manifested itself in the Americas. No explanation other than the arrival of voyagers from across the Pacific is plausible.
Grade: A
Sources: *Rickettsia prowazekii* – agent of louse-borne typhus (epidemic typhus)

Chin 2000, 372, 541–542. The body louse (*Pediculus humanus corporis*) is infected by feeding on the blood of a patient with acute typhus fever. People are infected by rubbing louse feces or crushed lice into the bite or into superficial abrasions. Humans are the reservoir during inter-epidemic periods. 372. The body-louse is involved in outbreaks of epidemic typhus caused by *Rickettsia prowazekii* and epidemic relapsing fever caused by *Borrelia recurrentis*.

Alchon 1991, 22. Disease before 1534. One can also build a strong case for the existence of both endemic (flea-borne) and epidemic (louse-borne) typhus in the New World, based on lice on mummies. Examinations of mummified human remains have revealed that head and body lice commonly infested native populations. Most native households in the Andes included several guinea pigs in the family's living quarters; these animals can be reservoirs for the typhus rickettsiae. Infected fleas can easily jump from rodent to human, transmitting the endemic form of the disease. There are pre-Conquest traditions of epidemics of some disease or other occurring during periods of social turmoil – wars, famines, and natural disasters – supporting the assertion that typhus existed in the

Americas before the sixth century. Guaman Poma described two
   epidemics long before the Spanish Conquest of Peru.
Cabieses 1979. Typhus was common in pre-Columbian Peru.
Guerra 1966, 330–2. The two most important aboriginal Aztec disease entities
   were *matlazahuatl* and *cocolitztli*. They caused major epidemics. Translation
   of the terms remains unclear. His analysis of the symptoms indicates that
   the former was exanthematic typhus, with a faint possibility that it was
   typhoid fever. On the contrary, Stutz 2006 reports that research by
   Acuña-Soto now identifies these two diseases as indigenous ebola-like
   infections.
Ackerknecht 1965, 32–43. Petechial typhus (spotted fever) is at least as old as
   1083 C.E. in Mexico, according to Aztec traditions. 53. The epidemic of
   1454 on the plateau of Mexico was in all probability typhus, not the
   yellow fever claimed by some.
Goldstein 1969. Ackerknecht, Bruce-Chwatt, and Sandison say typhus
   probably occurred in the Americas before Columbus, and Goldstein
   appears to agree.
Villacorta Cifuentes 1976. Exanthematic typhus was present anciently.
Fonseca 1970, 332–6. Nicolle (1932) drew attention to the distribution of
   typhus that supports the idea that pre-Columbian migrations reached the
   Americas from Oceania. 335. Cites a large literature (Mooser, Gay,
   Miranda, Gaitán, Nicolle) representing what Fonseca refers to as "most
   authors" who have written on this point and who have considered that
   exanthematic typhus existed in pre-Columbian America. Furthermore,
   several wild rodents in the Americas (*Sigmodon hispidus*, *Microtus mexicanus*,
   Geomys virginianus, *Neotoma fuscipes*) have been shown to be capable of
   acquiring typhus murin infection experimentally, which supports the idea
   that they could have constituted a reservoir.
Hare 1967, 118. This is probably a mutant of *R. mooseri* that ceased to infect
   the rat flea and became a parasite of the human body louse, citing Zinsser.
   This probably occurred in the sixth century. The first outbreaks [known in
   European medical history] were in Italy [only] in 1505. Epidemic typhus is
   therefore a comparatively modern disease and could not have come across
   Bering Strait.

Rickettsia rickettsii
Origin: Old World
Summary: Though disputed by many, there is significant evidence for the presence
of spotted fever. How and when it reached the Americas is unclear. By infected
persons on ancient transoceanic vessels is the most plausible scenario.
Grade: B
Sources: *Rickettsia rickettsii* – Infectious agent for various spotted fevers
   Chin 2000, 372. Rickettsioses are a group of clinically similar diseases caused
      by closely related rickettsiae [Rocky Mountain spotted fever is the only
      American version discussed]. They are transmitted by ixodid (hard) ticks,
      the tick species differing markedly by geographic area. 430–1. Rocky
      Mountain spotted fever is the prototype disease of the spotted fever

group rickettsiae. Reservoir: maintained in nature in ticks. Both the Rocky Mountain wood tick, *Dermacentor andersoni*, in the eastern and southern U.S., the American dog tick, *Dermacentor variabilitis*, and in Latin America, *A. cajennense*, are the principal vectors.

Woodbury 1965, 31–32. Maintained by ticks in relation to their hosts, principally rabbits and rodents. Humans are incidental victims. It is a very severe disease.

Saunders et al. 1992, 118. Newman (1985) considered that pre-European contact diseases included rickettsial and viral fevers. (Saunders seems to acquiesce.)

Newman 1976, 669. Rickettsial and viral fevers were present in pre-Columbian America and Europe.

Ackerknecht 1965. Petechial typhus (spotted fever) was at least as old as 1083 C.E. in Mexico, as he reads the Aztec traditions.

See also Alchon under *R. prowazekii* above.

Rickettsia typhi
Origin: Old World
Summary: See summary for the previous item.
Grade: A
Sources: *Rickettsia typhi* (ex. *Rickettsia mooseri*) – agent for typhus murine (i.e., endemic typhus).

Chin 2000, 544–5. Murine typhus is like louse-borne typhus, but milder. Found where humans and rats cohabit. Rats, mice, and other small mammals form the reservoir. Infective rat fleas (usually *Xenopsylla cheopis*) defecate rickettsiae while sucking blood, which contaminates the bite site and other skin wounds. Once infected, fleas remain so for up to their one year of life.

Laming-Emperaire 1980. Fonseca has convincingly demonstrated that typhus murine, among other parasite-caused diseases, was shared between Old World and pre-Columbian South American Indians.

Nicolle 1932. The typhus of Mexico and Guatemala was murine typhus, the same as in New Zealand, Australia, and Southeast Asia. Typhus murine might have come via the Vikings, but that is not very logical. He supposes that it reached the Americas via rats (see the material on *Rattus* sp. in the section below on larger, non-infective fauna) on Polynesian vessels.

Fonseca 1970, 333–6. Murine typhus was at first assigned primarily to two distinct geographic areas: certain regions of the Americas (Mexico, Guatemala, southern U.S.); the other area was the Far East and Pacific (India, Malaysia, China, Manchuria, Formosa, Australia, New Guinea, New Zealand, and Hawaii).

Alchon 1991, 22. Diseases before 1534. One can build a strong case for the existence of both endemic (flea-borne) and epidemic (louse-borne) typhus in the New World, based on lice on mummies. Examinations of mummified human remains have revealed that head and body lice commonly infested native populations. Most native households included several guinea pigs in the family's living quarters; these animals can be reservoirs for the typhus rickettsiae. Infected fleas can easily jump from rodent to human, transmitting the endemic form of the disease. Pre-Conquest traditions of epidemics occurring during periods of social turmoil—wars, famines, and natural disasters—support the assertion that typhus existed in the Americas before the sixth century. Chronicler Guaman Poma described two epidemics long before the Spanish Conquest.

Newman 1976, 669. Among diseases that were part of man's primate ancestry and that either crossed the Bering Strait cold-screen or "were acquired" in the Americas: "various rickettsial fevers such as Verruca and Carrion's disease, insect-borne and altitude localized." "This list could well include typhus on the grounds that the Aztecs had a name, *Matlazahuatl*, for the disease, and depicted it in conventionalized pictures of Indians with spots and nosebleeds, and the generally subclinical nature of the disease in the South Peruvian Sierra" (citing Ashburn). See now Stutz 2006 on another identification for *matlazahuatl*.

Hare 1967, 118. *Rickettsia mooseri* may be the oldest of the typhus group. Principal host is the rat flea, and Baker (1943) suggested that rats at the eastern end of the Mediterranean were the first to be parasitized. Hippocrates (ca. 400 B.C.E.) may describe this disease, but the first recorded cases clearly recognizable as typhus occurred in Spain in 1489.

Salmonella enterica serovar Typhi, or *S. typhi*
Origin: Old World
Summary: Evidence for presence of the typhoid bacillus in the New World is limited. More evidence would be needed before we could be confident of the pre-Columbian presence of *S. enterica* and thus of the possibility of a transoceanic transfer.
Grade: incomplete
Sources: *Salmonella enterica* – the typhoid bacillus

Chin 2000, 535–7. A new nomenclature for *Salmonella* has been proposed based on DNA relatedness. Only two species would be recognized, *S. bongori* and *S. enterica*. All human pathogens would be regarded as serovars within subspecies I of *S. enterica*. The proposed nomenclature would change *S. typhi* (italicized) to *S. enterica serovar* Typhi (last term not italicized), abbreviated S. Typhi (not italicized and beginning with a capital letter). The new nomenclature had not been officially approved as of mid–1999, but some official agencies have adopted it.

Alchon 1991, 20. Marvin Allison has suggested that typhoid fever may have existed in the Americas before 1492 (citing Allison 1979 in re. his finding of *Salmonella* antigens in Peruvian mummies; others doubt its presence).

Saunders et al. 1992, 118. Newman (1985) suggests pre-European contact diseases included *Salmonella* infection.

Hare 1967, 124. "There is no reason to doubt that this bacillus could have become established in Palaeolithic societies and might even have been taken to the Americas [via Bering Strait] .... [But the reference has to be to the *Salmonella* subspecies that caused gastroenteritis, for serovar Typhi

probably was not yet in existence.] None of this can be proved but all [organisms of this type] were causing disease in the Old World before the Christian era" [but how much before?]
Van Blerkom 1985, 67–8. A short treatment. S. Typhi was probably not indigenous [i.e., in existence in pre-Columbian times] to the New World, while other forms undoubtedly were.

Schistosoma sp.
Origin: Old World
Summary: Because Hoeppli believed that Schistosomiasis was in the New World before Columbus, the question should be studied about whether, when, and how this trematode reached the Americas.
Grade: incomplete
Sources: *Schistosoma haematobium* – cause of bilharziasis (snail fever) – liver fluke
   Chin 2000, 447–8. A blood fluke (trematode) infection with adult male and female worms living within mesenteric or vesical veins of the host over a life span of many years. Three major species cause human disease: *S. mansoni*, *S. haematobium*, and *S. japonicum*. Four other species are of importance only in limited areas. *S. mansoni* is found in Africa, Arabia, and eastern South America. *S. haematobium* is in Africa and the Middle East. *S. japonicum* is in China and Indonesia. None of the species is indigenous to North America. Epidemiologic persistence of the parasite depends on the presence of an appropriate snail as intermediate host, i.e., species of the genera *Biomphalaria, Bulinus, Oncomelania, Neotricula*, and *Robertsiella*. Infection is acquired from water containing free-swimming larval forms (*cercariae*) that have developed in snails. Transmitted usually while the person is working, swimming, or wading in water.
   Hoeppli 1969. "Some of the infections introduced by Africans already occurred in the New World in pre-Columbian time." Schistosomiasis was one.
   Millet et al. 1998, 99, 101, 104. *Schistosoma haematobium* is confirmed in a 3200-year-old Egyptian mummy by the presence of *S. (?haematobium)* ova.
   Sandison and Tapp 1998, 40. They accept that *S. haematobium* ova were found in the ROM I mummy (Egyptian).
   Kuhnke 1993, 456. Schistosomiasis. Described in Egyptian inscriptions and papyri. Ova found in Egyptian mummies from 1200 B.C.E. Snail hosts lived in slow-moving water, as in oases.

Shigella dysenteriae
Origin: Old World
Summary: New information would have to be found demonstrating shigellosis in the New World before this question could be considered seriously.
Grade: incomplete
Sources: *Shigella dysenteriae* (or *S. sonnei, S. flexneri, S. boydii*) – causes of bacillary dysentery
   Chin 2000, 451–3. Human reservoir. Transmitted by fecal/oral contamination. The *Shigella* genus is comprised of four species, or serogroups.

Saunders et al. 1992, 118. Newman (1985) suggests that pre-European contact diseases included bacillary dysentery.

Newman 1976, 669. Among diseases that were part of man's primate ancestry and that either crossed the Bering Strait cold-screen or were "acquired in the Americas: bacillary ... dysentery."

Kunitz and Euler 1972, 27–8. Turkeys have been implicated in the spread of *Shigella* organisms. Occurs among modern Indians of the Southwest U.S.

Hare 1967, 124. "There is no reason to doubt that this could have become established in Palaeolithic societies and might even have been taken to the Americas [via Bering Strait] .... None of this can be proved but all [disease organisms of this type] were causing disease in the Old World before the Christian era."

Van Blerkom 1985, 67–9. Could have come in Paleolithic hunting populations. There are no ethno-historical records of shigellosis, for it was only distinguished from other dysenteries in 1873.

Staphylococcus x aureus
Origin: Old World
Summary: As a first approximation (in the absence of much data) the hypothesis of transmission to the Americas via Bering Strait would be possible; however, transmission by voyagers at a later time provides an acceptable alternative explanation.
Grade: incomplete
Sources: *Staphylococcus x aureus*

Chin 2000, 460–2. Bacterial skin lesions are common: impetigo, carbuncles, abscesses, etc. There are various strains and many varied manifestations of staph infection. Reservoir: humans. Major site of colonization is the anterior nares. Transmission is through contact with a person who is a carrier of a pathogenic strain. Twenty to thirty percent of the general population (nowadays) are nasal carriers.

Newman 1976, 669. Among diseases that were part of man's primate ancestry and that either crossed the Bering Strait cold-screen or were "acquired in the Americas: a range of bacterial pathogens such as staphylococcus."

Saunders et al. 1992. Newman (1985) suggests that pre-European contact diseases included staphylococcus.

Hare 1967, 128. Commensal organisms such as *S. aureus* and *S. albus* are worldwide. "They have almost certainly accompanied man from his pre-hominid ancestor."

Van Blerkom 1985, 75–6. It is reasonably certain that staphylococcal infections were universally distributed through both hemispheres before Columbus. Some authors believe staphylococci were absent from the Americas, but she considers that they have ignored substantial evidence.

Streptococcus pneumoniae
Origin: Old World
Summary: That there was transfer between the hemispheres there is no doubt. When and how this came about is unknown. It could have been by Paleo Amerindians but equally well by voyagers.
Grade: incomplete
Sources: *Streptococcus pneumoniae*—cause of pneumonia
- Chin 2000, 387–8. The infectious agent for pneumonia. Reservoir: humans. Pneumococci are commonly found in the upper respiratory tract of healthy people throughout the world. Transmission is by droplet spread, oral contact, or indirectly through articles soiled with respiratory discharges.
- Newman 1976, 669. Among Amerindian native diseases: pneumonia.
- Allison, Pezzia, Hasegawa, and Gerszten 1974, 468. Cited by Newman as documentation for the presence of pneumonia.
- Verano and Ubelaker 1992, 213. "Studies of mummified human remains from the coastal desert of southern Peru and northern Chile have provided conclusive evidence for the presence of ... **pneumonia**." (Emphasis added.)
- Hare 1967, 119. This organism may persist for long periods in carriers, rendering it much more capable of surviving in scattered Palaeolithic populations. Pre-Columbian skulls have been found in the Americas showing evidence of acute infection of the mastoid from *S. pyogenes* [agent of 'strep' throat infection] or *Diplococcus* (=*Streptococcus*) *pneumoniae*. (Cites Hooton 1930, on Pecos). "... It would seem probable that one or both of [those two] organisms had become established in the Old World and were carried to the Americas before the land bridge over the Bering Strait was covered ...." 123. Related streptococcal infections likewise probably were this old.
- Van Blerkom 1985, 59–60. A variety of agents cause pneumonia: adenoviruses, parainfluenza viruses, respiratory syncytial virus, and others. Also pneuminia can be caused by various bacteria, many of them normal nose and throat inhabitants, pneumocystis (a protozoan), and a chlamydia. Cook (1946) reports that the Aztecs probably suffered from respiratory infections; some of these were most likely rhinoviruses and other cold viruses. Some were probably due to some of the causative agents of pneumonia. "In particular, there is evidence that pneumococci, *Streptococcus pneumoniae*, were present in the pre-Columbian New World because these micro-organisms also cause mastoiditis, ample skeletal evidence of which exists for prehistoric America (Moodie 1967, 43)." S. pneumoniae naturally infects wild primates and has a worldwide distribution in all climates and races. Found in mummies from Egypt and Peru.

Streptococcus pyogenes
Origin: Old World
Summary: It is evident that there was a transfer of this organism. Transfer via Bering Strait immigrants is possible, but so is transfer by voyagers. If no evidence of infection is found in Palaeoindian skeletons, scientists would have to turn to voyaging for an explanation.
Grade: incomplete
Sources: *Streptococcus pyogenes* – scarlet fever, strep sore throat, rheumatic fever
- Chin 2000, 470–3. Group A streptococci occur in approximately 80 serologically distinct types that vary greatly in geographic and time distributions. Skin infection sources are usually of different type from those associated with throat infections. Scarlet fever is one manifestation, as are erysipelas, impetigo, puerperal fever, and rheumatic fever. Reservoir: humans. Transmitted by large respiratory droplets or direct contact with carriers.
- Newman 1976, 669. Among diseases that were part of man's primate ancestry and that either crossed the Bering Strait cold-screen or were "acquired in the Americas: a range of bacterial pathogens such as streptococcus."
- Hare 1967. Pre-Columbian skulls have been found in the Americas showing evidence of acute infection of the mastoid from *S. pyogenes* or *Diplococcus pneumoniae*. (Cites Hooton 1930, on skulls from Pecos.) "... It would seem probable that one or both organisms had become established in the Old World and were carried to the Americas before the land bridge over the Bering Strait was covered ...." [As if it were not possible paddle in a boat in the open ocean or to walk on winter-ice across the Strait.]
- Van Blerkom 1985, 76–8. *S. pyogenes* was undoubtedly present in the New World before Columbus. Probably came across the Bering Strait.

Strongyloides sp.
Origin: Old World
Summary: Transfer is definite, and sea travelers are the most (only?) plausible means for it to be accomplished.
Grade: incomplete
Sources: *Strongyloides sp.* – hair worm, threadworm nematode
- Reinhard 1988, 359. From Antelope House (New Mexico) traces of this parasite were recovered from a coprolite. 362. It was also found in dog coprolites at this site, which suggests that dogs acted as a reservoir of infection for the human population.
- Sandison and Tapp 1998, 40. The (Egyptian) mummy Asru showed larval forms of this worm in the intestines.
- Verano 1998, 221. Once thought absent from New World, the presence of *Strongyloides* is now confirmed from (Peruvian) mummy study.
- Patterson 1993, 1016. Occurs around the world with a range similar to that of the hookworms. Like hookworms, the filariform *Strongyloides* larvae penetrate human skin, often through an unshod foot, reach heart and lungs, etc.

T-cell lymphotropic (retro) virus (HTLV-I)
Origin: Old World
Summary: Only a limited number of peoples in the Americas have this disease. To appeal to any early Bering-Strait explanation to account for that distribution is implausible. Voyaging would account for the observed facts; nothing else would.
Grade: A
Sources: HTLV-I.

> León, De León, and Ariza 1996, 132–6. The route by which the human T cell lymphotropic (retro) virus (HTLV-I) reached the Americas has been much discussed. Seroepidemiologic, genetic, virologic, molecular, anthropological, archaeological, and oceanographic data lead the authors to conclude that this virus could have arrived not only from Africa (as previously suggested, via colonial-era slaves), but also from Kyushu Island in Japan more than 5000 years ago through direct voyaging. The subjects of this study, the Noanama people, were Amerindians from the high mountains of southwestern Colombia; their geographical and social isolation reduces the chance of any contact with the slaves of African origin brought to Colombia by the Spaniards.
>
> A comparative study made some years ago utilized thirteen genetic markers to distinguish racial groups of the world. The study yielded one very interesting result—the Noanama had very close relations with Samoans on the one hand and Japanese—especially Ainu—on the other. This result suggests that HTLV-I was introduced to South America from the Far East thousands of years ago by a route other than the Bering Strait. Furthermore, recent genetic studies on native South Americans showed that their ancestors possessed genetic markers related to the histo-compatibility leucocyte antigen (HLA) like the Japanese of Kyushu (citing Sonoda et al.). A direct voyaging contact from Japan to Colombia would explain this relationship, because populations of North and Central America are totally without the HLA markers. At a mitochondrial DNA level, study of the deletion 9 bp in the human genome has shown it to be Asiatic, especially being found in North American Indians and Polynesians (citing Torroni et al., and Hanihara et al.). Yet, it is not present in the (Jomon-derived) Ainu, and the 9 bp deletion is also absent among the Noanama (as well as on the coasts of Chile and Peru a thousand years earlier). This suggests an intrusion of people from Japan. They cite the archaeological findings of Meggers et al. for the intrusive Valdivia culture of Ecuador as confirming their position.
>
> Finally, Japanese investigators have voyaged across the Pacific by the North Pacific route to Colombia, which the authors suppose was used anciently, and these experimental sailors/researchers used vessels similar to those of prehistoric times. This demonstrates that it was possible to make such a voyage (Errazurriz and Alvarado, 1993).
>
> Miura et al. 1994, 1124–7. Specimens of T-lymphotropic virus type I (HTLV-I) were phylogenetically analyzed from native inhabitants in India, Colombia, Chile, and Ainu of Japan (the last "regarded as pure Japanese

descendants from the pre-agricultural 'Jomon' period"). The phylogenetic tree for the 'cosmopolitan' type virus involved groupings into three lineages. One consists of some Caribbean, two South American, and some Japanese isolates, including that from the Ainu plus an (Asian) Indian isolate. This subtype implies a close connection of the Caribbean and two narrowly-defined South American peoples with the Japanese and "thereby a possible migration of the lineage to the American continent via Beringia in the Paleolithic era." [Their 1996 article expands upon and essentially supercedes this one. One cannot attribute a modern infection found in only a few limited areas in the Americas to communication across Bering Strait many millennia ago, which should have made it widespread.]

Treponema pallidum subspecies pallidum
Origin: Old World?
Summary: The single treponeme at the root of the whole range of manifestations called yaws, pinta, endemic syphilis, and venereal syphilis could have been and probably was present in both hemispheres very anciently. The diseases caused by the micro-organism depended upon environmental and social conditions in the lives of host humans. Nevertheless, hemispheric or regional sub-developments in the infection of a special nature could have been transmitted across the ocean by one or more of the voyaging parties now known to have made the trip. If so, only very special evidence of unusual virulence in a given location would have to be detected to demonstrate the connection. While the possibility is open, the likelihood of finding such evidence is unlikely [True, unless the disease leaves a distinctive trace on the bones.]
Grade: B
Sources: *Treponema pallidum* – the infectious agent producing syphilis, yaws, etc.
    Rose 1997, 24–5. Bruce and Christine Rothschild examined 687 skeletons from New World archaeological sites, ranging in age from 400 to 6000 years. Populations in New Mexico, Florida, and Ecuador proved to have syphilis, while those to the north (Ohio, Illinois, Virginia) had yaws. By contrast, 1000 Old World skeletons dated to before contact with the New World revealed no cases of syphilis. They had begun by analyzing collections of skeletons from Guam where the only treponemal disease predating 1668 was yaws. Also, they analyzed Near Eastern Bedouin for *bejel* and in both cases, as well as in North American cases of syphilis (diagnosed at autopsy), identified characteristic bone changes for each disease. The earliest New World yaws cases were at least 6000 years old, while the first syphilis cases were at least 800 and perhaps more than 1600 years old. This suggests that syphilis may be a New World mutation of yaws.
    Meanwhile, Olivier Dutour of Marseilles has recently claimed that a fourth-century C.E. skeleton of a seven-month-old fetus found in France has lesions from congenital syphilis, but B. Rothschild has examined the skeleton and contends that it is not a case of congenital syphilis but of lithopedion, calcification of a fetus, a rarity.

Anderson 1986, 341–50. Ninety-five Old World skeletons examined reveal bone conditions compatible with treponemal infection, suspected to be endemic syphilis. This occurrence dates earlier than 1531, the earliest known [historical] date for syphilis from Norway. No evidence has been reported previously from any part of Europe for this period for endemic syphilis. It appears that an impoverished segment of the Trondheim population suffered endemic (not venereal) syphilis in the sixth century.

Bogdan and Weaver 1992, 155–63. Summarizes the three competing theories for the evolution of treponematosis: (1) New World origin of syphilis, (2) Europe-to-New World, and (3) unitary or both-hemisphere presence. Advocates of the second maintain that venereal syphilis in Europe was not distinguished from a number of diseases grouped under the term 'leprosy,' including Roman, Greek, and later references to "venereal leprosy."

Goldstein 1969, 285–94. It is now known that treponematosis in one form or another has been present on every continent for thousands of years; "the old argument about whether Columbus' sailors brought syphilis to the New World or carried it back to Europe is moot."

Bullen 1972, 133–74. Recapitulates literature showing that treponemiasis was recognized in Florida skeletons 90 years ago and since. Evidence for syphilis is as early as the Archaic, ca. 3000 B.C.E.

Daws and Magilton 1980. They report a probable European case of syphilis dating before 1500 C.E.

El Najjar 1979, 599–618. Only one treponeme, *T. pallidum*, exists. European and New World strains were apparently interchanged at the time of the Conquest, with extreme virulence manifest in both areas as a result of the new introductions.

Goff 1967, 287–93. "Treponematous ancient bone lesions have been difficult if not impossible to identify scientifically in the light of our present knowledge." [DNA analysis ought to be possible to identify the significant variables.]

Hackett 1967, 152–69. A series of maps displays the author's inferences about probable geographical distributions of the four treponematoses—pinta, yaws, endemic syphilis, and venereal syphilis. Pinta, the earliest, was essentially worldwide by about 15,000 B.C.E. From about 3000 B.C.E. to the first century B.C.E. endemic syphilis existed throughout northern Africa and Arabia to Mongolia (as well as in central Australia and Bechuanaland). At the same period, yaws was present in tropical Africa and south and Southeast Asia through Oceania. Pinta was only American, essentially limited to Mexico through Brazil. [But it was supposed to have been world wide in 15,000 B.C.E.]

Hare 1967, 125. Depends chiefly on Hackett. About 7000 B.C.E., *T. pallidum* was evolved in the Old World and caused endemic syphilis. This was largely confined to the warm arid climates of North Africa, Southwest Africa, and ultimately, Australia. The same organism then about 3000 B.C.E. began to cause venereal syphilis in the mild form. The urban revolution facilitated this change. It continued to behave in this way but in the early years of the 16th century C.E. was supplanted by a more virulent mutant that produced the widespread epidemic of severe syphilis in Europe frequently considered to have been imported from the Americas by Columbus. [Hare says nothing about a duplicate mutation sequence in the Americas. Either that happened apart from the Old World sequence, or the venereal syphilitic organism had to have reached the New World via migrants after 3000 B.C.E., when, according to Hare, the venereal syphilis treponeme originated. Of course, the orthodox interpretation is that there were no migrants to the New World after 3000 B.C.E.]

Tisseuil 1974, 40–4. Endemic syphilis was widespread in Europe in the Middle Ages ("by cutaneous transmission"), mainly among the deprived classes. At the end of the 15th century, movements of armies and populations favored an epidemic explosion of venereal syphilis in Europe which was promptly carried to the New World.

Willcox 1972, 21–37. Considers that endemic syphilis was common in pre-Columbian Europe.

Hudson 1958. American pinta was essentially a variety of yaws, the latter somehow derived from the Old World in prehistoric times.

Hudson 1965, 885–901. The four syndromes of treponematosis are from one organism. Their manifestations form a continuum from yaws to venereal syphilis, variations dependent on local natural and social conditions. Lesions representing effects of the disease are evident in bones worldwide. No definitive indicator allows distinguishing in the bones of venereal syphilis from the other forms. It would have appeared in many places after it spread in relatively benign forms in Mesolithic/Neolithic times. Certainly, there is no merit in the theory that Columbus' crew carried syphilis to a previously untainted Europe.

O'Neill 1991, 270–87. Because of similarities of the early stages of leprosy and syphilis, syphilis may have been present in medieval Europe and mislabeled leprosy.

Livingstone 1991, 587–90. Treponemes were ubiquitous in human populations in both hemispheres but changed in different habitats. Epidemics of diseases were no longer present, but pathologies similar to modern treponemes no doubt occurred in the past. Syphilis in Europe may have come from the New World, but the tropical regions of the Old World, at that time being heavily contacted by Europeans for the first time, seem a more likely source. A non-venereal treponeme from Africa may have made the adaptation to venereal form at that time, hence syphilis is [still conditional: "may be"] one of the world's newest diseases. Increased occurrence of it in the Americas in post-Columbian times is evidence that a virulent strain was brought from the Old World (i.e., Africa) at the time of Columbus.

Weiss (1984, 35–37) considers three kinds of treponemal infections to have been present in pre-Columbian America—endemic syphilis (not the same as classic syphilis however) and 'pian' and 'mal del pinto'. Both these are rural infections. Syphilis is urban (today). "The fact is very significant that some of the traits that a comparative clinical study of treponemiasis seem properly to belong to the evolved characterization of *mal del pinto* have been noted also as traits of the so-called endemic syphilis known as '*bejel*' of the Bedouins of the Euphrates, the syphilis of the Arabs."

Van Blerkom 1985, 100–1. The causative agent of pinta is difficult to distinguish from that of yaws. Since yaws is a tropical disease (because growth of the spirochete in the skin requires warmth and humidity), it could not have been carried to the New World via early hunter groups across Bering Strait. There is one report of yaws in a pre-Columbian Mexican skull (Goff 1967, 291), but the evidence is questionable. The oldest evidence of yaws is in the Mariana Islands, from about 850 BP, and Iraq, dating to 500 C.E.

Goff 1967, 279–94. Many reliable investigators believe yaws was endemic in the New World at the Conquest. 291, 293. Bones from Mexico are illustrated and discussed showing what may be yaws (probably pre-Columbian).

Márquez Morfín 1997 (1998?), 11. Today, it is known that syphilis existed on both continents [i.e., Old and New Worlds] and that during the Conquest and mixing of populations a more resistant variety was formed that attacked the population.

Trichophyton concentricum
Origin: Old World
Summary: This fungus at least (as well as, perhaps, others of the genus) is manifest in Oceania and Southeast Asia, as well as in Tropical [but not Temperate] America. No explanation for the distribution is plausible other than movement by infected voyagers across the Pacific Ocean to the Americas.
Grade: B
Sources: *Trichophyton* spp. (includes *T. concentricum*) – ringworm of the body

Chin 2000, 147–53. Transmission is skin-to-skin or by indirect contact through shared objects. This is a fungal disease of the skin, other than of the scalp, bearded areas, and feet that characteristically appears as flat, spreading, ring-shaped lesions. Infectious agents: most species of *Microsporum* and *Trichophyton*

Regarding literature on distribution, see *Microsporum* spp.

Ainsworth 1993, 731. *Trichophyton concentricum* (*tinea imbricata*) is endemic in Southwest Asia and the South Sea Islands. It has other minor endemic centers in South America.

Ajello 1960, 30. *Trichophyton* spp. are some of the eleven species of fungi that are cosmopolitan, seven of which are anthropophilic. *T. concentricum* is recorded from Oceania, Asia, and North, Central and South America, but not north of Mexico or in Europe or Africa. 34. The geographic distribution of *T. concentricum* may be of anthropological significance. It is widespread among the inhabitants of Polynesia and the countries bordering the western shores of the Pacific Ocean; however, it is only a sporadic parasite of American Indians living in the tropical forests of Brazil, Guatemala, Mexico, and San Salvador. The disparity in prevalence between the Asian endemic areas and those of Latin America leads Ajello to speculate that the fungus was introduced from Asia into the New World.

Trichosporon ovoides
Origin: Old World
Summary: There is no explanation for the bi-hemispheric distribution except that voyaging humans conveyed it [across the ocean] from other tropical areas to the Americas.
Grade: A
Source: *Trichosporon ovoides* (or *T. inkin*; formerly *T. beigelii*)—a fungus causing a disease of the scalp and hair
> Fonseca 1970, 228–32. Known particularly from Brazil, but also Asia. Causes a group of nodular parasitic diseases of the hair and beard characterized by white or clear nodules on individual hairs. The fungus is of the genus *Trichosporon*, so he calls the disease *piedra tricospórica*; others have called it *piedra branca*. It stands in contrast to the disease piedra, for which see *Piedraia hortai*.

Trichuris trichiura
Origin: Old World
Summary: No explanation for the Asian/South American distribution is plausible except that humans brought the organism via voyaging.
Grade: A
Sources: *Trichuris trichiura* – whipworm
> Reinhard 1992, 231–45. He reprises South American incidence of the whipworm (*Trichuris trichiura*). The findings suggest direct transpacific contact, some think by way of Japan and Ecuador. Since both hookworms and whipworms require warm, moist conditions for the completion of their life cycles, finding human-specific parasites in the Americas is circumstantial evidence for transpacific contact.
> Verano 1991, 15–24. Coprolites from coastal Peru show the whipworm by 2700 B.C.E.
> Verano 1998, 221. *T. trichiura* is one of the parasites once thought absent from the New World, but now found.
> Ferreira et al. 1988, 65–7. Evidence was found in a cave site in Minas Gerais state, Brazil, dated between 3490 and 430 BP, consisting of eggs of *T. trichiura* and *Necator americanus*. The same parasites (i.e., *Trichuris trichiura* and *Necator americanus*), found at Unai, Minas Gerais have now been identified in human coprolites from Boqueirão do Sitio da Pedra Furada, Brazil, in a stratum radiocarbon-dated to 7320±80 BP. [Sitio has hearth charcoals stratified below the oldest record of C14 dating.]
> Patterson 1993, 1058. *Trichuris trichiura*. Archaeological evidence shows that this worm infected people in the Americas prior to the voyage of Columbus.

Trychostrongylus sp.
Origin: Old World
Summary: If Reinhard's find is accepted, then it is the only one in the Western Hemisphere. Such spotty distribution would not have resulted from an early spread via Bering Strait. That leaves a limited-destination voyage as the only theory, if one is needed. More data are needed.
Grade: incomplete
Source: *Trychostrongylus sp.* – a helminthic parasite
> Reinhard 1988, 359, 361. Found the organism in a coprolite from Antelope House, New Mexico. Other parasitologists dispute his identification (it is not clear whether they have actually examined the specimen), suggesting instead hookworm.

Tunga penetrans
Origin: New World
Summary: Blanchard's report is highly suggestive of a sudden intrusion if this organism into Africa. More historical evidence would have to turn up in Africa to establish the flea there and point to the inference that a pre-Columbian voyage was responsible.
Grade: incomplete
Sources: *Tunga penetrans* (syn. Pulex penetrans) – chigoe, chigger, nigua
> Blanchard 1890, II, 484–93. In 1324 C.E., according to chronicles, a caravan of Mansa Musa in Touat (In-Salah) (in the center of modern Algeria) was attacked by a strange disease. People suffered in their feet by a foot-penetrating parasite/flea (considered here to be *Pulex penetrans*), which is a particular species of Central America, perhaps *Sarcopsylla penetrans* (called *nigua* in Mexico, *pique* in Peru, and *pulga penetrante* in the Antilles). It was first medically observed in Africa in the year 1870.

> Weiss 1984, 19. A *nigua* is represented in a ceramic effigy in the Museo Amano, Lima.

> Karasch 1993, 537. *Tunga penetrans*, the chigger that burrows into the feet where it lays its eggs and causes painful foot ulcers, was native to Brazil.

Wuchereria bancrofti
Origin: Old World
Summary: Much more evidence than Hoeppli offers would have to appear before we could take a voyaging transmission of this organism seriously, but such evidence should be sought.
Grade: incomplete
Sources: *Wuchereria bancrofti* – a threadlike worm or nematode
> Chin 2000, 197–9. The cause of Bancroftian filariasis. Transmitted by the bite of a mosquito, the most important being several *Anopheles* and *Aedes* species.

> Hoeppli 1969. "Some of the infections introduced by Africans already occurred in the New World in pre-Columbian time." Elephantiasis [filariasis] was one.

Yersinia pestis
Origin: Old World
Summary: It might be said that *Y. pestis* is simply zoonotic in origin and as such has no relevance to the question of human distribution. But that dodges the question of exactly how the infectious organism, a bacillus, came to be in the Americas at all. Either an infected animal or an infected human bearing the bacillus crossed the ocean. (Bering Strait won't do if we are talking about small animals as carriers of the disease.) Van Blerkom's observations about *Y. pestis* orientalis involve a crucial consideration. We are not persuaded that an introduction of the plague by a human being in 1855 provides an adequate explanation for the occurrence of *Y. p. orientalis* a century and a half later for the bacillus infecting a wide variety of wild rodents over a good deal of the hemisphere. An introduction of the organism by voyagers from "Southeast Asian seaports" several millennia ago provides a far superior explanation.
Grade: B
Sources: *Yersinia pestis* (ex. *Pasteurella pestis*) – the plague bacillus
  Chin 2000, 381–3. Endemic in eastern and southern Asia and sub-Saharan Africa. Reservoir: wild rodents, especially ground squirrels, and also rabbits and hares. Transmission is as a result of human intrusion into the zoonotic (sylvan or rural) cycle, or by the entry of sylvatic rodents or their infected fleas into man's habitat. Domestic pets may carry plague-infected wild rodent fleas into homes. The most frequent source of exposure that results in human disease has been the bite of infected fleas (especially *Xenopsylla cheopis*, the oriental rat flea). Person to person transmission by *Pulex irritans* fleas, the 'human' flea, is presumed important in the Andes area.
  Stodder and Martin 1992, 55–73. Sylvatic plague probably occurred in the Southwest U.S. before the Spanish arrival (citing Van Blerkom 1985)
  Hare 1967, 115–131. *P. pestis* parasitizes many species of rodents, although most human infections are caught from the black rat. There is no evidence that the disease occurred at any time during the pre-Christian era. [Ergo, it would not have reached the Western Hemisphere via early settlers traversing the Bering Strait. The arctic lacked the rats, etc.]
  Van Blerkom 1985, 48, 50–9. Although human plague is more commonly zoonotic in origin, it can be transmitted from man to man, with or without the agency of vector fleas, and humans can act as a reservoir of the disease. Two forms are differentiated ecologically: sylvatic, the original form, and urban. Sylvatic, of course, is present in wild rodents and their fleas. The same organism can produce three different forms of plague, depending on the mode of transmission and climate: (1) bubonic, (2) pneumonic, and (3) septicemic. Pneumonic plague is more common in dry temperate zones and as a result of contact with infected wild rodents (usually contracted while skinning or otherwise handling the animal, or from a bite). Highly contagious, it localizes in the lungs and is rapidly fatal without medical treatment. It spreads rapidly to other humans via the respiratory route. Human fleas, *Pulex irritans*, can spread bubonic plague

without the involvement of rats, and *Xenopsylla cheopis* (the flea of R. *rattus*) also readily infests humans. Over 200 species of rodent, as well as other mammals, can carry plague. Most domesticated and commensal rodents do. 57. Many (Schwabe (1969, 282) calls it a consensus) believe that sylvatic plague is indigenous in the Americas. Several lines of evidence seem to support this conclusion. The most compelling evidence in favor of pre-Columbian plague is the existence of several extensive sylvatic foci in both North and South America, with the largest being in western North America in ground squirrels and other rodents. Also focussed in eastern Siberia and western Canada. This distribution suggests that plague is an ancient and widely distributed disease of rodents diffused across the Bering Strait. She disagrees. 58. There are three subspecies, *Y. p. orientalis*, endemic in India, Burma, and South China; *Y. p. antiqua*, carried by rodents in Central Asia and Africa; and *Y. p. mediaevalis*, of the Black Death and Europe and today found only in West Africa. If New World sylvatic plague were an indigenous disease of the rodents of this hemisphere, one would expect it to be the same strain found on the other side of the Bering Strait, *Y. p. antiqua*, the parent of the others. However, American plague is the same as the urban strain found in Southeast Asian seaports, *Y. p. orientalis* (Alland 1970, 101–2; Hull 1963, 534). This suggests that plague was carried by ship to the Americas from Southeast Asia during the last pandemic. She considers that to have been in China in 1855. Only later was plague found in wild rodents, and it seems to have spread rapidly into wild reservoirs from the original murine foci in seaports (Hull 1963, 547–54). [This presumes an unbelievable rate of spread to a wide variety of rodents (up to 200 species; see her p. 56) over a wide geographical range. The presence of *Y. p. orientalis* in the Americas can be explained much more economically by supposing its arrival on a pre-Columbian voyage from Southeast Asia, allowing time for a normal rate of dispersion.]

OTHER FAUNA

Alphitobius diaperinus
Origin: Old World
Summary: This species is present in parallel mortuary circumstances in ancient Egypt and Peru.
Grade: A
Sources: *Alphitobius diaperinus* (Panzer) – the lesser mealworm beetle
  Buckland and Panagiotakopulu 2001, 554. They note that Riddle and Vreeland (1982) report two species of Coleoptera, *Stegobium paniceum* and *Alphitobius diaperinus*, present in pre-Columbian Peruvian mummies examined in Lima. "Both species are recorded also from Pharaonic Egypt and Roman sites in Britain (e.g., Hall and Kenward 1990), and must therefore be of Old World origin."

Riddle and Vreeland 1982, 7. For discussion of the mummy bundles analyzed, see under *Stegobium paniceum*. *Alphitobius diaperinus* (Panzer) is known as the 'lesser mealworm.' It is a common pest of stored dried foods, such as grains, cereals, and seeds.

Panagiotakopulu 2000, 16, Table 3–3. *Alphitobius diaperinus* (Panz.). Earliest archaeological examples: British Isles, second century C.E. Also in Egypt ca. 1350 B.C.E. 110. Also recovered in the (Roman) Mons Claudianus (Egypt) samples. It is an omnivorous feeder, associated with a wide range of commodities, e.g. grains, flour, leather, bones, ground nuts, etc. The species has recently been recorded from Tell el-Amarna, Egypt. 12. An omnivorous feeder, associated with grains, flour, leather, bones, etc.

Alfieri 1976, 200. Collected from Alexandria, Cairo, El Wasta, Asyut, and Siwa areas.

Canis familiaris
Origin: Old World
Summary: One or more of the specialized varieties of dogs known in pre-Columbian America probably were, or could have been, imported to the hemisphere, but historical evidence is inconclusive.
Grade: C
Sources: *Canis familiaris* – the dog

Mair's data (1998) clarify the age of the domesticated dog. It turns out that the dog-in-the-company-of-humans, even in the Old World, is not as old as has commonly been assumed. The earliest domestication (or taming) was in the Near East (the Natufian era) only around 12,000 years ago. Dogs in the European Mesolithic period date to the order of 9000–6000 BP. 22–3. The earliest dogs we know of in China belong at around 6000 BP. Moreover, the common hypothetical root word for dog in ancestral language groupings, like Nostratic and Afro-Asiatic, appears to date "closer to 6000 B.C.E. than to 10,000 B.C.E." Taken at face value, these data mean that domesticated dogs would not have been available in northeastern Asia to accompany migrants to the New World until a number of millennia after the first settlement of the Western Hemisphere who crossed Bering Straits. .

Three varieties of canines may have been brought to the New World by voyagers from across the ocean:

(1) A voiceless, hairless dog

Coe (1968, 59) found physical evidence for small dogs having been eaten at San Lorenzo in southern Mexico around 1000 B.C.E.

Fiennes (1968. 26, 53–55, 103–110) wrote of the same special breed of hairless, 'toy' dogs that were kept and bred in China as well as in west Mexico and Peru as temple and sacrificial animals and for eating.

Campbell 1989, 385. Includes discussion of the place of hairless dogs in Mexico, Ecuador, and China. Dogs for eating appear in the Chorrera phase in coastal Ecuador, about 1500–500 B.C.E., alongside such Asiatic traits as house effigies, roller and flat stamps, and ceramic pillows.

Tolstoy (1974) saw the hairless dog of Mexico as derived from Asia (along with chickens and several plants).

Ling (1956) found what he considered "striking similarities" in a dog sacrifice complex that is ancient in Chinese archaeology, and that also occurs in parts of northern North America, South America, and Polynesia.

Roys 1931, 328. "Ah Bil, or Kik-bil. Canis caribaeus, L. (Gaumer 1917, p. 197). Perro mudo. [Barkless dogs.] 'Bil. Hairless dogs.' (Motul Dictionary.) 'These were used to hunt birds and deer and were also eaten.' (Rel. de Yuc. I, 63; Landa 1900, p. 400)." 340. Tzotzim-pek. "A dog of this land with very short hair." (Motul.) "Also the Indians have another sort of dogs which have hair, but they do not bark either, and are of the same size as the others (hairless dogs)." (Rel. de Yuc. I, 63). Lit. 'hairy dog.'

Latcham 1922, 37. Three varieties of domestic dog can be suggested as having been brought by voyagers from the Old World. The first is the small, hairless, often voiceless dog used for food. In general, Latcham (1922, 37) observes that such creatures were used for food in Mexico, Central America, the Antilles, and Peru. Coe (1968, 59) reports their skeletons at the Olmec site of San Lorenzo at the Isthmus of Tehuantepec in the late second or early first millennium B.C.E. He also notes that the bones give evidence that the dogs were eaten.

Covarrubias (1957, 93) observes that raising and eating voiceless, hairless dogs was a characteristic of ancient Chinese culture (as early as the Shang Dynasty in the late second millennium B.C.E., according to Simoons 1961).

(2) A possible European dog among the Inca of Peru

Friant and Reichlen (1950, 1–18) determined that "the Inca dog was not domesticated from a South American wild form but was brought from elsewhere already domesticated." Subsequently, Friant (1964–1965, 130–5) examined mummified dog remains and dog skulls in Inca burials and found that they compared closely with dog remains from Denmark in the late Neolithic. He postulated that the similarity must be due to the hybridization of Viking dogs with those of the "Indians," which type eventually reached the Inca area. This proposition, which seems fanciful at first glance, is supported by the existence of a surprising corpus of inscriptions of runic type from numerous sites in Brazil, Paraguay, and Argentina, reported and photographed by Mahieu (1988). DNA could now settle some of these questions about possible hybridization.

(3) A third variety documented by early naturalists visiting Northwest coastal Indian tribes

Lord (1866, 215; compare Vancouver 1798, I, 266; Kane 1859, 210) stated that "along the coast several tribes at one time kept dogs of a peculiar breed, having long white hair, that were annually shorn as we shear sheep, and the hair so obtained was woven into rugs." Kept on separate islets so as not to run away or mix with common canines, they differed "in every specific detail from all the other breeds of dogs belonging to either coast or inland Indians" (Lord 1866, 216). Kissell (1929, 85) further noted that the weaving of this dog hair was done on "a foreign loom" using an "archaic style of spinning found nowhere else in the world." This ethnographic anomaly was due, it was speculated, to possible contact with Asia. Lord observed, "Whence came this singular white long-haired dog?" His answer: "The ... probable supposition is that it came from Japan; and I am informed by a friend who has been there, that the Japanese have a small, long-haired dog, usually white, and from description very analogous to the dog that was shorn by the Indians of the coast and of Vancouver Island." The only other possible view (page 217) was that "it could have come ... from the north, which is far from likely." That the dog was not indigenous, he was quite sure.

Kissell 1929, 85. Among unique features of weaving in this area are a foreign loom (possibly from Colombia (sic)), an archaic style of spinning found nowhere else in the world, and a strange, domestic, fleece-bearing dog that furnished textile fiber and is thought to have come from Asia, being raised solely for its hair and kept in dog folds on islands away from domestic dogs. (Citing Kane 1859, 210 and Eells 1887, 630).

Vancouver 1798, I, 266. The dogs belonging to (certain Indians on the Puget Sound) were numerous and much resembled those of Pomerania, though in general somewhat larger. All were shorn as close to the skin as sheep in England. Their fleece was composed of a mixture of coarse wool with very fine long hair, capable of being spun into yarn. The abundance of garments woven from this wool amongst the people indicates the animal from whence the raw material is procured to be very common in this neighborhood, as they have no other animal domesticated excepting the dog. 284. A survey vessel went ashore and found "upwards of two hundred people, attended by about forty dogs in a drove, shorn close to the skin like sheep."

Kane 1859, 210. (Northwest coast tribe not identified.) "They have a peculiar breed of small dogs with long hair of a brownish black and a clear white. These dogs are bred for clothing purposes. The hair is cut off with a knife and mixed with goose down and a little white earth, with a view of curing the feathers." This is then "twisted into threads by rubbing it down the thigh with the palm of the hand ...." "These threads are then woven into blankets by a very simple loom of their own contrivance."

Cicada sp.
Origin: Old World?
Summary: The occurrence of cicadas in both hemispheres, according to Balser, and similarities in cultural practices in relation to the insect, raises the possibility of a

transfer of the genus to the Americas from East Asia by ancient voyagers. Or possibly the practices were transferred by Asian travelers when they discovered American cicada insects upon arrival in Central America. More research is desirable.
Grade: C
Source: *Cicada* sp. – cicada, harvest fly

>Balser 1988, 18. Cigarras, or chicharras, are of the sub-order *Homoptera*, known also by the Latin name cicadas. Their chirps are the song of the males. Females deposit their eggs in incisions made by them in the tender twigs of trees. These branches are broken off by even a gentle wind and fall to the ground. The larvae (wingless, scaly) thus reach the earth and enter the soil, where they live from four to twenty years (depending on the species and the latitude). The adult larvae feed on the fluids of roots. After a considerable time, they return to the surface of the earth. When fully developed, they climb the trunk of a tree to which they cling tightly. The larval skin then splits, and the adult insect emerges. It lives a little more than a week, during which time copulation is effected and a new life cycle begins. In the ancient cultures of China, the cicadas were a symbol of the resurrection. This is shown in a Han tomb (at Loyang) of the first or second century C.E., where a jade cicada was found placed in the mouth of the cadaver. Use of this insect as a funerary offering can be documented in China from the Eastern Chou Dynasty (770–256 B.C.E.) through the Ming Dynasty (until 1644 C.E.). It seems that in China the metamorphosis of the cicada is intimately related to the calendar by its coinciding with the summer solstice.

>Balser cont'd. In pre-Columbian America, we have little data on the cicada, except that "the great naturalist, Anastasio Alfaro, in his book *Investigaciones Científicos*, refers to ancient documents (traditions) that speak of the immortality of the spirits of the natives, indicating that they (the natives) in the first months of the rainy season noted that out of the soil came bees, 'sphinxes,' and cicadas." Balser reports several jade artifacts have been discovered in burials on the Nicoya peninsula of Costa Rica which are carved in the form of cicadas, very similar to those cicadas carved in jade in ancient China. He illustrates one of the Costa Rican examples (his Example No. 4 on p. 20). [Jades can now be identified by their chemical content, which could define this potentially as Chinese or not.]

Crax globicera
Origin: South Asia
Summary: Whitley's evidence for a South Asian source of this tropical American fowl is persuasive, but his argument involves so many disciplines that one wants confirmation of aspects of his hypothesis from relevant specialists before accepting it fully. Nevertheless, transfer by ships looks like the only credible mechanism.
Grade: B-
Source: *Crax globicera* (ex C. rubra) – the curassow

Whitley (1974b) argues that this large bird was first tamed in Southeast Asia, then was carried to Africa. The evidence comes from comparisons of the names for the bird and cultural traits associated with it. From Africa, it reached eastern South America, where some group speaking a language of the Tupí-Guaraní family (judging by names for it) domesticated it. From there, it spread to Mesoamerica, where it was a domesticated species around the time of the Spanish Conquest (Tozzer 1941, 202).

Dendrocygna bicolor
Origin: South Asia
Summary: Whitley's evidence in this case involves so many disciplines that confirmation of aspects of his argument needs to come from relevant disciplines before it deserves full acceptance, but again voyaging appears to be the sole credible mechanism for the movement.
Grade: B-
Source: *Dendrocygna bicolor* – fulvous tree duck
- Whitley (1974a) characterized this as one of eight species of a genus that originated in India. To the east of India, the East Indian Tree Duck has a relatively compact and coherent range extending through three subspecies to southern China, northern Australia, the Philippines, New Guinea, and Fiji. Westward, the fulvous tree duck reaches to Madagascar and East Africa. But it also has three loci in the New World: southern Brazil and Paraguay, Venezuela, and surrounding areas of northern South America and Mexico. (Leopold (1959) maps it along both coasts of Mexico.) In the Americas, it competes with an indigenous tree duck.
- Whitley maintains that man must have had a role in the distribution of this domesticated duck. When he compared local names, the terms appear to have spread from Africa to South America (he proposes that this took place via the Cape of Good Hope aboard vessels with humans). Separate names appear among the Arawak- and Tupí Guaraní-speaking peoples on the lower and middle Amazon. The Mexican name seems to have come from Paraguay.

Felis catus
Origin: Old World
Summary: At the Middle Preclassic archaeological site of Tlatilco, near Mexico City, excavations conducted over 30 years ago revealed the bones of the domestic cat. There is no actual evidence to suggest contamination of the archaeological remains by post-Castilian mixing of archaeological deposits for the faunal bones.
Transfer: Old World center (Mediterranean, Near Eastern, or Far Eastern) to Mexico.
Grade: incomplete
Sources: *Felis catus* (syn. domestica) – the domestic cat
- Álvarez 1976. This Middle Preclassic settlement and burial ground produced a single *Felis domestica* bone [as far as is reported all archaeological material from Tlatilco hitherto has been dated between ca. 800–400 B.C.E.] The single bone came from level "F", the sixth deepest sub-stratum (of nine)

within the III or deepest master stratum. [Although surface and intermediate strata, and a few deeper sub-strata, show the presence of horse, cattle, and goat bones.]

Álvarez and Ocaña 1999, 103. Bones of the domestic cat have appeared in five archaeological sites in Mexico. In two of them, at Tlatilco and Cuanalán, they were found in bottle-shaped pits. Three other sites with cat bones were of Colonial Spanish age. These authors suppose that the cat bones should be explained by either the pits being used after the Conquest when European cats had been introduced, or by the bones being introduced in the deposit "by accident," or by redepositioning of post-Conquest remains due to churning of the deposit by digging/tunneling rodents. [Both suggestions are not entirely realistic in the case of the bell-shaped pits, considering the relatively constricted top opening to such depressions through which rodents could have intruded. The question of whether the bones are modern or not could be resolved, of course, by geochronometric dating]

Gallus gallus
Origin: Southeast Asia
Summary: A variety of evidences from the American sources indicates that the distribution of Asiatic varieties of chickens in the Americas can only be accounted for by pre-Columbian voyages from Asia.
Grade: A-
Sources: *Gallus gallus* – chicken

The conventional position among ornithologists has been that chickens were first imported to the New World by the Spaniards. If that had been the case, the chickens in the hands of Amerindians immediately after the Conquest all ought to have been of Mediterranean type, but they were certainly not. Especially in the Andes, the native peoples soon after the Conquest had many chickens whose widespread name had no relation whatever to any name they might have learned from the Spaniards. Rather, various Asiatic-type chickens were manifest, that is, they were different in appearance, names, behavior, and uses from what the Spaniards knew (Carter 1971; 1998, 151–3; cf. Bright quoted in Hamp 1964). Multiple introductions of fowls across the Pacific are required to account for the disparate characteristics.

Latcham 1922, 175. He studied three kinds of chickens used now by Indians in Chile that were very distinct from those brought by the European conquerors. Those three types were present before the Spanish Conquest and are still represented among fowls kept by Araucanian Indians.

Castello 1924. He identified four varieties in Chile beyond the one brought by the Spaniards. The exotics all show Asiatic features; some are tailless and have multiple rows of comb on their foreheads as well as balls of puffy feathers at the sides and atop their heads, as do fowls in China. Some are melanotic in their combs, tongue and legs, with feathers on their toes and legs (Carter 1971; Finsterbusch 1931; Sauer 1952).

C. Sauer (1952) summarized some of the evidence for the presence in South America of a black-boned, black-meated (BB-BM) chicken. Its breast meat is dark, a melanotic sheath surrounds the bones, and it bears tufts on the sides of its head. It also has raised hackles, a black tongue and legs, and characteristic coloring of the feathers that mark it as distinctively Southeast Asian.

Johannessen and collaborators (Johannessen 1981; Johannessen and Fogg 1982; Johannessen et al. 1984) subsequently paid special attention to BB-BM chickens that are still found among various Indian groups in the Americas. This is a non-flocking chicken, displaying the social psychology characteristic of the chickens of Southeast Asia that leads them to stay apart from others when feeding.

At least among the groups that speak Mayan languages, Johannessen et al. found that the BB-BM chicken is not normally eaten, but is used in divination or medical treatments in essentially the same manner as recorded in China in the great encyclopedia of medicine about 1530. The Maya do sell some kinds of chickens to the Ladinos of their respective countries for comsumption. The treatments in China and the Americas are highly similar and esoteric. For instance, in highland Guatemala the chicken is cut sagitally, the cut surface is bound against the soles of a patient's feet, and the 'poultice' is left there for two or more hours. It is supposed to absorb pulmonary problems resulting from or causing an asthma attack. It is also used to cure 'women's problems.' The curer has specific incantations in a non-Mayan language that must be recited while candles and copal incense are burned and rum is blown onto the patient's bare skin (for shock effect?). Other rituals involving the BB-BM chicken take the fowl's life in order to protect a house, family members, tools, and even ships against hexes by painting all with the blood of the chicken. The South American groups who use the BB-BM chickens (Araucanians of Chile and the Chipaya of Bolivia) have been said to be tied linguistically to the Maya.

These beliefs and practices correspond to Chinese ways with BB-BM fowls. Transmission of these cultural matters must have involved careful teaching by Asian curing practitioners. Such rites and beliefs could not have been imported by such ephemeral contact as the natives had with people of the 17th- and 18th-century Manila galleons. And it is only speakers of Mayan languages who received, or at least have carried on, these practices.

Hartman's (1975) survey of the literature on the types of American chickens concluded that the Asian characteristics in American fowl can only be explained by voyagers' having introduced fowl to the New World across the Pacific Ocean before Columbus. She is the person who first emphasized that the eastern Mediterranean people selected for flocking habits of their chickens and pointed out the lack of that characteristic in traditional Southeast Asian chickens.

Most recently, linguist Soren Wichmann (1995, 76, 276) has reconstructed a term (*ce:wE(kV?)(n)) for 'chicken,' or 'hen,' in the Proto-

Mixe-Zoquean language of Mexico, which is believed to have been in use in the territory of the Olmec civilization of Mexico of the second millennium B.C.E. (Campbell and Kaufman 1976). He also reconstructed the expression *ná'w-ce:wy for 'cock.' Wichmann also gives nearly the same term for 'gallo/cock' for the Proto-Zoquean reconstructed language from the first millennium B.C.E. Both terms are distinct from words for 'turkey' in those tongues.

Guillemaud's (1947, 112) list of Mixe language terms in southern Mexico includes *tseuk* for 'gallina/hen,' and *tsag-naj* for 'gallo/cock,' the first of which is in general agreement with Wichman's term.

Archaeological specimens of purported chicken bones in the Americas have been reported; however, few have been tested positively to date before the time of Columbus. In at least one excavation, bones found at a Classic Maya site at Caracol, Belize where the site ranged in age between 200B.C.E. to 1,000 C.E. are accepted by the archaeologists as *Gallus gallus*, (Teeter 2004.177-191). Álvarez and Ocaña (1999, 100-102) have reported seven other archaeological sites in Mexico from which *Gallus* remains have been reported. Fifty chicken bones have been found in Chile dated before 1492. The DNA testing and C14 dating have been completed.

Lasioderma serricorne
Origin: the Americas (unclear)
Summary: The issue hinges on the place of origin of the species. It is well known now in the ancient Old World, but because it has been supposed connected with tobacco, it has also been supposed to come from the New World. If from the Old World, no transoceanic transport need be supposed.
Transfer: the Americas to Europe
Time of transfer: by the Egyptian Late Bronze Age, ca. 1400 B.C.E.
Grade: incomplete
Sources: *Lasioderma serricorne* – tobacco, or cigarette beetle

Jett 2002b. The species was first described in Europe in 1798, having been found on dried American materials, especially tobacco, and was first recorded in the United States in 1886. The beetle has also now been reported from the Late Bronze Age Minoan town of Akrotiri on the island of Thera in the Aegean, as well as at two Egyptian sites.

Panagiotakopulu 2000, 9. Noting the archaeological appearance in the Mediterranean region of this species, she thinks that "Its origin could be also Near Eastern." Its first archaeological record is from Akrotiri (Late Bronze Age). It has also been found in Tut's tomb in Egypt. But on page 6, Table 3–1, opposite *L. serricorne*, under "Place of origin," the column is left blank, meaning that she considers the place of origin to be undetermined.

Alfieri 1931. First report on the finding of *L. serricorne* in King Tut's tomb.

Alfieri 1976, 82. Seven species/varieties are recorded. *Lasioderma* (*Hypora*) *serricorne Fabricius*, specimens from Alexandria, Cairo, Delta, Faiyum, and Luxor regions. "Numerous individuals were found in an alabaster jar hermetically sealed in Tut Ank Amoun tomb 3500 years old."

Steffan 1982, 1985. *L. serricorne* was found in the mummy of Rameses II.

Steffan 1985. *L. serricorne* has several congeners, largely feeding on thistles, in the Old World. Hill (1994) considered the species of tropical origin. There are Mediterranean fossil records, which would support this explanation. Nevertheless, Steffan still relates the Rameses specimen to an unidentified species of *Nicotiana* from the mummy's visceral cavity. [Others have specified the leaf as *N. tabaccum*.]

Kislev 1991, 121. Origin of *L. serricorne*, Tropical America. 124. "The cigarette beetle" attacks mainly high value commodities such as cocoa and finished goods such as tobacco products and various processed foods. 128 (Table 11.2.) *L. serricorne* is listed as having archaeological manifestations in Egypt (only). "Among the seven beetles [listed], two of them should be excluded from this context: the find of *L. serricorne* in an ancient Egyptian site (Alfieri 1931) has to be considered as a modern intrusion because the beetle is known to originate in Tropical America."[sic] He repeats the point on page 129: "The absence of *L. serricorne* ... (which originated in the tropics) from the ancient Old World means that at least pulses were less likely to be damaged by pest beetles."

White 1990, 344. *L. serricorne* is "closely allied" with five species in North America. "In its native habitat" the species *L. haemorrhoidale* (Illiger), which he here reports, "exhibits a circum-Mediterranean distribution." The original host of *L. serricorne* was evidently the thistle, but at some time in the past it underwent an alteration of its feeding preference and became a pest of stored starches. There are more than 50 world species belonging to the genus *Lasioderma*, but the feeding preferences of fewer than 12 of these are known. There has never been a summary published of the genus. 347. Table 1 lists for *L. serricorne*'s distribution, "Cosmopolitan," with no reference to literature.

Munro 1966, 93. *Lasioderma serricorne* probably had a sub-tropical origin although it is now cosmopolitan.

Littorina littorea
Origin: Old World
Summary: Transatlantic transplantation would be impossible without voyagers being involved.
Grade: A
Source: *Littorina littorea* – a mollusc

Spjeldnaes and Henningsmoen 1938. They suggest that this mollusc was introduced to North America by Norse settlers about 1000 C.E. There is no other apparent way to account for its presence on the west side of the Atlantic. It is a hardy species that could survive for a long time in the bottom water (bilge) of open boats.

Meleagris gallopavo
Origin: New World
Summary: Archaeological, artistic, and historical documentation shows that the turkey reached and was in use in Europe and perhaps elsewhere in the Old World

before Columbus' first voyage. Only by voyages across the ocean can this distribution be explained logically.

Grade: A

Sources: *Meleagris gallopavo* – turkey

Hennig (1940) claimed that an American turkey could be seen in a painted frieze at Schleswig Cathedral, which had been built about 1280 C.E. (That claim was rebutted by Stresemann (1940; also Rieth 1967) who showed that the mural had been restored in the 1800s and 1900s, hence the turkey figure as it existed in 1940 could have depended on knowledge acquired after Columbus had brought knowledge of the turkey to Europe (the situation was reprised in Bökönyi and Jánossy (1959) and Varshavsky (1961)).

Meanwhile, Hungarian archaeologists have recovered turkey bones in the 14th-century royal castle at Buda. Turkey bones have also been excavated from a carefully-dated 14th-century site in Switzerland (Bökönyi and Jánossy 1959). Other sites in Hungary of the 10th–13th centuries have yielded signet rings engraved with images of this fowl, showing the fleshy pendent growth on the turkey's neck. In the light of these facts, it is possible that the Schleswig representation is authentically pre-Columbian.

Bökönyi and Jánossy (1959) reproduce a letter written in 1490 by Hungarian King Matthias, who died that same year, requesting through an envoy that the Duke of Milan send him turkeys – '*galine de Indie.*' (In post-Columbian Italy, the turkcy was termed '*gallo de Indie.*' 'Indie' refers to the Americas, 'the Indies,' while the common Mediterranean chicken was called 'fowl of Persia'). The Hungarian wished to acclimatize the turkey in his country. He asked that a man be sent who knew how to tend turkeys properly.

Apparent confirmation of the late medieval European distribution of the turkey is provided by a comment in a Relación (colonial report of inspection) from Mérida, Yucatan, from about 1579, which says: "There are many turkeys in the mountains which **differ little** from those in Spain, very good to eat, very timid birds" (Tozzer 1941, viii, 186; emphasis added). Traditionally, turkeys have been thought to have arrived in Spain from the Americas via conquistadors no earlier than 1523, and descendants of those fowl would not likely have multiplied so fast in Spain in the intervening half century as to be spoken of in the implied familiar manner.

Mus musculus

Origin: Asia

Summary: Bones were found in an 'offering' at the Aztec Templo Mayor of Tenochtitlan, the Aztec capital, as well as in a colonial Spanish waste deposit in Mexico City. That leaves some slight possibility that the mouse was present before the arrival of the Europeans.

Transfer: Asia, or some intermediate point, to Mexico?

Grade: incomplete

Source: *Mus musculus* - house mouse

Álvarez and Ocaña 1999, 103. A brief note about mouse bones ends with the explanation for their presence as either post-Conquest material or, in the case of the Templo Mayor specimen, *"una introducción anacrónica,"* which effectively means "no explanation." [The possibility that there was a pre-hispanic mouse perhaps would justify a radiocarbon dating of the Templo Mayor bones, although at best one could expect a date squarely, that is, unambiguously at the Aztec/Spanish boundary. Other mouse bones may have been found at Tlatilco.]

Mya arenaria
Origin: Western North Atlantic Ocean
Summary: Appearance of this mollusc in the ocean near Europe is unexplainable without involving humans and voyaging.
Transfer: from off the northeast coast of North America to the sea off Denmark
Grade: A-
Source: *Mya arenaria* – American soft-shell clam
> Petersen et al. 1992. They report that shells of this live clam have been discovered off the Danish coast. Until now the view had been that it was distributed only in the Americas. A radiocarbon date in the 13th century has been obtained for a specimen of shell that leaves only "very slight probability" of its dating after Columbus. Since the transfer had to have involved human voyaging (presumably involving the clam only inadvertently), it "could have been transferred from North America to Europe by the Vikings."

Oryctolagus cuniculus
Origin: Eurasia
Summary: The European rabbit (properly a hare), nominally introduced to Mexico during the colonial era, was found at Tlatilco, Mexico, in the excavation of a "troncocónica" formation, or bottle-shaped, debris pit. As in the case of the rat, the mouse, and the domestic cat, all of which were credited to the same location, this anomalous find deserves to be investigated further and properly dated, to place it unquestionably in the Preclassic time frame implied by this report, or to deny that.
Transfer: Europe, or some intermediate locus, to Mexico
Grade: incomplete
Sources: *Oryctolagus cuniculus* – the European rabbit
> Álvarez and Ocaña 1999, 100. They say the presence of bones of this "European rabbit" in a "bottle-shaped pit" at Tlatilco possibly can be explained by an "involuntary error" during the excavation or "perhaps it was introduced to the pit from a post-Conquest surface stratum by some burrowing animal." They say that more such bones have been found at Corral de Piedra, (at or near?) San Cristóbal de Las Casas, Chiapas.

> Álvarez 1976, Table I shows that the two specimens (bones) of this animal were found in stratum III (the lowest of three) of the excavation, in substratum IIIC (the third in descending order of nine substrata), not from a *"formacion troncocónica"*, but in the 1999 publication, they are said to have come from a *"formación troncocónica"*. In order to explain how these

bones of the European species came to be in the general excavation level from which they are said to have come, the author supposes (in general) that there was mixing in the contents of the bell-shaped pit from which they came, probably due to burrowing rodents (*tuzas*).

Rattus sp.
Origin: The *Rattus* genus is unquestionably Old World in origin. It has been generally supposed that rats were absent from the New World until European ships unintentionally brought them (*Rattus rattus* and *R. norvegicus*) in the 16th century. Summary: Recent studies of the spread of rats in the Pacific basin (Holdaway 1996; Matisoo-Smith et al. 1998; Matisoo-Smith and Robins 2004) have taken advantage of the obvious fact that the distribution of rats must be explained as a result of human voyaging, since rats do not swim at sea. Thus when we find that rat bones were excavated over 30 years ago from a grave at Tlatilco, a site in central Mexico that shows indications of Asian cultural influence, the explanation for their presence might come from a transpacific vessel on the Pacific coast of Mexico.
Transfer: from Oceania or Asia to Mexico
Grade: C
Sources: *Rattus* sp. – rat

 Álvarez 1976. Records of excavation show that bones identified as *Rattus* sp. were excavated at the site of Tlatilco, near Mexico City. [This Middle Preclassic settlement and burial ground has produced materials dated in the range of 1500-400 B.C.E. There is little reason to suspect post-1500 contamination in any Tlatilco remains.] Table I shows that all eight bones of this species came from the III stratum (deepest of three), and therein from the topmost of III's nine sub-strata.

 Álvarez and Ocaña 1999 say that bones of this species were recovered from a "*formación troncocónica*" (bottle-shaped pit) at Tlatilco, while in the 1976 report they were said to have come from general excavations, not from such a pit. Furthermore, the 1976 report calls these "rat" in general, while in 1999 (page 103) they were labeled *Rattus rattus*. On p.103 rat remains are said to have been found also in an offering at the (Aztec) Templo Mayor, in a colonial midden of a street in Guatemala [sic] (none of the extensive literature on the Templo Mayor site make reference to such a find), and at Tlalpizahuac in the state of Mexico (there is no other published information that we are aware of on this last site). [Despite the change in nomenclature between the 1976 and 1999 publications (from "*Rattus* sp." to "*Rattus rattus*") nowhere in the accessible literature is there indication that the rat remains were extensive enough and were examined expertly enough to assure whether they were of the *R. rattus* species, of indeterminate status, or possibly of *R. exulans*, which would show an Oceanic source.]

 Joaquin Arroyo-Cabrales of INAH, in an email to Carl Johannessen, 23 Nov. 2005, subject "*Rattus*", reports that he has checked with Patricia Ochoa, who has been working with the Tlatilco collection, and she assures him that the rat skeletons were found "*in situ*" at Tlatilco, which means that they were unlikely to have been buried by rodent activity.

Matisoo-Smith and Robbins 2004. An extensive sample (n=94) of the mtDNA of the Pacific rat, *R. exulans*, has abeen analyzed to examine the disputed question of the migrations in Near and Remote Oceania of the Lapita cultural complex and other cultural evidence for the development of the population of ancestral Polynesians.

Matisoo-Smith et al. 1998. Rat DNA phylogenies demonstrate that multiple contacts (voyages) took place between central Eastern Polynesia and New Zealand and Hawaii over a lengthy period of time. The rat also reached Easter Island.

In view of extensive evidence in the current paper of faunal and floral connections between the Americas and Oceania, it is not entirely unreasonable to postulate that the archaeological remains of *Rattus* sp? from Mexico derived from islander voyages to the Pacific Coast of Mexico. This could be settled by mtDNA and radiocarbon tests on the Mexico specimens, which they are investigating.

Rhyzopertha dominica
Origin: unclear
Summary: Some authors had apparently supposed this insect to be from South America. Kislev and Panagiotakopulu have stated that it came from India, without any supporting information (so said also by Potter, see below). If from the Old World, transoceanic transport in antiquity cannot be claimed, but if from South America, then an explanation is called for to account for its presence in Old World archaeological sites.
Transfer: Americas to the eastern Mediterranean?
Grade: incomplete
Sources: *Rhyzopertha dominica* – lesser grain borer

Panagiotakopulu 2000, 9, 62, 104, 110–11. Found at the Minoan site of Akrotiri on the Island of Thera as well as in a Roman site in Egypt. While commonly referred to as the 'South American lesser grain borer,' Panagiotakopulu lists the origin (in the table on page 9) as "India." Also known from Kahun in Egypt (1900–1800 B.C.E.), and in a vessel from Tut'ankhamun's tomb of 1345 B.C.E. 9. "The lesser grain borer." It is a usual pest on grain in warmer countries, and is also recorded from a wide variety of crops, such as wheat, barley, millet, rice, maize, and sorghum as well as other products. It was originally described from South America (Munro 1966, 95), but may have originated in India, citing Kislev (1991).

Kislev 1991, 121. Lists the place of origin of this insect as "India" (without any discussion or justification). 124. It was found at Nahal Yattir, Israel, from the second century C.E. 124, Table 11.2. He shows archaeological manifestations of this species in Spain, Israel, and Egypt.

Hill 1983, 433. *R. dominica*, the lesser grain borer, infests stored cereals. It was originally described from South America but now is cosmopolitan.

Potter 1935, 451. The original home of *R. dominica* is not known for certain, but the balance of opinion is that it is India or the Indian subregion. 452. It is known from Central America (1792 C.E.), Cuba (1857), and Mexico and Honduras (1883). (Potter's comprehensive survey of the literature makes it doubtful that it was "originally described from South America.")

Stegobium paniceum
Origin: Old World
Summary: This same species of beetle in both Egyptian and Peruvian burials can have no other explanation than transport by voyagers from the Old to the New World. (Cf. the presence of identical drugs in the burials in the same two areas, i.e., tobacco, coca, and hashish.)
Grade: A
Sources: *Stegobium paniceum* – the drugstore beetle

Riddle and Vreeland 1982. They speak of two species of Coleoptera, *Stegobium paniceum* and *Alphitobius diaperinus*, that come from pre-Columbian Peruvian mummies examined in Lima. Three bundles studied were radiocarbon dated to the Paracas (86 C.E.), Epigonal (1231 C.E.), and Huancho (1240 C.E.) periods. This beetle was found in the Paracas bundle between the innermost and the second-layer wrapping cloth, and on the surface of the fourth wrapping cloth, which lay directly beneath a wig of braided human hair, which had been placed over the top of the bundle. The Epigonal bundle showed adult *Alphitobius diaperinus*, associated with a cotton garment folded and placed over the area of the knees directly in front of the body. The Hunach (sic; Huancho) bundle showed adult *Stegobium paniceum* beetles in direct association with the fragments of cooked roots. "The possibility of post-exhumation contamination of the mummy bundles with modern insect populations was considered unlikely, because the outer wrappings showed no evidence of activity by boring insects, the storerooms in which the mummies had been located were periodically fumigated, and one of the Hunach (Huancho) mummy bundles was dissected just a few days after its excavation."

Buckland and Panagiotakopulu 2001, 6. *Stegobium paniceum* is commonly known as the 'drugstore beetle' or 'biscuit beetle,' a well-known pest which has been found in stored food of agricultural societies, including Old Kingdom Pharaonic Egypt (ca. 2700–2181 B.C.E.).

Panagiotakopulu 2000, 9. Breeds in starchy materials, including cereals and many other commodities such as spices, cocoa, beans, etc. Also known as the 'biscuit beetle.' It was recovered from deposits of 1399 B.C.E. and bread of 2049 B.C.E. from Egypt. 62. "The biscuit beetle" was found at Bronze Age Wilsford, Wiltshire, in England, and in Egypt ca. 3400 B.C.E.

Kislev 1991, 128, Table 11.2. Shows archaeological manifestations of stored-product pest, *S. paniceum*, at four sites in England and two in Egypt.

APPENDIX 2
Species Ordered by Uses

* indicates species for which we have definitive evidence
Unmarked species indicate those that have indicative evidence or ar
in need of further research

Foodstuffs

Grain Amaranths	*Amaranthus cruentus*
Grain Amaranths	*Amaranthus hypochondriacus*
Grain Amaranths	*Amaranthus caudatus*
Cashew Nut	*Anacardium occidentale*
Pineapple	*Ananas comosus* (sativa)
Custard Apple	*Annona squamosa*
Custard Apple	*Annona reticulata*
Custard Apple	*Annona cherimolia*
Custard Apple	Annona glabra
Peanut	*Arachis hypogaea*
Achiote	*Bixa orellana*
Pigeon Pea	Cajanus cajan
Indian Shot	*Canavalia edulis*
Jackbean, Swordbean	*Canavalia ensiformis*
Jackbean, Swordbean	*Canavalia obtusifolia*
Dog	Canis familiaris
Achira	Canna edulis
Chili Pepper	*Capsicum annuum*
Chili Pepper	*Capsicum frutescens*
Papaya	*Carica papaya*
Mexican Tea	*Chenopodium ambrosioides*
Coconut	*Cocos nucifera*
Dry-land Taro	Colocasia esculenta
Cannon-ball Tree	*Couroupita guianensis*
Curassow	Crax globicera
Chilacayote Squash	*Curcurbita ficifolia*
Crookneck Squash	*Curcurbita moschata*
Pumpkin	*Curcurbita pepo*
Hubbard Squash	*Curcurbita maximus*
Caigua	Cyclanthera pedata
Yellow Nutsedge	*Cyperus esculentus*
Edible Sedge	*Cyperus vegetus*
Fulvous Tree Duck	Dendrocygna bicolor
Yams	Dioscorea alata

Guinea Yam	*Dioscorea cayenensis*
Black Sapote	**Diospyros ebenaster*
Lablab Bean	*Dolichos lablab*
African Oil Palm	*Elaeis guineensis*
Chicken	**Gallus gallus*
Purple Mangosteen	**Garcinia mangostana*
Sunflower	**Helianthus annuus*
Sweet Potato	**Ipomoea batatas*
Bottle Gourd	**Lagenaria siceraria*
Common Periwinkle	**Littorina littorea*
Ribbed Gourd	**Luffa acutangula*
Lupine	*Lupinus cruickshanksii*
Tomato	**Lycopersicon esculentum*
Phasey Bean	**Macroptilium lathyroides*
Mango	*Mangifera indica*
Cassava	**Manihot esculentis*
Arrowroot	**Maranta arundinacea*
Turkey	** Meleagris gallopavo*
Monster Fruit	**Montera deliciosa*
Banana or Plantain	**Musa balbisiana × acuminata*
Chinese Banana	*Musa coccinea*
Soft-shelled Clam	**Mya arenaria*
Prickly Pear Cactus	**Opuntia dillenii*
European Rabbit	*Oryctolagus cuniculus*
Hawaiian Rose	**Osteomeles anthyllidifolia*
Jicama	**Pachyrhizus erosus*
Yam Bean, Jicama	**Pachyrhizus tuberosus*
Pearl Millet	*Pennisetum americanum*
Potato Bean	*Phaseolus adenanthus*
Phasey Bean	**Phaseolus lathyroides*
Lima Bean	**Phaseolus lunatus*
Kidney Bean	**Phaseolus vulgaris*
Ground Cherry	**Physalis lanceifolia*
Winter Cherry	**Physalis peruviana*
Guava	**Psidium guajava*
Sugarcane	**Saccharum officinarum*
Wapatoo	*Sagittaria sagittifolia*
Bulrush	**Schoenoplectus californicus*
Sesame Plant	*Sesamum orientale*
Sarsparilla	**Smilax sp.*
Naranjillo	**Solanum candidum*
Black Nightshade	**Solanum nigrum*
Potato	**Solanum tuberosum*

World Trade and Biologocal Exchanges Before 1492

Edible Tuber	*Solanum repandum*
A fruit tree	*Spondias lutyea*
Hogplum	*Spondias purpurea*
Tamarind Tree	*Tamarindus indicus*
Water Chestnut	*Trapa natans*
Cowpea	*Vigna sinensis*
Grape	*Vitis vinifera*
Corn, Maize	**Zea mays*

Fiber

Agave	**Agave* sp.
Kapok Tree	**Bombax malabaricum*
Kapok Tree	**Ceiba pentandra*
Dog	*Canis familiaris*
Coconut	**Cocos nucifera*
Cotton	**Gossypium arboretum*
Cotton	**Gossypium barbadense*
Cotton	*Gossypium brasiliense*
Cotton	*Gossypium drynaroides*
Cotton	**Gossypium gossypioides*
Cotton	*Gossypium herbaceum*
Cotton	**Gossypium hirsutum*
Cotton	*Gossypium religiosum*
Cotton	**Gossypium tomentosum*
Platonillo, Balisier	**Heliconia bihai*
Linden Hibiscus	**Hibiscus tiliaceus*
White Mulberry	**Morus alba*
White Mulberry	*Morus nigra*
White Mulberry	*Morus rubra*
Banana Plant	**Musa balbisiana x acuminata*
Bulrush	**Schoenoplectus californicus*
Bluegrass	**Sisyrhynchium augustifolium*
Sacramento Burbark Tree	*Triumfetta semitriloba*
Corn, Maize Plant	**Zea mays*

Fence Plants

Achiote	**Bixa orellana*
Linden Hibiscus	**Hibiscus tiliaceus*
Pink Hibiscus	*Hibiscus youngianus*
Prickly Pear Cactus	*Opuntia dillenii*
Fish Poisons	*Derris* sp.
Fish Poisons	*Lonchocarpus sericeus*

Fish Poisons .... *Tephrosia* spp.

Trees
Custard Apple	*Annona squamosa*
Custard Apple	*Annona reticulata*
Custard Apple	*Annona cherimolia*
Custard Apple	*Annona glabra*
Kapok Tree	*Bombax malabaricum*
Kapok Tree	*Ceiba pentandra*
Achiote..	*Bixa orellana*
Quinine Bark Tree.................................	*Chinchona officianalis*
Coconut Palm	*Cocos nucifera*
Cannon-ball Tree...................................	*Couroupita guianensis*
Black Sapote Tree.................................	*Diospyros ebenaster*
African Oil Palm...................................	*Elaeis guineensis*
Purple Mangsteen..................................	*Garcinia mangostana*
Linden Hibiscus.....................................	*Hibiscus tiliaceus*
Pink Hibiscus	*Hibiscus youngianus*
Magnolia Tree	*Magnolia grandiflora*
White Mulberry.....................................	*Morus alba*
White Mulberry.....................................	*Morus nigra*
White Mulberry.....................................	*Morus rubra*
Frangipanni...	*Plumeria rubra*
Guava Tree..	*Psidium guajava*
Soapberry Tree......................................	*Sapindus saponaria*
Toromiro Tree	*Sophora toromiro*
Tamarind Tree	*Tamarindus indicus*
Sacramento Burbark Tree	*Triumfetta semitriloba*

Drugs
Fly Agaric..	*Amanita muscaria*
Prickle Poppy	*Argemone mexicana*
Marijuana	*Cannabis sativa*
Jimsom Weed..	*Datura metel*
Datura, unknown...................................	*Datura sanguinea*
Thorn Apple..	*Datura stramonium*
Coca...	*Erythroxylon novagranatense*
Tobacco	*Nicotiana tabacum*
Tobacco	*Nicotiana rustica*
Blue Lotus	*Nymphaea caerulea*
Morning Glory.......................................	*Pharbitis hederacea*
Grape..	*Vitis vinifera*

Fish Poisons .... *Derris* sp.
Fish Poisons .... *Lonchocarpus sericeus*
Fish Poisons .... *Tephrosia* spp.

Weeds
Goatweed .... **Ageratum conyzoides*
Alligator Weed .... **Alternanthera philoxeroides*
.... *Alternanthera pungens*
.... *Alternanthera sessilis*
.... *Alternanthera tonella*
Amaranth .... **Amaranthus spinosus*
Three-awn Grass .... **Aristida subspicata*
Milkweed .... **Asclepias curassavica*
Air Potato .... *Dioscorea bulbifera*
A weed .... *Erigeron albidus*
A weed .... **Erigeron canadensis*
Purple Cudweed .... *Gnaphalium purpureum*
Pink Hibiscus .... *Hibiscus youngianus*
Phasey Bean .... **Macroptilium lathyroides*
Phasey Bean .... **Phaseolus lathyroides*
Sensitive Plant .... **Mimosa pudica*
Cowhage .... **Mucuna pruriens*
Bog Myrtle .... **Myrica gale*
Bluegrass .... **Sisyrhynchium angustifolium*
Nodeweed .... *Synedrella nodiflora*
Golden Crownbeard .... *Verbesina encelioides*

Religious
Fly Agaric .... *Amanita muscaria*
Pineapple .... **Anana comosus*
Amaranth .... **Amaranthus cruentus*
Kapok Tree .... **Bombax malabaricum*
Kapok Tree .... **Ceiba pentandra*
Cannon-ball Tree .... **Couroupita guianensis*
Coca .... **Erythroxylon novagranatense*
Chicken .... **Gallus gallus*
Sunflower .... **Helianthus annuus*
Magnolia Tree .... *Magnolia grandiflora*
White Lotus .... *Nymphaea ampla*
Morning Glory .... **Pharbitis hederacea*
Double Flowering Tuberose .... *Polianthes tuberosa*
Marigold .... **Tagetes erectus*
Water Chestnut .... *Trapa natans*

Grape	*Vitis vinifera*
Corn, Maize	*Zea mays*

Disease-Causing Organisms

Whooping Cough	**Bordetella pertussis*
Relapse Fever	**Borrella recurrentis*
Amoebic Dysentery	**Entamoeba hystolytica*
Yellow Fever	*Flavivirus* spp.
Giardia	*Giardia lamblia*
Herpes 3	**Herpes zoster* varicella-roster
Epstein-Barr	**Herpes (gamma)* herpes virus 4
Influenza	*Influenza* sp.
Leishmania	*Leishmania* sp.
Ringworm Fungi	**Microsporum tinea corporis*
Ringworm Fungi	**Microsporum tinea cruris*
Leprosy	*Mycobacterium leprae*
Tuberculosis	**Mycobacterium tuberculosis*
Onchocerciasis	*Onchocerca volvulus*
Piedra Negra	**Piedreaia hortai*
Malaria	*Plasmodium falciparum*
Acute Typhus	**Rickettsia prowazekii*
Spotted Fever	**Rickettsia rickettsii*
Endemic Typhus	*Rickettsia mooseri*
Typhoid	*Salmonella enterica* serovar Typhi
	Salmonella enterica serovar Typhimurium
Snail Fever	*Schistosoma haematobium*
Staph Infection	*Staphylococcus x aureus*
Pneumonia	*Streptococcus pneumonia*
Scarlet Fever	*Streptococcus pyogenes*
HTLV-I	**Human T-Cell Lymphotropic (retro) virus I*
Syphilis	*Treponema pallidum* pallidum
Ringworm	*Trichophyton* spp.
Piedra Branca	**Trichosporon ovoides*
Plague	**Yersinia pestis*

Parasites

Hookworm	**Ancylostoma duodenale*
Roundworm	**Ascaris lumbricoides*
Hookworm	**Necator americanus*
Human Lice	**Pediculus humanus capitis*

Human Lice .... *Pediculus humanus corporis
Human Flea .... Pulex irritans
Hair Worm .... Strongyloides sp.
Whipworm... *Trichuris trichiura
Helmintic parasite................................. Trychostrongylus sp.
Threadlike worm .... Wuchereria bancrofti
Rat Flea .... Xenopsylla cheopis

Pests
Lesser Meal Worm .... *Alphitobius diaperinus
Tobacco Beetle .... Lasioderma serricorne
Common Periwinkle .... *Littorina littorea
House Mouse .... Mus musculus
Soft-shelled Clam .... *Mya arenaria
Rat... Rattus rattus
Rat... Rattus exulans
Lesser Grain Borer.............................. Rhyzopertha dominica
Drugstore Beetle.................................. *Stegobium paniceum
Chigger... Tunga penetrans

Medicinals
Sweet Flag.. Acorus calamus
.... Adenostemma viscosum
Mexican Prickle Poppy .... *Argemone mexicana
Mugwort .... *Artemisia vulgaris
Achiote.. *Bixa orellana
Purging Cassia .... Cassia fistula
Mexican Tea .... *Chenopodium ambrosioides
Quinoa .... Chenopodium quinoa
Quinine Bark.. Chinchona officianalis
African Palm Oil.................................. Elaeis guineensis
Coca Plant.. Erythroxylon novagranatense
Chicken .... *Gallus gallus
Purple Mangosteen.............................. Garcinia mangostana
Bottle Gourd.. *Lagenaria siceraria
Vegetable Sponge .... *Luffa cylindrical
Vegetable Sponge .... *Luffa aegyptiaca
Arrowroot... *Maranta arundinacea
Cowhage .... *Mucuna pruriens
Morning Glory..................................... *Pharbitis hederacea
Tapertip Smartweed............................ *Polygonum acuminatum
Scarlet Sage .... Salvia coccinea
Sesame Plant .... Sesamum orientale

Sarsparilla	*Smilax* sp.
Black Nightshade	*Solanum nigrum
Chickory	*Sonchus oleraceus
Common Marigold	*Tagetes erectus
French Marigold	*Tagetes patula
Water Chestnut	Trapa natans
Golden Crownbeard	Verbesina encelioides

Spices

Mugwort	*Artemisia vulgaris
Turmeric Plant	*Curcuma longa
Hoary Basil	Ocimum americanum
French Basil	*Ocimum basilum
Sweet Basil, Holy Basil	Ocimum sanctum

Miscellaneous

Sweet Flag	Acorus calamus
Ageratum	Ageratum houstonianum
Whitewood	*Aster divaricates
Achiote	*Bixa orellana
Common Dog	Canis familiaris
Cicada	Cicada sp.
Domestic Cat	Felis catus
Indigo	Indigofera suffruticosa
Indigo	Indigofera tinctoria
Bottle Gourd	*Lagenaria siceraria
Lupine	Lupinus cruickshanksii
Ribbed Gourd	*Luffa acutangula
Carolina Desert-thorn	*Lycium carolinianum
Four o'clock Flower	*Mirabilis jalapa
Carpetweed	* Mollugo verticillata
White Mulberry	*Morus alba
White Mulberry	Morus nigra
White Mulberry	Morus rubra
Bog Myrtle	*Myrica gale
Frangipani	*Plumeria rubra
Double Flowering Tuberose	Polianthes tuberosa
Purslane	*Portulaca oleracea
Scarlet Sage	Salvia coccinea
West Indian Sage	Salvia occidentalis
Soapberry Tree	*Sapindus saponaria
A grass	Sisyrhynchium acre
Blue-eyed grass	Sisyrhynchium angustifolium

Toromiro Tree .... *Sophora toromiro*
French Marigold .... *Tagetes patula*

APPENDIX 3

Species of American Plants in South Asia, by Type of Evidence

Evidence type: Sanskrit name

Agave americana (syn. cantula/cantala)
Sources:
Balfour 1871–1873, I, 52. Sanskrit: *kala kantala*
Torkelson 1999, 1634. Sanskrit: *kantala*
Watson 1868, 250. Sanskrit: *kantala*
Nadkarni 1914, 23. Sanskrit: *kantala*
Pullaiah 2002, I, 34–5. Sanskrit: *kalakantala*
Parotta 2001, 40. Sanskrit: *kalakantala, kantala*

Agave angustifolia (syn. vivipera)
Sources:
Chopra et al. 1956, 9. *A. vivipera.* Sanskrit: *kantala*
Balfour 1871–1873, I, 52, 84. Sanskrit: *kala kantala*

Agave cantala (syn. americana, cantula)
Sources:
Chopra et al. 1969, 3. Sanskrit: *kantala*
Chopra et al. 1956, 9. Sanskrit: *kantala*
Balfour 1871–1873, I, 52. Sanskrit: *kala kantala.*

Ageratum conyzoides
Source:
Pullaiah 2002, I, 35. Sanskrit: *visamustih*

Ageratum philoxeroides
Source:
Pullaiah 2002, I, 47. Sanskrit: *matsyahi, lonika.*

Amaranthus caudatus
Sources:
Torkelson 1999, 1641. Sanskrit: *rajagiri*
Int. Lib. Assoc. 1996, 559. Sanskrit: *rajagirita*

Amaranthus spinosus
Sources:
Torkelson 1999, 1641. Sanskrit: *tanduliya*

Chopra et al. 1956, 15. Sanskrit: *tanduliya*
Int. Lib. Assoc. 1996, 559. Sanskrit: *alpamarisha, tandula*
Pullaiah 2002, I, 48. Sanskrit: *tandaluya, kataib, chaulai.*

Anacardium occidentale
Sources:
Nadkarni 1914, 32. Sanskrit: *shoephahara.*
Balfour 1871–1873, III, 409; I, 107. Sanskrit: *beejara sula. bijara sala.*
Pullaiah 2002, I, 52–53. Sanskrit: *kajutaka, anamnasam, bahunetraphalam*

Ananas comosus
Source:
Pullaiah 2002, I, 53. Sanskrit: *anamnasam, bahunetraphalam*

Annona reticulata
Sources:
Balfour 1871–1873, I, 125. Sanskrit: *Rama sita.*
Pullaiah 2002, I, 60. Sanskrit: *ramphal.*
Watson 1868 (citing Roxburgh 1814). Sanskrit: *luvunee.*
Torkelson 1999, 1646. Sanskrit: *ramphala.*
Chopra et al. 1956, 19–20. Sanskrit: *ramphala.*
Int. Lib. Assoc. 1996, 559. Sanskrit: *krishnabeejam, ramphal.*

Annona squamosa
Sources:
Nadkarni 1914, 38. Sanskrit: *shubhá, suda*
Watson 1868, 181, 527. Sanskrit: *gunda-gutra* or *gunda-gatra*
Parotta 2001, 70. Sanskrit: *gandhgataram, gandagatra, krishnabija.*

Arachis hypogaea
Sources:
Nadkarni 1914, 39. Sanskrit: *buchanaka*
Torkelson 1999, 1646. Sanskrit: *buchanaka.*
Chopra et al. 1956, 22. Sanskrit: *buchanaka.*
Pullaiah 2002, I, 65. Sanskrit: *buchanakah, mandapi.*
Krapovickas 1968, 527. Sanskrit: *andapi*
Balfour 1871–1873, I, 153–4. Sanskrit: *buchanaka.*

Argemone mexicana
Sources:
Nadkarni 1914, 41, 910. Sanskrit: *brahmadandi,* "*bramadundie*," and "*bramhadundie.*"
Watt 1888–1893, I, 305–6. Sanskrit: *srigála kantá, brahmadandi.*

Balfour 1871–1873, I, 177. Sanskrit: *"bramhie"* or *"bramh."*
Chopra et al. 1956, 23. Sanskrit: *srigala-kantaka.*
Torkelson 1999, 1646. Sanskrit: *satyanasi, srigala-kantaka.*
Int. Lib. Assoc. 1996, 559. Sanskrit: *bhramhadandi, swarnaksiri.*
Pullaiah 2002, I, 66. Sanskrit: *swarnakshiri, bhramadendi.*
Saraswat, Sharma, and Saini (1994, 262, 333, 334) report mention of this plant in the medical treatise Bhava Prakasha in the Sushruta Samhita (first/second century C.E.) where two Sanskrit names of the plant are given as *swarnakshiri* and *kauparni.*

Asclepias curassavica
Sources:
Int. Lib. Assoc. 1996, 560. Sanskrit: *kakatundi.*
Pullaiah 2002, I, 75–6. Sanskrit: *kakatundi.*
Parotta 2001, 122. Sanskrit: *kakatundi.*

Bixa orellana
Sources:
Balfour 1871–1873, I, 177. Sanskrit: *brahmi.*
Pullaiah 2002, I, 97. Sanskrit: *sinduri.*

Canavalia ensiformis (or *C. obtusifolia*)
Source:
Watt 1888–1893, II, 197. Sanskrit: *shimbi.*

Canna edulis (syn. *indica*)
Sources:
Nadkarni 1914, 77. Sanskrit: *sarvajaya*
Pullaiah 2002, I, 116. Sanskrit: *devakuli*
Balfour 1871–1873, I, 43. Sanskrit: *silarumba*

Capsicum annuum
Sources:
Watt 1888–1893, II, 134–9. Sanskrit: *marich-phalam*
Nadkarni 1914, 86. *Capsicum annuum* and *C. frutescens.* Sanskrit: *marichiphalam.*
Torkelson 1999, 1675. Sanskrit: *katuvira, marichi-phalam*
Pullaiah 2002, I, 121. Sanskrit: *katuvirah, rakta maricha*

Capsicum frutescens
Source:
Nadkarni 1914, 86. *C. annuum* and *C. frutescens.* Sanskrit: *marichiphalam.*

Carica papaya
Source:
Parotta 2001, 202. Sanskrit: *eranda karkati*

Ceiba pentandra
Sources:
Nadkarni 1914, 59. *Bombax malabaricum* (syn.?) Sanskrit: *shalmali, mocha*
Pullaiah 2002, I, 147. *C. pentandra*. Sanskrit: *swetha salmali*
Chopra et al. 1956, 61 and Torkelson 1999, 1684 both. Sanskrit: *vastuk*
Torkelson 1999. Sanskrit: *sugandhavastuk*
Int. Lib. Assoc. 1996, 562. Sanskrit: *kshetravastuk*

Cucurbita maxima
Sources:
Nadkarni 1914, 129. Sanskrit: *punyalatha, dadhiphala*
Pullaiah 2002, I, 194. Sanskrit: *pitakusmandah*

Cucurbita pepo
Sources:
Aiyer 1956, 57. Mentioned in the Atharvaveda, dating before 800 B.C.E. (name not in Aiyer)
Torkelson 1999, 1704. Sanskrit: *kurkaru, kushmanda*
Chopra et al. 1956, 83. Sanskrit: *kurkaru*
Watt 1888–1893, II, 641. Sanskrit: *kurkareu*

Cyperus esculentus
Source:
Pullaiah 2002, I, 203. Sanskrit: *bhadrmusta, nagaramustakah.*

Cyperus vegetus
Sources:
Chopra et al. 1956, 88. Sanskrit: *kaseruka*
Torkelson 1999, 1709. Sanskrit: *kaseruka*

Datura metel (syn. fastuosa, innoxia)
Sources:
Pullaiah 2002, I, 209. Sanskrit: *dhattura, dhatura*
Parotta 2001, 670. Sanskrit: *senmatla*

Datura stramonium (syn. *tatula, patula*)
Sources:
Chopra et al. 1958, 134. Sanskrit: *dhattura, unmatta, kanaka, Shivapriya*
Pullaiah 2002, I, 209. Sanskrit: *dhattura, madakara*

Erigeron canadensis
Source:
Torkelson 1999, 1726. Sanskrit: *jarayupriya, makshikavisha*

Gossypium barbadense
Sources:
Chopra et al. 1956, 127. Sanskrit: *maghani*
Kirtikar and Basu 1999, I, 348. Sanskrit: *maghani, purvam.*
Torkelson 1999, 1745. Sanskrit: *maghani*

Helianthus annuus
Sources:
Nadkarni 1914, 177–8. *Helianthus annuses* (sic) (i.e., *annuus*). Sanskrit: *suriya-mukhi.*
Pullaiah 2002, II, 282. Sanskrit: *adityabhakta, suryamukhi.*
Aiyer 1956, 67. Mentioned in Hindu Charaka Sahmita dated no later than the fourth century C.E.
Torkelson 1999, 1749. Sanskrit: *suriya-mukhi*
Chopra et al. 1956, 131. Sanskrit: *surya-mukhi.*
Watt 1888, IV, 209. Sanskrit: *Suria-mukhi*
Balfour 1871–1873, II, 492. Sanskrit: *suria mukhi*

Ipomoea batatas
Sources:
Aiyer 1956, 71. Sanskrit: "*Valli (Ipomoea batates?)*"
Pullaiah 2002, II, 307. Sanskrit: *pindalah, raktaluh.*

Lycopersicon esculentum
Sources:
Parotta 2001, 673. Sanskrit: *raktamachi, raktavardhak, ramphala, shak-stmeshdha*
Pullaiah 2002, II, 339. Sanskrit: *raktamachi*

Manihot esculenta
Source:
Pullaiah 2002, II, 346–7. Sanskrit: *darukandah, kalpakandah.*

Maranta arundinacea
Sources:
Aiyer 1956, 44. Sanskrit: *kuvai*
Pullaiah 2002, II, 348. Sanskrit: *tavakshiri, tugaksiri.*

Mimosa pudica
Sources:
Torkelson 1999, 1785. Sanskrit: *anjalikarika, lajja*
Chopra et al. 1956. Sanskrit: *lajja.*
Int. Lib. Assoc. 1996, 569. Sanskrit: *lajja*
Nadkarni 1914, 233. Sanskrit: *ajàlikalika, namaskâri.*
Pullaiah 2002, II, 358–9. Sanskrit: *lajjalu, namaskari.*

Mirabilis jalapa
Sources:
Torkelson 1999, 1786. Sanskrit: *krishnakeli*
Chopra et al. 1956, 168. Sanskrit: *krishnakeli.*
Int. Lib. Assoc. 1996, 569. Sanskrit: *krishnakeli.*
Pullaiah 2002, II, 362. Sanskrit: *Trisandhi, krsnakeli* [sic], *sandhya-raga.*
Balfour 1871–1873, III, 282. Sanskrit: *bahu-bumi, sundia-ragum*

Mucuna pruriens
Sources:
Nadkarni 1914, 242–3. Sanskrit: *atmagupta, kapikachchhu*
Torkelson 1999, 1788. Sanskrit: *atmagupta, kapikachchha*
Chopra et al. 1956, 171. Sanskrit: *atmagupta*
Int. Lib. Assoc. 1996, 569. Sanskrit: *atmagupta.*
Pullaiah 2002, II, 369–70. Sanskrit: *atmagupta, vanari.*

Nicotiana tabacum
Sources:
Pullaiah 2002, II, 380. Sanskrit: *tamakhu.*
Chopra et al. 1956, 176. Sanskrit; *tamakhu.*
Torkelson 1999, 1793. Sanskrit: *tamakkhu.* Arabic: *tanbak.* Pers.: *tanbaku*
Nadkarni 1914, 257. Sanskrit: *támrakúta*

Ocimum americanum (syn. canum)
Sources:
Pullaiah 2002, II, 384. Sanskrit: *vanabarbarika, aranyathullasi*
Parotta 2001, 438–9. (syn. basilicum). Sanskrit: *arjaka, arjakah, barbari*

Ocimum basilicum
Sources:
Chopra et al. 1958, 680. Sanskrit: *munjariki*
Pullaiah 2002, II, 385. Sanskrit: *barbari, munjariki.*

Ocimum sanctum
Sources:
Pullaiah 2002, II, 385. *Ocimum tenniflorum* (syn. sanctum). Sanskrit: *surasa, vrinda*
Parotta 2001, 441. Sanskrit: *ajaka, ramatulasi, tulasi, vriddhtulasi*
Gupta. 1996, 131–2. Sanskrit?: *tulasi, bhutagni* (?)

Opuntia dillenii
Sources:
Pullaiah 2002, II, 389. *Opuntia stricta* (syn. *dillenii*). Sanskrit: *vidara, visvasraka*
Torkelson 1999, 1798. (syn. *Cactus indicus*) Sanskrit: *vidara*
Chopra et al. 1956, 178. Sanskrit: *vidara*
Parotta 2001, 194. (syn. stricta). Sanskrit: *kanthari, vidara*

Pachyrhizus erosus
Source:
Watt 1892, VI, Part I, 3. (syn. angulatus). Sanskrit: *sankhálu*

Pharbitis hederacea
Source:
Chopra et al. 1956, 142. (syn. *Ipomoea hederacea*). Sanskrit: *krishnabija*

Phaseolus vulgaris
Source:
Levey 1973, 55 (see also Levey 1966, 16). "The medieval Arabic term for kidney bean [i.e., *P. vulgaris*] is *lubiya*. It is *lubbu* in Akkadian and LU.ÚB in Sumerian. ... In Sanskrit, however, it is *simbi* ...."

Physalis lanceifolia
Sources:
Chopra et al. 1956, 191. Sanskrit: *rajaputrika*.
Torkelson 1999, 1808. Sanskrit: *rajaputrika*.
Chopra et al. 1956, 192. Sanskrit: *lakshmipriya*.

Physalis peruviana
Sources:
Chopra et al. 1956, 191. Sanskrit: *rajaputrika*
Torkelson 1999, 1808. Sanskrit: *rajaputrika*.

Plumeria rubra (syn. acuminata, a variety of *P. rubra*)
Sources:
Pullaiah 2002, 2, 419. Sanskrit: *ksirachampaka*
Parotta 2001, 95. Sanskrit: *devaganagalu, kshira,* and four other names

Portulaca oleracea
Sources:
Chopra et al. 1956, 202. Sanskrit: *lonika*
Chopra et al. 1958, 521–3. Sanskrit: *mansala*
Pullaiah 2002, II, 426. Sanskrit: *ghotika, lonika*
Torkelson 1999, 1818. Sanskrit: *lonika*
Balfour 1871–1873, IV, 660. Sanskrit: *lonika*, or *loonia*
Parotta 2001, 598. Sanskrit: *brhalloni, ghotika, loni, lonika, lunia*

Psidium guajava
Sources:
Watt 1892, VI, Part I, 351–3. Sanskrit: *amrud*. Arabic, and Persian, both closely related
Chopra et al. 1956, 205–6. Sanskrit: *mansala*
Int. Lib. Assoc. 1996, 571. Sanskrit: *mansala*
Nadkarni 1914, 320. Sanskrit: *péràlà*. Hin.: *amrút*
Chopra et al. 1958, 683. Sanskrit: *amruta-phalam*.
Pullaiah 2002, II, 433. Sanskrit: *perukah, mansala*.
Aiyer 1956, 36. Mentioned in the Charaka Samhita, no later than the fourth century C.E.

Salvia coccinea
Source:
Watson 1868, 489, 201. Sanskrit: *rosea*

Sapindus saponaria
Sources:
Nadkarni 1914, 350. *Sapinda* (sic) *trifoliatus* (syn. *emarginatus*). Sanskrit: *phenila*
Int. Lib. Assoc. 1996, 572. *Sapindus trifoliatus* var. *emarginatus* (syn. *Sapindus emarginatus*). Sanskrit: *arishta*; *S. mukorosi*. Sanskrit: *urista*. (Species mentioned are probably syn. with *S. saponaria*.)

Spondias purpurea
Source:
Aiyer 1956, 19. (syn.?) *Spondias mangifera*, the Indian hog-plum; Sanskrit: *amrataka*

Tagetes erecta
Sources:
Pullaiah 2002, II, 492. Sanskrit: *sandu, sthulapushpa, ganduga*.
Torkelson 1999, 1853. Sanskrit: *zanduga*
Chopra et al. 1956, 239. Sanskrit: *zanduga*

Int. Lib. Assoc. 1996, 574. Sanskrit: *sthulapushpa*
Parotta 2001, 156. Sanskrit: *jhandu, zandu*

Tagetes patula
Source:
Pullaiah 2002, II, 493. Sanskrit: *taugla*

Zea mays
Sources:
Balfour 1871–73, V. s.v. *Zea mays*. Sanskrit: *yavanala*
While Monier Williams' standard Sanskrit dictionary lacks a word for maize, Watt (1888–1893, VI, Pt IV, 327) reported that in his day a certain (unspecified) publication by Williams "furnishes three [Sanskrit] words" that denote maize: *sasyam, stamba-kari, sasyavisesha*.
Chopra et al. 1956, 260. Sanskrit: *yavanala*
Torkelson 1999, 1874. Sanskrit: *yavanala*

Sanskrit Names of Plants of American Origin, in Alphabetical Order

adityabhakta	*Helianthus annuus*
ajaka	*Ocimum sanctum*
ajàlikalika	*Mimosa pudica*
alpamarisha	*Amaranthus spinosus*
amrud	*Psidium guajava*
amruta-phalam	*Psidium guajava*
anamnasam	*Anacardium occidentale*
andapi	*Arachis hypogaea*
anjalikarika	*Mimosa pudica*
aranyathulasi	*Ocimum americanum*
arishta (?)	*Sapindus saponaria*
arjaka	*Ocimum americanum*
arjakah	*Ocimum americanum*
arkakantha	*Helianthus annuus*
atmagupta	*Mucuna pruriens*
bahu-bumi	*Mirabilis jalapa*
bahunetraphalam	*Anacardium occidentale*
barbari	*Ocimum americanum, O. basilicum*
beejara sula	*Anacardium occidentale*
bhutagni (?)	*Ocimum sanctum*
bijara sala	*Anacardium occidentale*
brahmadandi	*Argemone mexicana*
brahmairandeh	*Carica papaya*

brahmi	Bixa orellana
bramh	Argemone mexicana
bramhie	Argemone mexicana
brhalloni	Portulaca oleracea
buchanaka	Arachis hypogaea
chaulai	Amaranthus spinosus
cheerapotha	Physalis spp.
dadhiphala	Cucurbita maxima
darukandah	Manihot esculenta
devaganagalu	Plumeria rubra
devakuli	Canna edulis
dhattura	Datura metel, & D. stramonium
dhatura	Datura metel, & D. stramonium
divaakaraha	Helianthus annuus
durdhura	Datura spp.
dusthara	Datura spp.
eranda karkati	Carica papaya
gandagatra	Annona squamosa
gandhgataram	Annona squamosa
ganduga	Tagetes erecta
ghotika	Portulaca oleracea
gunda-gatra	Annona squamosa
haridra	Curcuma longa
inamaskari	Mimosa pudica
jalakarika	Mimosa pudica
jarayupriya	Erigeron canadensis
jhandu	Tagetes erecta
kajutaka	Anacardium occidentale
kakatundi	Asclepias curassavica
kala kantala cantala	Agave americana, A. angustifolia, & A.
kalpakandah	Manihot esculenta
kanaka	Datura stramonium
kantala cantala	Agave americana, A. angustifolia, & A.
kanthari	Opuntia dillenii
kapikachchha	Mucuna pruriens
karrapendalamu	Manihot esculenta
kaseruka	Cyperus vegetus
kataib	Amaranthus spinosus
katuvira	Capsicum annuum
katuvirah	Capsicum annuum
kauparni	Argemone mexicana

khadiraka	*Mimosa pudica*
krishnabeejam	*Annona reticulata*
krishnabija	*Annona squamosa*, & *Pharbitis hederacea*
krishnakeli	*Mirabilis jalapa*
krsnakeli	*Mirabilis jalapa*
kshetravastuk	*Chenopodium ambrosioides*
kshira	*Plumeria rubra*
ksirachampaka	*Plumeria rubra*
kunayanah	*Cinchona officinalis*
kurkareú	*Cucurbita pepo*
kurkaru	*Cucurbita pepo*
kushmanda	*Cucurbita pepo*
kutashalmali	*Ceiba pentandra* (syn. *Bombax malabaricum*)
kuvai	*Maranta arundinacea*
lajja	*Mimosa pudica*
lajjalu	*Mimosa pudica*
lakshmipriya	*Physalis lanceifolia*
loni	*Portulaca oleracea*
lonika	*Portulaca oleracea*, & *Ageratum philoxeroides*
lunia	*Portulaca oleracea*
luvunee	*Annona reticulata*
madakara	*Datura stramonium*
maghani	*Gossypium barbadense*
makshikavisha	*Erigeron canadensis*
mandapi	*Arachis hypogaea*
mansala	*Portulaca oleracea*. & *Psidium guajava*
marichi-phalam	*Capsicum annuum*, & *C. frutescens*
marich-phalam	*Capsicum annuum*
matsyahi	*Ageratum philoxeroides*
mocha	*Ceiba pentandra* (syn. *Bombax malabaricum*)
mrdukunjika	*Physalis* spp.
munjariki	*Ocimum basilicum*
nagaramustakah	*Cyperus esculentus*
namaskari	*Mimosa pudica*
nisha	*Curcuma longa*
pérala	*Psidium guajava*
perukah	*Psidium guajava*
phenila	*Sapindus saponaria*
pindalah	*Ipomoea batatas*
pitakusmandah	*Cucurbita maxima*
punyalatha	*Cucurbita maxima*
puryam	*Gossypium barbadense*
rajagiri	*Amaranthus caudatus*

rajagirita	*Amaranthus caudatus*
rajani	*Curcuma longa*
rajaputrika	*Physalis lanceifolia*, & *P. peruviana*
rakta maricha	*Capsicum annuum*
raktaluh	*Ipomoea batatas*
raktamachi	*Ipomoea batatas*
raktavardhak	*Lycopersicon esculentum*
rakthapad	*Mimosa pudica*
Rama sita	*Annona reticulata*
ramatulasi	*Ocimum sanctum*
ramphal	*Annona reticulata*
ramphala	*Annona reticulata*, & *Lycopersicon esculentum*
rosea	*Salvia coccinea*
samanga	*Mimosa pudica*
samipatra	*Mimosa pudica*
sandhya-raga	*Mirabilis jalapa*
sandu	*Tagetes erecta*
sankhálu	*Pachyrhizus erosus*
sarvajaya	*Canna edulis*
sasyam	*Zea mays*
sasyavisesha	*Zea mays*
satyanasi	*Argemone mexicana*
senmatla	*Datura metel*
shak-stmeshdha	*Lycopersicon esculentum*
shalmali	*Ceiba pentandra* (syn. *Bombax malabaricum*)
shimbi	*Canavalia ensiformis*
shivapriya	*Datura stramonium*
shoephahara	*Anacardium occidentale*
shubhâ	*Annona squamosa*
silarumba	*Canna edulis*
simbi	*Phaseolus vulgaris*
sinduri	*Bixa orellana*
sinkona	*Cinchona officinalis*
srigála kantá	*Argemone mexicana*
srigala-kangtaka	*Argemone mexicana*
stamba-kari	*Zea mays*
sthulapushpa	*Tagetes erecta*
suda	*Annona squamosa*
sugandhavastuk	*Chenopodium ambrosioides*
sundia-ragum	*Mirabilis jalapa*
surasa	*Ocimum sanctum*
suria mukhi	*Helianthus annuus*
suriya-mukhi	*Helianthus annuus*

suryamukhi	*Helianthus annuus*
suuryakaanti	*Helianthus annuus*
suuryakamalaha	*Helianthus annuus*
sveta salmali	*Ceiba pentandra* (syn. *Bombax malabaricum*)
swarnakshiri	*Argemone mexicana*
tamakhu	*Nicotiana tabacum*
tamakkhu	*Nicotiana tabacum*
támrakúta	*Nicotiana tabacum*
tandula	*Amaranthus spinosus*
tanduliya	*Amaranthus spinosus*
tanduluya	*Amaranthus spinosus*
taugla	*Tagetes patula*
tavakshiri	*Maranta arundinacea*
tiktalabu	*Lagenaria siceraria*
trisandhi	*Mirabilis jalapa*
tugaksiri	*Maranta arundinacea*
tulasi	*Ocimum sanctum*
unmatta	*Datura stramonium*
upakunjika	*Physalis* spp.
urista (?)	*Sapindus saponaria*
valli (?)	*Ipomoea batatas*
vanabarbarika	*Ocimum americanum*
vanari	*Mucuna pruriens*
vastuk	*Chenopodium ambrosioides*
vidara	*Opuntia dillenii*
visamustih	*Ageratum conyzoides*
visvasraka	*Opuntia dillenii*
vriddhtulasi	*Ocimum sanctum*
vrinda	*Ocimum sanctum*
yavanala	*Zea mays*
zandu	*Tagetes erecta*
zanduga	*Tagetes erecta*

Evidence type: Representation in Indian Sacred Art

Anacardium occidentale
Source:
Gupta. 1996, 17

Ananas comosus
Source:
Gupta. 1996, 18

Annona squamosa
Sources:
Pokharia and Saraswat 1999, 97. Gupta. 1996, 19

Capsicum annuum
Source:
Gupta., 1996. 49–50

Capsicum frutescens
Source:
Gupta. 1996, 50

Couroupita guianensis
Source:
Gupta. 1996, 58

Helianthus annuus
Sources:
Johannessen and Wang 1998, 14–6. Gupta. 1996, 86

Monstera deliciosa
Source:
Gupta. 1996, 108–9

Ocimum sanctum
Source:
Gupta. 1996, 131

Zea mays
Source:
Johannessen and Wang 1998, 10-12

Evidence type: Archaeology

Amaranthus caudatus
Source:
Saraswat, Sharma, and Saini 1994, 282, 284, 331.

Annona sp.
Source:

Glover 1977

Annona squamosa
Sources:
Glover 1977, 43
Pokharia and Saraswat 1999, 101ff.

Arachis hypogaea
Sources:
Pokharia and Saraswat 1999, 101.
Glover 1977 (Timor)

Argemone mexicana
Source:
Saraswat, et al. 1981, 284.

Datura spp.
Source:
Pokharia and Saraswat, 1999, 90.

Erythroxylon novagranatense
Source:
Balabanova et al. 1992, 358

Macroptilium lathyroides
Source:
Pokharia and Saraswat 1999, 99

Mollugo verticillata
Source:
Chapman et al. 1974, 411–12

Ocimum spp.
Sources:
Saraswat, Sharma, and Saini 1981, 316
Pokharia and Saraswat 1999, 99

Phaseolus vulgaris
Source:
Pokharia and Saraswat 1999, 99.

Evidence type: Mention in Ancient Indian Documents

Annona reticulata
Source:
Bhishagratna 1907, 62. Sixth century B.C.E.

Argemone mexicana
Sources:
Saraswat, Sharma, and Saini (1994, 262, 333, 334) report mention of this plant in the medical treatise *Bhava Prakasha* in the *Sushruta Samhita* (first/second century C.E.).

Capsicum annuum
Source:
Gupta. 1996, 49. Mentioned in *Siva* and *Vamana Puranas* dated ca. sixth/eighth century C.E.

Ceiba pentandra
Source:
Tagare 1982, 408; 1983, 179. There are references to the silk cotton tree in the *Kurma Purana* of the fifth century and the *Brahmanda Purana* of the 10th century C.E.

Cucurbita maxima
Source:
Levey 1966, 315, in a medical handbook.

Cucurbita pepo
Sources:
Aiyer 1956, 57. Pumpkin is mentioned in the *Atharvaveda*, dating before 800 B.C.E. Also mentioned in the Buddhistic *Jatakas*.
Levey 1966, 315. In a medical text by Al-Kindi, ninth century C.E.

Datura stramonium
Source:
Chopra et al. 1958, 134-35. Known to ancient Hindu physicians; smoking seeds was a treatment for asthma and was known during the Vedic period. The drug is frequently mentioned in the literature in its use for suicidal and homicidal purposes.

Helianthus annuus
Source:
Aiyer 1956, 67. The sunflower, *H. annuus*, is mentioned in the Hindu *Charaka Sahmita* dated no later than the fourth century C.E.

Maranta arundinacea
Source:
Aiyer 1956, 44. Mentioned in the Tamil source *Malaipadukadam*, as well as in the *Mathuraikanji* (also Tamil), long preceding Portuguese arrival.

Mucuna pruriens
Source:
2002, II, 369–70. Described in texts in the tradition of Ayurvedic medicine.

Nicotiana tabacum
Source:
Ashraf 1985, 91–101

Ocimum sanctum
Source:
Gupta. 1996, 131

Phaseolus vulgaris
Sources:
Kramisch 1928, 50
Levey 1973, 55.

Psidium guajava
Sources:
Aiyer 1956, 36. Mentioned in the *Charaka Samhita*.
Sharma and Dash 1983, 518.

Spondias purpurea
Source:
Aiyer 1956, 19. *Spondias mangifera* (syn.? purpurea) is the Indian hog-plum; mentioned in the *Birhat Samhita* and *Mahabharatha*, previous to 400 C.E.

ILLUSTRATIONS

Figure 1
This wall sculpture from the Hoysala Dynasty Halebid temple at Somnathpur, Karnataka Pradesh, India, dates between the eleventh and thirteenth centuries. Among the numerous representations of maize ears, the shape of the ear, kernels offset in relation to those in adjacent rows, the presence of part of the husk, and other features ensure that no object other than an ear of maize could be represented. The *mudra* (sacred gesture) made by the figure's hand underlines the sacred significance of the context and thus of maize. (Photograph by C. Johannessen.)

Figure 2
A curl of maize silk is shown atop an unhusked ear of maize in a medieval sculpture from India. (Photograph by C. Johannessen.)

Figure 3
Artistic canons for showing maize changed over the centuries. This example is from the eighth century, in Udaipur Museum, Karnataka. Later images show buxom females holding maize ears (see Fig. 1); earlier art frequently shows an ear of corn held by a male. Here the stubby pyramidal ear resembles maize grown at high altitudes in Peru and Central America. (Photograph after Bussagli and Sivaramamurti 1971, 192, used by permission.)

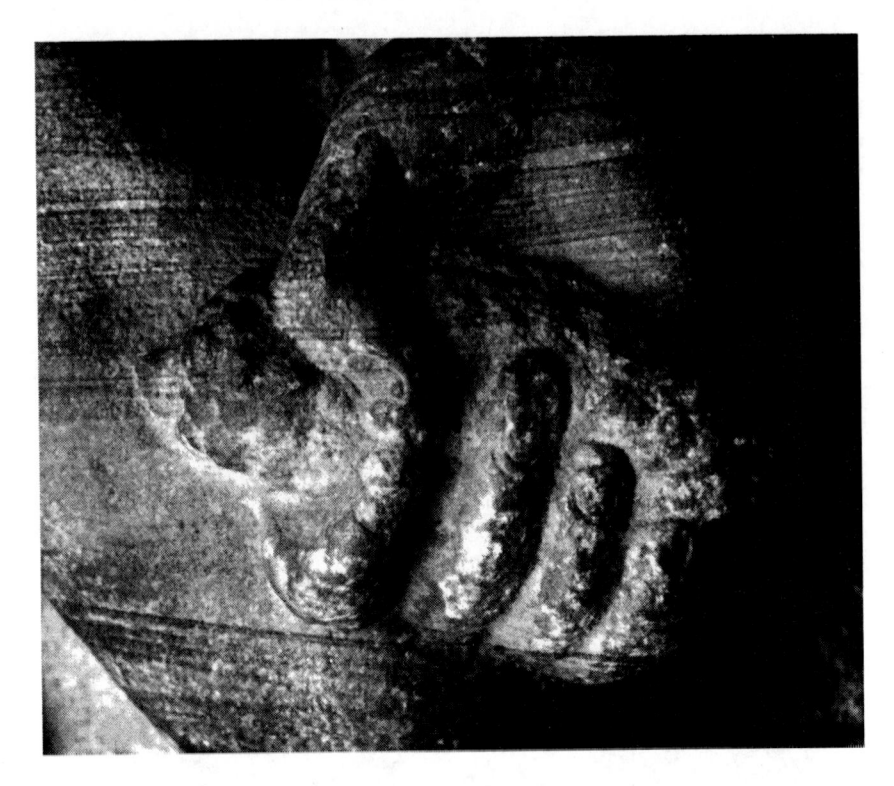

Figure 4
This earliest (Fifth Century C.E.) representation of maize so far known from India is held horizontally in the hand of the god Vishnu at Cave Temple III, Badami, India.
(Photograph by C. Johannessen.)

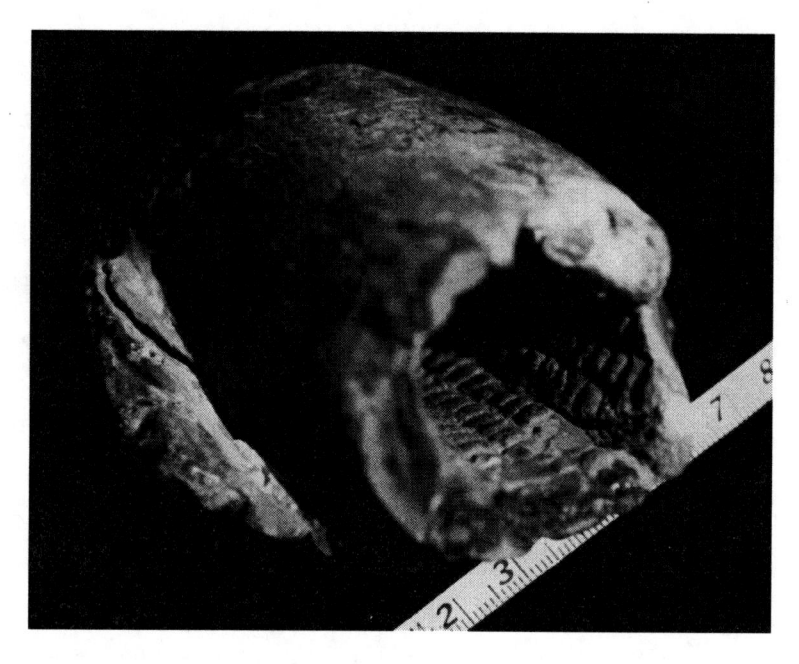

Figure 5
A pottery effigy of a bird, which is barely visible in this photograph, was formed of clay shaped around a maize cob; when the clay was fired, the cob was consumed, leaving on the interior of the clay object impressions where the maize kernels had been. The object was from a Han Dynasty tomb (no later than 200 A.D.) near Xinxiang, Henan, China, and is now in the Xinxiang Archaeological Museum. (Photograph by Cart L. Johannessen.)

John L. Sorenosn and Carl L. Johannessen

Figure 6
This bas-relief from a temple at Parambanan, Java, is over 1,000 years old. The row of plants shows leaves, tassels, and ears characteristic only of maize.
(Photograph by Evelyn McConnaughey, used by permission.)

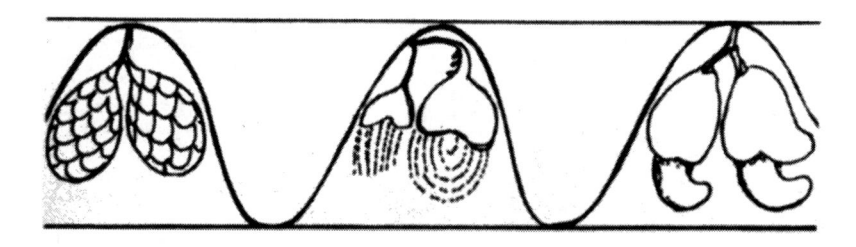

World Trade and Biologocal Exchanges Before 1492

Figure 7
Cashew nuts are represented on the balustrade of the Bharhut Stupa in Madhya Pradesh, India, dating to the second century B.C. Only this sketch now exists picturing this section of the ruin.
(Photo of the sketch courtesy of the American Institute for Indian Studies, copyright holder.)

Figure 8
Ananas comosus, the pineapple, is depicted at a cave temple at Udaiguri, India, dated ca. the fifth century AD. (Discussed in Gupta. 1996, 18. Photo courtesy of the American Institute of Indian Studies, copyright holder.)

Figure 9
Fruits of *Annona squamosa* were carved on the balustrade at Bharhut Stupa, Madhya Pradesh. Cunningham (1879) first identified these fruits which are from an American tree, but nobody then pursued the implication.
(Photo of the sketch courtesy of the American Institute for Indian Studies, copyright holder.)

Figure 10
An annona fruit is held in the hand of a goddess at the Durga Complex temple, Aihole, India. The date is medieval. (Photo by Carl L. Johannessen.)

Figure 11
A very explicit rendering of chile pepper plants is found on a wall at the temple at Parambanan, Java, adjacent to the bas-relief of maize plants shown in Figure 6. The structure is at least 1,000 years old. Representations of chile peppers have also been found in India (see Gupta. 1996, 50). (Photo by Evelyn McConnaughey, used with permission.)

Figure 12
This teapot in the shape of a green moschata squash is in Zhejiang Provincial Museum, Hangzhou, Zhejiang, China, and is assigned to the Song Dynasty (960-1279 A.D.) (Photograph by Carl L. Johannessen.)

World Trade and Biologocal Exchanges Before 1492

Figure 13
A sculpture of Nandi, the mythological bull associated with Shiva, bears this modeled sunflower between its ear and horn. Sunflowers at several positions on bull figures at Shiva temples mark sight lines from the lingam in the central sanctuary of the temple to the sun rising on the horizon on key days in the calendar. Here at a temple at Halebid, Karnataka, India, a live sunflower is juxtaposed with the sculpted stone. (Photograph by Carl L. Johannessen.)

Figure 14
At Pattadakal temple, Karnataka, a carving on a pillar shows a large sunflower seed-head. From its edge a perched parrot is eating seeds. No other plant bears a seed-head of this size nor has a stalk this strong. (Photograph by Carl L. Johannessen.)

Figure 15
Large dissected leaves of *Monstera deliciosa* appear on sculptures at Hindu and Jain temples in Gujarat and Rajasthan, India. This statue of Vishnu, from Jodhpur, is framed by the plant's foliage. The small personage on Vishnu's right holds a fruit of *M. deliciosa* on a plate. (Photo courtesy of the American Institute for Indian Studies, copyright holder.)

Figure 16
Pottery effigy of a chicken, Chimú culture (13th-14th centuries), National Museum, Lima, Peru. (Photograph by Carl L. Johannessen.)

BIBLIOGRAPHY

Ackerknecht, Erwin H. History and Geography of the Most Important Diseases. New York: Hafner, 1965.

Adelsteinson, S., and B. Blumenberg. "Possible Norse origin for two northeastern USA cat populations," Zeitschrift für Tierzüchtung and Züchtugsbiologie 100 (1983): 161–74.

Adauto de Araújo, J. G. Contribuição ao estudo de helmintos encontrados em material arqueológico de Brasil. Rio de Janeiro, 1980.

Aguilar, Manuel. "Ethnomedicine in Mesoamerica," Arqueología mexicana 10:59 (2003): 80–81.

Ainsworth, Geoffrey C. "Fungus infections (Mycoses)," The Cambridge World History of Human Disease. Ed. Kenneth F. Kiple. Cambridge: Cambridge University Press, 1993. 730–36.

Aiyer, A. K. Yegna Narayan. The Antiquity of Some Field and Forest Flora of India. Bangalore, India: Bangalore Press, 1956.

Ajello, Libero. "Geographic distribution and prevalence of the dermatophytes," Annals, New York Academy of Science.89. (1960) 30–38.

Alchon, Suzanne Austin. Native Society and Disease in Colonial Ecuador. Cambridge: Cambridge University Press, 1991.

Alexander, John. "The domestication of yams: a multi-disciplinary approach," Science in Archaeology: A Survey of Progress and Research, revised and enlarged edition. Ed. Don Brothwell and Eric Higgs. New York: Praeger, 1970. 229–34.

Alfieri, Anastase. "Les insectes de la tombe de Tutankhamon," Bulletin de la Société entomologique d'Egypte. 24 (1931): 188–89.

Alfieri, Anastase. The Coleoptera of Egypt. (Mémoires de la Societe Entomologique d"Egypte). Cairo: Atlas Press, 1976.

Alland, Alexander, Jr. Adaptation in Cultural Evolution: An Approach to Medical Anthropology. New York: Columbia University Press, 1970.

Allison, Marvin J., Daniel Mendoza, and A. Pezzia. "Documentation of a case of tuberculosis in pre-Columbian America," American Review of Respiratory Disease.107 (1973): 985–91.

Allison, Marvin J. "Paleopathology in Peru," Natural History 88:2 (1979): 74–82

Allison, M.J., Pezzia, A., Hasegawa, L., and Gerszten, E. "A Case of Hookworm Infestation in a Precolumbian American." American Journal of Physical Anthropology. 41 (1974):103-105.

Allison, Marvin J., E. Gerszten, J. Munizaga, C. Santoroto, and D. Mendoza. "Tuberculosis in Pre-Columbian Andean populations," Prehistoric Tuberculosis in the Americas. Ed. J. E. Buikstra. Northwestern University Archaeological Program, Scientific Papers No. 5, 1981. 49–61.

Alsar, Vital. La Balsa; the Longest Raft Voyage in History. New York: Reader's Digest Press/E. P. Dutton, 1973.

Alsar, Vital. Pacific Challenge. An 84-minute video, released by Concord Films (dba ALTI Publishers), La Jolla, California, 1974.

Álvarez, Ticul. "Restos óseos de las excavaciones de Tlatilco, Estado de México," Apuntes para la arqueología. 15 México: Instituto Nacional de Antropología e Historia, Departamento de Prehistoria, 1976. 3–18.

Álvarez, Ticul, and Aurelio Ocaña. Sinopsis de Restos Arqueozoológicos de Vertebrados Terrestres. Basada en Informes del Laboratorio de Paleozoología del INAH. (Colección Científica). México: Instituto Nacional de Antropología e Historia, 1999.

Álvarez Asomoza, Carlos. "Sacred mushrooms in Teotenango, State of Mexico," Arqueología mexicana 10:59 (2003). 83–84.

Anderson, Edgar. Plants, Man and Life, 2nd edition. Boston: Little, Brown, 1952.

Anderson, Edgar. "What is *Zea mays*? A report of progress," Chronica Botanica 9 (1945a): 88–92.

Anderson, Edgar. "A variety of maize from the Río Loa," Annals of the Missouri Botanical Garden 30 (1945b): 469–76.

Anderson, Edgar. "The evolution of domestication," Evolution after Darwin, Vol. 2: The Evolution of Man, Sol Tax, edition, Chicago: University of Chicago Press, 1960. 76–84.

Anderson, Edgar and Willaim Brown. "Origin of Corn Belt maize and its genetic significance." Heterosis. Ed. J. W. Gowen. Ames: Iowa State College Press. 1952: 124-48.

Anderson, T. "Suspected endemic syphilis (Treponarid) in sixteenth-century Norway," Medical History 30 (1986): 341–50.

Anthony, Irvin. Voyagers Unafraid. Philadelphia: Macrae Smith, 1930

Araújo, Adauto. "Paleoepidemiologia da Ancilostomose," Paleoparasitologia no Brasil, Eds. L. Fernando Ferreira, A. Araújo, and U. Confalonieri. Rio de Janeiro: Programa de Educação Pública, Escola Nacional de Saúde Pública, 1988. 144–51.

Araujo, A, Reinhard, KJ, Ferreira, LF, and Gardner, SL. "Parasites as probes for prehistoric human migrations?" in Trends in Parasitology 2008 Mar; 24(3):112-5

Arias, D. M., and L. H. Rieseberg. "Genetic relationship among domesticated and wild sunflowers (*Helianthus annuus, Asteraceae*)," Economic Botany 49:3 (1995): 239–48.

Arnold, Dean. "The evidence for pre-Columbian indigo in the New World," Antropología y Técnica 2 (1987): 53–84.

Ashraf, Jaweed. "The antiquity of tobacco (*Nicotiana tabacum*) in India," Indica 22: 2 Sept. (1985). 91–101.

Bailey, Liberty Hyde. The Standard Cyclopedia of Horticulture. 3 vols. New York: MacMillan, 1935.

Baker, Herbert G. Plants and Civilization. 2nd edition. Belmont, CA: Wadsworth Publishing, 1970.

Bakhuizen van den Brink, H. C. "De Indische flora en haar eerste Amerikaanse Indringster," Natuurk. Tijdschrifft Nederlanderische-Indië 93 (1933): 20–55.

Balabanova, Svetla. "Tabak in Europa vor Kolumbus," Antike Welt 3 (1994): 282–85.

Balabanova, Svetla, Boyuan Wei, and M. Krämer. "First detection of nicotine in ancient population of southern China," Homo 46 (1995): 68–75.

Balabanova, Svetla, F. Parsche, and W. Pirsig. "First report of drugs in Egyptian mummies," Naturwissenschaften 79 (1992a): 358.

Balabanova, Svetla, F. Parsche, and W. Pirsig. "Drugs in cranial hair of pre-Columbian Peruvian mummies," Baessler Archiv (NF) (1992b): 40.

Balabanova, Svetla, F. W. Rösing, G. Bühler, W. Schoetz, G. Scherer, and J. Rosenthal. "Nicotine and cotinine in prehistoric and recent bones from Africa and Europe and the origin of these alkaloids," Homo 48 (1997): 72–7.

Balfour, Edward G. Cyclopedia of India, 2nd edition. 5 vols. Calcutta, 1871–1873.

Balser, Carlos. "Jade de América Central con una possible influencia China," China Libre Magazine 6:6, Julio-Agosto (1988): 14–21.

Banerji, Sures Chandra. Flora and Fauna in Sanskrit Literature. Calcutta: Naya Prokash, 1980.

Barthel, Thomas S. "Pre-contact writing in Oceania," Current Trends in Linguistics 8. Linguistics in Oceania, Ed. T. A. Sebeok The Hague: Mouton, 1971. 1165–86.

Barthel, Thomas S. "Weiteres zu den hinduistischen Âquivalenzen im Codex Laud," Tribus 24 (1975a): 113–36.

Barthel, Thomas S. "Weiteres zur Frage der altmexikanischen Nactherren," Indiana 3 (1975b): 41–66.

Barthel, Thomas S. "Planetary series in ancient India and prehispanic Mexico: An analysis of their relations with each other," Tribus 30 (1981): 203–30.

Barthel, Thomas S. "Hindu-Maya syncretism: The Palenque focus," Ibero-Amerikanisches Archiv 11. Manchester: School of Geography, 1985. 51–63.

Barthel, Thomas S. "Hindu-Maya syncretism: The Palenque focus, (abstract only)" Abstracts of Papers, 44th International Congress of Americanists. Manchester: School of Geography, Manchester University, UK (1982).

Barthel, Thomas S. "Von Mexiko zum Indus," Tribus 33 (Festschrift für Bodo Spranz.) Stuttgart, (1984): 75–79.

Barton, Humphrey. Atlantic Adventures: Voyages in Small Craft. New York: Van Nostrand; and Southampton, England: Adlard Coles, 1962.

Bayard, D. T. "On Chang's interpretation of Chinese radiocarbon dates," Current Anthropology 16 (1975): 167–70.

British Broadcasting Corporation. "The lost pyramids of Caral." BBC2: 31 January 2002 text available on http://www.bbc.co.uk/science/horizon/2001/caraltrans.shtml.. 2003

British Broadcasting Corporation Channel 4. The Mystery of the Cocaine Mummies." http://www.druglibrary.org/schaffer/misc/mummies.html. Transcript of an interview with Dr. Balabanova, David Rosalie and others discussing Dr. Balabanova's discoveries. Video available at http://www.youtube.com/watch?v=izsym4bxeGA. Originally aired on BBC Channel 4. The video is only available through this site in the UK. http://www.channel4.com/programmes/the-mystery-of-the-cocaine-mummies/4od#2919495

Beaudry-Corbett, M. and S. McCafferty."'Spindle Whorls: Household Specialization at Ceren", Ancient Maya Women. Ed. T. Ardren. Walnut Creek, CA: AltaMira Press. 2002. 52-67.

Bednarik, Robert J. "The initial peopling of Wallacea and Sahul," Anthropos 92 (1997): 355–67.

Bednarik, Robert J. "Replicating the first known sea travel by humans: the Lower Pleistocene crossing of Lombok Strait," Human Evolution 16:3 - 4 (2001): 229–42.

Bellwood, Peter. Man's Conquest of the Pacific: The Prehistory of Southeast Asia and Oceania. Oxford University Press. New York. 1979.

Ben Shemesh, A., ed. and transl. Taxation in Islam, Vol. 1. Yahya Ben Adam's Kitab al Kharaj. Leiden: E. J. Brill, 1958.

Benz, Bruce F., and John E. Staller. 2006 The Antiquity, Biogeography, and Culture History of Maize in the Americas. In Histories of Maize, edited by J. E. Staller, R. H. Tykot, and B. F. Benz, pp. 665-673. Elsevier/Academic Press, Amsterdam.

Berry, Edward W. "A banana in the Tertiary of Colombia," American Journal of Science (5th ser.) 10 (1925): 530–37.

Bertoni, M. S. "Essai d'une monographie du genre ananas," Anales científicos paraguayos Asunción, 11 (1919): 280ff..

Bhishagratna, K. K., trans. The Sushruta Samhita, Vol. 3. Chowkhamba Sanskrit Series XXX. Varanasi, India, 1907.

Bird, Junius B. "America's oldest farmers," Natural History 57 (1948): 296–303, 334–35.

Black, Michael. "Diffusion of *Arachis hypogaea*." Unpublished seminar paper submitted to Prof. Carl Johannessen, University of Oregon; copy in Johannessen's possession, 1988.

Blanchard, Raphael A. E. Traité de zoologie médicale, Vol. 2. Paris: Livres J.-B. Baillière et Fils, 484–93, 1890.

Blumler, Mark A. "Independent inventionism and recent genetic evidence on plant domestication," Economic Botany 46:1 (1992): 98–111.

Blumler, Mark A. "Ecology, evolutionary theory and agricultural origins," The Origins and Spread of Agriculture and Pastoralism in Eurasia. Ed. David R. Harris. Washington: Smithsonian Institution Press, 1996. 25–50.

Bogdan, Georgie Ann, and David S. Weaver. "Pre-Columbian treponematosis in coastal North Carolina," Disease and Demography in the Americas, Eds. John W. Verano and Douglas H. Ubelaker. Washington: Smithsonian Institution Press, 1992. 155–63.

Bökönyi, Sándor, and Dénes Jánossy. "Adatok a pulyka kolumbusz ellötti Európai elöfordulás ához," Aquila: a Magyar Ornithologiai Központ Folyóirata Budapest. 65 (1959): 265–9.

Borah, Woodrow W. Silk Raising in Colonial Mexico. (Ibero-Americana 20.) Berkeley: University of California Press, 1943.

Borden, Charles A. Sea Quest: Global Blue-Water Adventuring in Small Craft. Philadelphia: Macrae Smith, 1967.

Borg, Jim. "The history within," Hawaii Magazine 14:1 February 1997: 326–41.

Bradburn, Anne S. "Botanical Index," A Dictionary of the Maya Language as Spoken in Hocabá, Yucatán, Eds. Victoria Bricker, Elentorio Po'ot Yah, and Ofelia Dzul de Po'ot. Salt Lake City: University of Utah Press, 1998. 320–28.

Brand, Donald D. "The sweet potato: an exercise in methodology," Man across the Sea: Problems of Pre-Columbian Contacts.Eds. Carroll L. Riley et al. Austin: University of Texas Press, 1971. 343–65.

Bretschneider, Emil. Botanicon Sinicum. Notes on Chinese Botany from Native and Western Sources. London: Trübner. 1882. (Simultaneously as Journal of the North-China Branch of the Royal Asiatic Society 16 (1881), Article III.)

Bretschneider, E. Botanicon Sinicum. Notes on Chinese Botany from Native and Western Sources, Part II. The Botany of the Chinese Classics, with Annotations, Appendix, and Index by Rev. Ernst Faber. Shanghai: Kelly & Walsh, Ltd, 1892.

Bretschneider, E. "Botanicon Sinicum, Part III. Botanical Investigations into the Materia Medica of the Ancient Chinese," Journal of the Royal Asiatic Society, Chinese Branch (n.s.) 29 (1896):1–623.

Breuer, Hans. Columbus Was Chinese: Discoveries and Inventions of the Far East. (trans. Salvator Attanasio). McGraw-Hill Book Company. New York. 1970, 1972.

Brockington, J. L. "Sanskrit," The Encyclopedia of Language and Linguistics, Vol. 7, Ed. R. E. Asher. Oxford: Pergamon, 1994. 3649–51.

Bronson, Bennet. "Roots and the subsistence of the ancient Maya," Southwestern Journal of Anthropology 22:3 (1966): 251–79.

Brown, Cecil H. 2006 Glottochronology and the Chronology of Maize in the Americas. In Histories of Maize, edited by J. E. Staller, R. H. Tykot, and B. F. Benz, pp. 647-663. Elsevier/Academic Press, Amsterdam.

Brown, Forest B. H. "Flora of Southeastern Polynesia, I. Monocotyledons". Bishop Museum Bulletin 84. Honolulu: B. P. Bishop Museum, 1931.

Brown, Forest B. H. "Flora of Southeastern Polynesia, III. Dicotyledons". Bishop Museum Bulletin 130. Honolulu: B. P. Bishop Museum, 1935.

Brubaker, C. L., and Jonathan F. Wendel. "Reevaluating the origin of domesticated cotton (*Gossypium hirsutum*: Malvaceae) using nuclear restriction fragment length polymorphisms (RFLPs)," American Journal of Botany 81 (1994): 1309–26.

Bruce-Chwatt, L. J. "Paleo-epidemiology of primate malaria," Bulletin, World Health Organization 32 (1965): 363–87.

Brücher, Heinz. Useful Plants of Neotropical Origin and Their Wild Relatives. Berlin: Springer-Verlag, 1989.

Bruman, Henry J. "Some observations on the early history of the coconut in the New World," Acta Americana 2 (1944): 220–43.

Bryan, E. H. Samoan and scientific names of plants found in Samoa: Compiled April 1935. Honolulu: The author, 1935.

Bucaille, Maurice. Mummies of the Pharaohs: Modern Medical Investigations. New York: St. Martins, 1990.

Buckland, P. C., and E. Panagiotakopulu. "Rameses II and the tobacco beetle," Antiquity 75 (2001): 549–56.

Buikstra, Jane E. "Introduction," Prehistoric Tuberculosis in the Americas. Ed. Jane E. Buikstra. Northwestern University Archaeological Program, Scientific Papers No. 5, 1981. 1–23.

Bullen, Adelaide K. "Paleoepidemiology and distribution of prehistoric treponemiasis (syphilis) in Florida," Florida Anthropologist 25:4 (1972): 133–74.

Burkill, Isaac H. A Dictionary of the Economic Products of the Malay Peninsula. Kuala Lumpur, Malaysia: Ministry of Agriculture and Cooperatives, 1966.

Burrows, Thomas. The Sanskrit Language. London: Faber and Faber, 1955.

Bushnell, Geoffrey H. S. "An Old World view of New World prehistory," American Antiquity 27 (1961): 63–70.

Bussagli, Mario, and Calembus Sivartamamurti. 5000 Years of the Art of India. New York: Harry N. Abrams, 1978.

Bustamente, Miguel E. La fiebre amarilla en México y su origen en América. Mexico: Instituto de Salubridad y Enfermedades Tropicales, 1958.

Byrne, R., and J. H. McAndrews. "Pre-Columbian purslane (*Portulaca oleracea* L.) in the New World," Nature 253 (1975): 727–29.

Cabieses, Fernando. "Diseases and the concept of disease in ancient Peru," Aspects of the History of Medicine in Latin America. Eds. John Z. Bowers and Elizabeth F. Purcell. New York: Josiah Macy, Jr., Foundation, 1979. 16–53.

Camp, W. H. "A possible source for American pre-Columbian gourds," American Journal of Botany 41 (1954): 700–1.

Campbell, Joseph. Historical Atlas of World Mythology, Vol. 2. The Way of the Seeded Earth, Part 3: Mythologies of the Primitive Planters: The Middle and Southern Americas. New York: Harper and Row, 1989.

Canals Frau, Salvador. "Las dioscoreas cultivadas (ñames) y su introducción en el Nuevo Mundo," Buenos Aires. Runa 8 (1956–1957): 28–42.

Carter, George F. "Plant evidence for early contacts with America," Southwestern Journal of Anthropology 6 (1950): 161–82.

Carter, George F. "Plants across the Pacific," Asia and North America: Transpacific Contacts, Ed. M. W. Smith. Society for American Archaeology Memoir 9, 1953. 62–71.

Carter, George F. "Pre-Columbian chickens in America," Man across the Sea: Problems of Pre-Columbian Contacts. Eds. Carroll L. Riley, et al. Austin: University of Texas Press, 1971. 7–22.

Carter, George F. "Domesticates as artifacts," The Human Mirror: Material and Spatial Images of Man, Ed. Miles Richardson. Baton Rouge: Louisiana State University Press, 1974. 201–30.

Carter, George F. "The chicken in America: Spanish introduction or pre-Spanish?" Across before Columbus? Evidence for Transoceanic Contact with the Americas Prior to 1492, Eds. D. Y. Gilmore and L. S. McElroy. Edgecomb, Maine: New England Antiquities Research Association, 1998. 151–60.

Carter, George F. "O. F. Cook, pioneer in the use of plants as evidence of transoceanic movements: a centenary appreciation," Pre-Columbiana: A Journal of Long-distance Contacts 2:4 (2002): 252–68.

Carter, W. E., M. Mamani P., J. V. Morales, and P. Parkerson. Coca in Bolivia. Research Report. La Paz, Bolivia, 1980.

Cartmell, L. W., A. D. Aufderheide, A. Springfield, C. Weems, and B. Arriaza. "The frequency and antiquity of pre-historic coca-leaf-chewing practices in northern Chile: Radioimmunoassay of a cocaine metabolite in human hair," Latin American Antiquity 2 (1991): 260–68.

Casella, Domenico. "The annona and the pineapple depicted at Pompeii," Pre-Columbiana: A Journal of Long-distance Contacts 2:4 (2002a): 322–23.

Casella, Domenico. "Concerning the depiction of pineapple and Annona squamosa in Pompeian paintings," Pre-Columbiana: A Journal of Long-distance Contacts 2:4 (2002b): 326–33.

Casella, Domenico. "More concerning depictions of pineapple, mango, and Annona squamosa in Pompeian paintings," Pre-Columbiana: A Journal of Long-distance Contacts 2:4 (2002c.): 337–41.

Castello, Salvador. "The *Gallus* inaureis and the hen which lays blue eggs," Second World Poultry Congress (Barcelona), Barcelona. 1924. 113–18.

Castelló Yturbide, Teresa. Presencia de la comida prehispánica. México: Fomento Cultural Banamex. 1987.

Chadwick, Robert E. Lee, Jr. The Archaeology of a New World Merchant Culture. Unpublished Ph.D. dissertation. Tulane University. 1974.

Chadwick, Robert E. Lee, Jr. Ca. Toward a Theory of Trans-Atlantic Diffusion. (An 82-page typescript summarizing his 1974 doctoral dissertation; copy in Brigham Young University library.) 1975.

Chang, Kwang-chih. "Chinese prehistory in Pacific perspective: some hypotheses and problems," Harvard Journal of Asiatic Studies 22 (1959): 100–149.

Chang, Kwang-chih. The Archaeology of Ancient China. New Haven: Yale University. 1963.

Chang, Kwang-chih. "The beginnings of agriculture in the Far East," Antiquity 44 (1970): 175–85.

Chang, Kwang-chih. "Radiocarbon dates from China: some initial interpretations," Current Anthropology 14 (1973): 525–28.

Chapman, J., R. B. Stewart, and R. A. Yarnell. "Archaeological evidence for pre-Columbian introduction of *Portulaca oleracea* and *Mollugo verticillata* into eastern North America," Economic Botany 28 (1974): 411–12.

Chard, Chester S. "New World migration routes," University of Alaska Anthropological Papers 7 (1958): 23–6.

Chekiang Province Cultural Properties Control. "Report on the first and second seasons of excavation at the site of Ch'ien-shan-Yang in Wu-hsing hsien, Chekiang," K'ao ku hsüeh pao 2 (1960): 84–87.

Chen Wenhua. 1994. Zhongguo nongye kaogu tu lu. Nanchang, China: Jiangxi kexue jushu chubanshe. (Page 60 has a summary in English.)

Chevalier, A. "Nouvelles researches sur l'arbre a beurre du Soudan," Revue internationade botanique applique et d'agriculture tropicale 28 (1949): 241–56.

Chiba, Tokuji. "Mindaibunken ni arawareta Chûgoku no tômorokoshi [Part I], Aichi-daigaku Bungaku-onsô 36 (1968): 79–96.

Chiba, Tokuji. "Mindaibunken ni arawareta Chûgoku no tômorokoshi [Part II], Aichi-daigaku Bungaku-onsô 40 (1969): 1–22.

Chiba, Tokuji. "Chûgoku ni okeru tômorokoshi no to sono chiriteki igi," Chirigaku-hyôron 43 (1970): 687–90.

Chin, James, ed. Control of Communicable Diseases Manual, Seventeenth edition. Washington: American Public Health Association. 2000.

Chopra, R. N., I. C. Chopra, K. L. Handa, and L. D. Kapur. Chopra's Indigenous Drugs of India, Second edition, revised and largely rewritten. Calcutta and New Delhi: Academic Publishers. 1958 (reprinted 1982).

Chopra, R. N., I. C. Chopra, and B. S. Varma. Supplement to Glossary of Indian Medicinal Plants. New Delhi: Council of Scientific and Industrial Research. 1969.

Chopra, R. N., S. L. Nayar, and I. C. Chopra. Glossary of Indian Medicinal Plants. New Delhi: Council of Scientific and Industrial Research. 1956.

Christian, Frederick W. "On the distribution and origin of some plant- and tree-names," Journal of the Polynesian Society 6 (1897): 123–40.

Christian, Frederick W. "Words and races: story of the kumara," Journal of Science and Technology Wellington, New Zealand. 6 (1924): 152–3.

Clark, George A., Marc A. Kelley, John M. Grange, and M. Cassandra Hill. "The evolution of mycobacterial disease in human populations: A reevaluation," Current Anthropology 28:1 February 1987: 45–62.

Clissold, P. "Early ocean-going craft in the eastern Pacific. An appreciation of part of 'American Indians in the Pacific,'" Mariner's Mirror 45 (1959): 234–42.

Cockburn, Aidan. "Disease," in Mummies, Disease, and Ancient Cultures. Eds. Aidan Cockburn and Eve Cockburn. Cambridge: Cambridge University Press. 1980. 157–70.

Cockburn, Aidan, Robin A. Barraco, William H. Peck, and Theodore A. Reyman. "A classic mummy: PUM II," in Mummies, Disease, and Ancient Cultures, 2nd edition. Eds. A. Cockburn, E. Cockburn, and T. A. Reyman. Cambridge: Cambridge University Press. 1998. 69 – 90.

Coe, Michael D. "San Lorenzo and the Olmec civilization," Dumbarton Oaks Conference on the Olmec. Ed. E. P. Benson. Washington: Dumbarton Oaks. 1968. 41–78.

Collins, G. N. "A new type of Indian corn from China," United States Department of Agriculture, Bureau of Plant Industry, Bulletin 161 (1909): 7–16, 24–25.

Collins, J. L. "Pineapples in ancient America," The Scientific Monthly 67 (1948): 372–7.

Collins, J. L. "Pineapples in ancient America," University of Hawaii Pineapple Research Institute, Miscellaneous Paper No. 46, 1951. (slightly modified.)

Compton, Todd. Leap into Fire and Rabbit in Moon: Auto-Sacrifice and World Age in Aztec, Indian and Native American Myth. Unpublished paper, copy in possession of John Sorenson. 1997.

Cook, O. F. "The origin and distribution of the cocoa palm," Contributions from the U.S. National Herbarium. Washington. 7 (1901): 247–93.

Cook, O. F. "Food plants of ancient America," Annual Report of the Board of Regents of the Smithsonian Institution . . . [for1903]. Washington. 1904. 481–97.

Cook, Orator Fuller, and Robert C. Cook. "The maho, or mahagua, as a trans-Pacific plant." Journal of the Washington Academy of Sciences 8 (1918): 153-170.

Covarrubias, Miguel. Indian Art of Mexico and Central America. New York: Knopf. 1957.

Cox, Paul Alan, and Sandra Anne Banack, eds. Islands, Plants, and Polynesians: An Introduction to Polynesian Ethnobotany. Portland, Oregon: Dioscorides Press. 1991.

Crawford, Michael H. The Origins of Native Americans: Evidence from Anthropological Genetics, Revised, English version. Cambridge: Cambridge University Press. 1998.

Crockford, Susan J. Osteometry of Makah and Coast Salish Dogs. Burnaby, British Columbia: Archaeology Press, Department of Archaeology, Simon Fraser University. 1997.

Cronk, Lynn Ellen. Mesoamerican and Indian Fire Gods and Ceremonies. Unpublished M.A. thesis, University of Calgary. 1973.

Cunningham, Alexander. The Stupa of Bharhut: A Buddhist Monument Ornamented with Numerous Sculptures Illustrat[ive] of Buddhist Legend and History in the Third Century B.C. London. 1879. (Reprinted Varanasi, India: Indological Book House. 1962.)

Dagodag, Tim, and Gary Klee. "A review of some analogies in sunken garden agriculture," Anthropological Journal of Canada 11 (1973): 10–5.

Danin, Avinoam, Irene Baker, and Herbert G. Baker. "Cytogeography and taxonomy of the *Portulaca oleracea* L. polyploidy complex," Israel Journal of Botany 27 (1978): 177–211.

Darling, Samuel T. "Observations on the geographical and ethnological distribution of hookworms," Parasitology 12:3 (1920): 217–33.

Darlington, Cyril D. Chromosome Botany and the Origins of Cultivated Plants, 3rd (revised) edition. London: George Allen and Unwin. 1973.

Davis, Nancy Yaw. The Zuni Enigma: A Native American People's Possible Japanese Connection. W.W. Norton & Company. New York. 2000.

Daws, J. D., and J. R. Magilton. The Archeology of York, Vol. 12, fasc. I: The cemetery of St. Helen-on-the-Walls. York, England. Aldwark, England: Archeological Trust. 1980.

De, D. N. "Pigeon pea," Evolutionary Studies in World Crops: Diversity and Change in the Indian Subcontinent, Ed. Joseph Hutchinson. Cambridge: Cambridge University Press. 1974. 79–88.

Degener, O. Ferns and Flowering Plants of Hawaii National Park. Honolulu. 1930.

Denevan, William M., ed. The Native Population of the Americas in 1492. Madison: University of Wisconsin Press. 1976.

Dennis, J. V., and C. R. Gunn. "The case against trans-Pacific dispersal of the coconut by ocean currents," Economic Botany 25 (1971): 407–13.

De Prez, Alfred S. "Observations sur la flore et la faune representies sur les bas-reliefs de quelques monuments indo-javanais," Revue des arts asiatiques 9 (1935): 57–62.

Desmond, Ray. The European Discovery of the Indian Flora. New York: Oxford University Press. 1992.

Dhamija, Jasleen. "The Geography of Indian Textile: a study of the movement of Telia Rumal, Asia Rumal, Real Madras Handkerchief, George Cloth & Guinie Cloth." Paper presented at "Real Madras Handkerchief: A Cross Cultural Perspective." Madras Craft Foundation. India. 1994

Dhawan, N. L. "Primitive maize in Sikkim," Maize Genetic Cooperation News Letter 38 (1964): 69–70.

Díaz, José Luis. "Hallucinogens in prehispanic Mexico," Arqueología mexicana 10:59 (2003): 78–80.

Dickinson, William R., Y. H. Sinoto, R. Shutler, Jr., M. E. Shutler, J. Garanger, and T. M. Teska. "Japanese Jomon sherds in artifact collections from Mele plain on Efate in Vanuatu," Archaeology in Oceania 34 (1999): 15–24.

Dillehay, Thomas D. The Settlement of the Americas: A New Prehistory. New York: Basic Books. 2000.

Dixon, E. James. Quest for the Origins of the First Americans. Albuquerque: University of New Mexico Press. 1993.

Dixon, E. James. Bones, Boats, and Bison: Archeology and the First Colonization of Western North America. Albuquerque: University of New Mexico Press. 1999.

Dixon, Roland B. "Review of Africa and the Discovery of America, Vol. l, by Leo Wiener." American Anthropologist 22 (1920): 178–85.

Dixon, Roland B. "Words for tobacco in American Indian languages," American Anthropologist 23 (1921): 19–50.

Dixon, Roland B. "The problem of the sweet potato in Polynesia," American Anthropologist 34 (1932): 40–66.

Donkin, R. A. "*Bixa orellana*: 'The eternal shrub,'" Anthropos 69 (1974): 33–56.

Doran, Edwin, Jr. "The sailing raft as a great tradition," Man across the Sea: Problems of Pre-Columbian Contacts, Eds. Carroll L. Riley, et al. Austin: University of Texas Press. 1971. 115–38.

Doran, Edwin, Jr. "Seaworthiness of sailing rafts," Anthropological Journal of Canada 16 (1978): 17–22.

Dressler, Robert L. "The pre-Columbian cultivated plants of Mexico," Harvard University Botanical Museum Leaflets, 16:6 (1953): 115–72.

Drisdelle, Rosemary. (9/28/2010). Old World Hookworm, New World Hookworm - Origins and History. Suite101 http://suite101.com/article/old-world-hookworm-new-world-hookworm---origins-and-history-a290966#ixzz2I5npJCwq. Accessed 1/15/2013.

DuBois, Constance Goddard. "The religion of the Luiseño Indians of Southern California." University of California Publications in American Archaeology and Ethnology 8:3 (1908): 69–186.

Dumont, Henri J., Christine Cocquyt, Michel Fontugne, Maurice Arnold, Jean-Louis Reyss, Jan Bloemendal, Frank Oldfield, Cees L. M. Steenbergen, Henk J. Korthals, and Barbara A. Zeeb. "The end of moai quarrying and its effect on Lake Rano Raraku, Easter Island," Journal of Paleolimnology 20 (1998): 409–22.

Dunn, Frederick L. "Malaria," The Cambridge World History of Human Disease. Ed. Kenneth F. Kiple. Cambridge: Cambridge University Press. 1993. 855–62.

Durbin, Marshall. "Review article: 'The evolution and diffusion of writing'", American Anthropologist 73:2 (1971): 299–304.

Dutt, Udoy Chand & Sir George King. The Materia Medica of the Hindus, compiled from Sanskrit medical works. Calcutta: Thacker, Spick, &Co. 1877 http://www.archive.org/stream/materiamedicahi00kinggoog/materiamedicahi00kinggoog_djvu.txt

Easton, N. Alexander. "Mal de mer above terra incognita, or, what ails the coastal migration theory?," Arctic Anthropology 29:2 (1992): 28–41.

Edwards, Clinton R. Aboriginal Watercraft on the Pacific Coast of South America. Berkeley: University of California Press. 1965.

Edwards, Clinton R. "New World perspectives on pre-European voyaging in the Pacific," Early Chinese Art and Its Possible Influence in the Pacific Basin; a Symposium Arranged by the Department of Art History and Archaeology, Columbia University, New York City, August 21–25, 1967, Ed. Noel Barnard in collaboration with

Douglas Fraser. Vol. 3: Oceania and the Americas. New York: Intercultural Arts Press. 1969. 843–87.

Edwards, Clinton R "Commentary: Section II," Man across the Sea: Problems of Pre-Columbian Contacts, Eds. Carroll L. Riley et al. Austin: University of Texas Press. 1971. 293–307.

Eells, Myron. "The Twana, Chemakum, Klallam Indians of Washington Territory," Smithsonian Annual Report for 1887. Washington. 1887.

Elkin, Adolphus Peter, and N. W. G. MacIntosh, eds. Grafton Elliot Smith: The Man and His Work. Sydney: Sydney University Press. 1974.

El-Najjar, Mahmoud Y. "Human treponematosis and tuberculosis: evidence from the New World," American Journal of Physical Anthropology 51:4 (1979): 599–618.

El-Najjar, M.Y. and T.M.J. Mulinksi. "Mummies and Mummification Practices in the Southwestern and Southern United States", Ed. A. Cockburn and E. Cockburn. Mummies, Disease and Ancient Cultures. Cambridge, U.K. Cambridge University Press: 1980. 103-117.

El-Najjar, Mahmoud Y., Thomas M. J. Mulinski, and Karl J. Reinhard. "Mummies and mummification practices in the southern and southwestern United States," Mummies, Disease and Ancient Cultures, 2nd edition. Eds. Aidan Cockburn, et al. Cambridge: Cambridge University Press. 1998. 121–137.

Engelbrecht, William E., and Carl K. Seyfert. "Paleoindian watercraft: evidence and implications," North American Archaeologist 15 (1994): 221–34.

England, Nora C. La autonomía de los idiomas Mayas: historia e identidad. Guatemala: Cholsamaj. 1992.

Erickson, David L., Bruce D. Smith, Andrew C. Clarke, Daniel H. Sandweiss, and Noreen Tuross. "An Asian origin for a 10,000-year-old domesticated plant in the Americas?," Proceedings, National Academy of Sciences of the USA 102:51 (Dec. 20, 2005): 18315–18320.

Erlandson, Jon M. "Anatomically Modern Humans, Maritime Voyaging, and the Pleistocene Colonization of the Americas." The First Americans, Ed. Nina G. Jablonski. Memoirs of the California Academy of Science, No. 27. San Francisco, CA: April 8, 2002. 59 – 92.

Erlandson, Jon M. and Rick C. Torben, eds. Human Impact on Ancient Marine Ecosystems: a Global Perspective. Berkeley: University of California Press, 2008.

Erlandson, Jon M., Michael H. Graham, Bruce J. Bourque, Debra Corbett, James A. Estes, & Robert S. Steneck. "The kelp highway hypothesis: Marine ecology, the coastal migration theory, and the peopling of the Americas." Journal of Island and Coastal Archaeology. 2 (2007):161-174.

Errazurriz, J., and C. Alvarado. "An archaeologic bridge over the Pacific: transpacific currents and Tumaco-La Tolita transpacific crossing." Audiovisual presentation, Tokyo, NHK(TV), July 29, 1993.

Estrada, Emilio, and Betty J. Meggers. "A complex of traits of probable transpacific origin on the coast of Ecuador," American Anthropologist 63 (1961): 913–39.

Evans, Jeff. The Discovery of Aotearoa. Auckland: Reed. 1998.

Faeggri, K. "Plantenes utbredelse som vitnesbyrd om menneskenes historie," Naturen. Bergen, Norway. 88:6 (1964): 344–51.

Fage, J. D. "Anthropology, botany, and the history of Africa; review article on G. P. Murdock, Africa; Its Peoples and Their Culture History", Journal of African History 3 (1962): 299–309.

Faria, Carmen. "El grupo Tumaco-Tolita a través de la colección de Torredembarra," Boletín americanista 27/35 (1985): 91–114.

Feinhandler, Sherwin J., H. C. Fleming, and J. M. Monahon. "Tobaccos," Economic Botany 33 (1979): 213–26.

Fernald, M. L. ed. (largely rewritten and expanded) Gray's Manual of Botany. New York: American Book Co. 1950.

Ferreira, Luiz Fernando, Adauto Araújo, and Ulisses Eugenio Confalonieri. "The finding of eggs and larvae of parasitic helminths in archaeological material from Unai, Minas Gerais, Brazil," Transactions, Royal Society of Tropical Medicine and Hygiene 74:6 (1980): 65–67.

Ferreira, Luiz Fernando, Adauto Araújo, and Ulisses Eugenio Confalonieri. "Os parasitos do homem antigo," Ciência Hoje 1 (3 Nov.-Dez., 1982): 63–67.

Ferreira, Luiz Fernando, Adauto Araújo, Ulisses Eugenio Confalonieri, M. Chame, and B. Ribeiro Filho. "Encontro de ovos de ancilostomideos em coprólitos humanos datados de 7,230±80 BP no estado de Piauí, Brazil," Paleoparasitologia no Brasil. Eds. L. Fernando Ferreira, A. Araújo, and U. Confalonieri. Rio de Janeiro: Programa de Educação Pública, Escola Nacional de Saúde Pública. 1988. 37–40.

Ferris, G. F. Contributions toward a Monograph of the Sucking Lice, Part 8. Stanford University Publications, Biological Sciences Series. 1935.

Ferris, G. F. The Sucking Lice. Memoirs of the Pacific Coast Entomological Society, Vol. 1. San Francisco. 1951.

Fiennes, Richard, and Alice Fiennes. The Natural History of Dogs. London: Weidenfeld and Nicholson. 1968.

Finan, J. S. "Maize in the great herbals," Annals of the Missouri Botanical Garden 35 (1948): 149–91.

Finsterbusch, C. A. "The Araucano, the blue-egged fowl of Chile," The Feathered World 85:2201 (1931): 465–70.

Fladmark, K. R. "Routes: alternative migration corridors for early man in North America," American Antiquity 44 (1979): 55–69.

Fladmark, K. R. "Times and places: environmental correlates of Mid-to-Late Wisconsin human population expansion in North America," Early Man in the New World. Ed. Richard Shutler. Beverly Hills: Sage Publications. 1983. 13–42.

Fladmark, K. R. "Getting one's Berings," Natural History 95 (1986): 8–19.

Fonseca, Olympio da. Parasitismo e migrações da parasitologia para o conhecimento das origens do homem americano. (Estudos de Pré-história Geral e Brasileira). Sao Paulo: Instituto de Pré-história de Universidade de São Paulo. 1970.

Forbes, Robert J. Studies in Ancient Technology, Vol. 4. Leiden: E. J. Brill. 1956.

Fosberg, F. R. "The American element in the Hawaiian flora," Pacific Sciences 5 (1951): 204–6.

Foster, Mary LeCron. "Old World language in the Americas: 1." Unpublished paper delivered at the annual meeting of the Association of American Geographers, San Diego, April 1992a. (Copy in the possession of John Sorenson; abstract appears in Sorenson and Raish, 1996, 326.)

Foster, Mary LeCron. "Old World language in the Americas: 2." Unpublished paper delivered at the annual meeting of the Language Origins Society, Cambridge University, September 1992b. (Copy in the possession of John Sorenson; abstract in Sorenson and Raish, 1996, 325.)

Friant, M. "Le chien des Incas précolombien et la découverte de l'Amérique," L'Ethnographie 58–9 (1964–1965): 130–5.

Friant, M., and Henry Reichlen. "Deux chiens préhispaniques du désert d'Atacama, Travaux de l'Institut Français d'Études Andenes 2 (1950): 1–18.

Fryxell, Paul A. "The correct name of 'kidney cotton," Baileya 19 (1973):91-2

Fuchs, Stephan. "Ancient cultural links between America, Asia, and Oceania," Journal of the Anthropological Society of Bombay 5 (1951): 51–75.

Furst, Peter T. "West Mexico, the Caribbean and Northern South America: some problems in New World inter-relationships," Antropológica 14 (1965): 1–37.

Gamble, Clive. Timewalkers: The Prehistory of Global Colonization. Phoenix Mill, England: Alan Sutton; and Cambridge: Harvard University Press. 1993.

García-Bárcena, Joaquín. "Tiempo Mesoamericano II: Preclásico Temprano (2500 a. C–1200 a. C.)," Arqueología mexicana 8 (41, Jul.–Ag., 2000): 12–7.

García-Payón, José. "Una cabecita de barro de extraña fisonomía," Boletín, Instituto Nacional de Antropología e Historia. México.6 (Oct. 1961.): 1–2.

The Garuda Purana. Ancient Indian Tradition and Mythology 14 (2). Delhi: Motilal Banarsidass. 1980.

Gates, William. Yucatan before and after the Conquest, by Friar Diego de Landa. (Maya Society Publication No. 20), 2nd ed. Baltimore. 1937.

Giesing, Kornelia B. Rudra-Siva und Tezcatlipoca: ein Beitrag zur Indo-Mexikanistik. Tübingen: Verlag Science und Fiction. Reihe Ethnologische Studien 1. 1984.

Gifford, Edward Winslow. "Review of The Native Culture in the Marquesas, by E. S. C. Handy," American Anthropologist 26 (1924): 549–53.

Glover, Ian C. "The Late Stone Age in eastern Indonesia," World Archaeology 9 (1 June, 1977): 42–61.

Glover, Ian C. Archaeology in Eastern Timor, 1966–67. Terra Australis #11. Department of Prehistory, Research School of Pacific Studies. The Australian National University, Canberra. 1986: 198–199, 229–230.

Goff, C. W. "Syphilis," Diseases in Antiquity. Eds. Don Brothwell and A. T. Sandison. Springfield, Illinois: C. C. Thomas. 1967. 279–94.

Goldstein, Marcus S. "Human paleopathology and some diseases in living primitive societies: a review of the recent literature," American Journal of Physical Anthropology 31 (1969): 285–94.

Gonzalez Calderón, O. L. The Jade Lords. Coatzacoalcos, Ver., Mexico: The author. 1991.

Gorner, Peter. "Plants as evidence for ancient contacts," Early Man 2 (1980): 19–22.

Gould, Stephen J. "In the mind of the beholder," Natural History 103 (1994): 14–23.

Gray, Asa, and J. H. Trumbull. "A review of De Candolle's Origin of Cultivated Plants, with annotations upon certain American species," American Journal of Science, 3rd series 25 (1883): 242–55.

Groves, R. H., and F. di Castri, eds. Biogeography of Mediterranean Invasions. New York: Cambridge University Press. 1991.

Guerra, F. "Maya medicine," Medical History 8 (1964): 31–43.

Guerra, F. "Aztec medicine," Medical History 10 (1966): 315–38.

Gunther, Robert T., ed. The Greek Herbal of Dioscorides. Oxford: Oxford University Press. 1934.

Guppy, Henry B. The Observations of a Naturalist in the Pacific between 1896 and 1899. 2 vols. London :Macmillan. 1906.

Gupta, D., and H. K. Jain. "Genetic differentiation of two Himalayan varieties of maize," Indian Journal of Genetics and Plant Breeding 33 (1973): 414.

Gupta, Shakti M. Plants in Indian Temple Art. Delhi: B. R. Publishing. 1996.

Guthrie, James L. "Observations on nicotine and cocaine in ancient Egyptian mummies," Pre-Columbiana: A Journal of Long-distance Contacts 2:4 (2002): 317–18.

Hackett, C. J. "The human treponematoses," Diseases in Antiquity. A Survey of the Diseases, Injuries and Surgery of Early Populations. Eds. Don Brothwell and A. T. Sandison. Springfield, Illinois: C. C. Thomas. 1967. 152–69.

Hadkins, E. S., R. Bye, W.A. Bramdemburg, and C.E. Jarvis. "Typification of Linnaean Datura names (*Solanaceae*)," Botanical Journal of the Linnean Society 125 (1997): 295–308.

Hall, A. R., and H. K. Kenward. Environmental Evidence from the Colonia. London: Council for British Archaeology, for York Archaeological Trust. Archaeology of York 14/6. 1990.

Hamblin, Nancy N. and Amadeo M. Rea. "Isla Cazumel Archaeological Avifauna." Prehistoric Lowland Maya Environment and Subsistence Economy. Ed. Mary Pohl. Cambridge: Peabody Museum of Archeology and Ethnology, Harvard University Press, 1985.

Hamp, Eric P. "'Chicken' in Ecuadorian Quichua," International Journal of American Linguistics 30 (1964): 298–99.

Handy, Edward S. C. III. Marquesan Legends. Bishop Museum Bulletin 69. Honolulu: B. P. Bishop Museum. 1930.

Hare, Ronald. "The antiquity of diseases caused by bacteria and viruses, a review of the problem from a bacteriologist's point of view," Diseases in Antiquity: A Survey of the Diseases, Injuries and Surgery of Early Populations. Eds. D. Brothwell and A.T. Sandison. Springfield, Illinois: C. C. Thomas. 1967. 115–31.

Harlan, Jack R., and J. M. J. de Wet. "On the quality of evidence for origin and dispersal of cultivated plants," Current Anthropology 14 (1973): 51–62.

Harms, H. "Übersicht der bisher in altperuanischen gräbern gefundenen Pflanzenreste," Festschrift Eduard Seler. Ed. W. Lehmann, Stuttgart: Strecker und Schröder. 1922. 157–88.

Harries, H. C. "The evolution, dissemination and classification of *Cocos nucifera* L.," Botanical Review 44 (1978): 265–320.

Harris, Hendon Mason. The Asiatic Fathers of America. Wen Ho Printing Co. , Ltd. Taipei, Taiwan R.O.C. 1973.

Hartman, Orar M. The Origin and Dispersal of the Domestic Fowl: A Study in Cultural Diffusion. Unpublished M.A. thesis, University of Oregon. 1973.

Hather, J., and P. V. Kirch. "Prehistoric sweet potato (*Ipomoea batatas*) from Mangaia Island, central Polynesia," Antiquity 65(1991): 887–93.

Hatt, Gudmund. "The corn mother myth in America and in Indonesia," Anthropos 46 (1951): 853–914.

Hawkes, J. G. "The introduction of New World crops into Europe after 1492," Plants for Food and Medicine. Eds. H. D. V. Prendergast, N. L. Detkin, D. R. Harris, and P. J. Houghton. Kew, England: Royal Botanic Gardens. 1998. 147–59.

Heine-Geldern, Robert von. "The problem of transpacific influences in Mesoamerica," Handbook of Middle American Indians, Vol. 4. Archaeological Frontiers and External Connections. Eds. G. F. Ekholm and G. R. Willey. Austin: University of Texas Press. 1966. 277–95.

Heine-Geldern, Robert von, and Gordon F. Ekholm. "Significant parallels in the symbolic arts of southern Asia and Middle America," The Civilizations of Ancient America. Selected Papers of the Twenty-ninth International Congress of Americanist (New York, 1949). Ed. Sol Tax. Chicago: University of Chicago Press. 1951. 299–309.

Heiser, Charles B., Jr. Of Plants and People. Norman: University of Oklahoma Press. 1985.

Heiser, Charles B., Jr. "Domestication of *Cucurbitaceae*: *Cucurbita* and *Lagenaria*," Foraging and Farming: The Evolution of Plant Exploitation. Eds. D. R. Harris and G. C. Hillman. London: Unwin Hyman. 1989. 470–80.

Heiser, Charles B., Jr., E. F. Schilling, and B. Dutt. "The American species of Luffa (*Cucurbitaceae*)," Systematic Botany 13 (1989): 138–45.

Helms, Mary W. Ulysses' Sail: An Ethnographic Odyssey of Power, Knowledge, and Geographical Distance. Princeton: Princeton University Press. 1988.

Hennig, R. "Eine rätselhafte Tier—Darstellung im Dom von Schleswig," Natur und Volk, Ornithologische Monatsberichte, Band 70 (1940): 100–1.

Herklots, G. A. C. Vegetables in Southeast Asia. London: George Allen & Unwin. 1972.

Hernández de Toledo, Francisco. Historia de las Plantas de Nueva España, 3 tomos. México: Imprenta Universitaria, 1942-1946.

Heyerdahl, Thor. Kon-Tiki: Across the Pacific by Raft. New York: Rand McNally. 1950.

Heyerdahl, Thor. "Prehistoric voyages as agencies for Melanesian and South American plant and animal dispersal to Polynesia," Plants and the Migrations of Pacific Peoples: A Symposium (Tenth Pacific Science Congress, Honolulu, 1961). Ed. Jacques Barrau. Honolulu: Bishop Museum Press. 1961. 23–35.

Heyerdahl, Thor. "Feasible ocean routes to and from the Americas in pre-Columbian times," American Antiquity 28 (1963a): 482–88.

Heyerdahl, Thor. "Archaeology in the Galapagos Islands," Galapagos Islands: A Unique Area for Scientific Investigations; A Symposium Presented at the Tenth Pacific Science Congress . . . (Honolulu, 1961). Occasional Papers of the California Academy of Sciences 44 (1963b): 45–51.

Heyerdahl, Thor. "Plant evidence for contacts with America before Columbus." Antiquity 38 (1964): 120–33.

Heyerdahl, Thor. "Notes on the pre-European coconut groves on Cocos Island," Reports of the Norwegian Archaeological Expedition to Easter Island and the East Pacific, Vol. 2: Miscellaneous Papers. Eds. Thor Heyerdahl and Edwin N. Ferdon, Jr. Monograph of the School of American Research and the Kon-Tiki Museum 24:2. 1965. 461–67.

Heyerdahl, Thor. The Maldive Mystery. Bethesda, Maryland: Adler and Adler. 1986.

Heyerdahl, Thor. Green Was the Earth on the Seventh Day. New York: Random House. 1996.

Heywood, V. H. Flowering Plants of the World. New York: Oxford University Press. 1993.

Hill, Arthur W. "The original home and mode of dispersal of the coconut," Nature 124:3117 (1929): 133–34, 151–53; 124 (3127): 507–8.

Hill, Dennis S. Agricultural Insect Pests of the Tropics and Their Control, 2nd edition. Cambridge: Cambridge University Press. 1983.

Hillebrand, W. Flora of the Hawaiian Islands. Heidelberg. 1888.

Hoeppli, Reinhard. Parasites and Parasitic Infections in Early Medicine and Science. Singapore: University of Malaya Press. 1959.

Hoeppli, Reinhard. "Parasitic diseases in Africa and the Western Hemisphere: early documentation and transmission by the slave trade," Acta Tropica, Supplementum 10. Basel: Verlag für Recht und Gesellschaft. 1969.

Holdaway, R. N. "Arrival of rats in New Zealand," Nature 384 (21 Nov., 1996): 225–26.

Holden, Constance. "Were Spaniards among the first Americans?," Science 286 (19 November, 1999): 1467–68.

Hooton, Earnest A. "The Indians of Pecos Pueblo." Papers of the Southwestern Expedition, No. 4. Andover, Massachusetts: Department of Archaeology, Phillips Academy. 1930.

Howe, R. W. "A laboratory study of the cigarette beetle *Lasioderma serricorne* F., with a critical review of the literature," Bulletin of Entomological Research 48 (1957): 9–56.

Hristov, Romeo H., and Santiago Genovés T. "Viages transatlánticos antes de Colón," Arqueología mexicana 6:33 (1998): 48–53.

Hristov, Romeo H., and Santiago Genovés T. "Mesoamerican evidence of pre-Columbian transoceanic contacts," Ancient Mesoamerica 10 (1999): 207–13.

Hudson, Ellis H. Non-Venereal Syphilis; A Sociological and Medical Study of Bejel. Edinburgh: E. and S. Livingstone. 1958.

Hudson, Ellis H. "Treponematosis and man's social evolution," American Anthropologist 67 (1965): 885–901.

Hull, Thomas G., ed. Diseases Transmitted from Animals to Man. 5th edition. Springfield, Illinois: C. C. Thomas. 1963.

Hutchinson, Joseph B. "The history and relationships of the world's cottons," Endeavour 21 (1962): 5–15.

Hutchinson, Joseph B. "Crop plant evolution in the Indian subcontinent," Evolutionary Studies in World Crops: Diversity and Change in the Indian Subcontinent. Ed. J. B. Hutchinson. London: Cambridge University Press. 1974. 151–60.

Hutchinson, Joseph B., R. A. Silow, and S. G. Stephens. The Evolution of Gossypium and the Differentiation of the Cultivated Cottons. New York: Oxford University Press. 1947.

Innes, Frank C. "Disease ecologies of North America," The Cambridge World History of Human Disease. Ed. Kenneth F. Kiple. Cambridge: Cambridge University Press. 1993. 519–35.

International Library Association (ILA), comp. and ed. Medicinal Plants Sourcebook India: A Guide to Institutions, Publications, Information Services and Other Resources. Switzerland: International Library Association; and Dehra Dun, India: Nahraj Publishers. 1996.

Jairazbhoy, Rafique A. Ramses III, Father of Ancient America. London: Karnak House. 1992.

Jaramillo-Arango, Jaime. The Conquest of Malaria. London: Heinemann Medical Books. 1950.

Jarcho, Saul. "Some observations on disease in prehistoric North America," Bulletin of the History of Medicine 38 (1964): 1–19.

Jeffreys, M. D. W. "The history of maize in Africa," Eastern Anthropologist 7 (1953a): 138–48.

Jeffreys, M. D. W. "Pre-Columbian maize in Africa," Nature 172 (1953b): 965–66.

Jeffreys, M. D. W. "Columbus and the introduction of maize into Spain," Anthropos 50 (1955): 427–32.

Jeffreys, M. D. W. "The banana in the Americas," Journal d'agriculture tropicale et de botanique appliqueé 10:5–7 (1963): 191–203.

Jeffreys, M. D. W. "Pre-Columbian maize in Asia," Man across the Sea: Problems of Pre-Columbian Contacts. Eds. Carroll L. Riley, et al. Austin: University of Texas Press. 1971. 376–400.

Jeffreys, M. D. W. "Pre-Columbian maize in the Old World: an examination of Portuguese sources," Gastronomy, the Anthropology of Food and Food Habits. Ed. M. L. Arnott. The Hague: Mouton. 1975. 23–66.

Jeffreys, M. D. W. "The Arab introduction of exotic domesticates into Africa," The New Diffusionist 6 (1976): 9–28.

Jennings, Jesse D. Prehistory of North America. New York: McGraw-Hill. 1968.

Jett, Stephen C. "Diffusion versus independent development: the bases of controversy," Man across the Sea: Problems of Pre-Columbian Contacts. Eds. Carroll L. Riley et al. Austin: University of Texas Press. 1971. 5–53.

Jett, Stephen C. "Introduction: Early watercraft and navigation in the Pacific," Pre-Columbiana: A Journal of Long-distance Contacts 1:1–2 (1998): 3–8.

Jett, Stephen C. "Nicotine and cocaine in Egyptian mummies and THC in Peruvian mummies; a review of the evidence and of scholarly reaction," Pre-Columbiana: A Journal of Long-distance Contacts 2:4 (2002a): 297–313.

Jett, Stephen C. "Archaeological hints of pre-Columbian plantains in the Americas," Pre-Columbiana: A Journal of Long-distance Contacts 2:4 (2002b): 314–16.

Jett, Stephen C. "Postscript on pineapple and annona," Pre-Columbiana: A Journal of Long-distance Contacts 2:4 (2002c): 342–43.

Jett, Stephen C. "More on nicotine and cocaine in Egyptian mummies: a précis of recent articles," Pre-Columbiana: A Journal of Long-distance Contacts 3:1–3 (2004): 46–50.

Jia Ming. "Yinshi xuzhi," Tush jicheng jianbian. Ed. Wang Yunwu. Taipei, Taiwan: Commercial Press. 1966 [1473].

Jiao, M., M. Luna-Cavazos, and R. Bye. "Allozyme variation in Mexican species and classification of Datura (Solanaceae)," Plant Systematics and Evolution 232 (2002): 155–66.

Johannessen, Carl L. "Folk medicine uses of melanotic Asiatic chickens as evidence of early diffusion to the New World," Social Science and Medicine 15D (1981): 427–34.

Johannessen, Carl L. "Distribution of pre-Columbian maize and modern maize names," Person, Place and Thing: Interpretive and Empirical Essays in Cultural Geography. Ed. Shue Tuck Wong. (Special issue of Geoscience and Man 31) 1992: 313–33.

Johannessen, Carl L. "Maize diffused to India before Columbus came to America," Across before Columbus? Evidence for Transoceanic Contact with the Americas Prior to 1492. Eds. D. Y. Gilmore and L. S. McElroy. Edgecomb, Maine: New England Antiquities Research Association. 1998a. 110–24.

Johannessen, Carl L. "Pre-Columbian American sunflower and maize images in Indian temples: Evidence of contact between civilizations in India and America," Mormons, Scripture and the Ancient World: Studies in Honor of John L. Sorenson. Ed. D. Bitton. Provo, Utah: Foundation for Ancient Research and Mormon Studies. 1998b. 351–89. Also printed in NEARA Journal, Volume XXXII, No. 1 Summer 1998.

Johannessen, Carl L., and May Chen Fogg. "Melanotic chicken use and Chinese traits in Guatemala," Revista de historia de América 93 (1982): 73–89.

Johannessen, Carl L., Wayne Fogg, and May Chen Fogg. "Distributional and medicinal use of the black-boned and black-meated chicken in Mexico, Guatemala, and South America," National Geographic Society Research Reports 17 (1984): 493–95.

Johannessen, Carl L., and Ann Z. Parker. "Maize ears sculptured in 12th and 13th century A.D. India as indicators of pre-Columbian diffusion," Economic Botany 43 (1989a): 164–80.

Johannessen, Carl L., and Ann Z. Parker. "American crop plants in Asia prior to European contact," Year Book 1988, Proceedings of the Conference of Latin Americanist Geographers 14 (1989b): 14–19.

Johannessen, Carl L., and Wang Siming. "American crop plants in Asia before A.D. 1500," Pre-Columbiana: A Journal of Long-distance Contacts 1 (1998): 9–36.

Johnson, B. L. "*Gossypium palmeri* and a polyphyletic origin of the New World cottons," Bulletin, Torrey Botanical Club 102 (1975): 340–49.

Johnson, Frederick, and Richard S. MacNeish. "Chronometric dating," The Prehistory of the Tehuacan Valley, Vol. 4, Chronology and Irrigation. Ed. Frederick Johnson. Austin: University of Texas Press. 1972. 3–55.

Johnson, Rubellite K., and Bryce G. Decker. "Implications of the distribution of names for cotton (*Gossypium* spp.) in the Indo-Pacific," Asian Perspectives 23:2 (1980): 249–307.

Jones, Peter N. "American Indian demographic history and cultural affiliation: a discussion of certain limitations on the use of mtDNA and Y chromosome testing," Anthro-Globe Journal. September 2002.

Kane, Paul. Wandering of an Artist among the Indians of North America. London: Longman, Brown, Green, Longmans, and Roberts. 1859.

Karasch, Mary C. "Disease ecologies of South America." The Cambridge World History of Human Disease. Ed. Kenneth F. Kiple. Cambridge: Cambridge University Press. 1993. 535–43.

Kaufman, Terrence. El Proto-Tzeltal-Tzotzil. Fonología comparada y diccionario reconstruido. México: UNAM, Centro de Estudios Mayas Cuaderno 5. 1972.

Kaufman, Terrence, and W. Norman. "An outline of proto-Cholan phonology, morphology and vocabulary," Phoneticism in Maya Hieroglyphic Writing. Eds. J. Justeson and L. Campbell. Institute for Mesoamerican Studies 9. Albany: State University of New York. 1984. 77–166.

Kehoe, Alice Beck. 2003 The Fringe of American Archaeology: Transoceanic and Transcontinental Contacts in Prehistoric America. Journal of Scientific Exploration 17(1):19-36.

Kelley, David H. Our Elder Brother Coyote: Evidence for a Mexican Element in the Formation of Polynesian Culture. Unpublished doctoral dissertation, Harvard University, Anthropology. 1957.

Kelley, David H. "Calendar animals and deities," Southwestern Journal of Anthropology 16 (1960): 317–37.

Kelley, David H. "*Wangkang, *kumadjang, and *Longo," Pre-Columbiana: A Journal of Long-distance Contacts 1:1/2 (1998): 72–77.

Kidder, Alfred V., Jesse E. Jennings, and Edwin M. Shook. Excavations at Kaminaljuyu, Guatemala. Washington: Carnegie Institution Publication 561. 1946.

Kidder II, Alfred V. "South American high cultures," Prehistoric Man in the New World. Eds. J. D. Jennings and E. Norbeck. Chicago: University of Chicago Press. 1964. 451–86.

Kiple, Kenneth F. "Yellow fever and the Africanization of the Caribbean," Disease and Demography in the Americas. Eds. J. W. Verano and D. H. Ubelaker. Washington: Smithsonian Institution Press. 1992. 15–24.

Kirch, Patrick V. On the Road of the Winds: An Archaeological History of the Pacific Islands before European Contact. Berkeley: University of California Press. 2000.

Kirchhoff, Paul. "The adaptation of foreign religious influences in pre-Spanish Mexico," Diogenes 47 (1964a): 13–28.

Kirchhoff, Paul. "The diffusion of a great religious system from India to Mexico," Proceedings, Thirty-fifth International Congress of Americanists (Mexico, 1962), Vol. I . México. 1964b. 3–100.

Kirtikar, K. R., and B. D. Basu. Indian Medicinal Plants. 5 vols. Allahabad: Sudhindra Nath Basu. Reprint edition 1935. 2nd ed., edited, rev., enl., and mostly rewritten by E. Blatter, J. F. Caius, and K. S. Mhaskar. Dehradun, India: International Books Distributors, 1987.

Kislev, M. E. "Archaeology and storage archaeoentomology," New Light on Early Farming: Recent Developments in Palaeoethnobotany. Ed. Jane M. Renfrew. Edinburgh: Edinburgh University Press. 1991. 121–36.

Kissell, Mary Lois. "Organized Salish blanket pattern," American Anthropologist 31(1929): 85–88.

Klepinger, Linda L. "Comment on Clark, et al. 1987," Current Anthropology 28 (1 February, 1987): 45–62.

Knoche, W. Die Osterinsel: eine Zusammenfassung der chilenischen Osterinseln Expedition des Jahres 1911. Concepción, Chile: Verlag des Wissenschaftlichen Archives von Chile. 1925.

Kosakowsky, Laura J., Francisco Estrada Belli, and Paul Pettitt. "Preclassic through Postclassic: ceramics and chronology of the southeastern Pacific coast of Guatemala," Ancient Mesoamerica 11 (2000):199–215.

Kramisch, Stella. A Treatise on Indian Painting and Image Making. The Vishnudharmottra, Part III. Calcutta: Calcutta University Press. 1928.

Krapovickas, A. "The origin, variability, and spread of groundnut (Arachis hypogaea)," The Domestication and Exploitation of Plants and Animals. Eds. Peter J. Ucko, and C. W. Dimbleby, eds., London: Duckworth; and Chicago/New York: Aldine–Atherton. 1969. 427–41.

Krauss, Beatrice H., compiler. Ethnobotany of Hawaii. Photocopy edition. Honolulu: University of Hawaii, Department of Botany. n.d.

Kroeber, Alfred L. "Native Culture of the Southwest." University of California Publications in American Archaeology and Ethnology 23:9 (1928): 375–98.

Kroeber, Alfred L. Anthropology; Race, Language, Culture, Psychology, Prehistory. Revised edition. New York: Harcourt, Brace. 1948.

Kuhnke, LaVerne. "Disease ecologies of the Middle East and North Africa," The Cambridge World History of Human Disease. Ed.

Kenneth F. Kiple. Cambridge: Cambridge University Press. 1993. 453–62.

Kulakov, P. A., H. Hauptli, and S. K. Jain. "Genetics of grain amaranth," Journal of Heredity 76 (1985): 27–30.

Kunitz, S. and R. Euler. "Aspects of Southwestern Paleoepidemiology." Prescott College Anthropology Prereports, No. 2. Prescott, Arizona. 1972.

Laming-Emperaire, Annette. Le problème des origins américaines; théories, hypothèses, documents. Lille: Editions de la Maison des Sciences de l'Homme, Presses Universitaires de Lille. 1980.

Lancaster, S. P. "The sacred plants of the Hindus," Bulletin of the National Botanical Garden, No. 113. Lucknow. 1965.

Langdon, Robert. "New World cotton as a clue to the Polynesian past," Oceanic Studies: Essays in Honour of Aarne A. Koskinen. Ed. Jukka Sükala. Finnish Anthropological Society Transactions No. 11. Helsinki. 1982. 179–92.

Langdon, Robert. "Manioc, a long concealed key to the enigma of Easter Island," The Geographical Journal 154 (1988): 324–36.

Langdon, Robert, and D. Tryon. The Language of Easter Island: Its Development and Eastern Polynesian Relationships. Laie, Hawaii: Brigham Young University – Hawaii Campus, Institute for Polynesian Studies. 1983.

Las Casas, Bartolomé de. Historia de las Indias. (Written in 1517). Madrid. 1875–1876.

Latcham, Ricardo E. "Los animales domésticos de la América pre-Colombiana," Museo de Etnología e Antropología, Publicación. Santiago: Chile 3:1 (1922): 1–199.

Latcham, Ricardo E. La Agricultura Precolombina en Chile y los Países Vecinos. Santiago: Ediciones de la Universidad de Chile. 1936.

Lathrap, Donald W. "Our father the cayman, our mother the gourd: Spinden revisited, or a unitary model for the emergence of agriculture in the New World," The Origins of Agriculture. Ed. C. A. Reed. Chicago: Aldine. 1977. 713–51.

Laufer, Berthold. "A theory of the origin of Chinese writing," American Anthropologist 9:1(1907): 487–97.

Laufer, Berthold. "The American plant migration," Scientific Monthly 28(1929): 230–51.

Laufer, Berthold. "Tobacco in New Guinea." American Anthropologist. 33 (1931): 138 – 140.

Lawler, Andrew. "Animal Domestication: In Search of the Wild Chicken." Science Vol. 338 no. 6110 pp. 1020-1024. DOI: 10.1126/science.338.6110.1020.

Layard, Austen H. Nineveh and Its Remains. 2 vols. London. 1849.

Leach, Helen M. "On the origins of kitchen gardening in the ancient Near East," Garden History 10 (1982): 1–16.

Leland, Charles G. Fusang, or the Discovery of America by Chinese Buddhist Priests in the Fifth Century. New York: J. W. Bouton. 1975.

Lels, Daniela, et al. "Molecular paleoparasitological diagnosis of Ascaris sp. From coprolites: new scenery of ascariasis in pre-columbian South America times". Memorias do Instituto Oswaldo Cruz. Feb 2008. Available at: http://www.scielo.br/scielo.php?script=sci_arttext&pid=S0074-02762008000100017&lng=en&nrm=iso. Accessed July 2009.

Lentz, David L., Mary E. D. Pohl, Kevin O. Pope, and Andrew R. Wyatt. "Prehistoric sunflower (*Helianthus annuus* L.) domestication in Mexico," Economic Botany 55:3 (2001): 370–76.

León, Fidias E., Amparo A. de León, and Adriana Ariza de León. "HLA, trans-Pacific contacts, and retrovirus," Human Immunology 42:4 (1995): 348–50.

León, Fidias E., Amparo A. de León, and Adriana Ariza. "El viaje transpacífico del virus de la leucemia de células T del adulto tipo I," Acta Neurológica Colombiana 10 (3 Júl.–Sept. 1996): 132–36.

Leopold, A. Starker. Wildlife of Mexico. The Game Birds and Mammals. Berkeley and Los Angeles: University of California Press. 1959.

Lepofsky, D. S., H. Harries, and M. Kellum. "Early coconuts on Mo'orea Island, French Polynesia," Journal of the Polynesian Society 101 (1992): 229–308.

Levathes, Louise. When China Rules the Seas: The Treasure Fleet of the Dragon Throne 1405-1433. Simon and Schuster. New York. 1994.

Levey, Martin. The Medical Formulary of Aqrabadhin of Al-Kindi, Translated with a Study of its Materia Medica. Milwaukee: University of Wisconsin Press. 1966.

Levey, Martin. Early Arabic Pharmacology. Leiden: E. J. Brill. 1973.

Levey, Martin, and Noury Al-Khaledy. The Medical Formulary of Al-Samarqandi. Philadelphia: University of Pennsylvania Press. 1967.

Lewis, Albert B. "Tobacco in New Guinea," American Anthropologist 33 (1931): 134–38.

Lindemann, Hannes. Alone at Sea. Ed. J. Stuart. New York: Random House. 1957.

Ling Shun-shêng. "The Formosan sea-going raft and its origin in ancient China," Bulletin of the Institute of Ethnology, Academia Sinica. Taipei. 1 (1956): 25–54.

The Linga Purana. Ancient Indian Tradition and Mythology 5 (1). Delhi: Motilal Banarsidass. 1973.

Livingstone, Frank B. "On the origin of syphilis: an alternative hypothesis," Current Anthropology 32 (1991): 587–90.

Long, Austin, B. F. Benz, D. J. Donahue, A. J. T. Jull, and L. J. Toolin. "First direct AMS dates on early maize from Tehuacan, Mexico," Radiocarbon 31 (1989): 1035–40.

Lord, John Keast. The Naturalist in Vancouver Island and British Columbia, Vol. II. London: Richard Bentley. 1866.

Lovell, Nancy C. "Comment on Clark et al. 1987," Current Anthropology 28 (1 Feb. 1987): 53.

Lowie, Robert H. "Some problems of geographical distribution," Südseestudien: Gedenkschrift zur Erinnerung an Felix Speiser. Basel: Museum für Völkerkunde, und Schweizerischen Museum für Volkskunde. 1951. 11–26.

Lozoya, Xavier. "Plants of the soul," Arqueología mexicana 10:59 (2003): 89–91. (In Spanish as "Las plantas del alma," pp. 58–63.)

Luna Cavazos, Mario, Mejun Jiao, and Robert Bye. "Phenetic analysis of Datura section Datura (Solanaceae) in Mexico," Botanical Journal of the Linnean Society 133 (2000): 493–507.

Luna-Cavazos, Mario, Robert Bye, and Meijun Jiao. 2009 The origin of Datura metel (Solanaceae): genetic and phylogenetic evidence. Genetic Resources and Crop Evolution 56:2.

Lunde, Paul. "The Middle East and the Age of Discovery," Aramco World 43 (3 May–June, 1992). 2–64.

Lundell, Cyrus L. The Vegetation of Peten. Carnegie Institution, Publication 478. Washington. 1937.

Lundell, Cyrus L. "Plants probably utilized by the Old Empire Maya of Petén and adjacent lowlands," Papers of the Michigan Academy of Science, Arts, and Letters 24:I (1938). 37–56.

Mackenzie, Donald A. Myths of Pre-Columbian America. London: Gresham. 1924.

MacNeish, Richard S. The Origins of Agriculture and Settled Life. Norman: University of Oklahoma Press. 1992.

MacNeish, Richard S., and C. Earle Smith. "Antiquity of American polyploid cotton," Science 173 (1964): 675–6.

MacNeish, Richard S., Annette Nelken-Terner, and Irmgard W. Johnson. The Prehistory of the Tehuacan Valley, Vol. 2. Nonceramic Artifacts. Austin: University of Texas Press. 1967.

Mahieu, Jacques de. "Corpus des inscriptions runiques d'Amerique du Sud," Kadath: Chroniques des civilizations disparues 68 (1988): 11–42. (Brussels.)

Maimonides, Moses. Moses Maimonides on the Causes of Symptoms. Berkeley: University of California Press. 1974.

Mair, Victor H. "Canine conundrums: Eurasian dog ancestor myths in historical and ethnic perspective," Sino-Platonic Papers 87. Philadelphia: University of Pennsylvania Department of Asian and Middle Eastern Studies. 1998.

Mangelsdorf, Paul C., R. S. MacNeish, and G. R. Willey. "Origins of agriculture in Middle America," Handbook of Middle American Indians, Vol. 1: Natural Environment and Early Cultures. Ed. R. C. West. Austin: University of Texas Press 1964. 427–45.

Manter, H. W. "Some aspects of the geographical distribution of parasites," Journal of Parasitology 53 (1967): 1–9.

Marcus, Joyce. "The plant world of the sixteenth- and seventeenth-century Lowland Maya," Maya Subsistence: Studies in Memory of Dennis E. Puleston. Ed. Kent V. Flannery. New York: Academic Press. 1982. 239–73.

Markham, Clements R. A Memoir of the Lady Ana de Osorio, Countess of Chinchon and Vice-queen of Peru (A.D. 1629–39), with a Plea for the Correct Spelling of the Chinchona Genus. London: Trübner. 1874.

Márquez Morfín, Lourdes. "Paleoepidemiología en las poblaciones prehispánicas mesoamericanas," Arqueología Mexicana 5 (1997): 4–12.

Marszewski, Tomasz. "The age of maize cultivation in Asia; a review of hypotheses and new ethnographical, linguistic and historical data," Folia Orientalia 4 (1963): 243–95. (Krakow, Poland.)

Marszewski, Tomasz. "The age of maize cultivation in Asia (further investigations)," Folia Orientalia 10 (1968): 91–192. (Krakow, Poland.)

Marszewski, Tomasz. "The problem of the introduction of 'primitive' maize into Southeast Asia, Parts I and II," Folia Orientalia 16 (1975–1978): 237–60 and 19 (1975–1978): 128–63. (Krakow, Poland.)

Marszewski, Tomasz. "Badania nad dawnoxcia uprawy kukurydzy no polnocnowshodnich kresach indii," O Polskich Badaniach Etnograficznych uv Afryce, Ameryce i Aazji 33 (1987): 193–203. (Warsaw.)

Martí, Samuel. Mudra: manos simbólicas en Asia y América. México: Litexa. 1971.

Martínez Muriel, Alejandro Claudio. Don Martín, Chiapas: inferencias económico-sociales de una comunidad arqueológica. Unpublished thesis, Escuela Nacional de Antropología e Historia, and Universidad Nacional Autónoma de México (UNAM). 1978.

Matisoo-Smith, E., R. M. Roberts, G. J. Irwin, J. S. Allen, D. Penny, and D. M. Lambert. "Patterns of prehistoric human mobility in Polynesia indicated by mtDNA from the Pacific rat," Proceedings of the National Academy of Sciences of the USA 95 (Dec. 1998): 15145–151500.

Matisoo-Smith, E., and J. H. Robins. "Origins and dispersals of Pacific peoples: evidence from mtDNA phylogenies of the Pacific rat," Proceedings of the National Academy of Sciences of the USA 101 (June 15, 2004): 9167–9172.

Matsumura, Jinzo. Nippon Shokubutsumaii. Tokio: Z. P. Maruya and Co. 1884.

Mattingly, David. "Making the desert bloom: the Garamantian capital and its underground water system," Archaeology Odyssey 3 (2000): 31–37.

McBryde, Felix W. "Cultural and Historical Geography of Southwest Guatemala." Smithsonian Institution, Institute of Social Anthropology, Publication No. 4. 1945.

Medvedov, Daniel. "Anatomía maya: el lenguaje simbólico de la mano." Abstracts of Papers, Forty-fourth International Congress of Americanists (Manchester, 1982). Manchester, England: School of Geography, Manchester University. 1982. 207.

Meggers, Betty J. "Yes if by land, no if by sea: The double standard in interpreting cultural similarities," American Anthropologist 78 (1976): 637–39.

Meggers, Betty J., Clifford Evans, and Emilio Estrada. "Early Formative period of coastal Ecuador; the Valdivia and Machalilla phases," Smithsonian Contributions to Anthropology 1. Washington. 1965.

Mellén Blanco, Francisco. Manuscritos y documentos españoles para la historia de la isla de Pascua: La expedición del Capitán D. Felipe González de Haedo a la isla de David. Madrid: Biblioteca C.E.HOPU. 1986.

Méndez Pereira, Octavio. (ed. by E. W. Hesse). Balboa. New York: American Book Co. 1944.

Menzies, Gavin. 1434: The Year a Magnificent Chinese Fleet Sailed to Italy and Ignited the Renaissance, William Morrow, New York. 2008.

Menzies, Gavin. 1421: The Year China Discovered the World. Bantam Press, London. 2003.

Menzies, Gavin. The Lost Empire of Atlantis: History's Greatest Mystery Revealed. William Morrow, New York. 2011.

Merriam-Webster, Inc. Merriam-Webster's Collegiate Dictionary, 10th edition. Merriam-Webster - Merriam-Webster: 1993.

Merrill, Elmer D. "The botany of Cook's voyages and its unexpected significance in relation to anthropology," Chronica Botanica 14 (1954): 165–385.

Merrill, Elmer D. "American fruit trees on murals at Pompeii," Pre-Columbiana: A Journal of Long-distance Contacts 2:4 (1954): 324.

Merriwether, D.A., et al. "Gene flow and genetic variation in the Yanomama as revealed by mitochondrial DNA," America Past, America Present: Genes and Languages in the Americas and Beyond, Ed. Colin Renfrew. Cambridge: McDonald Institute for Archaeological Research, University of Cambridge. 2000. 89–124.

Meyerhof, M., and G. P. Sobhy, eds. The Abridged Version of 'The Book of Simple Drugs" by Ahmad Ibn Muhammad al-Gaafiqii, by Gregorius Abu'l-Farag (Barhebraeus). Cairo: Al-Ettemad. 1932 [Written before 1160].

Milewski, Tadeusz. "La comparaison des systèmes anthroponymiques aztèques et indo-européens," Onomastica 5:1 (1959): 119–75. (Krakow, Poland.)

Milewski, Tadeusz. "Similarities between the Asiatic and American Indian languages," International Journal of American Linguistics 26 (1960): 265–74.

Milewski, Tadeusz. Nowe poglady na geneze kultury srodkowoamerykanskiej. Krakow, Poland: Oriental Commission of the Polish Academy of Science. 1961.

Milewski, Tadeusz. "Pochodzenie ludnmosci Ameryki przedkolumbijskiej w odbiciu jezykowym," Etnografia Polska 10. 1966.

Millet, Nicholas B., Gerald D. Hart, Theodore A. Reyman, Michael R. Zimmerman, and Peter K. Lewin. "ROM I: mummification for the common people," Mummies, Disease and Ancient Cultures, 2nd edition. Eds. A. Cockburn, E. Cockburn, and T. A. Reyman. Cambridge: Cambridge University Press. 1998. 91–105.

Miranda, Faustino. La vegetación de Chiapas. Parte primera y parte segunda. Tuxtla Gutierrez, Chiapas, México: Departamento de Prensa y Turismo, Ediciones del Gobierno del Estado de Chiapas. 1952–1953.

Missouri Botanical Garden (MOBOT). w3TROPICOS Nomenclatural Data Base. www.mobot.org. 2003.

Miura, Tomoyuki, and 19 others. "Phylogenetic subtypes of human T-lymphotropic virus Type I and their relations to the anthropological background," Proceedings of the National Academy of Sciences of the United States of America 91:3 (1994): 1124–27.

MOBOT. 2003 (See Missouri Botanical Garden.)

Moran, Hugh A., and David H. Kelley. The Alphabet and the Ancient Calendar Signs, 2nd edition. Palo Alto, CA: Daily Press. 1969.

Moseley, Michael E. "Assessing the archaeological significance of mahamaes," American Antiquity 34 (1969): 485–87.

Mukerji, Dhirendra Nath. "A correlation of the Maya and Hindu calendars," Indian Culture 2:4 (1936): 685–92.

Munro, J. W. Pests of Stored Products. London: Hutchinson of London. 1966.

Murdock, George Peter. Africa: Its Peoples and Their Culture History. New York: McGraw-Hill. 1959.

Nadkarni, K. M., ed. Indian Plants and Drugs with Their Medical Properties and Uses. Madras: Norton & Co. (Reprinted 1998). 1914.

Naudou, Jean. "A propos d'un eventual emprunt de l'art Maya aux arts de l'Inde extérieure," Proceedings, 34th International Congress of Americanists (Vienna, 1960). 1960. 340–47. (Vienna.)

Nayar, N. M., and Rajendra Singh. "Taxonomy, distribution and ethnobotany," Cucurbits. Eds. N. M. Nayar and T. A. More. Enfield, New Hampshire: Science Publishers. 1998. 1–18.

Needham, Joseph, Wang Ling, and Lu Gwei-djen. Science and Civilisation in China, Vol. 4: Physics and Physical Technology, Part III: Civil Engineering and Nautics. Cambridge: Cambridge University Press. 1971.

Needham, Joseph, and Lu Gwei-Djen. Trans-Pacific Echoes and Resonances; Listening Once Again. Singapore and Philadelphia: World Scientific. 1985.

Neher, R. F. "The ethnobotany of Tagetes," Economic Botany 22 (1968): 317–25.

Nerlich, Andreas G., Franz Parsche, Irmgard Wiest, Peter Schramel, and Udo Löhrs. "Extensive pulmonary hemorrhage in an Egyptian mummy," Virchows Archiv 427:4 (1995): 423–29.

Newcomb, Robert M., ed. and comp. Plant and Animal Exchanges between the Old and the New Worlds. (Notes from a Seminar at UCLA Presented by Carl O. Sauer) Los Angeles: privately printed. 1963.

Newman, Marshall T. "Aboriginal New World epidemiology and medical care, and the impact of Old World disease imports," American Journal of Physical Anthropology 45 (1976): 667–72.

Nicolle, Charles. "Un argument médical en faveur de l'opinion de Paul Rivet sur l'origine océanienne de certaines tribus indiennes du Nouveau Monde," Journal de la société des américanistes de Paris 24 (1932): 225–29.

Nicolson, Dan H., C. R. Suresh, and K. S. Manilal. An Interpretation of Van Rheede's Hortus Malabaricus. Königstein, Germany: Koeltz Scientific Books. 1988.

Norton, Presley. "El señorio de Salangone y la liga de mercaderes: el cartel spondylus-balsa," Arqueología y etnohistoria del sur de Colombia y norte del Ecuador. Comps. José Alcina Franch and Segundo Moreno Yánez. Miscelanea Antropológica Ecuatoriana, Monográfico 6, y Boletín de los Museos del Banco Central del Ecuador 6. Cayambe, Ecuador: Ediciones Abya-Yala. 1987.

O'Brien, Patricia J. "The sweet potato: its origin and dispersal," American Anthropologist 74 (1972): 342–65.

O'Neale, Lila M., and Thomas W. Whitaker. "Embroideries of the Early Nazca Period and the crop plants depicted on them," Southwestern Journal of Anthropology 3 (1947): 294–321.

O'Neill, Ynez Violé. "Diseases of the Middle Ages," History and Geography of Human Disease. Ed. Kenneth F. Kiple. New York: Cambridge University Press. 1991. 270–87.

Oviedo y Valdés, Gonzalo Fernández de. Historia general y natural de las Indias, islas y tierra-firme del mar Océano. 4 vols. Madrid. 1851–1855.

Oxford English Dictionary (OED). 2nd edition. Oxford and New York: Clarendon Press, and Oxford University Press. 1989.

Pal, Mohinder, and T. N. Khoshoo. "Grain amaranths," Evolutionary Studies in World Crops: Diversity and Change in the Indian Subcontinent. Ed. Joseph Hutchinson. Cambridge: Cambridge University Press. 1974. 129–37.

Panagiotakopulu, Eva. Archaeology and Entomology in the Eastern Mediterranean. Research into the History of Insect Synanthropy in Greece and Egypt. Oxford, UK: BAR International Series 836. 2001.

Pandey, D. S. "Exotics – introduced and natural immigrants, weeds, cultivated, etc.," Flora of India. Introductory Volume (Part II). Eds. N. P. Singh et al. Calcutta: Botanical Survey of India. 2000. 266–301.

Parker, Heidi G., Abigail L. Shearin, and Elaine A. Ostrander. "Man's Best Friend Becomes Biology's Best in Show: Genome Analyses in the Domestic Dog." Annual Review of Genetics Vol. 44: 309-336 (Volume publication date December 2010). First published online as a Review in Advance on August 25, 2010. DOI: 10.1146/annurev-genet-102808-115200. http://www.ncbi.nlm.nih.gov/pmc/articles/PMC3322674/

Parkes, A. "Impact of prehistoric Polynesian colonization: pollen records for Central Polynesa." Abstract of paper, Seventeenth Pacific Science Congress, Honolulu (as cited by Ward and Brookfield 1992). 1991.

Parotta, John A. Healing Plants of Peninsular India. New York: CABI Publishing. 2001.

Parsche, Franz. "Reply to 'Responding to First identification of drugs in Egyptian mummies'." Naturwissenschaften 80 (1993): 245–46.

Parsche, Franz, Svetla Balabanova, and Wolfgang Pirsig. "Drugs in ancient populations," The Lancet 341 (Feb. 20, 1993): 503.

Parsche, Franz, and A. Nerlich. "Presence of drugs in different tissues of an Egyptian mummy," Fresenius' Journal of Analytical Chemistry 352 (1995): 380–84.

Patiño, Victor Manuel. Plantas cultivadas y animales domésticos en América equinoccial. Tomo II. Plantas alimenticias. Cali, Colombia: Imprenta Departamental. 1976.

Patterson, K. David. "Ascariasis," The Cambridge World History of Human Disease. Ed. Kenneth F. Kiple. Cambridge: Cambridge University Press. 1993a. 603-4.

Patterson, K. David. "Strongyloidiasis," The Cambridge World History of Human Disease. Ed. Kenneth F. Kiple. Cambridge: Cambridge University Press. 1993b. 1016.

Pedraza, Cristobal de. Onduras y Higueras Colección de Documentos Inéditos Relativos al Descubrimiento de Ultramar, Segunda Serie. La Real Academía de la Historia. Madrid: Establecimiento Tipografía. Series II, 11:1 (1898 [1541]): 385-409.

Peng Shifan. Xiushui faxian yuanshi shehui wanqi luohuasheng zhongzi. Nanchang, China: Wenwu gongzuo ziliao. 1961.

Pérez de Barradas, José. Orfebrería prehispánica de Colombia. Madrid: Talleres Gráfico "Jura." 1954.

Petersen, K. S., K. L. Rasmussen, J. Heinemeier, and N. Rud. "Clams before Columbus?," Nature 359 Oct. 22, 1992.): 679.

Pevny, Charlotte D. and Tom Jennings. "The Fiber of Their Being: Direct Dating Fiber Artifacts." Mammoth Trumpet. 27:1. January 2012. pp. 10-11, 20.

Pickersgill, Barbara. "Pineapple," Evolution of Crop Plants. Ed. W. Simmonds. London and New York: Longman. 1976. 14-18.

Pickersgill, Barbara, and Charles B. Heiser, Jr. "Origins and distribution of plants domesticated in the New World tropics," Origins of Agriculture. Ed. C. A. Reed. The Hague: Mouton. 1977. 803-35.

Pike, A. M. "The recovery of parasite eggs from ancient cesspit and latrine deposits: an approach to the study of early parasite infections," Diseases in Antiquity, Eds. D. Brothwell and A. T. Sandison. Springfield, Illinois: C. C. Thomas. 1967. 184-48.

Piña Chan, Román, and Luis Covarrubias. Los Olmeca. México: Folletos del Museo Nacional de Antropología. 1964.

Ping-ti Ho. "The introduction of American food plants into China," American Anthropologist 57 (1955):191–201.

Piperno, Dolores. "Non-affluent foragers, resource availability, seasonal shortages, and the emergence of agriculture in Panamanian tropical forests," Foraging and Farming: The Evolution of Plant Exploitation. Eds. D. Harris and G. Hillman. London: Unwin and Hyman. 1989. 538–54.

Piperno, Dolores R. "The origins and development of food production in Pacific Panama," Pacific Latin America in Prehistory: The Evoluition of Archaic and Formative Cultures. Ed. Michael Blake. Pullman, Washington: Washington State University Press. 1999. 123–34.

Plowman, Timothy. "The origin, evolution, and diffusion of coca, Erythroxylum spp., in South and Central America," Pre-Columbian Plant Migration. Ed. Doris Stone. Papers of the Harvard University, Peabody Museum of Archaeology and Ethnology 76 (1984): 125–63.

Pokharia, A.K., and K. S. Saraswat. "Plant economy during Kushana period (100–300 A.D.) at ancient Sanghol, Punjab," Pragdhara [Journal of the U(ttar) P(radesh) State Archaeology Department] 9 (1999):75–104.

Pollmer, Udo. "Chemische Nachweise von Suchtmitteln des Altertums," Tagungsberichte Robert Freiherr von Heine-Geldern, Tagung anlässlich des 30. Todestages 30 April–3 Mai 1998. Ed. Christine Pellech. (Acta Ethnologica et Linguistica, Nr. 72, Series Generalis 19, Symposia 1.) Vienna: Föhrenau. 2000. 235–52.

Polunin, Nicholas U. Introduction to Plant Geography and Some Related Sciences. New York: McGraw-Hill. 1960.

Pope, Willis T. Manual of Wayside Plants of Hawaii. Rutland, Vermont: Tuttle. 1968.

Potter, C. "The biology and distribution of Rhizopertha dominica (Fab.)," Transactions of the Royal Entomological Society of London 83:IV (1935): 449–78.

Powell, Mary Lucas. "Health and disease in the late prehistoric Southeast," Disease and Demography in the Americas. Eds. J. W. Verano and D. H. Ubelaker. Washington: Smithsonian Institution Press. 1992. 41–53.

Pullaiah, T. Medicinal Plants in India. 2 vols. New Delhi: Regency Publications. 2002.

Purseglove, John W. Tropical Crops: Dicotyledons. London: Longmans. 1968.

Quigley, Carroll. "Aboriginal fish poisons and the diffusion problem," American Anthropologist 58 (1956): 508–25.

Ramírez, Elisa. "Toloache or devil's herb," Arqueología mexicana 10:59 (2003): 88. (Spanish as "El toloache o yerba del Diablo," pp. 56–57.)

Rands, Robert L. "The water lily in Maya art: A complex of alleged Asiatic origin," Smithsonian Institution, Bureau of American Ethnology Bulletin 151, Anthropological Papers No. 34 (1953):77–153.

Rands, Robert L., and Carroll L. Riley. "Diffusion and discontinuous distribution," American Anthropologist 60 (1958): 274–97.

Reinhard, Karl J. "Cultural ecology of prehistoric parasitism on the Colorado Plateau as evidenced by coprology," American Journal of Physical Anthropology 77 (1988): 355–66.

Reinhard, Karl J. "Parasitology as an interpretive tool in archaeology," American Antiquity 57:2 (1992): 231–45.

Reko, Blas Pablo. "De los nombres botánicos aztecas," El México antiguo 1 (5 Dic., 1919): 113–57.

Rensch, Karl H. "Polynesian plant names, linguistic analysis and ethnobotany, expectations and limitations," Islands, Plants, and Polynesians: An Introduction to Polynesian Ethnobotany. Eds.

Paul Alan Cox and Sandra Anne Banack. Portland, OR: Dioscorides Press. 1991. 97–111.

Reyman, Theodore, A., Henrik Nielsen, Ingolf Thuesen, Derek N. H. Notman, Karl J. Reinhard, Edmund Tapp, and Tony Waldron. "New investigative techniques," Mummies, Disease and Ancient Cultures, 2nd edition. Eds. A. Cockburn, E. Cockburn, and T. A. Reyman. Cambridge: Cambridge University Press. 1980. 353–94.

Rheede tot Drakenstein, H. A. van. Hortus Malabaricus. 12 vols. Amsterdam. 1678–1703.

Riddle, J. M., and J. M. Vreeland. "Identification of insects associated with Peruvian mummy bundles by using scanning electron microscopy," Paleopathology Newsletter 39 (1982): 5–9.

Rieth, Adolf. Vorzeit gefälscht. Tübingen, Germany: Verlag Ernst Wasmuth. 1967. (Stuttgart.)

Riley, Carroll L., J. Charles Kelley, Campbell W. Pennington, and Robert L. Rands. "Conclusions," Man across the Sea: Problems of Pre-Columbian Contacts. Eds. C. L. Riley, J. C. Kelley, C. W. Pennington, and R. L. Rands. Austin: University of Texas Press. 1971. 445–58.

Robinson, Eugenia J., Marlen Garnica, Patricia Farrell, Dorothy Freidel, Kitty Emery, Marilyn Beaudry-Corbett, and David Lentz. "El Preclásico en Urías: una adaptación ambiental y cultural en el Valle de Antigua," XIII Simposio de Investigaciones Arqueológicas en Guatemala, 1999, Vol. II, 2 vols. Eds. Juan Pedro Laporte, Héctor L. Escobedo, Ana Claudia de Suasnávar, y Bárbara Arroyo. Guatemala: Museo Nacional de Arqueología y Etnología. 2000. 841–46.

Robinson, Stuart. A History of Dyed Textiles. London: Studio Vista. 1969.

Rochebrune, A. T. de. "Recherches d'ethnographie botanique sur la flore des sépultures péruviennes d'Ancon," Actes de la Société Linnéene de Bordeaux 33 (1879): 343–58.

Rohde, Douglas L. T. On the common ancestors of all living humans. (Dated Nov. 11, 2003; unpublished but posted on the author's website at M.I.T.) 2003.

Rose, Mark. "Origins of syphilis," Archaeology 50 (1 (1997): 24–5.

Roullier, Caroline, Laure Benoit, Doyle B. McKey, and Vincent Lebota. "Historical collections reveal patterns of diffusion of sweet potato in Oceania obscured by modern plant movements and recombination." PNAS January 22, 2013. http://www.pnas.org/content/early/2013/01/16/1211049110?cited-by=yes&legid=pnas;1211049110v1#cited-by.

Roxburgh, W. Hortus Bengalensis. Serampore, India. 1814.

Royal Botanic Gardens at Kew. "Cumulated Index Kewensis: Original 2 volumes plus supplements 1-16:" Microfiche version of cut-up set in Kew Library.

Royal Botanic Gardens at Kew. http://www.kew.org/plant-cultures/plants/ (a study of 25 plants)

Roys, Ralph L. "The Ethno-Botany of the Maya," Tulane University, Middle American Research Series, Publication No. 2. 1931.

Sachan, J. K. S., K. R. Sarkar, and M. M. Payak. "Studies on distribution of constitutive heterochromatin in relation to origin, evolution, and diffusion of maize," Advances in Cytogenetics and Crop Improvement. New Delhi: Kalyani Publishers. 1982. 41–8.

Sachan, J. K. S., and K. R. Sarkar. "Sikkim primitive maize – an overview," Indian Journal of Genetics and Plant Breeding (supplement) 46 (1986a): 153–66.

Sachan, J. K. S., and K. R. Sarkar. "Discovery of Sikkim primitive precursor in the Americas," Maize Genetics Cooperative Newsletter 60 (1986b): 104–6.

Safford, William E. "The useful plants of the island of Guam," Contributions from the U.S. National Herbarium, Vol. IX. Washington. 1905.

Safford, William E. "Food plants and textiles of ancient America," Proceedings, Nineteenth International Congress of Americanists (Washington, 1915). Washington. 1917. 12–30.

Salo, W. L., A. C. Aufderheide, J. Buikstra, and T. Holcomb. "Identification of *Mycobacterium tuberculosis* DNA in a pre-Columbian mummy," Proceedings of the National Academy of Sciences (USA) 91 (1994): 2091–4.

Sanchez Castro, Alejandro. Luís Nicolas Guillemaud, Interesante Historia de un Buen Francés que Vino a México en 1830: Los Mixes, Historia, Leyendas, Música. México. 1947.

Sandison, A. T. "Parasitic disease," Diseases in Antiquity. A Survey of the Diseases, Injuries and Surgery of Early Populations," Eds. An Compls. D. Brothwell and A. T. Sandison. Springfield, Illinois: C. C. Thomas. 1967. 178–83.

Sandison, A. T., and Edmund Tapp. "Disease in ancient Egypt," in "ROM I: Mummification for the common people," Mummies, Disease and Ancient Cultures, 2nd edition. Eds. Aidan Cockburn, Eve Cockburn, and Theodore A. Reyman. Cambridge: Cambridge University Press. 1998. 38–58.

Sapper, Karl. "Geographie der altindianischen Landwirtschaft," Petermanns Geographische Mitteilungen 80 (1934): 119.

Saraswat, K. S., N. K. Sharma and D. C. Saini. "Plant economy at ancient Narhan (ca. 1300 B.C–300/400 A.D)." Excavations at Narhan (1984–1989), Appendix IV, by Purushottam Singh, Varanasi: Department of Ancient Indian History, Culture and Archaeology, Banaras Hindu University. 1994. 225–337.

Sarkar, K. R., B. K. Mukherjee, D. Gupta, and H. K. Jain. "Maize," Evolutionary Studies in World Crops. Diversity and Change in the Indian Subcontinent, Ed. Joseph B. Hutchinson. London: Cambridge University Press. 1974. 121–27.

Sasuke, Nakao, and Jonathan D. Sauer. "Grain amaranths," Land and Crops of Nepal Himalaya: Scientific Results of the Japanese Expeditions to Nepal Himalaya, 1952–1953, Vol. II. Ed. H. Kihara. Kyoto: Kyoto University Fauna and Flora Research Society. 1956. 141–46.

Sauer, Carl O. Agricultural Origins and Dispersals. (Bowman Memorial Lectures). New York: American Geographical Society. 1952. (2nd edition. Cambridge: Massachusetts Institute of Technology Press. 1969.)

Sauer, Carl O. "Maize into Europe," Proceedings of the 34th International Congress of Americanists (Vienna, 1960). Horn-Vienna, Austria: Verlag Ferdinand Berger. 1962. 777–788.

Sauer, Carl O. Seeds, Spades, Hearths, and Herds: The Domestication of Animals and Foodstuffs, 2nd edition. Cambridge: The MIT Press. 1969.

Sauer, Jonathan D. "The grain amaranths: a survey of their history and classification," Annals of the Missouri Botanical Garden 37 (1950): 561–632.

Sauer, Jonathan D. "The grain amaranths and their relatives: a revised taxonomic and geographic survey," Annals of the Missouri Botanical Garden 54 (1967): 103–39.

Sauer, Jonathan D. "Identity of archaeological grain amaranths from the Valley of Tehuacán, Puebla, Mexico," American Antiquity 34 (1969): 80–81.

Sauer, Jonathan D. Historical Geography of Crop Plants: A Select Roster. Boca Raton, Florida: CRC Press. 1993.

Saunders, Shelley R., P. G. Ramsden, and D. A. Herring. "Transformation and disease; pre-contact Ontario Iroquoians," Disease and Demography in the Americas. Eds. J. W. Verano and D. H. Ubelaker. Washington: Smithsonian Institution Press. 1992. 117–25.

Scaglion, R., and K. A. Soto. "A prehistoric introduction of the sweet potato in New Guinea?," Migration and Transformations: Regional Perspectives on New Guinea. Eds. A. Strathern and G. Sturzenhofecker. Pittsburgh. ASAO Monograph 15. 1994. 257–94.

Schafer, E. H. Shore of Pearls. Berkeley and London: University of California Press. 1970.

Schoenhals, Louise C. A Spanish-English Glossary of Mexican Flora and Fauna. Mexico: Summer Institute of Linguistics. 1988.

Scholes, France V., and Dave Warren. "The Olmec region at Spanish conquest," Handbook of Middle American Indians, Vol. 3. Archaeology of Southern Mesoamerica, Part 2. Ed. G. R. Willey. Austin: University of Texas Press. 1965. 776–87

Schwabe, Calvin W. Veterinary Medicine and Human Health. Baltimore: Williams and Wilkins. 1964.

Schuhmacher, W. Wilfried, F. Seto, J. Villegas Seto, Juan R. Francisco. Pacific Rim: Austronesian and Papuan Linguistic History. Bibliothek der allgemeinen Sprachwissenschaft: Reihe 2, Einzeluntersuchungen und Darstellungen. Heidelberg: Carl Winter Universitätsverlag. 1992.

Schumann, Karl, and Karl Lauterback. Die Flora der deutschen Schutzegebiete in der Südsee. Leipzig: Borntraeger. 1901.

Schwerin, Karl H. Winds across the Atlantic. (Mesoamerican Studies 6). Carbondale: University of Southern Illinois. 1970.

Science News. "Polynesian tools tout ancient travels," Science News 149 (March 2, 1996.): 135.

Service, Robert F. "Rock chemistry traces ancient traders," Science 274:5295 (1996): 2012–13.

Shady Solís, Ruth. La Ciudad Sagrada de Caral–Supe en los Albores de la Civilización en el Perú. Lima: Fondo Editorial, Universidad Nacional Mayor de San Marcos. 1997.

Shady Solís, Ruth and Carlos Leyva. La Ciudad Sagrada De Caral-Supe: Los Origenes De La Civilizacion Andina Y La Formacion Del Estado Pristino En El Antiguo Peru. Instituto Nacional de Cultura, Proyecto Especial Arqueologico Caral-Supe: 2003.

Shady Solís, Ruth, Jonathan Haas, and Winifred Creamer. "Dating Caral, a preceramic site in the Supe Valley on the Central Coast of Peru," Science 292 (2001): 723–26.

Sharma, R. K., and Bhagwan Dash. The Caraka Samhita, Vol. 1. Varanasi, India: Chowkhamba Sanskrit Series Office. 1983.

Sharpe, William D. "Essay-Review," Transactions and Studies of the College of Physicians of Philadelphia, Ser. 5 (1983): 278–81.

Silow, R. A. "The problem of trans-Pacific migration involved in the origin of the cultivated cottons of the New World," Proceedings, Seventh Pacific Science Congress 5 (1949): 112–8.

Simmonds, Norman W. Bananas, 2nd edition. London: Longmans. 1966.

Simmonds, Norman W., ed. Evolution of Crop Plants. London: Longmans. 1976.

Simoons, Frederick J. Eat Not This Flesh: Food Avoidances in the Old World. Madison: University of Wisconsin Press. 1961.

Sinoto, Yosihiko H. "The Huahine excavation: discovery of an ancient Polynesian canoe," Archaeology 36 (1983): 10–15.

Sivarajan, V. V., and Philip Mathew. Flora of Nilambur (Western Ghats, Kerala). Dehra Dun, India: Bishen Singh Mahendra Pal Singh. 1984.

Skottsberg, Carl J. F. "The phanerogams of Easter Island," The Natural History of Juan Fernández and Easter Island, Volume 1. Uppsala, Sweden: Almquist and Wiksells. 1920.

Skottsberg, Carl J. F. "Le peuplement des îles pacifiques du Chili," Journal de la société de biogeographie 4 (1934): 271–80.

Skvortsov, B. V. "On some varieties of peanuts grown in China," Journal of the North China Branch, Royal Asiatic Society 51 (1920): 142–5.

Smartt, J. "Evolution of American Phaseolus beans under domestication," The Domestication and Exploitation of Plants and Animals. Eds. P. J. Ucko and G. W. Dimbleby. Chicago: Aldine. 1969. 451–62.

Smith, G. Elliot. Elephants and Ethnologists: Asiatic Origins of the Maya Ruins. London: Kegan Paul, Trench, Trubner; and New York: Dutton. 1924.

Smole, William J. "Musa cultivation in pre-Columbian South America," Historical Geography of Latin America. Eds. W. V. Davidson and

J. J. Parsons. (Special issue of Geoscience and Man, Vol. 21.) 1980. 47–50.

Smole, William J. "Plantain (Musa) cultivation in pre-Columbian America: an overview of the circumstantial evidence," Pre-Columbiana: A Journal of Long-Distance Contacts 2:4 (2002): 269–96.

Soper, Fred L. "The report of a nearly pure 'Ancylostoma duodenale' infestation in native South American Indians and a discussion of its ethnological significance," American Journal of Hygiene 7 (1927): 174–84

Sopher, David E. Turmeric in the Color Symbolism of Southern Asia and the Pacific Islands. Unpublished M.A. thesis, University of California, Berkeley. 1950.

Sorenson, John L. "The significance of an apparent relationship between the ancient Near East and Mesoamerica," Man Across the Sea: Problems of Pre-Columbian Contacts. Eds. Carroll L. Riley et al. Austin: University of Texas Press. 1971. 219–41.

Sorenson, John L. and Carl L. Johannessen. "Biological Evidence for Pre-Columbian Transoceanic Voyages." In Contact and Exchanges in the Ancient World. ed. Victor H. Mair. University of Hawaii Press, Honolulu. pp. 238 – 297. 2006

Sorenson, John L., and Martin H. Raish. Pre-Columbian Contact with the Americas across the Oceans: An Annotated Bibliography, 2nd edition, revised. 2 vols. Provo, UT: Research Press. 1996.

Spinden, Herbert J. "Origin of civilizations in Central America and Mexico," The American Aborigines. Ed. D. Jenness. Toronto: University of Toronto Press. 1933. 217–46.

Spjeldnaes, Nils, and Kari E. Hinningsmoen. "*Littorina littorea*: an indicator of Norse settlement in North America," Science 141 (1938):275–6.

Spores, Ronald. "The Zapotec and Mixtec at Spanish contact," Handbook of Middle American Indians, Vol. 3, Archaeology of Southern Mesoamerica, Part 2. Eds. R. Wauchope and G. R. Willey. Austin: University of Texas Press. 1965. 962–87.

Spriggs, Matthew. "Early coconut remains from the South Pacific," Journal of the Polynesian Society 93 (1984): 71–76.

Sreekumar, P.V., D. B. Singh, and T. V. R. S. Sharma. "Occurrence of Annona glabra L.–a wild relative of custard apple in the Andaman Islands, India," Malayan Nature Journal 50 (2 (1996): 81–3.

Standley, Paul C. Trees and Shrubs of Mexico. Contribution from the United States National Herbarium 23. Washington, DC: Smithsonian Institution. 1920 – 1926.

Standley, Paul C. Flora of Yucatan. Field Museum of Natural History, Botanical Series, No. 279. Chicago, IL:Field Museum of Natural History. 3:3. September 11, 1930.

Standley, Paul C. Flora of the Lancetilla Valley Honduras. Field Museum of Natural History, Botanical Series, No. 283. Chhicago, IL:Field Museum of Natural History. 10. January 15, 1931.

Standley, Paul C., and Salvador Calderón. Lista Preliminar de las Plantas de El Salvador. San Salvador: Tipografía La Unión, Dutriz Hermanos. 1925.

Steffan, J. R. "L'Entomofaune de la momie de Ramsès II," Annales de la Société entomologique de France 18 (1982): 531–4.

Steffan, J. R. "L'Entomofaune de la momie," La Momie de Ramsés II. Contribution scientifique a l'Egyptologie. Eds. L. Balout and C. Roubet. Paris: Editions Recherches sur les Civilisations, Muséum National d'Histoire Naturelle & Musée de l'Homme. 1985. 108–15.

Steffy, J. Richard. "The Kyrenia ship: an interim report on its hull construction," American Journal of Archaeology 89 (1 January 1985): 71–101.

Steffy, J. Richard. Wooden Ship Building and the Interpretation of Shipwrecks. College Station, Texas: Texas A&M University Press. 1994.

Steffy, J. Richard. E-mail to John L. Sorenson. Subject: "Agave." 18 April 2001.

Stephens, S. G. "The cytogenetics of Gossypium and the problem of the origin of New World cottons," Advances in Genetics 1 (1947): 431–32.

Stephens, S. G. "Polynesian cottons," Annals of the Missouri Botanical Garden 50 (1963): 1–22.

Stephens, S. G. "Some problems of interpreting transoceanic dispersal of the New World cottons," Man Across the Sea: Problems of Pre-Columbian Contacts. Eds. Carroll L. Riley et al. Austin: University of Texas Press. 1971. 401–15.

Steward, Julian H. "South American cultures: an interpretive summary," Handbook of South American Indians, Vol. 5, The Comparative Ethnology of South American Indians. Ed. J. H. Steward. Smithsonian Institution, Bureau of American Ethnology Bulletin 143. 1949. 669–772.

Stewart, T. D. The People of America. New York: Scribner. 1973.

Stodder, Ann L. W., and Debra L. Martin. "Health and disease in the Southwest before and after Spanish contact," Disease and Demography in the Americas. Eds. John W. Verano and Douglas H. Ubelaker. Washington: Smithsonian Institution Press. 1991. 55–73.

Stonor, C. R., and Edgar Anderson. "Maize among the hill peoples of Assam," Annals of the Missouri Botanical Garden 36 (1949): 355–404.

Storey, Alice A. et al. " Radiocarbon and DNA evidence for a pre-Columbian introduction of Polynesian chickens to Chile." Proceedings of the National Academy of Science, United States of America. 104: 25 (2007). 10335 - 10339.

Stresemann, Erwin. "Die 'vor-columbischen' Truthähne in Schleswig," Ornithologische Monatsberichte No. 5 (1940): 154–9. (Berlin.)

Stutz, Bruce. "Megadeath in Mexico," Discover February 2006: 44–51.

Stutz, Bruce. "Megadeath in Mexico", Discover Magazine online publication. http://discovermagazine.com/2006/feb/megadeath-in-mexico/.

Suto, T., and Y. Yoshida. "Characteristics of the oriental maize," Land and Crops of Nepal Himalaya: Scientific Results of the Japanese Expeditions to Nepal Himalaya 1952–1953 Vol. 2. Ed. H. Kihara. Kyoto: Kyoto University Fauna and Flora Research Society. 1956. 375–430.

Symon, David E., and L. A. R. Haegi. "Datura (Solanaceae) is a New World genus," Solonaceae III. Taxonomy, Chemistry, Evolution. Eds. J. G. Hawkes, R. N. Lester, M. Nee, and N. Estrada. Richmond, Surrey, Eng.: Royal Botanic Gardens Kew, for the Linnean Society of London. 1991. 197–210.

Tagare, G. V., trans. The Bhagavata Purana. Ancient Indian Tradition and Mythology Series, 20 (4). Delhi: Motilal Banarsidass. 1976.

Tagare, G. V., trans. The Kurma Purana. Ancient Indian Tradition and Mythology Series, 20–21. Delhi: Motilal Banarsidass. 1982.

Tagare, G. V., trans. The Brahmanda Purana. Ancient Indian Tradition and Mythology Series 22 (1). Delhi: Motilal Banarsidass. 1983.

Teeter, Wendy G. "Animal utilization in a growing city, vertebrate exploitation at Caracol. Belize." Maya zooarchaeology: new directions in method and theory. Monograph 51. Ed. Kitty F. Emery, Los Angeles, Cotsen Institute of Archaeology, University of California, Los Angeles. 2004.

Tessman, Günter. Die Indianer Nordost-Perus. Hamburg. 1920.

Tessman, Günter. Menschen ohne Gott. Ein Besuch bei den Indianern des Ucayali. Stuttgart. 1928.

Tewari, Shitala P. Contributions of Sanskrit Inscriptions to Lexicography. Delhi: Agam Kala Prakashan. 1987.

Thapa, J. K. "Primitive maize with the Lepchas," Bulletin of Tibetology 3 Gangtok, India: Namgyal Institute of Tibetology. (1966): 29–31.

Thompson, Gunnar. Nu Sun: Asian-American Voyages 500 B.C. Pioneer Publishing Co. Fresno, CA. 1989.

Thompson, Gunnar. Secret Voyages to the New World: Nine True Adventures from the Forbidden Chronicles of American Discovery. Misty Isles Press: Seattle, WA. 2006.

Thompson, J. E. S. Maya History and Religion. Norman: University of Oklahoma Press. 1970.

Thompson, R. Campbell. A Dictionary of Assyrian Botany. London: The British Academy. 1949.

Thorarinsson, Sigurdur. "Winlandsproblemet; Några reflexioner med anledning av V. Tanners skrift," Ymer 62 (1942): 39–46.

Tisseuil, J. "Le syphilis vénerienne n'est pas d'origine américaine," Bulletin de la société de pathologie exotique 67 (1974): 40–4.

Tolstoy, Paul. "Cultural parallels between Southeast Asia and Mesoamerica in the manufacture of bark cloth," Transactions of the New York Academy of Sciences 25 (1963): 646–62.

Tolstoy, Paul. "Method in long-range comparison," Proceedings, Thirty-sixth International Congress of Americanists (Barcelona and Seville, 1964), I (1966), 69–89. (Barcelona.)

Tolstoy, Paul. "Transoceanic diffusion and nuclear Mesoamerica," Prehispanic America. Ed. S. Gorenstein. New York: St. Martin's. 1974. 124–44.

Torkelson, Anthony R. Common Names A-L. Vol. I, The Cross Name Index to Medicinal Plants. Boca Raton, Florida: CRC Press. 1999.

Torkelson, Anthony R. Common Names M-Z. Vol. II, The Cross Name Index to Medicinal Plants. Boca Raton, Florida: CRC Press. 1999.

Torkelson, Anthony R. Scientific Names A-Z. Vol. III, The Cross Name Index to Medicinal Plants. Boca Raton, Florida: CRC Press. 1999.

Torkelson, Anthony R. Plants in Indian Medicine A-Z. Vol. IV, The Cross Name Index to Medicinal Plants. Boca Raton, Florida: CRC Press. 1999.

Towle, Margaret A. "The pre-Columbian occurrence of Lagenaria seeds in coastal Peru," Harvard University Botanical Museum Leaflets 15:6 (1952): 171–84.

Towle, Margaret A. "The ethnobotany of pre-Columbian Peru," Viking Fund Publications in Anthropology 30. New York: Wenner-Gren Foundation for Anthropological Research. 1961.

Townsend, Charles H. T. "Ancient voyages to America," Brazilian American 12 (4 July 1925): five unnumbered pp.

Toxopeus, H. J. "On the origin of kapok, Ceiba pentandra," Mededelingen van het Algemeen Proefstation voor den Landbouw (Buitenzorg) 56 (1948): 1–19.

Tozzer, Alfred M., ed. and trans.. "Landa's Relacion de las cosas de Yucatan: A Translation." Harvard University, Peabody Museum of American Archaeology and Ethnology, Papers, Vol. 18. 1941 [ca. 1566]

Turner, Christy G., II. "Teeth, needles, dogs, and Siberia: bioarchaeological evidence for the colonization of the New World," Memoirs of the California Academy of Sciences 27 (2002): 123–58.

Tylor, Edward B. "On American lot-games as evidence of Asiatic intercourse before the time of Columbus," Internationales Archiv für Ethnographie 9:supplement (1896): 55–67.

Ugent, D., S. Pozorski, and T. Pozorski. "Archaeological manioc (Manihot) from coastal Peru," Economic Botany 40 (1986): 78–102.

University of Melbourne, Department of Botany. Multilingual Multiscript Plant Name Database (MMPND) at http://www.plantnames.unimelb.edu.au/Sorting/

Van Blerkom, Linda Miller. The Evolution of Human Infectious Disease in the Eastern and Western Hemispheres. Unpublished Ph.D. dissertation, University of Colorado at Boulder.

Vancouver, George. 1798. A Voyage of Discovery to the North Pacific Ocean and Round the World. 2 vols. London: Robinson and Edwards. 1985.

Varshavsky, S. R. "Appearance of American turkeys in Europe before Columbus," New World Antiquity 8:8 (1961): 104–5.

Various. Ayurvedic Medicinal Plants. http://ayurvedicmedicinalplants.com/index.php?option=com_zoom&Itemid=26 (web-based database of Ayurvedic Medicinal Plants with their names and uses)

Verano, John W. "Prehistoric disease and demography in the Andes," Disease and Demography in the Americas, Eds. John W. Verano and Douglas H. Ubelaker. Washington: Smithsonian Institution Press. 1991. 15–24.

Verano, John W. "Disease in South American mummies," in Mummies, Disease and Ancient Cultures, 2nd edition. Eds. A. Cockburn, E. Cockburn, and T. A. Reyman. Cambridge: Cambridge University Press. 1998. 215–34.

Verano, John W. and Douglas H. Ubelaker. Disease and Demography in the Americas. Washington, DC: Smithsonian Institution Press. 1992.

Villacorta Cifuentes, Jorge Luis. Historia de la Medicina, Cirugía y Obstetricia Prehispánicas. Guatemala: The author. 1976.

Vishnu-Mittre. "[The beginnings of agriculture:] Palaeobotanical evidence in India," Evolutionary Studies in World Crops: Diversity and Change in the Indian Subcontinent. Ed. Joseph B. Hutchinson. London: Cambridge University Press. 1974. 3–30.

Vishnu-Mittre, Aruna Sharma, and Chanchala [sic.] "Ancient plant economy at Daimabad," Daimabad 1976–79, Appendix II, Ed. S. A. Dali. Calcutta: Government of India Central Publication Branch. Memoirs of the Archaeological Survey of India 83. 1986. 588–627.

Von den Steinen, K. "Marquesanische Knotenshnüre," Correspondenz-Blatt, Deutschen Gesellschaft für Anthropologie 34 (1903): 108–14.

Von Hagen, Victor Wolfgang. The Aztec and Maya Papermakers. New York: J. J. Augustin. 1944.

Walker, Egbert H. Flora of Okinawa and the Southern Ryukyu Islands. Washington: Smithsonian Institution Press. 1976.

Ward, R. Gerard, and Muriel Brookfield. "The dispersal of the coconut: did it float or was it carried to Panama?," Journal of Biogeography 19 (5 September 1992): 467–80.

Wasson, R. Gordon. "Soma brought up-to-date," Journal of the American Oriental Society 99 (1 January–March 1979): 100–5.

Wasson, R. Gordon. Wondrous Mushrooms. Mycolatry in Mesoamerica. New York: McGraw-Hill. 1980.

Wasson, Valentina Pavlovna, and R. Gordon Wasson. Russia, Mushrooms and History. 2 vols. New York: Pantheon Books. 1957.

Watson, John Forbes. Index to the Native and Scientific Names of Indian and other Eastern Economic Plants and Products. London: India Museum. 1868.

Watson, William. "Early cereal cultivation in China," The Domestication and Exploitation of Plants and Animals. Eds. P. J. Ucko and G. W. Dimbleby. Chicago: Aldine. 1969. 397–402.

Watt, George. A Dictionary of the Economic Products of India. 6 vols. Calcutta: Superintendent of Government Printing, India. 1888–1893.

Watt, Sir G. The Wild and Cultivated Cotton Plants of the World. Longmans, Green, and Co., London. 1907.

The Wealth of India. "Maize in India," The Wealth of India. A Dictionary of Indian Raw Materials and Industrial Products, Vol. XI. New Delhi: Council of Scientific and Industrial Research. 1974. 25–83.

Weiss, Pedro. "Paleopatología americana," Boletín de Lima 33 (1984): 17–52.

Wells, Samuel A. "American drugs in Egyptian mummies: a review of the evidence." http://www.colostate.edu/Depts/Ent...urses/en570/papers_2000/wells.html. 2000.

Wendel, Jonathan F. "New World tetraploid cottons contain Old World cytoplasm," National Academy of Sciences USA, Proceedings 86 (1989): 4132–36.

Wendel, Jonathan F. "Cotton. Gossypium (Malvaceae)," Evolution of Crop Plants, 2nd edition. Eds. J. Smart and N. W. Simmonds. New York: Wiley. 1995. 358–66.

Wendel, Jonathan F., Andrew Schnabel, and T. Seelanan. "An unusual ribosomal DNA sequence from *Gossypium gossypioides* reveals ancient, cryptic, intergenomic introgression," Molecular Phylogenetics and Evolution 4 (1995): 298–313.

Whalen, M. D., D. E. Costich, and C. B. Heiser. "Taxonomy of Solanum section Lasiocarpa," Gentes Herbarum 12 (1981): 41–129.

Whistler, W. Arthur. "The other Polynesian gourd," Pacific Science 44 (1990): 115–22.

Whistler, W. Arthur. "Polynesian plant introductions," Islands, Plants, and Polynesians: An Introduction to Polynesian Ethnobotany. Eds. Paul Alan Cox and Sandra Anne Banack. Portland, Oregon: Dioscorides Press. 1991. 41–66.

Whitaker, Thomas W., and Julius B. Bird. "The identification and significance of the cucurbit materials from Huaca Prieta, Peru," American Museum of Natural History Novitates, No. 1426. 1949.

Whitaker, Thomas W., and George F. Carter. "Oceanic drift of gourds: experimental observations," American Journal of Botany 41 (1954): 697–700.

White, Richard E. "Lasioderma haemorrhoidale (Ill.) now established in California, with biological data on Lasioderma species (Coleoptera: Anobiidae)," The Coleopterists Bulletin 44:3 (1990): 344–48.

Whitley, Glenn R. "The fulvous tree duck as a cultural tracer," Anthropological Journal of Canada 12:1 (1974a): 10–7.

Whitley, Glenn R. "Tame curassow birds as indicators of cultural diffusion," Anthropological Journal of Canada 12:2 (1974b): 10–5.

Wichmann, Søren. The Relationships among the Mixe-Zoquean Languages of Mexico. Salt Lake City: University of Utah Press. 1995.

Wiener, Leo. Africa and the Discovery of America, 3 vols. Philadelphia and New York: Innes and Sons. 1920–1922.

Wiener, Leo. "The philological history of 'tobacco' in America," Proceedings, Twenty-first International Congress of Americanists (Gotenburg, Sweden, 1924), Part 2. 1924: 305–14. (Stockholm.)

Wiercinski, Andrzej. "Inter- and intrapopulational racial differentiation of Tlatilco, Cerro de las Mesas, Teotihuacan, Monte Alban and Yucatan Maya," Actas, Documetos y Memorias, 36a Congreso International de Americanistas, Lima, 1970, Vol. 1. Lima: Instituto de Estudios Peruanos. 1972. 231–248.

Wiercinski, Andrzej. "Afinidades raciales de algunas poblaciones antiguas de Mexico," Anales, Instituto Nacional de Anthropología e Historia, 1972–1973. México. 1975: 123-144.

Wilcox, Charlotte. Mummies, Bones, and Body Parts. Minneapolis, Charlrhoda Books. 2000.

Wilkinson, I. G. The Manners and Customs of the Ancient Egyptians. 3 vols. New York: Scribner and Welford. 1879.

Willcox, R. R. "The treponemal evolution," Transactions, St. John's Dermatological Society 58 (1972): 21–37.

Willey, Gordon R. An Introduction to American Archaeology, Volume 2. Englewood Cliffs, New Jersey: Prentice-Hall. 1971.

Willey, Gordon R. "Some continuing problems in New World culture history," American Antiquity 50 (1985): 351–63.

Witenberg, G. "Human parasites in archaeological finding" [sic], Bulletin, Israel Exploration Society 25 (1961): 86.

Wittmack, Ludwig. "Die Nutzpflanzen der alten Peruaner," Proceedings, Seventh International Congress of Americanists (Berlin 1888), 1888: 325–48.

Woodbury, Angus M. "Notes on the Human Ecology of Glen Canyon," University of Utah, Anthropological Papers, Department of Anthropology, No. 74. Glen Canyon Series No. 26. 1965.

Wulff, E. V. An Introduction to Historical Plant Geography. Waltham, Massachusetts: Chronica Botanica. 1943.

Wulff, Hans E. The Traditional Crafts of Persia: Their Development, Technology, and Influence on Eastern and Western Civilizations. Cambridge: M.I.T. Press. 1966.

Xu, H. Mike. Origin of the Olmec Civilization. Edmond, Oklahoma: University of Central Oklahoma Press. 1996.

Xu, H. Mike. "New evidence for pre-Columbian transpacific contact between China and Mesoamerica," Journal of the Washington Academy of Sciences 88 (1 March, 2002.): 1–11.

Yacovleff E., and F. L. Herrera. "El mundo vegetal de los antiguos peruanos," Revista del Museo Nacional 3 (1934–1935): 243–322.

Yarnell, Richard A. "Palaeo-ethnobotany in America," Science and Archaeology: A Survey of Progress and Research, revised and enlarged edition. Eds. D. Brothwell and E. Higgs. New York: Praeger. 1970. 215–27.

Yen, Douglas E. "Sweet-potato variation and its relation to human migration in the Pacific," Plants and the Migrations of Pacific Peoples, A Symposium Held at the Tenth Pacific Sciences Congress (Honolulu, 1961). Ed. J. Barrau. Honolulu: B. P. Bishop Museum Press. 1963. 93–117.

Yen, Douglas E. The Sweet Potato and Oceania: An Essay in Ethnobotany." Bishop Museum Bulletin 236. Honolulu: B. P. Bishop Museum Press. 1974.

Yen, Douglas E. "Subsistence to commerce in Pacific agriculture: some four thousand years of plant exchange," Plants for Food and Medicine: Proceedings of the Joint Conference of the Society for Economic Botany and the International Society for Ethnopharmacology, London 1-6, July 1996. Eds. H. D. V. Prendergast, N. L. Etkin, D. R. Harris, and P. J. Houghton. Kew, England: Royal Botanic Gardens. 1998. 161–83.

Zamora, Tomás, Vladimir Zaninovic, Masaharu Kajiwara, Haruko Komoda, Masanori Hayami, and Kazuo Tajima. "Antibody to HTLV-1 in indigenous inhabitants of the Andes and Amazon regions in Colombia," Japanese Journal of Cancer Research 8:8 (1990): 7; 15–9.

Zeven, A. C., and J. M. J. de Wet. Dictionary of Cultivated Plants and Their Regions of Diversity, Excluding most Ornamentals, Forest Trees and Lower Plants. Wageningin, The Netherlands: PUDOC, Centre for Agricultural Publishing and Documentation. 1982.

Zinsser, Hans. Rats, Lice, and History. New York: Bantam Books. 1960.

Zhejiang sheng wenwu guanlin weiyuanhui. "Wuxing qianshanyang yizhi ti 1, 2 ci fajue baogao," Kaogu Xuebao 1960:2 (1960): 73–91.

Zohary, Daniel. "The mode of domestication of the founder crops of Southwest Asian agriculture," The Origins and Spread of Agriculture and Pastoralism in Eurasia. Ed. David R. Harris. Washington: Smithsonian Institution Press. 1996. 142–58.

Zohary, Daniel, and Maria Hopf. Domestication of Plants in the Old World: The Origin and Spread of Cultivated Plants in West Asia, Europe, and the Nile Valley, 2nd edition. Oxford: Clarendon Press, and Oxford University Press. 1993.

Index

A

Achiote 112, 113
Ackerknecht, Erwin H. 58, 279, 280
Acorus calamus 81
Adauto de Araújo, J. G. 261
Adenostemma viscosum 81
Agave
    Agave americana 83
    Agave Americana 318
    Agave angustifolia 84, 318
    Agave cantala 84, 318
    Agave spp. 82
Ageratum conyzoides 84, 318
Ageratum houstonianum 85
Ageratum philoxeroides 318
Aguilar, Manuel 87
Ainsworth, Geoffrey C. 290
Aiyer, A. K. Yegna Narayan 16, 38, 123, 137, 170, 180, 184, 192, 211, 227, 242, 321, 322, 325, 333, 334
Ajello, Libero 61, 290
Alchon, Suzanne Austin 53, 54, 56, 57, 58, 59, 60, 263, 264, 265, 267, 268, 271, 275, 277, 278, 280, 281
Alexander, John 147
Alfieri, Anastase 295, 302
Alland, Alexander, Jr. 63, 294
Allison, Gerszten, et al. 56, 272
Allison, Marvin J. 273, 281
Allison, Mendoza, et al. 5, 56, 260
Allison, Pezzia, et al. 284
Alphitobius diaperinus 65, 294, 308
Alsar, Vital 9
Alternanthera
    Alternanthera philoxeroides 85
    Alternanthera pungens 86
    Alternanthera sessilis 86
    Alternanthera tonella 86
Álvarez and Ocaña 300, 302, 305, 306
Álvarez, Ticul 299, 305, 306
Amanita muscaria 87, 144
Amaranth
    Amaranthus caudatus 11, 88, 92, 318, 331
    Amaranthus cruentus 92
    Amaranthus hypochondriacus 11, 93

Amaranthus spinosus 12, 89, 95, 318
Anacardium occidentale 26, 95, 319, 330
Ananas comosus 26, 39, 97, 98, 99, 109, 194, 319, 330, 342
Ancylostoma duodenale 4, 5, 52, 260, 261, 265, 273
Anderson and Brown 13, 107, 259
Anderson, Edgar 13, 18, 91, 252, 259
Anderson, T. 288
Annatto 112
Annona
   Annona cherimolia 100
   Annona glabra 100, 101
   Annona reticulata 27, 99, 101, 102, 104, 319, 333
   Annona squamosa 12, 26, 27, 102, 319, 331, 332, 343
Anthony, Irvin 8
Arachis hypogaea 9, 12, 13, 104, 105, 319, 332
Araújo, Adauto 5, 261
Argemone mexicana 27, 108, 146, 319, 332, 333
Arias, and Rieseberg 171
Aristida subspicata 109
Arnold, Dean 175, 176
Artemisia vulgaris 27, 109, 110
Ascaris lumbricoides 52, 262
Asclepias curassavica 28, 111, 320
Ashraf, Jaweed 17, 204, 334
Aster divaricates 111

B

Bailey, Liberty Hyde 30, 46, 100, 101, 102, 118, 128, 131, 136, 140, 145, 151, 154, 172, 189, 192, 194, 213, 215, 222, 225, 226, 228, 240
Baker, Herbert G. 16, 149, 178
Bakhuizen van den Brink, H. C. 45, 123, 124, 223
Balabanova, Parsche, and Pirsig 17, 117, 153, 206, 332
Balabanova, Rösing, et al. 17
Balabanova, Svetla 207
Balabanova, Wei, and Krämer 206, 207
Balfour, Edward G. 19, 26, 28, 39, 41, 44, 46, 49, 83, 84, 85, 89, 95, 97, 100, 101, 108, 109, 112, 116, 150, 171, 193, 196, 197, 204, 219, 221, 223, 225, 226, 228, 239, 241, 247, 250, 318, 319, 320, 322, 323, 325, 326
Balisier 172
Balser, Carlos 298
Banana 180, 199, 202
Banerji, Sures Chandra 28, 41
Barthel, Thomas S. 16, 76, 88, 180
Barton, Humphrey 8
Bayard, D. T. 106

Beaudry-Corbett, M. and S. McCafferty 168
Bednarik, Robert J. 8
Ben Shemesh, A. 19
Berry, Edward W. 198, 199, 201
Bertoni, M. S. 98, 99
Bird, Junius B. 35, 140, 156, 218
Bixa orellana 28, 112, 113, 244, 320
Black, Michael 13, 107, 272
Blanchard, Raphael A. E. 292
Blumler, Mark A. 6
Bogdan, Georgie Ann, and David S. Weaver 288
Bökönyi, Sándor, and Dénes Jánossy 70, 304
Borah, Woodrow W. 40
Borden, Charles A. 8
Bordetella pertussis 52, 262
Borg, Jim 9
Borrelia recurrentis 53, 58, 263, 274, 278
Bradburn, Anne S. 89
Brand, Donald D. 15, 177, 178
Bretschneider, Emil.11, 12, 16, 30, 32, 39, 44, 46, 49, 89, 91, 92, 95, 96, 103, 104, 106, 108,
   110, 114, 116, 122, 125, 126, 131, 135, 138, 139, 150, 180, 185, 187, 195, 196, 213, 216,
   219, 220, 225, 239, 241, 242, 247, 248, 250, 259
Bronson, Bennet 15, 29, 33, 116, 118, 124, 135, 177, 191
Brown, Forest B. H.28, 29, 33, 44, 45, 46, 47, 84, 85, 97, 98, 109, 111, 116, 121, 122, 124,
   139, 163, 164, 180, 192, 220, 222, 226, 228, 229, 238, 243
Bruce-Chwatt, L. J. 58, 127, 277, 279
Brücher, Heinz 11, 15, 29, 32, 33, 36, 37, 40, 42, 44, 89, 96, 100, 101, 103, 116, 118, 121,
   125, 127, 133, 135, 137, 138, 140, 150, 155, 166, 171, 177, 182, 183, 184, 185, 186, 187,
   195, 196, 206, 214, 215, 217, 221, 222, 243
Bruman, Henry J. 128, 129, 202
Bucaille, Maurice 16, 205
Buckland, P. C., and E. Panagiotakopulu 17, 71, 294, 308
Buikstra, Jane E. 56, 272
Bullen, Adelaide K. 288
Burkill, Isaac H. 34, 39, 143, 146, 147, 149, 164, 170, 194, 195, 197, 207, 225, 229, 251
Bushnell, Geoffrey H. S. 9, 43
Bussagli, Mario, and Calembus Sivartamamurti 27, 103, 337
Bustamente, Miguel E. 266

C

Cabieses, Fernando 58, 277, 279
Cajanus cajan 113
Camp, W. H. 36, 181
Campbell, Joseph 66, 295
Canals Frau, Salvador 148

Canavalia sp. 113, 114, 115, 217
Canis familiaris 65, 66, 285, 295
Canna edulis 115, 116, 320
Cannabis sativa 17, 18, 65, 117, 146
Capsicum
   Capsicum annuum 28, 118, 119, 121, 320, 331, 333
   Capsicum frutescens 28, 119, 120, 121, 320, 331
   Capsicum spp. 28, 118, 120
Carica papaya 28, 121, 122, 321
Carter, George F. 35, 36, 67, 83, 93, 106, 123, 173, 181, 182, 183, 243, 300
Carter, W. E., et al. 153
Cartmell, L. W., et al. 154
Casella, Domenico 26, 27, 99, 100
Cashew 26, 95, 96, 97, 190, 319, 330, 341
Cassia fistula 122
Castelló Yturbide 245
Castello, Salvador 68, 300
Ceiba pentandra 29, 122, 321, 333
Chang, Kwang-chih 13, 43, 106, 107, 215
Chapman, J. et al. 39, 46, 194, 332
Chard, Chester S. 8
Chekiang Province Cultural Properties Control 106, 247
Chen Wenhua 13, 108, 217
Chenopodium ambrosioides 30, 125
Chenopodium quinoa 95, 126
Chevalier, A. 123, 183, 215
Chiba, Tokuji 18, 253
Chicken 67, 69, 300, 302
Chin, James 53, 54, 55, 56, 57, 58, 59, 62, 262, 263, 264, 265, 267, 268, 269, 270, 271, 274, 276, 278, 279, 280, 281, 282, 283, 284, 285, 290, 292, 293
Chopra, R. N., I. C. Chopra, and B. S. Varma 84, 318
Chopra, R. N., I. C. Chopra, et al...34, 46, 143, 150, 152, 184, 197, 203, 210, 225, 227, 234, 238, 321, 323, 325, 333
Chopra, R. N., S. L. Nayar et al...28, 30, 34, 35, 44, 50, 81, 82, 84, 85, 92, 95, 102, 103, 105, 109, 111, 117, 126, 138, 141, 142, 154, 162, 163, 167, 170, 174, 175, 180, 184, 192, 193, 195, 198, 203, 205, 211, 216, 218, 220, 222, 225, 227, 238, 244, 250, 318, 319, 320, 321, 322, 323, 324, 325, 326
Christian, Frederick W. 205
Christmasberry 186
Cicada sp. 297
Cichorium intybus 49, 126, 240, 241
Cinchona officinalis 127
Clark, George A., et al. 272
Clissold, P. 9
Coca Plant 17, 146, 153, 332
Cockburn et al. 52, 262

Cockburn, Aidan ... 260
Coconut ... 30, 127, 130, 131, 151, 180, 213
Cocos nucifera ... 30, 127, 131, 151, 213
Coe, Michael D. ... 66, 295, 296
Collins, G. N. ... 18, 108, 252, 259
Collins, J. L. ... 26, 98
Colocasia esculenta ... 132
Compton, Todd ... 76
Cook and Cook ... 173
Cook, O. F. ... 30, 92, 128, 129, 130, 131, 172, 173, 178, 197, 199, 201, 227, 284
Corn ... 1, 12, 14, 18, 76, 94, 104, 105, 209, 227, 249, 250, 251
Cotton ... 124, 158, 159, 160, 162, 163, 168, 169
Couroupita guianensis ... 31, 132, 331
Covarrubias, Miguel ... 66, 296
Cowhage ... 197
Crawford, Michael H. ... 261
Crax globicera ... 298
Cronk, Lynn Ellen ... 75, 76
Cucumis sp. ... 133
Cucurbita
    Cucurbita ficifolia ... 32, 33, 133
    Cucurbita maxima ... 33, 134, 321, 333
    Cucurbita moschata ... 32, 136
    Cucurbita pepo ... 135, 137, 321, 333
Cunningham, Alexander ... 26, 102, 104, 343
Curcuma longa ... 33, 138
Custard Apple ... 102
Cyclanthera pedata ... 139, 140
Cyperus esculentus ... 140, 321
Cyperus vegetus ... 140, 321

D

Dagodag, Tim, and Gary Klee ... 200
Danin, Avinoam et al. ... 46
Darling, Samuel T. ... 4, 5, 260, 273
Darlington, Cyril D. ... 179, 199
Datura
    Datura metel ... 34, 142, 145, 321
    Datura sanguinea ... 145
    Datura spp. ... 34, 141, 144, 146, 332
    Datura stramonium ... 142, 144, 145, 146, 321, 333
Daws, J. D., and J. R. Magilton ... 288
De Prez, Alfred S. ... 29, 124, 130, 154, 199
Degener, O. ... 98
Dendrocygna bicolor ... 299

Denevan, William M. 266
Dennis, J. V., and C. R. Gunn 31, 129, 131
Derris sp. 146
Desmond, Ray 25, 82, 213
Dhamija, Jasleen 212
Dhawan, N. L. 12, 18, 253, 259
Díaz, José Luis 118, 145, 208
Dickinson, William R. et al. 8
Dillehay, Thomas D. 9
Dioscorea
   Dioscorea alata 146, 147, 148
   Dioscorea cayenensis 149
Diospyros ebenaster 150
Diplococcus pneumoniae 264, 285
Dixon, E. James 8, 9
Dixon, Roland B. 15, 17, 205
Dog 65, 295
Dolichos lablab 151
Domestic Cat 66, 299, 305
Donkin, R. A. 28, 112
Doran, Edwin, Jr. 9, 237
Dressler, Robert L. 96, 100, 101, 114, 150, 212, 222
DuBois, Constance Goddard 34, 142
Dumont, Henri J. et al. 45, 47, 186, 224, 232
Dunn, Frederick L. 278
Durbin, Marshall 75

E

Easton, N. Alexander 8
Edwards, Clinton R. 9
Eells, Myron 297
Elaeis guineensis 151
Elkin, Adolphus Peter, and N. W. G. MacIntosh 8
El-Najjar, M.Y. and T.M.J. Mulinksi 57, 276
El-Najjar, Mahmoud Y. 288
Engelbrecht, William E., and Carl K. Seyfert 9
England, Nora C. 34, 41, 97, 207
Entamoeba hystolytica 53, 264
Enterobius vermicularis 265
Erickson, David L. et al. 8, 37
Erigeron albidus 152
Erigeron canadensis 152, 322
Erlandson, Jon M. 74
Erlandson, Jon M. and Rick C. Torben 74
Erlandson, Jon M. et al. 8, 9

Errazurriz, J., and C. Alvarado 61, 286
Erythroxylon novagranatense 17, 146, 153, 332
Estrada, Emilio, and Betty J. Meggers 9
Evans, Jeff 179

F

Faeggri, K. 47, 233
Fage, J. D. 179
Feinhandler, Sherwin J., H. C. Fleming, and J. M. Monahon 205
Felis catus 66, 299, 305
Felis domestica 299
Ferreira, Luiz Fernando, Adauto Araújo, and Ulisses Eugenio Confalonieri 5, 260
Ferreira, Luiz Fernando, et al. 5, 62, 261, 273, 291
Ferris, G. F. 57, 274, 275
Fiennes, Richard, and Alice Fiennes 66, 295
Finan, J. S. 19, 257
Finsterbusch, C. A. 68, 300
Fladmark, K. R. 9, 37
Flavivirus spp. 265
Fleabane 22, 152, 322
Fonseca, Olympio da ... 4, 5, 55, 57, 58, 59, 60, 61, 260, 261, 269, 270, 274, 276, 277, 279, 280, 291
Forbes, Robert J. 212
Fosberg, F. R. 6, 169
Foster, Mary LeCron 166
Friant, M. 66, 296
Friant, M., and Henry Reichlen 66, 296
Fryxell, Paul A. 160, 164
Fuchs, Stephan 138, 208
Fulvous Tree Duck 299

G

Gallus gallus 66, 67, 69, 300, 302
Gamble, Clive 8, 9
García-Bárcena, Joaquín 11, 119, 182
García-Payón, José 25
Garcinia mangostana 154
Gates, William 147
Giardia lamblia 267
Giesing, Kornelia B. 75
Gifford, Edward Winslow 29
Glover, Ian C. 12, 19, 27, 104, 105, 249, 331, 332
Gnaphalium purpureum 155
Goff, C. W. 271, 288, 290
Golden Crownbeard 247

Goldstein, Marcus S. 58, 277, 279, 288
Gorner, Peter 231
Gossypium
    Gossypium barbadense..........14, 157, 158, 159, 160, 161, 162, 165, 166, 167, 168, 175, 322
    Gossypium brasiliense..........163, 164
    Gossypium drynarioides..........161, 163, 164
    Gossypium gossypioides..........14, 164, 165, 166
    Gossypium herbaceum..........159, 160
    Gossypium hirsutum..........14, 157, 158, 159, 162, 163, 165, 166, 167, 168
    Gossypium religiosum..........162, 167, 168
    Gossypium spp...........13, 155, 161, 163, 164, 167
    Gossypium tomentosum..........158, 159, 161, 163, 164, 165, 166, 167, 168, 169, 170
Gould, Stephen J. 6
Grape 248, 249
Gray, Asa, and J. H. Trumbull 46, 225
Groves, R. H., and F. di Castri 212
Guava 46, 226, 227, 325, 334
Guerra, F. 58, 266, 279
Gunther, Robert T. 44, 48, 221
Guppy, Henry B. 6, 30, 130, 242
Gupta, D., and H. K. Jain 12, 18, 203, 253
Gupta, Shakti M...19, 26, 27, 28, 32, 35, 39, 96, 97, 99, 103, 119, 122, 125, 132, 171, 194, 208, 211, 253, 255, 324, 330, 331, 333, 334, 342, 345
Guthrie, James L. 154

H

Hackett, C. J. 288
Hadkins, E. S. et al. 141
Hall, A. R., and H. K. Kenward 71, 294
Hamblin, Nancy N. and Amadeo M. Rea 69
Hamp, Eric P. 300
Handy, Edward S. C. III 29
Hare, Ronald.52, 53, 54, 56, 58, 62, 262, 263, 264, 268, 269, 272, 273, 279, 281, 283, 284, 285, 288, 289, 293
Harlan, Jack R., and J. M. J. de Wet 12, 49, 106, 244
Harms, H. 30, 42, 115, 123, 129, 200, 201
Harries, H. C. 31, 129, 131, 132
Hartman, Orar M. 68, 301
Hather, J., and P. V. Kirch 16, 179
Hatt, Gudmund 148, 255, 257
Hawaiian Rose 213
Hawkes, J. G. 234
Heine-Geldern, Robert von 208
Heine-Geldern, Robert von, and Gordon F. Ekholm 208
Heiser, Charles B. et al. 184, 185

Heiser, Charles B., Jr. 36, 37, 48, 119, 183, 184, 231, 232, 235, 236
Helianthus annuus 34, 170, 171, 172, 322, 331, 334
Heliconia bihai 172
Helms, Mary W. 8
Hennig, R. 70, 304
Herklots, G. A. 140
Hernández de Toledo, Francisco 44, 47, 49
Heyerdahl, Thor..15, 29, 30, 31, 35, 38, 42, 44, 45, 47, 49, 97, 98, 118, 121, 122, 128, 129, 131, 132, 140, 147, 169, 171, 172, 173, 176, 178, 186, 190, 191, 192, 200, 204, 214, 218, 219, 222, 224, 230, 231, 232, 241, 247
Heywood, V. H. 211
Hibiscus 174
Hibiscus tiliaceus 173
Hibiscus youngianus 174
Hill, Arthur W. 30
Hill, Dennis S. 303, 307
Hillebrand, W. 45, 81, 84, 85, 111, 112, 142, 152, 155, 161, 162, 163, 164, 167, 170, 174, 176, 178, 197, 216, 222, 225, 232, 247
Hoeppli, Reinhard 274, 275, 277, 282, 292
Hog Plum 242, 325, 334
Holdaway, R. N. 306
Holden, Constance 9
Hookworm 260, 261
Hooton, Earnest A. 264, 284, 285
Hristov, Romeo H., and Santiago Genovés T. 25
Hudson, Ellis H. 289
Hull, Thomas G. 63, 294
Human (alpha) herpes virus 3 .... 54, 267, 268
Human (gamma) herpes virus 4 .... 54, 267, 268
Hutchinson, Joseph B. 43, 157, 160, 169, 235, 255, 256
Hutchinson, Joseph B., R. A. Silow, and S. G. Stephens 13, 14, 43, 159, 161, 162, 168, 169

I

Indigo 174, 175, 176
Indigofera suffruticosa 174
Indigofera tinctoria 174, 175, 176
Influenza viruses 268, 284
Innes, Frank C. 264
International Library Association...27, 28, 30, 34, 47, 50, 92, 95, 102, 109, 111, 117, 126, 142, 175, 193, 198, 227, 229, 238, 244, 318, 319, 320, 321, 323, 325, 326
Ipomoea acetosaefolia 176
Ipomoea batatas 15, 176, 322

J

Jaramillo-Arango, Jaime 277

Jarcho, Saul 277
Jeffreys, M. D. W. 14, 19, 106, 201, 207, 212, 240, 251, 254, 256, 257, 258
Jennings, Jesse D. 9
Jett, Stephen C. 8, 16, 17, 18, 99, 100, 117, 154, 175, 202, 207, 212, 302
Jia Ming 32, 136
Jiao, M., M. Luna-Cavazos, and R. Bye 145
Jicama 214
Johannessen, Carl L. 16, 18, 19, 26, 31, 34, 35, 46, 67, 68, 98, 107, 108, 112, 117, 120, 121,
    146, 148, 171, 187, 201, 244, 245, 250, 251, 254, 256, 257, 258, 301, 306
Johannessen, Carl L., and Ann Z. Parker 18, 19, 119, 120, 138, 251, 254, 258
Johannessen, Carl L., and May Chen Fogg 68, 301
Johannessen, Carl L., and Wang Siming 12, 18, 19, 26, 27, 28, 32, 35, 43, 93, 100, 103, 107,
    119, 135, 136, 170, 178, 186, 215, 250, 331
Johannessen, Carl L., Wayne Fogg, and May Chen Fogg 68, 301
Johnson, B. L. 156, 158, 159, 166, 168, 169
Johnson, Frederick, and Richard S. MacNeish 12
Johnson, Rubellite K., and Bryce G. Decker 14, 160

K

Kane, Paul 296, 297
Kapok 124
Karasch, Mary C. 56, 57, 272, 275, 292
Kaufman, Terrence 69
Kaufman, Terrence, and W. Norman 41
Kelley, David H. 15, 16, 45, 75, 76, 180, 223
Kidder II, Alfred V 9
Kidder, Alfred V. et al. 4
Kiple, Kenneth F. 266
Kirch, Patrick V. 132
Kirchhoff, Paul 76
Kirtikar, K. R., and B. D. Basu 13, 96, 105, 109, 112, 115, 125, 163, 198, 322
Kislev, M. E. 303, 307, 308
Kissell, Mary Lois 297
Klepinger, Linda L. 56, 264, 272
Knoche, W. 47, 49, 97, 118, 230, 241, 247
Kosakowsky, Laura J. et al. 37, 185
Kramisch, Stella 218, 334
Krapovickas, A. 13, 105, 107, 319
Krauss, Beatrice H. 98
Kroeber, Alfred L. 3, 34, 142
Kuhnke, LaVerne 52, 262, 282
Kulakov, P. A., H. Hauptli, and S. K. Jain 89
Kunitz, S. and R. Euler 283

L

Lagenaria siceraria 35, 37, 180
Laming-Emperaire, Annette 261, 270, 276, 280
Lancaster, S. P. 45, 133, 137, 141, 145, 189, 211, 223, 224, 244
Langdon, Robert.14, 28, 38, 47, 97, 111, 118, 126, 162, 168, 169, 174, 175, 177, 187, 190, 206, 230
Langdon, Robert, and D. Tryon 47, 177, 182, 229, 230
Las Casas, Bartolomé de 40, 196, 270
Lasioderma serricorne 302, 303
Latcham, Ricardo E. 67, 200, 296, 300
Lathrap, Donald W. 36, 158, 182, 183
Laufer, Berthold 15, 106, 206, 255, 257, 258
Layard, Austen H. 26, 98
Leach, Helen M. 46
Leishmania sp. 269
Lentz, David L. et al. 34, 170
León, Fidias E., de León, and Ariza 60, 286
León, Fidias E., de León, and de León 61
Leopold, A. Starker 299
Lepofsky, D. S., H. Harries, and M. Kellum 131
Lesser Mealworm 65, 294, 308
Levey, Martin 32, 33, 43, 135, 136, 138, 219, 324, 333, 334
Levey, Martin, and Noury Al-Khaledy 49
Lewis, Albert B. 206
Lindemann, Hannes 8
Ling Shun-shêng 9
Littorina littorea 69, 303
Livingstone, Frank B. 289
Lonchocarpus sericeus 183
Long, Austin et al. 12, 156, 158, 167
Lord, John Keast 66, 67, 296, 297
Lotus 207, 208, 209
Lovell, Nancy C. 56, 272
Lowie, Robert H. 4
Lozoya, Xavier 144
Luffa acutangula 183
Luffa cylindrica 37, 135, 184
Luna Cavazos, Mario, Mejun Jiao, and Robert Bye 34, 145
Lunde, Paul 130, 228
Lundell, Cyrus L. 39, 110, 122, 194, 196, 208, 223, 240
Lupinus cruickshanksii 185
Lycium carolinianum 186
Lycopersicon esculentum 187, 188, 322

M

Mackenzie, Donald A. 28, 110
MacNeish, Richard S. 30, 42, 49, 89, 131, 214, 245
MacNeish, Richard S. et al 14, 40, 167, 196
MacNeish, Richard S., and C. Earle Smith 158
Macroptilium lathyroides 43, 188, 332
Magnolia grandiflora 188
Mahieu, Jacques de 296
Maimonides, Moses 48, 239
Mair, Victor H. 46, 65, 295
Mair, Victor H. 1, 2
Maize 1, 12, 18, 76, 94, 104, 105, 209, 227, 249, 251, 257, 326, 331
Malaria 277, 278, 367
Mangelsdorf, Paul C. MacNeish, and Willey 36, 130, 253, 259
Mangifera indica 154, 176, 189
Mango 154, 176, 189, 190, 195, 196
Manihot esculenta 322
Manihot sp. 38, 190
Manioc 190, 191
Manter, H. W. 261
Maranta arundinacea 38, 191, 322, 334
Marcus, Joyce 100, 242
Marijuana 17, 18, 65, 117, 118
Markham, Clements R. 127, 178
Márquez Morfín, Lourdes 290
Marszewski, Tomasz 12, 18, 205, 252, 253, 254
Martí, Samuel 76
Martínez Muriel, Alejandro Claudio 30, 114, 120, 125, 148, 191, 204, 218, 239, 248
Matisoo-Smith, E. et al. 306, 307
Matisoo-Smith, E., and J. H. Robins 306, 307
Matsumura, Jinzo 89, 92, 95, 108, 126, 180, 187, 219, 250
Mattingly, David 256, 258
McBryde, Felix W. 41, 97, 112, 114, 134, 175, 187, 190, 201, 230, 239, 245
Medvedov, Daniel 76
Meggers, Betty J. 8
Meggers, Betty J., Clifford Evans, and Emilio Estrada 61, 286
Meleagris gallopavo 69, 303
Mellén Blanco, Francisco 33, 38, 48, 49, 136, 182, 191, 200, 257
Méndez Pereira, Octavio 132
Merrill, Elmer D. 14, 30, 42, 91, 94, 98, 99, 107, 128, 129, 148, 150, 157, 169, 173, 174, 178, 179, 200, 201, 202, 223
Meyerhof, M., and G. P. Sobhy 48, 239
Microsporum spp. 55, 269, 270, 290
Milewski, Tadeusz 75
Millet, Nicholas B. et al. 278, 282

Mimosa pudica...38, 192, 323
Mirabilis jalapa...38, 193, 323
Miranda, Faustino..........................12, 95, 114, 120, 123, 124, 125, 174, 191, 199, 204, 232, 248
Missouri Botanical Garden (MOBOT)39, 44, 83, 84, 85, 122, 174, 176, 184, 193, 202, 210, 211, 213, 214, 216, 220, 229
Miura, Tomoyuki et al. 286
Mollugo verticillata..39, 193, 332
Monstera deliciosa..39, 194, 331, 349
Moran, Hugh A., and David H. Kelley..75
Morus
  Morus alba..39, 195, 196
  Morus celtifolia...40, 196
  Morus rubra..40, 196
Moseley, Michael E..200
Mucuna pruriens..41, 196, 323, 334
Mukerji, Dhirendra Nath..76
Mulberry..39, 40, 194, 195, 196
Munro, J. W...303, 307
Murdock, George Peter..149, 178, 179
Mus musculus..304
Musa
  Musa balbisiana...41
  Musa coccinea...202
  Musa paradisiaca...41, 200
  Musa sapientum..41, 200, 202
  Musa spp..41
Musa Musa × paradisiaca..198
Mya arenaria..70, 305
Mycobacterium leprae..271
Mycobacterium tuberculosis...55, 56, 271, 272, 273
Myrica gale..42, 202

N

Nadkarni, K. M....17, 27, 28, 29, 33, 34, 36, 38, 41, 44, 47, 48, 83, 96, 103, 104, 105, 108, 116, 117, 120, 125, 135, 136, 141, 154, 170, 181, 193, 197, 207, 211, 220, 227, 229, 238, 244, 318, 319, 320, 321, 322, 323, 325
Naudou, Jean...208
Nayar, N. M., and Rajendra Singh 37, 138, 140, 181, 185
Necator americanus..5, 52, 260, 261, 273, 274, 291
Needham, Joseph et al..9
Needham, Joseph, and Lu Gwei-Djen..9
Neher, R. F. 49, 244, 245
Nelumbo sp..207, 208, 209
Nerlich, Andreas G. et al. 17
Newcomb, Robert M......19, 28, 33, 97, 112, 113, 115, 118, 124, 130, 134, 138, 139, 140,

148, 149, 150, 151, 159, 160, 169, 172, 179, 184, 199, 202, 209, 214, 217, 227, 245, 248, 257
Newman, Marshall T. 53, 59, 60, 264, 269, 280, 281, 283, 284, 285
Nicolle, Charles...59, 60, 279, 280
Nicolson, Dan H. et al. 27, 34, 41, 102, 103, 104, 118, 121, 123, 137, 142, 197, 198, 238
Nicotiana rustica 144, 203, 206, 207
Nicotiana tabacum..16, 17, 146, 203, 204, 206, 207, 323, 334
Norton, Presley..9
Nymphaea sp. 207, 208, 209

O

O'Brien, Patricia J. 15
O'Neill, Ynez Violé 289
Ocimum
   Ocimum americanum..210, 323
   Ocimum basilicum 210, 211, 323
   Ocimum sanctum...211, 324, 331, 334
   Ocimum spp. 210, 211, 332
Onchocerca volvulus 274
Opuntia dillenii 211, 212, 324
Oryctolagus cuniculus..62, 305
Osteomeles anthyllidifolia 213
Oviedo y Valdés, Gonzalo Fernández de...106, 170, 201, 243
Oxford English Dictionary (OED)..197

P

Pachyrhizus
   Pachyrhizus erosus 42, 213, 324
   Pachyrhizus spp. 42
   Pachyrhizus tuberosus 214
Pal, Mohinder, and T. N. Khoshoo...89, 91
Panagiotakopulu, Eva...65, 71, 102, 111, 295, 302, 307, 308
Pandey, D. S. 50, 84, 85, 96, 103, 109, 122, 142, 145, 152, 155, 193, 195, 213, 243, 244, 245, 248
Papaya..28, 29, 121, 122, 321
Parkes, A. 131
Parotta, John A....45, 103, 122, 145, 149, 188, 207, 210, 211, 212, 213, 216, 223, 225, 244, 318, 319, 320, 321, 322, 323, 324, 325, 326
Parsche, Franz...153
Parsche, Franz, Balabanova, and Pirsig...17, 117, 118
Patiño, Victor Manuel........15, 30, 36, 42, 106, 130, 148, 151, 170, 177, 182, 186, 192, 212, 242
Patterson, K. David 52, 262, 285, 291
Paullinia sp. 215
Peanut 9, 12, 13, 104, 105
Pediculus humanus 263

Pediculus humanus capitis...274
Pediculus humanus corporis..53, 278
Pediculus humanus spp. 56
Peng Shifan 12
Pennisetum americanum 215, 216
Pérez de Barradas, José 29
Petersen, K. S. et al. 305
Pharbitis hederacea..216, 324
Phaseolus
    Phaseolus adenanthus...216
    Phaseolus lunatus...113, 114, 115, 216
    Phaseolus spp...43
    Phaseolus vulgaris...43, 114, 218, 324, 332, 334
Physalis
    Physalis alkekengi 220
    Physalis indica 220
    Physalis lanceifolia 44, 220, 324
    Physalis peruviana 44, 221, 324
    Physalis philadelphica 221
    Physalis pubescens..221
    Physalis spp. 44
Physalis Physalis minima..221
Pickersgill, Barbara...98
Pickersgill, Barbara, and Charles B. Heiser, Jr. 43, 93, 106, 107, 120, 138, 166, 217, 218
Piedreaia hortai...57, 276
Pike, A. M..53, 54, 264, 265, 267
Pineapple 98
Ping-ti Ho..107
Pinta 288
Piperno, Dolores R. 38, 147, 192
Plasmodium falciparum..276, 278
Plowman, Timothy..17, 153
Plumeria rubra..45, 189, 223, 324
Pokharia, A.K., and K. S. Saraswat19, 26, 27, 34, 37, 43, 48, 102, 104, 105, 109, 141, 142,
    188, 217, 218, 249, 331, 332
Polianthes tuberosa...223, 224
Pollmer, Udo...17
Polunin, Nicholas U...6, 47, 233
Polygonum acuminatum...45, 47, 141, 224, 231, 232
Pope, Willis T. 243
Portulaca oleracea 46, 225, 325
Potter, C..307, 308
Powell, Mary Lucas..272
Psidium guajava..46, 226, 325, 334
Pullaiah, T....16, 29, 36, 38, 39, 45, 46, 81, 83, 85, 86, 95, 96, 99, 101, 103, 105, 109, 110,
    111, 112, 113, 116, 120, 121, 122, 125, 127, 133, 135, 140, 142, 154, 170, 175, 180, 181,

184, 188, 191, 192, 193, 198, 204, 208, 210, 211, 217, 223, 225, 227, 229, 238, 244,245, 318, 319, 320, 321, 322, 323, 324, 325, 326, 334
Pumpkin 135, 137, 333
Purple Cudweed 155
Purseglove, John W. 91, 156, 169, 180, 190
Purslane 46, 225, 325

Q

Quigley, Carroll 146, 183, 215, 230, 246
Quinoa 95, 126

R

Rabbit 305
Rands, Robert L. 208, 209
Rands, Robert L., and Carroll L. Riley 3
Rat 307
Rattus rattus 59, 280, 294, 306, 307
Reinhard, Karl J. 5, 62, 261, 267, 273, 285, 291, 292
Reko, Blas Pablo 34, 144
Rensch, Karl H. 16, 177
Rheede tot Drakenstein, H. A. van 85, 86, 198, 238
Rhyzopertha dominica 307
Rickettsia
   Rickettsia prowazekii 58, 274, 278
   Rickettsia rickettsii 59, 279
   Rickettsia typhi 59, 280
Riddle, J. M., and J. M. Vreeland 65, 71, 294, 295, 308
Rieth, Adolf 70, 304
Riley, Carroll L. et al. 72
Robinson, Eugenia J. et al. 31, 128, 130
Robinson, Stuart 212
Rochebrune, A. T. de 123, 124, 154, 199, 200
Rose, Mark 287
Roxburgh, W. 101, 112, 135, 212, 319
Royal Botanic Gardens at Kew 25, 50, 82
Roys, Ralph L...28, 30, 32, 38, 39, 41, 42, 44, 47, 48, 49, 57, 89, 91, 99, 100, 101, 104, 110, 111, 112, 116, 120, 121, 122, 125, 137, 148, 150, 160, 167, 175, 179, 182, 187, 191, 192, 193, 197, 202, 209, 212, 214, 218, 221, 226, 228, 230, 232, 234, 238, 240, 241, 242, 245, 247, 275, 296

S

Saccharum officinarum 227
Sachan, J. K. S., Sarkar, and Payak 258
Sacramento Burbark 247

Safford, William E. 13, 29, 85, 108, 111, 122, 124, 125, 142, 143, 186, 213, 216
Sagittaria sagittifolia...228
Salmonella enterica 281
Salo, W. L., et al. 56, 273
Salvia coccinea..228, 325
Salvia occidentalis..228
Sandison, A. T. 57, 58, 275, 277, 279
Sandison, A. T.. and Tapp 271, 278, 282, 285
Sapindus saponaria 47, 229, 325
Sapindus trifoliatus..229, 325
Sapper, Karl..41, 201
Saraswat, K. S., Sharma and Saini 12, 27, 91, 92, 109, 210, 320, 331, 332, 333
Sarkar, K. R. et al. 18, 259
Sasuke, Nakao, and Jonathan D. Sauer 94
Sauer, Carl O.....19, 33, 68, 81, 113, 114, 124, 134, 138, 140, 147, 149, 150, 158, 159, 163,
   169, 179, 199, 202, 209, 217, 228, 246, 257, 258, 300, 301
Sauer, Jonathan D...11, 12, 83, 89, 90, 91, 92, 93, 94, 95, 97, 105, 115, 126, 131, 151, 162,
   169, 180, 181, 190, 203, 215, 217, 218, 219, 248, 256, 257
Saunders, Shelley R., P. G. Ramsden, and D. A. Herring...................53, 59, 264, 280, 281, 283
Scaglion, R., and K. A. Soto...179
Schafer, E. H. 29, 123
Schistosoma sp. 282
Schoenhals, Louise C. 99, 136, 140, 141, 150, 228
Schoenoplectus californicus..47, 224, 230
Scholes, France V., and Dave Warren 201, 248
Schuhmacher, W. Wilfried et al. 275
Schumann, Karl, and Karl Lauterback 172
Schwabe, Calvin W..54, 62, 265, 294
Schwerin, Karl H. 36, 114, 158
Science News 8
Service, Robert F. 8
Sesamum orientale..232
Shady Solís and Carlos Leyva..113
Shady Solís, Ruth................14, 17, 100, 105, 115, 116, 118, 126, 137, 162, 177, 191, 214
Shady Solís, Ruth, Haas, and Creamer..15, 28, 154, 177, 226
Sharma, R. K., and Bhagwan Dash 46, 227, 334
Sharpe, William D. 272
Shigella dysenteriae 282
Silow, R. A. 157, 158, 169
Simmonds, Norman W. 41, 98, 199
Simoons, Frederick J. 296
Sinoto, Yosihiko H. 29
Sisyrhynchium acre 232
Sisyrhynchium angustifolium...47, 233
Sivarajan, V. V., and Philip Mathew...86
Skottsberg, Carl J. F. 45, 49, 141, 186, 200, 224, 231, 241

Smartt, J. 37, 188
Smilax sp. 233
Smith, G. Elliot 75, 271
Smole, William J. 41, 201, 202
Solanum
   Solanum candidum 48, 235, 236, 237
   Solanum nigrum 48, 220, 238, 239
   Solanum repandum 48, 235, 236, 237, 239
   Solanum sessiliflorum 237
   Solanum sessiliflorum 48, 236, 237
   Solanum sessiliflorum 237
   Solanum sessiliflorum 237
   Solanum sessiliflorum 239
   Solanum spp. 48, 235, 238, 239
   Solanum tuberosum 48, 239
Sonchus oleraceus 49, 126, 240
Soper, Fred L. 5, 261
Sopher, David E. 33, 139
Sophora toromiro 49, 241, 242
Sorenson, John L. 26, 67, 78, 204
Sorenson, John L., and Martin H. Raish 3, 7
Spinden, Herbert J. 72
Spjeldnaes, Nils, and Kari E. Hinningsmoen 69, 303
Spondias lutyea 242
Spondias purpurea 242, 325, 334
Spores, Ronald 42, 202
Spriggs, Matthew 129, 132
Sreekumar, P.V., D. B. Singh, and T. V. R. S. Sharma 101
Standley, Paul C. 142, 148, 214, 234, 235, 239, 242, 243
Standley, Paul C., and Salvador Calderón 134
Staphylococcus x aureus 283
Steffan, J. R. 303
Steffy, J. Richard 25, 82, 83
Stegobium paniceum 71, 294, 295, 308
Stephens, S. G. 14, 15, 156, 157, 158, 160, 163, 166, 167, 168, 169, 170, 219
Steward, Julian H. 30, 107, 215
Stewart, T. D. 135, 147, 272, 277
Stodder, Ann L. W., and Debra L. Martin 52, 53, 54, 261, 262, 264, 267, 293
Stonor, C. R., and Edgar Anderson 18, 255, 259
Storey, Alice A. *et al*. 69
Streptococcus pneumoniae 284
Streptococcus pyogenes 264, 285
Stresemann, Erwin 70, 304
Strongyloides sp. 285
Stutz, Bruce 60, 266, 279, 281
Sugarcane 227

Sunflower 34, 170, 171, 172, 322, 331, 334
Suto, T., and Y. Yoshida 18, 252, 253, 254
Sweet Potato 15, 176, 322
Swordbean 115
Symon, David E., and L. A. R. Haegi 34, 141
Synedrella nodiflora 243
Syphilis 289

T

T cell lymphotropic (retro) virus (HTLV-I) 60, 286
Tagare, G. V. 125, 251, 333
Tagetes erecta 49, 243, 244, 245, 325
Tagetes patula 49, 244, 245, 326
Tamarindus indicus 245
Teeter, Wendy G. 69, 302
Tephrosia spp. 215, 230, 246
Tessman, Günter 139, 202
Tewari, Shitala P. 172
Thapa, J. K. 255, 258
The Wealth of India 18, 254, 255
Thompson, J. E. S. 204
Thompson, R. Campbell 30, 48, 125, 140, 218, 238
Thorarinsson, Sigurdur 42, 47, 203, 233
Thorn Apple 143
Tisseuil, J. 289
Tobacco 204, 207
Tobacco Beetle 302, 303
Tolstoy, Paul 40, 66, 173, 195, 196, 296
Tomato 187, 188, 221, 322
Torkelson, Anthony R 27, 30, 34, 35, 39, 44, 83, 92, 95, 101, 103, 105, 109, 120, 126, 138, 141, 142, 152, 162, 163, 170, 174, 175, 184, 193, 196, 198, 205, 211, 220, 222, 225, 234, 238, 244, 250, 318, 319, 320, 321, 322, 323, 324, 325, 326
Towle, Margaret A 13, 18, 27, 32, 33, 36, 46, 47, 92, 100, 104, 106, 112, 115, 116, 120, 123, 124, 126, 133, 134, 135, 137, 140, 154, 163, 174, 175, 182, 191, 200, 212, 214, 217, 226, 230, 231, 252
Townsend, Charles H. T. 156, 174, 175, 212
Toxopeus, H. J. 123
Tozzer, Alfred M 40, 47, 49, 70, 110, 122, 147, 189, 196, 211, 226, 230, 234, 240, 242, 299, 304
Trapa natans 105, 246, 247
Treponema pallidum 287
Trichophyton concentricum 61, 290
Trichosporon ovoides 61, 291
Trichuris trichiura 61, 261, 274, 291
Triumfetta semitriloba 247

Trychostrongylus sp. 292
Tuberculosis 55, 56, 271, 272, 273
Tunga penetrans 292
Turkey 69, 70, 138, 171, 258, 303, 304
Turmeric 139
Turner, Christy G., II 65, 66
Tylor, Edward B. 4, 75
Typhus 279, 280

U

Ugent, D., S. Pozorski, and T. Pozorski 47, 116, 191, 230
Ulei 213

V

Van Blerkom, Linda Miller...52, 53, 54, 57, 62, 63, 263, 264, 265, 266, 268, 269, 271, 275, 277, 282, 283, 284, 285, 290, 293
Vancouver, George 296, 297
Varshavsky, S. R. 70, 304
Verano, John W. 52, 56, 62, 260, 262, 265, 273, 285, 291
Verano, John W. and Douglas H. Ubelaker 284
Verbesina encelioides 247
Vigna sinensis 248
Villacorta Cifuentes, Jorge Luis 266, 277, 279
Vishnu-Mittre 253, 256
Vishnu-Mittre, Aruna Sharma, and Chanchala 37, 43, 188, 217, 219
Vitis vinifera 248, 249
Von den Steinen, K. 29, 97, 122, 190
Von Hagen, Victor Wolfgang 40, 196

W

Walker, Egbert H. 43
Wapatoo 228
Ward, R. Gerard, and Muriel Brookfield 31, 131
Wasson, R. Gordon 87
Wasson, Valentina Pavlovna, and R. Gordon Wasson 88
Watson, John Forbes......27, 32, 33, 34, 38, 39, 41, 46, 49, 83, 96, 101, 104, 108, 136, 138, 142, 184, 193, 228, 241, 318, 319, 325
Watson, William 105, 247
Watt, George.......19, 26, 27, 28, 32, 33, 34, 35, 39, 41, 42, 46, 47, 48, 49, 97, 99, 102, 104, 108, 109, 111, 113, 115, 116, 120, 124, 126, 135, 136, 137, 138, 139, 143, 150, 154, 164, 167, 171, 185, 192, 195, 197, 203, 207, 212, 214, 219, 225, 226, 229, 239, 240, 250, 259, 319, 320, 321, 322, 324, 325, 326
Weiss, Pedro 269, 274, 289, 292
Wells, Samuel A. 17

Wendel, Jonathan F. 14, 155, 156, 159, 169
Wendel, Jonathan F. Schnabel, and Seelanan 14, 158, 163, 165
Whalen, M. D., D. E. Costich, and C. B. Heiser 48, 236, 237
Whistler, W. Arthur 36, 37, 48, 173, 181, 236
Whitaker, Thomas W., and George F. Carter 36, 181
Whitaker, Thomas W., and Julius B. Bird 36, 133, 134, 137
White, Richard E. 303
Whitley, Glenn R. 298, 299
Wichmann, Søren 69, 301, 302
Wiener, Leo 17, 205, 207
Wilkinson, I. G. 26, 98, 209
Willcox, R. R. 289
Willey, Gordon R. 3, 9, 72
Witenberg, G. 267
Wittmack, Ludwig 154, 174, 175, 199, 200, 201
Woodbury, Angus M. 280
Wuchereria bancrofti 292
Wulff, E. V. 6
Wulff, Hans E. 212

X

Xu, H. Mike 67, 166

Y

Yacovleff E., and F. L. Herrera 29, 42, 48, 49, 110, 116, 124, 139, 186, 214, 215, 231, 238, 241, 242
Yam 178
Yarnell, Richard A. 32, 33, 118, 135, 137, 156, 181, 191, 204, 217, 219, 240
Yen, Douglas E. 14, 15, 16, 43, 113, 115, 116, 133, 137, 156, 162, 163, 177, 178, 179, 218
Yersinia pestis 62, 293

Z

Zea mays 1, 9, 12, 14, 18, 19, 35, 44, 76, 90, 94, 104, 105, 126, 138, 147, 201, 209, 220, 227, 244, 249, 250, 251, 252, 255, 256, 257, 259, 272, 307, 326, 331, 337, 338, 339, 340, 345
Zeven, A. C., and J. M. J. de Wet 29, 39, 44, 47, 84, 105, 110, 113, 116, 117, 121, 123, 140, 150, 166, 176, 184, 185, 188, 190, 193, 194, 204, 206, 214, 217, 222, 229, 244, 245, 249
Zinsser, Hans 57, 275, 276, 279
Zohary, Daniel 6
Zohary, Daniel, and Maria Hopf 10

ABOUT THE AUTHORS

John L. Sorenson
Emeritus professor of anthropology at BYU, where he founded work in anthropology in the 1950s. He was attracted to anthropology from the physical sciences through his study of archeology. He earned his M.S. from Cal Tech and his Ph.D. in archaeology from UCLA. Professor Sorenson lives and works in Provo, Utah where he is a distinguished and respected professor at Brigham Young University.

Carl L. Johannessen
Emeritus professor of biogeography in the Department of Geography at the University of Oregon. He taught there from 1959 to 1994. His B.A. in Wildlife Conservation and management, M. A. in zoology and Ph. D. in geography came from the University of California at Berkeley. Professor Johannessen lives and works in Eugene, Oregon, where he was the Department Chair of the University of Oregon's Department of Geography.

Both professors are still actively involved in research at their respective universities.